F R O M M E R ' S

WONDERFUL
WEEKENDS
FROM BOSTON

BY MARILYN WOOD

D0104913

Macmillan • USA

About the Author

Marilyn Wood came to the United States from England to study journalism at Columbia University. The former editorial director of Macmillan Travel, she has also worked as a reporter, ranch hand, press officer, and book reviewer. In addition, Marilyn is the author of *Frommer's Wonderful Weekends from New York City, Frommer's Wonderful Weekends from San Francisco, Frommer's London from $60 a Day, Frommer's Toronto,* and a co-author of *Frommer's Canada.*

MACMILLAN TRAVEL
A Simon & Schuster Macmillan Company
1633 Broadway
New York, NY 10019

Find us on-line at **www.frommers.com**

ISBN 0-02861334-1
ISSN 1094-7671

Editor: Alice Fellows
Production Editor: Lori Cates
Design by Amy Peppler Adams—designLab, Seattle
Digital Cartography by Roberta Stockwell and Ortelius Design
Page Creation by Jenaffer Brandt, Bob LaRoche, and Dave Pruett

SPECIAL SALES

Bulk purchases (10+ copies) of Frommer's and selected Macmillan travel guides are available to corporations, organizations, mail-order catalogs, institutions, and charities at special discounts, and can be customized to suit individual needs. For more information write to Special Sales, Macmillan General Reference, 1633 Broadway, New York, NY 10019.

Manufactured in the United States of America

CONTENTS

VERMONT
—<o>—

MAPS

An Invitation to the Reader

In researching this book, we discovered many wonderful places—hotels, restaurants, shops, and more. We're sure you'll find others. Please tell us about them, so we can share the information with your fellow travelers in upcoming editions. If you were disappointed with a recommendation, we'd love to know that, too. Please write to:

Frommer's Wonderful Weekends from Boston
Macmillan Travel
1633 Broadway
New York, NY 10019

An Additional Note

Please be advised that travel information is subject to change at any time—and this is especially true of prices. We therefore suggest that you write or call ahead for confirmation when making your travel plans. The authors, editors, and publisher cannot be held responsible for the experiences of readers while traveling. Your safety is important to us, however, so we encourage you to stay alert and be aware of your surroundings. Keep a close eye on cameras, purses, and wallets, all favorite targets of thieves and pickpockets.

Abbreviations used in this book:

MAP   Modified American Plan
EP   European Plan
AP   American Plan

Introduction

Even if we do live in the most historic, humanly scaled, and fun city in the United States, by Thursday most of us harried city or suburban dwellers are looking forward to the weekend, eagerly anticipating a break from our busy work routine and the chance to get away from the tarmac, to relax, calm our jangled nerves, and rediscover who we really are. And that is what this book is all about: 2- or 3-day breaks among the lakes or the mountains or the forests or down along the shore—and all within a 2- to 4-hour drive from Boston.

There are thousands of miles of coastline to explore in Maine, Cape Cod, and the islands of Martha's Vineyard and Nantucket; miles and miles of hiking and mountain biking trails in New Hampshire and Vermont; and cultural festivals galore to enjoy in areas like the Berkshires and elsewhere throughout New England. There are all kinds of unique museums and art galleries to visit; historic homes filled with the personalities and the drama of the lives of those that have lived there; and artists' and writers' residences and studios to view. Whole areas of countryside, shore, and mountain wait to be explored by canoeing, cycling, gliding, hiking, kayaking, camping, fishing, golfing, skiing, sailing, swimming, or doing whatever you relish and enjoy. Or you can simply opt for a rocking chair, a cocktail, and a broad veranda overlooking a verdant garden or ocean or mountain vista.

And while you're enjoying all this, you can stay in old sea captains' homes, bracketed and gingerbread Victorian fantasies with turrets and lacy trimmings, sybaritic coastal retreats, or log-cabin lodges with huge stone hearths. Your choices are endless, and so, too, are the delights of the table—juicy, sweet lobsters from Maine; fresh clams, scallops, cod, and other seafood on Cape Cod and the islands; luscious Vermont dairy products and maple syrup— ingredients in the regional cuisine that can be savored in airy dining rooms overlooking mountain, lake, or ocean or at picnics on the beach, by a stream, or on a mountainside.

To arrange your weekend in a way that suits your particular needs and quirks of personality requires a certain amount of planning. When you only have 2 or 3 days, you need to know where you want to stay. And you can't waste precious moments trekking to a well-regarded restaurant at Saturday noon only to find that it's closed for lunch, or driving around looking for a perfect picnicking spot.

This guide has been researched and written to forestall such problems and to deliver you, the weekender, from any such headaches, leaving you free to concentrate on fully enjoying your weekend your way. *Wonderful Weekends from Boston* is designed to help you through every step in the planning process. Each destination opens with a section that includes details about getting there by car, estimated driving times, and a list of any ultraspecial seasonal events that you may want to plan your weekend around (or plan to avoid, depending on how you feel about crowds).

After these opening sections, you'll find a brief general introduction to highlights of the area and then a detailed description of what your weekend is really all about: what to see, what to do, and what to explore. Inevitably, it's a very personal choice. Therefore, I have described the many possibilities available to you, offered some guidance about how to organize your 2 or 3 days, and let you know what I consider the real highlights of each destination. You, of course, will pursue your own interests, whether they're architecture, historic houses, wine and food, antiques, graveyards, gardens, art galleries, museums, theater, bird watching, or more active pursuits from windsurfing to skiing, swimming, golf, or horseback riding. These last I have covered in an activities section at the end of each chapter (except in certain cases where it made more sense to place them at the end of each section in the chapter). In this section, I identify public sports facilities wherever possible but make no claims as to their quality and standards of service.

The problem of accommodations is tackled next, and while we're on the subject, I can't urge you strongly enough to make reservations—in peak summer, fall foliage, and winter seasons as much as 5 or 6 months in advance, *particularly* on weekends. I have selected what I consider especially appealing accommodations, including a great number of inns and bed-and-breakfast places. In each case, I have endeavored to convey the atmosphere and type of lodging and treatment that a visitor can expect to receive. Rates are included, but I urge you always to check before you leave—undoubtedly prices will have changed by the time this book reaches your hands. And do keep in mind that most inns have 2- and (increasingly in popular summer resort areas) 3-night minimums on weekends. Although this book does not pretend to be a camper's guide, I have included some camping ideas, usually in state parks and other wilderness areas. Commercial campgrounds and trailer parks are not listed.

Next, the problem of meals. I have included what I consider the best in each region for breakfast, lunch, and dinner. Often, on a balmy day, you'll want to take a picnic somewhere overlooking the ocean or a river. Unlike in France or England, where you can pull into a field and stretch out among the poppies with a fine bottle of wine, a baguette, and some garlic sausage, picnicking is not as easy to find in the United States. So I've tried to include information about state parks and other idyllic settings for your leisurely meal *en plein air* and also, wherever possible, the suppliers of your picnic fare.

And finally, although many of the country destinations that appear in this book lack any rousing nightlife (which is precisely why you've chosen to go there), I have tried to include some nightlife options, if it's only a quiet, cozy, convivial bar.

So let's weekend! T. H. White wrote, "The Victorians had not been anxious to go away for the weekend. The Edwardians, on the contrary, were nomadic." Let's mimic those Edwardians.

SIX IMPORTANT TOPICS

Prices and Hours: Although I've made every effort to obtain correct and current prices and hours for establishments and attractions, these can change swiftly and dramatically. Changes in ownership, changes in policy, and inflation can all affect this information. Prices in this book are given per room, unless otherwise noted. For prices beyond 1999, add about 5% to 10% to the given rates per year.

Reservations: Reservations are a must on weekends. For accommodations they should be made well in advance, particularly if you want to stay at a certain inn—in some cases, as much as 3 months ahead and in exceptional circumstances, when major festivals or events occur, as much as a year. Dinner reservations, especially for Friday and Saturday, should also be made well in advance to avoid disappointment.

Minimum Stays: Most places demand minimum stays of 2 or 3 nights on weekends and 4 nights on holiday weekends. This information has not always been included, so check ahead. Note, too, that in hotel listings the term *weekend* means Friday and Saturday. The term *weekdays* refers to Sunday night through Thursday night.

Deposits: Deposits are often nonrefundable, since they're the innkeepers only defense against those folks who don't show up, especially when the weather is inclement. Always clarify this point when you book—and don't be a no-show.

Taxes: Taxes are not included in the quoted rates.

Definitions: "Weekends:" In hotel and restaurant listings, "weekend" always refers to Friday and Saturday nights. In attractions listings it refers strictly to Saturdays and Sundays. **"In-Season/Off-Season":** On Cape Cod, the islands, the Maine coast, and in Newport, Rhode Island, in-season is summer, usually from the end of May or mid-June to Labor Day. In New Hampshire and Vermont, the only off-seasons are late fall (after the foliage season and before the snow falls) and early spring.

MASSACHUSETTS

Cape Cod—The Upper Cape

The Falmouths ◆ *Mashpee* ◆ *Woods Hole* ◆ *Bourne*
◆ *the Cape Cod Canal* ◆ *Sandwich*

Distance in miles from Boston: Sandwich, 60; Falmouth, 68.

Estimated driving times: 1⅛ hours to Sandwich, 1¼ hours to Falmouth.

Driving: Take Route 3 to Route 6. Cross the Sagamore Bridge and take marked exits for Sandwich. You can also take this route to Falmouth by taking Route 6 to the Bourne Bridge to connect with Route 28.

Alternatively, for Falmouth take Route 3 to Route 24, Route 495 to the Bourne Bridge, and then Route 28 to Falmouth.

◄o►◄o►◄o►◄o►◄o►

Bus: Call **Plymouth and Brockton Bus Lines** (☎ 508/775-5524) for service from Boston; **Bonanza** (☎ 800/556-3815) operates from Providence, Hartford, and New York to Bourne, Falmouth, and Hyannis.

Train: Amtrak from New York runs on weekends only.

Further Information: For further information, contact the **Cape Cod Chamber of Commerce,** Routes 6 and 132, P.O. Box 16, Hyannis, MA 02601 (☎ 508/362-3225).

Falmouth Chamber of Commerce, 20 Academy Lane, Box 582, Falmouth, MA 02541 (☎ 508/548-8500).

◄o►◄o►◄o►◄o►◄o►

The Puritans established their first trading post on the Cape at Bourne to do business with the French and the Indians. Today a replica of that trading post welcomes visitors to the town. Bourne is also the prime keeper of the Cape Cod Canal, that body of water that cuts through the shoulder of the Cape connecting Buzzard's Bay and Cape Cod Bay. The canal was a financial disaster for its developers, but today it affords great opportunities for all kinds of recreation—boating, canoeing, biking, in-line skating, or simply walking.

Sandwich is the oldest town on the Cape. An unspoiled village centered around a mill pond, it has a leisurely, very English air. Sandwich proudly displays the traces of its past, when windmills powered industry and the meetinghouse was both the religious and the community center.

Falmouth is also historic—but it has a much saltier air and very distinct

Events & Festivals to Plan Your Trip Around

March: Falmouth/Mashpee Heart Fund Buffet Dinner and Silent Auction. Call ☎ 508/775-2533 for information.

April: Sandwich Daffodil Festival when more than 500,000 bell-shaped flowers paint the town gold.

May: Herb Festival, Sandwich, with exhibits and garden walks at the Green Briar Nature Center. Call ☎ 508/888-6870.

Dexter Rhododendron Festival, Sandwich. Heritage Plantation (☎ 508/888-3300) sells offshoots of its botanical collection.

July: Mashpee Wampanoag Pow Wow is a major event in the Native American calendar, and tribes attend from all over the nation. Call ☎ 508/477-0208.

Barnstable County Fair, East Falmouth. An old-fashioned, 6-day agricultural fair with prize livestock and produce. Call ☎ 508/563-3200.

August: Falmouth Road Race over a 7.1 mile course from Woods Hole to Falmouth Heights. This race was founded by the legendary Bill Rodgers. In 1976, the race attracted 2,000 runners; it's now limited to 4,500. Call ☎ 508/540-7000.

Mentadent Champions Tournament to benefit cystic fibrosis and Willowbend Children's Charities at Willowbend, Mashpee. Call ☎ 508/539-5700.

October: Bourne Farm Pumpkin Festival, West Falmouth. Fun for everyone, with pumpkin picking and hayrides at a 1775 farmstead. Call ☎ 508/548-0711.

differences between its several villages. From Falmouth it's only a short distance to other communities with well-defined characters of their own—Mashpee, with its Indian heritage, and Woods Hole, the internationally famous oceanographic center. So there are plenty of wonderful weekend opportunities on the Upper Cape.

THE FALMOUTHS, MASHPEE & WOODS HOLE

Each of the several villages that make up the town of Falmouth has a very different flavor. Old historic Falmouth, settled in 1660, is arranged around a fenced triangular green (1749) in classic New England style. To the east, commercial Falmouth stretches all the way to residential East Falmouth. Falmouth Heights is a Victorian summer resort, and West Falmouth a quiet historic haven with a dignified Quaker heritage. Although they're different, they all savor

Cape Cod

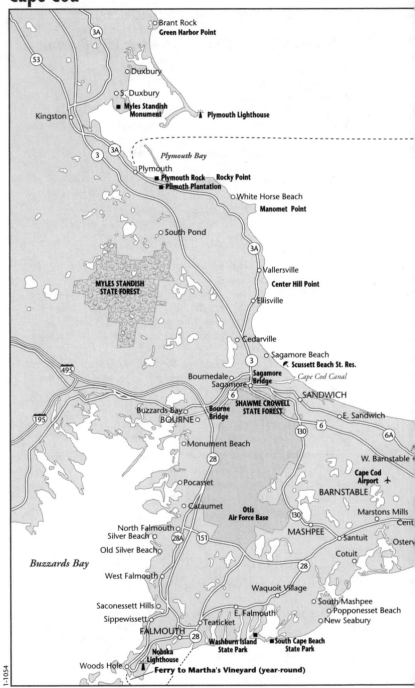

Brant Rock
Green Harbor Point

Duxbury

S. Duxbury

■ **Myles Standish Monument**

Kingston

☀ **Plymouth Lighthouse**

Plymouth Bay

Plymouth
■ **Plymouth Rock** — Rocky Point
■ **Plimoth Plantation**

White Horse Beach
Manomet Point

South Pond

MYLES STANDISH STATE FOREST

Vallersville
Center Hill Point

Ellisville

Cedarville

Sagamore Beach
⚓ **Scussett Beach St. Res.**

Bournedale
Sagamore **Sagamore Bridge**
Cape Cod Canal

SANDWICH

Buzzards Bay **Bourne Bridge**
BOURNE
SHAWME CROWELL STATE FOREST

E. Sandwich

Monument Beach

W. Barnstable

Cape Cod Airport ✈

BARNSTABLE

Pocasset

Cataumet

Otis Air Force Base

Marstons Mills
Cent

MASHPEE
Santuit
Oster

North Falmouth
Silver Beach
Old Silver Beach

Cotuit

Buzzards Bay

West Falmouth

Waquoit Village

South Mashpee
Popponesset Beach
New Seabury

Saconessett Hills
Sippewissett
Teaticket
E. Falmouth

FALMOUTH

■ **Washburn Island State Park**
■ **South Cape Beach State Park**

Nobska Lighthouse
Woods Hole
Ferry to Martha's Vineyard (year-round)

1-1054

4

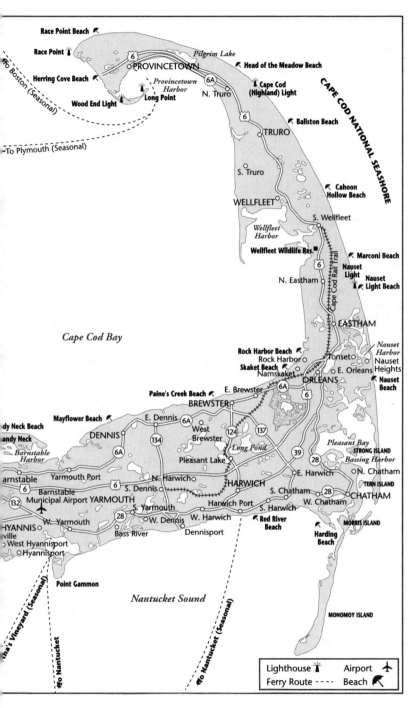

of the sea and have their own beaches, harbors, marshes, and seaside pastimes.

On the northern side of the historic green of old Falmouth stands the tall white-steepled **First Congregational Church.** When the church was built in 1796, it stood right on the green, but was moved to the present location in 1858. It is said that its bell was cast by Paul Revere. On the same side of the green are several historic homes, including the **Julia Wood House,** 55–65 Palmer Ave. on the Village Green (☎ 508/548-4857), which serves as the **Falmouth Historical Society** headquarters. It's open June 15 to September 15, Wednesday to Sunday from 2 to 5pm. Admission is $2 for adults, 50¢ for children. The **Conant House** (1724) next door is a weathered shingle house with the original glass windows.

On Main Street, browse the stores—the **Seven Winds** for antiques, a couple of galleries, **Maxwell's** for good quality casuals, **Eight Cousins** for children's books, **Colonial Candle,** and the **Quaker Bonnet** for ceramic and other gifts. Step into **Ben and Bills Chocolate Emporium,** with its overpowering aroma of chocolate and sugar, where the ice cream churns are turning in the window and dozens of assorted chocolates delight the eye and tempt the palate.

Another institution that lends cachet to Falmouth is the **Falmouth Playhouse,** which opened in 1949 with Tallulah Bankhead playing in *Private Lives,* produced by Richard Aldrich, husband of Gertrude Lawrence.

Before leaving town, turn right on Scranton Street and explore **Falmouth Harbor.** Return to 28 and, before coursing east along the shore, turn down the road that runs along the eastern rim of the harbor and through **Falmouth Heights,** one of the state's first-ever summering places and the site of a Christian Culture Camp in 1891. Here are grand old Victorian summer homes fronting the long sandy beach off Grand Avenue. Beach lovers who like to just fall out of bed onto the beach will want to anchor here at one of the inns.

Back on Route 28, if you continue east, you'll come to **East Falmouth** and eventually to Waquoit Bay, famous for its oysters. East Falmouth was settled by the Portuguese and has retained traces of their culture. They pioneered strawberry growing in the 1920s and 1930s and also picked the cranberries that were abundant in the local bogs. Visit the research facility at the **Waquoit Bay National Estuarine Reserve,** P.O. Box 3092 (☎ 508/457-0495), where you can hike the trails and camp on **Washburn Island.** It covers 2,250 acres in Falmouth and Mashpee and protects salt ponds, salt marshes, and barrier beaches and forest where piping plover, least tern, and osprey live. Also in East Falmouth, the Massachusetts Audubon Society operates the **Ashumet Holly and Wildlife Sanctuary,** north of Route 151 and Currier Road (☎ 508/563-6390). You'll find self-guided nature trails and a swallow colony here.

Beyond East Falmouth, **Mashpee** could be said to have been the first Indian reservation created in North America—the Wampanoags established a claim to their land with the help of a Christian priest, Richard Bourne, in 1660. A legend about the origin of the cranberry is attached to his name—according to the story, a medicine man once cast a spell on Bourne, miring his feet in a bog. There followed a contest of wills that lasted 2 weeks, and during his ordeal, Bourne received a little moisture from an occasional cherry brought

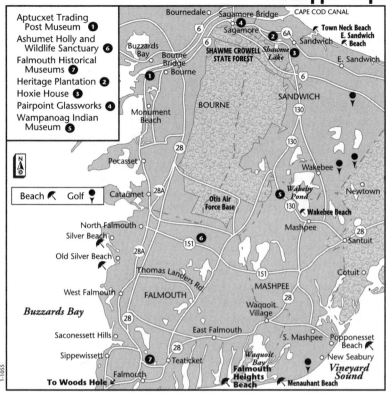

The Upper Cape

Aptucxet Trading Post Museum **①**
Ashumet Holly and Wildlife Sanctuary **⑥**
Falmouth Historical Museums **⑦**
Heritage Plantation **②**
Hoxie House **③**
Pairpoint Glassworks **④**
Wampanoag Indian Museum **⑤**

CAPE COD CANAL
Bournedale
Sagamore Bridge
Sagamore
Town Neck Beach
E. Sandwich Beach
Sandwich
Buzzards Bay
Bourne Bridge
SHAWME CROWELL STATE FOREST
Shawme Lake
E. Sandwich
Bourne
BOURNE
SANDWICH
Monument Beach
130
130
Pocasset
Wakebee
Newtown
Beach ☈   Golf ☇
Cataumot
28A
Wakeby Pond
130
Otis Air Force Base
Wakebee Beach
North Falmouth
Mashpee
28
Silver Beach
Santuit
Old Silver Beach
28A
151
Thomas Landers Rd
151
Cotuit
West Falmouth
FALMOUTH
MASHPEE
28
Buzzards Bay
Waquoit Village
28
Saconessett Hills
East Falmouth
S. Mashpee
Popponesset Beach ☈
Sippewissett
28
New Seabury
Teaticket
Waquoit Bay
Vineyard Sound
Falmouth
To Woods Hole
Falmouth Heights Beach
Menauhant Beach

to him by a dove. At the end of it all, the cherry fell into the bog, giving birth to the Cape Cod cranberry.

Today you can visit a couple of Native American sites. **Mashpee Wampanoag Indian Museum,** Route 130 (☎ 508/477-1536), displays assorted Indian artifacts. The **Old Indian Meeting House,** Route 28 (☎ 508/477-1536), which dates to 1684, is one of the oldest Indian mission churches still standing. See the interior with its box pews and organ gallery and other memorabilia of this mission to the Indians. The museum is open year-round, Tuesday to Saturday from 10am to 2pm; the meeting house is open only to groups and only by appointment.

Shopping gurus will want to visit **Mashpee Commons,** one of the proverbial contemporary outlet centers.

West Falmouth lies on Route 28A, northwest of historic Falmouth. The town is quiet and gracious, a typical New England village that was settled by Quakers who had fled persecution in Barnstable and Sandwich. Many of the settlers were whalers and merchants. You can browse in the cluster of antiques stores along Route 28 plus a gallery or two before meandering along the coastline that threads in and out, offering myriad beaches and sunset vista points. It's jagged and irregular like jigsaw-puzzle pieces, indented with inlets, coves, and ponds that are filled with water that seems to lap at the land so closely and intimately that you expect it to flood over at any moment. For a sweeping view of Buzzards Bay, find your way out to the **Knob.** To get there, take the road to the small, scenic Quisset Harbor and hike the path to the Knob. Farther north lies **Old Silver Beach** and North Falmouth.

Even if you have never heard of a Cape Codder, you are probably familiar with Ocean Spray cranberry juice, the juice of a fruit that is harvested from the bogs of New England. Although we associate cranberries with their rich crimson hue, they were in fact named after the crane, whose head the flowers (that bloom in June) were thought to resemble. Hence, they were called "crane berries," which later became cranberries. They grow through the summer, swelling and ripening in August and September until October, when they are harvested by a machine that rakes the fruit from the plants. The berries are sifted from the leaves and other contaminants, crated, and then lifted from the bog by helicopter. This so-called dry harvesting method is used to produce fresh or frozen berries. Fruit for juices and sauces is wet harvested. The bog is flooded and the crop is picked by eggbeaters, or water reels, that cause the berries to float to the surface, creating that beautiful palette of crimson that you will often see in harvest season. The berries are then corralled in and pumped ashore into a hopper that separates the fruit from other debris before delivering it to a truck that takes it to the packing plant.

Woods Hole lies a few miles southwest of Falmouth. On the way, take some time to detour off Woods Hole Road to **Nobska Light** (1829) just for the coastal view. Although Woods Hole is primarily known as the port where you catch the ferry to Martha's Vineyard, it has much more to offer the visitor. Here, in 1602, explorer Bartholomew Gosnold landed, and if you take School Street behind and around Eel Pond to Gosnold Road, you'll see a marker memorializing the event. The town was an old whaling and fishing port, and it continues to derive its living from the ocean. Gone are the candle factories and the once-stinking guano works. Here in their stead are several marine fishing institutions of international renown.

The **Marine Biology Laboratory** (☎ 508/548-3705 or 508/289-7623) is the oldest marine lab in America. It grew out of some informal gatherings of students in 1873, led by Harvard professor Louis Agassiz. The laboratory was formally established in 1888. It has been directed by many august scientists, including Dr. Frank Lillie, who was director from 1908 to 1926. It serves as an international center for teaching and research in biology or life science. Tours are given, but you'll need to reserve well in advance.

The **Woods Hole Oceanographic Institute** was founded in 1930. Perhaps its most famous employee is *Alvin,* the deep-sea diving two-person submarine that discovered a hydrogen bomb off the coast of Spain in 1966. Its most famous discovery, however, has to be the *Titanic* in 1985. Drop into the institute's **Exhibit Center** on School Street (☎ 508/457-2000, ext. 2252), which shows videos and has a display about *Alvin.*

The **National Marine Fisheries Aquarium**, Water Street (☎ 508/548-7684) is a small aquarium with only about a dozen tanks containing a variety of marine creatures. Fun for the kids. The aquarium is open from mid-June to mid-September, daily from 10am to 4pm; weekdays only the rest of the year.

On the main street, browse the stores. Among the more interesting are **Handworks,** 68 Water St. (☎ 508/540-5291), which stocks attractive craft items.

FALMOUTH LODGING

Right near the historic green, **Mostly Hall,** 27 Main St., Falmouth (☎ 508/548-3786), is sheltered from the road by rhododendrons and tall trees. The odd name is supposedly derived from an apocryphal story that tells of a visiting child who remarked spontaneously on stepping into the center hall, "Why Daddy it's mostly hall." Certainly the entrance hall is impressive.

The house is designed in an Italianate style with a cupola and was built in 1849 by Albert Nye. The wide front porch, furnished with wicker, wraps around the entire house and overlooks the lawn and a lovely flowering cherry and dogwood. The very elegant interior has high ceilings and floor-to-ceiling windows with shutters. The sitting room glows with peach-colored walls and is furnished with a mixture of rockers, Victorian sofas, gilded mirrors, and several antique clocks. The oriental rugs and the black marble fireplace add a dash of splendor. Breakfast is served at one end at a long, elegant Georgian table. Fruit, breads, and such dishes as eggs Benedict soufflé are the order of the day.

Two staircases lead up to the six spacious corner rooms, which are all handsomely decorated using fine wallpapers, wall-to-wall carpeting, and oriental rugs, plus pedestal or marble sinks in the bathrooms. In one room you might find a Tudor-style four-poster, in another a rice four-poster. Tucked away on the top floor is the cupola to which guests can retreat for a game of chess or to watch some TV.

The acre of grounds stretches far back, and guests can loll in the gazebo and admire the venerable shade trees that stand on the property. Bikes are available. Rates: May 23 to October 25, $115 to $130; off-season $95 to $105.

The Inn at One Main Street, 1 Main St., Falmouth (☎ 508/540-7469), stands on the corner of 28A. The elegant shingled Victorian with a witch's cap turret stands behind a picket fence and gardens and is run by friendly innkeepers Mari and Karen. All six rooms have been nicely decorated with floral or candy-stripe wallpapers; lace curtains; and furnishings such as oak dressers, trunks, wicker rockers, and braided rugs. Room 5, which has been spongepainted in lemon yellow, is very bright and appealing. Breakfast features dishes such as lemon soufflé pancakes or chili cheese soufflé. Rates: $90 to $125.

Village Green Inn, 40 Main St., Falmouth, MA 02540 (☎ 508/548-5621), occupies a very historic home that belonged to Braddock Dimmock, deacon of the First Congregational Church and son of the man who raised the militia and defended the town against the British in 1779. It's been a bed-and-breakfast since 1986 and is operated by Don Crosby, a former teacher, and Diane, who works as a nurse. Guests enjoy gathering around the fireplace in the small parlor. Furnishings are comfortable, and there's even a piano for the musically inclined. There are five rooms. The two ground-floor rooms have wood-burning fireplaces. The Crocker Room (the house was also in the Crocker family) has a beautiful inlaid marquetry floor as well as a brick fireplace. The Long Room's pencil four-poster is dressed with a wedding ring quilt, and the room is made even more striking by the tin ceiling and the square-panel mahogany wainscoting. All rooms have small cable TVs. Breakfast will bring an assortment of breads and perhaps a fresh cranberry compote followed by something like apple-cinnamon French toast. From the front porch of the house, there's a fine view of the green. The grounds are graced with a spectacular carriage house and dovecote. Bicycles, beach towels, and sand chairs are available. Rates: $95 to $155.

The **Palmer House Inn,** 81 Palmer Ave., Falmouth, MA 02540 (☎ 508/548-1230), just west of the green, occupies a turn-of-the-century turreted home and converted carriage house. The interior of the main house has architectural elements like stained glass windows and fine woodwork. There are 12 rooms. Those in the carriage house are more spacious and have larger bathrooms than those in the main house. They're furnished with rice four-posters with crocheted canopies, two wing chairs, and amenities such as small refrigerators, cable TVs, and telephones. Some have Jacuzzis. Walls are covered in bold floral papers. Rooms in the main house are idiosyncratic. One might contain a sleigh bed, another a canopied bed. The top floor rooms are tucked under the eaves and have great character. There's also a Tower Room decorated in burgundy and blue and furnished with a brass bed, wicker chairs, and table. All are very appealing. In addition, there's a suite at the back of the property, in a house (with deck and garden) that was moved here in 1925.

Guests enjoy reading or relaxing in the living room, in front of the brick fireplace or on the inviting window seat. The cockatoo, and Jamie, an African gray parrot with a 150-word vocabulary, are the entertainers. A full candlelit breakfast is served in a room decorated with all manner of historical souvenirs, tools, and kitchenware. Orange-strawberry or apricot-orange and other blended juices accompany dishes such as eggs with chives and cinnamon biscuits, plus fresh fruit and cereal. Rates: Mid-June to mid-October, $115 to $195; May to mid-June and mid-October to late October, $98 to $175; November to April, $88 to $160.

The **Captain Tom Lawrence House,** 75 Locust St., Falmouth, MA 02540 (☎ 508/540-1445) is named after a whaling captain who built it in 1861. On the road that leads to Woods Hole, it stands well shielded from the road by a privet hedge and some venerable maple trees. It's a handsome Italianate house with widow's walk and meticulous detailing, including carved scrolled brackets and an original spiral staircase with coffin nook. The rooms are well decorated with fine-quality linens and fabrics throughout. Mate's room is decked out in rich dark purple. Alto possesses a bed with a lace canopy. There's also an apartment that is ideal for families; it has an outside private entrance and a kitchenette.

Innkeeper Barbara Sabo-Feller was raised in Germany and comes from the Black Forest. At breakfast she prepares specialties such as German pancakes with apples and cinnamon or quiche Gisela and serves them at an elegantly set table. Guests can relax in the comfortable sitting room with its fireplace and even play the Steinway grand if so moved. Rates: June 16 to October 14, $108 to $145; January 1 to June 15 and October 15 to December 31, $95 to $105.

Right on the beachfront, the **Grafton Inn,** 261 Grand Ave. S., Falmouth Heights, MA 02540 (☎ 508/540-8688), is operated by friendly innkeepers Liz and Rudy Cvitan. The striking Victorian with a witch's hat turret was built by a wealthy Worcester manufacturer in 1850 as a summer home. The interior features details such as tongue-and-groove ceilings and wainscoting throughout. It's now filled with family heirlooms and art from Liz's days as a gallery owner. There are 11 rooms of all different sizes and shapes. Both Liz and her husband have traveled a lot and they are aware of the importance of details—

they provide everything that guests might need, even supplying noise eaters in the rooms to ensure an undisturbed sleep as well as amenities such as hair dryers, bathrobes, flashlights, nightlights, makeup mirrors, and full-length mirrors.

Each room is idiosyncratically and fetchingly decorated. Lace curtains adorn the windows, fine fabrics cover the furnishings, and heirlooms such as a drum table and trunk are found in the rooms. One room contains Liz's mother's dresser and Hitchcock bed plus a poem written by her above the bed. One of the appealing turret rooms has a wicker rocker that belonged to Liz's grandfather. Guests can relax around the hearth or play a game of backgammon or chess in the small living room. Wine and cheese are served at 5pm. The enclosed porch-breakfast room, where a buffet that might include eggs Benedict or waffles with strawberries is served, overlooks the ocean toward Martha's Vineyard. Rates: $105 to $179 summer; $85 to $145 winter.

Inn on the Sound, 313 Grand Ave., Falmouth Heights, MA 02450 (☎ 508/457-9666), is refreshingly different and yet right on the beach. It's modern, offers large rooms and bathrooms, and bucks the historic traditional New-England-waterfront kind of ambience. The innkeeper formerly owned an art gallery, and the house is full of original art—in the sitting room are some brilliant pencil drawings of wildlife by Terry Miller. Guests gather here around the river-stone fireplace. There are five light and airy modern rooms with baths, all large enough to include sitting areas. Penzance Point is decked out in black and cream and features wicker chairs among its furnishings. Fiddler's Cove has white pickled floors. One room on the ground floor is a study in white on white, with a four-poster bed plus a fireplace. Breakfast consists of fruit and cakes and pastries, plus a hot entree like stuffed French toast or herbed eggs. Rates: Mid-June to mid-September, $115 to $150; mid-April to mid-June and mid-September to October 31, $95 to $130; November to April, $75 to $120.

Inn at West Falmouth, 66 Frazar Rd., off Route 28A, P.O. Box 1208, West Falmouth MA 02574 (☎ 508/540-7696), is a very secluded place, high on a hill overlooking Buzzard's Bay. It's located in a turn-of-the-century shingled mansion that is extraordinarily comfortable and very tastefully decorated with a mixture of oriental, English, and European antiques. Fresh flowers add color and romance throughout, oriental lamps light the rooms, and Moroccan carpets cover the floors. Most of the six spacious rooms have fireplaces and private balconies. All are furnished with four-posters and have marble bathrooms with whirlpool tubs. Guests can relax in front of the pink granite fireplace in the bright airy living room or bask on the upholstered furniture on the large screened-in porch or flower-filled deck. The gardens are lovely, and they shelter a small pool and clay tennis court. Rates: January to March, $155 to $235; May to October, $185 to $310; November to December and April, $175 to $260.

Guests come to the **B & B of Waquoit Bay,** P.O. Box 638, Waquoit, MA 02536 (☎ 508/457-0084), because of its location and because they appreciate the warmth of delightful hosts Tom and Janet Durkin. The tone is set by the living room, where you'll find a grand piano that is often played and also serves to display family photographs. Walls are adorned with brilliantly colored landscapes painted by daughter Pattee. In winter folks gather 'round the fireplace. The four rooms are fairly ordinary but perfectly comfortable. The ground floor room has modern built-ins plus a private stone terrace overlooking the Child's River. Sloping ceilings add character to the upstairs rooms, which have their own decks. A full breakfast, selected from an à la carte menu featuring eggs, omelets, and pancakes, is served on the porch overlooking the river or in the sitting room. Rates: $85 to $135.

The **Coppage Inn,** 224 Waquoit Hwy., Waquoit MA 02536 (☎ 508/548-3228) is named after Hilda Coppage, a member of a prominent family in the region. It has great historic ambience but needs some sprucing up. The new owners are working on this. The indoor pool is an unexpected plus for this kind of establishment. Guests also enjoy access to an attractive private brick patio furnished with statuary. There are five rooms. One ground-floor room has a canopied bed with an eyelet lace canopy and painted floors enhanced by rugs. Wing chairs, table, desk, and dresser complete the furnishings. The suite contains a working fireplace and a spool bed, along with a Federal-style highboy and Shaker-style sconces. Homemade breads and muffins, fresh fruit, and dishes like quiche or tomato and basil tart compose the breakfast. Rates: Mid-May to mid-October, $95 to $145; mid-October to mid-May, $80 to $105.

FALMOUTH DINING

Regatta of Falmouth by the Sea, Clinton and Scranton avenues, Falmouth (☎ 508/548-5400), is the special place to dine. It's right down at the entrance to the harbor and is splendidly decorated with much regal purple—purple napkins, rose tablecloths, and very elegant dinnerware. The food is assertively prepared using superb ingredients. For an appetizer that will set you dreaming, choose the pan-seared New England sea scallops with smoked salmon cream sauce, black American caviar, and summer leeks or the New York foie gras with Madeira and shiitake mushroom sauce, fresh spinach, and sweet potato crisps. There will be eight or so entrees, ranging from seared halibut with lobster wonton ravioli, wasabi in butter sauce with Asian greens and sticky rice, or veal T-bone with a roasted sweet garlic and thyme au jus, portobello mushrooms, and risotto. Prices range from $24 to $28. Desserts include fruits and sorbets, but if it's available, have the chocolate seduction with a sauce framboise. Open from 4:30pm to closing. Closed off-season.

My favorite dining place in the area is the **Chappoquoit Grill,** Route 28A, West Falmouth (☎ 508/540-7794). The locals love it, too, because it's refreshingly different from the typical Cape Cod seafood shack or the historic inn serving traditional New England fare. The cuisine is innovative and excellent, featuring specials such as horseradish encrusted salmon with mango salsa served on a huge pile of mashed potatoes or roasted garlic- and herb-encrusted pork tenderloin with a balsamic-port reduction. There are good specialty pizzas, pastas, and other dishes. Prices range from $9 to $16. The wine list offers a wide selection by the glass as well as by the bottle. The menu changes frequently to keep the many regulars happy. Service is friendly but efficient, and the rooms are attractively decorated in salmon pink and jade with decorative wooden fish suspended from the ceiling. The place, as they say, has a buzz. There's also a cafe (☎ 508/540-2239) serving light fare and breads and pastries. Open daily from 5 to 10pm; cafe open Monday to Saturday from 8am to 5pm.

At **Oysters Too,** 876 E. Falmouth Hwy. (Route 28) (☎ 508/548-9191), revelers gather in the large and comfortable bar to listen to jazz on Saturday night. The emphasis here is clearly on seafood—seafood fra diavolo, swordfish with herb butter, fried oysters—leavened by such dishes as veal marsala and chicken Oscar. A raft of specials is also presented daily, often featuring several different lobster dishes. Prices range from $13 to $17. Open daily for dinner 5 to 9pm. Closed Monday and Tuesday in winter.

Although the decor at the **Flume,** Lake Avenue, Mashpee (☎ 508/477-1456), is very plain, the food is actually good, especially the fish dishes. It's out in the woods, and it's owned by the Wampanoags, as the decor's portraits and other artifacts suggest. Start with a bowl of clam chowder or some shellfish or fried smelts. Follow with one of the fish dishes—swordfish broiled with anchovy butter, scrod with lemon butter, or scrod Creole en casserole. Other dishes include steaks and pot roast or chicken pie. Prices range from $9 to $21 (the last for the lobster Newburg). This is the place to try some real Indian pudding. Open Monday to Saturday from 5 to 9pm, Sunday from noon to 8pm. Closed Thanksgiving to April 1. To get there from Route 28, at the Mashpee rotary circle, take Great Neck Road to Route 130. The restaurant is on Lake Avenue, just off Route 130; you'll see a sign.

Nimrod, 100 Dillingham Ave. (☎ 508/540-4132), is very Cape Cod. It's a fun place with jazz 6 nights a week. The menu offers a variety that will satisfy every palate. You can have grilled shrimp in a ginger citrus vinaigrette, or Szechwan chicken, or steaks. Prices range from $12 to $22. Open daily from noon to 1am.

Laureen's, 170 Main St. (☎ 508/540-9104), is a casual down-home place where the tables are spread with green gingham. A good lunch stop, it's known for its feta pizzas, topped with ingredients like pesto, tomatoes, black olives, and mozzarella, or meatballs. There are also sandwiches and salads. Prices range from 5 to $10.

The Quarter Deck, 164 Main St. (☎ 508/548-9900), is a typical seafaring-town restaurant—dark and polished with ships' wheel tables. The menu reflects a salty bias with regular seafood specials—the house specialty is a baked seafood platter of stuffed shrimp, scrod, scallops, clams casino, and oysters Rockefeller. More humble dishes, like fish and chips, also appear, along with a range of meat dishes from barbecue ribs to veal parmigiana. Prices range from $12 to $17. It's also a good lunch spot for soup and sandwiches. Open daily for lunch and dinner. Open Sunday to Thursday from 11:30am to 10pm, Friday and Saturday from 11:30am to 10:30pm.

Right down at the entrance to the harbor beside the Regatta, the **Clam Shack,** 227 Clinton Ave. (☎ 508/540-7758), is the place to pick up a lobster roll or a dish of fried or fresh clams. Take them outside and find a table dockside. Open Memorial Day to mid-September.

Billy Weaner's Silver Lounge, 412 Rte. 28A, North Falmouth (☎ 508/563-2410), is a casual publike restaurant where you can enjoy decent chili, fish and chips, burgers, sandwiches, steaks, ribs, and many shellfish and fish dishes such as baked scrod or scallops en casserole topped with Monterey jack cheese. Prices range from $10 to $17. The dining rooms have a nautical atmosphere created by model boats, ship's lanterns, and other effects, but most of the items are placed above the rafters so that the effect is not overwhelming or overdone. On cold days a fire burns in the stone hearth. This place has been going strong since the 1950s, and it's still popular. Open daily from 11:30am to 1am.

In Woods Hole there are several dining possibilities. For a real salty experience, go down the alley to **Shucker's Raw Bar,** 91 Water St. (☎ 508 /540-3850) and sit outside, overlooking the action on Eel Pond. Have a plate of fresh tangy littlenecks or quahogs or some great shrimp.

Landfall, Luscombe Avenue, Woods Hole (☎ 508/548-1758), is another very nautical place right down on Vineyard Sound by the ferry docks. Floats, buoys, pulleys, and block-and-tackle dangle from the ceiling, and the bar is part skiff. Much of the decor has been rescued from local landmarks, while the amphora that hangs from the rafters was actually pulled from the Aegean Sea. It's a fun place to enjoy the seafood delights that dominate the menu. Among the specialties, the halibut filet with sweet red pepper and pineapple chutney is particularly good, but then so is the pan-blackened red snapper with a citrus fruit compote. More traditional dishes, like baked stuffed lobster and broiled scrod, and a fisherman's platter brimming with scrod, scallops, clams, and shrimp are also offered. For those who don't like seafood, there are a couple of steaks and a chicken dish. Prices range from $15 to $23. Open mid-April to October, daily 11:30am to 10pm.

The Dome, Woods Hole Road (☎ 508/548-0800), is up the hill from town and is notable for having been designed by Buckminster Fuller. It's fancier in both style and cuisine than most other Woods Hole restaurants. Under the dramatic tented ceiling, you can sample from a menu featuring duck with black raspberry sauce, chicken Kiev, and prime rib and steaks. Prices range from $14 to $26. Open mid-April to mid-October, Tuesday to Sunday from 5:30 to 10pm.

BOURNE & SANDWICH

On your way to Falmouth, you will cross the Bourne Bridge over the Cape Cod Canal or the Sagamore Bridge on Route 6, which also brings you into Bourne. Either way, **Bourne** is the first community that most visitors encounter on the Cape, and it was the first place where the Plymouth Colony decided to set up a post, on the Manomet River, to trade with the Dutch in New Amsterdam and the French along the Connecticut River. Today there is little to draw the visitor to Bourne except for the **Cape Cod Canal** that affords opportunities for hiking, biking, and in-line skating along its banks and the replica of that early 1627 trading post, the **Aptucxet Trading Post Museum,** Aptucxet Road, Bourne (☎ 508/759-9487). The museum also features the small, private railroad station that was built in 1892 for President Cleveland, who used to summer at his nearby fishing lodge, Gray Gables. Open May 1 to Columbus Day, Tuesday to Saturday from 10am to 5pm; Sunday from 2 to 5pm.

The canal was dreamed of as early as 1624, but it wasn't until 1883 that a company actually started digging it. It took another 30 years to finance and complete the project. It opened in 1914, and while it did cut 70 to 100 miles off the route around the Cape, it was not deep enough to accommodate large vessels and so proved a financial disaster—an engineering feat that also was soon made obsolete by more advanced and cheaper forms of transportation.

Bourne was originally part of Sandwich, which lies east of Bourne on the bay side of the Cape. Sandwich is a delightful, historic town. Lacking a harbor, it's less of a seafaring place and more of a commercial manufacturing town than Falmouth, but the industries that flourished here were preindustrial and left no blight on this serene, beautiful village.

Sandwich was founded in 1637 by Edmund Freeman. Along with nine others, he trekked from the Plymouth Colony to carve out this settlement. At first it was called Manomet, but changed its name to Sandwich 2 years later. A Congregational church was established, but the colony was plagued by religious disputes between the Episcopalians, the Quakers, and the already-established church.

The settlers cleared the land and farmed and fished and also went "shore whaling"—dead whales sometimes washed ashore, and the settlers were able to make money from the oil. Soon they were driving the whales into the shore and turning shore whaling into a little business—until the whales departed.

There were two prime industries: glassmaking and vehicle manufacture. To get some idea of the role that glassmaking played in the history of Sandwich, head for the **Sandwich Glass Museum** (☎ 508/888-0251). Here you can see samples of the glass manufactured in the 19th century. Some good audio-visuals explain glassmaking techniques, and you can even try your hand at making it. Admission is $3.50 for adults, $1 for children 6 to 12. Open April to October, daily from 9:30am to 4:30pm; November, December, February, and March, Wednesday to Sunday 9:30am to 4pm. Closed January.

Glass lovers will want to visit the **Pairpoint Glass Works**, 851 Sandwich Rd., on Route 6A in nearby Sagamore (☎ 508/888-2344). The glassworks is open Monday to Friday from 8:30am to 4:30pm; the gift shop is open daily.

The village focuses on Shawme Lake, and around it are several historic homes including the house said to be the oldest on the Cape, **Hoxie House,** at 18 Water St. at School Street (☎ 508/888-1173), built in 1675. Its tiny windows and thick walls suggest that the early settlers lived in fear of attack. **Dexter's Grist Mill,** dating to 1654 stands beside the brook that feeds the lake. It has been restored and grinds the corn with its wooden mechanisms just as it did back then. Hoxie House is open from early June to mid-October, Monday to Saturday from 10am to 5pm and Sunday from 1 to 5pm. Dexter's Mill is open from mid-June to mid-September, daily from 10am to 4:30pm.

Next to the grist mill, the **Thornton Burgess Museum,** Water Street (☎ 508/888-6870), features memorabilia of the author who gave us "Peter Rabbit and the Briar Patch," among other *Bedtime Stories,* and also created characters such as Jerry Muskrat, Reddy Fox, Sammy Jay, Buster Bear, and Bowser the Hound. Burgess was born at 6 School St. in 1874. His first book, *Old Mother West Wind,* was published in 1910, but *Bedtime Stories* remained his most popular work.

The first parish meeting house, established in 1638 at Main and River streets is occupied today by the **Yesteryears Doll Museum** (☎ 508/888-1711). Doll fanciers will want to see this international collection of dolls, dollhouses, doll furnishings, and accessories. Open mid-May to October, Monday to Saturday from 10am to 4pm.

Although **Heritage Plantation,** Grove and Pine streets (☎ 508/888-3300) appears at first blush as hokey, it really isn't. This estate belonged to Charles Dexter, who commissioned landscape designer Paul Frost to lay out the gardens in 1916—the gardens alone are worth the visit. The owner lent his name to the Dexter Rhododendron, which bloom here from mid-May to mid-June. The museum, however, was established in honor of Josiah Kirby Lilly by the Lilly family and consists of a number of buildings and replicas that have been erected on the property. In the Round Barn, you'll find a dazzling display of antique cars. They positively glow with glamour—the icon of the jazz age, a 1915 Stutz Bearcat; the 1931 Duesenberg built for Gary Cooper; and Mrs. J. K. Lilly's 1962 Rolls Silver Cloud II convertible. Another building contains the restored Looff Carousel which used to be in Crescent Park, Rhode Island. Downstairs, there's a collection of stunningly beautiful Elmer Crowell's bird carvings and charming miniatures. Open mid-May to October, daily from 10am to 5pm. Admission is $8 for adults, $7 for seniors, $4 for children 6 to 18. Take Route 6A to Route 130.

There are also several sites worth visiting in East Sandwich. Hikers and nature lovers will enjoy the **Green Briar Nature Center,** off 6A on Discovery Hill Road (☎ 508/888-6870). There are nature trails open to the public. If you'd like to see how jams and jellies are made and purchase some on the spot, then go into the Green Briar Jam Kitchen, at the same location. Open Monday to Saturday from 10am to 4pm, Sunday from 1 to 4pm.

Several generations of the Nye family operated mills in the area and at 85 Old County Rd. (☎ 508/888-2368), you can visit the **Nye family homestead.** The original part of the house dates back to 1685, and the house is arranged to show visitors the additions and structural changes that have been wrought over the years. Don't miss the chimney room. Open mid-June to mid-October, Monday to Friday from noon to 4:30pm.

Another prominent family's home is the **Wing Fort House,** 69 Spring Hill Rd. (☎ 508/833-1540), which dates back to 1641. Stephen Wing was Sandwich's first Quaker. Open mid-June to late September, Tuesday to Saturday from 10am to 4pm.

On your way to Barnstable, the **State Fish Hatchery** on Route 6A is fun to visit, especially in the late fall when the fish are spawning.

SANDWICH LODGING & DINING

Seth Pope House, 110 Tupper Rd., Sandwich, MA 02563 (☎ 508/888-5916), sits high on a hill overlooking the pond. It's a fine historic home dating to 1699. Seth Pope was an itinerant peddler who did not have enough money or land to satisfy the town fathers. They asked him to leave, so he went to New Bedford, where he achieved financial and social success. He returned to Sandwich in 1699 and built this house for his son, and though he bought up much of the town, he spurned ever living there. The keeping room is loaded with atmosphere, featuring a paneled hearth with a beehive oven. The parlor was added in 1740 or 1750. It's a comfortable room, with a fireplace, a grandfather clock, and wing chairs or a sofa for reading or listening to music. A TV is available in an adjacent room, and an additional sitting room is upstairs. There are three sizable rooms, all with private baths. The Victorian room sports a Victorian period bed, a marble-topped pier-style dresser, and an old armoire. From the windows you have a view of the salt marsh. The Colonial room is more in keeping with the original house. It has slanting, uneven floors, gunstock beams, and a four-poster combined with a solid cherry bonnet chest. Here breakfast is served by candlelight at a long refectory table. Rates: Memorial Day to Labor Day, $95; otherwise $85.

Capt Ezra Nye House, 152 Main St., Sandwich, MA 02563 (☎ 508/888-6142), is right in the center of town. Built in 1829, it's named after the sea captain who commanded the *Independence* and won even earlier fame as the man who steered the Jewel liner *Amethyst* from Liverpool to Boston in 20 days. There are nautical references throughout the house along with artifacts from the China trade. Above the brick wood-burning fireplace in the Blue Room hangs a portrait of a schooner, while in the parlor there's a collection of blue Chinese porcelain on top of the piano as well as a similar collection of Chinese export plates in the dining room. The idea of the collection was inspired by the porcelain shards that were found in the house's garden. The seven rooms all have rice or pencil four-posters with canopies and are nicely decorated with design accents like sponge-painted walls, stenciling, colorful quilts, and lace curtains. The largest room is the Blue Room, which has a carved mahogany four-poster and a working fireplace. The smallest is the Yellow Room, which features an antique sleigh bed. Rates: June to October, $85 to 110; November to May $85 to $105.

The Summer House, 158 Main St., Sandwich, MA 02563 (☎ 508/888-4991), is admittedly a perfect summer place, but despite the name, it's also great in the winter when the hearths are blazing. The Greek Revival house was built in 1835 and has been carefully restored. It's made even more appealing by the enthusiasms of the innkeepers, Kevin and Marjorie Huelsman. Both are musicians—he plays trumpet and she flute. Guests enjoy the parlor (with TV and board games), the back sunporch, and the hammocks in the lovely gardens filled with roses, tulips, phlox, and other flowers in season. There are five rooms, four with fireplaces. In the ground-floor front room, you'll find an iron four-poster with silk rose decoration set on a wide-board floor that has been painted a sage green and enhanced by an oriental rug. In another room, a carpet has been painted on the floorboards. A full breakfast—fruits, pastries, and omelets or eggs Benedict—is served in an inviting, cranberry-colored breakfast room with a black-and-white checkerboard floor. Afternoon tea is also offered from 4 to 6pm. Rates: summer, $85 to $105; winter, $75 to $95.

Isaiah Jones Homestead, 165 Main St., Sandwich, MA 02563 (☎ 508/888-9115), was built in 1849 for Isaiah Jones, who owned a tack factory in town. It has been carefully restored and maintained and contains several splendid rooms. The Sam Beale Room is spacious, thanks to the bay window, and yet the beamed ceiling gives it a cozy feel. It has a richly carved four-poster, oriental rugs on the floor, and swag drapes at the windows. Another room contains a carved Eastlake bed, while the Lombard Jones Room features a fireplace that uses alternative fuel, a bed with a fringed-corona above, and windows with balloon treatments; wicker furnishings, and a Jacuzzi complete the amenities. The Jarvis Room is extraordinary with its burled birch bed dressed in floral linens and a huge pier mirror, plus two rockers set invitingly in front of the fireplace. This room, too, has a Jacuzzi. There's a small parlor that has the original fireplace and deep window seats (and a small TV). Guest conveniences include a refrigerator. A candlelit breakfast and afternoon tea are served in the dining room. The front porch provides additional space in summer. Rates: May 23 to October 31, $105 to $170; November 1 to May 22, $85 to $140.

The Daniel Webster Inn, 149 Main St., Sandwich, MA 05463 (☎ 508/888-3622), is a modern motor inn, right in the center of the village, that replicates a building that used to stand on this spot. Although some of its 46 rooms and suites are arranged motel style, the inn does have character, mainly because of its lovely gardens in the back.

The rooms are attractively furnished with colonial-style reproductions—canopied beds, wing chairs, ceramic oriental lamps, and stenciled walls. All have TVs, telephones, and clock-radios, along with turndown and room service and a complimentary newspaper. The inn also offers four suites in the historic Fessenden House, two with fireplaces, all with whirlpool tubs. Rooms in the Quince Tree House have fireplaces and share a colonial-style sitting room; the bedrooms have hoop-canopied beds and colonial decor. Facilities include an outdoor pool entered via a lych-gate and complimentary access to a health club nearby.

The dining rooms are popular with the locals who enjoy both the tavern, located in the gardens, and the more formal dining room. The cuisine is contemporary American with such items as pan-seared halibut with a tamari ginger glaze; grilled sirloin topped with smoked red peppers and caramelized onions drizzled with balsamic vinegar; roast breast of chicken with cranberry sage stuffing; and rack of lamb in a port-and-blackcurrant sauce. Prices range from $12 to $25. The wine list is well chosen and features a number of good wines by the glass. More casual fare is served in the tavern. Rates: MAP: late May to late October, $121 to $154 per person; late October to early April, $100 to $126; early April to late May, $107 to 135. Room only: late May to late October, $139 to $209; late October to early April, $109 to $169; early April to late May, $129 to $189.

Falmouth, Mashpee, Bourne & Sandwich
Special & Recreational Activities

Beaches: Bourne: Monument Beach off Route 28 is free. **Falmouth:** The best with public parking include Old Silver Beach, Quaker Road, North Falmouth; Menauhant off Route 28 in East Falmouth; and Surf Drive in Falmouth. **Sandwich:** East Sandwich Beach, North Shore Blvd.; Town Neck, off Route 6A; and Wakeby Beach, South Sandwich Road.

Biking: The **service roads along the Cape Cod Canal** from Sandwich to Bourne (8 miles) off 6A afford some great biking. You can access them on the north side from Scusset State Park, the east side of the Sagamore Bridge, or the northeast side of the Bourne Bridge. South-side access points are from Sandwich near the boat basin and the U.S. engineers observation station, Pleasant Street in Sagamore, or from the southeast side of the Bourne Bridge. Another good bike path is the **Shining Sea Bike Path,** which runs between Falmouth and Woods Hole for 3½ miles (off Route 28).

Rentals are available at **P & M Cycles** (☎ 508/759 2830) and **Village Cycles** (☎ 508/759-6773) on Main Street in Buzzards Bay; and also at **Cape Cod Bike Rental,** 40 Route 6A, Sandwich, MA 02563 (☎ 508/ 833-2453).

Birding: **Ashumet Holly and Wildlife Sanctuary,** East Falmouth off Route 151 (☎ 508/563-6390) offers a 45-acre bird sanctuary. Guided nature walks are given.

Cruises: From **Falmouth Harbor** the schooner *Liberté* sails between July and the end of August (☎ 508/548-2626) on 2-hour cruises. From **Hyannis,** the catboat *Eventide* leaves from Ocean Street Docks from May through November for 1½-hour cruises. From **Woods Hole,** *Oceanquest,* Water Street, (P.O. Box 316) (☎ 508/457-0508), a fully equipped research vessel sails on 90-minute trps with professional educators and scientists aboard. It operates from mid-June through Labor Day, 5 days a week. Tickets are available at the dock on Water Street.

You can also cruise the **Cape Cod Canal.** In fact, you can kick off a weekend with a TGIF cruise or enjoy a Sunday jazz cruise, a sunset cocktail cruise, or a moonlight-and-music cruise. These cruises operate, along with day cruises, from mid-June to the end of August from the Onset Bay Town Pier (☎ 508/295-3883). Prices range from $7 to $13.

Fishing: From **Woods Hole** Harbor, *Susan Jean* is operated by Captain John Christian (☎ 508/548-6901); or contact Falmouth Fishing (☎ 508/ 548-2626) or Captain Bob MacGregor and his *Hop Tuit.*

Golf: The two top courses in the area are **Ballymeade Country Club,** 125 Falmouth Woods Rd. (P.O. Box 367), North Falmouth (☎ 508/ 540-4005), which has recently been revamped by Pete Dye, Brian Silva, and Tom Fazio; and the two courses at the **New Seabury Country Club,** Shore Drive, New Seabury (☎ 508/477-9111), that are only open to the public off-season. Other courses include the **Cape Cod Country Club,** Route 151, Hatchville, off Sandwich Road, North Falmouth (☎ 508/ 563-9842); the **Falmouth Country Club,** 630 Carriage Shop Rd., East Falmouth (☎ 508/548-3211); and the **Paul Harney Golf Course,** Route 151, East Falmouth (☎ 508/563-3454).

Hiking: Call the Conservation Commission (☎ 508/888-4200) for information on trails. **Green Briar Nature Center** (☎ 508/888-6870) has 57 acres with trails. **Ashumet Holly and Wildlife Sanctuary** (☎ 508/563-6390) and **Waquoit Bay National Estuarine Research Reserve** (☎ 508/ 457-0495) also have trails.

Horseback Riding: **Fieldcrest Farm,** Falmouth (☎ 508/540-0626); **Haland Stable,** West Falmouth (☎ 508/540-2552).

Sailing: For sailing information, contact Falmouth Recreation Department (☎ 508/457-2567) or Sandwich Recreation Department (☎ 508/ 888-4361)

Tennis: There are courts at **Taft's Playground,** Bell Tower Lane, in Woods Hole and at Nye Park in North Falmouth.

Wildlife Refuges: See "Hiking," above.

Windsurfing: Falmouth is the windsurfing mecca on Cape Cod. Contact **New England Windsurfing Academy,** Old Silver Beach, North Falmouth (☎ 508/540-8106).

Cape Cod—The Mid Cape

Barnstable ◆ *Hyannis* ◆ *Yarmouth & Yarmouth Port* ◆ *Dennis* ◆
West Dennis ◆ *Osterville* ◆ *Cummaquid* ◆ *Centerville* ◆ *Cotuit*

Distance in miles from Boston: Barnstable, 72; Yarmouth Port, 76;
Dennis, 80.

Estimated driving times: 1½ hours to Barnstable; 1½ hours to Yarmouth
Port; 1½ hours to Dennis.

◄○►◄○►◄○►◄○►◄○►

Driving: Take Route 3 to Route 6. Cross the Sagamore Bridge and take marked
exits for Barnstable, Yarmouth, and other points.

Plane: Business Express/Delta Connection (☎ 800/345-3400) flies from Boston or New York to Hyannis; Colgan Air (☎ 800/272-5488 or 508/775-7077)
flies from Newark and LaGuardia to Hyannis; Cape Air (☎ 800/352-0714 or
508/771-6944) flies from Boston to Hyannis and Provincetown.

Bus: Call Plymouth and Brockton Bus Lines (☎ 508/775-5524) for service
from Boston; Bonanza (☎ 800/556-3815) operates from Providence, Hartford, and New York to Bourne, Falmouth, and Hyannis.

Train: Amtrak from New York on weekends only.

Further Information: For further information, contact the **Cape Cod Chamber of Commerce,** Routes 6 and 132, P.O. Box 16, Hyannis, MA 02601
(☎ 508/362-3225).

Hyannis Chamber of Commerce, 1481 Rte. 132, Hyannis, MA 02601
(☎ 508/362-5230).

◄○►◄○►◄○►◄○►◄○►

With the exception of Hyannis on the southern shore, this section of the Cape
is one of quiet historic towns—Barnstable, Yarmouth Port, and Dennis. You
can amble along Route 6A, the original Old King's Highway, past ancient Dutch
elms and ancient homes and taverns, stopping at the occasional antiques store
or gallery or ducking down to a secluded beach or harbor. History is writ large
in each of these towns. Each one has its own distinctive flavor and makes a
perfect weekend getaway.

€vents & festivals to Plan Your Trip Around

May: Hyannis's Great Race weekend when the **Figawi Sailboat Race** from Hyannis to Nantucket is held. Call ☎ 508/778-1691 for information.

June: Hyannis Harbor Festival with the blessing of the fleet, sailboat races, and maritime exhibits. Call ☎ 800/449-6647 for information.

Cape Cod Book, Print, and Paper Show in Hyannis. Call ☎ 508/888-6870.

August: Two concerts, **Jazz by the Sea** and **Pops by the Sea,** take place in Hyannis. Call ☎ 508/790-2787.

Festival Days, Dennis. Fun for the family activities, including a kite-flying contest, canoe races, and crafts. Call ☎ 800/243-9920.

October: Yarmouth Seaside Festival, Yarmouth. Parades, fireworks, and sporting events. Call ☎ 508/778-1008.

November: Hyannis Harbor Lighting and Boat Parade, Hyannis. The boats parade with twinkling lights, and Santa arrives via lobster boat to open the Christmas season. Call ☎ 508/362-5230.

December: Yarmouth Port Christmas Stroll, Yarmouth Port. Stroll along Old King's Highway for open houses and caroling. Call ☎ 508/778-1008.

BARNSTABLE & HYANNIS

The arm of Sandy Neck wraps Barnstable Harbor in a protective embrace, and behind the harbor stretch the Great Marshes north of West Barnstable. It's an inspiring sight, and one that remains much as it was since the days when the Cummaquid Indians gathered on Sandy Neck to feast on the abundant lobsters, clams, and oysters. Take Millway down to the picturesque harbor and stroll through the salt marshes, watching the shore birds glide and whirl overhead. A timeless place.

Barnstable includes several communities in its boundaries——Barnstable, Cummaquid, Hyannis, Hyannisport, Osterville, and Cotuit. Barnstable has long been the administrative center, Hyannis the commercial center, and Cotuit and Hyannisport the social meccas.

John Lothrop arrived in Barnstable in 1639. The colony flourished under this powerful minister who had been drummed out of England because he had sought reform of the church. If you go to the **Sturgis Library** on Route 6A, which incorporates his second home, you can view a genealogical chart showing all his descendants. What an amazingly diverse group of people they are, with differing personalities and talents: Eli Whitney, Benedict Arnold, Henry Wadsworth Longfellow, Lewis Comfort Tiffany, Franklin Roosevelt, Marjorie Meriwether Post, Benjamin Spock, Dina Merrill, and George Bush. All these famous names can be traced back to this one remarkable man. The library (☎ 508/362-6636), built in 1644, is the country's oldest public library building. Lothrop's home was bequeathed to the library by a later occupant, William Sturgis, a ship's captain who was also a book lover. Sturgis left his book collection and a sum of money for the endowment of a free library. Also in the library you can see the Bible that was used aboard the *Mayflower* for the swearing of the Covenant, with a hole in a Bible passage that was burned by the wax from a candle aboard the ship.

To gain some sense of this early history, visit the **West Parish Meeting House,** 2049 Meetinghouse Way (Route 149), in West Barnstable. It was built in 1717 and is the second oldest meeting house on Cape Cod. The bell cast by Paul Revere still tolls folks to services.

For more historical information, visit the **Donald G. Trayser Memorial Museum** (☎ 508/362-2092), housed in the old Customs House (1856) on Route 6A. It contains a melange of paintings, toys, maritime artifacts, and other local objects. The Old County Jail (1690) has been relocated here, too. Open July to August, Tuesday to Sunday from 1:30 to 4:30pm.

There are several stores and galleries worth your attention in Barnstable. **Cape Cod Art Association Gallery,** Route 6A, Barnstable (☎ 508/362-2909), mounts shows by local artists and offers classes in all art media. **Harden Studios,** 3264 Main St. (☎ 508/362-7711), has some very fine American furniture, oil paintings, oriental art objects, and terrific rugs, plus a gallery featuring Harden's appealing etchings and watercolors of great blue heron, fish, birds, and landscapes. **Salt & Chestnut,** Route 6A at Maple Street in West Barnstable (☎ 508/362-6085), displays some wonderful antique weathervanes, both outside in the yard and inside. Each weathervane is an individual piece of folk art: A horse, a rooster, a fish, a whale, a mermaid, an angel, and more are represented. Prices range from $200 to thousands. At **Tern Studio,** Route 149, West Barnstable (☎ 508/362-6077), Albert Barbour crafts beautiful bowls and other woodware from cherry, walnut, maple, apple, catalpa, and Siberian elm. A real artist, he'll even make a hand-carved piecrust tilt-top table for a price. **Packet Landing Iron,** 1040 Rte. 6A, West Barnstable (☎ 508/362-9321), makes wrought-iron decorative and functional objects— wood carriers, lamps, candleholders, fireplace accouterments, and more, fashioned in a very fluid and beautiful manner.

Don't overlook **Cummaquid,** although you might just miss its tiny post office. It's named after the Mattakeese tribe of Cummaquid, and the bones of one of its chiefs, Sachem Iyanough, who assisted the Pilgrims when they first landed on Cape Cod, is buried here. Today there are several galleries and crafts studios that are well worth stopping in. **Cummaquid Fine Arts** displays a variety of fine watercolors, drawings, pastels, and oils that are far from the usual run-of-the-mill-art so often displayed in seasonal galleries. The gallery is located in an inviting 18th-century home. Don't miss **The Glass Workshop** and **Samuell Day Gallery** where Caryn Samuell makes her glass and displays upstairs in the barn some terrific work by other craftspeople and artists. The quality of everything here is very high, and the prices are very reasonable. Browse for gifts among the jewelry, glass, ceramics, and woodware. Caryn is happy to explain stained glass techniques and other glassmaking techniques. The setting, too, is lovely, with wisteria and a goldfish pond.

The Mid Cape

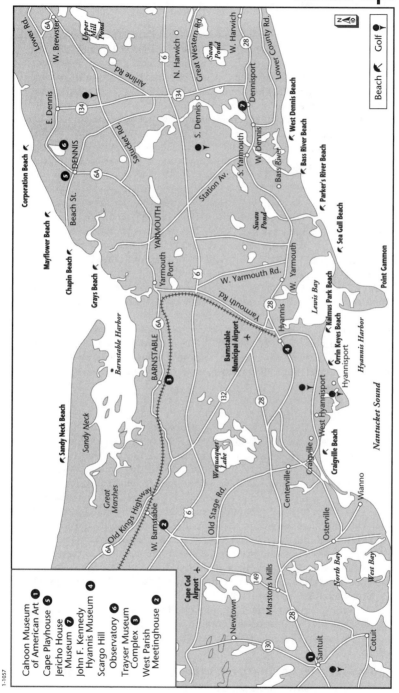

Beach � Golf ⛳

Cahoon Museum
of American Art ①
Cape Playhouse ⑤
Jericho House
Museum ⑦
John F. Kennedy
Hyannis Museum ④
Scargo Hill
Observatory ⑥
Trayser Museum
Complex ③
West Parish
Meetinghouse ②

1-1057

From West Barnstable, you can take Route 132 to Hyannis or the Old Stage Road south into Craigville/Centerville Harbor and Hyannisport. The southern strands of the Cape attracted summer visitors early on, and resorts developed around Centerville and Osterville and along the dramatic coastline overlooking Nantucket Sound. **Centerville** is a charming small village. It has a fine **historical museum** at 513 Main St. (☎ 508/775-0331), located in the historic home of Mary Lincoln, daughter of tinsmith Clark Lincoln. Its holdings include a fine collection of antique quilts and period costumes, marine and military objects, Sandwich glass, Elmer Crowell miniatures, paintings by Dodge MacKnight, and more. Open mid-June to September, Wednesday to Sunday from 1:30 to 4:30pm. Admission is $3 for adults, $1 for children 6 to 17.

Osterville is also a charming village. It's perhaps best known to the sailing community as the home of the boatyard that built the famous stabilized but fast *Crosby Cat*. Examples of these legendary wooden boats can be seen at the **Museum of the Osterville Historical Society,** West Bay and Parker roads. (☎ 508/428-5861). Antiques, art, and toys are also displayed, and special exhibitions arranged. Open Thursday to Sunday from 1:30 to 5pm.

A variety of shops along Main Street are worth browsing. Try the **Farmhouse** at 1640 Main St. and **Stanley Wheelock** at 870 Main St. for antiques.

Route 149 and Old Post Road will bring you south to Cotuit Bay, the source of the oysters of the same name. Also in Cotuit, the **Cahoon Museum of Fine Art,** 4676 Falmouth Rd. (☎ 508/428-7581), exhibits contemporary art. The core of the collection, however, has been built around works by American Impressionists and the primitive artists Ralph and Martha Cahoon. Open Tuesday to Saturday from 10am to 4pm. Admission is free. Cotuit also has its own **historical society** at 1148 Main St. (☎ 508/428-0461). It's open mid-June to mid-September, Thursday to Sunday from 2:30 to 5pm. Nearby **Marston's Mill** was the location of the first fulling mill on the Cape. Although the mill was destroyed, the herring run, the dam, and the site remain on Route 149.

Hyannis is a commercial center blighted by strip malls and highways. Kennedy fans will still want to visit the **John F. Kennedy Hyannis Museum** at 397 Main St. (☎ 508/790-3077 or 508/352-5230), which contains photographs, videos, and oral histories of the days that JFK and his family spent on Cape Cod. Open Monday to Saturday from 10am to 4pm, Sunday from 1 to 4pm. In addition, many visitors will want to pay their respects at the **memorial to John F. Kennedy** on Ocean Street—the presidential seal is set in a wall by a reflecting pool. The most dramatic part of the memorial is the setting, overlooking Lewis Bay, where the Kennedys did, and still do, sail. A summer attraction is the **Cape Cod Scenic Railroad,** which operates between Hyannis and Sandwich (☎ 508/771-3788).

For evening entertainment the **Cape Cod Melody Tent,** West Main Street (☎ 508/775-9100), hosts top-line comics and musical entertainers throughout the summer. It's been here since the 1950s, a major contributor to summer stock.

BARNSTABLE, CUMMAQUID & CENTERVILLE LODGING & DINING

A dignified sanctuary, **Ashley Manor,** 3660 Old King's Hwy. (P.O. Box 856), Barnstable, MA 02630 (☎ 508/362-8044), stands on 2 acres behind a privet hedge. Innkeeper Donald Bain is a retired attorney who has embraced the serenity of the Cape and uses some of his time to practice the art of furniture making. He's also a delightful host. The house was built in 1699 but has been added to in the 18th and the 20th centuries. It has a very comfortable air. Watercolors and plenty of books, along with the fireplace, grace the small parlor, which opens into a much larger second parlor with another open hearth. There are five rooms, four with fireplaces. All have coffeemakers and extras like fresh flowers and chocolates. The smallest room is the Federal. The Terrace does indeed have a terrace as well as a working fireplace. The Ashley Suite has a Georgian-style gaming table and other attractive antiques among the furnishings. Other rooms might have claw-foot lowboys or drop-leaf desks. Some of the furniture was crafted by Donald himself. Also on the property is a cottage suite with a wood-burning stove and a Jacuzzi tub. Breakfast is taken in the colonial-style dining room. A favorite spot is the terrace, set with umbrella tables and overlooking the large lawn and gardens with a fountain and a trellised gazebo. Facilities include a tennis court. Rates: $130 to $190.

The Acworth Inn, 4352 Old King's Hwy. (P.O. Box 256), Cummaquid, MA 02637 (☎ 508/362-3330) is terrific fun, thanks to owners Jack and Cheryl Ferrell, who really go out of their way for their guests. The cinnamon rolls and muffins that Cheryl produces at breakfast are legendary, and you can enjoy them in the kitchen or on the back deck along with a fabulous full breakfast. The inn occupies a 19th-century home with gardens and shade trees. The six rooms are refreshingly light, airy, and summery, all decorated in white or pastel palettes. The wide-board floors have been painted a gray-green; furnishings will likely consist of wicker and white-painted pieces. Watercolors by local artists hang on the walls. Bathrobes, sewing kits, and other extra amenities are nice touches. The most appealing room, with its own fireplace, is on the first floor. Guests may use the large, comfortably furnished sitting room, but most folks gravitate to the smaller den that has a large-screen TV with cable. No matter what, you're guaranteed a great weekend because Jack and Cheryl's enthusiasm is absolutely infectious. Bikes are available. Rates: mid-May to October $100 to $125; November to mid-May $85 to $115.

Set on 5 acres, **Waratah,** 4308 Main St. (P.O. Box 6), Cummaquid, MA 02637 (☎ 508/362-1469), is run by a warm, fun Australian-American couple, which helps explain the name. The *waratah* is in fact the state plant of New South Wales, and Garry and Nancy Hopkins have a dried sample on display in the living room in case you've never seen one. The 18th-century house stands behind stone walls surrounded by gardens and groves of Cape cedar. There are three rooms, two with baths. In the Blue Room, a scene showing a Dutch windmill was painted on the eaves by Basil Rathbone's wife when the Rathbones resided here. It has been comfortably furnished and has a small sitting area. There's also a very appealing two-bedroom cottage with a big, old raised fireplace in the living room. This is where Rathbone used to practice his lines. Personal collections adorn the common rooms. In the parlor, which has a fireplace with a beehive oven, you'll find a silver collection, family portraits, and some very good reading. A three-course breakfast (mangoes and kiwis, apricot muffins, Brie and herb omelets) is served either in the glassed-in porch or outside on the brick terrace. In the yard, hammocks invite some ease. A canoe is also available for use on Hallet's Mill Pond and Cape Cod Bay, which abuts the property. Rates: Memorial Day to Columbus Day, $95 to $230; less off-season.

The **Charles Hinkley House,** Old King's Highway at Scudder Lane (P.O. Box 723), Barnstable, MA 02630 (☎ 508/362-9924), is a most authentic colonial bed-and-breakfast in an 1809 Federal Colonial that was built by shipwright Charles Hinkley. The rooms feature lovely old paneling; sloping, creaking floors; and deep casement windows. The furnishings are fitting—oriental rugs, Martha Washington chairs, and wing chairs. All rooms have private baths, fireplaces, and four-posters. The Plum Suite contains a four-poster and has a separate plant-filled sitting room. Another room has a skylit cathedral ceiling and is decorated in muted mustard tones; it also has an antique brass bed. The Library Room contains a collection of fine old books and a couple of wing chairs in front of the fireplace for reading. A full breakfast—juices, breads, and items such as crab cakes with poached eggs—is served on plain wood tables in the dining room. Daffodils, grape hyacinths, and tulips blossom around the house in spring, and other seasonal flowers bloom the rest of the year under the tender care of the owners, Miya and Les Patrick, who have been innkeepers for 16 years. Rates: $129 to $159.

Only 2 miles from Sandy Neck Beach, **Honeysuckle Hill,** 591 Old King's Hwy. (Route 6A), West Barnstable (☎ 508/362-8418), is well named, given the large honeysuckle bushes that grow at the back of the property. It's a charming, well-kept shingled Victorian (ca. 1810) on 1.3 acres. Fieldstone walls and brick pathways add even more style to its appearance. There are four rooms (one is a two-bedroom suite), and all have hardwood floors covered with fetching rugs. Windsong has a light summery look with its jade painted floors and wicker loveseat. Sea Breeze is furnished with a wicker chest and a four-poster bed with quilt in pastel colors. Guests can relax on the stone porch or play some croquet on the lawn. Extra guest amenities include beach towels, beach chairs, and umbrellas plus a courtesy phone. The parlor has a terrarium of African violets, and books line its walls. Breakfast is served buffet style in the dining room. Egg dishes are supplemented by cereals, pastries, and breads. Rates: $125; $185 for the two-bedroom suite.

A magnificent 100-year-old weeping beech dominates the backyard of **Beechwood Inn,** 2839 Main St. (Route 6A), Barnstable, MA 02630 (☎ 508/ 362-6618). The house was built in 1853 in a Queen Anne style, with scallops, diamonds, and octagonal shingling and hints of Greek Revival. The interior has some great Eastlake styling. Some rooms have pressed tin ceilings or Palladian windows, while throughout the house you'll find beaded pine tongue-and-groove. Some of the six rooms have been dramatically furnished. For example, note the red velvet fainting couch in the Rose Room, and the glorious antique Italian mahogany armoire, not to mention the rice four-poster with a crochet canopy. The Marble Room overlooks the garden and is named after the beautiful marble fireplace. From the third floor, in Garrett, there's a view of Barnstable Harbor. Here a brass bed is covered with a unique and lovely quilt. Breakfast consists of three courses—muffins and breads, fruit, and dishes such as apple harvest pancakes or Hawaiian French toast, which combines Portuguese bread, chocolate chips, and pineapple. It's served in the dining room at individual lace-covered tables. Afternoon tea is also served. The parlor is arrayed in William Morris and Eastlake designs. Perennial gardens blossom over the 1¼ acres. Two golden retrievers will likely greet you when you arrive and take you past the porch, which is the most popular spot in the house. Rates: $135 to $160 summer; $100 to $140 winter.

The Inn at Fernbrook, 481 Main St., Centerville, MA 02632 (☎ 508/775-4334), is on a very quiet street in this very quiet village. The building stands back from the road behind shade trees and carefully groomed shrubs and hedges. Among the six rooms, the most remarkable is the one named in honor of Cardinal Spellman. It has its own private entrance and features large stained-glass windows, a tiled fireplace, and a pyramid-shaped ceiling. The canopied bed, antique bureau, and oriental carpets only add to its majesty. The Kalmus Suite, named after the inventor of Technicolor, has a sitting room in the turret. The Marston Room looks out on the rose garden and features a cherry four-poster. The third-floor suite has cathedral ceilings, two bedrooms, and a living room with a fireplace, plus a balcony overlooking the living room and a sundeck on the roof. There's also a cottage on the property with a wrap-around porch. A full breakfast of fruit, breads, and egg dishes is served in the formal dining room. The beautiful gardens include a trellis that's covered with wisteria blooms in the spring. Rates: summer, $145 to $205; winter, $115 to $175. The two-bedroom suite is $290 in summer and $230 in winter.

Inn at the Mills, 71 Cotuit Rd. (Route 149) at Route 28, Marston Mills, MA 02648 (☎ 508/428-2967), has some very appealing aspects, including the pool and the pond beyond it as well as the fine quality of the furnishings both in the rooms and in the public areas. There are six rooms, each furnished with lovely antiques. One has a maple serpentine canopied bed, a bull's-eye mirror, and a Federal lowboy. Another contains a highboy with a rich patina, finely upholstered wing backs, and some well-chosen original art. The large Hayloft Room has cathedral ceilings and a fully equipped kitchenette decorated with copper pots. In the parlor, a Victorian-style sofa, wing chairs, and a butler's table are all arranged around the fireplace. Another option for relaxing is the sunroom. An expanded continental breakfast is served in the dining room, which is, in fact, the converted stable. Rates: $95 to $135 (Note: The inn is so appealing that many couples hold their weddings here, and so weekends are often fully booked. If you can get away during the week, this is the one place to stay.)

Millway Fish and Lobster, Millway Harbor (☎ 508/362-2760) is a small operation down by the harbor and a terrific spot to secure some really good cuisine, believe it or not. Chef Ralph is an accomplished cook, and he displays some enticing dishes. The favorite is the seafood sausage, made with shrimp, lobster, and scallops. That's just a beginning. He has fashioned a dish that he calls "seafood bread," which is a hollowed-out, round Italian loaf layered with mushrooms, salmon, shrimp, and scallops, and finished with white wine. Other dishes include lobster manicotti, shrimp bisque, oysters Rockefeller, and salmon cakes with potato crust. They sell for $9 to $17 a pound. You can sit outside at one of the picnic tables or choose takeout and have a picnic nearby. Great food. Open from Memorial Day to Labor Day, daily from 10am to 7pm.

HYANNIS/COTUIT LODGING & DINING

Bill Putman, innkeeper at the **Simmons Homestead Inn,** 288 Scudder Ave., Hyannis Port, MA 02647 (☎ 800/637-1649 or 508/778-4999), injects a lot of fun into the business of innkeeping. He doesn't take himself too seriously, which makes for a very relaxing experience. Numerous sardonic signs are posted outside and inside—stating among other things that no dullards or miscreants are welcome. The inn was built in 1820 for Lemuel Simmons, a famous sea captain. It has all the original woodwork and the wide pine floors have been refinished. In the 10 bedrooms and the two-bedroom suite, Bill has come up with an unusual decorating theme. Every room is designed around a particular animal—giraffes in one, cats in another, and elephants or zebras in still others. Complementary furnishings include canopied or brass beds and other country pieces. Two of the rooms have working fireplaces, and one has a private deck. The back rooms, which were originally used as servants' quarters, are the largest accommodations. Here Bill serves a hearty breakfast that he doesn't pretend is gourmet. Swing seats await you on the wraparound porch, and hammocks are found in the garden. Guests gather for wine in the evening, and there's also a regulation-size billiard parlor and a sitting room with TV. Beer is available and so are gift vouchers for the local fast food outlets. Mountain bikes are available, plus beach chairs and towels. Rates: Mid-May through October, $150 to $185, suite $260; November to mid-May, $100 to $140, suite $170.

The **Regatta of Cotuit,** Route 28, Cotuit (☎ 508/428-5715) is located in the historic Crocker House and contains a series of small dining rooms. The menu is more extensive than you might expect, with eight or nine appetizers to choose from. They might range from a rewarding brandied lobster bisque crowned with chervil and crispy leeks, to a sauté of five wild mushrooms in a phyllo basket with a white wine sauce infused with shallots, marjoram, and sun-dried tomatoes. My choice among the entrees would be the roasted rack of lamb with the full-flavored pinot noir sauce, rosemary pesto, red onion jam, and buttermilk-chive whipped potatoes. Or on the lighter side, you might choose the seared sashimi tuna steak with a tamari and blood orange sauce, served with spring rolls and baby snap peas. It's adventuresome cuisine and those extra little touches—like the duck with a little balsamic vinegar in the orange sauce—make all the difference. Prices range from $19 to $25. The small bar up front has a pianist on weekends. Open daily from 5pm to closing.

The **Roadhouse Cafe,** 488 South St., Hyannis (☎ 508/775-2386), offers a fun dining experience. The restaurant hums in the piano bar on weekends. There is a warren of shiplike dining rooms, all with tongue-and-groove polished woodwork and brass. The fare is what you'd expect in this shoreline location: fresh oysters, littlenecks, and chowders plus grilled fish of all kinds, broiled scrod, baked salmon with a honey dill Dijon glaze, steaks, and some pasta dishes. Pizzas and sandwiches are also available. Prices range from $10 to $22; jazz is offered on Monday night. Open daily from 4pm.

Cooke's Seafood, 1120 Rte. 132, Iyanough Rd., Hyannis (☎ 508/775-0450), is the McDonald's of seafood. You order at the cash register and take the order of fried clams or crab rolls to your table.

The Paddock, West Main Street Rotary, Hyannis (☎ 508/775-7677), is a somewhat old-fashioned but atmospheric place that recalls the racetrack. The dining room and bar are dark and paneled. In the dining room, there's an odd mural that is placed outside the window, depicting a donkey feasting on oysters and shellfish. If nothing else, stop in the clubby velvet piano bar. The menu offers classic continental dishes—escargots and oysters or mussels to start, followed by dishes such as poached salmon with a beet vinaigrette and bearnaise sauce, sole Oscar, prime rib, lobster, rack of lamb with a gingered mint pesto, and several steak dishes. Prices range from $16 to $21. Open daily from 11:30am to 2:30pm and from 5pm until closing.

YARMOUTH & YARMOUTH PORT

This great seafaring town still has many of the historic homes that were built by its sea captains and shipwrights. The **Winslow Crocker House**, 250 Main St., Yarmouth Port (☎ 508/362-4385), was built in 1780 by Winslow Crocker who passed it to his son Watson in 1821; it was occupied by a member of the Crocker family right up to 1935, when Miss Mary Thacher purchased and restored it. Today it displays her collection of Federal furniture plus hooked rugs, ceramics, and pewter. The house itself is an architectural gem and the paneling and wainscoting of the interior is exceptional. Open June 1 to October 15, Tuesday, Thursday, Saturday, and Sunday from noon to 4pm. For information call SPNEA (☎ 617/227-3956).

The Greek Revival **Captain Bangs Hallett House**, 11 Strawberry Lane (off Route 6A), Yarmouth Port (☎ 508/362-3021), dates to 1840. The interiors contain antique furnishings and portraits of the owners, Captain Bangs and Anna Hallett. Open July and August, Thursday to Sunday from 1 to 3:30pm; June, September, and October, Sunday only.

Two other historic points of interest are the two windmills. **Baxter Grist Mill** on Route 28 in West Yarmouth (☎ 508/398-2231, ext. 292), was built in 1710 and worked until about 1900. It has been lovingly restored and functions with a turbine just as it did in 1860 when the wooden waterwheel was replaced. Open from June to September, Saturday and Sunday from 1 to 5pm. The **Judah Baker Windmill** on the Bass River in South Yarmouth was built in 1791 in Dennis and moved here later on, where it was used until 1890. It's currently being renovated and will eventually reopen to the public.

While you're in Yarmouth, do stop in and poke around the wonderful **Parnassus Book Service**, on Route 6A. It's an extraordinary place—books are piled everywhere, and the stock, which is vast, is not labeled, although it is organized. There's a good selection of titles in all fields, from local history to psychology and art. Other shopping musts include: **Kings Row Antiques**, 175 Main St. (☎ 508/362-3573), which sells fine early American furniture, paintings, pewter, china, and other decorative objects; **Minden Lane Antiques**, 175 Main St. (☎ 508/362-0220), which offers an eclectic array of objects including Victorian paintings; **Peach Tree Designs**, 173 Main St. (☎ 508/362-8317), a great place to browse for beautiful bed and table linens, cushions, photo frames, and other interior design accents; and **Wild Birds Unlimited** in the Hearth and Kettle Plaza on Route 28 in South Yarmouth for everything that a bird watcher or fancier covets, from binoculars to bird feeders—an ornithological orgy.

YARMOUTH PORT LODGING

The Inn at Cape Cod, 4 Summer St. (P.O. Box 96), Yarmouth Port, MA 02675 (☎ 800/850-7301) occupies a remarkable Greek Revival mansion with soaring Corinthian pillars supporting the front pediment. It stands on a small knoll right in old Yarmouth. The owners have decorated the common parlors with some grand European antiques—an antique French boule étagère, for example, and some fine art including some beautiful Dutch pastels. The 10 rooms, too, have been furnished exquisitely. In the Joshua Sears Room, you'll find a carved mahogany bed along with oriental rugs and floor-to-ceiling windows. The Library Room features a brass half-tester bed with a canopy. The Butler's Room is named after the walnut and bird's eye maple butler's chest and also contains a scrolled mahogany bed. One room has a fireplace. All have private baths, TVs, telephones, and bathrobes. A continental breakfast is served. Rates: Mid-June to Labor Day, $130 to $185; May 1 to mid-June and Labor Day to October 31, $110 to $160; November to April, $85 to $135.

    Wedgewood Inn, 83 Main St. (6A) Yarmouth Port, MA 02675 (☎ 508/362-5157) is surrounded by gardens filled with rhododendrons, tulips, daffodils, and more. The house was built in 1812. It has six rooms, all with private baths and all comfortably furnished. Several have fireplaces. Most have cherry-pencil four-posters decorated with antique quilts standing on wide-board floors. Furnishings range from acorn chests and treadle tables to chaise lounges, depending on the room. In the inviting parlor, oriental rugs cover the floor and ceramic lamps grace drop-leaf side tables. A full breakfast, featuring waffles, pancakes, or something similar is served at separate tables in the handsome dining room. Three rooms are being added in the barn on the property. Rates: $135 to $175.

    The **Captain Farris House,** 308 Old Main St., South Yarmouth MA 02664 (☎ 508/760-2818), is a 19th-century home with a porch running along the front facade. There are eight rooms, all with the following amenities: large private baths, cable TVs, phones with dataports, and hair dryers. Fresh flowers and original art are additional nice touches. The most extravagant room contains a carved maple bed combined with a large armoire and French-style sofa. Room 1 has an iron canopied bed, while Room 3 has a private entrance and a double Jacuzzi in the bathroom. Rooms 7 and 8 are loft style, with sundecks, fireplaces, and Jacuzzis. There's also a large one-bedroom suite with a double Jacuzzi, sundeck, and dining area with a small refrigerator. The public areas are more lavishly decorated than the rooms. French doors lead out into a picturesque courtyard set with metal tables, a statue or two, and a New Orleans–style fountain. Guests enjoy access to the open kitchen where spring water and cold drinks are always available, plus hot coffee. Breakfast is an elaborate three-course affair served on fine china and table linens. There's always fresh-baked breads and pastries, fruit, and main dishes such as stuffed French toast or a frittata. The marquetry sideboard and the chandelier add further elegance. The parlor, which features a grand piano and tasteful French-style antiques, is accented with a personal collection of tea cups. The 2-acre gardens are meticulously maintained. Rates: January 1 to mid-April, $110 to $125; mid-April to May 22 and mid-October to December 31, $125 to $150; May 23 to mid-October, $105 to $195.

Liberty Hill Inn, 77 Main St. (Route 6A), Yarmouth Port, 02675 (☎ 508/362-3976), was originally built by a whaling tycoon in 1825. The five rooms are attractively decorated with floral wallpapers and a mixture of wicker and other country pieces. You might find such nice accents as silhouettes on the walls or a striking stirrup lamp by the bed. The beds range from iron and brass to pencil four-posters, depending on the room. Top-floor rooms have a view of the bay. Breakfast—French toast with black raspberry sauce, fresh fruit, cereals, and pastries—is served at individual tables in the dining room. Guests have access to a refrigerator. Rates: Memorial Day to Columbus Day, $95 to $145; off-season, $75 to $120.

Crocker Tavern Bed & Breakfast, 3095 Old King's Hwy. Barnstable, MA 02630 (☎ 508/362-5115) is located in a historic 1754 tavern. The architectural detailing is extraordinary—paneling, window seats, iron door latches—and the furnishings only enhance the atmosphere. In the parlor stands a grandfather clock; above the mantel is a marine oil painting. The dining room has a lovely 18th-century antique painted hutch that houses a pewter collection. The rooms are all named after local historical figures. Julia Crocker features a rice four-poster with a crochet canopy, a fireplace, and such decorative accents as copper plates and candles with a snuffer. James Otis is decked out in deep colonial blue and furnished with an empire chest and reproduction highboy along with decoys, marine paintings, and more. Cornelius Crocker has an old wood stove and wooden icebox for decor. An expanded continental breakfast is served by candlelight at a harvest table set with fine china and crystal. The brick patio in the back is inviting and so are the lawn chairs on the 3.3 acres of wooded grounds. Beach towels and beach chairs are provided for guests. There's also a courtesy refrigerator. Rates: $95 to $120; some rooms are slightly less off-season.

YARMOUTH PORT DINING

abbicci, 43 Main St. Yarmouth Port (☎ 508/362-3501) occupies a 1755 building that has plenty of character. It's been made even more attractive by the addition of original art and sculpture in the several dining rooms. It offers fine contemporary Northern Italian cuisine. Some of the dishes are old favorites, like the veal Milanese with lemon and caper butter sauce or the saltimbocca alla romano; others are less common, like the sautéed calf's liver, balsamic-glazed sweet onions, and sautéed spinach; or the delicate spring rabbit braised in port wine with grapes and shallots and garnished with walnuts and garlic escarole. There is, of course, a full selection of pastas, from linguine with clams, spiced up with crushed chilies; and penne with roasted chicken, sun-dried apricots, thyme, spinach, walnuts, and cream. Prices range from $15 to $22. Open daily from 11:30am to 2:30pm and 5 to 10pm.

At the husband-and-wife-operated **Inaho,** 157 Rte. 6A, Yarmouth Port (☎ 508/362-5522), you can experience some of the freshest sushi and sashimi anywhere. If you enjoy Japanese cuisine, then have one of your dinners here. Try the fresh mackerel, octopus, and eel as well as the tuna—either at the sushi bar or at one of the wood tables separated by shoji screens. Other traditional Japanese dishes are also offered—tempura, teriyaki, and so on. Prices range from $13 to $21. Open Tuesday to Saturday from 5pm. Closed Sunday and Monday.

Aardvark, 135 Main St., Yarmouth Port (☎ 508/362-YUMM), occupies a remarkable Gothic revival home that has been painted in multicolored Victorian style. Here in the dining room where the wide-board floors have been retained and the high ceilings give an air of elegance, you can dine on good American fare modified by some distinct ethnic influences. For example, you might find a salmon that has been basted in miso sauce, grilled and served with oriental peanut noodles; however, you're just as likely to find a grilled swordfish with lemon scallion demiglace or a New York sirloin, both accompanied by delicious garlic "smashers." Pasta, kabobs, and sandwiches round out the menu. Prices range from $10 to $18. On one side of the building there's an old-fashioned cafe where you can pick up some terrific baked goods as well as light fare for breakfast or lunch. Open Monday from 7 to 10am, Tuesday to Saturday from 7am to 9pm, and Sunday from 9am to 9pm; off-season, Wednesday to Sunday for dinner and Sunday brunch.

A slice of real Americana awaits you at **Hallet's,** Main St., Yarmouth Port (☎ 508/362-3362). This soda fountain dates back a few decades as you can guess from its oak glass-fronted cabinets and pharmacy drawers. It serves some terrific ice cream, including black raspberry, plus floats, malteds, and ice cream sodas. Great breakfast spot, too. Open daily from 7:30am to 5pm.

DENNIS & WEST DENNIS

The Dennises (Dennis; East, South, and West Dennis; and Dennisport) straddle the Cape from the north shore to the south shore. On the north side, Dennis and East Dennis cluster around Scargo Lake and focus on such cultural institutions as the famous Cape Playhouse, while on the south shore the Bass River gives West Dennis and Dennisport their definition.

Dennis itself, on the north shore, was originally the east parish of Yarmouth. It was organized in 1721 and later incorporated and named after its first minister in 1793. Josiah Dennis, it seems, was well liked for his personality and whimsical humor even if he was somewhat absent minded. You can visit his **Manse** at Nobscuset and Whig streets (☎ 508/385-3528 or 508/385-2232), which was built in 1736. The oldest schoolhouse on the Cape (1770) stands on the same property. Open late June to August, Tuesday to Thursday from 2 to 4pm.

Dennis had its share of ancient mariners in the 19th century, who sailed the clippers and schooners, and their homes—half-Capes, Capes, saltboxes, and the grander sea captain's homes—can be found throughout the Dennises, representing a history of Cape architecture. Along 6A you'll find many such houses, identified by historic markers.

The Cape Cod Museum of Fine Arts, Route 6A, Dennis Village (☎ 508/385-4477), is part of a complex that includes the theater and cinema. The museum nurtures Cape Cod artists and is well worth visiting. The temporary show will doubtless be visually exciting, well displayed and interpreted. Downstairs, a very small portion of the permanent collection is on display. You'll find examples of works by contemporary Cape Cod artists and some of the Provincetown artists of the 1920s and 1930s. Open Tuesday to Saturday from 10am to 5pm, Sunday from 1 to 5pm.

The museum sponsors a **Secret Garden Tour** every year, usually at the end of June, which is a great way to view gardens and landscapes that visitors would not otherwise be privileged to see. In each garden, a horticulturist is on hand. Artists paint the garden scenes, too; their works are for sale and are also displayed at the museum. Reservations are required. Tickets go on sale on April 1, and the tour is quickly sold out, so book early.

It's worth going into the **Cape Cinema** (☎ 508/385-2503) next door just to see the 6,400-square-foot mural painted by Rockwell Kent. The **Cape Playhouse** (☎ 508/385-3838) is legendary among theater lovers. It was established by producer Raymond Moore in 1926, and many a famous performer has walked the boards here, including Henry Fonda and Anne Baxter, who made their professional debuts here. Gertrude Lawrence, who appeared here frequently between 1939 and 1950, was the most famous star associated with the theater. Other notables who worked here were Bette Davis, who was an usher, and Mel Ferrer, who was a stage manager. More recent stars include the late Jessica Tandy and Arlene Francis.

Do visit the **Grose Gallery**, 524 Rte. 6A (☎ 508/385-3434). Everyone in the family either paints, illustrates, or photographs. David Grose is famous for making limited edition prints of his watercolors of Cape Cod scenes, some of which are outstanding. I love his engravings and woodcuts. I also like his daughter Peggy's original oils. In addition, the gallery displays photographs by Margit, David's wife. You may be lucky enough to catch them silkscreening and observe the long process. Open daily year-round; winter from 10am to 4pm, from 10am to 5pm in summer.

Don't miss **Scargo Pottery**, off Route 6A (Box 956), Dennis (☎ 508/385-3894). It's a magical place set among the woods a short distance from the lake of the same name. It was started in 1952 by Harry Holl, who has since taught many apprentices. You can see the potters working, and under the trees in summer you'll find an outdoor display of brilliantly colored and designed tiles, vases, mirrors, pots, and plates, plus some fantasy ceramic, castlelike bird baths to place amid your garden's ground cover. It's a wonderful place to visit, and many of the pieces are quite affordable. Picnic tables are available on the grounds. Or, you can try to secure one of the six or so parking spots down by the lake and enjoy a picnic or rest there. Open daily from 10am to 6pm.

For a view of the area, climb the **Scargo Hill Observatory**, off Route 6A. On a clear day, you can see all the way to Provincetown.

Route 6A is an antiques-lover's dream and could be simply dubbed "antiques row." Some stores, though, do stand out. **Webfoot Farm,** 1475 Main St. in East Dennis (☎ 508/385-2334), has some stunning oriental pieces—ceramic lamps, figurines, occasional Buddhas, and tea containers. There are American pieces, too, lots and lots of silver and silverware. Everything is of very fine quality and fairly priced. In contrast, the **Dennis Antiques Center,** 243 Main St. (Route 6A) (☎ 508/385-6400), has mostly kitsch on the ground floor. Art books and larger pieces of furniture are found upstairs.

In West Dennis, **Jericho House Museum,** Trotting Park Road at Old Main Street (☎ 508/398-6736), incorporates an 1801 historic house built for sea captain Theophilus Baker. The barn houses a museum containing exhibits about salt making, cranberry farming, shipping, and shipbuilding. In addition, there's a whimsical collection of driftwood carvings fashioned by Sherman Woodward—animals, birds, fish, and people. Open July to August, Wednesday to Friday from 2 to 4pm. Admission free.

DEnnIS LODGING

Scargo Manor, 909 Main St. (Route 6A), Dennis, MA 02638 (☎ 508/ 385-5534), is a beautifully maintained home that is more than 100 years old and sits on 3 acres. The interior boasts details such as stained-glass windows and intricate woodwork. The two suites and one room are decorated with style. Floors have been painted and then spot covered with braided rugs. The Captain Howes Room is large enough to accommodate a king four-poster and a sitting room with a working fireplace and a TV. The grounds sweep down to Scargo Lake where you'll find a 55-foot-long dock, a private beach, and a boathouse. Guests appreciate the large, comfortably furnished living room and the small TV room where they will be warmed by a fire in winter. The expanded continental breakfast is served at individual tables in the dining room or on the glass-enclosed porch, furnished with wicker and hanging flower baskets. Rates: April 1 to mid-June, $90 to $130; mid-June to Columbus Day, $120 to $150; mid-October to December 31, $90 to $130.

Approached via a sweeping drive, **Four Chimneys Inn,** 946 Main St. (Route 6A), Dennis, MA 02638 (☎ 508/385-6317), is an imposing Victorian residence set well back from the road across from Scargo Lake. It was built in 1881 and has gracious architectural detailing—fine woodwork, plaster moldings and medallions, marble fireplaces, and extra-high ceilings. Among the nine rooms, Blueberry is particularly pretty. A collection of blue glass stands on the decorative marble mantel, setting off the blue wing backs and other pieces of blue decor. Teaberry is decked out in a green and pink stripe; the bathroom is small, but the room does have a deck of its own. Rosehip is the most sophisticated room, with its serpentine canopied bed with crochet netting and a marble fireplace. The third-floor rooms, tucked under the eaves, have skylights and views of Scargo Lake. Seven of the rooms have TVs. A continental breakfast—muffins, bagels, and fresh fruit—is served in the formal dining room. A guest phone is available. In addition to the comfortable living room, there is a library with a TV/VCR. In spring, more than a thousand bulbs paint the gardens; later in the year, the gardens bloom with more than 200 perennials. Rates: June 6 to September 7, $85 to $125; April 25 to June 5 and September 8 to October 19, $80 to $115.

Isaiah Hall, 152 Whig St., Dennis, MA 02638 (☎ 800/736-0160 or 508/ 385-9928), is run by Marie Brophy, who has been operating the business for many long years. As a consequence, she makes sure that her guests have all the conveniences and comforts they might need—witness the basket containing a hair dryer and other amenities you may have left at home. The farmhouse dates to 1857 and is named after the cooper who owned it. He was the originator of the cranberry barrel, and his brother Henry Hall cultivated the first cranberry bogs a short distance from the inn. The welcoming small parlor contains some eye-catching antiques and other pieces—a Shaker mommy rocker, a cuckoo clock, and models of sea birds. The tiles around the mantel commemorate the East Dennis Shiverick shipyard that turned out three-masted schooners in the last century. There are 10 rooms (5 in the main house). The main house rooms are furnished in a traditional style using tried and true palettes, like Williamsburg blue, and antique reproductions. Quilts grace most of the beds, which may be serpentine and canopied. Carriage house rooms are fashioned out of knotty pine and decorated with wall-to-wall carpet and painted cottage furniture, plus wicker chaise lounges. The carriage house also has its own living room, which focuses on an 1850s wood stove and is decorated with fraktur painting. Guests have their own refrigerator. An expanded continental breakfast is served at a long cherry table that seats 14. The lawns are nicely shaded by trees and shrubs. Rates: Mid-June to Labor Day, $95 to $127; off-season $98 to $127.

DEnnIS DInIng

Red Pheasant Inn, 905 Main St. (☎ 508/385-2133), is an elegant place to dine. The food is good, and you can expect to find such dishes as sesame-crusted halibut served with a delicious Thai curry and tamarind sauce, or roast duck with quince caramelized ginger and red wine sauce. Prices range from $16 to $25. Open late May to early September daily from 5 to 10pm. Closed 3 weeks in March and Monday and Tuesday in winter.

    Scargo Cafe, Route 6A (☎ 508/385-8200), is light and airy and offers fine-quality seafood and other dishes. Among the appetizers, try the barbecue shrimp in a delicious tangy barbecue sauce with grilled pineapple and a piquant mustard sauce for dipping. Other dishes are also well prepared. Open mid-June to mid-September, daily from 11am to 11pm; off-season daily from 11am to 3pm and from 4:30 to 10pm.

    The **Sundae School Ice Cream Parlor,** 381 Lower County Rd., Dennisport (☎ 508/394-9122), sells all kinds of ice cream flavors and sundaes, but the far-out favorite is the giant banana split.

    Gina's by the Sea, 134 Taunton St., Dennis (☎ 508/385-3213), has the air of a smuggler's den. Tucked away in the dunes a short distance from Chapin Beach, Gina's has been in business since 1938. There are two low-ceilinged cozy dining rooms and a tavern room with booths and a bar hung with hard hats. All are redolent with the scent of garlic, which flavors many of, if not all, the dishes—terrific scampi, veal à la Milanese, veal parmigiana, and rich cannelloni. Prices range from $13 to $21. Open June to September, Monday to Friday from 11:30am to 3pm and daily from 5 to 10pm; call for off-season hours.

Barnstable, Hyannis, Yarmouth & Dennis
Special & Recreational Activities

Beaches: The best beaches with public parking include **Barnstable:** Craigville Beach, on the south shore, Craigville Road; Sandy Neck, a magnificent barrier beach off Route 6A in West Barnstable on the north shore. **Hyannis:** Kalmus Park, Ocean Street; Orrin Keyes, Sea Street; and Veteran's Park, Ocean Street. **Dennis:** Chapin Beach, Howes Street Beach, and Mayflower Beach are all off Route 6A in Dennis; Sea Street Beach is off Route 6A in East Dennis. **Dennisport:** Depot Street Beach; Haigis Beach, Inman Road

Beach, Raycroft Parkway Beach, and Sea Street Beach are all off Route 28. **Yarmouth:** Bass River, Parker River, and Seaview are all along South Shore Drive off Route 28.

Birding: The **Great Salt Marsh Conservation Area**, Sandy Neck Road, Barnstable, is a great place to observe water birds.

Canoeing/Kayaking: Contact **Cape Cod Boats** (☎ 508/394-9268) in West Dennis.

Fishing: Barnstable Harbor has several party boats operating. The *Sea Witch* (Capt. Bob Singleton; ☎ 508/776-1336 or 413/283-8375); *Annie B* (Capt. Bob Bolduc; ☎ 508/398-2486); and *Drifter* (Capt. John Crompton; ☎ 508/362-8635) sail from Barnstable Harbor. **Hyannis:** *Rosie S* (Capt. Les Schwom; ☎ 508/775-8517) sails from Hyannis Harbor. **Dennis:** Two party boats, *Bluefin* (Capt. Pete Veroni; ☎ 508/697-2093) and *Albatross* (Capt. Dave Hoss; ☎ 508/385-3244 or 508/385-2063) operate from Sesuit Harbor.

Golf: Olde Barnstable Fairgrounds Golf Course, 1460 Rte. 149, Marstons Mills (☎ 508/428-1142), is one of the Cape's great public courses. In Yarmouth, **Bass River Golf Course**, High Bank Road, South Yarmouth (☎ 508/398-9079), offers some challenges but is best for beginners; **Tara Hyannis Golf Course**, West End Circle (☎ 508/775-7775, is a highly rated par-3 course. Other courses include Bayberry Hills Golf Course, West Yarmouth Road, (☎ 508/394-5597; Blue Rock Golf Course, off High Bank Road, South Yarmouth (☎ 508/398-9295); King's Way Golf Course, Old King's Highway, Yarmouth Port (☎ 508/362-8870). Dennis Highland Golf Course, 825 Old Bass River Rd. (☎ 508/385-8347); Dennis Pines Golf Course, Golf Course Road (off Route 134), East Dennis (☎ 508/385-8347); Hyannis Golf Club, Route 132 (☎ 508/362-2606).

Hiking: In Barnstable the **Sandy Neck Peninsula** is great for exploring dune and marsh. It offers 4,000 acres with trails. **Fresh Pond Conservation Area** is another 27 acres of marsh and woodland off Route 134.

Parasailing: Contact **Aquaray Parasail Charters**, Red Jacket Beach Resort, South Yarmouth (☎ 508/398-6941).

Sailing: For information contact **Barnstable Recreation Department** (☎ 508/790-6345); **Cape Cod Sailing Inc.**, Hyannis (☎ 508/771-7918); **Yarmouth Recreation Department** (☎ 508/398-2231).

Tennis: There are courts at **Cape Cod Community College**, Route 132, West Barnstable, and at **Flax Pond**, North Main Street, South Yarmouth.

Whale Watching: Hyannis **Whale Watcher Cruises** (☎ 508/362-6088) operate from Barnstable Harbor starting in April.

Cape Cod—The Lower Cape

Harwich ◆ Chatham ◆ Brewster ◆ Orleans ◆
Monomoy National Wildlife Refuge

Distance in miles from Boston: Brewster, 87; Orleans, 92.

Estimated driving times: 1¾ hours to Brewster; 1¾ hours to Orleans.

◄o►◄o►◄o►◄o►◄o►

Driving: Take Route 3 to Route 6. Cross the Sagamore Bridge and take marked exits for Brewster, Harwich, and Orleans. For Chatham, take Exit 11 to Route 137 to Route 28.

Bus: Call Plymouth and Brockton Bus Lines (☎ 508/775-5524) for service from Boston.

Further Information: For further information, contact the **Cape Cod Chamber of Commerce,** routes 6 and 132, P.O. Box 16, Hyannis, MA 02601 (☎ 508/362-3225).

　　Chatham Chamber of Commerce, P.O. Box 793, Chatham, MA 02633 (☎ 508/945-5199); **Orleans Chamber of Commerce,** P.O. Box 153, Orleans, MA 02653 (☎ 508/255-1386).

◄o►◄o►◄o►◄o►◄o►

At Cape Cod's elbow the land narrows to only 8 miles and turns to face the Atlantic Ocean. Here, particularly in the towns of Orleans and Chatham, you will encounter the sea that is constantly re-forming and redrawing the coastline, flooding the islands, and moving beaches with its never-ceasing tides. This is where the most dangerous shoals lie and where Chatham Light stands sentinel against the ocean.

　　Clipper ship captains and sailors were the main residents here in the 19th century, and they have left behind the many striking homes that line the lanes of all the towns in the area, particularly Brewster. Each town has its delights for the visitor: Chatham is a lively outpost and gateway to the Monomy Wildlife Refuge; Brewster, in addition to its historic homes, offers the Museum of Natural History, the Stoney Brook Mill and Herring Run, and Nickerson State Park, with all kinds of recreation; Orleans has magnificent Nauset Beach and many watery nooks and crannies; while Harwich's Wychmere Harbor is one of the most picturesque on the Cape.

Events & Festivals to Plan Your Trip Around

April: Brewster in Bloom, with arts, a craft parade, and open houses to view. Call ☎ 508/896-8088 for information.

June: Brewster Historical Society Antiques Fair, features around 80 top antiques dealers in an outdoor setting. Call ☎ 508/896-7389.

August: Sails around Cape Cod at Saquatucket Harbor Harwich Port. Call ☎ 508/432-1600.

September: Cranberry Festival, Harwich. Nine days of events celebrating the colorful harvest. Call ☎ 508/430-2811.

November: Chatham's Christmas by the Sea. Ten days of events: historic inn tours, open houses, and carolers. Call ☎ 508/945-5199.

HARWICH & CHATHAM

Harwich lives in the shadow of two other Cape towns—Chatham on one side and Dennis on the other. Harwich is not as developed as adjacent Dennis, but it has its share of commercialism along Route 28. It possesses a couple of attractive harbors—the prettiest is Wychmere; the other, Saquatucket, is the port for the steamer to Nantucket. It also has a historical museum, **Brooks Academy Museum,** routes 39 and 124 (☎ 508/432-8089), where you'll find exhibits on cranberry farming, textiles, and china and glass, plus paintings by C. D. Cahoon and bird carvings by Elmer Crowell. Open mid-June to mid-September, Thursday to Sunday from 1 to 4pm.

Chatham is a world unto itself. William Nickerson of Yarmouth founded Chatham. He purchased the land from the Indians in 1656, but it took 16 years for him to secure his claim at Plymouth. Geographically, Chatham bulges out, forming the elbow of the Cape, and is intricately linked to the ocean and the ebb and flow of the winds and the tides. Myriad inlets, ponds, and harbors cut their patterns into the land that shelters behind the spit of the National Seashore. To get the flavor of the sea, go down to the **fish pier** on Shore Road Boulevard at Barcliff Avenue and watch the fishermen unload the catch after 2pm. Drive down to the **Chatham Light,** also off Shore Road Boulevard, for some glorious ocean vistas. This is not the first light that has been here. Many lighthouses have been destroyed by the ocean breaking through the outer beach, as it did in November 1870 during a hurricane. Shore Road Boulevard leads south to Stage and Morris Islands. Off this coast lies the **Monomoy National Wildlife Refuge.**

Chatham is a town rich in history. The **Old Atwood House Museum,** 347 Stage Harbor Rd. (☎ 508/945-2493), is certainly worth visiting just to see the Stallknecht murals and the Frederick Wight Gallery. Other exhibits focus on maritime art, artifacts, and history, shells, parian ware, Sandwich

The Lower Cape

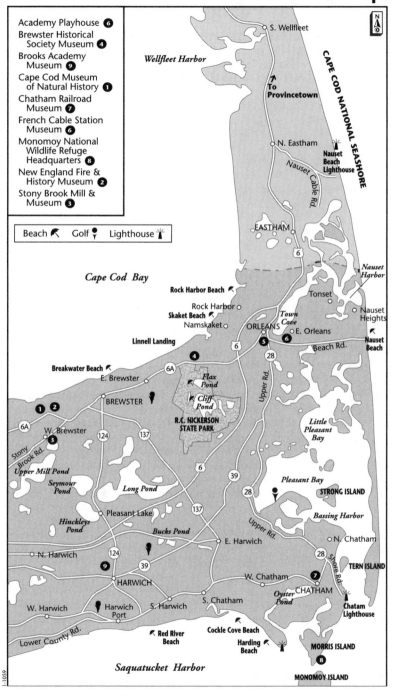

Academy Playhouse ➏
Brewster Historical
  Society Museum ➍
Brooks Academy
  Museum ➒
Cape Cod Museum
  of Natural History ➊
Chatham Railroad
  Museum ➐
French Cable Station
  Museum ➏
Monomoy National
  Wildlife Refuge
  Headquarters ➑
New England Fire &
  History Museum ➋
Stony Brook Mill &
  Museum ➌

Beach 🏖   Golf ⛳   Lighthouse 🗼

S. Wellfleet

Wellfleet Harbor

CAPE COD NATIONAL SEASHORE

To
Provincetown

N. Eastham

Nauset
Beach
Lighthouse

Nauset Cable Rd.

EASTHAM

6

Cape Cod Bay

Rock Harbor Beach

Rock Harbor
Skaket Beach
Namskaket

Linnell Landing

Breakwater Beach

E. Brewster
6A

BREWSTER

W. Brewster
6A

124   137

Stony Brook Rd.

Upper Mill Pond

Seymour
Pond

Long Pond

Hinckleys
Pond

Pleasant Lake

Bucks Pond

N. Harwich

124

HARWICH

39

W. Harwich   Harwich
Port

Lower County Rd.

S. Harwich

Red River
Beach

Saquatucket Harbor

Flax
Pond

Cliff
Pond

R.C. NICKERSON
STATE PARK

6

39

137

E. Harwich

Town
Cove

ORLEANS

6

28

E. Orleans

Beach Rd.

Tonset

Nauset
Harbor

Nauset
Heights

Nauset
Beach

Upper Rd.

Little
Pleasant
Bay

Pleasant Bay

STRONG ISLAND

Bassing Harbor

N. Chatham

28

Upper Rd.

W. Chatham

S. Chatham

Oyster
Pond

CHATHAM

Shore Rd.

TERN ISLAND

Chatam
Lighthouse

Cockle Cove Beach

Harding
Beach

MORRIS ISLAND

MONOMOY ISLAND

J-1059

glass, and more. The museum is located in the home built in 1752 by Captain Joseph C. Atwood, a merchant mariner, and extended in the 1830s. Open mid-June to September 30, Tuesday to Friday from 1 to 4pm.

Railroad buffs will want to see the **Railroad Museum,** Depot Road (no phone), that displays hundreds of railroad memorabilia, including a NYCRR caboose and a diorama of Chatham Railroad Yard around 1915. Only for enthusiasts.

Chatham has some of the best shopping on the Cape. Just outside of town on Route 28, glass or craft enthusiasts should not miss **Chatham Glass,** 758 Main St. (☎ 508/945-5547), operated by Jim Holmes and Deborah Doane. They design wonderfully organic-looking bud vases, candlesticks, and bowls in bold vibrant colors like tangerine and cobalt blue. All pieces have intense color and range in price from $60 for a bud vase to thousands for the larger items. Across the street, **1736 House Antiques,** 1731 Main St. (☎ 508/945-5690), specializes in pine furnishings, but it also displays some fine watercolors by local artists, notably Linda George. **Amazing Lace,** 726 Main St. (☎ 508/945-4023), has stunning retro clothes from the '30s and '40s plus linens, runners, tablecloths, and much more. Stop by **Cape Cod Cooperage,** 1150 Old Queen Anne Rd. (☎ 508/432-0788), if you're looking for choice barrels to use as planters or unfinished country furniture. On Main Street you'll find **Spyglass,** which stocks telescopes plus navigational and other marine antiques, **Chatham Cookware, Pentimento,** and many other stores worth browsing.

HARWICH LODGING & DINING

Dunscroft by the Sea, 24 Pilgrim Rd., Harwich Port, MA 02646 (☎ 508/432-0819), is special because it's only 500 feet from your very own beach and it's operated by warm and vivacious Alyce Cunningham. She has decorated this delightful Dutch gable home in a very light and feminine manner using lace, ruffles, and flowers. There are eight rooms. One has a king canopy that has been wrapped in tulle; it also has a Jacuzzi in the bathroom. Another contains a serpentine canopied bed draped with a rose-motif fabric that is matched with a curtained, kidney-shaped dresser. Still another has a sleigh bed set against plain cream walls. The Dresden China Room has its own private entrance and is very summery, thanks to its blue and white palette that picks up the china's blue, and it features a spindle four-poster with a lacey canopy. The Cottage Room has a wood-burning fireplace. All of the rooms have the romantic touch of candles and a silver-framed "love letter," addressed to renowned love couples, informing guests where things are. The living room is very large, divided into a sitting area around the brick fireplace and a well-stocked reading area that also has a grand piano. The room opens out into a glass-enclosed porch. At breakfast, the table will be set with lace, and guests will enjoy a delicious full breakfast of gourmet pancakes and egg dishes plus breads and fruit. Rates: High season, $145 to $235; low season, $105 to $195.

The **Beach House Inn,** 4 Braddock Lane, Harwich Port, MA 02646 (☎ 508/432-4444), is right on the beach. It's different from most of the other bed-and-breakfast and inn accommodations covered here. It has a real coastal feel and doesn't affect any colonial style. Built in the 1950s, it's light, airy, and modern. At the back of the house, there's a large octagonal porch that spills down onto another large deck right on the beach, where you can loll on a chaise lounge and tan to your heart's content. It's a combination hotel/bed-and-breakfast. There are 14 rooms, 7 with whirlpool tubs. Room 11 is a suite with a small sitting room; it's decorated with lighthouse-motif wallpaper and a fabric with a shell design. All rooms have fine views and contain wall-to-wall carpeting, pine furnishings, leather-studded chairs, and brass lamps. All have air-conditioning, refrigerators, and TVs. A continental buffet-style breakfast is served. Rates: June 16 to September 15, $175 to $285. January 1 to February 25, April 12 to June 15, and September 16 to December 31, $120 to $195;

Cape Sea Grille (☎ 508/432-4745) is only a few blocks from the beach. It offers innovative cuisine, and that's why the locals appreciate it. There's a small bar and a light-filled dining room. The cuisine is superb. With such signature dishes as the Sea Grille—a mixed grill medley of swordfish wrapped in applewood smoked bacon, half a roasted lobster, salmon with herb butter, and barbecue shrimp—it's little wonder that people descend on this restaurant in droves. Certainly the fish dishes are the lures—crispy sole piccatta with lemon capers and plum tomato or Chatham cod seared and braised bouillabaisse style with herbs, fennel, potatoes, leeks, and tomato and finished with sofrito and grilled bread. You've never tasted cod like this. The meat dishes, too, excite the taste buds, from the grilled tenderloin with Roquefort butter and toasted pecans to the grilled leg of lamb with a sweet pepper/garlic sauce, but there's definitely an emphasis on seafood. Prices range from $15 to $23. Open April to Columbus Day, daily 5 to 10pm.

CHATHAM LODGING

Technically the **Wequassett Inn,** Pleasant Bay Road, Chatham, MA 02633 (☎ 800/225-7125 or 508/432-5400), is not in Chatham, but it doesn't really matter because it occupies an inspiring 22-acre setting overlooking Pleasant Bay and Round Cove. Here you'll likely spy heron and egrets and other waterbirds hooking their own meals. At this lovely resort, there are 104 rooms located in roughly 20 buildings. The cottage-style accommodations are well furnished, with cannonball pine beds covered with floral spreads, plus couches and wicker chairs. Each room has a full range of amenities—a minibar, iron/ironing board, coffeemaker, hair dryer, umbrella, telephone, TV, clock-radio, and gas fireplace. Waterfront cottages have their own decks. The tennis villas located near the five courts have more of a country look. Facilities include an outdoor pool surrounded by grass; tennis courts; a fitness center with treadmill and stair-climbing machine; and equipment for sailing, windsurfing, and fly-fishing. A launch takes guests to the outer beach. This is one of the few really quiet, sophisticated resort-style retreats on the Cape. Open mid-April to mid-November. For dining, see below. Rates: June 26 to August 31, $265 to $505; May 1 to 22 and October 13 to 31, $185 to $375; May 23 to June 25 and September 1 to October 12, $220 to $405; April and November, $105 to $210.

Chatham Bars Inn, 297 Shore Rd., Chatham, MA 02633 (☎ 508/945-0096), has magnificent views of the bar. It's a large resort with accommodations in a series of cottages arranged around the grand central building featuring a long pillared lobby and library and a full verandah where you can sit out and enjoy the perfect view. The 155 rooms (which include cottages and suites) are attractively decorated with wall-to-wall carpeting and maple chests and desks. Beds might be half-posters. Some rooms have fireplaces and decks; all have TVs and telephones. The cottages have refrigerators. There are two dining rooms: the main dining room and the North Beach Tavern and Grille. The first serves a traditional New England menu featuring grilled swordfish, broiled cod, roasted chicken, and rack of lamb (prices ranging from $18 to $25). In summer, there's also a beach house grill down by the ocean, and guests are treated to clambakes and themed dinners. Facilities include an outdoor pool, tennis courts, a fitness center, and a private beach. Rates: Summer, $200 to $375, suites from $415; early spring and late fall, $120 to $240, suites from $285; late spring and early fall, $150 to $310, suites from $335; winter, $95 to $190, suites from $190.

George and Linda Watts make the **Moses Nickerson House Country Inn,** 364 Old Harbor Road, Chatham, MA 02633 (☎ 508/945-5859), a special place. It's a striking house surrounded by lawns and gardens. There are seven very fetchingly decorated rooms using strong palettes of dark green, Ralph Lauren–style bed linens and fabrics, and oriental rugs. In Room 7, decoys and a horse collar add decorative accents and a lovely star quilt covers the rice four-poster. Room 5 has a serpentine canopied bed and a richly carved armoire, plus a wood-burning fireplace. The parlor is very comfortable indeed with its wing backs, loveseats, and sofa. Breakfast is served in a pleasant room made bright by the French doors and furnished with wrought iron tables and chairs. Dishes such as quiche or stuffed French toast, plus fruit and pastries are offered. Rates: Memorial Day to Columbus Day, $139 to $179; off-season, $105 to $145

Captain's House Inn, 369-371 Old Harbor Rd., Chatham, MA 02633 (☎ 508/945-0127), is a meticulously kept inn, operated by Jan and Dave McMaster. The building is set on 2½ acres of beautifully landscaped grounds bordered by a perfectly trimmed privet hedge. There's an ornamental herb garden. The white Greek Revival home positively sparkles and is furnished throughout with the finest antiques. There are 19 elegant guest rooms, all with phone, hair dryer, iron, and clock radio. Some have fireplaces and other amenities. In Lady Hope, you'll find a mahogany four-poster with a crochet canopy covered with an antique quilt, combined with a luxurious serpentine dresser. Swagged drapes adorn the windows. In Clarissa, drop-leaf tables stand beside the serpentine canopied bed. There's a leather-topped desk and a lovely ceramic lamp as well as silhouettes for a decorative accent. Cambridge is a room filled with light from windows on three sides. There are four rooms in the carriage house, all with fireplaces. The most lavish rooms are in the stables. The Lydia Harding Suite is a two-room suite with a double whirlpool tub, a large balcony, and two fireplaces. All three rooms in the stables have TV/VCR, refrigerator, and coffeemaker. A full breakfast is served in the Spanish-tiled conservatory at individual tables set with fine china and napery, or you can enjoy a continental breakfast in your room. Afternoon tea is also served, and a beverage and light snack tray is placed in the kitchen in the evening. There's a very comfortable sitting room for guests, furnished with fine antiques in an appropriate Williamsburg style. Bikes are available. Rates: $145 to $285; Lydia Harding Suite, $335.

At the **Carriage House Inn,** 407 Old Harbor Rd., Chatham, MA 02633 (☎ 800/355-8868 or 508/945-4688), you will most likely be welcomed by one of the golden retrievers who will escort you into the welcoming front parlor, complete with fireplace flanked by book-filled bookcases. The six rooms are attractively decorated. One might have a wicker bed set against magnolia-pink walls, another might contain a cannonball-style bed with a floral coverlet set on a rose colored carpet. The nicest rooms are in the carriage house. They have private entrances and sliding glass doors to small patios. The largest is flooded with light from a large fan window and has a wood-burning fireplace and a Shaker four-poster with a lace canopy. A continental breakfast is served in the formal dining room or out on the sunporch, which is adorned with many colorful window boxes. Guests have access to a refrigerator, and there is TV in the living room and a courtesy phone. Six bicycles are also available. Rates: May to October, $120 to $185; November to April, $95 to $145.

Old Harbor Inn, 22 Old Harbor Rd., Chatham, MA 02633 (☎ 508/945-4434), is run by warm and friendly innkeepers Judy and Ray Braz. There are eight rooms, all prettily decorated in Laura Ashley style. The most luxurious is the South Beach, which has cathedral ceilings, a gas fireplace, and a four-poster without a canopy. The gathering room is comfortable and offers games as well as a grand piano. An expanded continental breakfast is taken in a light-filled room furnished with round wicker tables. The back deck looks out over the parking area. Rates: Spring, $115 to $180; summer, $155 to $205; fall, $145 to $195; winter, $115 to $165.

The **Cyrus Kent House Inn,** 63 Cross St., Chatham, MA 02633 (☎ 508/945-9104), is located just outside Chatham off Main Street in an 1877 home. The heart of the house is the graciously decorated sitting room with its white carpeting, grand piano, and white wing chairs arranged around the marble fireplace. There are 11 tastefully decorated rooms, all with phones and TVs. Some are in the carriage house where no. 8 is a favorite, thanks to its cathedral ceiling, Palladian windows, and a couch and canopied bed facing the double fireplace. In other rooms, the decor might include a maple four-poster with a fabric canopy, wing chairs, and a butler's table. Watercolors, stenciling, and fresh flowers add decorative accents to the rooms. A continental breakfast is served. Rates: Mid-June to mid-October, $145 to $160; mid-April to mid-June, $120 to $210; mid-October to mid-April, $105 to $190.

The Cranberry Inn, 359 Main St., Chatham, MA 02633 (☎ 508/945-9232), is located on the main street. Even though it's not a quiet ocean-front or country retreat, it still has many comforts to recommend it. It's furnished throughout with antique reproductions. There's a full bar that has some gaming tables, a large sitting area with grand piano, and a pretty breakfast room. The 18 accommodations are spacious, and some have cathedral-style ceilings. All are furnished with pine armoires and pencil four-posters and feature TVs, phones, and private baths. Some have fireplaces, wet bars, or balconies. A buffet breakfast with hot dishes is served. Rockers on the porch invite guests to watch village life pass by. A trail leads back to the Old Mill Pond. Rates: May 10 to June 13, $105 to $210; June 14 to September 16, $165 to $255; September 17 to December 1, $145 to $199; December 2 to May 1, $100 to $160.

Port Fortune, 201 Main St, Chatham, MA 02633 (☎ 508/945-0792), is also on the main street, but it's tucked away on the road to the lighthouse. The main building is set back from the road and has a brick terrace in front with the ocean only about 100 yards away. It's furnished with good-quality antique reproductions—pencil four-posters, wing chairs, and so on. All rooms have telephones for outgoing calls. There are two homey sitting rooms, one with a gas fireplace. A buffet breakfast is offered. Rates: Mid-June to mid-September, $140 to $180; May 1 to mid-June and mid-September to October, $120 to $165; November to April, $95 to $120.

CHATHAM DINING

The **Eben Ryder House** at the Wequassett Inn (☎ 508/432-5400), overlooks Pleasant Bay, and the tables in the dining room as well as the Garden Terrace take full advantage of the view. The cuisine is contemporary American and offers a full panoply of seafood that has been delicately and carefully prepared. The grilled swordfish is married with a cilantro, pineapple, and red pepper salsa and served with dikon salad and crispy plantains; the grilled Nantucket scallops are served in a creamy lobster sauce. For a more Asian twist, the Thai marinated duck breast grilled with a spicy peanut and coconut sauce is a perfect balance of hot, sweet, and sour. Prices range from $18 to $32. Open daily from 11am to 2pm and from 6 to 10pm.

Upstairs in a small mall, **Vining's Bistro**, 595 Main St. (☎ 508/945-5033), is the town's one innovative restaurant. Here the chef toils in an open kitchen, turning out daily specials such as salmon steamed in a foil with herbs and white wine, plus a broad range of dishes inspired by different traditions, from North African vegetable curry to lobster tacos. Prices range from $14 to $19. There's a carved bar up front. Open April through December, Wednesday to Sunday from 5pm to closing.

The **Impudent Oyster,** 15 Chatham Bars Ave. (☎ 508/945-3545), is a favorite of the locals who come in for luncheon and dinner. The food is good and reasonably priced. Soups are piping hot, and salads are made with a variety of greens and well dressed, while the hot dishes are well prepared. To start, there are plenty of shellfish dishes including clams casino and oysters Bienville plus Portuguese mussels and chourisco sausage steamed in a spicy tomato diablo sauce. Main courses run to steak au poivre, roast duck with orange or some other fruit, and sole with Cajun crab and shrimp stuffing. Prices range from $15 to $21. It's not stylish. The room has cathedral ceilings, a square polished pine bar, and some stained glass accents. Open Monday to Saturday from 11:30am to 3pm, Sunday from noon to 3pm, daily from 5 to 10pm.

Marley's, 1077 Main St. (Route 28; ☎ 508/945-1700), is a typical seafood restaurant with tables covered with oil cloth, captain's chairs, and a woodsy decor. The majority of the dishes are seafood dishes—broiled haddock with lemon parsley and white wine, broiled cod with tomatoes and basil, and bluefish seasoned with a hint of Dijon mustard plus some pasta dishes. Prices range from $9 to $12. Open daily from 11:30am to 2:30pm and 5pm to closing.

BREWSTER & ORLEANS

Brewster is named after Elder William Brewster who arrived on the Mayflower and settled here in 1659. It has a long history as a wealthy seafaring town where hundreds of packet ships stopped at Breakwater Beach en route between Boston and New York and where salt making and other early, wind-mill-powered industries flourished. Today, many of the homes of captains that sailed on the clippers have been converted into welcoming inns, and the whole place exudes a self-confident charm that makes it very appealing.

If you have kids in tow, the **Cape Cod Museum of Natural History,** Route 6A (☎ 508/896-3867), is one place to take them when they get tired of the beach. Here you can learn about local ecology and nature, from whales to barrier beaches. The museum has salt- and freshwater aquariums. There are also walking trails and picnicking facilities. Open year-round, Monday to Saturday from 9:30am to 4:30pm, Sunday from 12:30 to 4:30pm. Admission is $5 for adults, $4.50 for seniors, $2 for children 5 to 12.

Two historical attractions are also here for a rainy day. The **Brewster Historical Society Museum,** Route 6A, East Brewster (☎ 508/896-9521), displays local historical artifacts. Among the exhibits are a turn-of-the-century barbershop and an old post office. The museum is located in the Harris-Black house. Open July and August, Tuesday to Friday from 1 to 4pm; call for off-season hours. The **New England Fire and History Museum,** Route 6A (☎ 508/896-5711), has a collection of fire trucks dating from the late 18th to the 20th century. It also displays an apothecary and blacksmith shop. Open Memorial Day to Labor Day, daily Monday to Friday 10am to 4pm; Labor Day to Columbus Day, Saturday to Sunday from noon to 4pm, weekends only. Closed from Columbus Day to Memorial Day.

For me, the most atmospheric historical spot to visit here is the **Stoney Brook Mill** on Stoney Brook Road. It's as if you've stepped into another century. The pond stretches mirrorlike beside the mill while water gushes down a herring run across the road. It's thrilling to see when the herring are running. The gulls whirl and shriek above the brook, diving down into the water and occasionally plucking out a fish. Locals may come by and scoop the glistening shad out in nets. The mill was originally used to finish cloth. It was one of several mills—a carding mill and a tannery among them. Today the mill grinds corn in May and June, Thursday to Saturday from 2 to 5pm; and July and August, Friday only 2 to 5pm. There's also a museum upstairs.

Brewster has some notable studios and shops. **Sydenstricker Glass,** Route 6A, Brewster (☎ 508/385-3272), demonstrates a glass-fusion process. Open April to December, daily from 10am to 5pm and for demonstrations Tuesday to Saturday from 10am to 2pm. At **Kemp Pottery,** 258 Main St., West Brewster (☎ 508/385-5782), Steven Thomas Kemp uses oriental throwing techniques to make pottery that he then decorates in a variety of ways using a variety of techniques—sgraffito, wax resist, and brushwork. He also creates sculpted teapots, tureens, and fountains; lovely glazed sinks; plus some fantastic architectural garden ornaments. The **Underground Art Gallery,** 673 Satucket Rd., Brewster (☎ 508/896-3757), displays watercolors and other works of art that are more eye-catching than the usual standard Cape Cod landscapes seen at many other galleries.

William Baxter Antiques (☎ 508/896-3998) stocks some very fine antiques worth thousands—Asian and oriental objects, English furniture, and more. Open by appointment only. **The McCloud House,** 2095 Main St., Brewster (☎ 508/896-2513), has wonderful decorative objects for the garden, from urns and benches to statuary and birdbaths. **Shirley D. T. Smith,** 2926 Main St., Brewster (☎ 508/896-4632), stocks fine silver, furniture, paintings, china, and early American country items. **Works of Art Antiques,** 3799 Main St., Brewster (☎ 508/255-0589), has some quirky, interesting objects including dollhouses and lighthouses, fine portraits and early American primitive and folk paintings, plus other collectibles. **Breton House Antiques,** 1222 Stony Brook Rd., Brewster (☎ 508/896-7431), is a collector's dream. It's filled with all kinds of stuff—games, toys, tin farm animals, model cars and boats, canes, fans, hats, lamps, French puppets, and other theater-arts items. **Kingsland Manor Antiques,** Route 6A, West Brewster (☎ 508/385-9741), has an array of stunning antiques, many of them large pieces. They range from a mahogany bar taken from an English club to rococo sculptures, massive torchères, and a walnut Eastlake bed, all displayed very attractively in a series of rooms set around a brick courtyard with a fountain.

In the evening, you can take in one of the outdoor performances of the **Cape Cod Repertory Theater.** Call ☎ 508/896-1888 for information.

The mystery of **Orleans's** Frenchified name remains a mystery. Until 1797 it was the southern satellite of Eastham. In history Orleans is famous for being the defiant Cape town that refused to pay the British a ransom during the War of 1812. The British frigate *Newcastle* challenged the town but ignominiously ran aground. Determined to exact revenge, the British commander seized several sloops in Orleans, but he made the mistake of impressing a local man to pilot one of them. His name is not known, but he had the wit to run the sloop aground in Yarmouth. Orleans is also famous for being the only place touched by World War I, when a German U-boat fired 146 shots at a tug and several barges in July 1918.

Here at Orleans the elbow of the Cape turns, and beaches face out to the Atlantic Ocean. In fact, Orleans is home to one of the Cape's most famous beaches—Nauset Beach. This stretch of coast was the site of many a shipwreck, including pirate Black Bellamy's *Whidah*. Although the locals will deny that there ever was such a game as "mooncussing"—when ships were lured aground on moonless nights by false lanterns—some men certainly did make a living from salvaging the cargo from shipwrecks. Surrounded by coves, ponds, inlets, and with Pleasant Bay on the south side, Orleans gives plenty of access to water and water-related pastimes. At one time, Orleans was famous for its shellfish, especially scallops, and it's still great for scalloping. Additional stories relating to the town can be gleaned at the **Museum of Orleans Historical Society** in the Meeting House on Main Street (☎ 508/240-1329). Open July to August, Monday to Friday from 1 to 4pm.

At Cove Road and Route 28, you'll encounter another piece of Orleans history at the **French Cable Station Museum** (☎ 508/240-1735). It was built in 1891 to house the cables that reached from here to Brest, France, and was at the time the source of international news. You can see how the cable operation worked. Open June 1 to Labor Day, Monday to Saturday from 10am to 4pm.

The **Academy Playhouse,** 125 Main St. (☎ 508/255-1963), produces a long season of comedies and musicals that kicks off in March.

BREWSTER LODGING

High Brewster, 964 Satucket Rd., Brewster, MA 02631 (☎ 508/896-3636), is a superb accommodation and one of my favorites on the entire Cape. It stands on 2½ acres with a lovely view of Lake Adirondacks. Its restaurant is one of the best on the Cape (see below), but it also has exceptional rooms. Built in 1738, it has a truly seasoned flavor that has been enhanced by the creative decoration. The Red Room has super-wide (18 to 20 inches) wide-board floors. Here you'll find a maple four-poster, a fine antique chest, and desk, plus strictly red-only accents. My favorite accommodation is the Summer Cottage, available only in the summer because it lacks heat. It has two decks, one that is screened and another that is open, with a sweeping view of the lake. The barn is equally wonderful, with soaring ceilings and a brick hearth in the common area. There are two bedrooms here, one with an outdoor private stone patio and another up in the loft. It also has a large galley-style kitchen. Brook House is another accommodation with a brick fireplace overlooking the herring run to the Lower Mill Pond. It too has a large comfortable deck, full kitchen, and two bedrooms. A full breakfast is served in the dining room. Rates: Summer, $90 to $110, cottages $150 to $210. Closed December to March.

The Ruddy Turnstone, 463 Main St., Brewster, MA 02631 (☎ 508/385-9871), is a delightful bed-and-breakfast. The house and the setting are idyllic, overlooking a salt marsh, and they're made even more so by the hospitality of Sally and Swanee Swanson and the delicious breakfast that emerges from the kitchen in the mornings. Some rooms are located in an old barn that was shipped over from Nantucket. The rooms here are extra large and very nicely furnished, with pencil four-posters and decorative accents such as decoys and iron sconces. The best room in the main house is very large and has a wood-burning fireplace (TV, too) and great views of the grounds and the marsh beyond. Furnishings include an antique bed, two easy chairs, a Shaker bench, and a pine chest. The sitting room is a feast for the eye with numerous bird decoys and carvings, original paintings, and assorted roosters, which Swanee has been collecting for years. It has a great view of the marsh. Guests gather around the fire for conversation or to watch TV. Birders will appreciate the many visitors that alight on the feeders—cardinals, Baltimore orioles, gold finches, and many more. Rates: Mid-June to Columbus Day, $105 to $160; at other times $90 to $135. Closed January and February.

Lodgings at the **Bramble Inn,** 2019 Main St. (P.O. Box 807), Brewster, MA 02631 (☎ 508/896-7644), are located in two 19th-century buildings where the rooms are decorated with great panache. One room sports bird-of-paradise wallpaper. Room 2 is called the "cockerel room" because it has portraits of roosters on cushions and ceramics plus Currier and Ives very own *Ride a Cock Horse.* A brass-and-iron bed, oak dresser, and wood table plus wing chairs complete the furnishings. Room 3 is decorated in a very floral Victorian style. There's a skylit living room with a large TV for guests. Breakfast is served in a series of small rooms or out on the patio. Among the special dishes, the eggs Santa Fe are made with chili, cheese, and salsa—a great way to start the day. The first floor is given over to a restaurant, which is one of the finest in the area (see below). Rates: $105 to $135.

The **Captain Freeman Inn,** 15 Breakwater Rd. (off Route 6A), Brewster, MA 02631 (☎ 508/896-7481), occupies a handsome 1860s Victorian adjacent to The Egg (a landmark hollow in town) and the church. The entrance hall is striking for its mahogany and maple herringbone-pattern floor, carved staircase, and ornate plaster moldings. There are nine rooms; three have hot tubs. Barnstable is one of the luxury rooms that has a TV/VCR, a refrigerator stocked with soft drinks, a phone, a working fireplace, and a hot tub on an enclosed deck. The furnishings are primarily oak, and the room is spacious enough to accommodate a canopied bed and sitting area. The three rooms on the third floors share a bath and are available only in summer. Guests are asked to make their breakfast choices—omelets, other egg dishes, and pancakes—the night before. There's a large sitting room furnished in Victorian style. At the back of the house, there is an outdoor pool and a large lawn with chaise lounges. The front and side porches are great, too. Rates: June to October, $110 to $235; November to May $100 to $205.

Beechcroft Inn, 1360 Main St., Brewster, MA 02631 (☎ 508/896-9534), has a welcoming down-to-earth innkeeper and the additional attraction of on-the-premises meals. It's a warm cozy place that once served as the meeting-house of the Universalist Society. The 10 rooms are refreshingly different, decked out in strong colors. The Marsh Rosemary has raspberry-colored walls, setting off its four-poster with a lace canopy and peony-motif quilt. Queen Anne's Lace is tucked under the eaves and has a small deck of its own. Columbine rambles around the central brick chimney but has room for a loveseat, chest, and Windsor chair. Guests can enjoy the TV/VCR in the den or the living room, where conversational pieces include the scientific balance and telescope that belonged to the owner's father. Breakfast is included as well as evening cocktails. Dinner is available also. There's a bar, warmed in winter by a fire. Bikes are available. Rates: $75 to $155.

Brewster Farm House Inn, 716 Main St., Brewster, MA 02631 (☎ 800/892-3910 or 508/896-4232), offers five comfortable guest rooms, all equipped with TVs, terrycloth bathrobes, and hair dryers. The Garden Room has floors painted pale blue, a floral canopy on the rice four-poster, two wing chairs, and a private deck. The Acorn, under the eaves, is raspberry pink and has an impressively high maple four-poster. Breakfast is a rather splendid affair that might include Belgian pecan waffles with sautéed peaches and baked pears, or herbed eggs with eggplant and mango salsa and wild mushrooms. In winter, breakfast is served at the harvest table in a room with a cathedral ceiling and rugs spread over Mexican tile; in summer, it's served on the deck. Innkeeper Carol Concors, it seems, likes to collect rabbits, and they appear throughout as decor, often needlepointed by Carol herself. Guests like to relax in the sitting room around the fireplace or enjoy a game of chess. The outdoor hot tub and the pool, landscaped with hydrangeas, are bonus features. Rates: summer $160 to $230; winter $145 to $200.

Great Vacations Ocean Edge Resort, 2660 Rte. 6A, Brewster, MA 02631 (☎ 800/626-9984), is indeed on the ocean but it's not at the very edge as the name implies because this is a big resort with winding roads and stop signs so that it's quite a walk to the ocean from the main building. It was once the Nickerson Estate, and the central building (1912) exhibits some grand architectural features—a carved staircase, leaded-glass windows, and parterres. Today it functions as a resort-conference center. The main building houses the Ocean Grille dining room and a pub with a billiard table. Accommodations are in several buildings, including two- and three-bedroom villas, near either the private beach or the fairways. Villas have living and dining rooms and fully equipped kitchens with washer/dryers. Facilities include private beach, two indoor and four outdoor pools, 11 clay tennis courts, an 18-hole golf course, and a fitness center. Bike rentals are available, and kids programs are offered. Special golf and tennis packages are available. Rates: Summer, rooms $235 to 320, two-bedroom villas $500 to $550; fall, rooms $200 to $260, two-bedroom villas $410 to $450; winter, rooms $105 to $160, two-bedroom villas $200; spring, rooms $150 to $265, two-bedroom villas $300 to $470.

The Inn at the Egg, 1944 Main St., Brewster, MA 02631 (☎ 508/896-3123), stands opposite the Brewster General Store and the First Parish Church. The building once served as the parsonage and was at one time the residence of the parish preacher, Horatio Alger Jr. The Egg referred to in the name is the hollow across the street. You'll find comfortable rooms, all with TVs, that are furnished with antique reproductions. Among the room furnishings you might find a brass bed, painted dresser, a rolltop desk, or a maple chest. A two-room suite is ideal for families. A full breakfast includes pancakes, omelets, and similar dishes. There's also a sitting room for guests. The inn is within walking distance of the beach. Rates: Mid-June to mid-October, $95 to $160; mid-October to mid-June $85 to $125.

Isaiah Clark House, 1187 Main St. (Route 6A), Brewster, MA 02631 (☎ 508/896-2223), occupies a 1780s home that stands on 5 acres planted with many fruit trees. Traces of the families who lived here early on can be seen—a signature of Isaiah Clark's son Jeremiah on one of the bedroom doors and even remnants of an 1836 newspaper that the family used to line the closet. The house has seven guest rooms, several with working fireplaces. All are pleasantly furnished in colonial style. Deborah contains a pencil four-poster with a crochet canopy, a Hitchcock rocker, a wicker chair, and a chest. Some of the rooms, like the Jeremiah Clark, are tucked under the eaves. A full breakfast featuring, for example, Belgian waffles with strawberry sauce, plus fruit and breads is served in the stenciled dining room at a table in front of the brick fireplace. Guests can relax in the upstairs library or on loveseats and wing chairs in the living room. Rates: Memorial Day to Columbus Day, $108 to $130; off-season, $92 to $115.

Pepper House Inn, 2062 Main St., Brewster, MA 02631 (☎ 508/896-4389), occupies a sea captain's home that was built in 1793. The four guest rooms are decorated in fine style, with bold floral wallpapers, rice four-posters dressed with white lacy linens, lace curtains, and leather wing chairs. One room is decked out in dark green and has a canopied bed and two wing chairs upholstered with fine fabrics. The most dramatic room is on the first floor. It has cream-colored wainscoting and a colorful wallpaper with a bird motif. An oriental rug lies on the wide-board floor, and among the furnishings is a kidney-shaped dresser embellished with a bouillon-fringed fabric. The bathroom has a claw-foot tub. A full breakfast is served in the sitting room. There are afternoon refreshments also. The deck overlooks the lawn with its shade trees on the ⅔-acre property. Rates: Memorial Day to Columbus Day, $119 to $149; off-season, $99 to $129.

The **Candleberry Inn,** 1882 Main St. (Route 6A), Brewster, MA 02631 (☎ 508/896-3300), is operated by warm hosts David and Gini Donnelly. It stands on 2 acres of lovely grounds filled with perennials—lilies of the valley, camellias, forsythia, iris, and more. The six rooms, three with fireplaces, are very tastefully decorated in colonial style and are all equipped with bathrobes and hair dryers. Swag drapes adorn the windows, tables and beds are covered with attractive top-quality fabrics, and accents might run to a banjo clock or Federal-style mirror. Gini is a photographer, and her work can be seen on the staircase leading to the rooms. The Snow Room has a Shaker-style pencil four-poster set on a black-painted wide-board floor that is dressed with rugs, as well as a gas fireplace. In the suite, an iron-and-brass bed is set against raspberry walls. Breakfast is served by candlelight in an elegant dining room, at a table set with fine china and sterling silver. Dishes might be poppy-seed pancakes with hard cider syrup or eggs Florentine, accompanied by breads, pastries, and fruits. Several oriental rugs cover the parlor floor, and seating arrangements include couches and wing chairs. Conversation pieces include the grandfather clock and the pump organ as well as the original art on the walls. The room is warmed by a wood-burning stove. The brick patio in the back is very inviting, and folks compete for the glider on the back lawn. A guest refrigerator is stocked with soda. Rates: July to Labor Day, $105 to $135; May, June, September, and October, $100 to $125; November to April, $90 to $110.

BREWSTER DINING

Chillingsworth, 2449 Main St. (☎ 508/896-3640), is the place to go if you want to dress up in the evening and dine on premier French cuisine. Here you will be treated to a perfectly presented and orchestrated seven-course meal that offers choices for every course. Among the appetizers there might be foie gras, French bean jicama, and arugula salad with warm truffle vinaigrette or richly flavored crab cakes with cucumber julienne, lemon chive sour cream, golden roe, and pepper oil. Soup and salad and sorbet will follow. There will be a choice of 10 or so entrees, ranging from grilled swordfish with eggplant ragout, olive, caper, and tomato relish balsamic vinaigrette to a roasted tenderloin of beef with Dauphinoise potatoes, roasted shallots, French beans, and a truffle sauce. For dessert, the tart with blueberry and kiwi is a wonder. The price for all this will be determined by the price of the entree and will range from $50 to $60.

Chillingsworth also has a more casual bistro with Breuer chairs and Mexican tile floors. Here a different menu, featuring such dishes as grilled chicken with warm mushroom vinaigrette, salmon with a chive lemon-butter sauce, and grilled New York steak with a tarragon lemon butter sauce is priced from $11 to $23. Open July and August, 11:30am to 2:30pm and 6 to 9:30pm. Call for off-season hours. Closed late November to mid-May.

The dining rooms at the **Bramble Inn** (☎ 508/896-7644) are extremely fetching and some very fine food is available—the current chef migrated from Chillingsworth. He prepares a wonderful four-course dinner that might begin with brandied escargot and field mushroom gratinée with leek cream or delicious chilled shrimp-stuffed sea scallops with nori wrappers, pickled ginger, and wasabi cream. For a main course, the roast rack of lamb with oven caramelized spring vegetables in a Pinot noir consommé is a winning dish and so is the seafood curry studded with lobster, cod, scallops, and shrimp with grilled banana, toasted almonds, coconut, and chutney. The price of the meal is determined by the entrees, which range from $42 to $52. Open June to mid-October, Tuesday to Sunday from 6 to 9pm. Closed January to April.

Brewster Fish House, 2208 Main St. (☎ 508/896-7867), is so popular that in season you can expect a wait of an hour or more for a table or a spot at the bar. It's a small place but the chef knows how to prepare the bounty from the sea, and that's why folks flock here. Start with the thick and wonderful chowder. Then select any of the perfectly cooked fish dishes—grilled halibut with plum tomatoes, garlic, and fresh herbs; baked cod with a cranberry and ginger relish and herb stuffing; or grilled red snapper in a Spanish-style marinade, with grilled onion and pineapple. Prices range from $12 to $22. Open June to early September, Tuesday to Saturday from 11:30am to 3pm and 5 to 10pm, Sunday noon to 3pm and 5 to 9:30pm. Closed mid-December to mid-April.

High Brewster, 964 Satucket Rd. (☎ 508/896-3636), with its inspiring James Hansom murals depicting sun, moon, sky, and trees is a most romantic place to dine. The cuisine is equally thrilling. The menu is limited. Among the small selection of appetizers, there might be grilled shrimp over marinated summer vegetables with roasted red pepper coulis or a vegetable pace with lemon thyme infused vegetable broth. The main courses range from grilled beef tenderloin with red wine sauce to grilled Atlantic salmon with port wine reduction. The price of the four-course meal is determined by the entrees, which range from $36 to $46. Open late May to mid-September, daily from 5:30 to 9pm; call for off-season hours. Closed from December to March.

ORLEANS LODGING

Nauset House Inn, Beach Road (P.O. Box 774), East Orleans, MA 02643 (☎ 508/255-2195), occupies a farmhouse that was built in 1819. It's only a 10-minute walk from Nauset Beach and has some spectacular features, including the charming obviously artistic innkeepers, Al and Diane Johnson. There are 14 rooms (8 with private bath), all attractively decorated. Sundew features furniture painted by innkeeper Al Johnson's mother-in-law, plus wall stenciling that is also her work. Mayflower has an intensely blue stained-glass window created by innkeeper Diane Johnson and a hand-painted Jenny Lind bed among its furnishings. More painted furniture can be found in Bayberry, along with some decorative floral designs hand-painted on the walls. Four rooms are located in the carriage house, and there is one cottage. The barn has been converted into four lovely rooms that are my favorites. They have beamed ceilings and are furnished with pencil four-posters, oriental rugs, and such pieces as an Empire chest. The large common room is welcoming with its fireplace and glass coffee table, featuring a collage of seashells, tiles, wine labels, and other items, all arranged on a sand base. Breakfast is served at long tables that sit 10 in front of a big old hearth. The conservatory/solarium is magical. Filled with rhododendron, weeping cherry, and camellias and furnished with wicker, the setting is inspirational. Guests can also enjoy the picnic tables set out in the backyard under the huge old apple trees. Breakfast is included and hors d'oeuvres and wine are served in the evening. Rates: $65 to $138. Closed November through March.

The **Parsonage Inn,** 202 Main St., East Orleans, MA 02643 (☎ 508/255-8217), an attractive 18th-century former parsonage, is operated by an Englishman, Ian Browne, and his wife, Elizabeth. He spent many years in East Africa, and you'll find a cache of African artifacts throughout the house—Masai sculptures, batik fabric depicting flamingos, and a carving of an African dhow. There are eight rooms furnished traditionally. The one on the first floor has a canopied pencil four-poster, an acorn chest, and wicker chair. Braided rugs decorate the floors. My favorite is the Oak Room, which has sloping ceilings and arranges itself around the crooked chimney. There's a star quilt on the bed, and the floor has been painted rust red. The largest room is the Barn Room, which has a sitting area and is equipped with fridge and coffeemaker. A full breakfast is served at individual tables, and there's wine and appetizers in the evening; in summer, both are served on the brick terrace beside the entrance. Don't be surprised if you hear the strains of a Brahms waltz or Chopin nocturne—Elizabeth is a serious pianist and a piano teacher. Rates: $95 to $125.

ORLEANS DINING

Captain Linnell House, 137 Skaket Beach Rd. (☎ 508/255-3400), is a spectacular dining room in an off-the-beaten-track location in a striking mansion that has soaring Ionic columns, a resplendent cupola, and is draped in wisteria. Surprisingly, there is no dress code, and all diners are welcome. It was once the home of Captain Linnell, one of Orleans great mariners, who never lived to enjoy this beautiful home. There are three dining rooms decorated in an elegant French style. The signature dishes are the rack of lamb with an herbed mustard crust in a pinot noir sauce and the pork tenderloin with maple demi glaze and caramelized onions. Other selections might include veal Milanese, chicken with a pommery mustard sauce, and a variety of fish dishes. Prices range from $16 to $24. Open daily 5 to 10pm.

    Barley Neck Inn, 5 Beach Rd. (☎ 508/255-3626), has a warm, welcoming atmosphere. On one side of the building there's a large bar with a huge stone fireplace where a pianist entertains on weekends. On the other side are two formal dining rooms dripping with elegance, down to the pristine white tablecloths and the swag drapes at the windows. Start with one of the great soups—seafood bisque flavored with fennel and saffron, or clam chowder finished with sherry and cream. The rest of the menu is well rounded, offering a full choice of fish—broiled salmon on red pepper coulis, trout in a brandy sauce, and lobster with wild mushroom stuffing served with a champagne sauce—and meats from roasted pork in a mushroom port wine sauce to filet mignon with a peppercorn sauce. Prices range from $13 to $22. Open June to early September, daily 5 to 10pm.

    Nauset Beach Club, 222 E. Main St., East Orleans (☎ 508/255-8547), is a comfortable, inviting restaurant consisting of two small rooms painted in glowing peach and jade tones. It's stylish and casual at the same time. The food is bistro style. You'll find pork chops served with smothered onions, grilled steak, and braised lamb shank with Mediterranean spices served with baked beans. Pasta dishes are also available. Prices range from $14 to $19. Open late May to mid-October, Sunday to Thursday from 5:30 to 9pm, Friday and Saturday from 5:30 to 9:30pm; mid-October to May, Tuesday to Saturday 5:30 to 9pm.

    The **Old Jailhouse,** 28 West Rd. (☎ 508/255-5245), is a large boisterous pub. A grill separates the stone jailhouse from the newer dining room where steaks, broiled fish, and barbecue chicken are served at dinner. Peel-it shrimp, steamed mussels, and oysters are served anytime. Prices range from $15 to $18 for dinner entrees. Sandwiches, pizzas, and salads are much less. Open daily from 11:30am to 1am.

The Lobster Claw, Route 6A (☎ 508/255-1800), is a typical seafood restaurant swathed in fishing nets and lobster pots and lanterns. You can secure a 1¼-pound lobster here for $17 as well as other broiled seafood dishes (haddock, bluefish, sole, or swordfish) which are priced from $10 to $15. Open May to October, daily 11:30am to 9pm. Closed November to April.

If you want to have a picnic, **Fancy's Farm,** Route 28, West Chatham (☎ 508/945-1949), has picnic supplies. A branch is also located at 199 Main St., East Orleans.

Harwich Chatham, Brewster, & Orleans
Special & Recreational Activities

Adventure Outfitters: Goose Hummock Outdoor Adventure Program offers lessons, trips, and rentals for fly-fishing, canoeing/kayaking, biking, hiking, and camping. Write to Dept 63, P.O. Box 57, Orleans, MA 02653 (☎ 508/255-2620), for more information.

Art, Antiques, and Crafts: Chatham and Brewster have some of the very best shopping on the Cape; see above.

Beaches: The best beaches with public parking include **Brewster:** Breakwater Beach, Breakwater Road; Robbins Hill Beach off Lower Road, off Route 6A; and Saint's Landing, Robbins Hill Road, off Lower Road, off 6A; in East Brewster, Crosby Landing on Crosby Lane, Ellis Landing on Ellis Landing Road, and Linnell's Landing on Linnell Road; Paine's Creek, West Brewster. **Chatham:** Cockle Cove and Ridgevale, both in South Chatham; Hardings Beach, in West Chatham; Oyster Pond in Chatham is free. All are off Route 28. **Orleans:** Facing the Atlantic, Nauset Beach, is one of the finest beaches on the East Coast, off Route 28 or 6A; Skaket Beach, Namskaket Road, is on the bay.

Biking: This is great biking territory. The **Cape Cod Rail Trail** goes from South Dennis to Eastham via Harwich and Orleans (20 miles). It's off Route 134, with parking facilities at Nickerson State Park on Route 6A in Brewster, Route 124 in Harwich, and at Salt Pond Visitors' Center off Route 6 in Eastham. Rentals are available from **Orleans Cycle,** 26 Main St. (☎ 508/255-9115).

Birding: Bells Neck Conservation Area is in West Harwich; **Monomoy Island National Wildlife Refuge,** Chatham, includes a bird sanctuary on its 2,700 acres.

Boating: For rentals, contact **Jacks Boat Rentals,** Brewster (☎ 508/896-8556)

Camping: Nickerson State Park, Brewster (☎ 508/896-3491), has campsites.

Canoeing/Kayaking: The following rent canoes and kayaks: **Jack's Boat Rentals,** Nickerson State Park, Brewster (☎ 508/896-8556); **Cape Cod Paddle Ventures,** Brewster (☎ 508/896-2610); **Cape Water Sports,** Harwich Port (☎ 508/432-7079); **Goose Hummock Outdoor Center,** Orleans (☎ 508/255-2620);

Clamming: You'll need a permit; then head for **Brewster Flats** on Cape Cod Bay or **Dowest Point,** Osterville.

Cruises: The ketch *Sabbatical* sails from **Harwich**'s Saquatucket Harbor (☎ 508/432-3416).

Fishing: In **Orleans** the largest fleet, with about 20 charter boats, operates from Rock Harbor (☎ 508/255-9757); also the *Striper* (☎ 508/432-4025). **Harwich:** *Fish Tale* ☎ 508/432-3783) and *Arlie X* (☎ 508/430-2454) sail from Saquatucket Harbor.

Golf: Cranberry Valley Golf Course, 183 Oak St., Harwich (☎ 508/430-7560), is rated among the top 75 courses in the nation; **The Captain's Golf Course,** 1000 Freeman's Way, Brewster (☎ 508/896-5100), is another highly rated course. Other courses include **Harwich Port Golf Course,** South Street (☎ 508/432-0250); **Chatham Seaside Links,** 209 Seaview St., Chatham (☎ 508/945-4774); and **Ocean Edge Golf and Tennis Club,** Route 137, Brewster (☎ 508/896-5911).

Horseback Riding: Contact **Deer Meadow Riding Stable,** East Harwich (☎ 508/432-6580) or **Woodsong Farm,** East Brewster (☎ 508/896-5555).

Sailing: Arey's Pond Boat Yard, South Orleans (☎ 508/255-0994) rents sailboats.

State Parks: Two-thousand-acre **Roland C. Nickerson State Park,** Brewster (☎ 508/896-3491), offers camping, bike paths, and eight kettle ponds.

Tennis: Courts can be found at **Brooks Park,** Route 39 and Oak Street, Harwich; **Depot Road,** Chatham, and **Eldredge Park,** Route 28, Orleans.

Windsurfing: Rentals and instruction are available from **Monomoy Sail & Cycle,** Route 28, North Chatham (☎ 508/945-0811); **Cape Water Sports,** Route 28, Harwich Port (☎ 508/432-7079); **Nauset Sports,** Route 6A, Orleans (☎ 508/255-2219); **Jacks Boat Rentals,** Brewster (☎ 508/896-8556).

Cape Cod—The Outer Cape

Eastham ♦ *Wellfleet* ♦ *Truro* ♦ *Provincetown* ♦
Cape Cod National Seashore

Distance in miles from Boston: Eastham, 96; Wellfleet, 108; Truro, 112; Provincetown, 121.

Estimated driving times: 1¾ hours to Eastham; 2⅛ hours to Wellfleet; 2¼ hours to Truro; 2¼ hours to Provincetown.

◄o►◄o►◄o►◄o►◄o►

Driving: Take Route 3 to Route 6. Cross the Sagamore Bridge and take to marked exits for Eastham, Wellfleet, Truro, and Provincetown.

Plane: Cape Air (☎ 800/352-0714 or 508/771-6944) flies from Boston to Hyannis and Provincetown.

Bus: Call Plymouth and Brockton Bus Lines (☎ 508/775-5524) for service from Boston.

Further Information: For further information, contact the **Cape Cod Chamber of Commerce,** routes 6 and 132 (P.O. Box 16), Hyannis, MA 02601 (☎ 508/362-3225).

   Wellfleet Chamber of Commerce, P.O. Box 571, Wellfleet, MA 02687 (☎ 508/349-2510); **Provincetown Chamber of Commerce,** 307 Commercial St. at Macmillan Wharf (P.O. Box 1017), Provincetown, MA 02657 (☎ 508/487-3424).

◄o►◄o►◄o►◄o►◄o►

For centuries the dunes, ocean, bay, beaches, harbors, and an unmatched National Seashore have drawn people to Cape Cod, the finger of land jutting out into the Atlantic, and here on the Outer Cape is where you can see the beauty of the topography most clearly along the windswept and ever-changing coastline of the National Seashore. This is the place to come for contemplation while enjoying the thousand and one recreational delights, from canoeing and kayaking to whale watching, hiking, and biking. And then, of course, there's Provincetown, still the frontier town at the tip of the Cape, as melodramatic as ever, at its most commercially frenetic in summer and its most alluring in winter.

Events & Festivals to Plan Your Trip Around

June: Provincetown Blessing of the Fleet. Fishing boats decorated with flags and bunting sail past the downtown wharf, and the bishop blesses the bow of each boat. It's followed by mass and evening celebrations (usually the last weekend of the month). Call ☎ 508/487-3424.

  Provincetown Portuguese Festival, celebrating the town's Portuguese heritage with music, dancing, and a parade, along with the traditional blessing of the fleet. Call ☎ 508/487-3424.

August: Eastham Antiques Fair. Call (☎ 508/255-0788).

  Carnival Week in Provincetown. An extravagant flamboyant carnival celebration in summer with full parade. Call ☎ 508/487-3424.

  Beach Plum Music Festival in Provincetown, with top jazz and folk acts. Call ☎ 508/349-6874.

September: Provincetown Art Festival, complete with a major auction sponsored by the Provincetown Art Association and Museum. Artists open their studios, and the galleries hold many openings and special events. Call ☎ 508/487-1750.

October: Provincetown's Fantasia Fair. The fashionable women that sashay along the streets during this 10-day festival are stunning. A transvestite celebration.

  Women's Week in Provincetown, when the town fills up with lesbians to celebrate their lives and loves.

December: Holly Folly in Provincetown. A gay and lesbian holiday festival with balls, carols, house tours, concerts, and a reindeer race.

EASTHAM, WELLFLEET & TRURO

Eastham, just above the elbow of the Cape, is where the National Seashore begins. For information and also to see natural history exhibits and a film on the region's ecology and natural life, stop at the Salt Pond Visitor Center on Route 6. Open in summer, daily from 9am to 6pm; spring and fall, daily from 9am to 4:30pm; and January to mid-February, on weekends only. From here, Coast Guard Beach is easily accessed.

On the bay side in Eastham, take Samoset Road to a lovely beach that is also historic. Here, in the winter of 1620, Myles Standish and a party of Pilgrims camped on the beach and encountered the Nauset Indians. A fight ensued, and ever since the spot has been referred to as "First Encounter Beach." The encounter sent the Pilgrims west to Plymouth. However, in 1644 one Thomas Pence set out from Plymouth to establish a settlement called "Nauset." He purchased land from the Indians for a few hatchets. By 1646 Nauset had

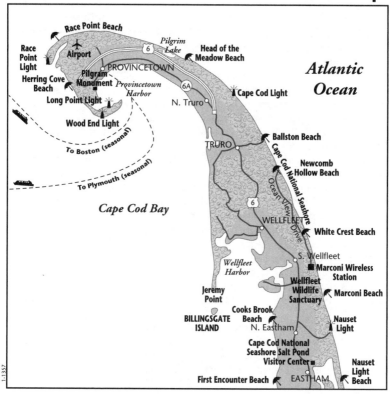

Race Point Beach
Pilgrim Lake
Head of the Meadow Beach
Race Point Light
Airport
PROVINCETOWN
Pilgrim Monument
Herring Cove Beach
Provincetown Harbor
N. Truro
Long Point Light
Wood End Light
To Boston (seasonal)
To Plymouth (seasonal)
Cape Cod Bay
TRURO
Ballston Beach
Newcomb Hollow Beach
Atlantic Ocean
Cape Cod Light
Cape Cod National Seashore
Ocean View Drive
WELLFLEET
White Crest Beach
S. Wellfleet
Wellfleet Harbor
Marconi Wireless Station
Jeremy Point
Wellfleet Wildlife Sanctuary
Marconi Beach
Cooks Brook Beach
BILLINGSGATE ISLAND
N. Eastham
Nauset Light
Cape Cod National Seashore Salt Pond Visitor Center
Nauset Light Beach
First Encounter Beach
EASTHAM

1-1357

become a town, and in 1651 it took the name Eastham. Eastham prospered, and a couple of homes built by its many wealthy residents over the years can still be seen.

The **Captain Edward Penniman House,** Fort Hill Road, off Route 6 (☎ 508/255-3421), is a splendid Victorian that was built by a retired whaling captain in 1867. The **Swift Daley House,** Route 6 (☎ 508/240-1247), which stands next to the post office, was built in 1741. There's also a tool museum here. The houses are open July and August, Monday to Friday from 1 to 4pm; in September on Saturday only, 1 to 4pm.

If you turn off Route 6 down Cable Road, you'll come to the much heralded **Nauset Beach.** This is where the great sweep of coastline to Race Point at the tip of the Cape can best be experienced. It has been said of this coastline that if all the wrecks that have taken place here were arranged bow-to-stern against each other, they would create a wall from Chatham to Provincetown. Here on the bluff, there's an incredible canvas of ocean and shore, and if you peer out on a clear day, you'll likely see the distant speck of a ship on the horizon. A cable station (1879) once stood here, on land that is now eroded; it was able to send messages 3,000 miles across the ocean to Brest in France, via Newfoundland, using a submarine cable. The station was later moved to Orleans and continued operating until the 1950s. In 1838, three lighthouse towers, known as the Three Sisters, stood 150 feet apart on this treacherous coastline. They were eventually swept into the ocean and replaced in 1923 by the light that you see standing today. This light carried on the tradition of the Three Sisters by flashing three times every 10 seconds, alternating between red and white.

On the bay side, before you reach the turnoff to Wellfleet village, you can visit the **Massachusetts Audubon Sanctuary.** Its 600-plus acres incorporate salt marsh, pond, shore, and upland. More than 200 species have been spotted. The society sponsors special seal and seabird cruises in spring and fall that leave from Wellfleet Harbor aboard the *Navigator* for around $25. Call ☎ 508/349-2615 for information.

On the ocean side, before you reach the turnoff to Wellfleet village, you can visit Wellfleet's **Marconi Beach.** At the north end of the beach is the site of the Marconi station. The inventor of the telegraph, Guglielmo Marconi, built two towers here that were blown down by a nor'easter in 1901. He rebuilt the station and successfully transmitted telegraph signals to Cornwall on January 19, 1903, conveying messages between Teddy Roosevelt and King Edward VII. It was an astonishing moment. The station was closed in 1917 and scrapped in 1920, and today there are only interpretive displays to recall the event. Just north of the turnoff to Marconi, you can enjoy another scenic drive by turning off at Le Count Hollow Road and traveling along **Ocean View Drive** past several beaches to Newcomb Hollow Beach. Gross Hill Road loops back to Route 6.

Wellfleet has retained its character and an unspoiled main street. In earlier days the town was famous as an oystering and whaling center and later as a commercial fishing port. Duck Creek was lined with wharves. If you want to know more about the town and its characters in those days, read Thoreau's portrait of oysterman John Newcomb in *Cape Cod* (1864). Among Wellfleet's more famous seamen was Captain Lorenzo Dow Baker, a schooner skipper who brought back Jamaican bananas on one of his trips to the Caribbean. He and his brother-in-law built a banana fleet and organized the Boston Fruit Company, which became the United Fruit Company in 1899. Back then, the place-names Billingsgate, Great Griffiths, and Bound Brook referred to islands. Today only the first is still an island.

To get some perspective on the town's history, visit the **Wellfleet Historic Society Museum,** 266 Main St. (☎ 508/349-9157), which exhibits old photographs, maps, and documents as well as agricultural, marine, and other commercial implements and artifacts. Open late June to mid-September, Tuesday and Friday from 10am to noon. Admission is free.

Today, Wellfleet has less of a reputation as a port and more of a reputation as an art center. The town has a number of fine art galleries and could be said to have taken over the role that Provincetown used to play as the center of the region's very best contemporary art. Turn left as you come into Wellfleet down Commercial Street. It leads to the harbor, but along the way are several galleries well worth visiting. The **Cove Gallery** (Box 482) (☎ 508/349-2530) in particular has some great work by local artists, from John Grillo to Judy Shahn and many others, including Leonard Baskin. **Left Bank Gallery** at no. 25 (☎ 508/349-9451) also puts on good shows by fine contemporary artists.

Go back to Main Street and take Chequesett Neck Road out to **Jeremy Point** and the **Grand Island Trail.** Billingsgate Island used to lie just off Jeremy Point, but it has long since sunk back into the ocean.

From Wellfleet, Route 6 sweeps around past the **Truros** to Provincetown. The dunes begin to loom around North Truro. Windswept and lonely, the Truros are small villages without any real centers. Blink and you will have missed them.

Today Truro is a hideaway for seekers of solitude and serenity. In North Truro, you may well want to visit **Highland Light** (1795), which faces the Atlantic. Often referred to simply as "Cape Cod Light," it's the first light that a Boston-bound ship from Europe sees and is one of the most powerful lights on the East Coast. To the northeast are the treacherous Peaked Hill Bars, which wrecked many a vessel. The **Truro Historical Museum** (☎ 508/487-3397) is practically next door in what once served as a small hotel on the bluffs. The shipwreck exhibit here would unnerve anyone and helps explain the importance of the lighthouse. The museum also features works by local artists (Edward Wilson, Courtney Allen) as well as collections of tools and firearms, plus some period rooms. Open June to September, daily 10am to 5pm.

Head of the Meadow Beach plus **High Head** at the south end of Pilgrim Lake are two highlights of the National Seashore.

EASTHAM & WELLFLEET LODGING

At the **Whalewalk Inn,** 220 Bridge Rd., Eastham, MA 02642 (☎ 508/255-0617), accommodations are located in five buildings on the 3-acre grounds. All 16 rooms and suites are delightfully decorated in elegant country fashion, using country antiques and reproductions. All have a hair dryer, clock radio, and iron. Some have a fireplace, refrigerator, and stocked pantry. The second-floor suite in the barn is particularly attractive. It has a living room with dining area and fireplace and a deck overlooking the meadows. Each of the four rooms in the carriage house has a fireplace, double Jacuzzi, and deck. The beds are mostly pencil four-posters or cannonball four-posters swathed in linens and ruffles and pillows. Innkeeper Dick Smith is the creator of breakfast, and his waffles with strawberry sauce are just great for getting you going in the morning. Adirondack chairs await on the lawns, and there's an outdoor flagstone patio with umbrella tables. Bikes are available. Rates: $150 to $250.

The **Penny House Inn,** 4885 County Rd. (Route 6), Eastham, MA 02642 (☎ 800/554-1751 or 508/255-6632), occupies a 1690 shingled home that has been restored and modernized. The great room where guests gather around the hearth has a cathedral ceiling that makes it light and airy in contrast to the dining room, which has retained its low, beamed ceilings. There are 11 rooms furnished in a country style with a mix of wicker and Eastlake and oak pieces. The largest and most lavish room has knotty-wood paneling around a working fireplace, a brass bed, and a wing chair. There are 2 acres of grounds for guests to enjoy and a back patio for relaxing. Rates: $95 to $165.

The **Inn at Duck Creek,** 70 Main St., Eastham, MA 02642 (☎ 508/349-9333), is located in a historic building owned by a sea captain. The rooms are simply furnished in colonial style. In any given room you might find a Jenny Lind bed matched with an acorn chest, a Hitchcock rocker, and a sofa or loveseat. The bathroom will more than likely feature an old-fashioned tub with shower. Some rooms are on the drab side. Guests can relax in the sitting area off the lobby around the fireplace. Breakfast is a substantial continental meal. Rates: Summer, $65 to $75; spring and fall, $55 to $65 with private bath; $45 to $55 with shared bath.

EASTHAM & WELLFLEET DINING

Aesop's Tables, Main Street (☎ 508/349-6450), is located in a historic house. The cuisine is modern American. Among the dishes, you might find a succulent halibut with roasted-red-pepper puree, cilantro oil, and mango habañero sauce or duck breast marinated in balsamic vinegar and rosé and grilled with dried cranberry cassis sauce. Rack of lamb comes with a port wine demiglace. Prices range from $16 to $21. Start with the clam chowder or the crab cakes. The tavern on the terrace offers a menu featuring sandwiches, barbecue ribs, steamed mussels, and similar fare. Open July and August, Wednesday to Sunday from noon to 3pm, daily from 5:30 to 9pm; call for off-season hours.

    Painter's, 50 Main St., Wellfleet (☎ 508/349-3003), is a cool place. It displays striking contemporary art and has a convivial bar. Upstairs there's a jazz bar. Fire blazes in the hearth on cool nights. The cuisine is up-to-the-minute. Wraps on the menu are delicious and very filling; for example, you might find red bliss potato–wrapped salmon with spinach and lemon parsley beurre blanc. Dishes are more likely to be on the seafood side, like the hearty Portuguese clam stew with linguica and chorizo or the blackened swordfish with grilled leeks, spinach, and basmati rice. Meat dishes tend to bistro-style filet of beef with delicious garlic mashed potatoes and horseradish cream sauce. Prices range from $15 to $19. Open May to October, Wednesday to Monday from 5 to 11pm. Closed Tuesday and from November to April.

    The **Blacksmith's Shop,** off Route 6A, Truro (☎ 508/349-6554), has an appropriate decor of oxen yokes and other rustic artifacts. There's a garden room in back. The menu tilts to Mediterranean and offers a selection of pastas, including an arresting linguine with pancetta and Gorgonzola. Other specialties are Asian five-spice pork tenderloin served with mango pear chutney and monkfish sauced with a spicy Sicilian tapenade. Prices range from $4 to $19. Open late May to early September, Saturday and Sunday 8am to 1pm, daily 4:30 to 10pm.

    For live jazz and other entertainment plus casual dining (catch of the day, chicken burrito, steak kabobs, and burgers), head to the **Duck Creek Tavern,** Main Street, Wellfleet (☎ 508/349-7369). The old tavern room has a fireplace, a beamed ceiling, and a bar made from a collection of period Coors and marine charts. Prices range from $10 to $17. Open late May to mid-October, daily from 5 to 11pm. off-season.

PROVINCETOWN

Even though **Provincetown** is awash in tourist trinkets, it still has its moments, as they say, but you'll have to peer beyond the T-shirt and souvenir stores to find what the artists who came here loved so much. You can't help but be inspired by the quality of the light that seems to resonate with brilliance and color and is especially affecting in the late afternoon and early evening. The dunes that surround the town lure visitors with their mystery. Here, ocean and desert meet. Drive out to Race Point to see them in all their magnificence. The narrow streets lined with Capes and half Capes, often surrounded by fences covered in roses, charm the passerby, and there are still traces of the art colony to be found out at the east end of town, where you can go in and out of one gallery after another.

Provincetown still has a creative, anything-goes edge, and the dunes and beaches are only a short ride away if you need relief from the 45,000 people that may gather here in a single day. And finally, you can't help but love the free-wheeling openness of a town where anything goes and there is a welcome to one and all no matter what the lifestyle. This warm welcome accounts for Provincetown's importance as a gay and lesbian resort, where the individual is free to be as "out" as he or she pleases.

Even though much of its history has been physically wiped away, some does remain or has been memorialized. Provincetown is where Icelander Thorvold may have arrived sometime early in the 11th century, and explorer Bartholomew Gosnold passed this way in 1602. However, the first documented landing was the arrival of the Pilgrims on November 11, 1620. Here they anchored and signed the famous Covenant before migrating on to Plymouth.

EXPLORING THE TOWN

Start in the east end and stroll down Commercial Street. This is where the art and theater colony began, and there are still plenty of art galleries to visit, beginning around Howland Street. The **Provincetown Art Association and Museum,** 460 Commercial St. (☎ 508/487-1750), played a major role in nurturing the art colony and is still going strong. Today you can view the works of local artists and look at the paintings in the permanent collection. The sculpture garden outside is a pleasant place to stop for a rest. Open Memorial Day to July 4 and September, daily noon to 5pm, Friday and Saturday 8am to 10pm; July to Labor Day, daily 8am to 10pm; October to May, Saturday and Sunday noon to 4pm. Admission is a $3 donation. $1 for seniors and children.

If you want to get a sense of Provincetown's history and what it used to be like before and after it became fashionable, then visit the **Provincetown Heritage Museum,** 356 Commercial St. at Center St. (☎ 508/487-0666). The community started out as a den of smugglers, buccaneers, and fishermen until it was incorporated in 1727. Around 1820, some of the fishermen moved out to Long Point to be closer to the fishing, but around 1850 the fish migrated (for whatever reason) and the settlers floated their houses on scows and rafts from the point to Provincetown. The last house was moved in 1867. As you walk around town, look for the blue-and-white plaques showing a house on a boat that indicates a house's historic status. Most of these plaques are now in the west end.

Provincetown Harbor, meanwhile, had become a thriving whaling port, second only to Nantucket and New Bedford, and a major commercial fishing port inhabited by a large Portuguese community. Close to 100 wharves existed along Commercial Street. The museum has many photographs of those bustling days, when fish flakes lined the wharves and the shoreline, and schooners and the 100-strong fishing fleet jammed the harbor. An exhibit focuses on the Portuguese community, which has fished these waters for more than a century and set the tone of the town in the 19th century. Today only 15 or so fishing boats are still operating, and their owners are fast opting for the government repurchase program because they can no longer make a living from the depleted waters with the now-restrictive rules.

Another exhibit documents the community of artists and writers. The arts colony was created at the turn of the century when Charles Hawthorne set up his school in 1899. An inspiring teacher, he attracted painters such as Max Boehm, Richard Miller, George Elmer Browne, and John Noble. The famous theater colony followed. The Provincetown Players was founded in 1915. Eugene O' Neill joined in 1916, and he and other figures such as Susan Glaspell, George Cram Cook, and Mary Heaton Vorse contributed to its reputation and success, which continued until the 1950s and 1960s at different playhouses along the wharves.

The artists and writers clustered at the east end of town, but some of them chose to live in shacks on the dunes. Mabel Dodge started the trend when she converted the Peaked Hill Coast Guard Station into a residence that she later rented to Eugene O'Neill. Sadly, it was swept into the sea in 1931. Nevertheless, writers and artists continued to settle into the dune shacks. You can see photographs of these shacks in the museum and visit them later on a tour. Writer Hazel Hawthorne occupied Euphoria, built in the 1930s. Other famous residents who were drawn to Provincetown were John Dos Passos, Edmund Wilson, and Paul Cadmus; in the 1950s, Jack Kerouac came. Perhaps the most romantic dune-shack figure was Harry Kemp, a drunken poet who had been an amateur fighter, hobo, and vagabond before settling into his shack—a tiny triangular room with bed, stove, desk, and typewriter, where you could reach everything sitting in one place—it's replicated right here in the museum. For many years, Kemp directed the yearly reenactment of the Pilgrim Landing on November 21. Today some of the shacks have been leased to renovators or artists-in-residence by the National Park Service.

One Provincetown character has an entire exhibit devoted to him—Peter Hunt. On display are examples of this man's peasant art—brilliantly painted tables, chairs, and hutches. Hunt arrived in the 1920s and swept into town wearing a long black cape, with two Afghans and a dwarf trailing behind him. His real name was Frederick Lowe Schnitzer, and he had been born in New Jersey, but he had reinvented himself. He opened an antiques store in Provincetown. During the Depression and World War II, people couldn't afford to buy new furniture, so he began painting old furniture to give it a new look, and in so doing, he set off a trend.

Upstairs, practically the entire floor is occupied by a huge, half-scale model of the schooner *Rose Dorothea,* the Grand Banks fishing schooner that won the Lipton Cup during the Old Home Week Celebration in the Boston-Gloucester fishermen's race in 1907. The museum is open daily 10am to 5:30pm. Admission is $3 for adults, no charge for children under 12.

MacMillan Wharf (named after native son Admiral MacMillan, who accompanied Peary to the Arctic) is still at the center of town life. This is the place to go for information and to sign up for ocean-going trips. Behind it stands **Pilgrim Monument,** High Pole Hill Road (☎ 508/487-1310). Provincetowners like to remind the folks down at Plymouth that it was at Provincetown that the Pilgrims first landed and signed their Covenant. The granite Pilgrim Monument soars 350 feet above the town and gives a great view of the surrounding area. The bas relief at the base depicts the landing on November 11, 1620 (a plaque at the west end of Commercial Street marks the exact spot). Open daily April 1 to November 30, daily from 9am to 5pm (9am

Provincetown

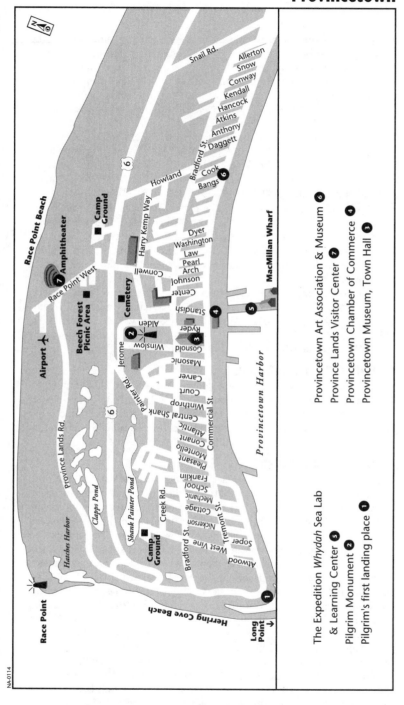

The Expedition *Whydah* Sea Lab & Learning Center ❺
Pilgrim Monument ❷
Pilgrim's first landing place ❶

Provincetown Art Association & Museum ❻
Province Lands Visitor Center ❼
Provincetown Chamber of Commerce ❹
Provincetown Museum, Town Hall ❸

NA-0114

63

to 7pm in July and August). Admission (which includes admission to the Provincetown Museum) is $5 for adults, $3 for children 4 to 12.

Continue through the west end and follow 6A round to Province Land Road, which loops through the dunes with turnoffs to Race Point Light and Race Point Beach. For information, drop into **Province Lands Visitor Center,** Race Point Road (☎ 508/487-1256), open daily in summer from 9am to 6pm, in spring and fall 9am to 4:30pm.

If you want to experience the dunes take a dune tour with Art Costa. Art began the dune-shack tours in 1946, and they've been going ever since. The ORVs take you through the dunes and past the dune shacks to the Coast Guard Station. For information, call **Art's Dune Tours** or stop by at Commercial and Standish streets (☎ 508/487-1950 or 508/487-1050).

Galleries One of the galleries that is particularly appealing to me is the **Julie Heller Gallery** at 2 Gosnold St. (☎ 508/487-2169). The gallery shows the works of early Provincetown artists, including Milton Avery, W. M. Chase, Arthur Diehl, Charles Hawthorne, Oliver Chaffee, Tod Lindenmuth, William Mekitt, and William Zorach. Other notable galleries are the **Berta Walker Gallery**, 208 Bradford at Howland St. (☎ 508/487-6411); the **Rising Tide Gallery**, 494 Commercial St. (☎ 508/487-4037); the **Long Point Gallery**, 492 Commercial St. (☎ 508/487-1795); the **Rice/Polak Gallery**, 430 Commercial St. (☎ 508/487-1052); **Albert Merola Gallery**, 424 Commercial St. (☎ 508/487-4424); and the **DNA Gallery**, 288 Bradford St. (☎ 508/487-7700).

PROVINCETOWN AFTER DARK

Unlike many other towns on the Cape, Provincetown doesn't close up at night. For a start, check out who's performing at **Town Hall**, 260 Commercial St. (☎ 508/487-6400). For information about theater, clubs, bars, and other entertainment, also check with **Provincetown Reservations Systems** at its office at 293 Commercial St., or call ☎ 508/487-6400.

PROVINCETOWN LODGING

Six Webster Place, 6 Webster Place, Provincetown, MA 02657 (☎ 508/487-2266), is in the heart of town, but it is tucked away down a dead-end lane so that it enjoys some privacy. It's a very winning 1750s house whose owners have great flair—when I visited in October, the exterior had artfully been wrapped in thin strands of artificial cobwebs for Halloween. The sitting room is super comfortable and so too are the dining room and kitchen. The owners are very welcoming. There are five rooms, one suite, and three apartments, most with a private bath and working fireplace and all with cable TV. Most are decorated in high style with four-posters, antique furnishings, gilt-framed art, and wing chairs. Breakfast is served in a beautifully paneled dining room that's warmed on cold days by a blazing fire. At the back is an enclosed deck for sun bathing and lounging in a nine-person Jacuzzi. Rates: Spring and fall, $90 to $175; summer, $100 to $155; winter, $75 to $120; apartments, rented weekly only in summer, one bedroom $1,000 and two bedrooms $1,350.

The Brass Key, 9 Court St./12 Carver St., Provincetown, MA 02657 (☎ 508/487-9005), has a lot to recommend it and is often fully booked a year in advance. It's one of Provincetown's most special places. The accommodations are arranged around a brick courtyard with an outdoor pool and hot tub that's been landscaped with a waterfall. The rooms are elegantly furnished. All have private baths, phones with voicemail and dataports, TV/VCRs, refrigerators, and extras like bathrobes and hair dryers. The most luxurious rooms also have Bose radios, wet bars, additional TVs in bedrooms and baths, fireplaces, and/or Jacuzzi tubs. A continental breakfast is served in an attractive breakfast room with a fireplace. Great attention is paid to service. The Brass Key is located 1 block from Commercial Street towards the west end. Its friendly owner is Michael MacIntyre, who also operates a property under the same name in Key West. Rates: April to mid-June and mid-September to November, weekends $135 to $200, midweek $85 to $200; mid-June to mid-September $175 to $275. Closed December to March.

The Tucker Inn, 12 Center St., Provincetown, MA 02657 (☎ 508/487-0381), is a very lovely accommodation in the heart of town but almost a block off Commercial Street. It's located in a handsome Victorian and has eight very tastefully decorated rooms. Throughout the house, owners Katherine Bishop and Denise Karas have used fine fabrics and original art to bring a touch of luxury to the rooms. All rooms have cable TV; some share a bath. A two-bedroom, two-bath cottage with full kitchen and deck is also available for weekly rental. A continental breakfast is served in the living room or on the private tree-shaded patio at the side of the house. Beach chairs and towels are available. Rates: Spring and fall, $80 to $110; summer $100 to $130; cottages $1,000 (per week) in spring and fall and $1,500 in summer.

The Bradford Gardens Inn, 178 Bradford St., Provincetown, MA 02657 (☎ 508/487-1616), is located in the east end of town away from the hubbub. The house dates to around 1825, and it has a historic ambience with its wide-board floors and low ceilings. There are eight rooms with private baths and TV/VCRs in the inn; six have wood-burning fireplaces. Rooms are decorated in a pretty way. For example, Room 5 has a white-painted four-poster with an eyelet lace canopy combined with a white-painted chest and bold floral wallpaper. There are four cottages in the back (three with fireplaces). Two of the cottages are furnished in a rustic manner and have sleeping lofts. The two-bedroom townhouses are modern; each has a fully equipped kitchen, living room with fireplace, dining area, and canopied beds. Guests love to sit around the brick hearth in the living room; the strawberry-and-mustard color scheme gives it a warm glow. Books, art, and a glass collection make it feel very homey, and classical music provides background. Breakfast is served on trays in the sitting room—shirred eggs, broccoli and cheese omelets, or similar dishes. The gardens in front and around the property add a touch of romance to the place. Rates: Memorial Day to Labor Day, $125 to $148, two-bedroom units, $195 to 260; off-season, $85 to $145, two-bedroom units $165 to $205.

The Inn at Cook Street, 7 Cook St., Provincetown, MA 02657 (☎ 508/487-3894), is an 1836 charmer standing behind a white painted fence and gardens in the quieter east end of town. It's operated by Paul Church and his partner, Dana Miton. Guests enter to find an attractive living room furnished with a comfortable sofa and easy chairs arranged around a brick hearth. The three rooms and two suites are all well appointed, each with private bath and TV. The suites have TV/VCRs, refrigerators, and either private or shared decks. One suite has a sitting area with a loveseat and a chair with footrest. A double has a sleigh bed standing under the dormer window and floors covered with oriental rugs. Another room with a four-poster is decked out in Laura Ashley style. Breakfast—fresh fruit, muffins, and other baked goods—is served at a long table from the open kitchen. There's a nice back garden retreat too. Rates: June to mid-September, $100 to $135; mid-September to October, $75 to $85; November to May, $60 to $75.

Plums, 160 Bradford St., Provincetown, MA 02657 (☎ 508/487-2283), is located in a brightly painted Victorian on quieter Bradford Street. Pretty gardens extend alongside the house, filled in season with lilies, irises, and dahlias. The rooms are decked out with lace, flowers, and country antiques. For example, in one room you'll find an antique bed set against bold floral wallpaper combined with a large armoire and wicker furnishings. Breakfast is served at a table set with lace and silver in a dining room lit by a crystal chandelier. Fresh fruit and baked goods accompany French toast stuffed with cream cheese and strawberries or something similarly delicious. Rates: Memorial Day to mid-September, $122; off-season, $92.

Located at the quiet east end, **Windamar House,** 568 Commercial St., Provincetown, MA 02657 (☎ 508/487-0599), occupies a gracious 1840s home on property that extends from Commercial to Bradford streets. The six rooms have been individually decorated in different palettes. Sloping ceilings and skylights add character to many of the spaces. The most lavish is the Studio, which has a cathedral ceiling and an entire wall of glass overlooking the gardens and grape arbor. The bed is a carved Victorian matched with a claw-foot loveseat and armoire. It's one of the two rooms that have private baths and the only one with a TV. There are also two apartments, both with fully equipped kitchens. A continental breakfast is served in the Common Room where guests also gather to watch TV or the VCR. Rates: Late May to mid-September, $90 to $120; mid-September to mid-October, $80 to $105; mid-October to late May, $70 to $95. Mid-season and summer, apartments rent by the week, $650 to $900; and from late October to May by the night, $95 to $105.

The Masthead, 31–41 Commercial St., Provincetown, MA 02657 (☎ 508/487-0523), is in the west end in a great location, right down on the waterfront. In fact, the tides wash the deck that fronts the lawn at the back of the property. The accommodations are in cottages/apartments and motel units, many of them trellised with morning glories or other climbers. Cottages are equipped with kitchens, baths, refrigerators, and TVs. In some, sliding doors open to private decks. They are furnished in an eclectic way, mostly with rather old-fashioned 1950s-style pieces, although some rooms have oriental rugs and more stylish, country-comfortable furnishings. Some have attractive pine dining alcoves and painted furniture by the late Peter Hunt. The main reasons to stay here are the beachfront location, the kitchen facilities, and the oceanfront decks. Rates: July to Labor Day, rooms $87 to $167, efficiencies $168 to $191, cottages/apartments $228 to $316; June and Labor Day to mid-September, deduct $5 to $10; mid-September to May, rooms $65 to $100, efficiencies $82 to $98, cottages/apartments $126 to $170.

Watermark Inn, 603 Commercial St., Provincetown, MA 02657 (☎ 508/487-0165), is also located in the quieter east end, right down on the waterfront. It's a modern establishment where the 10 well-designed suites have cathedral ceilings, skylights, decks, and sleek contemporary furniture. All have TVs, phones, and private baths. One suite has a full kitchen, while the rest have kitchenettes with sinks, small refrigerators, coffeemakers, and toasters. Two have fireplaces. Some have full ocean views; others have oblique water views. Rates: Late May, June, and September, $115 to $230; July to August, $135 to $300. October to late May, $90 to $175.

PROVINCETOWN DINING

Dancing Lobster Cafe/Trattoria, Mariners Wharf (☎ 508/487-0900), is the best place to dine in Provincetown. It's on the waterfront at the east end. Lit by Shaker lanterns and warmed by a brick hearth on cool evenings, it's a romantic place. Folks gather at the long bar that incorporates a boat hull before dining. Start with the clams and mussels, teamed with garlic, fresh herbs in lemon, and wine, or choose an antipasto of seafood—shrimp, squid, and lobster with lemon vinaigrette. There's a selection of salads and pastas to follow. Specialties of the house are the delicious Basque stew, a festive collection of littlenecks, chicken, shrimp, linguica, squid, and mussels steamed with white beans; and the *tonno scottatao,* thinly sliced rare tuna served over cold sautéed fennel. For meat lovers, there are several filet mignon dishes, from steak Diane to steak bosco, with a red-wine reduction. Prices range from $12 to $21. There's a good wine list with several choices by the glass. Open July to September, Tuesday to Sunday from 6 to 11pm; call for off-season hours. Closed December to April.

Ciro and Sal's, 4 Kiley Ct. (☎ 508/487-0049), has been here for many years, and it's still one of the town favorites, with a cozy retro ambience. Posts and beams and seasoned wood tables give it warmth; a few Chianti bottles hang from the ceiling. The menu is very comprehensive, offering a dozen pasta dishes and as many meat and fish dishes. All the traditional Italian favorites are here, along with some less common northern Italian dishes, like the delicious chicken livers sautéed with prosciutto, marsala, and sage; or the fresh fish of the day, broiled with fresh mint, olive oil, and red-wine vinegar. Among the pastas, why not select the spaghetti served with garlic, anchovies, pine nuts, and raisins for a change? At least three daily specials are also offered. Prices range from $11 to $21. Open late May to September, daily from 6 to 10pm. Call for off-season hours.

Martin House, 157 Commercial St. (☎ 508/487-1327), offers some of the town's finest dining in a series of charming and snug dining rooms. The cuisine is innovative and makes use of the best local fish and shellfish. You might start with Wellfleet oysters on the half shell with ponzu dipping sauce, wasabi and pickled ginger, or steamed Provincetown littlenecks in a saffron sherry broth with romesco sauce. Main courses might run to pan-roasted sea bass in a miso and pickled ginger broth with mixed Asian greens and a wakame and Asian pine nut topping; or venison tournedos with a juniper herb crust, blueberry coulis, and a quince and Eastham turnip puree. Prices range from $15 to $27. Open June to October, daily from 6 to 11pm; call for off-season hours.

Napi's, 7 Freeman St. (☎ 508/487-1145), is a fun restaurant, a good choice for vegetarians, and a great place for casual dining. It's decorated with a variety of artwork, stained glass, and objects that include a carousel horse. The menu has something for everyone. Vegetarian dishes include vegetable burrito filled with onion, peppers, broccoli, spinach, and cheese and served with black beans and rice. Try the Brazilian shrimp that is sautéed in garlic herbs and fresh lime and then served with a banana fritter, black beans, and rice. Brazilian steak is done in the same zippy way, and there are plenty of other seafood and chicken dishes ranging from $13 to $29. Open May to October, daily from 11am to 4:30pm and 5 to 10pm; November to April, daily from 5 to 10pm.

Front Street, 230 Commercial St. (☎ 508/487-9715), is located in the cellar of a Victorian building and has a very intimate atmosphere. The menu changes weekly. The food is always simple, but intensely flavored in a traditional bistro style. Among the entrees there might be lime-grilled swordfish with a tequila beurre blanc or a grilled veal rib chop with a mushroom sauté and pinot noir demiglace. There's likely to be a bacon-crusted filet mignon, and rack of lamb is always available. Prices range from $19 to $24. A real treat. Good wine list. Open daily 6 to 10:30pm.

In the morning, join the lines at **Provincetown Portuguese Bakery,** 299 Commercial St. (☎ 508/487-1803), a local favorite for delicious breads and pastries—a Provincetown tradition. Closed November to March. For a picnic, try **Box Lunch,** 353 Commercial St. (☎ 508/487-6026), for "rollwiches," pita bread packed with a variety of fillings.

Eastham, Wellfleet, Truro, & Provincetown
Special & Recreational Activities

For additional information, contact each of the local chambers of commerce. Note, too, that the Cape Cod Chamber of Commerce publishes a *Sportsman's Guide to Cape Cod* and other information (☎ 508/362-3225).

Beaches: The **National Seashore** includes Coast Guard and Nauset Light in Eastham; Marconi in Wellfleet; Head of the Meadows in North Truro. In Provincetown, Race Point on the ocean side is the rougher and more exciting; Herring Cove is calmer and tends to be a haven for same-sex couples. Note that at all these beaches there's a daily parking fee as well as a charge for those who arrive on foot or by bike.

    Outside the Seashore: Cook's Brook in North Eastham and First Encounter are two bay beaches. Most beaches in Truro and Wellfleet require resident stickers. An exception is White Crest, off Ocean View Drive in Wellfleet, a great Atlantic beach.

Biking: The **Cape Cod Rail Trail,** which is part of the state park system, runs for 25 miles from Dennis via Harwich, Brewster, Orleans, and Eastham to Wellfleet. For information, call Nickerson State Park (☎ 508/896-3491).

    The **National Seashore** also offers great biking opportunities. Pick up maps at the Eastham's Salt Pond Visitor Center or Provincetown's Visitor Center. You can bike the 1⁶/₁₀-mile **Nauset Trail** from Eastham along the Nauset Marsh to the old Nauset Coast Guard Station, or you can ride from the Salt Pond Visitor Center to Coast Guard Beach. In North Truro, the 2-mile **Head of the Meadow Trail** passes along the edge of the Salt Meadow. In Provincetown, **Province Lands Trail** winds for 7¼ miles through the dunes and marshes, providing access to Herring Cove Beach and Race Point

Beach. In Provincetown, rentals are available at Arnold's, 329 Commercial St. (☎ 508/487-0844), for as little as $10 a day.

Birding: Wellfleet Bay Wildlife Sanctuary, South Wellfleet (☎ 508/349-2615), has a bird sanctuary. **First Encounter Beach** in Eastham is a good place to see sea birds; **Fort Hill** in Eastham also offers great birding.

Boating: Flyer's Boat Rental, 131A Commercial St., Provincetown (☎ 800/750-0898 or 508/487-0898), rents power boats (from $90 a day), sail boats (from $95 a day), canoes ($40 a day), and jet skis ($45 for ½ hour). Sailing lessons are available. Jack's Boat Rentals, Wellfleet (☎ 508/349-9808), also rents boats.

Cruises: In Provincetown, the schooner *Bay Lady II* (☎ 508/487-9308) leaves from Macmillan Wharf on 2-hour cruises from May to October. Tickets range from $10 to $15, depending on the time of day. There are many other possibilities. **Capt'n Mike's Seafari** (☎ 508/48-SHARK) also runs cruises.

Fishing: Several boats sail from Wellfleet town marina: *Jac's Mate* under Captain George Ministeri (☎ 508/255-2978 or 508/240-8310); *Erin-H* skippered by Captain Robert Hussey (☎ 508/349-9663 or 508/349-3524); the *Snooper* by Captain Joe Dominico (☎ 508/349-6113); and the *Naviator* with Captain Rick Merrill (☎ 508/349-6003). Charges average $20 or so, including equipment and bait. Trips are daily in July and August and weekends in May, June, and September.

Golf: Highland Links Golf Course, Highland Road, North Truro (☎ 508/487-9201), is a fine challenging course; in addition, there's the **Chequessett Yacht and Country Club,** Chequessett Road, Wellfleet (☎ 508/349-3704).

Hiking: There are 11 self-guided nature trails at the National Seashore; some tours are more scenic than others. The 1½-mile **Fort Hill Trail** off Route 6 in Eastham at Governor Prence Road provides great views of Nauset Marsh and the ocean. The 1-mile **Nauset Marsh Trail,** by the Salt Pond Visitor Center, winds along the edge of Salt Pond and Nauset Marsh. In Wellfleet, the 8-mile **Great Island Trail** to Jeremy Point Overlook is the most difficult, but is well worth exploring for the bay vistas. It's mostly soft sand, and at high tide some is submerged. It's accessed via Chequesset Neck Road. The 1¼-mile **Atlantic White Cedar Swamp Trail** off Route 6 in South Wellfleet, loops through the swamp. Follow the signs. Pick up information about the trails at the Salt Pond Visitor Center (☎ 508/255-3421) in Eastham.

Horseback Riding: Nelson's Riding Stable, 43 Race Point Rd., Provincetown (☎ 508/487-1112), offers several daily guided trail rides plus a 2-hour sunset ride for more advanced riders.

Nature Trips: The **Cape Cod National Seashore** sponsors many ranger-led activities—hikes, bird watching, and even canoeing. Call or ask at the information centers in Eastham (☎ 508/255-3421) and Provincetown (☎ 508/487-1256).

Parasailing: Contact **Aqua Ventures Parasailing,** Macmillan Wharf, Provincetown (☎ 800/300-3787 or 508/487-6386).

Sailing: Flyer's Boat Rental, 131A Commercial St., Provincetown (☎ 800/750-0898 or 508/487-0898), rents sail boats (from $95 a day). Sailing lessons available, too.

State Parks: Nickerson State Park, with 1,961 acres, offers 400 campsites; 13 miles of hiking and biking trails; plus swimming, boating, and fishing.

Whale Watching: The **Stellwagen Bank,** which is the center of the whale feeding grounds in Massachusetts Bay, is only 6 miles or so off Provincetown, so you shouldn't miss taking a whale-watching trip here. You might see humpback, right, fin, and minke whales. From Provincetown, the **Dolphin Fleet** (☎ 508/349-1900) operates several trips daily that are led by scientists from the Center for Coastal Studies in Provincetown. Other whale-watching boats include the *Portuguese Princess* (☎ 508/487-2651) and *Ranger V* (☎ 508/487-3322). Tours operate usually from April to October; tickets cost around $17 to $18 for adults and $15 for children 7 to 12. Dress warmly—it can be cold out on the water.

Windsurfing: Places for rentals are **Jack's Boat Rentals,** Route 6, Wellfleet (☎ 508/349-9808) and **Windsurfing Unlimited,** Commercial Street, Provincetown (☎ 508/487-9272).

Martha's Vineyard

Vineyard Haven ◆ *Oak Bluffs* ◆ *Edgartown* ◆ *the Tisburys*
◆ *Chilmark* ◆ *Menemsha* ◆ *Gay Head*

Distance in miles from Boston: 85.

Estimated driving time: 1½ hours plus ferry time

◄O►◄O►◄O►◄O►◄O►

Ferry: The **Steamship Authority** (☎ 508/477-8600 or 508/693-9130) operates a car-passenger ferry from Woods Hole to Vineyard Haven year-round (45 min.). In peak season, from mid-May to mid-October, round-trip tickets cost $88 for a car, $10 for adults, and $5 for children 5 to 12. There's a small charge for bicycles.

The following operate passenger-only ferries from May to October. **Hy-Line Cruises** (☎ 508/778-2600) sails from Hyannis to Oak Bluffs (1¼ hr.; $11 round-trip). The **Island Queen** (☎ 508/548-4800) sails from Falmouth to Oak Bluffs (35 min.; $10 round-trip). **Cape Island Express** (☎ 508/997-1688) operates a ferry from New Bedford to Vineyard Haven (1½ hr.; $16 round-trip). **Falmouth Ferry Service** (☎ 508/548-9400) operates from Falmouth to Edgartown (1 hr.). **Viking Ferry Lines** (☎ 516/668-5700) sails from Montauk to Vineyard Haven (5½ to 6 hr.; $80 round-trip).

Hy-Line operates a ferry from Oak Bluffs to Nantucket in summer (2¼ hr.; $22 round-trip).

Air: Cape Air (☎ 800/352-0714 or 508/771-6944) flies from Boston, New Bedford, Hyannis, and Nantucket to Martha's Vineyard. Flying time is 20 to 30 minutes.

Further Information: For further information, contact **Martha's Vineyard Chamber of Commerce**, Beach Road, Vineyard Haven, MA 02568 (☎ 508/693-0085).

◄O►◄O►◄O►◄O►◄O►

In many people's imaginations, Martha's Vineyard is that glamorous island where celebrities, writers, and the well connected maintain homes. And, indeed, that image is accurate, and has been ever since Emily Post settled in Edgartown and Katherine Cornell arrived at Lambert's Cove, but it's only part of the story. The island is blessed with a diversity, both geographical and

71

Events & Festivals to Plan Your Trip Around

April: **Easter Morning Sunrise Service** held at the inspirational Gay Head Cliffs.

June: **A Taste of the Vineyard,** Edgartown's Whaling Church. Restaurateurs offer samplings of their specialties to benefit the Martha's Vineyard Preservation Trust. Call ☎ 508/627-8017.

July: **Chilmark Road Race;** the course is 3.1 miles and is limited to 1,500 runners.

Edgartown Regatta; for information call ☎ 508/627-4361.

August: **Possible Dreams Auction,** held on the Harborside Inn's lawn, Edgartown, benefits the Martha's Vineyard Community Services. Resident celebrities often take part. Call ☎ 508/603-7900.

Agricultural Society Livestock Show and Fair, a traditional country carnival and fair held at the West Tisbury fairgrounds. Call ☎ 508/693-4343.

Illumination Night, held at the Oak Bluffs Campground. Around 9pm, the first candle is lit at the tabernacle, and shortly afterwards hundreds of Japanese lanterns are lit—a tradition since 1869. Call ☎ 508/693-0085.

Oak Bluffs Fireworks, a spectacular show that is introduced by band concert in Ocean Park. Call ☎ 508/693-5380.

October: Cranberry Day, the second Tuesday in October, is an important day for the Wampanoags who celebrate with special events

socioeconomic, that allows you to make it your very own. Only 20 miles long and 6 miles wide, Martha's Vineyard offers a remarkable range of terrain and six very different towns to explore.

On the northern coast, the West and East Chops protect the island's two harbors. The southern coastline is indented with a series of ponds protected by a long barrier beach. Behind them, forest and meadow stretch out across the center of the island. At the west end, the Gay Head cliffs rise up, while at the east end floats Chappaquiddick Island. Three towns face Nantucket Sound—Vineyard Haven (actually in the town of Tisbury), Oak Bluffs, and Edgartown. "Up island," a nautical term that is still used by the locals and off islanders alike, you'll find first West Tisbury, then Chilmark, and Gay Head. Each of these towns has a very distinct flavor and history of its own.

When early explorer Bartholomew Gosnold visited and named the island, he noted strawberries, blueberries, and raspberries, but more often than anything else, he saw grapes, and so he named the island after the predominant fruit and his daughter Martha. In 1641, Thomas Mayhew bought Martha's Vineyard, along with Nantucket and the Elizabeth Islands, for a mere 40 pounds from two English aristocrats who had conflicting claims. His son, Thomas Junior, established a settlement in 1642 at Edgartown, or Great Harbor as it was then called. Thomas began a mission to the local Indians and succeeded

Martha's Vineyard

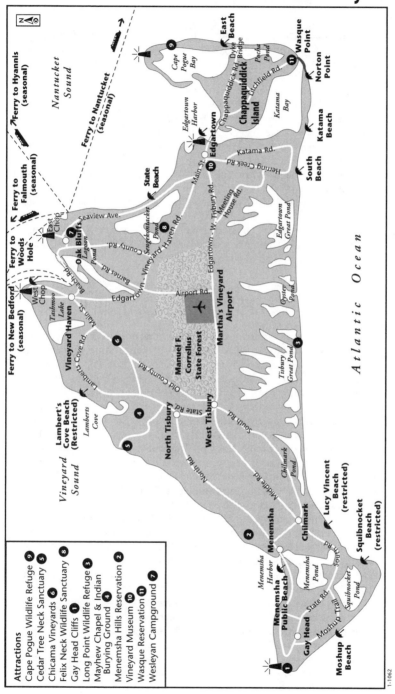

Attractions

Cape Pogue Wildlife Refuge ⑨
Cedar Tree Neck Sanctuary ⑤
Chicama Vineyards ⑥
Felix Neck Wildlife Sanctuary ⑧
Gay Head Cliffs ①
Long Point Wildlife Refuge ③
Mayhew Chapel & Indian Burying Ground ④
Menemsha Hills Reservation ②
Vineyard Museum ⑩
Wasque Reservation ⑪
Wesleyan Campground ⑦

in building a congregation of "praying Indians" at Christiantown. Sadly, he was killed on a return trip to England. Today you can visit the chapel and memorial to him, built by the Indians on Christiantown Road.

The early settlers engaged in farming and mercantile trade between the West Indies and the colonies, exchanging their cranberries, wool, salt cod, clay, and salt for sugar, rum, and slaves. The Revolutionary War, though, interrupted this economic prosperity; the British raided the island in September 1778, carrying away more than 10,000 sheep and hundreds of cattle. It took a long time for the island to recover. It was whaling that brought salvation. From 1820 to 1860, whaling, centered in Edgartown, dominated island life. Again war intervened. This time the Civil War interrupted commerce, an interruption from which the island didn't recover; the whaling industry was at the end of its heyday. Finally, tourism led the island to recovery in the late 19th century.

Today the year-round population of about 14,000 swells to 70,000 during the summer. President Clinton's vacations here in 1993, 1997, and 1998 have drawn more attention than usual to the island.

VINEYARD HAVEN & OAK BLUFFS

This is where most visitors arrive and form their first impression of the island. **Vineyard Haven** is a busy small town, with few historic features. Originally it was called Holmes Hole, a safe haven for the thousands of ships that passed through Vineyard Sound before the opening of the Cape Cod Canal in 1914. Here they could wait out bad weather or pick up a pilot who knew the treacherous tides and shoals of the sound. From the harbor, you can walk up to Main Street, which is lined with a variety of stores. The whole town looks distinctly modern unless you take a detour down one of the side streets. This is because a fire swept through town on August 11, 1883, destroying three-quarters of the buildings. If you want to see the surviving older buildings, walk down William Street, or a couple of other side streets. On Main, many of the shops are worth browsing. The **Bunch of Grapes Bookstore** is a place where the locals meet, and it's also a really terrific bookstore.

While you're in town you may want to visit **Seaman's Bethel**, 15 Beach Rd. (☎ 508/693-9317), which has hosted and helped seamen who visit or reside on the island for more than 100 years. In return, they have donated the items on display here—ships' models, scrimshaw, historic photographs, seashells, and even a life belt from the *Titanic*. Open Monday to Friday from 9am to 1pm. Admission free.

Return to Main Street and you can continue walking or driving out past Owen Park, which provides access to the waterfront. Eventually you'll reach the **West Chop Light,** first built in 1817 and then replaced in 1838. The road then leads around into Franklin Street, which passes Mink Meadows Pond and the golf course. If you're looking for evening entertainment, Vineyard Haven is home to the island's major professional theater, the **Vineyard Playhouse,** at 24 Church St. (☎ 508/696-6300).

If you turn left instead of right at the famous Five Corners in Vineyard Haven, you'll be traveling along Beach Road, which runs along a narrow spit of land with harbor and sound on one side and lagoon and pond on the other. It will bring you to East Chop and Oak Bluffs. On the way, you may want to stop at **All Things Oriental**, 123 Beach Rd. (☎ 508/693-8375), which stocks some fine antiques. Like West Chop, East Chop has a lighthouse, built in 1875. If you want to visit it, continue along Beach Road and turn left down Temahigan Avenue and another left onto Highland Drive, which runs into East Chop Drive. Alternatively, you can turn right off Beach Road onto Eastville Avenue and then right again on County Road to Shirley Avenue to visit the **State Lobster Hatchery** before entering the chock-full-of-character town of Oak Bluffs.

To head to **Oak Bluffs,** continue from Beach Road onto Temahigan Avenue; the road swings sharply right on New York Avenue and then drops down to Lake Avenue, which runs past the Wesley House along Oak Bluff harbor. At the junction of Lake, Circuit, and Oak Bluffs avenues stands one of the town's landmarks, the **Flying Horses Carousel**, 33 Circuit Ave. (☎ 508/693-9481). It's one of the nation's oldest, dating back to 1876. It was brought here from Coney Island in 1884 and still provides visitors with the classic thrill of riding one of the 22 magical horses for $1 a ride. Open Easter Sunday to Columbus Day, daily 9:30am to 10pm in summer and fall, weekends only until mid-May.

The outstanding attraction at Oak Bluffs, though, is the famous **Methodist Camp Ground** established here in August 1834. You can access it from Circuit Avenue via a passageway through the Arcade Building. Entering it for the first time is a delightful experience. Narrow streets are lined with dollhouse cottages painted in brilliant colors and pastels. They're loaded with scrollwork and gingerbread, dainty balconies, and gothic or star-shaped windows. Most of these charmers have porches decorated with flower baskets, where the residents rock in their chairs.

At the center of the colony stands the **Trinity Park Tabernacle** (☎ 508/693-0525), a steel structure erected in 1879. The first camp was held in 1835, and people set up tents to listen to all-day gospel sessions. By the mid-1850s more than 12,000 people were attending the camp. In 1859 the first cottage was built. By the 1870s, there were 1,000 of them. If you want to see inside one of the cottages and view memorabilia relating to the camp, visit the **Cottage Museum,** 1 Trinity Park (☎ 508/693-0525). It's open mid-June to mid-September; admission is free. Every year, to mark the closing of the camp, lamps were lit as a reminder to carry the light abroad. This tradition continues today. In August on **Illumination Night** (the date is traditionally supposed to be a secret), Japanese lanterns flicker from the porches, casting their glow across the water.

Oak Bluffs also has a rich African-American history and a year-round African-American community, which today includes such notable residents as Dorothy West, last surviving member of the Harlem Renaissance, and film maker Spike Lee. The **Shearer Cottage** (1909) is the oldest African-American guesthouse on the island, and over the years it has hosted Adam Clayton Powell, Martin Luther King, Paul Robeson, and Ethel Waters.

Circuit Avenue is the commercial heart of the town. One end of it opens into Lake Avenue, which skirts the harbor. From here, take Sea View Avenue past **Ocean Park,** which is overlooked by some wonderful Queen Anne–style

Victorians. On summer Sundays, concerts are given at the bandstand at the center of the green, and this is also the place where the spectacular fireworks display is given in August. Seaview sweeps along **Oak Bluff Town Beach** and Farm Pond before becoming Beach Road and passing along a wonderful strip of coastline. On one side, the great swath of **Joseph A. Sylvia State Beach** faces Nantucket Sound. On the other stretches the large **Sengekontacket Pond**, frequented by lots of shore birds, many of which reside at the Felix Neck Wildlife Sanctuary on the pond's western shore. State Beach runs into Edgartown Beach, and Beach Road becomes Oak Bluffs Road before it leads into Edgartown.

VINEYARD HAVEN LODGING & DINING

The **Lothrop Merry House,** Owen Park (P.O. Box 1939), Vineyard Haven MA 02568 (☎ 508/693-1646), is right down by the harbor at Owen Park in a small historic home and has its own little beach. A sailboat and a canoe are available to guests, who also have the opportunity to charter the 54-foot ketch *Laissez Faire* from owners John and Mary Clarke. Among its distinguished features are the original works of art that hang in each room. Six rooms are available in winter; seven in summer. Each of the three rooms in the main house has a private bath, and the three in the adjacent 1790 house share a bath. The Blue Room has a view of the harbor; a wood-burning fireplace; and an ebony four-poster, an elegant desk, and a pier mirror set against the Williamsburg blue walls. Landscapes and portraits by Mary's grandfather, Charles Hopkinson, add a touch of luxury. The main sitting room is also the breakfast room. A continental breakfast is served on trays that can be taken down to the waterside or wherever you like. Guests appreciate being able to relax on the brick patio trellised with a grape arbor or down at the beach where they can watch the panorama of the harbor. Rates: Mid-June to mid-October, $139 to $205; mid-April to mid-June and mid-October to early December, $98 to $175; and early December to early April, $78 to $135.

The **Black Dog Tavern,** Beach Street Extension (☎ 508/693-9223), a well-known Vineyard icon, is a prime destination for many guests. It's an atmospheric sea-dog kind of place, rather hard to find as it's tucked away right down on the harbor's edge. Visitors love this rough-hewn tavern with its open kitchen and polished wood tables. The menu changes daily but you might find items such as yellowfin tuna with mango salsa; codfish with mixed peppers, scallions, and oyster sauce; or a hearty dish like grilled pork chops with braised onions and smoked bacon. Prices range from $22 to $26. Open June to early September, Monday to Saturday 7am to 2:30pm and 5 to 10pm, Sunday 7am to 1pm and 5 to 10pm. Call for off-season hours.

Dry Town Cafe, 70 Main St. (☎ 508/693-1484), is a small storefront casual restaurant offering fine innovative cuisine. Among the delicious starters, you might enjoy warm Maine lobster over creamy polenta with wild baby ramps and lobster basil beurre blanc. The menu leans toward fish that is exquisitely prepared, like the striped bass marinated in sake-ginger and cooked over very high heat in Japanese style. Meat lovers will relish the pan-roasted rack of lamb in a lamb reduction and mint oil. Prices range from $19 to $28. BYOB. Open June to October, daily 10:30am to 2:30pm (juice bar) and 6 to 10pm (dinner). Closed late February to late March.

Le Grenier, 96 Main St. (☎ 508/693-4906), is upstairs in a townhouse and is a classic French dining room where the chef prepares traditional classic French cuisine. You'll find a shrimp Pernod, duck a l'orange, and many other classics along with some little surprises like the scallops Barcelona sautéed with almonds and flamed with amarettto. Prices range from $19 to $30. July to August, daily 6 to 10pm. Closed January and February.

OAK BLUFFS LODGING & DINING

Oak House, Seaview Avenue at Pequot Avenue (Box 299), Oak Bluffs, MA 02557 (☎ 508/693-4187), overlooks the state beach. An architecturally interesting residence that was built in 1872, it served as the summer residence for the governors of Massachusetts. It has wide front porches, and the interior features rich oak paneling. When the governor purchased it in the early 1900s, he is supposed to have cut the building in half and added a second floor in between the original floors.

The 10 rooms all have private baths, air conditioning, and TVs. They are furnished in a warm country style. The Jenny Lind Room has an iron-and-brass bed with a floral coverlet, a maple dresser, and a wing-back chair plus books in the built-in shelves. The most striking rooms are the President Ulysses Grant Suite, which has a beamed ceiling, and the Governor Claflin Room, which is a study in oak and contains a brass bed, two window seats, and a tiny balcony. On the third floor the Captain's Room has a sloping ceiling of gleaming oak (as do the other rooms up here) and a view of the ocean from its balcony. The Tiffany Room has fringed lamps and a stained glass window. Ginger jar lamps and other accents give China Seas its oriental look.

The living room has some extraordinary antiques—elaborately carved tables and chairs and an unusual female cigar-store Indian. There's a glassed-in front porch plus a large outdoor porch overlooking the ocean and a brick patio with a grill in the back. Afternoon tea is also served, and the innkeeper, an ex pastry chef, assures that it's an extra-special spread. A continental breakfast is included. Open May through October. Rates: Early May $110 to $185; late May to early September $150 to $255; early September to October $125 to $195.

Oak Bluffs Inn, 167 Circuit Ave. at Pequot Avenue, Box 2477, Oak Bluffs, MA 02557 (☎ 508/693-7171), is a turreted Victorian that has been painted in Victorian style, using 21 exterior colors. It's right in town. There are nine rooms, all different shapes and sizes, and furnished in a cottage Victorian manner. Room 4, for example, has a cottage bed and dresser plus a table and chairs in the bay window. There are also three rooms in the carriage house. Guests are invited to climb up into the tower, which offers a fine view. Rates: Spring and fall, $120 to $160; summer, $130 to $175 midweek and $145 to $200 weekends

Wesley Hotel, 1 Lake Ave., Box 2370, Oak Bluffs, MA 02557 (☎ 508/693-6611), looks out over the harbor. It's the last of the large Victorian shingle-style hotels in town, complete with turret and front porch extending the length of the facade. Inside, the large, long lobby has a historic look and air. Here Victorian-style couches upholstered in plush burgundy are arranged around the big river-stone fireplace, and the room is lit with chandeliers. The 62 rooms are all furnished in similar uninspired style. Cane rockers line the front porch. Rates: May to early June and mid-September to mid-October, $105 to $120; mid-June to mid-September, $145 to $185.

Sea Spray Inn, 2 Nashawena Park, Box 2125, Oak Bluffs, MA 02557 (☎ 508/693-9388), is owned by artist Rayeanne King, and it's an original with a distinct Bohemian flair. It overlooks the park at the end of which is the ocean. Traditionalists may not appreciate its inventiveness, but freer souls will find it refreshingly different. The seven rooms contain original furnishings by local artists. For example, in one of the rooms there's a driftwood chest, in another a carved headboard. Rooms are painted in various colors—peach, lilac, and jade. In one, for example, the floorboards are jade and the door is a pale green. The furnishings include a remarkable gentleman's dresser and a large California king bed draped with a floral quilt. Hand-painted rugs adorn the bathroom floor, and the walls are pale sky blue. The largest accommodation is the garden suite, which has its own porch. A continental breakfast is served buffet style. Open April to October. Rates: May 20 to October 10, $100 to $150; off-season $75 to $100.

The **Sweet Life Cafe,** 168 Circuit Ave. (☎ 508/696-0200), is one of my favorite places to dine on the island, and also a local favorite. It's right in town in a historic townhouse that offers intimate dining rooms and a delightful courtyard dining area. The cuisine is superb, fresh, and imaginative. The menu changes seasonally but you might start with a goat cheese terrine that is enhanced with roasted eggplant and peppers and a parsley coriander sauce or with a tangy fresh mussel saffron soup with tomato concasse.

It's hard to choose a main course. The fire-roasted chicken with braised carrots, roasted garlic mashed potatoes, and onion broth is deeply satisfying, but both the tenderloin of lamb with a Provençale sauce and the pan-roasted salmon with shiitake-mushroom risotto, wilted spinach, and red wine herb au jus are both perfect. Prices range from $20 to $28.

If you can't make dinner then come for brunch, when you'll find dishes such as frittata made with smoked bacon, sautéed potatoes and onions, banana nut pancakes, and many other tempting items. Open Memorial Day to Columbus Day, daily 5:30 to 10:30pm; Columbus Day to January 1 and April and May, Wednesday to Sunday 5:30 to 10:30pm. Closed January to March.

Lola's, Beach Road (☎ 508/693-5007), is a sassy, fun, somewhat noisy and frantic kind of place. Come here for huge portions and also to catch some jazz in the late evening. The food is as spicy as the atmosphere. To start, try the grilled blackened shrimp with a pineapple mango cilantro salsa, or the house specialty—barbecue riblets with a smoky Jack Daniels barbecue sauce. Among the entrees is rib-eye steak—from hell or heaven, depending on whether or not you request the jalapeño demi glace. The menu is always supplemented by a raft of up-to-the-minute specials like seafood étouffée or steamed lobster. Prices range from $20 to $24. To finish, don't miss out on either the key lime pie or the bread pudding with a warm bourbon sauce. Open mid-May to mid-September, daily from 5 to 9pm, and for lunch on Sunday from 10am to 2pm. Call for off-season hours.

Brasserie, 162 Circuit Ave. (☎ 508/693-3300), is a sleek and stylish place that hums at night. People come for the contemporary cuisine, which ranges from a simple linguine with white clam sauce to grilled rack of lamb with pomegranate glaze and pinot sauce. Try the shrimp martini, spice rubbed, seared, and served atop garlic mashed potatoes and garnished with oysters, mushrooms, and fresh carrot ginger splash. The garlic mash is so good some people order it separately. To start, the lobster chowder is good, and there's a whole raw bar to explore, too. Prices range from $24 to $29. Open May to October, daily from 6 to 10pm.

Zapotec, 10 Kennebec Ave. (☎ 508/693-6800), is a small plain dining room with wooden tables. The warm colors of the art that adorns the walls and the colored lights on the ceiling suggest a Mexican flavor. The food is a cut above typical Mexican, but it's not outstanding. You can order the standard burritos, enchiladas, and fajitas along with dishes such as crab cakes served with two salsas or chicken with mole sauce, plus daily specials. If you want spicy food, order some sliced jalapeños. Prices range from $11 to $18. Open daily from 5 to 9pm, and for lunch on weekends from noon to 3pm.

Linda Jean's, Circuit Avenue (☎ 508/693-4093), is where everyone heads for a hearty breakfast. Great pancakes and other classic egg dishes in a typical down-home atmosphere. Expect to wait outside. Open year-round, daily from 6am to 8pm.

A fun new place to hang your hat year-round is the **City Ale and Oyster,** 30 Kennebec Ave. (☎ 508/693-2626), a microbrew pub that offers eight or so special brews. The fare goes with the beer—calamari fried in a graham-cracker batter and served with a red pepper aioli, plus fish dishes that include lobster, a clambake, and brick oven pizzas. Prices range from $12 to $24. Open June to September, from noon to midnight. Call for off-season hours.

EDGARTOWN

Edgartown is the grand dame of the island—historic, moneyed, and well coifed. This is where the whaling money was made, and you can see it in the grand residences that line the streets—Greek Revival beauties with Doric columns, fanlights, and Federal balustrades and porticos. They were painted white to simulate stone, and indeed if you visit the old Whaling Church, it's hard to conceive that those pillars out front are really made of wood. Money still lives here, but it's also buttressed by fame. This is the town, after all, that raises money for community services by auctioning items such as a sail with Walter Cronkite, tennis with Mike Wallace, and a performance by Carly Simon in your own home. The auction is held every August in the gardens of the Harbor Side Inn. Humorist Art Buchwald wields the gavel. Even if you can't afford to bid $86,000 to secure Carly Simon's appearance in your living room, it's fun to attend and watch the rich in action.

Wander around the lanes and streets and admire the homes and their gardens. Many are enclosed by white fences draped with rambling roses. At 99 Main St. stands the classic Federal style **Dr. Daniel Fisher House** (☎ 508/627-8017), which was built in 1840 at the height of the whaling era. He was a doctor-surgeon and entrepreneur who made a fortune from whale oil, banking, and manufacturing. At one time his factory produced 60 tons of candles per year for all the lighthouses. He also owned and operated a grist mill. The interior of the **Old Whaling Church,** 89 Main St. (☎ 508/627-4442), can be seen only on a tour given by the Preservation Trust. It is a splendid, imposing edifice. Built in 1843 to show the Congregationalist landed gentry just how powerful and wealthy the Methodists had become, thanks to their whaling profits, it certainly made its point well. Surprisingly, given its sizable exterior appearance, it's only a two-story building. The lower floor was and is used for administration, while the upper floor contains the church. The church has box pews for approximately 540 people, and each pew has a different size and style of prayer book rack. The church also possesses a great organ, and today it is the town's major performance space, hosting concerts, lectures, plays, and films.

Behind the church stands the **Vincent House,** a 1672 Cape that has two front rooms and a back keeping room. It was moved from its original site on the Great Pond and restored by the Preservation Trust. Visitors can see how the walls were made with wattle and daub using nary a nail. One room has been furnished in Federal style and has some striking marbleized paneling on the doors. The large fireplace in the keeping room is 3½ feet deep, and behind one of the cupboards there's a dangerously steep staircase (such steep staircases were the cause of many deaths in the early colonies). Open Memorial Day to Columbus Day daily from 10:30am to 3pm. Walking tours of the town are also given by the Preservation Trust, starting from the Vincent House Museum. For information call ☎ 508/627-8619.

Stroll down Main Street. There are plenty of fine shops to browse, including the bookstore **Bickerton and Ripley** that labels some of its books with recommendations. On South Summer Street you can search out the old building that houses the offices of the *Vineyard Gazette,* the venerable island newspaper. Today it's owned by the Restons, but Henry Beetle Hough is still the editor, and you might like to pick up one of his books about the island. From Main Street, South Water Street cuts off to the right and north to the left. Both are worth exploring. North Water Street leads round to the harbor. On South Water Street, don't miss **the pagoda tree,** which was brought from China as a seedling by Captain Thomas Milton. Farther along the street is the home of Captain Valentine Pease, master of the *Acushnet,* the ship on which, in 1841, Herman Melville took on his first and only whaling trip. The prime keeper of the town's history is the **Martha's Vineyard Historical Society,** which has its headquarters at the corner of School and Cooke streets (☎ 508/627-4441). On the grounds, the **Thomas Cooke House** (1765) contains 12 rooms displaying furniture; scrimshaw; marine art; and whaling, fishing, and farming tools. The Fresnel lens that was taken from the Gay Head Lighthouse in 1952 is also located here. Wagons and boats occupy the carriage shed. The **Foster Maritime Gallery** is in the **Dale Huntington Library.** Other historical exhibits are found in the **Captain Francis Pease house,** open mid-June to Columbus Day, Tuesday to Saturday 10am to 5pm; off-season, Wednesday to Friday 1 to 4pm and Saturday 10am to 4pm.

Chappaquiddick Island is part of Edgartown, and on any weekend you should take the tiny ferry across, preferably with a bicycle, and ride around this totally uncommercialized piece of land. Be sure and take a picnic because there is no place to purchase food or drink out here. Many people take their ORVs across to the **Cape Pogue Refuge** and beaches to see the Cape Pogue Lighthouse.

The hot ticket for nighttime entertainment on the island is the **Hot Tin Roof,** Carly Simon's place out near the airport.

EDGARTOWN LODGING

The **Charlotte Inn**, 27 S. Summer St., Edgartown, MA 02539 (☎ 508/ 627-4751) is *the* place to stay, and you know it from the minute you enter the handsome doorway into the foyer with its 19th-century oil paintings. The gracious house was built in 1864 and has served as an inn since the 1920s. The inn also incorporates four other buildings, making it a veritable warren of true comfort and sumptuousness, surrounded by beautiful gardens. Throughout, guests will find authentic and priceless English antiques, fine fabrics, wallpapers, and carpets. Even the hallways are delightful, decorated with books and blessed with the occasional window seat or little alcove.

The main house has 12 extraordinarily lavish accommodations, but the most dramatic accommodation is the Coach House Suite. Climb the stairs from the carriage area (it does still shelter a handsome wicker carriage, along with two more modern chariots), and you'll find a luxurious sitting area furnished with plush armchairs and a window seat in front of the Palladian window that offers glimpses of the harbor. A Chippendale table stands in front of the fireplace, flanked by bookcases filled with leather-bound volumes, and gilt-framed original art graces the walls. Green velvet tiebacks lead into the bedroom, which has a mahogany half-poster and a chaise lounge. The other rooms are decorated with a great sense of style and comfort and appointed with items such as sterling silver dresser sets, brass and crystal lamps, silk and linen draperies, and vases of fresh flowers. Most but not all rooms have a TV, telephone, and air-conditioning. Brick pathways, bordered by perfectly trimmed hedges and meticulously cared for shrubs, wind through the property. Once you settle in here you may never decide to leave. See below for dining at the inn. Rates: summer, rooms $260 to $460, suites $510 to $675; interim season, rooms $175 to $410, suites $410 to $575; winter, rooms $135 to $410, suites $375 to $560.

Right in the middle of town, the **Tuscany Inn**, 22 N. Water St. (P.O. Box 2428), Edgartown, MA 02539 (☎ 508/627-5999), is another stunning place to stay— with a unique mood and style. It's decorated in a warm and wonderful way by Laura Sbrana, an interior decorator from Florence, Italy, who has transformed the house. The sumptuous cherry colored couches and chairs in the living room invite guests to sink into them. A Chinese silk rug covers the floor, while the walls are sponge-painted in a rich ocher shade. There are eight rooms. One has an iron canopied bed, matched with a marquetry inlay boule chest, an armoire, and a couch and fine china and ceramic accents. Other rooms are beautifully decorated in high style. You might find turquoise candy-stripe wallpaper combined with painted cottage furnishings or a lace-canopied bed and rug-covered tile floors. Two of the rooms have whirlpool tubs under skylights. The breakfast room will inspire even the most jaded morning risers, with its gorgeous Italian tile floors, antique chairs, tables clad in blue gingham tablecloths, and the sheen of copper pots. The food will inspire, too. Expect to enjoy tasty frittatas and freshly baked breads. The formal dining room functions as La Cucina restaurant, with outdoor dining on a stone patio where the tables are arranged around a sculpted birdbath. Handsome silver peacocks grace the tables. Rates: Mid-June to September 1, $210 to $335; mid-May to mid-June and early September to late October, $160 to $255; late October to mid-May, $100 to $155.

Victorian Inn, 24 S. Water St., Box 947, Edgartown, MA 02539 (☎ 508/627-4784), occupies a glorious 1820 bracketed Victorian in the center of town. Inside the entrance and to the right there's a comfortable living room with a fire blazing. It's a wonderful, unstuffy place where you really can relax and enjoy yourself. Innkeepers Stephen and Karyn Caliri are both very hospitable, and Steve is an exceptionally entertaining, humorous host. There are 14 rooms, all with private baths. The front rooms have decks with great views. Room 10, for example, has two balconies, both with views of the harbor. A pencil-style canopied bed with lace ruffles stands on wall-to-wall rose-colored carpeting. A small drop-leaf desk, two wing-back chairs, and other antique reproductions complete the furnishings. A decanter of sherry is placed in every room. The bathrooms are exceptionally well designed with extra storage space and nice amenities such as china soap dishes. The breakfast is excellent and offers a choice of muffins, plus egg dishes such as Greek frittata, and delicious sour cream banana waffles. In summer, breakfast is served in the pretty back brick courtyard at umbrella tables. There's also an afternoon tea. Rates: Memorial Day to Columbus Day, $135 to $275; off-season $95 to $208.

The Daggett House, 59 N. Water St., Box 1333, Edgartown, MA (☎ 508/627-4600), consists of three buildings in garden settings. The Daggett itself is a genuine historic home, which actually has a secret room, located at the top of a spiral staircase accessed from the dining room via a door hidden behind a series of shelves beside the hearth. The room is furnished with a four-poster bed, an Empire chest, and wing chair and has a fine view of the harbor. Out back, there's a brick patio and a long lawn that extends down to the water's edge. A couple of rooms, available only in summer, are located in a cottage that once served as a schoolhouse. Fifteen rooms and three suites are located across the street at the Greek Revival Captain Warren House, which was built in 1850. Accommodations in the Captain Warren House are nicely furnished with marble-top chests, wing chairs, and four-posters with crochet canopies. Each room also has a TV and telephone. The most attractive room in the house has a 40-by-15-foot roof deck with a spectacular view of the harbor, South Beach, and Chappaquiddick; a hot tub; and a kitchen with stove.

In the dining room, plank tables and Windsor chairs stand on wide-board floors in front of a huge 1660 brick beehive fireplace. Here a full breakfast is served plus lunch and dinner. Dinner features traditional fare such as baked cod in lemon caper butter sauce or hazelnut mustard pork chop au jus. Prices range from $18 to $23. Rates: Mid-May to mid-October, rooms $155 to $215; suites $240 to $410; mid-October to mid-May, rooms $90 to $125, suites $125 to $295.

Enter the small gate and go past the croquet lawn to the reception area of the **Point Way Inn,** 104 Main St., Box 5255, Edgartown, MA 02539 (☎ 508/627-8633). Here whaling displays, navigational charts (used by the innkeepers on their many voyages), and the harpoon over the door that leads into a comfortable living room emphasize the maritime flavor of this rambling inn. The library, which is adjacent to the living room, has a variety of books, custom-made puzzles, and games for guests to enjoy. French doors lead out to a brick patio that is a veritable sun trap.

The inn offers 15 rooms, 11 with a fireplace. The suite in the back is very appealing. It has window seats on both sides of the fireplace and a private deck. The skylit bedroom has a cannonball bed, a small desk, and Hitchcock chairs. The five rooms in the main house are smaller, but comfortably furnished with beds that have crochet canopies, wing chairs, and iron floor lamps. Among my favorite rooms is the attic room, which is painted a brilliant lemon yellow and has a cathedral ceiling and a canopied bed covered with a handsome quilt. Another favorite is the deck room, with its wood stove and superlarge private deck.

Breakfast is served in the nautical dining room where the walls are covered with photographs of innkeepers Ben and Linda Smith on their travels around the world. It's warmed by a wood stove and made even more eye-catching by its drip-painted floors. The inn is famous for its croquet tourney in August. Ben will also take you clamming. Guests have their own refrigerator. Rates: April to mid-June, $110 to $175; mid-June to mid-September, $160 to $295; mid-September to October, $145 to $200; November to March, $100 to $155.

The **Edgartown Inn,** 56 N. Water St. (P.O. Box 1211), Edgartown, MA 02539 (☎ 508/627-4794), is a 1798 house that has seen many celebrity visitors. Daniel Webster was once turned away because of his dark complexion but returned later as a guest, and Nathaniel Hawthorn stayed nearly a year. The rooms are far from fancy, but it's a warm and friendly place. Furnishings are in a simple country style with an assortment of wicker, painted chests, and Ethan Allen beds. The King's Room has a glorious ocean view and is sponge-painted a deep blue. Among the older furnishings are an Eastlake couch and old trunk. Some rooms have a TV. The decor, though, is notable for the quirky humorous art—for example, morning and night portraits of famous characters and Napoleon holding a baby. Some works, like the collage boxes on the top floor, are created by owner Earle Radford. Anyone who has this sense of humor gets our vote. The breakfast room is fun, too, filled with all kinds of interesting, entertaining objects. In summer, breakfast can be enjoyed on the secluded patio-garden out back. Breakfast is not included in the rates. Rates: Late May to late September, $140 to $190; April to late May and late September to late October, $95 to $130.

The **Arbor Inn,** 222 Upper Main St. (P.O. Box 1228), Edgartown, MA 02539 (☎ 508/627-8137), is on the edge of town. It's refreshingly different and made very welcoming by Peggy Hall, who has realized her dream of operating an inn on the island for the last 15 years. It's a delightful place. The old part of the house, with its low ceilings, has great character and dates back to 1880. Here, you'll find a small dining room that has been enhanced by a wonderful mural depicting a flower-filled garden with blue sky above. The main dining room was added later, and the living room, which has soaring cathedral ceilings, was added by Peggy herself. She has decorated it with lavish couches and rugs and fetching lamps. She loves gardening, and the house is full of plants. There are 10 attractively furnished rooms. You'll likely find brass beds, painted side tables, and stenciled walls. One room is papered with photographs of the island. The front porch has rush-seated rockers for guests' pleasure, but for privacy you can't beat the back courtyard-garden, furnished with wrought iron. A continental breakfast is served buffet style by candlelight. Rates: Mid-June to September, $110 to $160; May to mid-June and October, $90 to $120.

The **Shiverick Inn,** 5 Peases' Point Way (P.O. Box 640), Edgartown, MA 02539 (☎ 508/627-3797), is located at the head of Main Street in a striking 1840 residence with a wonderful cupola. The common rooms have been elaborately decorated by the friendly, helpful innkeeper, Denny Turmelle. Rose-colored swag drapes adorn the windows, and there are several comfy couches. The breakfast room has nine windows, and outside it, the stone patio with its fountain is a lovely summer dining spot. The 10 rooms all have private baths and are furnished with rice four-posters and antique reproductions. One might have a scallop-shell bed combined with a wing chair, or a Martha Washington chair, and set off by a floral wallpaper and Chinese rug on wide-board floors. Another might have a four-poster with a taffeta or lace canopy. Breakfast— granola, fresh fruit, breads, and pastries—is served buffet style. Guests have use of a library, which houses the TV (tucked away in a cupboard), plus books, games, and other pastimes. A large porch, furnished with a swing sofa and chaise lounge, offers a great view of the whaler's church. Rental bikes are available. Rates: Mid-June to mid-October, $205 to $260; mid-October to mid-June, $130 to $180.

EDGARTOWN DINING

L'Etoile, at the Charlotte Inn (☎ 508/627-5187), consistently offers the best dining experience. The green room has a formal ambience with its mahogany paneling and equestrian art. Chippendale chairs are set around tables furnished with fine crystal and silver and decorated with a single perfect rose. In summer, the brick terrace with its sculptured fountain is a perfect romantic dinner setting. The $56 fixed-price menu offers a full selection of appetizers, entrees, and desserts. To begin, you might choose galantine of fresh rabbit saddle filled with watercress, pistachio, and morel mushroom mousseline with roasted garlic and basil sauce or the sevruga caviar with mascarpone on dandelion greens, with spring onions and potato galettes. An intermezzo will follow—perhaps a blood-orange-and-champagne sorbet. Among the five or so entrees, there will always be a fish and often a game dish—étouffée of lobster with parsnip and chive custard, champagne, lobster and saffron sauce; or roasted pheasant breast on sautéed broccoli rabe with roasted corn and quinoa melange, sour cherry, pinot noir, and sage sauce.

Savoir Faire, 14 Church St. (☎ 508/627-9864), is small, intimate, and tucked away down a side street off Main. It's a chic spot with comfortable banquettes and an outside terrace in summer. The food is superb, especially the fish. The menu changes daily, but if it's available, try the orange-crusted halibut over artichokes, arugula pesto, and blanched garlic broth (a wonderful melding of flavors); or the roast codfish wrapped in bacon with Napa cabbage and cooked in a double chicken stock with a lemon thyme and balsamic glacé. The meat dishes—for example, the grilled rack of lamb with risotto, asiago shards, and cipolline onion sauce—are also well prepared. Prices range from $24 to $30. Open July and August daily from 6:30 to 9:45pm; call for off-season hours and closings.

O'Briens, 137 Upper Main St.(☎ 508/627-5850), is the kind of place you go when you just want to unwind, enjoy a good meal, and come away feeling content and satiated. Start with the sautéed crab cakes in a spicy rémoulade sauce or the grilled portobello mushrooms served on a bed of greens and topped with a port balsamic syrup. To follow, there might be baked stuffed sole with lobster sauce, rack of lamb with a lovely mint apple au jus, or filet mignon on red onion confit. Prices range from $24 to $29. Open July 4 weekend to Labor Day, daily from 6 to 10pm; off-season, Thursday to Saturday from 6 to 9pm.

Newes from America, 23 Kelly St. (☎ 508/627-4397), is a cozy pub with good food. The fish and chips are some of the best anywhere; there are also a few Mexican-inspired dishes, as well as burgers and sandwiches. Prices range from $8 to $10. There's a good selection of beers. Expect to wait—the value attracts a crowd.

THE TISBURYS

From Vineyard Haven—which is, in fact, in the town of Tisbury—you can take the State Road southwest. Turn right on Lambert's Cove Road, which loops over to **Lambert's Cove** and James Pond before linking back up with the State Road again. A short distance beyond this linkup, Indian Hill Road leads into Christiantown Road, named after the Praying Indian congregations that were nurtured here by Thomas Mayhew, Jr. At the end of the road, you can visit the **Mayhew Chapel** and the **Indian Burial Ground** that serves as the congregation's memorial. Farther along Indian Hill Road you can reach the dirt road turnoff to **Cedar Tree Neck Wildlife Sanctuary.** In this 216-acre refuge, trails lead down through woodlands to North Shore beach on Vineyard Sound. It's a beautiful and largely undiscovered spot where you can walk and turn your face to the sun just as the cormorants will likely be doing on the shoreline rocks. No picnicking, swimming, or fishing is allowed.

If you want to visit the island's only winery, then don't take the first turnoff to Lambert's Cove, but instead, stay on the State Road until you come to Stoney Hill Road on the left. This dirt road will bring you to **Chicama Vineyards** in West Tisbury (☎ 508/693-0309). The vineyard makes some decent wines, and you can take a tour of the establishment and taste some samples. The vinegars make great buys, too.

Also in West Tisbury, stop in at the **Field Gallery** (☎ 508/693-5595). Don't overlook the statuary created by owner Tom Maley in the adjoining field.

TISBURY LODGING & DINING

Lambert's Cove Country Inn, Lambert's Cove Road (P.O. Box 422), Vineyard Haven MA 02568 (☎ 508/693-2298), is up island in West Tisbury. It has a really secluded location on 7½ acres at the end of a wooded road. Apple trees, rhododendrons, and perennials, plus an English garden filled with lilac, make this an elysian spot. There's a nice variety of accommodations plus a large deck and a tennis court. The most appealing rooms, in my opinion, are in the barn. They are the largest and most private. The Blue Room, for example, contains a pine four-poster, an oak chest, and wicker chairs and has a large deck. In the main house, the library has floor-to-ceiling bookcases and comfortable seating where guests can relax and read in front of the fire. The parlor also has a fireplace and functions as an entertainment room with a TV/VCR (there's a movie library on hand), 3-D puzzles, and games. Breakfast is served in the garden room in winter or on the deck in summer. The dining room is decorated in a pretty country style with white and rose tablecloths. At dinner a select menu is served, featuring American cuisine and offering such dishes as horseradish-crusted poached salmon with rémoulade sauce or grilled loin lamb chops with raspberry-blackberry mint vinegar. Prices range from $22 to $26. Beach passes for Lambert's Cove, a 15-minute walk, are available. Rates: Mid-May to mid-October $145 to $185; mid-October to early December and mid-March to mid-May, $100 to $145; early December to mid-March, $85 to $130.

CHILMARK, MENEMSHA & GAY HEAD

At North Tisbury, North Road goes directly down into **Menemsha,** a fishing village that is separated from Gay Head by Menemsha Creek. Menemsha still lives by the sea and has an authentic and salty air. Pleasure boats are not moored in the small harbor, but fishing and lobster boats are—it's a working harbor that has not been prettified. Lobster pots and shrimp traps are piled high on the wharves, along with empty shells and other flotsam and jetsam.

The State Road continues into **West Tisbury,** a village with a typical white, steepled church, general store, and post office. At one time the town was known for the manufacture of satinet, a fabric that was used for whaler's jackets. Here the road splits into Middle Road and South Road. Both lead to Chilmark—the first via Middle Road Sanctuary and Peaked Hill and the second leading past the fairgrounds, Chilmark Pond, and Lucy Vincent Beach. **Peaked Hill,** by the way, is the highest point on the island at 311 feet, and the 70-acre reserve has trails that offer some great ocean views. The rolling hills and stone-fringed fields are all that is left of the sheep farms that once thrived around here before the summer colony arrived.

Chilmark has many art associations. Thomas Hart Benton settled and taught here. Among his students was Jackson Pollock. Other Chilmark artists have included Edward Hopper and photographer Alfred Eisenstaedt, who visited the island regularly from the 1950s until his death in 1995. He had been introduced to the island by a member of the Larsen family who worked at *Time*. (The Larsen's fish business is still here, and you can pick up some fresh fish or shellfish there.) Eisenstaedt loved in particular to photograph Menemsha.

From Chilmark, the State Road winds out to Nashaquitsa cutting between Menemsha Pond and Squibnocket Ponds to **Gay Head.** This is the stronghold of the Wampanoag Tribe, who have lived on the island for more than 600 years and who formally claimed the peninsula as their tribal lands in the 1970s. Their tribal government was recognized by the Federal government in 1987. The tribe has about 800 members, but only 300 of them live on the island. The brilliantly colored cliffs that drop starkly to the beach below are considered sacred by the Indians. These ancient cliffs carry the fossil life of the island's early history, and they are a beautiful sight. Ignore the trinket stands that line the route to the **lighthouse** (☎ 508/693-4922), which has been perilously perched on the cliffs since 1844. There are lovely vistas of the cliffs and the ocean from the park area at the base. Another road loops around the head— the Moshup Trail, which travels along Zacks Cliffs and Philbin Beach to Gay

Head Cliffs and then loops around (on Lighthouse Road) to **Lobsterville**, where there's a great beach, but no place to park. Go there by bike.

CHILMARK, MENEMSHA & GAY HEAD LODGING & DINING

The **Inn at Blueberry Hill**, North Road, Chilmark, MA 02535 (☎ 508/645-3322), is very different from a traditional New England inn. It's modern and also one of the few, if not the only, place on the island to offer a full range of facilities—fitness room equipped with Sybex and Stairmaster, outdoor lap pool, tennis court, massage, and facials. It also has nature trails. It's a place that is meant to help you restore both body and soul. Set back from the road and up a long drive, the inn was originally a farm. Today the property covers 56 acres. The main building, from the 1940s, has been completely renovated. The 25 rooms are furnished in an understated and modern fashion and may not appeal to everyone. Some are on the second floor in the central building; the rest are arranged on both sides of it. Rooms are studies in serene whites and contain pine beds furnished with duvets, plain chests, and chairs. Room 4 has more style, with its painted bed, table, and mirror. Some rooms have wall-to-wall carpeting; others have polished wood floors. The inn has a health-conscious attitude, and the amenities include Neutrogena soap and other health-oriented products. Extra touches are bathrobes, penlight flashlights for evening strolls, an ice cooler, and chocolates at turndown. Guests gather around the brick fireplace in the sitting room; there's a grand piano, as well as a TV room. Breakfast is served buffet style. Lunch is provided on request.

Theo's, the on-premise restaurant, has an excellent reputation. It offers a four-course fixed-price dinner, featuring some innovative American cooking. A sample meal might start with cured salmon nori maki served with soy, wasabi, and pickled ginger or with a delicious Maine crab margarita—a blend of crab, avocado, and mango. Among the five or so main courses, there could be a tuna steak with an orange-ginger reduction or a richly flavored vegetarian dish like the roasted eggplant-, mushroom-, and basil-filled ravioli served with a red wine tomato sauce and niçoise olive garnish. Prices range from $38 to $50. Open daily 6 to 9pm. Rates: June 21 to Labor Day, $150 to $220, suites $260 to $380; May 1 to June 20 and Labor Day to Columbus Day, $123 to $189, suites $198 to $325; Columbus Day to November 1, $100 to $157, suites $160 to $269.

The Outermost Inn, Lighthouse Road, RR 1, (P.O. Box 171), Gay Head, MA 02535 (☎ 508/645-3511), stands within sight of the Gay Head light, a perfectly remote hideaway at the center of a stirring landscape. It's a warm and welcoming place, operated by a friendly couple, Hugh and Jeanne Taylor. Hugh will occasionally entertain on his guitar or xylophone. Each of the seven light and airy, modern rooms has a TV, telephone, and private bath. Each room has a different wood flooring for which it is named—oak, cherry, hickory, and so on. On a good day, the Ash Room has a view of the ocean. It's furnished simply with a pine table and chairs, a desk, and a bed with a headboard made from cypress. A colorful hooked rug is on the floor. Dhurries brighten the living room, where guests can enjoy books and games and the folk art that decorates the room. A full breakfast of waffles, omelets, or similar fare is served. Dinner is also available, spring through fall. There's a wide porch overlooking rolling hills, with very distant views of the ocean, where you can just sit and watch the birds whirling and chanting overhead. Rates: summer, $260 to $295; winter, $200 to $220.

Menemsha Inn & Cottages, P.O. Box 38-C, Menemsha, MA 02552 (☎ 508/645-2521), is located on 10½ acres and has views of Vineyard Sound. There are nine rooms, six suites, and 12 cottages. The most comfortable accommodations are the six suites in the carriage house. Each has a bedroom, sitting area, writing desk, minibar, and sundeck and is decorated with wall-to-wall carpeting and pine furnishings. Guests share a living room with a stone fireplace. The cottages have fully equipped kitchens, living rooms with wood-burning fireplaces, screened porches, outside decks, outdoor grills, and TVs. They are available only in season and only for weekly rentals. The breakfast room has a large deck and sun room. Rates: Mid-June to late September, rooms and suites $125 to $180, one-bedroom cottage $1,075 weekly, two-bedroom cottage $1,500; late April to mid-June and late September to November 1, rooms and suites $95 to $110, cottages $750 and $850, respectively.

The Home Port, Menemsha (☎ 508/645-2679), is a casual place where you can sit outside and watch the sun go down while you feast on one of the many lobster preparations and fresh broiled scrod, bluefish, salmon, and scallops. Fish platters and full shore dinners are available, along with some steaks to keep everyone happy. There's a take-out window, too. Prices range from $18 to $30. Open June to September, daily from 6 to 10pm. Closed mid-October to mid-April.

On the Menemsha Harbor go to **Larsen's** (☎ 508/645-2680) for steamers and for the best lobster roll anywhere. You can eat at picnic tables or take them with you.

Martha's Vineyard
Special & Recreational Activities

Beaches: Even though the island has 100 miles of shoreline, sadly most of the beaches are private or restricted to residents or renters. Permits for town beaches can be secured at the town hall of the community in which you're staying. Some up-island inns provide temporary passes to parking at Chilmark, Squibnocket, West Tisbury, and Lambert's Cove beaches. The beaches on the northern and eastern shores are shallow and well protected; those on the southern shore offer pounding surf.

Public beaches are as follows:

Chilmark: Menemsha Public Beach right next to Dutchers Dock. Great sunsets. Other Chilmark beaches such as Lucy Vincent and Squibnocket are open to residents only.

Edgartown: East Beach on Chappaquiddick Island, part of Cape Pogue and Wasque Reservation, is a great beach that is open to four-wheelers; otherwise, it's unadulterated. Lighthouse Beach is right in town at Starbuck's Neck, off North Water Street, and is best for strolling and watching sunrises or sunsets; nearby, at the end of Fuller Street, is Fuller Street Beach, around from the lighthouse; Katama Beach, also known as South Beach, lies at the end of Katama Road; it's a sandy beach extending for 3 miles—one end attracts families; the other, college kids and teens.

Gay Head: Moshup Beach stretches from Philbin Beach to the cliffs. It's a 10-minute walk from the parking lot ($15 fee in summer). Lobsterville Beach offers 2 miles of beach and dunes but very limited parking.

Oak Bluffs: Town Beach offers a long strand of sand from the Oak Bluff steamship dock, ending at the state beach. Joseph Sylvia State Beach stretches for 2 miles between Oak Bluffs and Edgartown; *Jaws* was filmed here. Eastville Beach on Beach Road is a quiet bay beach on the Oak Bluffs side of the drawbridge.

Vineyard Haven: Lake Tashmoo Town Beach at Herring Creek, accessed via Daggett Avenue and Herring Creek Road, is quiet and calm and offers fishing, too; Owen Park Beach is on the harbor, in town off Main Street, and is good for kids and boat watching; Tisbury Town Beach is located at the end of Owen Little Way next to the yacht club.

West Tisbury: Lambert's Cove, a lovely beach, is open only to West Tisbury residents.

Biking: The island is great for biking, since it has miles and miles of bike trails and numerous rental stores in each community. In Edgartown, Wheel Happy on South Water Street rents bikes for $15 a day. Other rental operations include Edgartown Bicycle, 190 Main St. ☎ 508/627-9008. In Vineyard Haven, try Martha's Vineyard Scooter & Bike, Union Street ☎ 508/693-0782. In Oak Bluffs, go to Anderson's Bike Rentals, Circuit Avenue Extension ☎ 508/693-9346.

Birding: The Massachusetts Audubon Society maintains the **Felix Neck Wildlife Sanctuary** (☎ 508/627-4850), which projects into Sengekontacket Pond. It's a lovely place to walk the trails, spotting osprey and other birds as you cross pond, meadow, and marsh. The entrance is on the Edgartown-Vineyard Haven Road. Admission is $3 for adults, $2 for children. Call about special programs. Another great place is **Cedar Tree Neck Reserve** (see below).

Canoeing/Kayaking: There are good opportunities in the lagoons and on the ocean for both. Canoes and kayaks are available at **Winds Up,** just outside Vineyard Haven (☎ 508/693-4252). Canoes cost $15 an hour or $40 a half day; kayaks $13 and $40. You can also try **Kayaks of Martha's Vineyard** (☎ 508/693-3885) and **Martha's Vineyard Kayaks** (☎ 508/627-0151), both in Vineyard Haven.

Cruises: There are plenty of opportunities for taking cruises. In **Menemsha Harbor,** the *Arabella* (☎ 508/627-0243 or 508/645-3511) is one of the most thrilling. It's a catamaran that sails to Cuttyhunk and the Elizabeth Islands twice daily in summer. The cost is $60 for the 6-hour day cruise and $43 for the shorter sunset cruise. In **Vineyard Haven,** *Laissez Faire* (☎ 508/693-1646) is a 54-foot ketch that charges $100 per person (maximum six) for day sails. *Shenandoah* (☎ 508/693-1699), *Ayuthia* (☎ 508/693-7245), and *Liberty* (☎ 508/693-4400) also sail from here. In **Edgartown,** *Vela* (☎ 508/627-1963) is a 50-foot ketch that sails on 2-hour trips for $60 per person. *Mad Max* (☎ 508/627-7500) also operates from Edgartown.

Fishing: Striped bass and bluefish are prime game fish in these waters, but there are many other species. **Cape Pogue Gut, Lambert's Cove Beach,** and **Dogfish Bar,** off Lighthouse Bar, are prime spots favored by the locals.

There's also good fishing at the **Wasque Reservation.** *The Skipper* (☎ 508/693-1238) is a fishing boat that operates from Oak Bluffs harbor; the charge is $25 per person for a 4-hour trip. Guided fishing trips are offered by **Larry's Tackle Shop,** 258 Upper Main St., Edgartown (☎ 508/627-5088).

Fruit Picking: Pick your own strawberries and raspberries at **Thimble Farm** (☎ 508/693-6396) in Vineyard Haven.

Golf: Farm Neck Golf Course (☎ 508/693-3057) in Oak Bluffs is where President Clinton played on his two trips to the island. The other course is **Mink Meadows** in Vineyard Haven (☎ 508/693-0600).

Hiking: Good hiking and nature trails are found at several reserves, notably **Poucha Pond and Wasque Reservations** on Chappaquiddick; **Peaked Hill,** off Tabor House Road in Chilmark; **Felix Neck Sanctuary,** off the Edgartown-Vineyard Road; **Cedar Tree Neck** in West Tisbury off Indian Hill Road; and **Menemsha Hills Reservation,** off North Road, which takes you to the second highest point on the island.

Horseback Riding: For trail rides, contact **Scrubby Neck Farm** in West Tisbury, across from the airport (☎ 508/693-3770), or **Misty Meadows** (☎ 508/693-1870). For additional information contact the **Martha's Vineyard Horse Council** at ☎ 508/645-3723.

Sailing: Wind's Up, 199 Beach Rd. (P.O. Box 238) in Vineyard Haven (☎ 508/693-4252), offers rentals and lessons. Sailboat rentals cost $20 to $30 per hour, depending on size and type, or $50 to $85 for a half-day.

Tennis: Courts are available at **Edgartown Town Courts,** Robinson Road; **Oak Bluffs Town Courts,** Niantic Avenue; **Vineyard Haven Town Courts,** Church Street; and **Chilmark Community Center,** Beetlebung Corner. Also call **Martha's Vineyard Tennis Center** at ☎ 508/696-8000, which is open to the public.

Wildlife Watching & Refuges: Cape Pogue Wildlife Refuge and **Wasque Reservation** (☎ 508/627-7260) are on Chappaquiddick. You really need an ORV to explore here. If you don't have one, you can take one of the four-wheel safaris or canoe trips that are offered at the refuge or explore on bike. **Long Point Wildlife Refuge** (☎ 508/693-7392) and **Cedar Tree Neck Sanctuary,** Indian Hill Road (☎ 508/693-5207), are both in West Tisbury and afford fine bird and nature watching. **Menemsha Hills Reservation,** off North Road (☎ 508/693-7662), has 4 miles of trails and a scenic lookout on Prospect Hill.

Windsurfing: Wind's Up, 199 Beach Rd., Vineyard Haven (☎ 508/693-4252), offers lessons and rentals. Rentals cost $15 an hour, $40 a half day.

Nantucket

Nantucket Town ◆ Siasconset ◆ Coskata Coatue Wildlife Refuge

Distance in miles from Boston: To Hyannis, 80.

Estimated travel time: 1½ hours plus ferry time.

◄○►◄○►◄○►◄○►◄○►

Car/Ferry: To reach Hyannis (80 miles) take Route 3 south to the Sagamore Bridge, Route 6 to Exit 6, and Route 132 into Hyannis.

Ferry: Freedom Cruise Line (☎ 508/432-8999) operates passenger ferries from Harwich Port from May to October. The trip takes about 1½ hours.

   Hy-Line (☎ 508/778-2600) operates passenger ferries from May to October from Hyannis and Oak Bluffs. It also operates a year-round high-speed catamaran (☎ 508/778-0404) that takes about an hour. The **Steamship Authority** (☎ 508/477-8600) operates a year-round car ferry from Hyannis. Approximate time is 2¼ hours. It costs $101 from mid-May to mid-October to take your car across, $77 at other times. Adult passengers are $11 one way.

Plane: Flights are available from Boston, Hyannis, and New Bedford, as well as from LaGuardia and Newark. **Cape Air** (☎ 800/352-0714) flies from Boston, Martha's Vineyard, and New Bedford. **US Airways Express** (☎ 800/428-4322) flies from Boston, Martha's Vineyard, and La Guardia. **Colgan Air** (☎ 800/272-5488) flies from Hyannis, LaGuardia, and Newark. **Island Airlines** (☎ 800/248-7779) and **Nantucket Airlines** (☎ 800/635-8787) both fly from Hyannis. In summer only, **Continental Express** (800/525-0280) operates from Newark.

Bus: Bonanza Bus Lines operates from New York City (☎ 212/947-1766) and Providence (☎ 800/556-3815); **Plymouth & Brockton Bus Lines** also operates from Logan Airport and Boston (☎ 508/746-0378).

Rail: Amtrak (☎ 800/872-7245) operates to Hyannis in summer only.

Further Information: For further information, contact the **Nantucket Island Chamber of Commerce**, 48 Main St., Nantucket, MA 02554 (☎ 508/228-1700).

◄○►◄○►◄○►◄○►◄○►

Events & Festivals to Plan Your Trip Around

April: Daffodil Weekend when 3 million or more daffodils herald the spring. There's also an antique car parade and tailgate picnics. Usually the last weekend in April, but call ☎ 508/228-1700 for exact date.

May: Figawi Boat Race from Hyannis to Nantucket and back on Memorial Day weekend. Call ☎ 508/778-1691.

June: Harborfest. This festival includes a chowder contest, maritime history walks and a host of other events; call ☎ 508/228-1700 for information.

   The Iron Man Race. This challenging race has been run for 18 years. It combines running, surfboard paddle, swimming, biking, and more running. It starts and finishes at the Muse on Surfside Road.

   Nantucket Film Festival, a new festival, includes showings of short and feature films and documentaries, staged readings, panel discussions, and a screenplay competition. Call ☎ 212/642-6339 for information.

July: July 4 fun and frolics include blueberry pie eating contests plus a competition for the best decorated bike. Call ☎ 508/228-1700.

August: Annual House Tour. Sponsored by the Nantucket Garden Club, this event allows visitors to see six historic homes and gardens. Call ☎ 508/257-4434.

   The **Opera House Cup** is the name for this classic for wooden hulled sailboats. Call ☎ 508/228-5977.

   Sand Castle and Sand Sculpture Day. This fairly serious contest has entries for all ages. Call ☎ 508/228-1700.

October: Cranberry Harvest Weekend. During this weekend you can tour the bogs, watch the cookery and window decorating contests, and just relish the good fruit of the season. Call ☎ 508/228-1700.

   Nantucket Arts Festival. A weeklong event with gallery exhibitions, art demonstrations, concerts, a mini-film festival, and more. Call ☎ 508/228-3424.

December: Nantucket Noel begins right after Thanksgiving with the tree lighting and caroling on Main Street and continues until Christmas. Book ahead, as lodgings tend to fill up. Call ☎ 508/228-1700.

   Christmas Stroll. Tours of traditionally decorated historic homes and inns plus caroling and other seasonal festivities—the top event of Nantucket Noel.

Remote, eerie, and sirenlike, Nantucket lies 22 miles, 2¼ hours by steamer, off the southeast coast of Massachusetts. The Indians called it "Far Away Island" and believed it to have been created by a giant Indian chief who tossed

his great moccasin full of sand out to sea. In bland contrast, science explains that the island was caused by an immense glacier that ripped it from the mainland and deposited it in the sea. From the ferry, as you pull into the harbor, you can make out the contours of a long, low slither of an island. If you fly in, you'll see its crescent or hammock shape and its 55 miles of beaches, a summer playground of great beauty. Here the seasons are short. Spring is 1 week, a summer of about 2½ months ushers in a brief fall before the onset of winter, when the island is at its most magical, especially during the Christmas season. Then "Grey Lady" seems an appropriate name, when any splashes of color stand out against the somnolent bluish gray of the snow. In the off-season you can hear your own footsteps, so quiet are the streets.

It's a magical place and one that stays in the memory, as many people have discovered, ever since summering there began in the 1870s. Sadly, the allure of the island has led to considerable overdevelopment. Today there are more year-round residents—7,000—than ever, many of them occupying the modern, shingled, cookie-cutter homes that are particularly prevalent at the west end of the island. In summer the crowds are overwhelming, with day-trippers from Harwich Port and Martha's Vineyard adding to the already substantial throng. If you can, come to see the island in spring or fall or even winter.

Nantucket has a rich and deep history lodged in the landscape, the architecture, and the lives of the islanders, many of whom can trace their roots to the original founding settlers. Indeed, if you open the phone book today, you can find listed 30 Mayhews, 30 Coffins, and 25 Gardners, all descendants of the island's first families. Even though a fire swept through town in 1846, destroying three-quarters of the houses (it was finally stopped by the brick Jared Coffin House), there are still 800 pre–Civil War buildings on the island. For a bird's-eye view of the island before you explore the town, climb up the tower of the Old North Church at 62 Centre St. (open mid-June to mid-October, Monday to Saturday from 10am to 4pm, plus Wednesday from 6am to 8pm in July and August).

EXPLORING NANTUCKET TOWN

Although explorers Verrazano and Bartholomew Gosnold had both discovered the island, it was first settled in 1659 by nine settlers who purchased it from Governor Mayhew for £30 and two beaver hats. The new owners settled around Hummock Pond, where they attempted to establish a farming community. Because the land was not suitable for farming, the settlers kept sheep for wool and supplemented their income by fishing. They built windmills—four of them—to process the wool and the corn. Today you can visit the **Old Mill** at South Mill and Prospect streets, one-half mile southwest of town (☎ 508/228-1894). The mill was constructed in 1746 by Nathan Wilbur, using lumber salvaged from shipwrecks, of which there were many in Nantucket Sound. Cornmeal is still ground and sold here. Open daily 10am to 5pm June to September; call for off-season hours.

A good number of the settlers were Quakers, and they set the moral tone of the early community before the advent of whaling. Nantucket had become a refuge for Quakers in the late 17th century, but it was not until 1708 that the first Quaker group was formally organized by the "great woman," Mary Coffin Starbuck, and her husband, Nathaniel. Today the only traces of this Quaker heritage can be found at the **Old Quaker Meetinghouse** (1838), at 7 Fair St. and at the **Quaker cemetery** at Madaket and Quaker roads. The first was built as a school and later converted. It is still used by the Friends for services on Sunday at 10am. Open daily June to September 10am to 5pm.

Island politics didn't always go smoothly in the early days. The original proprietors of the island had recruited fishermen and tradesmen to work on the island and had granted them half-shares in the colony. It didn't take long for the "half-share men," as they were called, to rebel against this restriction. They were led by John Gardner, who carried on a longstanding feud against Tristram Coffin. In 1680 the half-share men's appeal to the provincial government was granted, and the agreement was finally cemented by the marriage of Mary Gardner to Jethro Coffin, Tristram's grandson. A portrait of Mary, by the way, hangs in the Foulger Museum. She had a strong chin and a straight nose, but she was surely no great beauty. The oldest house on the island, the **Jethro Coffin House,** was given as a wedding gift to the couple. It still stands today.

From 1725 to 1825, Nantucket was the leading whaling port in the world. Between 1668 and 1869, 4,344 whaling voyages were made from Nantucket harbor. Originally, whaling was performed from the shore. When the first sperm whale (which produces a superior oil) was found in deep water by a man named Hussey in 1712, whaling became the island's major industry. Nantucket town had already begun to develop in its present location, but in 1716 it took a great stride forward when the first wharf was built, followed by Straight Wharf in 1723.

Whaling thrived until it was disrupted by the American Revolution, when the islanders were forced to choose between their economic partner, England, and the rebels. Most of the islanders tried to maintain neutrality and carry on trade, but they were blockaded by both the Americans and the British and their whaling fleet was decimated. The conflict divided the community, with Tim Foulger and Will Rotch on the side of preserving trade with England, while others sided with the Americans and accused Foulger and Rotch of treason.

In 1791 the sperm whale was spotted in the Pacific, and the legendary long whaling voyages began taking place—voyages that lasted as long as 5 years. At the bottom of Main Street you can see the **Pacific Building** (originally the counting house), the location of a club that was formed in 1854. Members were required to have rounded Cape Horn and to have knowledge of sailing the Pacific Ocean. Whaling had already produced great wealth for many islanders, and as early as 1782, when Crevecoeur visited the island, he described it as "this happy settlement, a sandy spot of 23,000 acres with neither stone nor timber resources nor arable land nor meadows, yet boasts a handsome town of 500 houses, 200 sailing vessels, employing 2,000 seamen; 15,000 sheep, 500 cows, 200 horses, and citizens worth then an astounding £20,000." It's quite a picture, which even today you can imagine if you take a moment.

The whaling industry was also interrupted during the War of 1812 but revived and boomed again. In 1820 a Nantucket whaler became the inspiration for Herman Melville's *Moby Dick*, when the vessel *Essex* was sunk by an enraged bull whale. At its height around 1840, the island's population was about 10,000. The whaling ships went forth to harvest whales for the oil and for whalebone, which was made into stays for corsets and umbrellas. Ambergris, a stomach secretion, was used in the preparation of perfume.

From 1840 on, whaling slowly declined. A newly formed sandbar made it difficult for the large whalers to get into Nantucket; New Bedford took over the lead in the industry—it had a deep harbor and immediate access to the continent via the railroad. Nantucketers tried to revive the industry by developing an ingenious boat called a camel to help float the whale boats over the shallow bar to the entrance to Nantucket Harbor, but the discovery of oil in Pennsylvania in 1859 effectively ended the importance of whale oil as a fuel. The last whaler, *Oak,* sailed in November 1869.

Whaling generated great wealth. The early whaling captains were the equivalents of oil-company CEOs, playing a role in an industry that was as significant then as the oil and petroleum industry is to our economy today. The results of that wealth can be seen along many of the island's streets. Just take a stroll up Main Street to nos. 93, 95, and 97 to see the **Three Bricks**, as they're called, that were built by Joseph Starbuck for his sons in 1838. No. 96, the **Hadwen House**, is perhaps the grandest mansion of all, built in 1845 by William Hadwen, owner of a candle factory. You can see the lavish lifestyle maintained by its residents. It's open to visitors from June to September, daily from 10am to 5pm. Admission is $3 for adults, $2 for children. The **Macy-Christian House,** also on Main Street, reflects the more modest wealth that was earned before the Revolution by island merchant Nathaniel Macy. It too can be visited; open daily June to September, from 10am to 5pm.

All these houses stand in stark contrast to the simple **Jethro Coffin House,** Sunset Hill Road, off West Chester (☎ 508/228-1894), which is the oldest house on the island. Built in 1686 by Tristram Coffin and John Gardner as a wedding gift for their children, it's a 1½ story lean-to with a center chimney and very small and few windows. Open daily June to September from 10am to 5pm. Another Coffin memorial, the **Coffin School,** 4 Winter St., is a fine example of Greek Revival architecture. Built in 1852–54, it served as an academy. Today it is home to the Egan Institute of Maritime Studies, which presents exhibitions and programs relating to the history of the island and the school. It's open Memorial Day to Columbus Day, daily from 11am to 3pm; admission is $1.

Another splendid building that owes its grandeur to whaling wealth is the **Nantucket Athenaeum,** 1 Lower India St. (☎ 508/228-1110). It was established as a private literary institution in 1834 with 3,200 volumes and became a public library in 1900. This impressive Greek Revival building, designed by Frederick Brown Coleman in the 1840s, hosts a variety of lectures and other events carrying on the tradition that began when Ralph Waldo Emerson, Henry David Thoreau, Horace Greeley, Frederick Douglass, and Lucretia Mott spoke here. Open in summer, Tuesday to Saturday from 9:30am to 8pm or 9:30am to 5pm; in winter, Wednesday and Saturday 9:30am to 5pm and Thursday and Friday noon to 5pm.

Wealth, population growth, and 60 grog houses along the waterfront also brought problems—crime and drunkenness among them. After two bank robbers escaped from the island's only jail, the islanders built a new jail in 1805 to deal with offenders. Eerily tucked away at the end of a grassy lane between two residences, you can visit this **Old Gaol,** made out of 2½ tons of thick iron bolts and straps, at 15R Vestal St. (☎ 508/228-1894). It contains four cells— two up and two down—equipped with toilet and fireplace. Escapes still occurred—one prisoner squeezed out of the chimney, another fashioned a key from a pewter spoon. The last escapee was Luther Rose, a murderer, who used a brick from the fireplace to knock out the jailer. Open June to September, daily from 10am to 5pm. Admission free.

Women have always played strong roles on Nantucket. Perhaps because the whaling captains and sailors were away for years at a time, women were forced to assume responsibilities that they might otherwise not have taken on. The island's redoubtable women are legion. Benjamin Franklin's mother, Abiah Foulger (1667–1752), is recalled by the **fountain** on the Madaket Road near Crooked Lane. Keziah Coffin profited mightily from smuggling during the Revolution; Lucretia Coffin Mott (1793–1880) labored as an abolitionist and women's rights activist; and Anna Gardner (1816–1901) worked in the suffrage, temperance, and abolitionist movements and taught freed slaves in North Carolina after the Civil War.

Perhaps the most famous female Nantucketer, though, is Maria Mitchell, an astronomer who discovered a comet in 1847, earning international renown for herself. She became the first woman elected to the Academy of Arts and Sciences and the first female professor of astronomy at Vassar College. You can visit the **Maria Mitchell** birthplace at 1 Vestal St. (☎ 508/228-2896); it contains family portraits, scientific instruments, and other personal items such as her opera glasses. The decor is also extraordinarily advanced for its time.

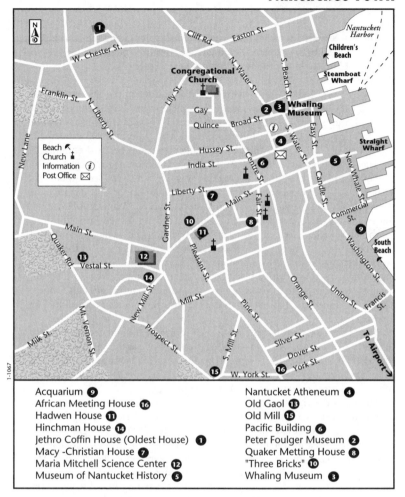

Acquarium **9**
African Meeting House **16**
Hadwen House **11**
Hinchman House **14**
Jethro Coffin House (Oldest House) **1**
Macy -Christian House **7**
Maria Mitchell Science Center **12**
Museum of Nantucket History **5**

Nantucket Atheneum **4**
Old Gaol **13**
Old Mill **15**
Pacific Building **6**
Peter Foulger Museum **2**
Quaker Metting House **8**
"Three Bricks" **10**
Whaling Museum **3**

See the swirl-painted floors and stenciled "peep at the moon" frieze (admission $3 for adults, $1 for children). Adjacent is the **observatory** (☎ 508/228-9273 or 228-9198) where she studied the stars with her father William, who taught celestial navigation to whaling captains in what is now the **library**, across the street. It features her manuscripts, along with 19th-century science books and other book and journal collections and also serves as the association's headquarters. It's at 2 Vestal St. at Milk (☎ 508/228-9219). Two other sites are under the aegis of the Maria Mitchell Association. They are the **Loines Observatory**, Milk Street Extension (☎ 508/228-9273), where the public can view the stars, and the small **Aquarium** (☎ 508/228-5387), which sits in a shack down on the waterfront between the Town Pier and the Commercial Wharf.

The **Hinchman House**, 7 Milk St. (☎ 508/228-0898), part of the Maria Mitchell Science Center, serves as the natural history museum and the headquarters for bird and wildflower walks and other nature-oriented programs.

It's one place to get a sense of the environmental issues facing the island. The science center/library is open Memorial Day to mid-September, Tuesday to Saturday 10am to 4pm, otherwise Wednesday to Friday 2 to 5pm and Saturday 9am to noon.

About 3,000 Indians were living on the island when the first settlers arrived. By 1874, only 125 years later, the population had been reduced to 35, largely through yellow fever and other diseases. If you want to see a portrait of Abrom Quary, the last male Indian on the island, who died November 25, 1854, visit the Nantucket Atheneum. His likeness hangs near the entrance.

The island has a rich black heritage. The black community was clustered at the southern edge of town in an area that was referred to as New Guinea. As early as 1716, the Quakers declared their opposition to slavery, and some of them actually went so far as to free their slaves. In 1773 William Rotch committed the revolutionary act of actually paying a slave, named Prince Boston, for the work he had done for Rotch aboard a whaler. The owner of the whaler tried to collect the money via the courts, but the courts ruled in the slave's favor. Absalom Boston, Prince Boston's grandson, went on to become a whaling captain, operating with a black crew. A man of courage, he also sued the local government so that his daughter could attend Nantucket High School. Another member of the black community, Lewis Temple, also contributed to the success of whaling by creating the effective Temple toggle harpoon. Frederick Douglass made his first speech to a mixed audience here at the Atheneum. Today the **African Meeting House,** at Pleasant and York streets (currently being restored), is a proud reminder of the community that once lived here. This post-and-beam building dating to the 1820s was the church, school, and meetinghouse for the black community.

Much more of the story of the island is told at the **Peter Foulger Museum** on Broad Street. Here you can see exhibits about the island's geology and its history from early Indian and colonial life up to today. Peter Foulger was Ben Franklin's grandfather and one of the first settlers. One of the more fascinating items on display is the journal of Susan Veeder, kept while she sailed on the whaler *Nanticon* in 1848–53 to Tahiti, Hawaii, and Hong Kong, among other ports of call. Also see the sailor-boy whirligigs created by island woodcarver William H Chase. Open year-round daily, June to September from 10am to 5pm; limited hours other times of year.

Next door the **Whaling Museum,** 13 Broad St. (☎ 508/228-1736), is filled with a broad variety of fascinating exhibits. Here you can see portraits of the many whaling captains and the treasures that they brought back from the Pacific—masks, war clubs, and tapa cloth. The Whale Room contains an immense skeleton of a finback whale that is 43 feet long.

For many visitors the highlight will be the Scrimshaw Room, which displays one of the finest collections—1,500 pieces—anywhere. All the scrimshaw pieces are exquisitely beautiful—from the clocks, boxes, bird cages, and canes to the utilitarian objects like rulers, dippers, rolling pins, jagging wheels, pestles, and fids (for separating rope). A whaleboat shop, sail loft, and shipsmith round out the displays. A good lecture is also given. This whole collection is a must-see, even if you have to go on a beautiful sunny day. Open year-round daily, June to September from 10am to 5pm; limited hours in spring, fall, and winter. Admission is $5 for adults, $3 for children 5 to 14. *Note*: The best way to see all of the historic properties plus the Whaling and Foulger museums is to secure a $10 National Historical Association visitor pass, $5 for children.

Shopping Main and Centre streets plus the **wharves** have some very fine shopping. For beautiful miniature Nantucket baskets crafted in solid gold with a top and plaque fashioned from recycled ivory, along with other stunning jewelry, step into **Diana Kim England,** 56 Main St. (☎ 508/228-3766). Prices range from $80 to thousands. Almost next door is **Murray's Toggery,** 62 Main St. (☎ 508/228-0437), the source of the famous "Nantucket reds"— cotton clothing that starts out tomato-red and fades to salmon pink. Murray's also stocks good country clothing, corduroy, flannel, cashmere, and tailoring by Austin Reed.

Other stores worth browsing on Main Street are **The Spectrum** at no. 26, which offers beautiful ceramics, glass, baskets, boxes, and a large selection of fine lighthouse baskets, and **Wolfhound** at no. 21 (☎ 508/228-3552) for fine-quality natural fiber domestic and international clothing. **Wayne Pratt Antiques,** 28 Main St. (☎ 508/228-8788) has an array of charming lamps, fine highboys, Nantucket lightship baskets, clocks, and other furniture and art. **Tonkin of Nantucket,** 33 Main St. (☎ 508/228-9697) has prime English, French, and country furniture plus silver, china, marine paintings, models, and more. **The Hub** at no. 31 (☎ 508/228-3868) is where locals pick up their newspapers and gather for morning gossip.

More stores line Centre Street—**Nantucket Glassworks** at no. 28 (☎ 508/228-7779) offers large, dynamic glass sculptures and vases, candlesticks, and glasses; **Sweet Inspirations** is the place to purchase some cranberry-orange marmalade or raspberry-cranberry preserves and boxes of fresh cranberries; **Vanessa Noel** displays fashions and accessories with cutting-edge chic. Off Centre Street, **Lynda Willauer** at 2 India St. (☎ 508/228-3631) has marvelous quality English majolica plus Staffordshire, Chinese export porcelain, and other lovely objects. **Nantucket House Antiques and Interior Design Studio,** 1 S. Beach St. (☎ 508/228-4604) offers fine American and French country furniture as well as folk and marine art. Next door, **Nantucket Gourmet** at 4 India St. (508/228-6447) sells jams, jellies, mustards, honeys, and vinegars, plus other cooking-oriented items.

By the way, the story behind the signature Nantucket baskets is interesting. They evolved from both Indian baskets and baskets made as early as the 1820s from rattan, recently discovered in the Pacific. The original lighthouse baskets, with their familiar wooden bottoms, were made by the crews aboard the floating lighthouses that were anchored offshore for months at a time. The covered baskets with lids decorated with scrimshaw plaques, which are primarily used as purses, were first made by Jose Reyes, who came here from the Philippines in the 1940s. If you purchase a basket, make sure it bears the authentication of the Nantucket Basket Makers Association and has been signed by the basket makers with the place of origin. Two places to start your comparative quality shopping are **Michael Kane's Carvers Guild,** 18½ Sparks Ave. (☎ 508/228-1548), and the **Lightship Shop,** 20 Miacomet Ave. (☎ 508/228-4164).

Having explored Nantucket town, you'll want to bike or drive out to Siasconset, a picture-perfect village of tiny homes, often covered with rambling roses, and very little else except a post office and a general store. This is the quiet side of the island. On the way, you can stop at the **Nantucket Life Saving Museum,** 57 Old South Rd. (☎ 508/228-1885), where the drama inherent in the lifeboat crews' motto, "You have to go out, but you don't have to come back," becomes clear. See the surfboats, beach carts, and a video and photographs of the many shipwrecks and disasters caused by the shoals off Nantucket, "the graveyard of the Atlantic." Open mid-June to Columbus Day, daily 9:30am to 4pm. Admission $3 adult, $2 children over 5.

NANTUCKET AFTER DARK

Nantucket supports a number of cultural organizations. The **Actor's Theatre of Nantucket,** 2 Centre St. (☎ 508/228-6325), performs in the Methodist church at the top end of Main Street. It celebrated its 13th anniversary in 1998. The season runs from Memorial Day to Columbus Day. **Theatre Workshop of Nantucket** (☎ 508/228-4305) stages plays, dance programs, and movies, while **Island Stage,** 115 Cliff Rd. (☎ 508/228-5570) performs musical revues. There are two cinemas on the island with the great names of Dreamland and Gaslight.

Fun places to hang your hat at night include the following piano bars: **The Club Car,** 1 Main St. (☎ 508/228-1101); **Brant Point Grill** at the White Elephant (☎ 508/228-1500); and the **Summer House,** in Siasconset (☎ 508/257-9976). For live entertainment head for the following: **The Hearth** at the Harbor House on South Beach Street (☎ 508/228-1500); the **Tap Room** at the Jared Coffin House (☎ 508/228-2400), and **Vincent's,** 21 South Water St. (☎ 508/228-0189).

NANTUCKET LODGING

The **Union Street Inn,** 7 Union St., Nantucket, MA 02554 (☎ 508/228-9222), is a delightful place and has much to recommend it. First, it's located on the quiet residential side of town; second, it has a commercial kitchen so that guests receive a full breakfast; third, it has the expertise of ex-hotelier Ken Withrow and his wife, Deborah, who make sure that every guest is comfortable; and fourth, it has great ambience. The inn was built in 1770. There are 12 rooms (6 with wood-burning fireplaces). All rooms have a private bath and TV and all are very well furnished with antiques. Room 3, for example, contains a rice four-poster, a marble dresser, and two wing chairs. Lace curtains adorn the windows, chintz wallpaper covers the walls, and exquisite fruitwood paneling surrounds the fireplace. Room 9 is large enough to accommodate a little sitting room, which has a TV/VCR. Scrambled eggs and bacon or apple cinnamon pancakes will be served at breakfast in the dining room or on the back patio. Rates: January to late April and late October to December, $100 to $170; late April to late May and early October to late October, $110 to $195; late May to early October, $150 to $245.

The **Jared Coffin House,** 29 Broad St. (P.O. Box 1580), Nantucket, MA 02554 (☎ 508/228-2400), is the island's historic inn moniker. It was built in 1845 as the residence for shipowner Jared Coffin and his family. It stands at the corner of Centre and Broad streets.

From the portico, you enter a hallway with the magnificent staircase. Thirty of the 60 rooms are in the main house; the remainder are in several historic buildings across the street. Each is decorated with fine antiques or antique reproductions. In the main house, Room 302, for example, is furnished with a four-poster with a crocheted canopy, a marble-top dresser, wing chairs, a desk, and an oriental rug and houses a decorative carved marble fireplace. Some of the nicest rooms are in the Harrison Gray Building, which has its own lavishly furnished sitting room. Tea-canister lamps grace the side tables beside the serpentine canopied beds, and marine or ornithological prints decorate the walls. The main dining room, Jared's, is open for dinner from late April until mid-October; the Tap Room stays open 365 days a year and is a local favorite. It has a cozy low-beamed ceiling ambience and a salty air imparted by ships lanterns and old marine paintings. In summer, the patio is appealing. There's also a serene garden across the street where guests can gather under the wisteria-covered arbor. Rates: January to early April, $95 to $105; early April to early May, $120 to $155; early May to late June, $155 to $185; late June to early October, $160 to $210; early October to October 30, $155 to $185; October 31 to late December, $105 to $120.

The Martin House Inn, 61 Centre St. (P.O. Box 743), Nantucket, MA 02554 (☎ 508/228-0678), offers one of the best values on the island. It was built in 1803 and has a more spacious ambience than some of the other in-town inns. It stands behind a fenced garden filled with flowers. The columned portico leads into a spacious living room with rich blue walls hung with gilt-framed landscapes and portraits. Here, on cold days, a fire invites guests to relax. There are 13 rooms (9 with private bath). Room 2 is sponge-painted in jade and has a rice four-poster covered with a floral pattern eiderdown, plus an armoire and a dresser. Room 22 is the largest room; it has a wood-burning fireplace and strawberry-colored sponge-painted walls, plus such lovely touches as a velvet-tufted black Empire chair. All the rooms are attractively and comfortably furnished. Even the smallest room has charm, with its four-poster sans canopy and hot-pink bathroom. The attic rooms share a bath. A small room with a small private bathroom that rents for only $95 in summer is a great buy. For only $60 you can rent a small room, under the eaves, that has a bed, a wicker chair, and an acorn chest and shares a bathroom. The continental breakfast is served at an attractively set table in the dining area. A favorite spot for guests is the hammock on the side porch. Closed January to February. Rates: Mid-June to mid-October, $90 to $180; mid-October to mid-June, $80 to $145.

White Elephant Inn & Cottages, Easton and Willard streets (P.O. Box 359), Nantucket, MA 02554 (☎ 508/228-2500), is a modern accommodation overlooking the harbor. The accommodations are arranged around an outdoor pool, with 22 rooms in the main building, 26 in the nearby Breakers, and one-, two-, and three-bedroom cottages on the grounds. They're spacious and modern and filled with white furnishings. Most rooms have a pullout couch, too. All of them have a TV in a pine cabinet, telephone, hair dryer, and clock radio. The largest and most attractive rooms are located in the Breakers. They have extra amenities like CD players and refrigerators; some have a balcony. In summer, the Brant Point Grill offers innovative cuisine with a great harbor view. Closed in the winter. Rates: Spring and fall, $210 to $335, cottages $260 to $510; summer, $260 to $520, cottages $295 to $750.

The Centerboard Guesthouse, 8 Chester St. (P.O. Box 456), Nantucket, MA 02554 (☎ 508/228-9696), is a Victorian home that has been decorated with great flair. It also offers guests a full range of amenities in all six rooms.

The first floor features a honeymoon suite, which is decorated in dark purple-rose. The marquetry floors are covered with oriental rugs. The bedroom has a four-poster with a crocheted canopy and is dressed with an antique quilt. The bathroom features a Jacuzzi tub sunk into a marble surround, with candles provided for romance. Wall-to-wall carpeting adds luxury. Each of the rooms is decorated creatively, and each has telephone, a refrigerator, and a TV. The bathrooms are particularly well designed. Guests enjoy using the parlor with its overstuffed chairs and oriental rugs. A continental breakfast is served. Rates: Mid-June to Columbus Day, $195, suite $335; off season, $120, suite $195.

The **Westmoor Inn**, Cliff Road, Nantucket, MA 02554 (☎ 508/228-0877), is located west of town en route to Madaket. It's a very lovely Colonial Revival mansion set well back from the road. It was built in 1917 by a Mr. Voss for his new bride, Miss Alice Vanderbilt. Wide-board floors covered with oriental rugs are in the foyer. Wine and cheese is served in the parlor in the evening. It's a very comfortable parlor with overstuffed sofa and easy chairs, arranged around a brick hearth, and a grand piano. There are 14 rooms, all with telephones. The most luxurious is a suite with a Jacuzzi bathroom. It's furnished with a wicker bed and sofa and chair and has floor-to-ceiling windows on all sides. It also has a small sitting area with a fireplace and a TV. Other rooms are furnished with iron-and-brass beds combined with wicker and pine pieces and accented with ornithological prints. Third-floor rooms are tucked under the eaves. The King Suite has a Palladian window and a view of the ocean beyond the modern beach homes. The beach is a short walk away. Single-speed bikes are available. Rates: Memorial Day to late October and during Christmas Stroll, $145 to $265; off-season, $115 to $195.

The Roberts House Inn, 11 India St. (P.O. Box 1436), Nantucket, MA 02554 (☎ 508/228-0600), is right on the corner of Centre Street in the heart of town. The rooms are nicely furnished with antiques. Some share baths. Your room might feature a high, rice four-poster with a lace canopy and a stool to help you climb up and down, a table swathed in fabric, and two rockers, plus amenities such as a TV, telephone, and small refrigerator. A buffet continental breakfast is served in the parlor. Rates: Mid-June to mid-October and holidays, $135 to $285; mid-May to mid-June and mid-October to late October, $105 to $200; late October to mid-May, $60 to $110.

The **Manor House Inn**, 11 India St. (P.O. Box 1436), Nantucket, MA 02554 (☎ 508/228-0600), which is next door and under the same ownership, has a very alluring brick patio surrounded by lovely gardens where guests can sit in Adirondack chairs and enjoy the beautiful surroundings. The house has two porches, one enclosed and the other open, overlooking the gardens. The most charming and private accommodation is the Linden Cottage in the old Carriage House. It has been converted into a pastel-colored light and airy summer accommodation furnished with wicker. It has a kitchen with a three-burner stove plus a microwave, coffeemaker, and refrigerator. In the main house, there are 15 rooms, 2 with fireplaces. They're furnished with a mixture of antiques and reproductions. Some are tucked under the eaves. Rates: Mid-June to mid-October and holidays, $135 to $285, cottage $375 to $400; mid-May to mid-June and mid-October to late October, $105 to $200, cottage $200 to $300; late October to mid-May, $60 to $110, cottage $125 to $150.

Away from Main and Centre streets, the **Sherburne Inn,** 10 Gay St., Nantucket, MA 02554 (☎ 508/228-4425), is very quiet. It occupies an 1835 building that was the headquarters of the Atlantic Silk Company before being converted into a guesthouse in 1872. The parlor here is very inviting with its cranberry-colored walls, fireplace, and gilt-framed paintings. There are eight rooms, all attractive and all with private baths—some baths are tiny but still functional. Some rooms have a fireplace; others have a small balcony. Room 6 features a queen half-poster, maple dressers, and porcelain lamps on side tables, plus a needlepoint chair, all set against William Morris–design wallpaper. Room 5 sports wallpaper with an unusual turtle-dove motif as a backdrop for a serpentine canopied bed, a marble-top dresser, and a wing chair. A parlor on the second floor has TV and a fireplace, too. A continental breakfast, consisting of fruit, muffins, and breads, is served in the first-floor parlor. Rates: Mid-June to mid-October, $130 to $200; April to mid-June and mid-October to December 31, $80 to $150; January to March, $70 to $100.

Harbor House Wharf Cottages, New Whale St., Nantucket, MA 02534 (☎ 508/228-1500 or 508/228-4620), is one of the island's largest accommodations with 114 rooms. Each is decorated in a modern way and has a full range of amenities, including a TV, telephone, and clock radio. The furnishings are usually pine and wicker. Some rooms, especially those on the third floor, have sizable balconies with great views of the harbor and bay. The townhouses, reached through some pretty gardens, have extra-large rooms with pull-out couches and pine furnishings. The studios and the one- to three-bedroom cottages are modern and have fully equipped kitchens. Facilities include an outdoor heated pool. For dining, the Hearth at the Harbor House has a huge hearth in the pub area plus a stylish dining room. It offers a terrific brunch ($19.95) on weekends featuring a carvery as well as omelet and waffle stations. Open April to the first week in December. Rates: Spring and fall, $135 to $225, summer, $235 to $285, winter, $125 to $150; cottages, spring $220 to $405; summer and fall $260 to $535.

76 Main Street, 76 Main St., Nantucket, MA 02554 (☎ 508/228-2533), occupies an 1883 house built by Captain William Swain, who was a sea lion hunter in the Northern Pacific. The interior is lavishly finished in redwood and fir from the Pacific, carved with mallow rose, hart and hound, and other motifs. The house stands on a quiet section of Main Street. The 18 rooms are spacious, clean, and simply furnished, and there's plenty of room for the guests' own things. Six accommodations, located across a small courtyard at the back of the property, are ideal for families, and have TVs and small refrigerators. They might contain a pencil four-poster and wing chairs and feature blue oriental-style wallpaper. Some of the bathrooms are small with shower only. Breakfast is served from 8:30 to 10am. Guests can relax in the comfortable parlor, which is warmed on cold days by a wood-burning stove. An ice machine and telephone are available for guests. Rates: Summer, $155 to $165; off-season, $100 to $110. Closed January.

Although it looks historic, **Seven Sea Street,** 7 Sea St., Nantucket, MA 02554 (☎ 508/228-3577), is in fact modern. It was built of red oak in the 1980s and designed with guest convenience and comfort in mind. There are nine rooms, all furnished with canopied beds, plus one suite-apartment on the top floor. The rooms have modern furnishings and contain all a guest needs—chest, side table, desk, rocker, and TV in a custom-made Shaker-style cabinet. Amenities include terry-cloth bathrobes, hair dryers, refrigerators, and telephones. The library is warmed by a wood-burning stove, and has a sofa, easy chairs, and plenty of reading material. A continental breakfast is served at the long harvest table in the keeping room, which has a brick hearth. Facilities include a spa-whirlpool. Rates: January to late April, $80 to $130; late April to late May, $110 to $170, suite $205; late May to late June and early September to early October, $130 to $200, suite $245; late June to early September, $160 to $240, suite $275; mid-October to late December, $110 to $170, suite $205.

The **Anchor Inn,** 66 Centre St., Nantucket, MA 02554 (☎ 508/228-0072), welcomes guests into its low-ceilinged, colonial-paneled, sage green parlor with a brick hearth. The inn is a historic place. The 11 rooms are all sizes and shapes, but they all manage to accommodate queen-size beds. Each room is named after a whaling ship. The Morgan wraps around the central chimney and has a sleigh bed standing on wide-board floors with spot rugs and a Federal lowboy. Cyrus has a serpentine four-poster with a crocheted canopy. Extra guest amenities include ice packs for picnics, telephones, beach towels, and a kettle and refrigerator for use anytime. Guests also enjoy relaxing on the patio in the side pocket garden. Rates: mid-June to mid-September, $125 to $170; mid-May to mid-June and mid-September to late October, $85 to $140; late October to mid-May, $65 to $110.

The **Corner House,** 49 Centre St. (P.O. Box 1828), Nantucket, MA 02554 (☎ 508/228-1530), is a center-hall colonial, and flanking the entrance you'll find two very lovely parlors both with low beamed ceilings, fine paneling, and fireplaces, furnished with antiques and paintings. One parlor features a TV; the other is extended by an enclosed side porch furnished with wicker and baskets of ferns. The rooms are plain and simple, furnished variously with, say, a Jenny Lind bed or wicker bed combined with braided rugs and pine or painted cottage chests. Nothing fancy, but serviceable; plus, you can expect to find good reading lights. A continental breakfast is served and an afternoon tea features scones, sandwiches, cookies, and cakes. Rates: July to September $105 to $195; mid-May to late June and October $90 to $140; late October to mid-May $75 to $120.

The **Periwinkle,** 9 N. Water St. (P.O. Box 1436), Nantucket, MA 02554 (☎ 508/228-9267), has some good-looking rooms and a little quieter locale. There are 17 rooms (11 with private bath). Room 1, for example, has a rice four-poster with a fabric canopy as well as an Empire dresser and sofa, a fireplace, and decorative porcelain lamps. Less elaborate rooms, most sharing baths, are located in the adjacent cottage. All rooms have a phone; some have a refrigerator. A continental breakfast is served. Rates: mid-June to mid-October and holidays, $120 to $215, cottage rooms $105; mid-May to mid-June and mid-October to late October, $85 to $170, cottage rooms $85; late October to mid-May, $60 to $105, cottage rooms $60.

nAnTUCKET DInInG

If you really want to treat yourself to an extra special dining experience, then make a reservation at the **Company of the Cauldron,** 7 India St. (☎ 508/228-4016), for its wonderful fixed-price dinner. The meal is served in an intimate and woodsy dining room that will be decorated with seasonal bounty and is accompanied by a classical harp. The menu changes nightly, but you might start with Nantucket vinewood roasted salmon in pastry with vidalia onions, spring asparagus, and red lentil wild rice. This could be followed by filet of sole stuffed with crabmeat, avocado, spinach, and leeks with a lime beurre blanc. Dinner could finish with lemon pound cake with summer fruit and Grand Marnier cream. The main course on another day could be grilled leg of lamb with mild curry sauce with fresh mango chutney and ginger fried rice. Great attention is paid to the garnishes so that the entire dish is pleasing to the eye as well as the palate. Prices range from $46 to $50 depending on the menu. Two dinner seatings every evening at 7 and 9pm.

21 Federal, 21 Federal St. (☎ 508/228-2121), is located in a historic building and attracts a knowledgeable food crowd to its series of elegant, intimate dining rooms. The cuisine draws plenty of rapturous reviews. The menu changes weekly. It might feature appetizers such as parma ham with aged balsamic vinegar and parmesan, or carpaccio with arugula and roast peppers. Among the main courses you might find spit-roasted duck with mashed potatoes and asparagus, grilled veal chop with wild mushroom fricassee and porcini au jus, or grilled swordfish with a traditional corn pudding mole and sweet potatoes. Desserts range from pumpkin bread pudding with cinnamon ice cream to tiramisu. Prices range from $21 to $32. Open April to mid-December, daily from 11:30am to 2:30pm and 6 to 10pm. Closed Sunday in spring and fall and sometimes other nights, too.

The dining room at **Oran Mor,** 1 S. Beach St. (☎ 508/228-8655), has a delicious Tuscan feel. It offers some good cuisine that emphasizes the bounty of the sea and also features game. Among the main dishes you might find loin of elk with eggplant, potato rosti, and demiglace, or sea scallops with roasted peppers, fennel, and Pernod jus. The lobster and crab cake served with wasabi is excellent, and the rack of pork is well balanced by sun-dried fruits and a brandade. To start, try the simple caviar creme fraiche or the black bean soup with tomato salsa and sour cream. Prices range from $22 to $34. Open summer, daily from 6 to 10pm and Sunday from 11am to 2pm (seasonal dates vary; call for information). Closed mid-October to mid-May.

Locals seem to rate **Le Languedoc,** 24 Broad St.(☎ 508/228-2552), their favorite restaurant, which gives it a very clublike air. They gather here downstairs in the low-ceilinged cafe at the blue gingham-covered tables or the small convivial bar. Upstairs the dining rooms are more formal, but in either place the food is excellent. Try the lobster bisque, which is full of flavor, or the oyster sampler with cucumber mignonette. Among the main courses, seafoods are top class; try the pan-seared roasted lobster scallop corn fritter with champagne essence or poached halibut with early morels, spring favas, ramps, and pancetta in a tarragon broth. Meat is not overlooked, and the grilled filet of beef with sauce Périgordine will certainly satisfy. Prices range from $20 to $30. Open May to December for dinner and for lunch from September to Christmas Stroll.

If Le Languedoc is the number-one choice among the locals, **Cioppino's,** 20 Broad St. (☎ 508/228-4622), is number two. They gather around the small convivial bar or in the light and airy dining room, casually furnished with Windsor chairs and white-clothed tables. The food is fresh and of high quality. Fish in particular stands out, like the hazelnut-crusted salmon fillet with raspberry vinaigrette or the signature dish cioppino, which combines local seafood with lobster and shrimp served over a bed of linguini. The meat dishes are also well prepared. Try the rack of lamb Provençale with tomato mint sauce, or the filet mignon with Madeira. Start with the smooth flavorsome lobster bisque or the chilled Nantucket oysters with a red wine mignonette sauce. Prices range from $20 to $30. Open May to October, daily from 11:30am to 2:30pm and 5:30 to closing.

Diners enter the **Club Car,** 1 Main St. (☎ 508/228-1101), via the club car, a cozy, sophisticated cocktail lounge in a car that once operated on the Nantucket railroad company's line from Nantucket town to 'Sconset. Here the chef prepares a wide range of dishes from a variety of cuisines. For example, you might start with octopus or squid Bangkok, made with Asian peppers, mint, cilantro, lime, tomato concasse, scallions, and fish sauce. Follow with a more traditional dish like scampi dijonnaise in a sauce enriched with shallots, garlic, brandy, mustard, and vermouth; or almond and walnut-crusted swordfish served with a pecan beurre blanc; or a more surprising lamb curry. For a real treat, try the broiled sesame eel with sweet potato, scallion, frissé, pickled ginger, and soy sake glaze. Prices range from $26 to $36; with special tasting menus offered for $65. The dining room exhibits simple good taste, with tables covered in crisp white tablecloths and cane-back chairs. Open May to December, daily from 11am to 3pm and 6 to 10pm.

American Seasons, 80 Centre St. (☎ 508/228-7111), has a funky, innovative air and a casual elegance. Plain painted kitchen chairs are set at the painted wood tables in a room with antiqued walls and colorful murals. Or you can dine on the outdoor patio, a perfect spot on a warm summer evening. The contemporary regional American cuisine is assertively flavored and ranges from New England with flair to Pacific Rim. If you seek the first kind of experience, then you can select the feathery mille-feuille of Hudson Valley foie gras with warm fig vinaigrette and oyster mushrooms, followed by pheasant with root vegetables and a Gouda tart or codfish with roasted tomato, fennel, and olive chutney, pancetta, and aioli in leek broth. On the Pacific side, you might try seared rare yellowfin tuna with a crispy sesame rice cake, or a marinated vegetable and ginger salad in a marin, soy, and lemongrass broth with fried noodles. Prices range from $20 to $25. A five-course tasting menu $65. Open April to December, daily from 6 to 10pm.

Brant Point Grill at the White Elephant, Easton Street (☎ 508/228-2500), is operated by Drew Nieporent of Tribeca Grill and Nobu fame. He has installed Chef Pat Trama from the Tribeca Grill in this Nantucket outpost. The room has great water views and needs no embellishment. The cuisine is fresh and assertive in flavor and makes the most of the natural bounty of the ocean. Dishes include horseradish-crusted cod with couscous, spinach, and chive oil; grilled yellowfin tuna with smoked onion mashed potatoes and pesto; braised rabbit wrapped with pancetta and served with whipped carrot and black olives; or a variation on classic grilled loin of lamb with puree of white beans, eggplant, and lemon mint. Prices range from $18 to $34. Open mid-May to October.

The **Boarding House,** 12 Federal St. (☎ 508/228-9622), offers atmospheric dining in its cellarlike dining room and a more casual experience in the light and airy bar. Prices range from $22 to $28 for dishes such as tarragon grilled chicken breast in a wild mushroom broth, swordfish flavored with lemon basil aioli, or beef tenderloin in a thyme flavored au jus. The appetizers, such as the crispy Chinese pot stickers and the grilled portobello mushroom with balsamic-marinated roast peppers, are extra appealing. Open in summer, daily from noon to 2pm and 6 to 10pm; winter, Thursday to Saturday, from 6 to 9:30pm.

You can't get closer to the waterfront than at **Straight Wharf Restaurant,** Straight Wharf (☎ 508/228-4499). In summer, the bar is full of bustle and marine muscle. The dining room is hopping, too. Folks come for the atmosphere and the fresh and varied cuisine with its hints of Asian flavor in some dishes. Try the steamed lobster with lemongrass, saffron sauce, and potato lasagna; the seafood cassoulet with fennel broth; or the shell of beef with vidalia onion and potato puree. Prices range from $22 to $34. Open June to September, Tuesday to Sunday from 6 to 10pm.

Arno's at 41 Main St. (☎ 508/228-7001) is a comfortable place where you can secure a good meal for a reasonable price by Nantucket's standards. Tables are set with floral cloths and glass tops, and the decor runs to brick walls accented with art and vintage portraits. You can start with a delicious chowder and follow with one of the often-spicy dishes—for example, the jerk-spiced grilled pork medallions with a roasted red pepper cream sauce and grilled onion chutney or the less fiery shrimp and scallop florentine served over angel-hair pasta. The crab cakes are great, and the rosemary grilled leg of lamb is another favorite. The garlic mashed potatoes is a comfort to the soul. Prices range from $14 to $19. Open year-round for breakfast (from 8am to 2pm), lunch (11am to 5pm), and dinner (from 5pm).

Moona, 122 Pleasant St. (☎ 508/325-4301), has a country but cool air with its tile bar and folk art–decorated walls. It's a casual, comfortable place with a glow. The floors are painted, and the copper-top tables gleam. The cuisine is exciting and innovative and features a broad range of dishes, including some fine vegetarian options. For example, you might start with a goat cheese and wild mushroom strudel with roasted beet and mâche salad, grilled tomato, and sage dressing. To follow, the halibut filet with a black olive and arugula pesto and a yellow tomato tapanade offer assertive flavors. For a delicious simple meat dish, the spit-roasted chicken with a sauce of red wine, tarragon and fennel, and oven-dried tomato risotto hits the spot. Prices range from $15 to $24. Open year-round, daily from 5 to 9pm; later on weekends.

Kendrick's, at the Quaker House, 5 Chestnut St. (☎ 508/228-9156), has two intimate, casual but elegant dining rooms with a small counter/bar. The cuisine is refreshingly contemporary and focused on the pure flavors of the prime ingredient in each dish. You'll likely enjoy a grilled rare tuna with bok choy and udon noodle cake or pan-roasted salmon with warm portabello mushroom and arugula salad. On the meat side, the dish could be a plain grilled veal chop with pan-fried herbed spaetzle. Prices range from $16 to $28. For an appetizer, two dishes in particular draw accolades—the potato pancake with smoked salmon and crème fraiche and the charred beef carpaccio, pickled tomatoes, and aged balsamic vinegar. Brunch is made more piquant than usual by the appearance of dishes such as Portuguese baked eggs with linguica and scallion potatoes or French toast served with sautéed bananas and rum-raisin sauce. Open year-round. July and August, Monday to Friday from 11:30am to 4pm, Saturday and Sunday from 8am to 2pm, daily 6 to 10pm; May, Thursday to Monday only; June, Thursday to Tuesday. The bar menu is offered until 11pm.

India House, 37 India St. (☎ 508/228-9043), as you'd expect, combines Eastern spices with the ingredients of classic cuisine in some of its dishes. Try the curried Cornish hen, the confit of duck leg and grilled duck breast with green peppercorn and peach pear syrup, or the swordfish with lime and thyme beurre blanc. The appetizers are always tempting: Hudson valley foie gras blackened with citrus zest crust and served with a vidalia onion marmalade, or crab cake with sweet corn, dried cranberry relish, and chive mustard sauce. The restaurant has two intimate dining rooms in a historic house as well as a pleasant outdoor dining area. Prices range from $19 to $30. Good brunch, too. Open April to December, daily from 6:30 to 9:30pm, Sunday 9:30am to 1pm.

West Creek Cafe, 11 W. Creek Rd. (☎ 508/228-8893), is a small, casual but very inviting dining room. On one side there's a small bar; another room contains a fireplace and banquettes with cushions at tables covered with floral or check tablecloths. A contemporary menu is featured, with dishes such as salmon with creamy parsnips, chili-glazed pork with smoky collard greens, or beef tenderloin with pancetta and baby onions in a mustard sauce. Prices range from $21 to $25. You might start with oysters on the half shell or beef satay with peanut vinaigrette. Open year-round, Wednesday to Monday from 6 to 9:30pm.

The **Woodbox,** 29 Fair St. (☎ 508/228-0587), is located in a 1709 house and offers romantic dining in low-ceilinged, beamed historic dining rooms lit by candlelight. Windsor comback chairs are placed at polished wood tables, arranged around a brick hearth. The cuisine is classic—beef Wellington with duck pâte and mushroom duxelle, duck with black cherry sauce, or rack of lamb with a rosemary infused jus. To start, try the delicious jumbo scampi with tarragon Dijon sauce, or the carpaccio with red pepper tapenade and horseradish crème fraiche. Open June to December, Tuesday to Sunday from 8:30am to 11pm, with two dinner sittings at 6:30 and 9pm; winter and spring, Thursday to Saturday only.

DeMarco, 9 India St. (☎ 508/228-1836), is a handsome, inviting restaurant where produce and food take pride of place. The Northern Italian cuisine is fresh and tempting, and the herbal blends are wonderful. The grilled dishes are examples of this fine, but often poorly executed, art. Among the main courses, you might find braised lamb with white wine and fresh herbs served with vegetables and orange rosemary, or salmon over celery root puree with braised lentils in honey and balsamic vinegar. The stuffed breast of veal is extraordinary, flavored with fennel, tomato, and Chianti and served with glazed root vegetables. So too is the potato horseradish–crusted salmon with beets and port wine sauce. For an appetizer, try the clam chowder that has been enriched with pancetta, savoy cabbage, and potatoes or the portobello mushrooms tossed with watercress in lemon and olive oil and flavored with pecorino and romano cheeses. Prices range from $19 to $29. Open April to December, daily from 6 to 10pm.

American Bounty, 60 Union St. (☎ 508/228-3886), is a substantial walk from town. It's a small, casual country-style dining room where copper pots give a glow to the entrance and a trellis adds a gardenlike air. Soft background music adds to the ambience in the beamed dining room. Here you'll find contemporary regional cuisine at fairly modest prices for the island. Start with the thick roasted corn and clam chowder; follow with pan-seared pork tenderloin, served with figs, caramelized shallots, and port sauce, or bay scallops prepared with tomato coriander and Madeira sauce. Prices range from $18 to $24. Open April to December, daily from 8am to 1pm and 6 to 9:30pm.

Jared's, 29 Broad St. (☎ 508/228-2400), is the formal dining room at the inn, which is known for its Wednesday and Sunday seafood buffets that assemble all the fish from the sea, it seems—clam chowder, clams, oysters, shrimp, plus swordfish piccata, seafood Newburg, and shrimp scampi. For good measure there's a beef or chicken dish. It's $26, and you can help yourself as often as you like. It's presided over by the august historic portraits on the wall. On other days you'll find such heartening dishes as roast pork tenderloin with peach chutney and Schnapps sauce, or pepper-crusted tenderloin of beef with grilled portabello mushrooms and cognac sauce. Prices range from $18 to $25. For a refreshing change, try the twin crab cakes with roasted chili sauce and scallion butter to start. Open April to mid-October, daily for breakfast and Wednesday to Monday from 5pm.

You won't find fresher sushi anywhere than that at **Sushi by Yoshi,** 2 E. Chestnut St. (☎ 508/228-1801). It's a tiny place with only three or four tables where the chef keeps creating the sushi and sashimi for satisfied customers. He calls some of the combinations by such names as Mitchell (tuna, avocado, asparagus, scallions, and caviar) or Rainbow (tuna, salmon, and whitefish or squid over a California roll). Prices start at $4.75 for two pieces of sushi and three pieces of sashimi. The combination prices are higher. The menu is rounded out by some noodle dishes, appetizers like shumai and gyoza, and chicken teriyaki. Open April to December, daily from 11:30am to 10pm.

The Tap Room at the Jared Coffin House, 29 Broad St. (☎ 508/ 228-2400), is one of the few places that stays open 365 days a year. It's a cozy pub with an outdoor dining area at the Jared Coffin House. The menu is typical—sandwiches, fish and chips, chowder, burgers, clam rolls, and dinner dishes such as baked stuffed sole, chicken saltimbocca, and teriyaki sirloin steak. Hearty, and there when you need it. Prices range from $12 to $20 at dinner. Open daily from 11:30am to 9pm.

Black Eyed Susan's, 10 India St., is the place to go for breakfast. It's a typical stool-and-counter place with some tables too. It's also open for dinner, but some folks can't get past the ambience to the food, which is always inspirational and different. For example, the closest thing to chowder on the menu will be Indian corn chowder with lentils and pappadums, and this dish might be one among appetizers that include things like wild boar sausage. The entrees range from scented pork confit topped with caramelized onion, served in a spicy mole and orange ancho chili sauce, to Thai shrimp cakes in a sweet curry sauce. Prices range from $15 to $20. BYOB. No credit cards. Open daily from 6:30am to 1pm and Monday to Saturday from 6 to 10pm. Closed 6 weeks in winter.

For brunch go to **The Hearth at Harbor House,** S. Beach Street (at the center of town; ☎ 508/228-1500), which puts on quite a spread in its waterfront dining room. You'll find a carvery, omelets made to order, rafts of fresh shellfish and seafood, fresh fruits, and loads of desserts. It's served Sunday from 10:30am to 2pm.

And finally, on any day, enjoy something fancy from the old-fashioned soda fountain at the **Nantucket Pharmacy** at 45 Main St. (☎ 508/228-0810).

SIASCONSET & NEARBY LODGING & DINING

The **Summer House,** 17 Ocean Ave. (P.O. Box 880), Siasconset, MA 02564 (☎ 508/257-4577), is around the corner from Siasconset village center. It's a delightful place, a perfect hideaway with a handful of rose-trellised cottages and its own beach across the narrow road. There are only eight cottages, but they are charmers. All the one-bedrooms have Jacuzzi bathrooms. Each has been decorated with whimsy, too. In Barclay, which has a lovely pickled-pine ceiling, you'll find a bedroom with a painted bed dressed with Battenburg lace. The floors are painted, too, watercolors adorn the walls, and the whole is stylish and romantic. Ketch has two bedrooms and a kitchenette with a two-burner stove and a fridge. Penrose has a wood-burning fireplace. The lush lawn in front of the cottages is dotted with Adirondack chairs.

Below the bluff, across the street, there is a pool, where lunch is served in summer. The restaurant is stylishly funky. It's decked out with a green marbleized decor and has white tables and chairs. The cuisine is fresh, stimulating, and eclectic with a definite lean to Northern Italy. Try the artichoke and fontina bruschetta with smoked beef carpaccio as a starter. Some of the fish dishes are wonderful—the red snapper with a ragout of jumbo lump crab, baby artichokes, capers, and lemon thyme; or the grilled lobster over warm marinated new potatoes and haricots vert, with a black truffle sauce. Prices range from $30 to $42. It's open daily in summer from noon to 2pm and 6:30 to 9:30pm. Closed from the end of October through Mother's Day.

Facilities include the beachside pool. The cottages are open from the end of April to the end of October. Rates: summer (mid-June through Labor Day), $425 to $550; mid-season (after Memorial Day to June 12, and after Labor Day to late September) $295 to $450; winter (before Memorial Day and after late September) $235 to $325.

Wauwinet (P.O. Box 2580), Nantucket, MA 02584 (☎ 508/228-0145), is the place to stay if you want a small resort in a fabulous but secluded beach location, where you can enjoy first-class service and amenities and a dining room that serves some of the finest food on the island. Wauwinet is located at the less developed east end of the island facing Head of the Harbor and the Atlantic Ocean.

There are 26 rooms in the main house, plus eight cottages. They are decorated in high style—beds with tufted headboards, large armoires, comfortable easy chairs with footstools, pine chests, and extra accents such as books, binoculars, botanical prints, and porcelain lamps. Even the smallest room accommodates a queen-size bed and a sitting area.

Amenities include CD players plus a music library to choose from. The rooms on the third floor have glorious ocean views. The cottages are lovely. Idelwild has a stone fireplace in a comfortable, well-furnished sitting room; Willet has the most privacy and includes a brick patio with an umbrella table and loungers. Guests appreciate the library and game room where the pickled-pine floor, the large brick fireplace, and comfortable seating make it a stylish but comfortable room for unwinding. A broad porch, furnished with green wicker, looks out across the lawn to the beach and bay beyond. The gardens are also well tended, and the chef maintains his own herb garden. In summer the marble tables on the brick patio are favorite dining places; there's also an outdoor dining/cocktail deck. Cheese, port, and sherry are served in the late afternoon in the library.

Facilities include two clay tennis courts, 30-plus mountain bikes, a croquet lawn, and two beaches—one a 2½-mile strand on the Atlantic; the other on the bay. Beach towels and lounge chairs are provided. Services include a concierge and twice-daily maid service. A regular jitney service is provided to and from town. Open early May to late October. For dining information see below. Rates: mid-May to mid-June and mid-September to late October, $200 to $550; cottages $425 to $1200; mid-June to mid-September $230 to $725, cottages $575 to $1,500.

The Chanticleer Inn, 40 New St., Siasconset 02564 (☎ 508/257-6231), is the premier dining place on the island. And a lovely place it is, indeed, in an ivy-covered shingled home dating to 1909, set around a courtyard garden where, in summer, you can enjoy an aperitif at tables set out under a rose-covered trellis. Very romantic. There are differently styled dining rooms: a formal dining room with an atrium-style extension and the more casual Grill Room with a decor of thematic art relating to Napoleon. The room features a solid cherry bar, and cigar smoking is allowed. Both rooms have handsome fireplaces. Tables in both are set with beautiful custom-made Limoges china from France. You can dine from a fixed-price or an à la carte menu. Either way, the cuisine of Jean-Charles Berruet will be super-memorable. The menu changes frequently, but you can always count on Beluga caviar being among the appetizers. Other sterling appetizers are the Wellfleet oysters on the half shell with a shallot vinegar sauce and a delicious lobster and truffle soup baked in puff pastry.

Among the main courses there might be rack of lamb roasted with spices and served with Provençe-style vegetable stew and beans, or roast duck with currant sauce. Of course, there's lobster, served triumphantly with a champagne butter. The fixed-price menu is $65; the à la carte from $30 to $40. The desserts are sublime, from the hot Valrhona chocolate soufflé served with a bitter chocolate sauce to a simple but delicious hot apple tart glazed with Calvados. The 30-page wine list is extraordinary: 1,200 to 1,400 selections from a cellar containing 40,000 bottles. Open from early May until late October, Tuesday to Sunday from 6:30 to 8:30 or 9pm; closed Monday.

Topper's at the Wauwinet (☎ 508/228-0145) is the other place to dine. It's not nearly as formal as Chanticleer, but the service is attentive, the ocean setting beautiful, and the cuisine quite wonderful. There are several rooms, all embellished with colorful floral bouquets, elegant silver lanterns, and original art. Here, some of the most delicately flavored and extraordinary fish and shellfish dishes are prepared. For a truly great seafood orgy, start with the steamed littleneck clams with champagne scallions and tomato and follow with some seared Nantucket Bay scallops with mâche and truffle vinaigrette. Then enjoy an arugula salad with blue cheese pancetta and cider vinaigrette just to clear the palate for the Nantucket lobster stew with salsify leeks and tomalley croutons, a dish the likes of which you will rarely enjoy ever again. If this stew is on the menu, skip the steamed lobster, for the former is a much better choice. And then finish with toasted brioche with poached pears and caramel sauce. Superb. Open May through December, Monday to Saturday from noon to 11pm, Sunday from 10:30am to 2pm and 5 to 11pm.

In & Around Nantucket
Special & Recreational Activities

Beaches: The whole 110-mile shoreline is open to the public. **North Shore** beaches are generally calmer and better for swimming: Children's Beach, Harbor View Way, is well named. It's on the harbor and ideal for young tots. Jetties Beach on North Beach Street has full facilities—lifeguards, a playground, showers, rest rooms, and restaurants and is popular with families. Dionis Beach on the Sound is a dune-backed beach about 3 miles from town. Brant Point has treacherous currents and is best for viewing the lighthouse and watching the boats round the point.

South Shore beaches have higher surf. Madaket Beach is 6 miles out of town. It has good surf and great sunsets. The shuttle takes you there, or you can bike to it. Cisco Beach, Hummock Pond Road, has heavy surf. Surfside, at the end of Surfside Road, 3 miles from town, has good surf but can be windy.

On the **Eastern Shore** Siasconset is a great beach also with heavy surf. The shuttle will take you there.

Biking: Rentals are readily available from **Young's Bicycle Shop**, Steamboat Wharf (☎ 508/228-1151), **Nantucket Bike Shop** on Broad Street (☎ 508/228-1999), and **Affordable Rentals**, 6 S. Beach St. (☎ 508/228-3501). (These outfits also rent scooters, cars, and 4×4s.) You can cycle to the best beaches. It's only 3.5 miles to Surfside, 8.2 to Siasconset, and 6.2 miles to Madaket.

Birding: Maria Mitchell Association (☎ 508/228-0898) offers tours three times a week.

Boating: Nantucket Boat Rental, Straight Wharf (☎ 508/325-1001) rents skiffs and sailboats. Prices start at $200 for a small skiff.

Canoeing/Kayaking: Contact **Sea Nantucket** (☎ 508/228-7499), which rents both canoes and kayaks. Half-day rates for kayaks start at $35; full day at $45. Canoes are $55 for a half day. Tours available. **Forces Watersports**, 37 Main St. (☎ 508/228-5358) also rents kayaks for $45 a half day.

Cruises: The captain who sails *The Endeavor* (☎ 508/228-5585) built the vessel and has been operating here for 15 years. It's docked at Straight Wharf and sails on 1 and 1½ hour trips. Fares range from $25 to $35. **Nantucket Adventures** (☎ 508/325-5917) puts you aboard the *Adventurer,* a high-speed catamaran that can accommodate 49 passengers for morning and sunset sails, a mystery cruise that includes hors d'oeuvres and a lobster clambake, and a reggae cruise with music and refreshments. Sailing times range from 2 to 4 hours. **Nantucket Harbor Cruises** (☎ 508/228-1444) operates lobstering, sunset, and harbor cruises. Tickets range from $15 to $22.50 for adults for cruises that range from 45 minutes to 1½ hours.

Fishing: Deep-sea charters leave from Straight Wharf for bluefish, striped bass, and other sport fishing. Among the operators, try **Just Do It Too** (☎ 508/228-7448), which operates daily 2½ hour trips, or **Monomoy Charters** (☎ 508/228-6867), which offers ¼-, ½-, and full-day trips. Also try **Albacore** (☎ 508/228-1439). Average price is $50. Surf fishing is also popular.

Golf: **Siasconset Golf Club,** Milestone Road (☎ 508/257-6596), allows visitors to play in the fall only; **Miacomet Golf Club,** 12 W. Miacomet Rd. (☎ 508/325-0335), is the only other nine-hole course, and it's not exactly PGA.

Ice Skating: If you're visiting in winter, try it at **Lily Pond,** near the Old North Cemetery, or at **Sesachacha Pond** off Polpis Road.

Nature Tours: Great Point Natural History Tours (☎ 508/228-6799) operates 3-hour tours led by naturalists along the barrier beaches of the **Coskata Coatue Wildlife Refuge,** the habitat of piping plover, least and roseate terns, oyster catchers, great blue herons, ospreys, and many more shore birds. The trip goes to Great Point Lighthouse. Seating is limited so reservations are needed. Price is $30 adult. Tours leave from the Wauwinet from June to October.

Sailing: Forces Watersports, 37 Main St. (☎ 508/228-5358), rents sunfish for $70 a half day and also provides lessons.

Tennis: There are six courts at **Jetties Beach,** open mid-June to mid-September. For information call the Park and Recreation Commission at ☎ 508/325-5334 or 508/228-7213.

Tours: Gail's Tours (☎ 508/257-6557) will familiarize you with the island. Tours last 1½ hours and are given in a van that holds 10 people. **Robert Pitman Grimes,** 22 Pleasant St. (☎ 508/228-9382), gives his tours a definite historic slant.

Whale Watching: Trips leave from Straight Wharf from June to September. Call **Nantucket Whalewatch** (☎ 508/283-0313) or Nantucket Whaleboat Adventures (☎ 508/228-5585). Average price is $70 per adult.

Windsurfing: Forces Watersports, 37 Main St. (☎ 508/228-5358), rents windsurfers for $65 a half day and also offers lessons.

The Central Berkshires

Lenox ◆ *Tanglewood* ◆ *Lee* ◆ *Stockbridge* ◆ *West Stockbridge* ◆
The Egremont Area ◆ *Great Barrington* ◆ *Sheffield* ◆
Pittsfield-Dalton & the Northwestern Corner ◆ *Jacob's
Pillar* ◆ *Williamstown* ◆ *Hancock Shaker Village* ◆
Mount Greylock ◆ *Adams & North Adams*

Distance in miles from Boston: Pittsfield, 137; Great Barrington, 164; Williamstown, 158; Springfield, 92; Deerfield, 114.

Estimated driving times: 2½ hours to Pittsfield; 2¾ hours to Great Barrington; 2¾ hours to Williamstown; 1½ to 1¾ hours to Springfield; 2 hours to Deerfield.

◄◦►◄◦►◄◦►◄◦►◄◦►

Driving: For Great Barrington, Lenox, Lee, and the Egremonts, take Exit 2 off the Massachusetts Turnpike. Route 7 north will take you to Williamstown. For Deerfield, take the Massachusetts Turnpike to I-91 north to the Deerfield exit.

Bus: Bonanza (☎ 800/556-3815) travels to Great Barrington, Lee, Lenox, Stockbridge, Pittsfield, and Williamstown. **Peter Pan** (☎ 800/343-9999) also services these towns plus Springfield and Deerfield.

Train: Amtrak services Springfield and Pittsfield from Boston. Call ☎ 800/872-7245.

Further Information: For further information about Massachusetts in general, contact **Massachusetts Office of Travel & Tourism**, 100 Cambridge St., Boston, MA 02202 (☎ 800/447-6277 or 617/727-3201).

For specific information about the area: **Berkshire Visitor's Bureau,** Berkshire Common Plaza Level, Dept. MA, Pittsfield, MA 01201 (☎ 413/443-9186); **Stockbridge Chamber of Commerce,** P.O. Box 224, Stockbridge, MA 01262 (☎ 413/598-5200); **Lenox Chamber of Commerce,** P.O. Box 646, Lenox, MA 01240 (☎ 800/25LENOX or 413/637-3646); **Southern Berkshire Chamber of Commerce,** 362 Main St., Great Barrington, MA 01230 (☎ 413/528-1510).

For Deerfield area information: **Pioneer Valley Convention & Visitor's Bureau,** 56 Dwight St., Springfield, MA 01103 (☎ 413/787-1548); **Mohawk Trail Association,** P.O. Box 7, Dept. MA, North Adams, MA 01347 (☎ 413/664-6256).

The Berkshires

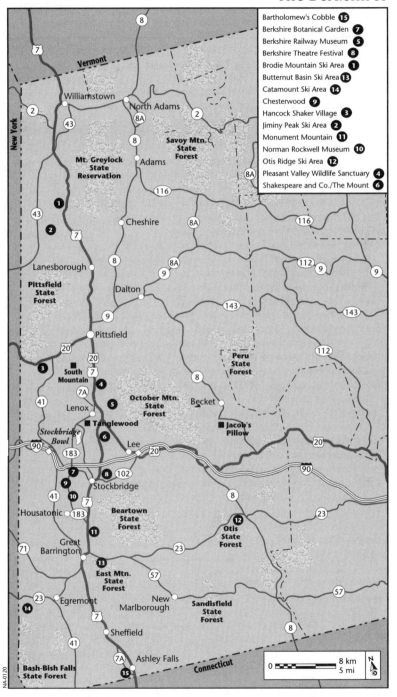

Bartholomew's Cobble **15**
Berkshire Botanical Garden **7**
Berkshire Railway Museum **5**
Berkshire Theatre Festival **8**
Brodie Mountain Ski Area **1**
Butternut Basin Ski Area **13**
Catamount Ski Area **14**
Chesterwood **9**
Hancock Shaker Village **3**
Jiminy Peak Ski Area **2**
Monument Mountain **11**
Norman Rockwell Museum **10**
Otis Ridge Ski Area **12**
Pleasant Valley Wildlife Sanctuary **4**
Shakespeare and Co./The Mount **6**

Vermont

New York

Williamstown

North Adams

Savoy Mtn.
State
Forest

Mt. Greylock
State
Reservation

Adams

Cheshire

Lanesborough

Pittsfield
State
Forest

Dalton

Pittsfield

South
Mountain

Lenox

October Mtn.
State
Forest

Becket

Peru
State
Forest

Tanglewood

Stockbridge
Bowl

Jacob's
Pillow

Lee

Stockbridge

Housatonic

Beartown
State
Forest

Great
Barrington

Otis
State
Forest

East Mtn.
State
Forest

Egremont

New
Marlborough

Sandisfield
State
Forest

Sheffield

Ashley Falls

Bash-Bish Falls
State Forest

Connecticut

0   8 km
      5 mi
N

NA-0120

Events & Festivals to Plan Your Trip Around

End of June through Labor Day: Summer Festivals

    Jacob's Pillow Dance Festival. Call ☎ 413/243-0745 for tickets.

    Williamstown Theatre Festival. Call ☎ 413/597-3400 for tickets.

    Berkshire Theatre Festival, Stockbridge. Call ☎ 413/298-5576 after June 1; 413/298-5536 at other times.

    Tanglewood. For tickets, which go on sale in early April, call ☎ 800/274-8499. Call ☎ 413/637-1666 for information or write to Boston Symphony Orchestra, Symphony Hall, Boston, MA 02115 (☎ 617/266-1492).

July: Aston Magna Festival, Great Barrington (☎ 800/875-7156 or 413/528-3595), features 17th- and 18th-century works performed on original instruments at various locations on weekends.

September: Josh Billings Race combines a 26-mile cycle trip from Great Barrington to the Stockbridge Bowl, two laps by canoe around the lake, and a 6-mile run to Tanglewood (usually mid-September).

    That same weekend the **Lenox Tub Parade** celebrates an earlier tradition. Horse-drawn carriages or "tubs" decorated with the harvest of the season parade through the streets, recalling the way the "cottagers" used to say their good-byes before heading back to the city.

September/October: South Mountain Chamber Concerts, South Mountain, Box 23, Pittsfield, MA 01201 (☎ 413/442-2106).

October: Harvest Festival at the Berkshire Botanical Garden in Stockbridge. Call ☎ 413/298-3926.

December: The **Annual Holiday House Tour** gives visitors the opportunity to view privately owned historic properties that are not usually open to the public.

◄○►◄○►◄○►◄○►◄○►

It would take a lot of weekends to "do" the Berkshires because the events and attractions are so many and so varied. First, of course, there are all those outstanding cultural events—Tanglewood, the Williamstown Theatre Festival, the South Mountain concerts, the Jacob's Pillow Dance Festival—that bring people flocking to this scenic area of lakes and wooded hills. And there's the history of the region that yields all kinds of attractions, some literary or artistic, like the homes of Herman Melville, Edith Wharton, Nathaniel Hawthorne, William Cullen Bryant, Daniel Chester French, and Norman Rockwell. Others are from a more worldly past, like the sumptuous mansions that line the streets and dot the countryside around Lenox and Stockbridge—Blantyre,

Bellefontaine, Wheatleigh, and Naumkeag. And last but far from least, there is the landscape—Mounts Greylock, Everett, and Monument, and the forests that surround them, with all kinds of opportunities for hiking, skiing, blueberrying, birding, picnicking, and just plain basking in the beauty of it all. In short, it's a very rich area to mine for many weekends or longer stays.

The first settlers of the Berkshires were the Mahkeenac Indians. Driven by the Iroquois from the Hudson Valley, the Mahkeenac found the lush streams, lakes, and wooded hills around Stockbridge and Great Barrington to be abundant hunting and fishing grounds. As pioneers moved west from the Massachusetts Bay Colony, they, too, entered into the area, establishing thriving farming and trading communities—the first at Sheffield in 1733 and the second at Stockbridge in 1735. Some of the settlers attempted to convert the Mahkeenacs to Christianity, as did the Reverend John Sergeant, whose Mission House can still be seen in Stockbridge. During the Revolutionary War, Berkshire County supported the patriots' cause, and indeed, as early as 1774 the townsfolk of Great Barrington showed their resistance to British rule by refusing to allow royal judges to sit in court. The domestic turmoil that followed the Revolution was also experienced here—in 1787 Daniel Shay led his famous farmers' rebellion against the Articles of Confederation, an event recalled today by a marker on Route 23 in South Egremont, where he supposedly surrendered to Colonel John Ashley of Sheffield. Soon after the Revolution the Shakers arrived. This community of pacifist celibates who dedicated their lives to hard work established their City of Peace in 1790 at Hancock, and it is a fascinating place to visit today.

Less simple folk soon followed. First to arrive was Boston financier Samuel Gray Ward. Such figures as Nathaniel Hawthorne, Herman Melville, Henry Wadsworth Longfellow, and James Russell Lowell came soon after. But these early comers were folks of modest means compared to the superrich who turned the area into a playground for the wealthy. These people represented the great fortunes that had been made from steel, milling, railroads, and other industries in the 19th century, and they looked for places to vacation and display their wealth. They built ever more lavish and ostentatious mansions and mock palaces in imitation of the European aristocracy. Those who liked the ocean summered at resorts such as Newport, Cape May, and Bar Harbor, while the Berkshires and Saratoga Springs attracted those who preferred the mountains. Edith Wharton, tired of Newport and marriage, built her $40,000 mansion here in 1901. She used to drive the dusty roads in her large automobile, with her frequent visitor, Henry James, often at her side. Harley Proctor of Proctor & Gamble built a "cottage" in Lenox, and other industrialists like George Westinghouse, the Vanderbilts, and Andrew Carnegie established great estates in the area.

From about 1880 to 1900 the Berkshires experienced their heyday. After that their popularity declined with the advent, among other things, of the automobile and later of the airplane, both of which afforded increased mobility to the younger generation. The mansions stood empty and unused, and most of them were sold off and converted into schools, camps, or guesthouses. Bellefontaine, for example, which had been copied from Louis XV's Petit Trianon and reputedly cost $1 million to build in 1899, sold for a mere $70,000 in 1946.

Despite the wealthy influx, the Berkshires always retained their image as a creative arts colony. Nathaniel Hawthorne wrote his *Tanglewood Tales* looking out over Lake Mahkeenac (the Stockbridge Bowl). In 1850 he met Herman Melville at a Monument Mountain picnic, and after that they visited each other often. Melville even dedicated *Moby Dick* to Hawthorne. William Cullen Bryant, editor of the *New York Post*, the jurist Oliver Wendell Holmes, the poet Henry Wadsworth Longfellow, and James Russell Lowell are just a few of the writers and intellectuals associated with the Berkshires. The artist Daniel Chester French built his Chesterwood in 1898, and much later Norman Rockwell, chronicler of America's small-town life, came to the Berkshires.

The artistic tradition of the area was further entrenched with the establishment of major cultural events like the Berkshire Music Festival, founded in 1936 when Sergei Koussevitsky conducted the first concert at Tanglewood; the Jacob's Pillow Dance Festival, established by Ted Shawn and Ruth St. Denis 5 years later; and the Berkshire Theatre Festival, which helped to establish the careers of such legendary actors as James Cagney, Ethel Barrymore, and Katharine Hepburn.

These summer events still draw enormous crowds, but no matter what time of year you choose to visit the Berkshires, they will always delight. In winter they present the idyllic winter scenes captured in Norman Rockwell's famous seasonal illustration of Stockbridge. There's skiing at Catamount, Jiminy Peak, Brodie, Berkshire East, and Butternut, cross-country skiing everywhere, skating on the lakes, and hot toddies and blazing fires in quaint old-fashioned inns to help you recover from outdoor exertions. Whether you come to ski or nod by the fireside in winter, to wander amid the mountain laurel in spring, to view the fantastic palette of the trees in fall, or to spread out your blanket and picnic under the stars at Tanglewood to the sounds of Beethoven or Mozart, you'll experience a deep thrill and contentment that will leave you wanting to return time and time again.

LENOX

Today, you can stay in many of the old mansions that were once the summer retreats for such industrial magnates as Harley Proctor, George Westinghouse, and Andrew Carnegie, who were drawn to the Berkshires's unspoiled beauty, and the tidy farms and streets of Lenox in particular.

Besides these wonderful mansions, the main attraction for visitors is, of course, the **Berkshire Music Festival at Tanglewood,** just outside Lenox, overlooking the lovely Stockbridge Bowl, which inspired Nathaniel Hawthorne to write his *Tanglewood Tales*. Although the festival may have lost some of its earlier seriousness and serenity, it still attracts dedicated listeners to its shaded lawns and large music shed and is still a very pleasant way to spend some of your time in the Berkshires. (For detailed information, see "Cultural Events in the Berkshires," below.)

A walk around the village past the rambling old clapboard houses is always a pleasure. On your way, at the corner of Walker and Main streets, you'll pass the old **Curtis Hotel,** a noted 19th-century stage stop that welcomed such illustrious guests as Chester Alan Arthur, Franklin Delano Roosevelt, Dwight

Eisenhower, Jenny Lind, and Sergei Koussevitzky. Today it has been remodeled into a home for the retired.

From here, be sure to walk to the top of the hill on Main Street to see the **Church on the Hill,** a very fine New England Congregational church erected in 1805.

At the junction of routes 7 and 7A, you can tour **The Mount** (☎ 413/637-1899), an impressive mansion with a dramatic widow's walk, an octagonal cupola, and a terrace with balustrade. The Mount was built in 1901–02. Modeled on Belton House, a 17th-century estate in Lincolnshire, England, it shows how accomplished Edith Wharton was when it came to architecture, interior design, and gardening. Wharton lived here while she wrote her novel *The House of Mirth* (1905) and where she was inspired to write *Ethan Frome* (1911), which is set in the Berkshire countryside. From the end of May through October, tours are given daily from 9am to 2pm. Admission is $6 for adults and $4.50 for children 13 to 18. After the tours, Shakespeare and Company offers theater at the Mount.

For a change of pace, the **Pleasant Valley Wildlife Sanctuary,** West Mountain Road (☎ 413/637-0320), maintained by the Massachusetts Audubon Society, offers miles of nature trails. Admission is $3 for adults, $2 for children 3 to 12. It's located just off Route 7 north of Lenox.

LENOX LODGING

Although there are plenty of wonderful accommodations within a 30-minute drive of Tanglewood (which I'll describe later), Lenox is the closest place to stay, and the village is full of notable hosteleries. You'll have to book well in advance, pay ahead, and probably stay a minimum of 2 or 3 nights. Tanglewood operates an **accommodations hotline,** providing rooms in local homes. Call the festival number: ☎ 413/637-1600.

The true connoisseur stays house-party style at **Blantyre,** 16 Blantyre Rd., Lenox, MA 01240 (☎ 413/637-3556 after May 1, 413/298-3806 off-season), built in 1902 for Robert Paterson, the president of W. J. Sloane, director of a Manhattan Bank, and a friend of Carnegie. Costing $135,000 ($300,000 if you add in the furnishings), it was the most expensive and lavish villa in the Berkshires (The Mount cost only $40,000.) It was modeled after his wife's Scottish ancestral home.

In its heyday, when the summer set walked to and from each other's houses attended by maids with lanterns, it was the scene of tea parties, games, charades, and formal balls and dinners. Thereafter it experienced a checkered but nevertheless fascinating history. In 1925 it, along with 250 acres, was sold for a mere $25,000; it served briefly as a country club before being bought by D. W. Griffith, who dreamed of turning it into an East Coast studio but died before he could do so. Various owners tried to make something of it until finally Senator and Mrs. Fitzpatrick, the inspiration behind the Red Lion in Stockbridge, bought it and created this luxurious accommodation.

So magnificent—veritably museum quality—are the furnishings that the proprietors have had to close the house to uninvited visitors because too many appeared to gawk at the splendor. In the main hall, lit by shimmering chandeliers, Elizabethan and Jacobean pieces and oriental vases are arrayed before the ornately carved fireplace. The similarly furnished music room also features a priceless Coromandel screen and a grand piano. There are 4 rooms and

4 suites in the main house and 12 additional, beautifully appointed rooms in the carriage house, out by the open-air swimming pool.

The suites are spectacular. The Cranwell has a dramatic four-poster and the various furnishings are all beautiful, genuine antiques—ormolu mirrors, inlaid tables, porcelain lamps, and couches and chairs covered with fine fabrics. The ceilings are at least 14 feet high, with elegant moldings. A pink fireplace, gilt-framed portraits, a pencil poster with a dusky-rose eiderdown, a silver brush set on a mahogany desk, and even a bathroom with crystal light fixtures and a marble sink are just a few of the highlights of the Laurel Suite. All bathrooms contain shampoo, conditioner, lotions, bath salts, and Crabtree & Evelyn soaps.

Note that there are only 20 accommodations, and so you may well be unable to secure a room without reserving at least 1 year ahead. Please don't harass the staff—this is simply a fact which is beyond their control.

In the paneled dining room, hung with rich tapestries, guests sit at a long Tudor refectory table bearing a lace tablecloth and impressive table settings of crystal and fine china. Here, a $70 per person, three-course dinner is served. Among the seven or eight entrees, you might find pan-seared halibut with little neck clams served with chervil and brown butter vinaigrette; sautéed lobster with chanterelles, haricots vert and lemon verbena; or roast rack of lamb with zucchini, eggplant, pistou, and red wine. For breakfast, the conservatory makes a beautifully bright setting. Other facilities include the aforementioned swimming pool and four tennis courts.

Rates: Late June to Labor Day and late September to late October, main suites $525 to $700, rooms $325 to $500; carriage house rooms $300, suites $375; cottages from $430. Rates are slightly less at other times. A 2-day minimum stay is required on weekends and in July, August, and October.

Canyon Ranch, 165 Kemble St., Lenox, MA (☎ 413/637-4100) is of course the outpost of the famous Tucson establishment of the same name. It's the place to go to restore your health and well being, to learn ways to relieve stress, change old unhealthy habits, and lead a more healthful life. The setting will certainly help to restore some lost vitality, for it occupies the marble-and-brick mansion, Bellefontaine, which is surrounded by 120 acres of woodland. It consists of the Mansion, the Spa, and the 120-room inn, all connected by covered glass walkways. The Mansion houses the elegant dining room, the medical and behavioral consultation areas, and the beautiful library with its ornately carved marble fireplace, Palladian windows, carved ceiling, and floor-to-ceiling bookcases. The spa offers every conceivable form of exercise and body therapy—exercise rooms, indoor and outdoor tennis, racquetball and squash, indoor and outdoor pools, and a suspended indoor running track. There are, in fact, 30 fitness classes each day. Treatments include mud and salt, herbal and aroma wraps, as well as a variety of massages, facials, and other salon services. On hand is a professional staff to assist you in developing a healthful diet and regimen with techniques ranging from biofeedback to hypnotherapy. In the dining room, the menu lists nutritional information. Besides eating healthfully here, guests can learn how to continue the habit outside. Rates: $440 per person per night. In summer, 3-night weekend packages, including a series of health-services packages, start at $1,470.

Overlooking a lake, **Wheatleigh,** West Hawthorne Road (P.O. Box 824), Lenox, MA 01240 (☎ 413/637-0610), the magnificent former home of the Countess de Heredia, has 22 acres of lawn and gardens. Modeled after a 16th-century Italian palazzo, it was built on the site of the Gideon Smith tavern; he was a Tory who was hanged for his folly. The gravel driveway ends in a circular courtyard with a central marble fountain standing in front of the wrought-iron and glass canopy. Inside, the most striking features of the great entry hall are the huge white marble fireplace, sculpted with cupids and flowers, and the grand staircase, also of marble.

Upstairs are 11 very spacious rooms and 4 smaller accommodations, each possessing its own flavor and mood. They all have extremely high ceilings, marble fireplaces, and large, old-fashioned bathrooms. Some have canopied beds, while the furnishings are a combination of English and French antiques. The rooms in the rear have lovely views of the lake. All have air-conditioning, telephones, and TV/VCRs. The house also has a unique accommodation in the former aviary—a duplex that Leonard Bernstein always chose to stay in when he was conducting at Tanglewood.

The restaurant at Wheatleigh is also a gem with its swag drapes, Chippendale chairs, fine table settings, and unique Dalton wall plaques. The $68 fixed-price menu includes two main dishes like sautéed halibut with fresh saltwater shrimp and loin of lamb with garlic flan and rosemary infused jus. This menu is supplemented by a low-fat, vegetarian menu and a menu degustation. Breakfast offers an interesting array of egg dishes, including poached eggs and mornay sauce served on an English muffin. Breakfast hours are from 8 to 10:30am daily; dinner daily from 6 to 9pm.

On the 22-acre grounds landscaped by Frederick Law Olmsted are a serene rock garden, a pool surrounded by fragrant pine and conifers, and a tennis court. In winter the grounds have cross-country skiing. Rates: $185 to $435.

The beautiful residence now known as the **Gateways Inn,** 71 Walker St., Lenox, MA 01240 (☎ 413/637-2532), was once Harley Proctor's mansion (of Proctor and Gamble). Wrought-iron gates mark the entrance to the drive that leads to the classical white-columned portico; a balustrade runs along the top of the front facade. Inside, a sweeping staircase leads to 12 large elegant accommodations (one suite), three with fireplaces, all furnished with large Victorian pieces, most often of mahogany. Some feature canopied beds; others sleigh beds. The bathroom in the Victorian room contains the oversize tub that was custom made for Mr. Proctor. All rooms have telephones, TVs, air-conditioning, and private baths, many featuring old-fashioned pedestal sinks.

The Gateways is known for excellent cuisine, served in elegant surroundings. On the seasonal menu you might find entrees such as a delicately flavored rack of lamb Provençale, penne alla arrabbiata (one of a dozen pastas), veal marsala, or a grilled pavé of salmon finished with an olive sauce. Prices range from $18 to $25. The restaurant is especially noted for its desserts: apfelstrudel, luscious Black Forest torte, and strawberries Gateways—fresh strawberries with kirschwasser, whipped cream, and Melba sauce, all blended together into one super taste treat. Dinner hours in summer are daily 5:30 to 9pm; closed Tuesday in winter. *Note:* If you stay at the Gateways, you can use the pool, bicycles, and tennis court at the Haus Andreas, nearby in Lee, under the same management.

Rates (including continental breakfast): June to October, Thursday to Sunday $215 to $250, Monday to Wednesday $130 to $170; November to May, $170 to $185, and $120 to $135, respectively.

Idyllically situated diagonally across from the west entrance to Tanglewood, the **Apple Tree Inn,** 334 West St. (P.O. Box 699), Lenox, MA 01240 (☎ 413/ 637-1477), does in fact stand on 22 acres in the midst of a fragrant apple orchard bordering the 750-acre Pleasant Valley bird sanctuary. The rooms in the 110-year-old house with its dormers and classical portico offer spectacular views over the Stockbridge Bowl and daisy-dappled fields to the hills beyond. There are 11 rooms and two suites in the main house. Room 4 has eyelet lace pillowcases on the bed, attractive Schumacher flower-and-bird wallpaper, ruffled curtains, and an inviting window seat. Room 2, or the Blue Room, affords a large pineapple bed with a step stool, two armchairs, a small ormolu mirror placed over a chest, and lace-curtained French doors that lead to a private terrace with a magnificent view. Room 3 is where Leontyne Price used to stay, a pretty country room of celery and pink hue, with a brass bed, marble-top side tables, and a fireplace. Rooms 5 and 6 have skylights, while the suite (no. 8) has books and records as well as a fireplace, a TV, and other amenities. Third-floor rooms come in odd, interesting shapes. Brass beds, quilts, wing chairs, and braided rugs continue the country theme. A newer guest lodge has 20 motel-style rooms, which are clean and tasteful, and some people prefer them because they're closer to the pool. All the accommodations are air-conditioned and have private baths.

The pool is spectacularly located and reached via a trellised walkway covered in roses and clematis. It has a flagstone apron, which is bordered by flower beds of roses, poppies, stocks, and more. From here there's a marvelous view over the valley to distant hills. There's also a clay tennis court for tennis enthusiasts, plus cross-country ski trails and miles of hiking.

For guests' comfort there's a parlor furnished with plush couches and armchairs, small chess and backgammon tables, and a piano where you might be lucky enough to find one of the featured Tanglewood artists "rehearsing."

There are two dining rooms. The Tavern, the former billiard room, with a large brick fireplace, oak beams and paneling, serves late-night snacks in summer and full meals in winter. It's ideal for dessert and coffee after a concert. The circular Gazebo is lighter in ambience, furnished in dusky rose with white bentwood chairs. The tented ceiling is strung with tiny lights. In summer you can dine to the symphonic melodies wafted here by the evening breezes from Tanglewood. There's also a deck for outdoor dining brightened by colored umbrellas and also by some of the 350 varieties of rose that the innkeeper cultivates. The food is continental/American—shrimp Dijon, duckling with cherry sauce, veal saltimbocca, and filet mignon with rosemary sauce. Several pasta dishes are also available. Desserts include profiteroles, pie of the day, and seasonal fruits. Brunch varies. Dinner prices range from $12 to $23. Dinner hours are Thursday to Sunday from 5:30 to 9pm (daily from 5 to 9:30pm during the Tanglewood season); Sunday brunch from 10:30am to 2pm year-round.

Rates: Summer (late June to Labor Day and from October 1 to 24) $140 to $310, the lower price for room with shared bath. Mid-April to late June and early September to October 1 and New Year's (shoulder season), $105 to $250;

winter $65 to $175. Reduced midweek rates are offered during shoulder and winter seasons.

The **Birchwood Inn,** 7 Hubbard St., Lenox, MA 01240 (☎ 413/637-2600), is a tastefully decorated and impeccably run accommodation. Set halfway up the hill, across from the Church on the Hill, it was originally built in 1776 by Israel Dewey. Later it became a veteran's home before being converted into a stunning inn. There are 12 very distinctively decorated guest rooms (all with telephones, 10 with private baths) with antique reproductions and beautiful wallpapers. Three rooms have four-poster canopied beds. Downstairs, the sunken living room is especially charming with its inviting window seats, gilt mirrors, and bookcases filled with interesting volumes; a smaller den makes a cozy stopping place for late-night conversation before retiring. Additional accommodations, consisting of one-bedroom efficiency apartments, are located in the carriage house. Rates (including continental breakfast): July and August $100 to $210; October $70 to $160; winter $70 to $150.

Across the street from the Birchwood Inn, **Whistler's Inn,** 5 Greenwood St., Lenox, MA 01240 (☎ 413/637-0975), is named after the second owner of the house, Whistler's nephew. There's a charming air about this French/ English Tudor mansion built in 1820 with its mansard roof and lattice windows, approached via a lovely lych-gate. On the ground floor, the music room has a grand piano and a marvelous library complete with comfortable wing chairs and a marble fireplace; the formal dining room has a large table and Chippendale chairs seating eight. Upstairs, there are 11 rooms, all with private baths (most with air-conditioning). Six rooms have dormer windows, sloping ceilings, and painted chests; there are two doubles with brass beds and three others with cannonball or pineapple bedsteads. The two master bedrooms, which have fireplaces and couches, are particularly welcoming. On sunny days, you can take a light breakfast of muffins and coffee or tea out on the back veranda overlooking the 7 acres of gardens. Rates: June 16 to October 31, $100 to $235 weekends, $90 to $190 midweek; otherwise, $90 to $170 and $80 to $150, respectively.

Garden Gables, 141 Main St. (P.O. Box 52), Lenox, MA 01240 (☎ 413/ 637-0193), is a delightful accommodation surrounded by 5 acres of beautiful gardens. The original house was built in 1780 but extensions were added in 1909. The Canadian owners are extremely relaxed and friendly. The 18 rooms all have air-conditioning and telephones; some have cable TV/VCRs. All are comfortably furnished in an unpretentious manner and have chintz or floral wallpapers. You might discover a maple bed or a maple dresser combined with a brass bed or, as in Room 15, a brick fireplace, a Shaker pencil four-poster, and wing chairs. Room 15 also has a large bathroom with whirlpool tub and a small porch. Room 9 is a favorite with its rose quilt and solid, carved four-poster. It too has a deck furnished with wicker and also a Jacuzzi bathtub and separate shower. There are two large and tastefully decorated sitting rooms for guest use. One features a copper-hooded fireplace, a Steinway grand, comfortable slip-covered chairs and couches, plenty of books, and some fine art on the walls. Fresh flowers are found throughout the house—a romantic touch. Fine crystal, candles, and Sheraton-style chairs set the scene in the dining room where a full breakfast is served buffet style—croissants, muffins, bagels, fruit, yogurt, cereal, and a hot dish like smoked salmon quiche. Facilities include a 72-foot-long outdoor pool. Rates: $140 to $235 summer weekends. Slightly less at other times.

Peggy and Richard Houdek, who migrated from California—where he was an arts administrator and music critic and she was managing editor of *Performing Arts* magazine—naturally sought a culturally rich area in which to relocate as innkeepers. They found an 1804 landmark building, **Walker House,** 64 Walker St., Lenox, MA 01240 (☎ 413/637-1271), only minutes from Tanglewood. Being music lovers, they have decorated all eight of the spacious rooms (all with private baths, five with working fireplaces), in honor of a particular composer. In the somber-colored ground-floor Beethoven Room, which has a fireplace, are portraits and a bust of the genius himself. Upstairs, there's a lighter, sunnier Chopin Room; a brilliant-blue Tchaikovsky Room; a summery green-and-white Verdi Room; rooms named after Handel, Puccini, and Mozart; and an intimate room honoring Debussy. Downstairs, there's a large parlor with a grand piano, a cozy hearth, plenty of reading material, and some astonishingly healthy plants. Equally beautiful plants share the long wide veranda with the comfortable wicker furniture. Breakfast conversation flows easily at the tables, and fast friendships are sometimes made. Cards and addresses may be exchanged over a morning repast of fresh juice or baked fruit, Peggy's home-baked muffins, cereal, hard-boiled eggs, and plenty of piping-hot, freshly ground coffee. And then, of course, the special delight of a stay here is the sound of glorious classical music that usually fills the house throughout the day. On cold winter nights, films, operas, and sports are shown on the 7-foot-screen TV. There are also 3 acres of wooded grounds for guests to explore. This inn has a nonsmoking policy. Rates: Late June to Labor Day $120 to $200 on weekends (Thursday to Sunday), $90 to $130 midweek (Monday to Wednesday); Labor Day to mid-September and November 1 to late June, weekends $90 to $130, midweek $80 to $100; mid-September to October 31, weekends $120 to $170, midweek $80 to $130.

Seven Hills Country Inn and Restaurant, 40 Plunkett St., Lenox, MA 01240 (☎ 413/637-0060), is a lavish, gracious resort. The public rooms are extravagantly furnished; the 27 acres include two tennis courts, a large pool, and very well-kept landscaped gardens. Some of the service personnel are selected from the major music schools—Juilliard, Mannes, Manhattan, and Peabody—and when they're not waiting tables they perform. The nightclub is most elegant with softly lit mauve-pink tented ceiling and low plush sofas and features a variety of Broadway and jazz artists such as Natalie Lamb and Ed Linderman on weekends. On Monday, Tuesday, and Wednesday, local artists perform.

The whole place is built on a grand scale. The so-called living room is more like a baronial hall, with floor-to-ceiling gilt mirrors, intricately carved and needlepointed Charles II chairs, and a central double fireplace of carved wood on one side and wedding cake stucco on the other, ornamented with cherubs and gryphons. Other features include another grand piano, handsome large carved sideboards, and dragon-decorated chairs. Window seats look out over the wide balustered flagstone terrace set with umbrella tables and marble benches. The balustrade supports a series of sculpted marble lions. Gravel paths lead between carved pillars and vine arbors down to the pool. The gardens are filled with peonies, shrubs, and trees.

Every Monday and Tuesday there are concerts in the Music Room, and although the management doesn't like to publicize particular names, many famous artists have performed here. Folk and square dancing are also enjoyed once a week during the summer, and the Emmy Award–winning "News in Revue" performs 6 nights a week.

The 52 rooms are located in either the main building or in motel-style units. A carved, paneled staircase decorated with two compelling landscapes leads to what, to me, are the nicest rooms. Room 1 has a fireplace, a large mahogany bed and chest, and a Williamsburg cane eagle chair, all set on a slate-blue carpet against similarly colored walls, ball fringe curtains, and eyelet-lace linens. Room 3 also has a fireplace and a small balcony. Room 7 possesses a high Victorian bird's eye maple bed and marble-top dresser coupled with bold floral-and-bird wallpaper. It, too, has a fireplace.

The 100-seat restaurant offers contemporary continental cuisine, for example, muscovy duck breast braised in balsamic vinegar and ruby red grapes, topped with porcini mushrooms, or breast of chicken stuffed with sun-dried tomatoes in a sauce of port wine and sage, topped with a grilled portobello. Main courses are priced from $19 to $27. The carved walnut Italian chairs, the oriental-style Van Luit wallpaper, and the bronze and porcelain chandelier make an elegant setting for the food.

For additional entertainment there's a library with TV and a small lounge with a grand piano and a wood fireplace. Seven Hills is definitely an experience. It's a chance to taste the opulent way of life that used to exist in the Berkshires but with a refreshing lack of excessive pretense. Rates (including breakfast): Summer and fall, $114 to $260; off-season $94 to $160. MAP is also offered.

Cliffwood Inn, 25 Cliffwood St., Lenox, MA 01240 (☎ 413/637-3330), occupies a large mansion set back from the road only 2 blocks from the center of town. An impressive semicircular drive leads to the oval portico supported by classical Ionic columns. The detailing of this building designed by Arthur Rotch—carved shell and urn moldings above the windows, some of which are oval—is quite fine and certainly worthy of being the summer home of Edward Livingston, the American ambassador to France, for whom it was built in 1889. An Italian alabaster statue of a woman on a marble column holding an illuminate globe lights the entry hall. To the right, there's a favorite little corner anchored by a fireplace with window seats.

The inn is filled with the antiques and antique reproductions collected by owners Joy and Scottie Farrelly, who are also dealers in Eldred Wheeler's fine-quality colonial reproductions. Floor-to-ceiling gilded mirrors and a handsome marble fireplace add to the grand atmosphere of the living room. French doors lead to a wide back veranda where baskets of begonias hang and rockers overlook the pool and gazebo. The oval dining room features a magnificent 400-year old sideboard and is lit by Venetian chandelier. Here or on the veranda, a continental breakfast of fresh fruit, muffins, and breads is served. There are seven guest rooms, all with baths and air conditioning, six with working fireplaces. Each is named after a Farrelly ancestor. The Jacob Gross Jr. Room has a four-poster canopied bed and easy chairs in front of the fireplace. Facilities include an indoor swimming pool and spa.

The owners also offer guests a computerized up-to-date calendar of cultural events, chairs and cushions for the lawn at Tanglewood, and easy access to the concert venue just down the street by a less heavily trafficked entrance. Foreign visitors will appreciate the owners' knowledge of French, Spanish, and Italian. Rates: July to August and foliage season, $133 to $223; $88 to $151 November to mid-May.

The **Village Inn,** 16 Church St. (P.O. Box 1810), Lenox, MA 01240 (☎ 800/253-0917 or 413/637-0020), is the one place where you can stop for a formal English Devonshire cream tea, consisting of homemade scones and preserves, plus desserts accompanied by a pot of fine tea of your choice. It is served in the dining room from 3 to 4:30pm. At this friendly, comfortable place, run by Clifford Rudisill and Ray Wilson, there are rooms to satisfy every pocketbook. The public areas are, perhaps the most lavishly appointed, furnished with family antiques. The reception desk, which doubles as a small bar, faces the small parlor where armchairs near the hearth are ideal for chatting over a glass of sherry. Across the hall there's a larger parlor with a grand piano and antique furnishings. There's also a separate TV room. Over the years, the innkeepers have furnished the 32 comfortable rooms, all with private bath, telephone, and air-conditioning, in an eclectic and unpretentious way. The standard and superior rooms are a little more "furnished," while the economy rooms contain homey, old-fashioned pieces. Some have canopied beds. The dining room has an excellent reputation for value. Menu selections might include pan-seared swordfish drizzled with a cucumber-yogurt sauce on a bed of couscous; black Angus sirloin with a wild mushroom sauce; or roast chicken with a pineapple mango salsa, priced from $12 to $19. There's also a downstairs tavern for after-concert snacks. Dinner hours in summer and fall are Tuesday to Sunday from 5:30 to 9pm; breakfast and tea served daily in summer, weekends only the rest of the year. Rates: Summer, $100 to $220; fall, $90 to $185; winter, $80 to $175; spring, $65 to $145. In winter and spring 30% discount midweek. Three-night minimum weekends in July, August, and holidays.

Brook Farm Inn, 15 Hawthorne St, Lenox, MA (☎ 413/637-3013), just down the hill from Lenox center, occupies a century-old house. What makes this place special is the keen pleasure the innkeepers Anne and Joe Miller take in literature and music. One wall of the living room is devoted to books, many of them poetry, and the strains of all kinds of music—Mozart, light opera, or Broadway musicals—waft through the house. A poem of the day starts each day, and Joe reads poetry during Saturday afternoon tea. There are 12 rooms, all with private baths, and six with fireplaces. Room 2 features a canopied bed, wing chairs, and the romance of a fireplace and small balcony. The coziest if not the grandest rooms are tucked under the eaves. One is decked out in deep purple and mauve lit by a skylight from above. Furnishings might include a brass bed, Hitchcock rocker, cottage dresser, and similar country pieces. Out back, guests can relax in the hammock or enjoy the pool. A full breakfast is served buffet style, and on Sunday mornings a quartet from the Tanglewood Institute provides music at breakfast. Rates: $100 to $210 double; less in midweek and spring and fall.

If you prefer modern accommodations with all the razzmatazz of TVs, phones, bars, and lounges, then there are plenty around, like the **Berkshire Quality Inn,** 390 Pittsfield/Lenox Rd. (Route 7), Lenox, MA 01240 (☎ 413/637-4244), which has an outdoor pool and tennis courts; or the **Susse Cha-**

let, routes 7 and 20, Lenox, MA 01240 (☎ 413/637-3560), which also has a pool. Rates are around $65 to $169 double, depending on the season.

LENOX DINING

Besides the outstanding restaurants at the establishments already mentioned, there are several other fine dining options.

Lenox 218, 218 Main St. (Route 7A; ☎ 413/637-4218), is spanking modern. The up-front bar is boldly decorated with black-and-white tile with a purple scaffoldlike sculpture above the bar itself. The two dining rooms are dramatically designed in black, featuring Milan-style chairs, walls accented with Japanese prints, and tables set with gray tablecloths and black napkins. The cuisine ranges from nutty chicken, which is prepared with almonds, sesame seeds, and sunflower seeds, to roast duck with raspberry chambord sauce and scrod florentine served on a bed of spinach and flavored subtly with pesto. There are also half a dozen simple pasta dishes. Prices range from $13 to $22. For an appetizer I recommend the roasted garlic soup or the polenta with tomato and basil sauce. The menu is supplemented by daily specials. The shrimp cocktail is extra tangy with its horseradish and chili sauce accompaniment. Desserts tend to be popular favorites—pies and shortcakes and hot fudge sundaes. Light snacks are available in the bar. Open daily from 11:30am to 2:30pm, and 5 to 10pm.

The **Pillars Carriage House,** Route 20, New Lebanon (☎ 518/794-8007), has two dining rooms. One is modestly decorated with tables set with forest green tablecloths and captain's chairs; the other is slightly more formal. There's also a bar area warmed in winter by a fire. The cuisine is modern American with a menu that offers traditional favorites such as rack of lamb, filet mignon with a mushroom sauce, veal Oscar, and filet of sole Nantua, which is baked with lobster, butter and cream and garnished with lobster meat and Hollandaise. Prices range from $15 to $24. Open Tuesday to Saturday 5 to 10pm, Sunday 4 to 9pm. Closed from Dec 31 through mid-February.

Antonio's Restaurant, 15 Franklin St. (☎ 413/637-9894), is a comfortable, casual California-style place that sports a miscellaneous collection of postcards, bank notes, business cards, and buttons covering one entire wall in the front. Here you can tuck into oversize portions of Italian specialties— *paglia e fieno* (with peas and proscuitto), linguine with clam sauce, veal marsala, shrimp primavera, or chicken bianco sautéed in white wine with garlic, pimentos, scallions, and capers in a brown sauce. Prices range from $12 to $18. Open Monday to Saturday from 4 to 10pm; off-season closes a little earlier.

The **Church Street Cafe,** 69 Church St. (☎ 413/637-2745), is a local favorite for soups, salads, burgers, and pasta dishes, all priced under $10 and served in a pleasant light-wood-and-plants atmosphere. For dinner there's always a fresh fish and pasta of the day, plus six or so entrees like pan-roasted chicken breast with pancetta, wild mushrooms, and a potato chestnut cake; crab cakes with a dilled tartar sauce; or rustic beef stew with wild mushrooms, caramelized carrots, shallots, and mashed potatoes. Prices range from $15 to $19. Open summer, daily from 11:30am to 2pm and 5:30 to 9pm; spring and fall Monday to Saturday from 11:30am to 2pm, Monday to Thursday from 5:30 to 8:30pm, Friday and Saturday 5:30 to 9pm. Closed Sunday and Monday in winter.

Just across the street, the **Cafe Lucia,** 90 Church St. (☎ 413/637-2640), is a fine lunch choice, serving soups, sandwiches, and salads; including caponata—an eggplant-and-tomato salad garnished with hard-boiled eggs, black olives, tomato, basil, and mozzarella. Egg dishes like zucchini frittata (made from eggs, cheese with mushrooms, and zucchini), pâte plate, and chilled mussels in white wine complete the selections. Pasta and good Italian dishes like osso buco, wild rabbit ragout, veal, and fish of the day are served at dinner, priced from $13 to $29. There's a pleasant outdoor patio under an awning. Open summer and fall, Tuesday to Sunday from 5:30 to 10pm; winter and spring, Tuesday to Saturday from 5:30 to 9:30pm. Closed Sunday and Monday.

Cheesecake Charlie's, 60 Main St. (☎ 413/637-3411), serves breakfast from 8 to 11am, but the prime attraction are the 13 flavors of cheesecake plus daily specials. If you order in advance you can choose from 50-plus flavors.

PICNIC SUPPLIES

Obviously, you'd expect to find many picnic suppliers in Lenox for all those bountiful Tanglewood spreads. Here are some of them.

Crosby's, 62 Church St. (☎ 413/637-3396), offers gourmet food to go. There are two different picnics a week to choose from and also a full range of deli and salad items. In summer it's open Sunday to Wednesday from 10am to 6pm, Thursday to Saturday to 8pm; winter, Sunday from 11am to 3pm, Thursday to Saturday 11am to 5pm; closed for several weeks in February and March.

Special desserts can be found at **Suchele Bakers,** 27 Housatonic St. (☎ 413/637-0939), open daily in July and August from 7am to 6pm and Sunday until 12:30pm, the rest of the year Tuesday to Saturday from 7am to 4pm.

LEE

Although Lee has lived largely in the shadow of Lenox as a down-to-earth town, somewhat careless of its beauty, recently it has shown much greater interest in preserving its past, as you'll see from the descriptions of accommodations below. Still, the main attraction here is the superb Jacob's Pillow Dance Festival just east of Lee in Becket.

LEE & SOUTH LEE LODGING & DINING

Devonfield, 85 Stockbridge Rd. (R.R. 1, Box 605B), Lee, MA 01238 (☎ 413/243-3298), is a 200-year-old mansion with a lovely pastoral view. Originally built by a Revolutionary War soldier, it was modernized by George Westinghouse Jr. and was briefly, in 1942, the residence of Queen Wilhelmina of the Netherlands, her daughter, Princess Juliana, and her granddaughters, Beatrix (now the queen) and Irene. The public areas include a large comfortable living room, a good reading area with a fireplace, and a TV room. Although all of the 10 rooms (4 with fireplace, 5 with TV) are furnished differently, you might find an intricately carved mahogany bed or a marble-top chest in yours. The penthouse suite features a Jacuzzi and so does the guesthouse/cottage, which also has a fireplace and kitchenette among its attractions. It's a lovely, quiet place, and it has a pool, bicycles for guest use, and a tennis court. Rates (including full breakfast): Summer/fall, midweek $120 to $200, weekends $165 to $270; winter/spring, midweek $80 to $165, weekends $110 to $200 (lower prices are for rooms with shared baths). In July and August, a minimum stay of 3 nights is required.

The **Federal House Inn,** Main Street (Route 102), South Lee, MA 01260 (☎ 413/243-1824), offers lavish settings and furnishings in the public areas of this classically proportioned, restored Federal house. The dining rooms have been a smash hit on the Tanglewood dining scene for years. Two elegant rooms, each with only about seven tables, are the setting for some classic continental cuisine—filet of salmon baked in a potato crust with herbed beurre blanc; roast tenderloin of pork with a balsamic glaze on caramelized onions and pureed potatoes; and roast duckling with fresh pear chutney sautéed with wild rice pancakes and preserved currant- and English-mustard sauce. Start with the delicious house smoked trout with warm cornmeal blinis, freshly grated horseradish sauce, red onions, chive oil, and leeks; or the galantine of goose breast, dried apricots, and figs with lingonberry sauce. Prices run from $17 to $24. In summer a special $38 four-course prix fixe is served. Open July to August, daily from 5:30 to closing; winter, Thursday to Sunday from 5:30 to closing.

Upstairs there are 10 rooms, all with private baths and air-conditioning. They are furnished in country style with chintz wallpapers and rugs on wide-plank floors. A couple have canopied beds. Rates: $195 in season $175 off-season.

If you stay at the **Historic Merrell Inn,** Main Street (Route 102), South Lee, MA 01260 (☎ 800/243-1794 or 413/243-1794), just down the street, you'll be overnighting in a truly historic hostelry. Among its authentic features is the original 1817 circular birdcage bar (no longer in use). Now listed in the National Register of Historic Places, this brick Federal building (1794) with double balcony was bought in 1980 by Faith and Charles Reynolds, two ex-teachers who have carefully restored it according to architectural and historical records. It looks as much like a stagecoach stop as it ever did, from the small entry hall featuring a tall case clock, Federal mirror, and candlesticks to the old tavern room with fireplace, pewter, and appropriate period furniture. The original iron latches have been retained throughout the house. Upstairs the nine rooms, all with private baths, air-conditioning, and telephones, have been exquisitely decorated with colonial-period furnishings, most with canopied beds. Guests have use of a TV room, but best of all is the gazebo down by the river for relaxing on a summer afternoon. Swimming is available at Benedict Pond in Beartown Mountain State Park, only a 10-minute drive away. Rates (including full breakfast): mid-June to October 31, weekends $145 to $175 double, midweek $100 to $125; November 1 to mid-June, $85 to $125, and $80 to $115, respectively.

Chambery Inn, 199 Main St., Lee, MA 01238 (☎ 800/537-4321), is an unusual accommodation. It occupies a former school, and the people who converted it had the wit to retain the blackboards, which provide a wonderful outlet for a variety of commentary. As you can imagine, the six rooms are extra large (about 500 square feet) and have very high ceilings. Each is a suite, possessing a sitting area with a fireplace and a king canopied or queen bed. Every room has a TV, telephone, and whirlpool bath. Furnishings are comfortable. Floors are covered with thick pile carpets; windows are draped with lace curtains, and you might find an elegant peer mirror in your room. Chippendale-style tables, desks, and sofas complete the picture. The largest room, Le Lycee, has five huge windows looking out onto the street. The bed is covered in a Ralph Lauren Indian design coverlet, and there's a glass table with a capital as its base. Le Aubusson is decorated with tapestries, as you would expect, and also contains a handsome rolltop desk. There's also a well-equipped room for guests with disabilities. Rates: Summer and fall, weekends $135 to $260, midweek $109 to $145; mid-June to July 1 and September, weekends $135 to $230, midweek $85 to $160; mid-October to mid-June, weekends $135 to $230, midweek $85 to $160.

The **Morgan House Inn,** 33 Main St., Lee, MA 01238 (☎ 888/243-0188 or 413/243-0181), is not a well-seasoned rural New England inn for the well-heeled traveler. Instead, it's a historic coaching inn standing on the main street of Lee. Built in 1817 as a private residence, it was converted into a stagecoach inn in 1853 and received such renowned visitors as Ulysses Grant and George Bernard Shaw, whose carefully preserved signatures can be seen on the wall by the reception desk. The 11 rooms are furnished in a country style. In the tavern bar, you'll find locals as well as travelers. The low-ceilinged tavern dining room is unpretentious, warm, and comfortable with its polished wood tables and paneling. It offers contemporary American cuisine featuring such dishes as pistachio-crusted swordfish with candied ginger and lime beurre blanc or hazelnut-crusted rack of lamb with tomato mint chutney. For an appetizer, try the lobster, scallop, and sweet potato cakes with roasted red pepper sauce. Prices range from $13 to $24. It's also a convenient popular lunch spot where prices and quality are hard to beat for such dishes as chicken and mushrooms in a popover or pasta primavera, plus salads and sandwiches priced from $5 to $10. The paintings that grace the walls are works of owner Lenora Bowen. Open Monday to Saturday 11:30am to 2:30pm, Monday to Thursday 5 to 9pm, Friday and Saturday 5 to 9:30pm, Sunday noon to 9pm (brunch 10:30am to 2:30pm). Rates: June to October, $90 to $115 midweek, $100 to $170 weekends; November to May, midweek $65 to $90, weekends $75 to $110.

Sullivan Station, Railway Station Lane (☎ 413/243-2082), housed in a converted railway station, is a good Saturday luncheon spot and also convenient at the beginning or end of the scenic ride that leaves from here. The menu features a daily pasta, fish, and quiche special plus sandwiches, burgers, and barbecue ribs priced from $5 to $7. At dinner the menu features such traditional favorites as baked scrod with lemon butter, veal parmigiana, and chicken almondine (from $13 to $17). Open daily from noon to 4pm and 5 to 9pm. Open Wednesday to Sunday only from late October to May 1.

STOCKBRIDGE

The name most often associated with Stockbridge is that of Norman Rockwell. His pictures and magazine covers captured the essence of life in an earlier, more innocent America. Born in New York City in 1894, Rockwell moved to Stockbridge in 1953, and he remained here until he died in 1978. He is buried in Stockbridge cemetery. In his life he produced more than 4,000 pictures, many of them covers for the *Saturday Evening Post* and *McCall's*, and here at the Norman Rockwell Museum, Route 183 (☎ 413/298-4100), you can see a good many of them. You may well see his first *Saturday Evening Post* cover (it appeared in 1916) of the schoolboy pushing a baby carriage, or one of my favorites, a family seen heading off for a day trip or vacation, children hanging out the window in their excitement, grandma sitting under her hat like a solemn stooge, and the same family returning, children downcast and grandma still stolid, stern, and unmoved. Open May to October, daily from 10am to 5pm; November to April, weekdays from 11am to 4pm, weekends 10am to 5pm. Rockwell's studio is open also from May to October. Closed major winter holidays. Admission is $9 for adults, $2 for children 6 to 18.

Along Main Street, stop in at the **Mission House** (☎ 413/298-3239) built in 1739 and home of the Reverend John Sergeant, first missionary to the Stockbridge Indians. The house has a fine collection of furnishings, and the garden is also interesting, displaying plants only from that period. Open Memorial Day to Columbus Day, daily from 10am to 5pm (last tour 4:15pm), Sunday and holidays, from 11am to 3:30pm only. Admission is $5 for adults, $2.50 for children 6 to 12.

Across the street from the Red Lion, **St. Paul's Episcopal Church** has some famous associations—McKim was the architect, the baptistery was created by Auguste St. Gaudens, one of the nave windows is by Tiffany, and the chancel window is by LaFarge.

Farther along Main Street you'll come to the **Children's Chimes**, erected on the site of the original mission church by David Dudley Field, as a memorial to his grandchildren. The chimes are played every evening at sunset from "apple blossom time until frost."

The modest cottage where Hawthorne wrote *Tanglewood Tales* can be seen on Hawthorne Street near Tanglewood. Of the view (still unchanged) across the Stockbridge Bowl, he wrote: "I cannot write in the presence of that view."

The marvelous house on Prospect Hill, **Naumkeag** (☎ 413/298-3239), was designed by Stanford White in 1886 for Joseph H. Choate, President McKinley's ambassador to the Court of St. James. The 26 sumptuous rooms and the formal gardens with fountains and Chinese pagodas give a good insight into the opulent lifestyle of the time. Open Memorial Day to Columbus Day, daily from 10am to 5pm (last tour 4:15pm). Admission is $7 for both the house and the garden, $5 for the garden only, and $2.50 for children 6 to 12.

A must in Stockbridge is a visit to the **Berkshire Botanical Garden**, routes 102 and 183 (☎ 413/298-3926), a glorious place in any season. From spring to early fall, the spectacular 15 acres display an array of annuals and perennials—delphiniums, clematis, azaleas—plus such flowering shrubs and trees as rhododendron and dogwood, roses of all hues, ornamental and other herbs. Specialty collections include crabapples, primroses, and day lilies; there's also a shady pond garden and woodland trail. The greenhouses with permanent collections are open through the winter. The gift shop offers interesting garden-related items. Open May to October, from 10am to 5pm. Admission is $5 for adults, $4 for seniors, free for children under 12.

Daniel Chester French referred to his summer home, **Chesterwood,** off Route 183 (☎ 413/298-3579), as "heaven," and certainly the view of Monument Mountain, both from the house and from his radiant 23-foot-high studio, does warrant such a description. The skylit studio, where he worked from 1898 to 1931, is most remarkable for the floor-to-ceiling double doors through which he rolled his sculptures on a small railroad trestle out into the daylight to examine them. One can also imagine his taking a break to entertain guests in the adjoining reception area furnished with fireplace, library, and piano. The studio contains sketches, plaster casts, and bronze models of his sculpture, including his seated Lincoln. From the house and studio, you can wander through the gardens. In the barn there are sketches and working models of many of his other famous works—*Brooklyn* and *Manhattan*, formerly at the entrance to the Manhattan Bridge, *Alma Mater* at Columbia University, and the *Minuteman* at the Concord North Bridge. Chesterwood is about 2 miles west of Stockbridge. Take Route 102 west to Route 183; turn left and drive for about a mile and follow the signs. Open May 1 to October 31, daily from 10am to 5pm. Admission is $7 for adults, $3.50 for children 13 to 18, $1.50 for children 6 to 12.

Stockbridge is the home of the respected **Berkshire Theatre Festival,** which takes place from June to August. For details, see "Festivals in the Berkshires" later in the chapter.

STOCKBRIDGE LODGING & DINING

The large country inn, the **Red Lion,** Main Street, Stockbridge, MA 01262 (☎ 413/298-5545), whose porch faces the main street, has become a symbol of hospitality in Stockbridge and the Berkshires. Many vacationers come expressly to visit the Red Lion, flocking into the front parlor where the fires blaze, and overflowing into the snug tavern or downstairs into the Lion's Den pub for a cocktail and nightly entertainment. The original structure, which served as a small tavern on the Albany-Hartford-Boston stage route in 1773, was destroyed by fire in 1896. A string of celebrities has bedded down here, among them Presidents William McKinley, Teddy Roosevelt, Calvin Coolidge, and Franklin Roosevelt; William Cullen Bryant; and Henry Wadsworth Longfellow.

At the Red Lion, you'll be living amid the charm of Staffordshire china, colonial pewter, and 18th-century furniture. There are 111 air-conditioned guest rooms including 26 suites. Most are in the main inn but some are located in seven smaller guesthouses nearby. Each room is individually decorated in a country style. In summer, the courtyard, colorfully decorated with impatiens and other flowers, makes a lovely dining spot. A swimming pool, fitness room (massage therapist available) completes the facilities.

The dining room specializes in seasonal New England favorites—herb-and-mustard–crusted prime rib served with a Stilton popover; roast turkey with a sage cornbread dressing; or New England bluepoint oyster stew—ranging from $18 to $24. Two remarkable features of the Red Lion are the friendly personnel and the quality of the food, which are sustained even when 1,200 people are served per day (200 at breakfast, 500 at lunch, and 500 at night). At a recent meal, the caramelized sea scallops were perfectly tender and well complemented by the accompanying bacon and thyme–flavored kraut.

Crystal chandeliers, large ornate gilt mirrors, willow-pattern china, damask tablecloths, and a posy of fresh flowers on each table set an elegant tone.

Dining hours: Breakfast: Monday to Friday 7 to 10am, Saturday and Sunday 8 to 10am. Lunch: Monday to Saturday noon to 2:30pm. Dinner: Monday to Thursday 6 to 9pm, Friday and Saturday 6 to 9:30pm, Sunday noon to 9pm. Jacket and tie for men required at dinner; no jeans permitted. Rates: Mid-April to late October $125 to $175, $97 room with shared bath; $195 to $365 suites; late October to mid April $97 to $140, $82 with shared bath; and $177 to $335 suites.

A discreet wooden sign hangs out front of the **Inn at Stockbridge,** 30 East St. (Route 7, Box 618), Stockbridge, MA 01262 (☎ 413/298-3337). Step onto the classical portico and into the plushly furnished parlor-hall graced with a grand piano and comfortable wing chairs set around the hearth. Although the 12 rooms (all with private bath, air-conditioning, and telephone) are not as lavishly decorated with antiques, they are all very prettily furnished with antique reproductions. The Chinese Room has Asian accents in the wallpaper and accessories, while the Rose Room sports cabbage rose wallpaper and an antique English armoire. The Terrace Room has a private terrace and whirlpool tub under a skylight in the bathroom. A separate building contains four specially themed junior suites, each with fireplace, canopied bed, whirlpool tub, and TV/VCR. They are decorated to reflect Provence, Kashmir, St. Andrews, and "Out of Africa." Hosts Alice and Len Schiller also serve a full breakfast on fine china. Alice turns out some extraordinary fare—fresh fruit cup, cheese-and-ham soufflé, cinnamon coffee cake, and a very special brew. Sunday breakfasts are extra-special, consisting of a mimosa followed by eggs Benedict and banana bread. At the back of the house, the garden's lilacs and other flowering shrubs provide a welcome retreat. So does the pool. Rates: July to October 31, weekends $205 to $270, midweek $185 to $230; November to June, weekends $180 to $215, midweek $150 to $200.

Set on a quiet back road not far from Stockbridge, the **Williamsville Inn,** Route 41, West Stockbridge, MA 01266 (☎ 413/274-6118), has all the pleasures of an English country inn. It has the physical makings of a delightful accommodation, a small and cozy 1797 farmhouse with wide-plank floors, fireplaces throughout the public areas, comfortable wing chairs, and antiques. There are 16 rooms, 2 with fireplaces, some with four-posters, country furniture, and private bathrooms. There's also a pool and tennis court.

The four dining rooms offer modern American cuisine. Try such dishes as salmon basil roulade with pesto sauce served with corn pudding; tenderloin of beef with red wine sauce and portobello mushrooms; or roasted breast of duck with peaches and balsamic glaze. Prices range from $15 to $23. For dessert, try the chocolate truffle cake or hazelnut *daquoise* or the varied pies and tarts. The inn has become popular for its Sunday-night storytelling and dinner series, which is given during the winter season. Dinner hours July to October, Wednesday to Monday from 5 to 9pm; November to June, Thursday to Sunday from 6 to 9pm. Rates: July to October, $130 to $195; November to June, $115 to $170. A 3-night minimum is required on summer weekends.

Roeder House, Route 183, Stockbridge, MA (☎ 413/298-4015), is a lovely accommodation occupying a Federal-colonial–style house that was built in 1856 and is surrounded by 4 acres of well-tended gardens. Owners Diane and

Vernon Reuss have hung numerous Audubon prints throughout the house. There are six rooms all with private baths and all furnished with antiques in fine taste and fetching colors. The Red Bird Room sports Lambeth wallpaper with a peafowl design, a luxurious silk fabric on the wing-back chairs, while the bed is covered with a handmade log cabin quilt. Ben's Room contains a four poster with a crocheted canopy. A room on the ground floor boasts a hoop canopy with Laura Ashley linens, a Chinese rug, and wing backs with iron floor lamps well placed for comfortable reading. A bell will summon you to a breakfast table set with crystal and fine English china and lit by candlelight. The fare might include blueberry coffeecake, fruit compote, a frittata, peach juice, and hazelnut coffee. Guests can use the well designed and landscaped pool and enjoy the screened in porch and the trellised gardens. Rates: Summer weekends, $205 to $215 double; spring and fall, $185 to $205; less in winter.

Other Stockbridge choices include **Main Street Market Cafe,** on Main Street (☎ 413/298-0220), which serves great breakfasts, a wide variety of luncheon items—soups, salads, sandwiches, grilled vegetables, hummus, and pretty much whatever you want to select in the market. You can eat in the comfortable, cheery cafe or assemble a picnic. Dinner is served on Thursday and Friday nights by reservation only. Open daily from 7:30am to 7pm (later on Thursday and Friday).

WEST STOCKBRIDGE

West Stockbridge has been touted as the in-the-know place in the Berkshires because of the many potters, painters, glassmakers, and other artisans who have been attracted to this area. If you want to learn about the work of some of the area's more important artisans and where it can be found, pick up the pamphlet, "The Art of West Stockbridge," available in display racks throughout the area.

The **Berkshire Center for Contemporary Glass,** 6 Harris St. (☎ 413/232-4666), is a new enterprise in a new building that contains both a showroom and a large work area. Classes and workshops are scheduled. It's located in the heart of the village; open May to October daily from 10am to 10pm; November to April from 10am to 6pm.

The town has a number of artificially old shops and boutiques, but there's really little else here except for a couple of good restaurants.

WEST STOCKBRIDGE DINING

The story of Luy Nguyen and wife, Trai Thi Duong, is very moving. After they escaped from Vietnam and came to this country, they first went to Hartford and then were invited to West Stockbridge to open the **Truc Orient Express,** Harris Street (☎ 413/232-4204). Their photograph album, which is proudly displayed, tells the story of their family—and how Senator Ted Kennedy helped to reunite them with their son after a 6-year separation.

Try the crab-and-asparagus soup first, then choose among such main dishes as shrimp with straw mushroom, sweet-and-sour chicken, or a delicious duck with lemongrass, all priced from $12 to $17 at dinner. The atmosphere is extremely pleasant, with bamboo chairs and wicker-based, glass-top Parsons tables set on tile floors in a light and airy space. Open daily from 11:30am to 3pm; Sunday to Thursday from 5 to 9pm, Friday and Saturday 5 to 10pm; closed Tuesday in winter.

La Bruschetta, 1 Harris St. (☎ 413/232-7141), offers a fresh approach to the ingredients in its up-to-the minute Italian cuisine. It's hard to choose among the appetizers, most of which lean to vegetarian tastes. The grilled radicchio is enhanced with smoked pancetta with Rawson Brook chèvre, sun-dried tomatoes, oil, and balsamic vinegar, while the delicious timbale of wild mushrooms is served with a fresh tomato herb coulis. These can be followed by one of several pastas—orecchiette with grilled shrimp, oven-roasted tomatoes, beet greens, garlic, and basil, for example—or one of the *secondi piatti* like the double center-cut pork chop served with apple leek compote and a cider pepper glaze or the poached salmon with fresh fennel, grilled potatoes, Prince Edward Island mussels, and fall greens. Prices range from $16 to $20. Open Thursday to Tuesday from 6 to 9pm.

WEST STOCKBRIDGE AFTER DARK

Shaker Mill Tavern, on Albany Road (routes 102 and 41), in West Stockbridge (☎ 413/232-4369), attracts a young crowd. A deck cafe is open in summer, and jazz, Latin, and comedy entertainment are offered Thursday through Sunday nights. There's a huge roster of international beers for sale. Open daily from Memorial Day to Columbus Day; closed Wednesday at other times.

THE EGREMONT AREA

South Egremont is a lovely, quiet village worth stopping in to browse through the several antique stores, bookshops, and the old-fashioned general store. Located on Route 23, it is surrounded by some dramatic scenery and provides access to Mount Everett and BashBish Falls. Other great antique hunting grounds are also nearby in Ashley Falls and Sheffield, along routes 7 and 7A. If you continue west along Route 23, you'll come to Catamount, crossing the border into New York, where there are a couple of renowned restaurants.

SOUTH EGREMONT LODGING

The **Egremont Inn,** Old Sheffield Road (P.O. Box 418), South Egremont, MA 01258 (☎ 413/528-2111), is a charming old place, originally built in 1780, with a wrap-around veranda. Inside, the tavern is especially alluring with its curved brick fireplace, low ceilings, and colonial-style furnishings. The dining room offers new American cuisine. Prices range from $15.50 for a boneless chicken breast stuffed with prosciutto, spinach, and fontina to herb-crusted rack of lamb with braised brussels sprouts. Other appealing dishes might include seared salmon filet with lemongrass beurre blanc, or breast of duck with a cabernet reduction. The tavern menu offers burgers, pasta, and salads. Dinner hours are Wednesday to Sunday from 5:30 to 9:30pm. Facilities include a pool and two tennis courts. None of the 21 rooms has a telephone or TV, but all have a private bath. Live jazz or similar in the tavern on Saturdays. Rates: Spring/summer/fall, weekends $110 to $175, midweek $100 to $130;

winter, weekends $105 to $145, midweek $90 to $120. Special packages available.

At the **Weathervane Inn,** Route 23 (P.O. Box 388), South Egremont, MA 01258 (☎ 413/528-9580), seasonal potted flowers bloom on the side porch of this attractive white clapboard house with black shutters, into which you'll be welcomed by the Murphy family. There are 10 rooms, all with private baths. Room 6 is tucked over the kitchen under the eaves, which gives it an interesting shape and feel. It's large enough to accommodate two brass beds, a marble-top dresser adorned with dried-flower arrangement, a maple side table, a desk, and an armchair. All rooms have electric blankets and air-conditioning, and at night you'll find a miniature nightcap—amaretto perhaps. Breakfast is served in a skylit room, decorated with Hitchcock chairs and tables, that overlooks the back lawn. You'll most likely tuck into Irish soda bread, freshly squeezed juice, and eggs of your choice with home fries, sausage or bacon, and toast. Afternoon tea is also served. Adjacent to the dining room is a sitting area with a small service bar in the corner. There's also a lounge with TV, books, and games. The outdoor pool has a good deck for sunning. Rates: Late June to early September, weekends (3 nights only) $475 for two; midweek $105 to $160 double per night; early September to mid-June, weekends $135 to $160; midweek $125 to $145.

A large white clapboard house, where you can sit on the porch and look over toward the lush greens of the Egremont Country Club, the **Windflower Inn,** Route 23 (Egremont Star Route, Box 25), Great Barrington, MA 01230 (☎ 413/528-2720), offers warm hospitality in antique-style surroundings. There are 13 rooms, all with private baths, some with fireplaces. Each is decorated in a Laura Ashley country style. There's an outdoor pool. Golf and tennis facilities are conveniently located across the road. Rates (including full breakfast): $110 to $180.

SOUTH EGREMONT DINING

For breakfast and an experience that probably recalls your childhood if you're over 25, head for the **Gaslight Store** (☎ 413/528-0870) in South Egremont. Here a few tables have been placed in the center of an old-fashioned general store that sells everything from aspirin to salami, newspapers to candy, complete with real wooden counters, scratched and burnished with use.

The **Old Mill,** Route 23, South Egremont (☎ 413/528-1421), is famed for its picturesque setting overlooking a small brook and has an excellent local reputation for consistently fine meals. The ambience is romantically country. The room is lit by a Shaker-style chandelier and little copper lanterns on the tables that make the white linens and wide-board floors glow. The menu offers a diverse range of bistro-style dishes. There will likely be pan-roasted cod wonderfully enriched with a roasted tomato vinaigrette, a New York steak with truffle butter and fries, and several daily specials. Prices range from $16 to $23. To start, I'd select either the caramelized onion tart with greens or garlicky pan-roasted shrimp. Among the desserts, my favorites are the profiteroles, but you might prefer crème brûlée, apple walnut tart, or peach Melba. Open June to October, Sunday to Thursday from 5 to 9:30pm, Friday to Saturday from 5 to 10:30pm. Closed Mondays from November to May.

Farther along Route 23 you'll come to **John Andrew's,** South Egremont (☎ 413/528-3469), which is a refreshing change from the traditional, cozy

New England-style restaurants that abound in the Berkshires. White tablecloths, the original black chairs from the Copacabana, and track lighting provide an art deco ambience. Among the appealing appetizers are the grilled shrimp with avocado; mango with lime, chilis, and cilantro; and the whole roasted garlic with peasant bread, goat cheese, sun-dried tomatoes, and black olives. The main courses are made with the freshest of ingredients, and free-range poultry is used. You might find grilled yellowfin tuna with lemongrass, ginger, cilantro, scented coconut milk, and baby bok choy; loin of elk with a cracked peppercorn sauce accompanied by Black Mission fig compote and hazelnut Indian pudding; or grilled leg of lamb with red wine and roast garlic jus. Prices range from $15 to $24. Desserts change daily. Cocktails or meals can be taken on the pleasant deck out back. Open July to August, daily from 5pm; closed Wednesday in winter.

NORTH EGREMONT LODGING & DINING

Some locals recommended the dining room at the **Elm Court Inn,** Route 71, North Egremont, MA 01252 (☎ 413/528-0325), more highly than any other in the immediate area. Floral curtains, a fireplace, and polished wood tables with place mats and a sprig of fresh flowers complete the decor. There's also a small cozy bar with a brick hearth. Dishes might include grilled swordfish with wasabi soy sauce, roasted duck with orange-ginger sauce, and a rack of lamb Provençale. The chef trained in Zurich, and certain dishes, such as the veal à la suisse, are accompanied by those delicious rosti potatoes. Prices range from $18 to $24. Open Wednesday to Saturday from 5 to 9pm, Sunday from 4 to 8:30pm.

The three simply furnished rooms (one with private bath) feature chenille bedspreads, chintz curtains, painted chests, and braided rugs. In my opinion, Room 4 is the nicest, with its corner cupboard, small captain's desk, blue-and-white braided rug, burgundy curtains, and sink with a marble surround. Rates: $65 to $75.

GREAT BARRINGTON & SHEFFIELD

Great Barrington is the largest town in the southern Berkshires, a major crossroads and commercial center. Just outside town, you can explore the **Albert Schweitzer Center,** 50 Hurlburt Rd. (☎ 413/528-3124), where you'll be greeted by this quotation: "The meaning of maturity which we should develop in ourselves is that we should strive always to become simpler, kinder, more honest, more truthful, more peace-loving, more gentle, and more compassionate." You can wander along Philosopher's Walk, by the brook, or in the universal children's garden. Lecture and concert series are given through the summer at this special haven. The grounds are open June to August, Tuesday to Saturday from 10am to 4pm, Sunday from noon to 4pm; September, November and March to May, Thursday to Saturday from 10am to 4pm; December to February by appointment only.

Inveterate shoppers and browsers will stop at **Jenifer House,** on Stockbridge Road, about a mile north of Route 23 on Route 7 (☎ 413/528-1500). This complex houses two antiques centers (with about 150 dealers), an art and print gallery, and a microbrewery. Open Monday to Saturday from 9am to 5:30pm, Sunday from 10 am to 5pm.

GREAT BARRINGTON LODGING

Little John Manor, 1 Newsboy Monument Lane, Great Barrington, MA 01230 (☎ 413/528-2882), is certainly one of Great Barrington's most secluded bed-and-breakfasts. I missed it several times. It's on Route 23 but tucked on a quiet loop, behind the statue of the Newspaper Boy, a gift presented to Great Barrington in 1895 by Colonel William L. Brown, publisher of the *New York Daily News.*

Owners Paul and Herb have four rooms sharing two baths. They've run resorts before, and their experience shows. The four rooms are immaculately kept and pleasingly decorated in harmonious colors. The twin, for example, has rose carpeting, Wedgwood-blue curtains, and a colorful floral bedspread. Fresh flowers stand on a chest. A small double features a bed with eyelet pillow cases and dust ruffle, a white eiderdown, an oak dresser, a bishop's chair, and Japanese prints. The living room is comfortably cluttered with a number of Toby jugs, among other things. Couches, rockers, and other chairs cluster around the white brick fireplace and the TV.

In the morning a full breakfast is served in the dining room, English style. Tea and coffee and juice are placed on the sideboard and piping-hot scrambled or fried eggs, ham, English sausages, mushrooms, broiled tomatoes, and potatoes in jackets emerge from the kitchen. English muffins or crumpets can be spread with homemade jams and marmalade. An afternoon tea of scones, Scottish oatcakes, banana bread, and fruit butters is either served in the lounge or taken out to the porch or the benches scattered through the garden.

A hutch in the dining room is filled with oils and vinegars, which Paul makes from the 55 to 60 varieties of herbs that he cultivates in the garden. You'll smell the aroma of everything from marjoram and horseradish to Egyptian onion. In summer the borders are also blooming with peonies, lilies, roses, and other flowers. Rates: Memorial Day through October, $90 to $110 double with fireplace; November to Memorial Day, $80 to $95.

At **Green Meadows,** 117 Division St., Great Barrington, MA 01230 (☎ 413/528-3897), owners Frank Gioia and Susie Kaufman have created a self-contained bed-and-breakfast wing by converting several rooms at the back of an 1880 Victorian farmhouse, which stands on 6 acres looking out over the fields. All four rooms have private baths and air-conditioning, and they are pretty and sparkling. The ground-floor room contains a brass bed with a navy-blue floral comforter, an oak dresser, and side table, all set against pink walls. Rooms upstairs are similar, with wide pine floors—the colors of rose and celery predominate in the decor. Breakfast is satisfying, likely to begin with berries or melon followed by an omelet or French toast with local maple syrup. Rates: $90 to $100.

Irv and Jamie Yost, owners of the **Turning Point Inn,** Route 23 at Lake Buel Rd. (R.R. 2, Box 140), Great Barrington, MA 01230 (☎ 413/528-4777), really bring the personal touch to their business by sending guests handwritten notes with their brochures. They have restored an old stagecoach stop right near Butternut (east of Great Barrington) and offer six rooms, two with shared bath. There are a couple of parlors to relax in, and the whole place has a distinct home-away-from-home feeling. There's also a two-bedroom housekeeping cottage available for $210 a night. The full breakfast consists of eggs (with dishes like pancakes), cereal, breads, fruit, and more. Rates: $95 to $115 double.

Seekonk Pines, 142 Seekonk Cross Rd. (Route 243), Great Barrington, MA 01230 (☎ 413/528-4192), a little farther west along Route 243, represents great value in this area. Innkeepers Bruce, Roberta, and Rita Lefkowitz bring their own personalities and ideas to this homey accommodation filled with their antiques and collectibles. The house was built between 1830 and 1832 as a farmhouse and remained in the same family for three generations. One of the previous owners was a friend of Thomas Edison, and Edison's portrait hangs in the entrance hall. There are six rooms, all with private baths and all named after previous owners. In the largest, the Harry G. Treadwell, the lace-canopied bed is covered by a colorful quilt; Chinese paintings adorn the walls; and a chest of drawers, side tables, a blanket chest, and two comfortable chairs complete the furnishings. Quilts are found in every room and stenciling appears in many.

The dining-room table supported a vase of purple Canterbury bells when I visited. A breakfast of fresh fruit, homemade muffins, and a hot entree is served, along with juice and coffee or tea. The garden is quite lovely—filled with foxgloves, lupines, sweet williams, and pansies. There's an outdoor pool, secluded by a private hedge and fence, and for indoor entertainment a TV/VCR, books, and games are available in the living room. Bikes also available. Rates: Memorial Day to October, $110 to $145; in winter, $90 to $125.

GREAT BARRINGTON DINING

Castle Street Cafe, 10 Castle St. (☎ 413/528-5244), occupies a large high-ceilinged storefront where the brick walls are accented with pieces of art portraying food ingredients in all their wondrous colors and shapes. There's a small bar in back and jazz is usually playing quietly in the background. The cuisine is carefully prepared and uses many locally grown and produced products. The flavor of the grilled breast of chicken is set off with a wild mushroom sauce; the cedar-planked salmon with maple glaze is wonderfully moist; and the rack of lamb has a fine garlic rosemary sauce. For the less hungry, there's a simple burger served with straw potatoes as well as a couple of pasta dishes. Among the desserts, the chocolate mousse cake rates high. Good, reasonably priced wine list. Open Sunday, Monday, Wednesday, and Thursday from 5 to 9pm, Friday and Saturday from 5 to 10pm.

Martin's, 49 Railroad St. (☎ 413/528-5455), offers good healthful cuisine. You'll find items such as veggie burgers; scrambled tofu (which really does substitute for eggs); apple pancakes; and omelets made with hot peppers, salsa, and cheese. The tables are plain wood, and the nice thing is that Martin's serves breakfast all day. Open daily from 6am to 3pm.

La Tomate, 293 Main St., Great Barrington (☎ 413/528-8020), will introduce you to Provençal cuisine, which is lighter than traditional French cuisine and uses olive oil rather than butter as the cooking medium. The limited menu emphasizes fish and shellfish. There might be a wonderful grilled salmon with wild mushroom risotto or a trio of salmon, sole, and scrod braised in a lemon beurre blanc. On the meat side, there might be roasted half chicken brushed with olive oil and garlic or veal scallopini with caramelized apples and calvados sauce. There are also several delicious pasta dishes, the most characteristic being the penne Provençal made with tomatoes, basil, black olives, garlic, capers, olive oil, and a dash of red-wine vinegar. To start, there's a classic caramelized onion tart; roasted goat cheese with mushrooms, thyme, and garlic; and mussels in white wine, tomatoes, and garlic. Prices range from $16 to $22. Finish with crème brûlée, chocolate mousse, or any one of the delicious tarts. Open Tuesday to Thursday and Sunday from 5 to 9pm, Friday to Saturday from 5 to 10:30pm.

20 Railroad Street, whose name is its address (☎ 413/528-9345), is a classic tavern-restaurant possessing a 28-foot-long Victorian carved mahogany bar and oak booths. The menu is broad, ranging from philly steaks and tuna melts and burgers to a hot turkey platter, pasta with seafood and sun-dried tomatoes, and grilled sirloin, priced from $7 to $14. The brunch menu provides good value and offers cooked-to-order choices among omelets, French toast, quiche, and other egg dishes plus selections from the regular menu. Open daily from 11:30am to 11pm.

Daily Bread Bakery, 278 Main St. (☎ 413/528-9610), has tempting breads, cookies, and pies made of seasonal fresh fruits. Delicious and fun, and they "contain no refined sugar unless marked." Open Monday from 8am to 1pm, Tuesday and Wednesday 8am to 3pm, Thursday to Saturday 8am to 4pm.

SHEFFIELD LODGING

From the minute you see **Ivanhoe Country House,** Under Mountain Road (Route 41), Sheffield, MA 01257 (☎ 413/229-2143), you are struck by how neat and trim the white clapboard house with black shutters is kept, and so, too, are the lawns and flowers. The oldest part of the house dates to 1780. Dick and Carole Maghery have nine rooms, all with private baths. There are two rooms on the first floor: One large room has a fireplace and a porch that accommodates a private Ping-Pong table along with wicker furnishings; the room itself contains a bed with a white eiderdown, an armoire, and a bathroom with claw-foot tub. Locally made rag rugs are found throughout. The Sunrise Room has a country painted bed and rust-and-blue chintz wallpaper. The Lakeview Room (which does indeed have a view) is decorated in dusky rose. The Willow Room has a sleigh bed, a Windsor rocker, and other appealing pieces. There's also a two-bedroom unit with a kitchenette and a porch that is very private—ideal for families or two couples. Both bedrooms have a fireplace and brass bed.

The living room is comfortably large and welcoming, with Victorian sofas, chestnut paneling, a brick fireplace, wing chairs, and plenty of books and magazines spread out on top of an early piano as well as a TV. French doors lead to a brick terrace with umbrella tables. Begonias and other flowers brighten the gardens. You'll probably meet the four golden retrievers (Dick and Carole used to raise them). The pool is beautifully located on the crest of a hill, where chaise lounges are lined up for sun worshippers. From the grounds there's a serene view of Berkshire Lake. Continental breakfast is served or will be delivered to your room. Rates: May through October, weekends $119 to $125, midweek $100 to $110; winter, $70 to $90. The two-bedroom unit for four with private bath costs $195 in summer, $145 in winter.

Staveleigh House, South Main Street, Sheffield, MA 01257 (☎ 413/ 229-2129), is a private home set back from Route 7 that is operated by two widows, Dorothy Marosy and Marion Whitman. Throughout the house feminine touches are evident. Many of the quilts on the beds or the walls, including the large one on the staircase wall, were crafted by Marion, while the rugs were hooked by Dorothy. Plants brighten the rooms, and the landing is inhabited by teddy bears. There are five rooms (three upstairs and two downstairs), two with private baths. The most charming one features a dresser (with mirror), rocker, and chaise lounge, all made of wicker, and plank wood floors; a quilt hangs over the bed rail. In the bathroom the floor has been decorated with sponge painting. Another favorite, on the ground floor, has a private entrance at the back. It's radiantly decorated in yellow and white and has maple furnishings.

In the living room, the name Staveleigh is carved above the grate, although neither owner knows the exact provenance. The center hall walls have been opened so that the living room flows into the dining room. Here, on a table spread with a lace tablecloth, a full breakfast is served—juice, fresh fruit, a hot dish like puffed oven pancakes, and homemade muffins and jams. Afternoon tea is also served. The room is personalized by a cobalt-blue glass collection and a display case containing a glass candlestick collection. Rates: $115 with private bath, $105 with shared bath.

When Ronald and Judith Timm had the task of furnishing **Centuryhurst**, Main Street (Route 7), Sheffield, MA 01257 (☎ 413/229-8131), they had the distinct advantage of owning and operating the antiques store located in the barn behind the main house. It's no surprise, then, that the four rooms sharing two baths are furnished with early 19th-century American pieces; many also feature clocks collected by Ron. You'll find tiger maple cannonball beds, grain-painted dressers and blanket chests, mirrors with reverse-painted glass, and many other decorative pieces. The house was built in 1800 and still has its original hardware, unique keystone archways, and an unusually large fireplace with beehive oven. There are two large sitting rooms, both with fireplaces, overlooking the 3 acres of landscaped grounds. Guests can also relax in the old New England rockers on the porch. Clock mavens will love the store, which specializes in Wedgwood and offers two floors of American country furniture. Rates: $66 to $88.

The **Stagecoach Hill Inn**, Route 41, Sheffield, MA 01257 (☎ 413/229-8585), exudes history. The rambling old brick building on 160 acres dates back to 1794. By 1802 there was a barn on the property, which is now the dark, beamed MacDougall's Tavern. The bar is decorated with car badges and other auto insignia—the place is frequented by many Lime Rock drivers and fans. It's made cozy by the double-brick hearth tiled on one side with Delft. Oil lamps hang from the beams. There's even a comfortable raised section with couches and TV. The brick building was constructed in 1820, and the smaller building in back was erected in the mid-1800s as a poorhouse. The place has since functioned variously as a summer house, guesthouse, and since 1946, as an inn. The previous owners were English and certain traces of their influence remain. A sign invites lords, ladies, and gentlemen to follow the pointer past the tavern into the dining rooms. Here a varied menu is offered at dinner—featuring, for example, rack of lamb with rosemary merlot demi glace; filet of salmon with roasted red pepper coulis; game hen with cabernet braised vegetables; and steak-and-mushroom pie. Prices range from $10 to $24. To start, try the portobello mushrooms with greens drizzled with balsamic vinaigrette or the corn and crabmeat wontons with green chili sauce. Pub fare is available in the tavern daily except Wednesday. Dinner hours are Sunday to Tuesday and Thursday from 5:30 to 9:30pm, Friday and Saturday 5:30 to 10:30pm.

The 11 rooms, most with private baths and all with air-conditioning and telephones, are located in the main house and cottage annex. They are furnished with an eclectic mix of antiques and antique reproductions. The nicest rooms, to my mind, are in the addition out back. Room 5, for instance, has a rope four-poster covered with a red-blue old quilt, a side table draped with a floor-length tablecloth, wing chairs, a dresser, and a chest. Room 4 is even brighter, thanks to the fantail light. Facilities also include an outdoor pool. Rates: Summer/fall, $85 to $155; winter/spring, $65 to $135. Lower prices are for shared bath.

The **Ramblewood Inn,** Under Mountain Road (P.O. Box 729), Sheffield, MA 01257 (☎ 413/229-3363), is located in an unusually spacious log house tucked away in the pine woods. All rooms have private tiled baths and are attractively furnished with pine beds, polished pine floors, ruffled curtains, and pinkish-gray wall-to-wall carpet. The ground-floor room has a high cathedral-style ceiling and light-filled atrium. One room has a private deck adorned with flower-filled tubs. Upstairs rooms are also prettily and variously decorated, with one wall sporting chintz wallpaper, cream-and-rust curtains at the windows, and a Hitchcock rocker. Quiche, blueberry pancakes, omelets, and sausage and eggs are likely breakfast dishes, along with home-baked items. Guests may use the canoe on the lake across the road. Rates: $100 to $135 double.

Orchard Shade, 84 Maple Ave. (P.O. Box 669), Sheffield, MA 01257 (☎ 413/229-8463), is the name given to this beautiful 1840 house standing on 10 acres with well-tended gardens and a swimming pool. There are seven rooms sharing three baths. All are furnished tastefully with antiques. In one you might find, for example, an Empire-style chest and bull's-eye mirror, along with a camelback sofa and wicker chair. Another might have painted cottage-style furniture. The guest parlors with fireplaces are very comfortable and decorated with good rugs, interesting objects, family portraits, and a good selection of books, art, and sculpture. A breakfast of breads and pastries is served. Rates: $70 to $135.

HARTSVILLE DINING

The **Hillside Restaurant,** a few miles southeast of Great Barrington on Route 57 (off Route 23) in Hartsville (☎ 413/528-3123), is in an old farmhouse set on the crest of a hill with a beautiful Berkshire Valley view. It serves such continental-Italian specialties as veal francese or veal piccata, filet of sole Oscar, and fettuccine Alfredo, all priced from $15 to $22. Staffordshire china is used for service; the two dining rooms are warmed by fires in winter, while in summer there's a porch that takes full advantage of the view. Open in summer, Sunday from noon to 2pm, Tuesday to Sunday from 5 to 9pm; in winter, Sunday from noon to 2pm, Wednesday to Sunday 5 to 9pm.

NEW MARLBOROUGH/SANDISFIELD LODGING & DINING

At the **Old Inn on the Green & Gedney Farm,** Route 57, New Marlborough, MA 01230 (☎ 413/229-3131), the Old Inn is set back behind a green in an

18th-century building with a classic double-porch facade. There are five rooms, all with private baths and air-conditioning. Each one is eclectically furnished in a very country style. The rooms might contain iron-and-brass beds, desks, armoires, wing chairs, or perhaps a white-painted table and chair. Some rooms have access to the long front balcony. Gedney Farm is located a short distance down the road. The 16 accommodations here are in a magnificent turn-of-the-century Normandy-style barn, and the interior decoration is refreshingly different from the traditional New England inn. Rooms are painted in brilliant Southwestern colors. All have private baths, and some have granite fireplaces and tiled whirlpool baths.

At the Old Inn, the four colonial-style dining rooms have fireplaces and are lit entirely by candlelight. Here, a fixed-price dinner is served on Saturday. Dinner specialties vary from week to week, but a typical sample menu might begin with oyster and crab bisque, followed by a choice between seared Arctic char *en croute* with a roasted pomodoro sauce or beef tenderloin with red wine mushroom jus. The finale might bring lemon chiffon tart or caramel pear ice cream. A fine repast, indeed, and well worth the $48 price tag. During the week, an à la carte menu is served in the dining rooms or on the canopied terrace by candlelight. Prices range from $18 to $23. You will always find a fish of the day as well as sea scallops in a tarragon infused fume and loin of pork with roasted onion cider sauce. The wine list is extensive. Breakfast is served in the room with a refectory table. The Courtyard Cafe at Gedney Farm is open for lunch on summer weekends. The Gallery at Gedney Farm features a variety of art shows during the year, including outdoor sculpture in summer and fall. Rates: Old Inn, $150 to $185 double; Gedney Farm, $185 to $215, suites from $235.

The oldest section of the **New Boston Inn,** 101 N. Main St. (routes 8 and 57, Village of New Boston), Sandisfield, MA 01255 (☎ 413/258-4477), dates to 1735. Today it serves as the tap room (open for guests only) of this zesty country inn. There are eight guest rooms, all with private baths. The floors are bleached wood; the decor soft florals. Room 4 is stenciled with a Tree of Life, done by a local artist. It also possesses a cottage-style Victorian suite and a striking turkey-red rush-seat chair and desk. The cove-ceilinged ballroom now serves as a place where guests gather to talk or to play billiards. According to local legend, Pearl Buck wrote *The Good Earth* here, Horowitz played in the ballroom, and Mrs. Anne Morrow Lindbergh wrote *Gift from the Sea* here. A full breakfast of bacon, sausage, and French toast is served. Rates: $105 double.

PITTSFIELD-DALTON
& THE NORTHWESTERN CORNER

Pittsfield and Dalton, with their more extensive commercial development, present a different face from the picturesque villages that have been explored thus far. Neither one is pretty, but they do possess several attractions. You may wish to begin at the **Berkshire Museum,** 39 South St. (☎ 413/443-7171), in the center of **Pittsfield,** where some of the displays will help you come to grips with the history of the area. There are some fine paintings from the

Hudson River School. Other exhibits concentrate on ancient civilizations and nature (including an aquarium featuring local and other aquatic specimens). Open Tuesday to Saturday from 10am to 5pm, Sunday from 1 to 5pm; July and August daily. Admission is $3 for adults, $2 for seniors, $1 for children 12 to 18. Free Wednesday and Saturday 10am to noon.

Just south of Pittsfield lies **Arrowhead,** at 780 Holmes Rd., Pittsfield (☎ 413/442-1793), where Herman Melville lived from 1850 to 1863. As you stand in the room where he wrote *Moby Dick, Pierre, The Confidence Man, Israel Potter,* and the *Piazza Tales,* you can imagine how often he must have contemplated the grim visage of Mount Greylock with despair, for his novels were failures and he was dogged by debt. Three rooms are devoted to his life and works and other memorabilia. The house is also the headquarters of the Berkshire County Historical Society. Open Memorial Day to Labor Day, daily from 10am to 5pm; Labor Day to October 31 Friday to Monday 10am to 5pm; November to May, by appointment. Admission: $5 adults, $4 children 6 to 16.

From Pittsfield you can travel 5 miles along Route 20 to a really fascinating attraction, best visited in good weather; don your boots and slickers on rainy days, for a visit involves a lot of outdoor walking. This is the **Hancock Shaker Village,** Route 20 (P.O. Box 898), Pittsfield, MA 01202 (☎ 413/443-0188). Allow at least 3 hours to tour this fascinating living museum dedicated to the Shakers, a communal religious sect that in 1790 established Hancock, the City of Peace, as the third of 18 Shaker communities settled in the United States.

Founded by Mother Ann Lee, the Shakers were dedicated to celibacy, simplicity, and equality. They were known for their excellence in agriculture and industry, and for their lively dance-worship, which gave the sect its name. Celibates, they took children and orphans into their community; the children were free to leave if they wanted to and many did. You can see the dorms where the men and women slept separately, their separate staircases, and the corridors where two narrow strips of carpet were placed—one for the women to walk on, the other for the men. In summer they rose at 4:30am, at 5am in winter, to begin their daily round of farming, craftsmaking, and cooking. You can tour 20 original Shaker buildings, and along the way can watch the old crafts being demonstrated—cooking that follows Shaker recipes, furniture making, box making, weaving, sewing, spinning, etc. There's also a Discovery Room where you can try your hand at spinning and weaving or try on Shaker-style clothing. The Village also has a working farm with historic breeds of livestock and vegetable and herb gardens. The museum shop sells fine crafts—their famous wool cloaks, tables, chairs, candleholders, boxes, vinegars, and herbs. It's a delightful outing. Open May 23 to October 18, 9:30am to 5pm daily. Admission: $13.50 for adults, $5.50 for children 6 to 17. April 1 to May 23 and October 18 to November 1, there are guided tours on the hour from 10am to 3pm. Tours are $10 for adults and $5 for children 6 to 17.

To get there: Don't go to Hancock Village itself—the Shaker Village is separated by a mountain barrier. Coming from the north, take Route 7 south to Route 20 west. From the south, take Route 22 to Route 295 and then east to Route 41 north.

The **South Mountain Chamber Concerts** are also given about 1 mile south of Pittsfield.

Due east of Pittsfield lies the industrial town of Dalton, where you can explore part of its heritage at the **Crane Museum**, South Street (☎ 413/684-2600), located off Route 9, by viewing the exhibits that document the art of fine papermaking since 1801. Unfortunately, this one will have to be done on a weekday. Open June to mid-October Monday to Friday from 2 to 5pm.

PITTSFIELD-DALTON LODGING

The **White Horse Inn,** 378 South St. (routes 7 and 20), Pittsfield, MA 01201 (☎ 413/442-2512), is a beige clapboard home with cream shutters and an elegant portico supported by classical pillars. All eight rooms have private baths, TVs, and telephones. They are neat and clean, and furnished with oak desks, beds, and dressers. The breakfast room overlooks the lawn and trees in back. Fresh flowers adorn the glass-topped tables. An ample continental breakfast of fruit, cereal, homemade muffins, and quiche is served here. Rates: July to Labor Day, $120 to $180 double, off-season, $100 to $145 double.

The **Dalton House,** 955 Main St., Dalton, MA 01226 (☎ 413/684-3854), will always have seasonal flowers in bloom, for owners Gary and Bernice Turetsky are enthusiastic gardeners. The main house was built by a Hessian soldier in 1810 and contains five comfortable rooms. The six rooms in the carriage house out back are especially nicely decorated to achieve a country look. All rooms have private baths, air-conditioning, and telephones. The public areas in the house itself are warm and cozy; the sitting room has a large fireplace and also contains a piano; you can retire to the loft area above to play cards or watch TV, especially after a day's skiing—this is a popular spot with skiing groups. Breakfast is served buffet style in the skylit Shaker-style dining room. In summer, loungers and tables are placed out on the deck. There is a large pool for guests. Rates (including breakfast): July and August, $95 to $125; spring/fall, $78 to $95; winter, $60 to $80.

PITTSFIELD DINING

An entrance surrounded by Chianti bottles welcomes you to the homey **Giovanni's,** located on Route 7 just south of Pontoosuc Lake (☎ 413/443-2441). Tiffany-style lamps, a few hanging plants, and pictures of Venice set the scene for tasty Italian dishes. Typical appetizers—gnocchi, calamari fritti—are priced from $5. Pastas run from $10 for ravioli with meat or marinara sauce to $18 for a linguine with sea scallops and shrimp in a basil pesto sauce. Main courses encompass everything from veal marsala and chicken cacciatore to Giovanni's sirloin finished with sautéed mushrooms and caramelized onions in a garlic sauce. In addition to the menu, there are always daily specials. Prices range from $13 to $20. Open Monday to Saturday from noon to 3pm, Monday to Thursday 4:30 to 9pm, Friday to Saturday 4:30 to 10pm, Sunday noon to 8pm.

JUST OVER THE NEW YORK BORDER

The **Inn at Shaker Mill,** Cherry Lane (off Route 22), Canaan, NY 12029 (☎ 518/794-9345). Idyllically situated by a flowing brook and waterfall, this lovely 1824 stone grist mill affords peace and quiet. Here you can sit in the living room, actually listening to the water running over the rocks. The couches are modern and so are the wood stoves; Shaker stools serve as coffee tables. Ingram Paperny, who has lived here for 30 years, restored the mill, handcrafting most of the built-in furniture himself. Some people may find the 20 rooms too austere, for the Shaker inspiration is strong. Rooms have wood side tables, chests, wide-board floors, and beams. The most appealing accommodation to my mind is a top-floor skylit apartment with wicker furnishings and a kitchen. There's a TV in the living room. The best pastimes are sitting out by the brook and looking across the fields dotted with cows or walking through the countryside. The prime reason for visiting the inn is the warm welcome given by Ingram, who relishes conversation and obviously has a warm interest in and affection for his guests. Meals are obligatory on weekends during the summer season. Rates: B&B $45 to $70 per person (the lower price off-season). Add $20 to $25 per person for MAP. Bring your own wine.

The **Sedgwick Inn,** Route 22, Berlin, NY 12022 (☎ 518/658-2334), is an exquisite home filled with antiques personally collected by Robert and Edith Evans, who restored and opened this inn as "a retirement project" after long careers in psychology. Accommodations consist of four rooms with private baths, a two-room suite, and six motel-style units. The one room I viewed contained two brass beds and a bird's-eye maple dresser. If the others reflect the quality of the public areas, they ought to be beautiful. The place is full of interesting artifacts. In the living room is a case filled with ivory pieces, figureheads, Toby jugs, and other small collectibles and a number of stone sculptures, the work of Edith Evans. A sofa, wing chairs, an oriental rug, and a fireplace ensure comfort. A Will Moses, given to the Evans by the artist, graces the walls. A marvelous etched-glass door depicting peacocks—a great find—leads to the porch breakfast room that has a view of the garden out back and is fittingly furnished with white metal chairs and tables on a brick floor. The library offers magazines, books, and comfortable chairs. In the corner, the cupboard is filled with jewelry and small antique items for sale. In a separate building that once served as a Civil War recruiting station, guests can enjoy a game of pool on the antique table. A gift shop and gallery are behind the inn. Wicker chairs line the front porch.

The Coach Room Tavern is a very popular restaurant for which you'll certainly need a reservation on weekends. The kitchen is supervised by Edith, and the menu changes weekly but will feature five entrees and a vegetarian choice. There might be oven poached haddock with a creole pepper sauce, baked chicken with artichokes and sun-dried tomatoes, or char-grilled filet mignon. Prices range from $13 to $22. The chef also turns out many soups, such as roasted eggplant and vidalia onion. Edith is Viennese, and desserts are her specialty—frozen cappuccino mousse pie covered with a dark chocolate glaze, bananas Foster, or four-berry coupe flavored with cointreau and served over vanilla ice cream. A pianist plays on Friday and Saturday evenings. Dining hours are Wednesday to Saturday from 11:30am to 2pm and 5 to 9pm, Sunday 1 to 8pm. Rates: June to October, $105 to $115 double, suite $135, motel $88; November to May, $95 to 105 double, suite $120, motel $78.

It's not surprising that the **Mill House Inn** (P.O. Box 1079, Hancock, MA 01237), on Route 43 in New York's Stephentown (☎ 518/733-5606), really does look like a Central European mountain chalet, for one of the owners, Romana Tallet, hails from Slovenia. She will welcome you into her cozy living room with its large arched stucco fireplace that throws out much-needed heat on winter days. The Tallets go to great lengths to ensure that everyone is content, and they are very well versed and forthcoming about the attractions of the area. There's a small game room, croquet is available, and there's a small swimming pool in back. All rooms have air-conditioning and private baths with continental-style showers; they're eclectically furnished, some with pine. In summer, breakfast is served on the terrace. The inn is only 10 minutes from Mount Greylock. Rates: $95 to $105 double, suites $115 to $150. Three-night minimum in July, August, and holiday weekends.

Les Pyrenees is off Route 295 in Canaan, NY (☎ 518/781-4451). Master chef Jean Petit has been attracting patrons to this secluded restaurant for 30 years. A stone stairway covered by a red, white, and blue awning leads to the restaurant; flowers bloom on either side. The front room is a dimly lit bar. The dining room behind glows. Gilt portraits, many of family and friends, adorn the Chinese-lacquer pink walls. The atmosphere is relaxed. Dishes are primarily French classics—chicken in burgundy, poached halibut in white wine and cream sauce, *escalope de veau viennoise, poulet au champagne,* or frogs' legs. They are priced from $12 to $27, the higher price for pheasant with pâté de foie gras and truffles. Among the desserts, the crème brûlée is extra special. Cash or personal check only. Open in summer Tuesday to Saturday from 5 to 10pm, Sunday 5 to 10pm; winter and spring Friday to Saturday from 5 to 10pm, Sunday from 4 to 9pm.

HANCOCK & JIMINY PEAK LODGING & DINING

The **Hancock Inn,** Route 43, Hancock, MA 01237 (☎ 800/882-8859 or 413/738-5873), is a highly idiosyncratic kind of place—an expression of Ellen and Chester Gorski. A small cement path lined with iris and marigolds leads to the small porch-foyer filled with ferns and cane rockers. Open the door into the hall, and you'll discover a very Victorian hallway. Stern Victorian portraits stare down from the walls; a Victorian-style couch and sideboard stand imperiously. To the right, a doorway surmounted with a semicircular stained-glass window leads into the dining room, where tables are set with white tablecloths and napkins, a sprig of fresh flowers, and glass candleholders. A large wall clock ticks away. Grapevine wreaths and cream ball-fringe curtains add a country touch. In winter it's warmed by a fire in the wood-burning stove. The food has been highly rated by the *Albany Times Union* critic. The limited menu features eight or so dishes—duckling braised in port wine with figs; filet mignon with shallots, red wine, and cognac; fish of the day; or chicken breast sautéed in a light apricot sauce. Prices run $16 to $20. Desserts are created by Ellen—homemade ice creams, white-chocolate mousse cheesecake, crème brûlée with strawberries. They'll be served on fine Depression glass of a harmonious color: cobalt blue, green, or burgundy. Open Friday to Sunday from 5 to 10pm.

Eight rooms with private baths are very idiosyncratically styled, and not in a lushly decorated way. Room 1 has stenciled walls, a country pine dresser and bed, a side table, a wardrobe, a desk with a handful of old books, and a costumed doll in the corner. The bathroom has wainscoting, while the room has bold pink- and white-rose wallpaper. Other rooms might have an old country teardrop dresser, a bird's-eye maple or Jenny Lind bed, a comfortable chair such as an old carpet-chair rocker, or a rare Larkin desk. The place has great charm, and Ellen is a warm, entertaining hostess. Rates: Late May to August and October, $80 double; September and November to early May, $60 double; $12 for additional person.

Jiminy Peak Inn and Mountain Resort, Corey Road, Hancock, MA 01237 (☎ 413/738-5500), is a well-designed, very attractive resort complex at the base of the mountain of the same name. All the accommodations are suites. Each is modern, containing a kitchen fully equipped with dishwasher, stove, fridge, and toaster; a living room with a couch that makes up into a queen-size bed, TV hidden in a cabinet, plus comfortable seating and a service bar. A bathroom with two sinks (a vanity outside) and bedroom with brass bed and pine furnishings complete the layout. The six-on-six and eight-on-eight windows give each an old-fashioned air. The dining room, Founders Grill, has a full view of the mountain, while the bar area has a stone fireplace and comfy wing chairs to rest in après-ski. The food is typical American/continental fare— chicken parmesan, chicken and seafood kebabs, prime rib, and baked scallops, priced from $10 to $20. The Founders Grill is open for lunch and dinner daily; breakfast depends on season.

The list of facilities is long. There are six tennis courts and an outdoor pool from which you can see tree-covered mountains. Facing the mountain is another outdoor heated pool that's used year round. Just off this pool area is a Jacuzzi and a fitness room with Universal equipment, sauna, and resident masseuse. The game room on the lower level, furnished with video games, is only one area that the kids enjoy. The Alpine slide is thrilling fun in summer ($4 a ride, $13 for a five-ride book, or 1½ hours' worth for $9.75). Laser trap shooting is also available. The miniature golf here is beautifully landscaped, and each hole is a scale reproduction of a famous hole. Trout fishing is offered at the stocked pond. Patio and picnic tables stand outside the round house, which is the tavern in winter, a sandwich place in summer. The grounds are well kept—colorful window boxes, fences with rambling roses show the extra attention to detail that has made Jiminy Peak the prime skiing and summer resort in the Berkshires.

Rates: One-bedroom, weekends $105 ($45 for a third night to a weekend), midweek $90; two-bedroom, weekends $140,($60 for a third night), midweek $120; three-bedroom, weekends $190 ($85 for a third night), midweek $170. These prices require a 2-night minimum stay.

WILLIAMSTOWN

Originally established in 1753 as a plantation called West Hoosuck, it was renamed after Colonel Ephraim Williams in 1755. When he left an estate for founding a free school with the proviso that the township's name be changed to Williamstown, of course, it was. And that's why **Williams College,** whose buildings are scattered along Main Street against a mountain backdrop, is here in this pretty town of rolling hills and dales. If you like, you can tour the college; ask at the Admissions Office in Hopkins Hall. The college's museum of art (☎ 413/597-2429) in Lawrence Hall on Main Street and the Hopkins Observatory are also worth visiting. But the outstanding attractions here are really the Clark Institute and the Williamstown Festival.

The **Sterling and Francine Clark Art Institute,** 225 South St. (☎ 413/458-9545), houses a distinguished personal art collection purchased between 1912 and 1955. Most famous for a room of Renoirs and paintings by Monet,

Degas, and Pissarro, and other 19th-century French impressionists, the collection also contains some other fine works—Mary Cassatt pastels; Venetian scenes by John Singer Sargent; several Winslow Homers, including his *Undertow* (1886), a luminous picture of lifeguards pulling two girls from the waves; a Remington bronze; some glorious Corots; Turner's *Rockets and Blue Lights*; and two Berthe Morisots, along with representatives from many other schools and periods.

What makes the collection so remarkable is that Clark only bought what he liked, and his taste was impeccable. His favorite work among them all was Renoir's *Onions*, because he especially appreciated the artistry that could transform the mundane onion into a shimmering object of beauty. Part of the museum is set aside for special exhibits. Open July 1 to Labor Day, daily from 10am to 5pm; September to June, Tuesday to Sunday from 10am to 5pm; open Memorial, Labor, and Columbus days, but closed Thanksgiving, Christmas, and New Year's Day. Admission: Free.

The Adams Memorial Theatre (☎ 413/597-3400) is home to the **Williamstown Theatre Festival,** premier summer theater in the Berkshires. See "Festivals in the Berkshires," below for information.

WILLIAMSTOWN LODGING & DINING

The Orchards, 222 Adams Rd. (Route 2 East), Williamstown, MA 02167 (☎ 800/225-1517 or 413/458-9611), stands on the site of an old apple orchard. It's a tasteful modern lodging with plenty of atmosphere. The design is extremely pleasing, laid out as it is around a large triangular garden with a rockery and goldfish pond. Here you can relax on the deck with its umbrella tables and enjoy cocktails or after-theater supper. Guests also appreciate the large living room where a full afternoon tea of finger sandwiches and pastries is served. The fireplace is fashioned from Vermont marble with a mantel from England, while oriental rugs grace the floors. Bookshelves span each side of the mantel, and the elegance is further underlined by the grand piano, large crystal chandelier, antique furnishings, and what will certainly be a bounteous bouquet of fresh flowers. A personal touch is revealed in the glass cases containing the owner's collections of antique silver teapots and of model soldiers ranging from a French Algerian cavalryman to a Norman knight.

The 47 extra-large rooms have been carefully designed and handsomely decorated in smoky blues and dusty pinks with wallpaper panel moldings. Fifteen rooms have fireplaces. The marble-floored bathrooms are fully tiled and have the added convenience of double sinks, a separate tub and shower, as well as many extra touches like bathrobes and extra-fine amenities. The rooms feature solid-wood closet doors, telephones, TV in armoires, nightlights, refrigerators, and a bar with a basket of fruit and bottles of Perrier. There's also plenty of working and seating space. The so-called smaller rooms (hardly small) lack the separate tub and shower and the refrigerator. The Tennessee Williams Suite is huge, decked out in Wedgwood blue with a pencil four-poster without a canopy.

Plush dark-green walls, pastel-patterned banquettes, Queen Anne chairs, dusty-rose napkins and tablecloths, fresh flowers in stem vases, and fine china settings provide the appropriate backdrop for fine food in the dining room. Start with the smoked Scottish salmon served with either the mixed greens, asparagus, and curry olive oil dressing or the house Caesar salad with extra-special cheese croutons. There will be about seven main courses to choose from—perhaps grilled swordfish with cilantro butter or honey, sesame roasted duck breast with plum sauce, or tenderloin of beef with caramelized onions. Prices range from $24 to $28. Desserts are carefully prepared and so good it's hard to select just one. Still, the vanilla crème brûlée with an orange confit is certainly up there. The dining room is open daily from 7 to 10am and noon to 2pm. Dinner hours are Sunday to Thursday from 5:30 to 8:30pm, Friday and Saturday 5:30 to 9pm.

Facilities include an outdoor pool and a well-equipped fitness room. The lounge draws a crowd and is particularly attractive in winter when a fire roars in the large stone fireplace. It's also well equipped with board and other games for those long, dark evenings and, of course, with comfortable lounge chairs. Rates: Memorial Day to mid-November, $170 to $235; mid-November to May, $135 to $185. Special packages are available.

River Bend Farm, 643 Simonds Rd. (Route 7) Williamstown, MA 01267 (☎ 413/458-3121), rewards guests with an authentic historic experience in a warm, hospitable atmosphere. The house was built in 1770, and when you stand in the tap room, it's as if time had stood still. The wood paneling, the iron door latches, and the cupboard filled with pewter all make it seem real. So does the paneled keeping room with its great hearth, numerous hutches, copper sink, and bunches of herbs hung up to dry. Here a breakfast of granola, breads, and fruit is served. There are four rooms, each furnished with appropriate antiques and accents like wrought iron or Shaker-style tin lamps. The ground floor room features Williamsburg blue paneling and is furnished with a double bed, a blanket chest, a wing-back chair and maple chest. Oriental rugs embellish the plank floors in all the rooms. The grounds are entrancing, too. Open April to October. Rates: $90 double.

Field Farm House, 554 Sloan Rd., Williamstown MA (☎ 413/458-3135), is a refreshing surprise. It was formerly the home of art collector and Williams College librarian Lawrence Bloedel. Some of his collection, including a striking sculpture called *Sandy Seated in a Square* by Richard A. Miller, can still be seen on the grounds and in the house. The house and the interior design are 1940s modern. Although Mr. Bloedel discussed the project with Frank Lloyd Wright, Ned Goodell was the original architect.

The rooms have a minimum of furnishings, mostly built-ins—dressers, drawers, closets. Where there are furnishings, they're Danish modern, like the glass-top tables and the chairs found in the North Room. This room also features a fireplace with brilliant tiles painted with butterfly designs and a small deck. The seamless carpet is original to the house, and the pinch-pleat track curtains are designed to shut out all light. The master bedroom is a study in serenity—cream white carpet, teak dresser, and a fireplace with tiles depicting bluebirds are the crucial elements, along with a huge deck that commands views of the mountains. The woodwork in the living room is stunning, and the cork parquet floor is certainly unique today. Books and sculptures add interest to the room, and there are great views of the mountains, the beaver pond, and the grounds—all 296 acres. In summer, guests may use the lovely kidney-shaped pool and the tennis court. There are marked trails for hiking in the summer and cross-country skiing in winter.

An eye opener, this place certainly made me see Danish modern in a new light. To reach the property take Route 7 south to Route 43. Turn right onto 43 south and take an immediate right onto Sloan Road. Field Farm is 1 mile up on the right. Rates: $110 double.

WILLIAMSTOWN DINING

Two miles south of Williamstown on routes 2 and 7, **Le Jardin** (☎ 413/458-8032), serves excellent food in elegant surroundings. You may begin your meal with caviar, or less extravagantly, with a fine homemade soup, and follow with one of the daily specials on the blackboard menu. Among the favorite dishes are duckling with a Bing cherry sauce, poached salmon with a Dijonnaise sauce, and a fine rack of lamb. Prices range from $15 to $24. Open July and August, Sunday to Friday from 5 to 9pm, Saturday from 5 to 10pm, Sunday from 10:30am to 2pm; September to December and May and June, Sunday, Monday, and Wednesday to Friday 5 to 9pm, Saturday 5 to 10pm; Sunday 10:30am to 2pm.

There are also six accommodations (four with fireplaces) available here in this lovely country-house atmosphere. Rates: $80 to $100. Closed January 1 to April 1.

The **Mill on the Floss,** Route 7 (P.O. Box 718), New Ashford, MA 01237 (☎ 413/458-9123), has country charm and serves some fine, if traditional, French cuisine. The limited menu offers classics such as chicken amandine, tournedos Bearnaise, poached salmon hollandaise, and rack of lamb, priced from $18.50 to $27. Start with the escargot with garlic butter or the crab cake with a piquant Dijon sauce. Open Tuesday to Sunday from 5pm to closing.

MOUNT GREYLOCK

While you're in the Berkshires, climb or drive to the summit of Mount Greylock and ascend the spiral stairway to the top of the tower. From here you have a 360-degree vista looking more than 50 miles to the Catskills and more than 100 miles to the distant Adirondacks.

You can even sojourn here at **Bascom Lodge,** P.O. Box 1800, Lanesboro, MA 01237 (☎ 413/443-0011 for advanced reservations; 413/743-1591 for current week), built in the 1930s to accommodate hikers. Lodgings are in four bunkrooms sleeping six to nine or in four private rooms sleeping two each. Note though that all share corridor baths. A family-style breakfast ($6) and dinner ($12) is served daily. Snacks and sandwiches are also available from a counter and can be eaten at the refectory tables. Open from mid-May to late October. Rates are discounted for members of the Appalachian Mountain Club: August and weekends bunk rooms $30 for nonmembers, $20 for members; at other times $25 for nonmembers, $15 members. Private rooms are $65 per room for nonmembers, $55 for members.

The Berkshires
Festivals in the Berkshires

Classical Music: Tanglewood, West Street (Route 183), Lenox, MA 01240 (☎ 413/637-1600). Spread your picnic on the lawn on this 210-acre site overlooking the lovely Stockbridge Bowl. Fuchsias and begonias make the scene even lovelier in summer, when the festival runs for 9 weeks, from early July to the end of August. Get there 2 hours before if you want space near the Music Shed. Evening performances are given on Friday at 7 and 8:30pm, Saturday at 8:30pm, with matinees on Sunday at 2:30pm and open rehearsals on Saturday mornings. For information before June 15, call Symphony Hall in Boston (☎ 617/266-1492).

South Mountain Concerts, P.O. Box 23, Pittsfield, MA 01202 (☎ 413/442-2106), features such chamber music greats as the Beaux Arts Trio and the Tokyo and Guarneri string quartets. Schedules vary, but concerts are usually held on Sunday afternoons from the end of August to mid-October, approximately every 2 weeks. Tickets run $20 to $25. Performances are given in a concert hall built in 1918 by the concert's founder, Mrs. Elizabeth Sprague Coolidge.

Dance: Jacob's Pillow, P.O. Box 287, Lee, MA 01238 (☎ 413/637-1322), is the superb 10-week dance festival founded by Ted Shawn and Ruth St. Denis in the 1930s when modern American dance was considered beyond avant garde. It's the oldest dance festival in America. Martha Graham performed some of her earliest works here. More recently, it has featured such greats as the Merce Cunningham Dance Company, the Mark Morris Dance Group, Paul Taylor Dance Company, and Trisha Brown Company. In addition, enjoy the Pillow Cafe and Pub and free showings on the Inside/Out stage prior to performances. Tickets range from $15 to $50. The festival runs from the end of June to Labor Day. Jacob's Pillow is located off Route 20 on George Carter Road in Becket, east of Lee. Call ☎ 413/243-0745 for tickets.

Theater: The **Williamstown Theatre Festival,** under the direction of producer Michael Ritchie, has established itself over the last 44 years as the premier summer theater in the Berkshires. The festival's stars have included Richard Chamberlain, Blythe Danner, Richard Dreyfuss, Christopher Walken, Roberta Maxwell, Christopher Reeve, Maria Tucci, and many, many more. The festival's Main Stage features classics by Williams, Brecht, Chekhov, Shaw, Ibsen, and others; on the Other Stage new works by Albert Innaurato, Edvardo Machado, and Donald Margulies and others are performed. For information, call ☎ 413/597-3400 or write to the festival at P.O. Box 517, Williamstown, MA 01267.

MacHaydn Theater, Route 203, Chatham, NY 12037 (☎ 518/392-9292). Here some of the best authentic summer stock can be found—refreshing, enthusiastic productions of *My Fair Lady*, *Sweet Charity*, and *Oklahoma!*

The **Berkshire Theatre Festival,** Main Street, Stockbridge, MA 01262 (☎ 413/298-5536, or 413/298-5576 after June 1 for the box office), offers a four-play season from the end of June to the end of August in a Stanford White–designed building constructed in 1886 as a casino. Such figures as Katharine Hepburn and James Cagney started their careers here.

Shakespeare & Company, The Mount, Plunkett Street (off Route 7), Lenox, MA 01240 (☎ 413/637-1199, or 413/637-3353 after May 10 for the box office). Bring a picnic before the outdoor performance at this dramatic mansion setting. The season runs from late May to the end of October.

The Berkshires
Special & Recreational Activities

Antiquing: South Egremont is an excellent hunting ground and so is Route 7 around Sheffield and Route 7A through Ashley Falls. Other stores are dotted throughout the Berkshires.

Boating: Laurel Lake is in Lee on Route 20. In Pittsfield, at **Pontoosuc Lake,** water-sports equipment is available for rent by the hour—motorboats cost $12.50 with a 10-hp engine, $21 for 50 hp, and $29 for 75 hp; waterskis are $5; canoes, $7; rowboats, $6, and paddleboats, $7; wave runners rent for $30 per 20 minutes; and sailboats are available. For information, contact **U-Drive Boat Rentals,** 123 Burke Ave. in Pittsfield or 1551 North St. (Route 7) at Pontoosuc Lake (☎ 413/442-7020). The **Ponterril YMCA** in Pittsfield (☎ 413/499-0647) also has boats for rent at its Pontoosuc Lake facility. Canoes rent for $8 an hour, Sunfish for $15 an hour, and a sailboat with a mainsail and jib for $20 an hour. Call the marina at ☎ 413/499-0694. Open from Memorial Day to September 1.

Camping: In the Lenox area, **Woodland Hills Family Campground,** Austerlitz, NY 12017 (☎ 518/392-3557), offers camping convenient to Tanglewood at 160 sites with water, electricity, and sewer hookups and a full range of facilities. Open from May 1 to Columbus Day. It charges $16 to $20.

    Prospect Lake Park, Prospect Lake Road, North Egremont, MA 01252 (☎ 413/528-4158), only 6 miles from Great Barrington, is ideal for families because of the great number of facilities—boat rentals (paddleboats, canoes, and rowboats), tennis, lake fishing, and two swimming beaches. Open from mid-May to October. From $24.

    Pittsfield State Forest, Cascade Street (☎ 413/442-8992), has 31 sites at various locations throughout the park. In **Windsor State Forest,** River Road, Windsor (☎ 413/684-9760), there's camping in the scenic Windsor Jambs area.

Canoeing: The Connecticut, Battenkill, Hoosic, or Upper Housatonic rivers will provide some easy paddling. The more experienced will want to try the Westfield or Deerfield rivers after a good rain. For information, rentals, and sales, contact **Berkshire Outfitters Canoe and Kayak Center,** Route 8, Cheshire Harbor, Adams, MA 01220 (☎ 413/743-5900); or **Riverrun/North,** Route 7, Sheffield, MA 01257 (☎ 413/528-1100).

Cross-Country Skiing: You can ski the trails on Mount Greylock. Ski and snowshoe rentals are available at **Berkshire Outfitters Canoe and Kayak Center,** Route 8, Cheshire Harbor, Adams, MA 01220 (☎ 413/743-5900). In Lenox, there's cross-country skiing in Kennedy Park. **Brodie Mountain,** Route 7, New Ashford, MA 01237 (☎ 413/443-4752), has 16 miles of trails and also offers snowboarding. Cross-country is available at **Notchview** in Windsor. **Canterbury Farm,** Fred Snow Road, Becket, MA 01223 (☎ 413/623-8765), has 11 miles of ski trails plus rentals and instruction. It is really secluded, located on a dirt road off Route 8 about 1 mile south of Becket.

Fishing: Laurel Lake has a fishing ramp off Route 20. In Pittsfield, **Pontoosuc Lake** has a ramp off Hancock Road near Route 7. **Onota Lake** is known for trophy-size bass and lake trout. The **Stockbridge Bowl** has a ramp off Route 183.

Golf: Egremont Country Club, Route 23 (☎ 413/528-4222), has a course with 18 holes; near Lenox, **Cranwell Golf Course,** 55 Lee Rd. (☎ 413/637-2563), has an 18-hole par 71 course. **Pontoosuc Lake Country Club,** Ridge Avenue, Pittsfield (☎ 413/445-4217), has an 18-hole par 70 course. **Oak 'n' Spruce Resort,** South Lee, (☎ 413/243-3500), has a 9-hole pitch and putt. **Taconic Golf Course,** Meacham Street, Williamstown (☎ 413/458-3997), has an 18-hole par 71 course; **Waubeeka Golf Links,** on routes 7 and 43, South Williamstown (☎ 413/458-5869), has an 18-hole, par-72 course.

Hiking: There's plenty of mountain terrain hiking. Lanesboro is the gateway to **Mount Greylock.** A visitors center is located on Rockwell Road, just off Route 7, although the most scenic route up the mountain is probably via Notch Road from North Adams. **Pleasant Valley Wildlife Sanctuary,** off Route 7 between Lenox and Pittsfield (☎ 413/637-0320), offers 7 miles of hiking trails. It's owned by the Massachusetts Audubon Society, which also operates a nature museum. Berry Mountain in the **Pittsfield State Forest** is great for blueberrying, viewing the azalea fields, picnicking, and camping, as well as just plain walking. Walk the path to the summit of 2,626-foot **Mount Everett** for fine views of New York, Massachusetts, Vermont, and Connecticut. Access is from Route 23 or 41 via South Egremont or from Route 22 via Copake Falls. Just south of Sheffield and west of Route 7, **Bartholomew's Cobble** gives prime views of the Housatonic.

Hike to the summit of **Monument Mountain** (1,642 feet), on Route 7 between Great Barrington and Stockbridge. **Hopkins Memorial Forest,** Bulkey Road off Route 7, has 25,000 acres on the slopes of the Taconic Mountains, plus miles of trails, including self-guided nature trails. Museum also. **Notchview** has 15 miles of hiking trails. For info about the **Appalachian Trail,** write to Pittsfield State Forest, Cascade Street, Pittsfield, MA 01201 (☎ 413/442-8992).

Horseback Riding: In Lenox, **Under Mountain Farm** (☎ 413/637-3365), offers 1-hour trail rides with an instructor for $45.

Picnicking: See the Lenox and Stockbridge dining sections for picnic suppliers. Tanglewood is not the only spot for picnicking; other places abound— **Berry Mountain** (in the Pittsfield State Forest), **Mount Everett** (reached from routes 23 or 41 via South Egremont) at the bottom of **Monument Mountain,** or **Mount Greylock,** and at **Windsor Jambs** in Windsor State Forest (☎ 413/684-0948).

Skiing: The Berkshires offer five skiing areas. Tallest and toughest of the five is **Berkshire East,** P.O. Box S, Charlemont, MA 01339 (☎ 413/339-6617), in a lovely setting on the Mohawk Trail. It has 34 trails served by one triple and three double chairs and a J-lift. **Butternut,** Route 23, Great Barrington, MA 01230 (☎ 413/528-2000), has a vertical drop of 1,000 feet; 22 trails with dramatic views; one poma and six chair lifts (one quad, one triple, four double) that can accommodate 10,000 skiers per hour; 98% snowmaking capacity; and a base lodge. The terrain is about 20% beginner and advanced and 60% intermediate. Cost is about $40 per day. There are also about 6 miles of cross-country. **Jiminy Peak,** Corey Road (off routes 7 or 43), Hancock, MA 01237 (☎ 413/738-5500), offers day and night skiing on close to 40 trails accessed by eight chair lifts and one tow. It also has a summer slide.

Catamount, Hillsdale, NY 12529 (☎ 518/325-3200 or 413/528-1262), offers fine skiing for beginners, intermediates, and experts on over 24 trails serviced by four double chairs and one J-bar. The steepest trail, dropping 500 feet over a 1,700-foot distance, is the Flipper Dipper. The mountain offers a 1,000-foot vertical drop and 96% snowmaking capacity. There's a modernized base lodge with cafeteria, cocktail lounge, and picture windows looking out onto the mountain. Also offered is a mountain coaster in summer. **Brodie Mountain**, Route 7, New Ashford, MA 01237 (☎ 413/443-4752), has 40 trails serviced by six lifts including four double chairs and two tows. Day rates range from $24 to $39.

State Parks & Forests: East Mountain State Reservation, Route 7 (☎ 413/528-2000), has hiking and skiing at Butternut. **Mount Greylock State Reservation**, Rockwell Road (☎ 413/499-4263 or 413/499-4262), offers bicycling, camping, fishing, hiking, picnicking, cross-country skiing, and snowmobiling. **October Mountain State Forest**, Woodland Road (☎ 413/243-1778 or 413/243-9726), has bicycling, camping, fishing, hiking, horseback riding, cross-country skiing, and snowmobiling. **Beartown State Forest**, Blue Hill Road (☎ 413/528-0904), has bicycling, boating, camping, fishing, hiking, horseback riding, picnicking, skiing, snowmobiling, and swimming. **Mount Washington State Park** and **Mount Everett**, East Street (☎ 413/528-0330), offers BashBish Falls along with 15 wilderness camping sites, hiking, horseback riding, and snowmobiling. **Toland State Forest**, Route 23 (☎ 413/269-6002), has boating, fishing, hiking, cross-country skiing, and snowmobiling; **Pittsfield State Forest**, Cascade Street (☎ 413/442-8992), has bicycling, boating, camping, fishing, hiking, picnicking, cross-country skiing, snowmobiling, and swimming. **Windsor State Forest**, River Road (☎ 413/684-9760), offers bicycling, camping, fishing, hiking, picnicking, cross-country skiing, swimming, and snowmobiling.

Swimming: Egremont Country Club (☎ 413/528-4222) has an outdoor pool. **Pittsfield State Forest** (☎ 413/442-8992) has a beach with lifeguards; **Pontoosuc Lake** has a free supervised beach. **Oak 'n' Spruce Resort** (☎ 413/243-3500) has outdoor and indoor pools; no children under 16. At **Stockbridge Bowl** you can swim off West Street. **Sand Springs**, off Route 7 near the Vermont line, has a 50-by 70-foot mineral pool with year-round temperature of 74. You can swim in the **Windsor Jambs**.

Tennis: Brodie Mountain, Route 7, New Ashford, MA 01237 (☎ 413/443-4752), has a racquet club featuring five indoor tennis and five racquetball courts. **Prospect Lake Park**, Prospect Lake, 3 miles west off Route 71, has two courts. **Berkshire West Athletic Club**, Tamarack Road, Pittsfield (☎ 413/499-4600), has eight outdoor and five indoor courts ($15 admission plus $18 to $20 an hour). **Egremont Country Club** (☎ 413/528-4222) has four courts; **Oak 'n' Spruce Resort**, South Lee (☎ 413/243-3500) has two clay courts. **Williams College** (☎ 413/597-3151) has 12 clay and 12 hard courts.

RHODE ISLAND

Newport

Distance in miles from Boston: 70.

Estimated driving time: 1¼ hours.

Driving: Take 95 south to Providence, then 195 to Fall River, and then routes 24 and 114 into Newport.

Bus: Greyhound (☎ 800/231-2222) travels to Providence, where you can change to a local Rhode Island bus into Newport.

Train: Amtrak (☎ 800/872-7245) services Providence via its Northeast Corridor route.

Further Information: For general information, contact the **Rhode Island Department of Economic Development,** Tourism Division, 1 West Exchange St., Providence, RI 02903 (☎ 401/277-2601).

For specific Newport information, contact the **Newport County Convention & Visitor's Bureau,** 23 America's Cup Ave., Newport, RI 02840 (☎ 800/976-5122 or 401/849-8098), or the **Newport County Chamber of Commerce,** 45 Valley Rd., Middletown, RI 02842 (☎ 401/847-1600).

When Verrazano first discovered Aquidneck Island, he named it Rhodes because the quality of the light reminded him of that mysterious Greek island. Today when one approaches the town from the west across the high-arching bridges, one is awestruck by the beauty of the bay, especially on a sunny day when white, blue, and red sails bobbing on the water make kaleidoscopic patterns on the deep-blue background of the ocean—hundreds of them—adrift as if in a romantic dreamy idyll.

To a visitor, Newport offers the perspective of an island, the excitement of a port, and world-class events—a wonderful blend of contemporary and past delights. The town represents two great eras of American history. Downtown reflects the original, boisterous 17th-century mercantile community, and the mansions on Bellevue Avenue show the extravagance and outrageous fantasy and spectacle of the Gilded Age. It's a wonderful place to be.

In summer, it swarms with life. The wharves are filled with sleek yachts and millions of dollars worth of powerboats, clinking and rocking in the harbor, their bronzed captains and crews crowding into harborside restaurants, bars, and stores, eyeing and vetting each other as they go. Behind the harbor, the stately 18th-century clapboard houses, painted muted grays and sage greens, line the narrow streets and add character and grace to the scene. Their shades must wonder at the parade of chic that now inhabits their lusty old port. Up

Newport

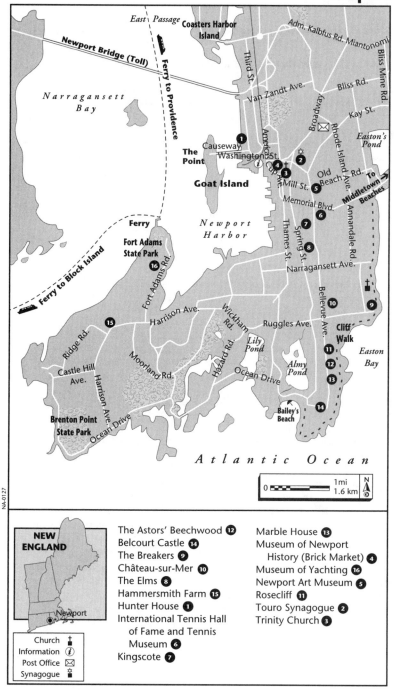

The Astors' Beechwood **12**
Belcourt Castle **14**
The Breakers **9**
Château-sur-Mer **10**
The Elms **8**
Hammersmith Farm **15**
Hunter House **1**
International Tennis Hall
   of Fame and Tennis
   Museum **6**
Kingscote **7**

Marble House **13**
Museum of Newport
   History (Brick Market) **4**
Museum of Yachting **16**
Newport Art Museum **5**
Rosecliff **11**
Touro Synagogue **2**
Trinity Church **3**

Church ✝
Information ⓘ
Post Office ⊠
Synagogue ⛎

NEW
ENGLAND

Newport

Events to Plan Your Trip Around

July: **Newport Music Festival.** Two weeks of chamber music concerts are held among the opulent mansions. Contact the Newport Music Festival, Box 3300, Newport RI 02840 (☎ 401/846-1133).

The **Miller Hall of Fame Tennis Championships.** For tickets and information, contact the Tennis Hall of Fame (☎ 401/849-3990).

Virginia Slims Tennis Tournament on grass courts at Newport Casino, Tennis Hall of Fame.

August: The **JVC Jazz Festival and Ben & Jerry Folk Festival** in Fort Adams State Park. For information call ☎ 401/847-3700.

The **Wooden Boat Show.** A Victorian-style boat show. Call the **Newport County Convention & Visitor's Bureau** (☎ 800/976-5122) for information.

September: The **Outdoor Art Festival** (usually early September) makes a colorful splash on Bowen's Wharf.

December: **Christmas in Newport** with wassail parties, Bach and Handel in the churches, and climaxed by a reading of "The Night before Christmas" and a bonfire in Washington Square.

on the hill, the mansions stand empty, except for busloads of visitors who come to stare at the gilt, the marble, and the lavish rooms where great balls once were held. In these opulent, gilded surroundings, the 400 members of fashionable society once cavorted—daughters were pledged to dukes, insults were hurled, even the dogs sat down to dinners of stewed liver, rice, and fricassee of bones.

In the beginning, Newport was first and foremost a colonial town, a mecca for ambitious 17th-century merchants, who risked their money, chances, and sometimes their lives, by engaging in the Triangular Trade between Africa, Europe, and the Caribbean, carrying slaves, molasses, rum, and sugar; defying the British; and taking advantage of European wars to increase their share of world trade. Newport's early merchants were fiercely independent souls, who had fled the narrow-mindedness of Massachusetts, and their ranks included dissidents of every sort—Methodists, Quakers, Jews, and all manner of those who chafed under the restrictions of British rule. The people of Newport were the first to declare their independence, an act that brought a contingent of Redcoats into their city and led to its occupation and the wanton destruction of 300 buildings during the Revolution. When the French arrived in July 1780, they found a beleaguered town that continued to languish for many years thereafter.

Newport's life and reputation as a resort began in the mid-1800s, when many southern planters discovered its pleasant climate and sought refuge from malaria and the oppressive southern heat. They spent their summers here in pleasant cottages like Kingscote. Julia Ward Howe's literary set and the moneyed folk from New York and Philadelphia soon followed. The latter built "cottages" on a palatial scale, imitating the aristocracy of Europe, and vying with each other in their extravagance and display. William K. Vanderbilt spent $11 million on the Marble House, a residence that he used only 2 months of the year. Society flocked to Newport, and days were spent languidly among luxurious surroundings.

Breakfasts were followed by tennis or riding. Lunches were taken aboard yachts. Lavish dinners and balls followed afternoons of polo. The "cottages" that the rich used for the season have been preserved and now stand as witnesses to this era of incredible wealth, ostentation, fantasy, and spectacle.

Society also brought to the island the two sports that are synonymous with Newport to this day—yachting and tennis. The America's Cup Challenge was moved from New York to Newport in 1930, and the cup remained here until 1983, when it was carried off by the Australians only to be returned triumphantly to the United States in 1987. The U.S. National Tennis Championships were held at the Newport Casino from 1881 until they moved to Forest Hills, New York, and if you like, you can play on those hallowed grass courts.

Mansions; extravagant hostesses; melodramatic scenes; and colonial tales of free-booting merchants and pirates, ships and yachts, elegant pastimes—Newport has it all—chic, beauty, history, romance, the ocean, and the nerve to remain a prestigious East Coast resort, a role bestowed on it by many generations.

THE GREAT MANSIONS

Plan to see only two or three mansions in a day. Tours last 1 hour, and you'll soon be exhausted and surfeited. On weekends, you'll want to get there early, because the crowds and busloads of people can be horrendous. I would see Kingscote (1839), an example of the earlier cottages that preceded the Gilded Age, and the Château-sur-Mer (1852), both of which have an added charm because they still seem lived in. The more extravagant era of the 1890s can be captured at The Breakers, Marble House, The Elms, or Rosecliff.

Kingscote (1839), Bellevue Avenue, was built by Richard Upjohn for George Noble Jones of Savannah, Georgia, and later was acquired by William Henry King, a China trader, after whom it is named. The house is furnished with fine oriental export pieces. Most dramatic is the dining room, designed by Stanford White and added in 1881. Light shimmers over the opalescent Tiffany brick tiles that surround the Siena marble fireplace at one end of the room, while an intricate spindle-work screen encloses the other. The paneling is mahogany, while the ceilings and upper walls are of cork. The tour is intimate and interesting.

Château-sur-Mer, Bellevue Avenue, was originally built in 1852 and transformed by Richard Morris Hunt into a grand chateau 20 years later. Owner William Shepard Wetmore, another China trader, entertained lavishly. At one of these affairs, held for George Peabody of London in 1857 and attended by 3,000 guests from both sides of the Atlantic, Wetmore served woodcocks, plovers, and snipes among the entrees, and confections that were molded in the shapes of Washington and Lafayette. To some the house may appear austere and somber, with its granite exterior; extensive use of Eastlake ash paneling in the entrance hall, staircase, and morning room; and heavy butternut furnishings in the bedrooms. Note the extravagantly carved Italianate overmantel in the dining room depicting Bacchus.

The Breakers (1895), Ochre Point Avenue, was built for Cornelius Vanderbilt II and is the most lavish and Italianate of the cottages. It contains 70 rooms, 33 being used for the 40-strong army of servants. The most striking attributes are the beautiful multicolored (rose to gray-green) marbles used throughout; the arched double loggia with mosaic ceilings, which provides dramatic ocean vistas; the music room, which was constructed in Europe and shipped here for reassembly; faucets that deliver salt and fresh water in the bathrooms; a two-story kitchen, sealed off so that none of the odors escaped; and a billiard room of gray-green marble, yellow alabaster, and mahogany. The house was used only 2 months of the year.

Rosecliff (1902), Bellevue Avenue, was the chosen setting for scenes in the films *The Great Gatsby* and *The Betsy*, and certainly it does have a romantic aura with its heart-shaped staircase, well-tended rose garden, and fountains. Theresa Fair Oelrichs, daughter of James Graham Fair, who struck the Comstock Lode, was one of the three top hostesses of Newport. She was a stickler for perfect cleanliness and was even known to scrub the floor herself if it did not meet her standards. Designed by McKim, Mead, and White after the Grand Trianon, Rosecliff contains the largest ballroom in Newport, where Tessie staged such extravagant balls as the White Ball, at which all the flowers and decorations were white, the guests were also all in white, while outside on the ocean floated several white-sailed ships, just to complete the effect.

Marble House (1892), Bellevue Avenue, was where Alva Belmont held court when she was the wife of William K. Vanderbilt. A dashing woman, she was the first of her set to cycle in bloomers, to own a car of her own, to cut her hair at the shoulders, and to divorce (she married O. H. P. Belmont). The $11-million cottage was modeled after the Petit Trianon by Richard Morris Hunt and contains the most ornate gilt-encrusted ballroom you'll ever see, where daughter Consuelo debuted and became engaged to the ninth Duke of Marlborough in 1895. The dining room is furnished with bronze chairs that weighed so much they required a servant's help whenever a guest wanted to sit or rise. The Chinese Teahouse was added in 1913 by Alva, who also had a tiny railroad constructed to ferry the footmen bearing tea from the main house. Later, she was one of the first to open the house to the public to raise funds for the suffragettes.

The Elms (1901), Bellevue Avenue, was built for coal magnate Edward J. Berwind by a relatively unknown Philadelphia architect, Horace Trumbauer, who adapted the design of the Chateau d'Asnieres, near Paris, creating a low-key classically symmetrical mansion. The grounds, dotted with bronze statuary, gazebos, and fountains and planted with an amazing variety of trees, shrubs, and colorful sunken gardens, are the most remarkable aspect of the house.

Open: In summer, May to October 31, all mansions are open daily from 10am to 5pm and sometimes later in the evenings. In winter you do best to check ahead. Usually only Marble House, The Elms, and Château-sur-Mer are open and only on weekends from 10am to 4pm. The Elms, Chateau-sur-Mer, and the Breakers are decorated for the holiday season. In April, The Breakers,

Marble House, and Rosecliff are open daily from 10am to 5pm; the others, on weekends only. For information, contact the **Preservation Society of Newport County,** 424 Bellevue Ave., Newport, RI 02840 (☎ 401/847-1000).

Admissions: Your best bet is to purchase a strip ticket good for two ($14 for adults; $5.50 for children 6 to 11), three ($19 and $7.50), four ($24 and $9.50), five ($27 and $10.50), six ($30 and $11), seven ($33 and $13) or eight ($35.50 and $14) mansions.

Hunter House, a colonial house (1748), and **Green Animals,** a topiary garden with 80 sculptured trees in Portsmouth are included in this combination ticket. Individual admissions range from $8 at seven of the mansions to $10 at The Breakers (plus $3.50 for the Breakers stable).

MORE MANSIONS

Besides the mansions maintained by the Preservation Society, several others are also open to the public.

Belcourt Castle, Bellevue Avenue (☎ 401/846-0669), was built for Oliver H. P. Belmont and Alva, former wife of William K. Vanderbilt. It was designed in 1891 by Richard Morris Hunt in the style of Louis XIII's palace at Versailles. The most dramatic displays here are the 23-karat-gold coronation coach, the armor collection, and the stained-glass windows in the grand Gothic hall. Costumed guides lead the way through the house, and ghost tours are given on Wednesday and Thursday in season. It's open Memorial Day to mid-October, daily from 9am to 5pm; February to March, weekends and holidays from 10am to 4pm; April to May, daily 10am to 5pm; November to January, weekends and by appointment. Closed Thanksgiving, Christmas. Admission is $7.50 for adults, $4 for children 6 to 12.

Beechwood (1855), Bellevue Avenue (☎ 401/846-3772), was the home of William B. Astor where the doyenne of Newport society, Mrs. William Backhouse Astor, the former Caroline Schermerhorn, held court. With the help of a southern gentleman, Ward McAllister, she devised the famous Four Hundred, a list of 213 families and individuals whose lineage could be traced back at least three generations. It was also the number of guests who could comfortably fit into the ballroom of her New York residence. So resplendent were her gowns and jewels that Mr. McAllister once remarked that she resembled a spectacular chandelier. Here at Beechwood, you'll find no roped-off rooms or historic lectures, but a re-creation of the lifestyle that the Astors brought to Newport in the 1890s, reenacted every day by the Beechwood Theater Company. Open mid-May through November, daily from 10am to 5pm, Friday to Sunday from 10am to 4pm, except during Christmas when hours vary. Closed January. Admission $8.75 for adults, $6.75 for children 6 to 13.

Hammersmith Farm, Ocean Drive (☎ 401/846-7346), was the summer cottage of John W. Auchincloss and family, where the daughter of Mrs. Hugh Auchincloss, Jacqueline Bouvier, and John F. Kennedy held their wedding feast. It's a beautiful seaside retreat, and the tour tells charming details of the time spent here by the Kennedy family. The gardens are also worth exploring. Open April to mid-November, daily from 10am to 5pm. Admission is $8 for adults, $3 for children 6 to 12. *Note*: At press time, Hammersmith farm is up for sale, so you should call first to see if it's still open to the public.

COLONIAL-ERA ATTRACTIONS

Walking tours of Historic Newport are offered by the Historical Society (☎ 401/846-0813) on Thursday, Friday, and Saturday at 10am and 3pm, mid-May through October, at a cost of $7. They leave from the Museum of Newport History at Touro and Thames streets. Cliff Walk tours are also offered.

Downtown, **Washington Square** is the center of colonial Newport. At the west end is the **Brick Market** (1762), which is now occupied by the **Museum of Newport History** (☎ 401/ 841-8770). At the other end is the **Old Colony House,** dating from 1739, which was used by the Rhode Island General Assembly until 1900. From the balcony here, Rhode Island issued its own Declaration of Independence on May 4, 1776. This act of defiance brought the wrath of the British Redcoats down on the city; when they occupied it during the Revolution they left it in ruins. Today you can only view the building's exterior. The interior is closed while work is done to bring it up to the fire code. The museum, which tells the city's story, is open year-round—April to December, Monday and Wednesday to Saturday from 10am to 5pm, Sunday from 1 to 5pm; in winter, Friday and Saturday from 10am to 5pm and Sunday from 1 to 4pm. Admission is $5 for adults, $4 for seniors, $3 for children 6 to 16.

An independent town founded by dissidents from Massachusetts in 1639, Newport attracted a great number of diverse religious groups and their houses of worship can still be seen. Most famous is probably the **Touro Synagogue,** 72 Touro St. (☎ 401/847-4794), built in 1759 (although the first member of the community arrived in the 1650s). Open July 4 to Labor Day, Sunday to Friday from 10am to 4pm; Memorial Day to July 4 and Labor Day to Columbus Day, Sunday from 11am to 3pm and Monday to Friday from 1 to 3pm; in winter, Sunday from 1 to 3pm, and by appointment Monday to Friday at 2pm.

A little way down Broadway from the synagogue stands the oldest house in Newport, the **Wyman Wanton-Lyman-Hazard House** (☎ 401/846-0813), which was built in the 1690s and is authentically furnished for the period. It also has an interesting colonial garden. Open June 1 to Labor Day, Friday to Sunday noon to 5pm. Admission is $3 for adults.

Back on Touro Street at no. 82, the **Newport Historical Society** (☎ 401/ 846-0813) has changing exhibits of furniture, colonial silver, toys, dolls, and other decorative arts. The **Seventh Day Baptist Meeting House** (1729) is also part of the museum. Open in summer, Wednesday to Saturday from 9:30am to 4:30pm (until noon only on Saturdays). Admission is free.

A few blocks away, in Queen Anne Square, you can see the spire of the 1726 **Trinity Church** (☎ 401/846-0660), inspired by the work of Christopher Wren and also by the Old Boston Church. The bells ring quite beautiful changes. Open May to June, Monday to Friday from 10am to 1pm; June to October, daily from 10am to 1pm; after the second service on Sunday only in winter.

From here, the whole area between Spring Street and Bellevue Avenue, Touro Street, and Mill Street is known as **Historic Hill,** and it's well worth wandering around to view the old clapboard buildings of this once-thriving seaport community.

The other historic area, **The Point,** is down along Washington Street on the harbor front, where the **Hunter House** is located at 54 Washington St. (☎ 401/847-1000). This Tory residence survived the occupation by the British, served as the headquarters for Admiral de Ternay when the French naval forces arrived in July 1780, and is worth visiting today to see the Townsend Goddard furniture and the floor-to-ceiling pine paneling. Open April, Saturday and Sunday from 10am to 5pm; May to October, daily from 10am to 5pm. Admission is $8 for adults, $3.50 for children 6 to 11.

OTHER NEWPORT ATTRACTIONS

Two absolute musts after (or even before the mansions): Drive or cycle **Ocean Drive,** stopping for a picnic at Brenton Point State Park; and walk along the back of the mansions on the 3-mile **Cliff Walk** (which stubbornly remains a public thoroughfare) to see the rocky coastline to full advantage. Downtown, you'll want to explore the many dining, shopping, yachting, and people attractions at harborside complexes such as **Bowen's** and **Bannister's Wharves.**

The **International Hall of Tennis Fame,** located in the Newport Casino at 194 Bellevue Ave. (☎ 401/846-4567), exhibits trophies, art, videos, and memorabilia. The casino building, designed by Stanford White, was commissioned by James Gordon Bennett Jr., publisher of the *New York Herald,* after a good friend of his was thrown out of the Bellevue Men's Club for riding a horse through the building. The casino with its horseshoe piazza, turreted porches, and breezy verandas instantly became the place to be seen and became the focal point of society, where people played croquet, court tennis, cards, and billiards and attended many special events. The United States Tennis Championships were played on the casino courts from 1881 until they moved to Forest Hills. Open daily from 9:30am to 5pm; admission $8 for adults, $6 for seniors, $4 for children 6 to 18.

Newport Art Museum, 76 Bellevue Ave. (☎ 401/848-8200), puts on a variety of exhibits by artists associated with Newport. The shows range from the works of artists who painted in and around Newport in the 19th century to avant-garde virtual reality pieces and photographs. The exhibits are staged in the Griswold House (1862), which was designed by Richard Morris Hunt, and in the Cushing Gallery. Open in summer, Monday, Tuesday, and Thursday to Saturday from 10am to 5pm, Sunday from noon to 5pm; in winter it closes at 4pm. Admission is $4 for adults, $3 for seniors, free for children 5 and under.

Sailing enthusiasts will want to visit the **Museum of Yachting** in Fort Adams State Park on Ocean Drive (☎ 401/847-1018), which offers a gallery of small craft, an exhibit about the history of yachting in Newport and the Americas Cup, and a slide show of 12-meter craft. Open May to October, daily from 10am to 5pm. Admission is $3 for adults, $2.50 for seniors, $1 for children.

Military buffs will want to visit the **Naval War College Museum,** Coasters Harbor Island (☎ 401/841-4052), which traces the history of naval warfare and the history of the naval presence in the Narragansett Bay region. Open year-round Monday to Friday from 10am to 4pm. June to September also open Saturday and Sunday from noon to 4pm. Closed holidays. Admission is free.

NEWPORT LODGING

Castle Hill Inn & Resort, Ocean Drive, Newport, RI 02840 (☎ 401/ 849-3800), has to be the most picturesque Newport accommodation, with a commanding view of Narragansett Bay, Newport Harbor, and the ocean. It's a prime vantage point from which to watch the sailing and fishing craft in the bay. In summer you can dine outside on the terrace, at the top of the grassy bluff that sweeps down to the water, or you can opt for the dining rooms where the fresh, innovative American cuisine will surprise and please everyone's palate. You won't forget an appetizer like the pan-seared foie gras served atop triangles of French toast with bourbon-flavored peach ginger jam or the Grand Marnier marinated oysters pan fried in a cornmeal crust. Main dishes run from the traditional and wonderful soft shell crabs or lobster Thermidor to chicken with a rich bourbon gravy or grilled sirloin and Cajun andouille sausage served with mashed Yukon golds flavored with blue cheese. Prices range from $18 to $28. Brunch dishes are just as thrilling—ranging from poached eggs and hash made with sausage, onion, and sweet pepper to a crispy salmon paillard served with whipped sweet potatoes.

The inn was built in 1874 by Alexander Agassiz, son of naturalist Louis Agassiz, and many an illustrious person has stayed here. The accommodation in the turret was inspirational for Thornton Wilder, who wrote that he could "see the beacons of six lighthouses and hear the booming and chiming of as many buoys." The 10 rooms are all different in size and shape. Some have exquisite paneling, some are oddly shaped, with dormer windows. Some, like Rooms 1 and 2, are undistinguished. Room 4, though, is beautifully paneled and sports a bold floral-and-bird-patterned wallpaper. Room 8 is tucked under the eaves, with wicker furniture. Harbor House rooms have such extras as whirlpool tubs, fireplaces, and French doors leading to a semiprivate deck with great views of the bay. There are also some rustic unheated efficiencies available for weekly rental. Rates: mid-June to mid-September, weekends $260, midweek $235; May to mid-June and mid-September to mid-November, weekends $260, midweek $175; mid-November to early May $175 to $205 weekends and $135 to $145 midweek. The efficiencies rent for $900 to $1,100 a week. Dining hours: Friday to Saturday and Monday noon to 3:30pm; Wednesday, Friday, Saturday 6 to 10pm; Sunday 11:30am to 3:30pm.

Sanford-Covell Villa Marina, 72 Washington St., Newport, RI 02840 (☎ 401/847-0206), is a spectacular place with a marvelous view of the harbor. The house, which was built for Milton Sanford, a New York City industrialist, was completed in 1870, before the Newport mansions were built. It was designed by William Emerson, cousin of Ralph. Step inside, and you'll be transported to an earlier more elegant era. In the soaring foyer, which retains the original gas lamps, stands a peacock, a bust of Sanford, and a grandfather clock among other period furnishings. The walls are brilliantly painted and decorated with "pouncing," a technique that pounds the paint into the walls creating a blistered but brilliant effect. There are only four guest rooms. My favorite is the Kate Field Room on the third floor. It has a window seat and a deck overlooking the water, a fine selection of books in the built-in bookcases, rocking chair, and a nonworking fireplace. Dolls, a blackboard, and the oak slat paneling add more charm. The room shares a bathroom that has a claw-foot tub, pull-chain toilet, and two marble sinks. The Cuvalier Room faces the

Newport Bridge and has plenty of character, too, thanks to the coffered ceiling, old books, ship's model on the mantel, tiny parasol, and an authentic Windsor chair. The Play Room is remarkable for its little balcony that extends out over the central lobby, its stained glass window, and its contents, which include many antique toys and the diaries of William King Covell from 1919 to 1972. The most spectacular is the Covell Room, which has a working fireplace, French-style furniture, and a large sitting room filled with antiques, oriental carpeting, books, and TV. Throughout the house there are fine decorative objects, including many clocks and dolls, to admire. A continental breakfast is served in the handsome dining room with a converted oil chandelier. The parlor features two baby grands, two fireplaces, and plenty of comfortable seating. Complimentary sherry is served in the evening. In summer the most glorious feature of the house is the broad porch furnished with wicker and below it the heated saltwater pool. Beyond stretches the entrance to Newport Harbor. A magnificent nostalgic retreat. Rates: Summer, $135 to $235; winter, $85 to $160.

The Ivy Lodge, 12 Clay St., Newport, RI 02840 (☎ 401/849-6865), is a gorgeous place to stay. Architecturally, the shingled house is extraordinary with its gables and chimneys and curving veranda. Step inside the front door, and an impressive entrance/hallway rises in front of you. The woodwork is glorious. An oak staircase zigzags its way to the third-floor landing directing your eye to the stained glass ceiling that glows above. There are seven rooms, all with private bath. Each is handsomely decorated with brass beds, wing chairs, wicker, and some painted pieces. Room 1 has a spectacular high-back Victorian bed. The Turret Room is among the most charming with its coral-colored sitting area with boudoir-style chairs and a bathroom with pull-chain toilet. Another favorite is the Under the Staircase Room, which boasts a mahogany sleigh bed, a fireplace with the original Delft tiles, a large bay window, and a double Jacuzzi in the bathroom. The public areas are lavishly decorated. A breakfast buffet is served at the long table that seats 14 in a paneled room with floor to ceiling windows lit by a striking silk floral chandelier. There's a small sitting area off the lobby and a larger sitting room furnished with a baby grand, comfortable sofas, and chairs arranged around the central fireplace. My favorite spot in summer is the swing seat on the wide porch, overlooking the colorful gardens complete with fountain. Rates: April 1 to October 31, $145 to $185, November 1 to March 31, $100 to $140.

Cliffside Inn, 2 Seaview Ave., Newport, RI 02840 (☎ 401/847-1811), would be my other choice for a Newport accommodation, even though it's located out toward Middletown. The lovely Victorian residence was built in 1880 by a governor of Maryland and later occupied by the family of artist Beatrice Pastorius Turner. The 15 rooms (12 with fireplace and double whirlpools) have all been personally and authentically furnished with great flair. In your room you might find a large four-poster spread with eyelet linens and pillow cases or a cannonball bed dressed with a floral design comforter. The Governor's Suite offers lavish comforts—king-size four-poster, two-sided fireplace, whirlpool bath, antique Victorian birdcage shower, and double pedestal sink. Miss Beatrice's Room features a Lincoln bed, Eastlake chairs, and marble-top tables as well as a black marble fireplace and an appealing window seat in the bay window. The bathroom contains whirlpool bath and double-headed shower. Several third-floor rooms have skylights. The bi-level Garden Suite has two fireplaces, double whirlpool bath, and a private patio. All rooms have air-conditioning and a TV; some have a VCR.

The day begins with coffee and juice delivered to your room and ends with turndown accompanied by a homemade pastry. A full breakfast is served in a comfortable parlor crammed with Victorian couches, love seats, and objets d'art. The innkeepers employ a pastry chef who prepares the splendid afternoon tea that has been ranked up there with the Ritz's. The porch is a favorite gathering place, arrayed with turquoise wicker chairs on canvas-painted flooring. Rates: $195 to $295 rooms; $295 to $360 suites.

Elm Tree Cottage, 336 Gibbs Ave., Newport, RI 02840 (☎ 401/849-1610), is a lovely romantic accommodation located away from the waterfront. What makes the bed-and-breakfast special are the innkeepers, Priscilla and Tom Malone, who have decorated their 1882 home with flair and style and who welcome their guests with warmth. The house is situated on an acre of landscaped property 2 blocks from the beach. Each of the six rooms—all with private bath—have been individually decorated in a rich tapestry of fabrics and wallpapers. The Windsor Suite is the largest and most elaborate. It contains a carved French Louis XV bed with a partial crown canopy, a fireplace with a gilt mirror above and a ceramic French clock on the mantel, a sofa and a French side chair. The bathroom is spectacular, too, with its vanity dressing table with fabric skirting and the sink that stands on gleaming crystal legs. The Harriman Room is more masculine with striped wallpaper with heraldic borders, paisley purple quilt, and hunting prints. The bathroom is mirrored and there's even a cushion in the deep tub. The former owner of the house was the heiress to a Pennsylvania railroad fortune, and the bar that she installed is still here, studded with hundreds of 1921 silver dollars, as well as the stained-glass porthole windows and the crest that she designed symbolizing the Pekinese, which she regarded as the result of crossing a lion and a monkey! Other public spaces are comfortably and lavishly furnished. The sun room is filled with wicker. The living room with grand and upright piano offers a variety of seating—camelback sofas and wing backs—and is accented with putti and a mirror that was rescued from a mansion. In winter there's a view of First Beach from the property. A full breakfast (pear stuffed crepes, orange waffles) is served in the elegant dining room. Afternoon hors d'oeuvres and iced tea or hot chocolate are served. The pergola and the statuary add panache to the gardens, too. Rates: $145 to $220, $235 to $360 suite.

The **Francis Malbone House**, 392 Thames St., Newport, RI 02840 (☎ 401/846-0392), is right downtown on the waterfront, but it manages to retain a quiet air thanks to a serene landscaped garden in the back where Adirondack chairs are set under the trees and on the flagstone patio. The house itself is supremely stylish with dentil moldings, wainscoting, and glorious scallop-shell corner cupboards. It was built in 1760 for shipping merchant Francis Malbone and designed by the architect responsible for both Touro Synagogue and the Redwood Library. The nine rooms are decorated in colonial colors like Wedgwood blue or slate gray and elegantly furnished with colonial reproductions—rice four-posters, oriental rugs, highboys, pier mirrors, and Martha Washingtons in front of the fireplace. Seven have working fireplaces. The curtains are swagged, and in some rooms there are inviting window seats under the casement windows. The Counting House Suite behind the main house offers a bedroom, living room, and dining room plus a Jacuzzi in the bathroom. The staff is extremely helpful and friendly. There are two parlors for guests to use plus a library that has TV and some good books to read. The sumptuous breakfasts—peach granola pancakes or Belgian waffles, for example—are graciously served in a colonial-style formal dining room at a lace-covered table lit by candlelight. A great place to stay. Rates: May 1 to October 31, $185 to $265; $305 to $365 suite; November 1 to April 30, $155 to $205; $235 to $285 suite.

One of the friendliest and most attractive places to stay—and also very conveniently located—is the **Admiral Benbow Inn,** 93 Pelham St., Newport, RI 02840 (☎ 401/846-4256), built in 1855. The vibrant innkeeper, Maggie, has a wonderful way of tending to guests and a genuine enthusiasm for what she's doing.

The 15 rooms in this handsome Victorian home, all with private bath, are large and comfortable. For example, the room I stayed in contains brass twin beds, dresser, wing chair, and couch. Curtains at the Palladian-style bay windows are cinched back; an old-fashioned gas lamp and chandelier provides light. Above the fireplace hang oriental prints, all reminiscent of an earlier era. Other rooms are furnished variously with fish-net canopy beds, satin eiders, and a mixture of antiques and reproductions. Room 2 has a kitchenette and Room 12 has its very own large deck for sunning with a view of the harbor. The room itself is small, but furnished with oak dresser, brass bed, side table, and Mission rocker, it's comfortable enough. Room 9 has a handsome hooped canopy. Some rooms have air-conditioning—ask.

Breakfast is served in the basement, decked out with colorful kites that serve as wall hangings. Muffins, cinnamon-raisin toast, cereals, and fresh fruit are spread out for you to help yourself. Guests gather here in the evenings if they want to watch TV or warm themselves in front of the woodstove. A collection of old barometers is on display and also for purchase. Rates: May 1 to October 31, $120 to $235; November 1 to April 30, $80 to $155.

At the **Brinley Victorian,** 23 Brinley St., Newport, RI 02840 (☎ 401/849-7645), there are 17 rooms, 13 with private bath. It's a large, rambling place occupying two houses (joined by a breezeway) situated a little distance from the immediate downtown area. It possesses much character, and each room is carefully and personally furnished with those extra touches, like fresh flowers and magazines. On the ground floor, Room 5 has a stucco fireplace, plus a double-poster bed set with Laura Ashley pillows and coverlets. In Room 4, a cherry bed is matched with a handsome Madame Recamier sofa against a beige chintz wallpaper. My favorite is Room 17, featuring a high oak bed, Eastlake chairs, and a brick colonial fireplace. Room 12 sports striped floral pink-and-brown wallpaper, oak furnishings, and two brass beds. The iron bed in Room 13 is covered with a pink lace-trimmed coverlet. The second house also has a comfortable parlor furnished with books and marble fireplace. Room 6 has a large double bed set in the bay window and a single; other furnishings include a wicker sofa, kneehole dresser, and armoire. Third-floor rooms with knee walls are smaller and attractively furnished with oak and wicker. There's a fridge on each floor for guests' use.

A breakfast of fresh-baked goods is served in the Victorian-style parlor furnished with a love seat and an Empire-style sofa set in front of the fireplace. Windows are covered with cream swag drapes. In summer breakfast is served in the brick courtyard. There's also an information/library area where guests can peruse books and menus of local restaurants or enjoy an assortment of games. Both houses have porches with swings and wicker furnishings. Rates: May 1 to October 31, $115 to $160 double with private bath, $100 to $125 with shared bath; November to April, $95 and $79, respectively.

Melville House, 39 Clarke St., Newport, RI 02840 (☎ 401/847-0640), is a charming 1750s shingled home, located on one of the quieter downtown historic area's streets. It's run by two enthusiastic innkeepers, Vincent DeRico and David Horan. In the country parlor, you'll find comfortable wing chairs and rockers set in front of an old pine fireplace, home to a basket of cones and gleaming copper tea kettles. Breakfast—buttermilk biscuits, Rhode Island johnnycakes, stuffed French toast, and so on—is served at polished wood tables in a sunny room adjacent to the parlor. There are seven rooms (five with private bath). Flowers and fruit are placed in every room, and each is nicely decorated in a colonial style. Ceilings are low, and all of the rooms have character. In the winter a romantic fireplace suite is available, and guests who stay in this room are welcomed with champagne and served breakfast in bed. Games and books are available in the corridor leading to the rooms. Afternoon tea is served (hot soup on cold days), and complimentary sherry is available when guests gather to chat in the evenings. An hospitable, warm, and friendly place. Rates: May 1 to October 31, $120 to $155; November to April $95 to $135; fireplace suite $185.

The **Inntowne,** at Mary and Thames streets, Newport, RI 02840 (☎ 401/846-9200), very conveniently located in the historic section, takes a contemporary approach to the interior of its two colonial-style buildings. The place is very nicely kept. There are 24 rooms, all with air-conditioning and phones, and all clean as a whistle and prettily decorated, often with matching floral prints on walls and curtains. By far the most interesting accommodations to me are in the Mary Street house—the Rathskeller, in particular—so named because of the rounded pine door frames and doors, brick, and tile. It has a mirrored bedroom, a cozy sitting room with a couch and armchairs, and a full kitchen. It costs $250 in season. Other rooms in this house are also very attractively furnished with antique reproductions, and often with coordinated wallpaper and bedspreads. An expanded continental breakfast of fresh-squeezed juice, quiche and ham, baked muffins, rolls, and beverage is served in the pretty dining room with polished wood table and ladder-back chairs. Afternoon tea is also served. Rates: $105 to $195 double.

Wayside, Bellevue Avenue, Newport, RI 02840 (☎ 401/847-0302), was built by Elisha Dyer, one of the "400" and cotillion dance master for the Astors and Vanderbilts. It's certainly imposing and lavish. In the entrance hall, a large molded stucco fireplace is carved with cherubs and a coat of arms that includes the fleur-de-lis. A staircase of quarter-cut oak leads to the huge rooms. In fact, some of the rooms are so large that they seem a trifle bare. Each has a small TV. Room 1 has a double canopy bed along with a single bed, both covered with candlewick spreads. A wicker chaise lounge, wicker table, and drawers are among the furnishings in this room hung with blue-rose wallpaper. Broken-scroll-decorated doors lead into the ground-floor room that was formerly the library. Even though there's an oriental-style bed, couch, love seat, armchair, and oriental chest, there's still masses of space. This room, decorated in bold blue floral wallpaper, also contains a handsome carved stucco fireplace. Coffee and pastries are put out in the morning for guests to help themselves. Facilities include an in-ground pool. For what you get, rates are reasonable. Rates: May 1 to October 31, $150 to $160 double; off-season $95 to $115 double.

Admiral Farragut Inn, 31 Clarke St., Newport, RI 02840 (☎ 401/846-4256), is located in an authentic colonial but it has been decorated in a fresh and entertaining way that is clear from the minute you enter the hallway, which boasts a large mural depicting a heron. There are 10 rooms, all with private bath and telephone. The rooms are charmingly decorated. For example, the atmospheric low-ceilinged Admiral's Quarters contains a Shaker four-poster, fireplace made of Dutch tiles, and walls that are sponge painted to resemble pale green marble. The bathroom has a lovely ceramic tile sink with decorative floral motif. In other rooms you might find oak or pine furnishings and wing chairs and other nice pieces. The Ensigns Quarters on the third floor has a skylight, wooden beams, enchanting sloping ceiling, and small fireplace. The Marquis Quarters holds one of the inn's most beguiling pieces: a gray and red folk art chair depicting two cats. A continental breakfast is served in the dining room at a long harvest table. Rates: May 1 to October 31, $95 to $185; November 1 to April 30, $75 to $135.

Admiral Fitzroy Inn, 398 Thames St., Newport, RI 02840 (☎ 401/846-4256 [same as the Farragut]), is in the heart of the waterfront district. The inn that occupies this redbrick building, dating to 1890, is named after the admiral who developed the barometer, and several modern versions decorate the front hallway and are for sale. There are 18 rooms, all with private bath, cable TV, refrigerator, coffeemaker, and hair dryer. You'll likely find a sleigh or iron and brass bed combined with various furnishings and color schemes. In Room 1, for example, the walls are painted moss-gray-green, and a large Eastlake dresser dating to 1853 is among the furnishings. Room 9 is particularly airy and bright, and roses and orchids are hand painted on the walls. In Room 10 the walls are adorned with a marvelous apricot tree. Rooms on the top floor have skylights and views of the harbor from their private decks. A continental breakfast is served in the basement breakfast room. There's also a sitting room in the basement with TV and VCR. Rates: May 1 to October 31, $135 to $235; November 1 to April 30, $95 to $175.

Victorian Ladies Inn, 63 Memorial Blvd., Newport, RI 02840 (☎ 401/849-9960), occupies a large Victorian with steep dormer roof. There are nine rooms, all with private bath, air-conditioning, and TV. Some have a telephone. The nine rooms are attractively furnished with a variety of antiques—carved Victorian, Shaker canopy, or iron and brass beds combined with loveseats and Queen Anne chairs or oak pieces. Room moods are created by dramatic use of color—forest green in one combined with silver gray fabrics, burgundy and rose and jade in another. Guests have access to a comfortable sitting room with fireplace; a full breakfast is served in the dining room. Rates: $105 to $205. Closed January.

Hydrangea House, 16 Bellevue Ave., Newport, RI 02840 (☎ 401/846-4435), is a small attractive bed-and-breakfast occupying an 1876 house. It offers six rooms, all with private bath. Each is very attractively and tastefully furnished. The Rose Dutchess Room is gussied up with tasseled window treatments, candy-stripe wallpaper, and wall-to-wall rose carpeting. Joshua Reynolds prints from the 1790s adorn the walls. My favorite, even though it's the smallest, is La Petite Rouge with its lush plum-red walls and hand-painted Edwardian chest of drawers, fireplace, and French cartoons. The Hydrangea Suite is the most lavish with its fine paneling, plush fabrics, and oriental rugs plus a double whirlpool bath. There's a deck on the back of the house where breakfast (fresh-squeezed juice and home-baked breads, plus raspberry pancakes or seasoned scrambled eggs) is served in summer. Otherwise, it's served in the downstairs gallery, where you can enjoy a full breakfast and look at the collection of works by local artists. Afternoon tea is also served, as well as chocolate chip cookies at the end of the day. A sundeck on the third floor has barbecue facilities. Rates: May 1 to October 31, $110 to $175, suite $290; November to April $85 to $135, suite $205.

Stella Maris Inn, 91 Washington St., Newport, RI 02840 (☎ 401/ 849-2862), was given its name by the Sisters of Cluny who occupied it in the 1920 when it was a convent. This stone mansion, built in 1853, stands down in the Point. There are eight rooms, all with private bath. Several, like the Lady Gregory Room, have marble fireplaces. This room also contains a Victorian bed, marble-top side tables, and a camelback sofa among its furnishings. The bathroom has delightful porthole windows. Most rooms are large enough to have small sitting areas. The window seat in the J. M Synge Room, which is furnished with a wicker bedroom suite and two wing-backs, offers a fine view of the bay. There's a comfortable parlor with TV. In the dining room, in addition to the table and Chippendale chairs, there's a Yamaha baby grand piano. A continental breakfast is served here or out on the wide porch, which affords a peek of the harbor between the houses across the street. Rates: May 1 to October 31, weekends $135 to $205, weekdays $120 to $135; otherwise, $105 to $135 and $85 to $105.

Cliff Walk Manor, 82 Memorial Blvd., Newport, RI 02840 (☎ 401/ 847-1300), is located just outside of town (about a 10-minute walk) en route to Middletown, right on Eastons Beach. It was built in 1855, and the rooms are large and the ceilings lofty. It was originally owned by the Chanlers, relatives of the Astors. Many of the 22 rooms overlook the ocean. So does the terrace adjacent to the restaurant-bar. Rooms have wall-to-wall carpeting, marble-top dressers and side tables, rockers, and often Renaissance Revival–style beds with Marseilles coverlets. Some have Jacuzzis, and all are air-conditioned and have a TV. Rates: Weekends $165 to $310; midweek $150 to $285.

Pilgrim House Inn, 123 Spring St., Newport, RI 02840 (☎ 401/846-0040), a gray clapboard with a steep mansard located in Newport's historic area, functions as a simple bed-and-breakfast guesthouse. There are 11 rooms, 3 with shared bath. They are unpretentious and simply decorated with chintz wallpapers, ruffle-trimmed curtains, painted drawers, and occasional pieces of wicker. In each you'll find a plant. At breakfast, muffins, fruit, coffee, and juice are served either inside or on the roof-top deck, with a view of the harbor. The hosts, the Messerlians, are native Rhode Islanders and will help you plan your local sightseeing and activities. Rates: $75 to $165 double in season.

If you're looking for modern accommodations in the historic area, then the **Mill Street Inn,** 75 Mill St., Newport, RI 02840 (☎ 401/849-9500), may be for you. It's a converted redbrick mill in which 23 suites are available, including eight two-story "town houses," as they're called, featuring a downstairs sitting room and an upstairs bedroom with a sliding door that leads to a deck with a view across the rooftops to the harbor. Facilities include TV and telephone. Furnishings are strictly modern IKEA. The living room has a bar area and fridge, pullout sofa, TV, telephone, and track lighting. All rooms have air-conditioning. Guests have use of the large communal roof deck for sunning and relaxing. The one-level units have bar/fridge, pullout sofa, and other amenities. A continental breakfast is served at tables set with pretty pink tablecloths in a room with rough hewn-stone walls. Tea is also served in the afternoon. Rates: In summer, $165 to $265; off-season, $135 to $165.

The **Doubletree Islander Inn**, Goat Island, Newport, RI 02840 (☎ 401/849-2600), is reached by a causeway. There are incredible views of the harbor in all directions. Parking is available (which is extremely important in this town), and you're a 5-minute drive or 15-minute walk away from the center of town. The accommodations are spacious and modern. Double sinks are an added convenience. Phones and cable TV are standard facilities. There are two dining rooms, a lounge-entertainment room, an indoor pool and outdoor salt-water pool, and tennis courts. Rates: January to mid-April, $109 to $184; mid-April to mid-June, $169 to 259; mid-June to late September, $209 to $309; late September to mid-November, $179 to $269; mid-November to December, $119 to $174.

Harborside Inn, Christie's Landing, Newport, RI 02840 (☎ 401/846-6600), is a modern accommodation with 14 rooms right down in the center of the seaport action. The furniture is modern pine (workbench style). Suites have a skylit loft bedroom reached by a ship's ladder (in a water-view suite) or by a regular staircase (in land-side accommodations). Rooms are beamed, beds covered with Tattersall-style comforters, and amenities include telephones, TVs, air-conditioning, refrigerators, and full baths. Water-view rooms and suites have small decks. There's a breakfast and sitting-room area furnished with director's chairs overlooking the dock and harbor. Help yourself to continental-style items at breakfast and to hors d'oeuvres and tea in the afternoons (in winter only). Parking is available. Rates: July to mid-September, weekends $265 to $295, midweek $165 to $195; spring/fall, weekends $165 to $205, midweek $95 to $145; winter, weekends $75 to $115, midweek $65 to $95.

Covell House, 43 Farewell St., Newport, RI 02840 (☎ 401/847-8872), has five rooms, all with private baths in a beige clapboard colonial with a pretty front porch and attractive breakfast room and pleasant gardens, too. Rates: Summer, $120 to $140; off-season, $85 to $90.

The **Jenkins Guest House**, 206 S. Rhode Island Ave., Newport, RI 02840 (☎ 401/847-6801), is an authentic European-style guesthouse. In this house the Jenkins's raised their eight children, and today they open two homey rooms to guests. A continental breakfast is put out in the morning. Sally understands that some folks want their freedom and others want convivial conversation, and she respects your wishes. Guests tend to gather in the kitchen or on the back deck overlooking the garden for their morning coffee. It's a relaxed, casual place. Sally and Dave, who have lived all their lives in Newport, will regale you with tales of the town and its history and give you the rundown on what's going on. Rates: $75 double. Open in season only.

NEWPORT DINING

The **Black Pearl,** Bannister's Wharf (☎ 401/846-5264), is one of Newport's leading restaurants. The tavern is a cozy gathering place; the patio is great for a meal or drink and a sea breeze, and the intimate Commodore Room, decorated in dark forest green with brass accents and polished wood, is known for its classic French cuisine. Prices range from $18 to $25 for dishes such as paillard of chicken with lemon butter, sautéed duck with green-olive sauce, medallions of veal with morels and champagne sauce, filet mignon au poivre, and more. Among the desserts there might be cheesecake, homemade ice creams, and profiteroles. To start, lobster mousse and escargots are a fine choice. In the tavern, prices range from $9 to $20. The chowders are so good I've seen people ask for several large bowls in the tavern, where the menu also includes burgers, omelets, and daily specials like bluefish with lemon caper butter. Open daily from 11:30am to 3pm and 6 to 11pm (10pm in winter). Jackets are required in the dining room.

Away from the bustle of the wharves, another of my favorites is the **White Horse Tavern,** at Marlborough and Farewell streets (☎ 401/849-3600), an old 1673 tavern that has a series of dining rooms with romantic ambience. The food is superb and ranges from traditional European to contemporary American. For example, you may start with either the iced shellfish (littlenecks, oysters, and shrimp) or the sauté of wild mushrooms served in puff pastry with a Madeira and herb reduction. Follow with the sautéed lobster with a cream sauce; baked salmon with chive butter sauce; tournedos of beef served over a morel and porcini reduction; or rack of lamb served with a mint and lingonberry jus. Prices range from $23 to $33. Similar finely prepared dishes are offered at lunch and Sunday brunch. Open Wednesday to Monday from noon to 2:30pm, Sunday to Thursday from 6 to 9:30pm, Friday and Saturday from 6 to 10pm. Jackets are required in the evening.

The **Clarke Cook House,** Bannister's Wharf (☎ 401/849-2900), for my money, is one of Newport's finest dining places. Located in an old colonial building are two dining rooms: the formal room, delightfully colonial with solid posts and beams, plank floors, and tables set with brass candlesticks, where black-tied waiters provide attentive service; or the Candy Store Cafe, which is more like a tavern-bar despite the marble tables. Models of ship's hulls and wood-framed pictures of sailing ships are the major decoration.

At dinner, start with ravioli of lobster and wild mushrooms with morels, or gravlax on a crisp potato galette with crème fraiche and oscietra caviar. Follow with a selection from dishes such as tuna steak with sweet-and-sour sherry vinegar glaze, rack of lamb with minted tarragon glaze, or filet mignon with a balsamic port sauce. Prices run $24 to $30. Finish with crème caramel or Locke Ober's famous Indian pudding. The cafe menu offers lighter dishes—pastas, pizzas, and a variety of wood-grilled dishes—burgers, fish, and pork tenderloin with ancho chilies and plum chutney, priced from $7 to $18.

Brunch offers an interesting array of egg dishes, plus such dishes as nachos with salsa, guacamole, and cheese; grilled shrimp and Cajun sausage en brochette; angel-hair pasta Bolognese; codfish cakes served with baked beans; Mexican pizza (delicious, and served on taco shell), or Irish lamb-and-stout stew. Save room for a delicious dessert, especially the Snowball in Hell—chocolate roulade, vanilla ice cream, and hot fudge sauce with a sprinkling of coconut, served in an iced wine glass coated with chocolate. Open Saturday and Sunday from 11:30am to 3pm; Wednesday to Sunday from 6 to 10:30pm. The cafe is open from 11:30am to 10:30pm on weekdays, until 11pm on weekends.

La Petite Auberge, 19 Charles St. (☎ 401/849-6669), is considered by many to be one of the city's top three restaurants. The service is gracious, the ambience romantic, and the food good, although not as memorable as the prices might suggest. The menu is very traditional French. Among the appetizers, you might start with a lobster bisque, goose liver pâté, or escargots bourguignons. Main courses, priced from $21 to $33, range from seafood—lobster tails with truffles, trout with hazelnuts—to meats, including tournedos Rossini, filet mignon au poivre, châteaubriand béarnaise, and saddle of lamb with garlic sauce. For dessert there are similar classics—crêpes suzette, banana flambé, peach Melba, and strawberries Romanoff. Tables are set with lovely lace tablecloths, lanterns, and fresh flowers. A classical music background, low lighting by wall sconces, and a handsome fireplace complete the romantic atmosphere. Open Monday to Saturday from 6 to 10pm, Sunday from 5 to 9pm.

Some exciting cuisine can be found at **Yesterday's Ale House Bar & The Place,** 28 Washington Sq. (☎ 401/847-0116). It may not look like the domain of fine food, but it certainly is. On one side there's a popular wine bar; on the other is the restaurant, with both booth and table seating. Among the 10 or so entrees there might be a maple-glazed duck with chipotle cherry barbecue sauce; lamb loin in a pecan crust with a balsamic vinegar sauce; and pan-seared Chilean sea bass served on a port wine reduction. Appetizers are similarly inspired—mussels with sake and lime, or chilies relleños with black-bean venison. Prices range from $18 to $28. Those who appreciate wine will enjoy the opportunity to taste several wines from a so-called flight, containing four 3-ounce glasses of different wines. Absolutely your first dinner stop. Open Sunday to Thursday from 11:30am to 10pm, Friday and Saturday from 11:30 to 11pm. The Place is open daily, Sunday to Thursday from 11am to 10pm, Friday and Saturday from 11am to 11pm.

At **Elizabeth's,** Brown and Howard Wharf (☎ 401/846-6862), Broadway show tunes set the pace, and old and new movies add to the fun, although don't be surprised if the hostess, Elizabeth Burley, an ex-film producer, launches into song too. The food is as theatrical as the ambience. You'll be served huge platters for two, piled high with treats such as shrimp and piselli (shrimp sautéed with garlic and oil and topped with pesto sauce) plus pasta of the day; roasted hot-herb sausage; and mushrooms, peppers, and onions; and the vegetable of the day, accompanied by piselli sauce and olives. Or there's the barbecue feast, which includes chicken spareribs with sweet potato pie, beans, and apples; mushroom hot-dog sausage; corn bread; and several vegetables. Prices range from $30 to $40 for the platters. The decor is charmingly eccentric and theatrical with assorted chairs and tables covered in exotic fabrics. In summer, there's a great deck for dining. Bring your own wine. Open in summer, daily from 5:30 to 10pm; in winter, Wednesday to Saturday from 5:30 to 10pm. Usually closed January and February.

Puerini's, 24 Memorial Blvd. W. (☎ 401/847-5506), is a delightful small Italian restaurant with a cozy ambience. The two dining rooms—upstairs and downstairs—contain tables spread with black plastic cloths covered with butcher paper. The walls are decorated with evocative art photographs of Italy. The food is good and reasonably priced, too. Start with the sweet roasted peppers in oil and garlic with provolone or the delicious portobello mushrooms sliced and sautéed with spinach, zucchini, roasted red peppers, pignoli nuts, and a touch of balsamic vinegar. Follow with a pasta like the ravioli stuffed with ricotta and Parmesan with pesto sauce or with one of the fine chicken dishes, marsala or fiorentina (with spinach). Prices range from $12 to $15. Beer and wine are available. Open Tuesday to Thursday from 5 to 9pm, Friday and Saturday from 5 to 10pm.

Muriel's, Spring and Touro streets (☎ 401/849-7780), is fun for break-fast, lunch, or dinner. Walls are covered with Maxfield Parrish posters; tables sport floral and lace-trimmed table cloths under glass; and ficus trees set off the jade-colored walls. For breakfast, choose the huevos rancheros or the French toast in spiced butter with walnuts and syrup. At lunch, salads, pasta, sandwiches, omelets, and entrees under $10 are offered. At dinner, the room is transformed by candlelight. The extensive seasonal menu might offer anything from vegetable stir fry and lasagna to chicken Bombay with bananas, raisin, and walnuts; shrimp Louisiana; and grilled porterhouse with caramelized onions. Prices range from $10 to $17. My favorite dessert is the chocolate bread pudding with vanilla ice cream, chocolate sauce, and walnuts. Beer and wine are available. Open on weekends year-round and weekdays in summer, daily from 5pm to closing.

Scales and Shells, 527 Thames St. (☎ 401/846-3474), is the quintessential waterfront fish restaurant. Up front is an open kitchen, and here chefs cook the produce of the sea. The choices are many. You can start with the cherrystones, liitlenecks, and oysters on the half shell or the calamari or grilled shrimp. Follow with lobster fra diavolo or any one of close to 20 mesquite-grilled fishes—swordfish, salmon, tuna, bluefish, red snapper, mahimahi, and so on. Prices range from $15 to $20 (market price for the lobster). Although there's little decor to speak of, the crowds create a charged atmosphere. The second-floor dining room, known as Upscales, offers more intimate dining with the same great seafood. The main restaurant is open in summer, Monday to Thursday from 5 to 10pm, Friday to Saturday 5 to 11pm, Sunday 4 to 10pm; in winter, Sunday to Thursday 5 to 9pm, Friday to Saturday 5 to 10pm. Closed Monday from January to May. Upscales is open May to September, Sunday to Thursday 6 to 10pm and Friday and Saturday from 6 to 11pm. No credit cards.

Christie's, Christie's Landing (☎ 401/847-5400), is home to the powerboat crowd and also a hangout for local politicos who like to drink and dine on steaks and seafood priced from $18 to $28. There's veal Oscar, salmon, lobster (stuffed, broiled, or served with tenderloin), swordfish, bouillabaisse, scallops, scrod, sole, and more; also, a clam boil of lobster, steamers, corn, potatoes, and onions; plus steaks and lamb chops. The dining room is large and crowded, and a warm atmosphere prevails. In winter, it's warmed by the large stone hearth. The long bar, separated from the dining room, is usually filled with locals anxiously watching the outcome of one of the Boston team's games. Luncheon brings salads, sole, seafood pie, scrod, and other dishes for $6 to $10. Many famous faces line the entryway here. Open daily from 11:30am to 3pm, Sunday to Thursday from 5 to 9pm, Friday and Saturday from 5 to 10pm.

The yachting crowd as well as the locals favor the **Mooring,** on Sayer's Wharf (☎ 401/846-2260), off America's Cup Avenue, which has a multilevel deck smack over the water and a large outdoor bar. The menu features steaks, lobsters, and fresh fish priced from $12 to $25. Favorite dishes are the seafood stew (lobster, shrimp, scallops, mussels and fish poached in cream with aromatics and herbs), baked stuffed jumbo shrimp, and crabmeat baked en casserole. The chowders are famous; sandwiches and salads are also available. Open daily from 11:30am to 10pm.

The Pier, Howard Wharf (☎ 401/847-3645), is another Newport tradition for steaks, seafood, and lobster served in half a dozen or so ways. Prices range from $13 to $20. In summer, there's nightly entertainment and dancing on weekends. Open daily from 11:30am to 10pm (in winter, lunches on weekends only).

Le Bistro, Bannister's Wharf (☎ 401/849-7778), offers classic bistro fare including a worthy steak and frites plus some really fine seafood dishes. Try the sea scallops with sherry vinegar sauce, broiled mahimahi with champagne sauce, or steamed lobster. To start, try the charcuterie selection of sausages and prosciutto or the escargots bourguignonne. Prices run $15 to $27. The dining room is comfortable country French. At lunch there are omelets, sandwiches, and salads, although if you wish the kitchen will prepare dinner items. Open daily from 11:30am to 11pm.

NEWPORT AFTER DARK

For the most current information, ask at the Convention and Visitor's Bureau for its nightlife paper. Sunday-afternoon jam sessions are held at the **Newport Harbor Hotel** on America's Cup Avenue (☎ 401/847-9000).

Christie's of Newport (☎ 401/847-5400) and the **Clarke Cooke House,** Bannister's Wharf (☎ 401/849-2900), offer bands and dancing on weekends.

For light entertainment, the **Newport Playhouse & Cabaret Restaurant,** 102 Connell Hwy. (☎ 401/848-7529), mounts a variety of productions year-round. Most tend to be comedies. A buffet dinner is served before the play, and afterwards you can return to the dining room for a cabaret performance.

In season, an exciting evening can be spent at the **Newport Jai Alai,** 150 Admiral Kalbfus Rd. (☎ 401/849-5000), watching the fast-paced Basque game of jai alai and wagering on the teams. The facility also offers simulcast horseracing and more than 400 video-lottery machines featuring blackjack, poker, and other games with payoffs up to $6,000.

Newport
Special & Recreational Activities

Antiquing: There are plenty of stores in Newport, although they're most concentrated along Franklin Street between Thames and Spring.

Beaches: Bailey's Beach, at Ocean Drive and Bellevue Avenue, is where the "400" park in their monogrammed parking spaces to frolic in private. **Gooseberry Beach** (☎ 401/847-3958) on Ocean Drive is attractive and open for a parking fee of $12 or so. **Fort Adams State Park,** Ocean Drive, also has a beach with a lifeguard. Other beaches are **Newport Beach,** at the eastern end of Memorial Boulevard; **Second Beach** (☎ 401/846-6273) in Middletown on Sachuest Beach Road; **Third Beach** is around the corner at the mouth of the Sakonnet River.

Biking: Rentals are available at **Ten Speed Spokes,** 18 Elm St. (☎ 401/847-5609). Daily charges average $25. Open April through October, daily; off-season Monday to Saturday.

Boating: Oldport Marine Services, Sayer's Wharf (☎ 401/847-9109), offers harbor cruises mid-May to mid-October. **Newport Sailing School** (☎ 401/848-2266) gives lessons and offers 1- and 2-hour tours for $18 and $25.

Cruises: Viking Tours, 184 Thames St. (☎ 401/847-6921), runs cruises of the harbor from its Goat Island dock six times daily in season. From mid-May to Columbus Day, a 1-hour narrated cruise to Jamestown costs $8.50 for adults, $3 for children 4 to 11.

Golf: In Portsmouth, a 10-minute drive from Newport, you can choose from two courses: **Green Valley** (☎ 401/847-9543) and **Montup** (☎ 401/683-9882).

Hiking: The **Cliff Walk** is a marvelous coastal experience, from the end of Newport Beach to Bellevue and Coggeshall avenues. **Norman Bird Sanctuary,** 583 Third Beach Rd. (☎ 401/846-2577), has 7½ miles of hiking trails to marsh, ridge, and pond. Open Tuesday to Sunday from 9am to 5pm; admission $4 for adults, $1 for children.

Polo: Take along a picnic and watch the game, played during late August and early September at **Glen Farm,** off Route 114 in Portsmouth.

State Parks: Brenton Point State Park (☎ 401/846-8240) is mainly a parking area off Ocean Drive with access to a fishing pier and rocky inlets. **Fort Adams State Park** has swimming and picnicking.

Swimming: The pools at the **YMCA,** 792 Valley Rd. (☎ 401/847-9200), and also at **Howard Johnson's,** 351 W. Main Rd., Middletown (☎ 401/849-2000), are open to the public for a small charge (from $7 to $10). Or you can head for the beaches mentioned above.

Tennis: The big thrill is to play on the courts at the **Casino Indoor Racquet Club,** 194 Bellevue Ave. (☎ 401/849-4777), for which the charge is $25 per hour, or on the grass courts at the **Tennis Hall of Fame** (☎ 401/849-3990), which will cost about $35 per person per 1½ hours. You can also watch or try to play the forerunner of tennis, "court tennis" (☎ 401/849-6672) at the Tennis Hall of Fame ($30 per person per hour).

Windsurfing: Island Sports, 86 Aquidneck Ave. (☎ 401/846-4421), offers rentals for $50 a day at Third Beach. It also rents kayaks and surf boards.

MAINE

Portsmouth & Maine's Southern Coast

Portsmouth, N.H. ◆ *Kittery* ◆ *York* ◆ *Ogunquit* ◆ *Perkins*
Cove ◆ *Rachel Carson National Wildlife Refuge* ◆
Wells ◆ *Kennebunkport* ◆ *Cape Elizabeth* ◆ *Portland*

Distance in miles from Boston: Portsmouth, 60; York, 62; Ogunquit, 70; Kennebunkport, 88; Portland, 109.

Estimated driving time: 1 hour to Portsmouth; 1 hour to York; 1¼ hours to Ogunquit; 1½ hours to Kennebunkport; 2 hours to Portland.

Driving: Take I-95 to Exit 6 or 7 for Portsmouth. For other destinations take I-95 to their appropriate exits: 1 for the Yorks, 2 for Wells and Ogunquit, 3 for the Kennebunks, and 7 or 8 for Portland.

Further Information: For further information, contact the **Greater Portsmouth Chamber of Commerce,** 500 Market St. Portsmouth, NH 03802 (☎ 603/436-1118); **Kittery Information Center** (☎ 207/439-1319); **York Chamber of Commerce,** P.O. Box 417, York, ME 03909 (☎ 207/363-4422); **Ogunquit Welcome Center,** P.O. Box 2289, Ogunquit, ME 03907 (☎ 207/646-5533); **Kennebunk-Kennebunkport Chamber of Commerce,** P.O. Box 740, Kennebunk, ME 04043 (☎ 207/967-0857); **Kennebunkport Information Center** (☎ 207/967-8600).

Convention and Visitor's Bureau of Greater Portland, 305 Commercial St., Portland, ME 04101 (☎ 207/772-4994).

Although this is not the quintessential coastline of Downeast Maine, there are some truly rewarding experiences here for any weekend visitor. Some parts of the southern coast may be overcommercialized, but they can easily be avoided or enjoyed for what they are—great beaches or great shopping, where people let their hair down and relax.

Portsmouth, in New Hampshire, right on the border, is the gateway to Maine. It makes a wonderful weekend stopover—you can spend a day or so at one of the finest and most authentic historical sites in the country and dine at some very fine restaurants. You can explore the harbor and cruise to the islands or even hop over to the old town of York, which is filled with the history

Southern Maine Coast

5
26
117
Winthrop
North Waterford
Turner
5
118
South Paris
4
202
11
Norway
Lovell
117
Mechanic Falls
Auburn
Lewiston
Richmond
302
Bridgton
Long Lake
11
196
Lisbon Falls
201
495
95
Saco R.
Casco
26
136
Bath
Naples
Bradbury Mountain ▲
Brunswick
5
117
11
Sebago Lake
Gray
Wolfneck Woods State Park
Freeport
South Freeport
Hiram
N. Windham
Harpswell Center
209
Cornish
35
Yarmouth
South Harpswell
5
25
302
202
Bailey Island
Casco Bay
Limerick
Westbrook
Portland
Hollis Center
4
South Portland
11
95
TNPK.
1
Shapleigh
5
Cape Elizabeth
Old Orchard Beach
Alfred
111
Saco
Saco Bay
109
Biddeford
Sanford
1
9
202
4
109
MAINE
Kennebunk
Cape Porpoise
9
Kennebunkport
North Berwick
Wells
Rochester
Berwick
9
95
South Berwick
Somersworth
Ogunquit
Perkins Cove
Dover
Cape Neddick
New Hampshire | **Maine**
91
York Beach
Durham
York Village
1
York Harbor
Kittery
108
Portsmouth
North Hampton
1A
■ Odiorne State Park
Rye Harbor

Atlantic Ocean

| Mountain ▲ |

0 ▭▭▭▭ 16 km / 10 mi.

N

NA-0138

Events & Festivals to Plan Your Trip Around

February: **Winter Carnival** in Kennebunkport brings ice skating and snow sculpture contests, and dog sled demonstrations, plus other amusements. Call ☎ 207/967-0857.

March: **Maine Boatbuilders Show** in Portland, ME. More than 200 exhibitors, and a great place to meet boatbuilders and other boat aficionados. Late March. Call ☎ 207/772-4994.

April: **Patriot's Day** weekend in Ogunquit features a bazaar, food, and entertainment plus a casino under tents at Ogunquit Beach. Call ☎ 207/646-5533.

May: **Portsmouth Children's Day** in Portsmouth, NH, brings out cartoon characters, puppets, hands-on arts and crafts, theater, and other entertainment for the kids. First Sunday in May.

June: **Portsmouth Chowderfest** is the day in Portsmouth, NH when you can taste a zillion different versions of this rich and satisfying seafood soup, served by area residents who compete for the title of best. Usually the Saturday of Memorial Day weekend or the first Saturday in June.

Old Port Festival in Portland, ME. A daylong block party in the historic district. Call ☎ 207/772-2249.

Portsmouth Market Square Weekend in Portsmouth, NH. A street festival with arts, crafts, food, and entertainment. Usually the second Saturday in June. Call ☎ 603/436-2848 for information.

Boat Parade and Blessing of the Fleet Weekend in Kennebunkport, plus sandcastle building, kayak slalom, and sailboat races, and other entertainment. Call ☎ 207/967-0857.

Portsmouth Jazz Festival. This weekend festival in Portsmouth, NH brings local and regional jazz groups together for one big jamming session. Last weekend in June. Call ☎ 603/436-1118 for information.

Chamber Music Festival in Ogunquit brings a whole weekend of chamber music to a variety of venues. Call ☎ 207/646-5533.

July: The summer-long (July and August) **Portsmouth Prescott Park Arts Festival** takes place on the banks of the river, featuring 60 free events—musicals, art shows, children's theater, and concerts. Call ☎ 603/436-1118 for information.

of early Maine. Ogunquit, of course has long been a coastal resort with a reputation as an art colony. It's still that, although it's become rather commercial, and for this reason, I recommend visiting slightly off-season if you can. Kennebunk is more tony than Ogunquit is, thanks to its current associations

York Summerfest on the Village Green in York village is a combination crafts and collectibles show plus food and house tours. Call ☎ 207/363-4422.

Ogunquit Beach Sand Building Contest is a sight to see— amazing what you can do with sand. Call ☎ 207/646-5533.

August: York Days offers a mixture of activities and entertainment in and around York. It includes a craft fair and fireworks and is spread over several weekends. Call ☎ 207/363-4422.

Annual auction of the Ogunquit Art Association. Call ☎ 207/646-4909.

Sidewalk Art Show features 80 artists who display their works along the streets of Ogunquit. Call ☎ 207/646-5533.

Kennebearport Teddy Bear Show in Kennebunkport, is where you can see all kinds of bear artists and collectors, and even learn how to make a bear. Call ☎ 207/967-0857.

September: Ogunquit Antiques Show at the Dunaway Center. Call ☎ 207/646-5533.

Fiddle Contest and Oldtime Country Music Show in Kennebunkport brings the state's best fiddlers to town for a jamboree. Call ☎ 207/967-0857.

November: Victorian Holiday. The Old Port in Portland, ME is decorated in a Victorian Christmas theme, with hayrides, window displays, and caroling. Late November to Christmas. Call ☎ 207/772-6828.

December: Portsmouth Winter Solstice Celebration starts with a parade and continues with candlelight strolls (see below), performances of the *Nutcracker,* and more. Call ☎ 603/436-1118.

Christmas Prelude, Kennebunkport. Santa's arrival in a lobster boat marks the beginning of Christmas with street shows, pancake breakfasts, and tours of the town's inns. Call ☎ 207/967-3286.

Candlelight Stroll, Portsmouth, NH. Historic Strawbery Banke lights more than 1,000 candles on its 10-acre grounds. Call ☎ 603/433-1100.

Christmas by the Sea in Ogunquit is a 3-day festival celebrating the season with caroling and tree lighting, a chowderfest, and other entertainment. Call ☎ 207/646-5533.

with George Bush and others who made this a prime summer resort. It is crowded and commercial to a degree, especially in summer, but it has much to recommend it—a rocky coastline and some fine inns and dining places. I'd anchor at the still-quiet Cape Porpoise north of Kennebunk proper. And finally, Portland is a great city to visit. There's plenty to do—the Old Port to shop, the art museum to explore, and all kinds of dining experiences. From the city you can also visit the Portland Light and several state parks around and south of Cape Elizabeth. All four of these make great weekend destinations at any season of the year.

PORTSMOUTH

Portsmouth is a quintessential seafaring town with a rich history. It stands at the mouth of the Piscataqua River which, along with the ocean, was the source of its great wealth in its early history. It was the first major port in New Hampshire and home to the Portsmouth Naval Yard, which opened in 1800. The town itself was settled in 1623.

EXPLORING THE TOWN

Today, if you want to experience what it was really like in colonial times, visit **Strawberry Banke Museum,** Marcy Street (☎ 603/433-1100), an extraordinary historical complex that is unique because most of the buildings in the complex are in situ—meaning they were built in the specific location that they occupy today. Consequently, their relationships to each other and to the communal life that they supported along these streets and lanes can be really imagined. This community grew up around Puddle Dock, the grassy area at the center marked by an old anchor. In 1630, the area was called Strawberry Banke because of the wild berries that grew abundantly here on the river banks. Later, in the 19th century, when the area changed and became an immigrant community, it was called Puddle Dock. The 42 buildings trace 300 years of history. Some of the buildings contain special exhibits devoted to particular subjects or collections.

The **Sherburne House** (1695), for example, has been arranged to demonstrate 17th-century architecture and construction methods. The **Lowd House** focuses on the talents and skills of New Hampshire woodworkers. The **Joshua Jackson House** (1790) has been left deliberately unrestored to reveal its structure and how it was changed over the years. The layers have been peeled back from the walls to reveal the different decorations applied to them in different periods, right back to the original construction. Here you can see how the house, once occupied by a colonial family, was eventually transformed into a rental property for immigrants in the 19th century. Some of the characters who lived in the house and community are profiled on the walls—Georgie Gould who ran the general store; Beanpot Kennett who played harmonica at any spontaneous dance; Mary Baker, a madam who had diamonds set in her two front teeth; and Cappy Stewart, owner of an oyster saloon and a brothel as well as an antiques dealer.

The **Drisco House** has been furnished to contrast the 1790s with 1950s style, complete with kitchen. The **Winn House** (1795) shows how buildings were framed and sheathed and how shingles were made—it also demonstrates the different patterns of masonry construction—Flemish, English and American—used in the doors, windows, and paneling. The creation of spiraled balusters and chair-rail moldings and other woodworking details are all

Portsmouth

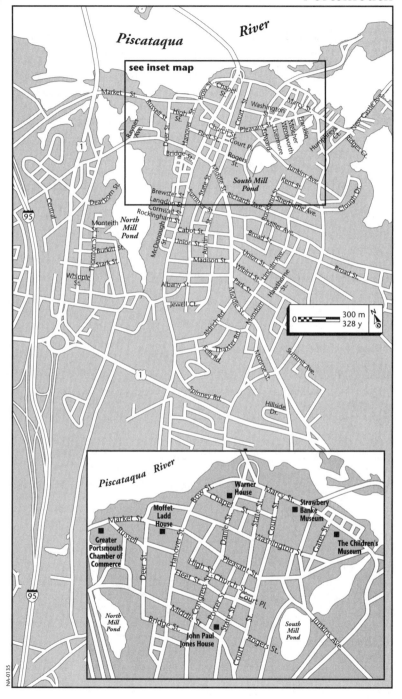

demonstrated, and there's a discussion of how interior decoration—painted woodwork, wallpaper, rugs, drapes, and upholstery—were made and applied.

The **Widow Rider House** tells the fascinating story of Mary Rider, who originally purchased the house with her husband in 1809 for $1,000. They came from Devon, England. Nine years later she was widowed and survived alone until she died in 1863. The inventory of her $13,366 estate makes fascinating reading. It includes such items as the house, which had risen in value to $1,258; a pew in St. Johns worth $5; and a sofa ($6) and table ($2). These amounts may seem small in comparison to today's average estate, but in her own time, Mary must have been remarkably enterprising to have amassed such a sum as a widow.

In contrast, the **Chase House** shows all the wealthy appurtenances of a successful merchant—a grand staircase with triple baluster, carved wood and stucco decoration, and a four-poster swathed in French chintz. At the **Walsh House,** Captain Walsh himself appears to tell the story of the seizure of his ship and how he was forced to winter in Jamaica. At the corner, you can step into a store (1943) that stocked only 400 items—in contrast to contemporary supermarkets where people can choose among more than 20,000 products. Surprisingly, many of the same product names are still with us: Hershey, Muellers pasta, and Salada tea, for example.

Kids especially enjoy meeting the characters and watching the coopering and other craft demonstrations that are given at some of the sites. In the first two weekends in December, there's a candlelight stroll; the theme is the evolution of Christmas festivities from the 18th century to the 1950s. Open from late April to early November, daily from 10am to 5pm. Admission is $12 for adults, $8 for children 7 to 17.

A good way to get a sense of the town is to follow the **Portsmouth Harbor Trail** (pick up the booklet for $2 at the Chamber of Commerce), beginning at Market Square, which is anchored by the North Church (1854) and the Athenaeum (1805), and continuing through the surrounding commercial streets of Market and Merchants Row. Among the highlights on the route is **The Moffatt-Ladd House**, 154 Market St. (☎ 603/436-8221), built in 1763 by Captain John Moffatt as a wedding gift for his son. It has an impressive three-story facade crowned by a captain's walk. Amateur interior designers will appreciate the 1815 Dufour wallpaper in the great hall, which takes up a third of the ground floor. Many of the furnishings are original to the house, including portraits of the Moffatt family that were painted by Gilbert Stuart, Joseph Blackburn, and Albert Gallatin Hoit, and others, as well as a set of carved Chinese Chippendale furniture that was purchased by the family from the last Royal Governor of New Hampshire, John Wentworth. The terraced gardens are a blissful oasis and feature some plantings that date back to the 18th century. The enormous horse chestnut was planted by General William Whipple, Revolutionary War hero and signer of the Declaration of Independence, who married one of the Moffatts. Open from mid-June to mid-October, Monday to Saturday from 10am to 4pm and Sunday from 2 to 5pm.

Farther along Market Street, the *USS Albacore*, 600 Market St. (☎ 603/436-3680), lies stranded in a park. It's a navy submarine that was built here and served from 1953 to 1972 as a testing lab for control systems, dive brakes, sonar systems, and more. Open from May 1 to Columbus Day, 9:30am to

5pm. Admission is $4 for adults, $2 for children 7 to 17.

The walking tour will also clue you in to another industry that gave the city fame and fortune—brewing, the city's dominant industry from the end of the Civil War to Prohibition. John Swindell, an English innkeeper, started the industry when he built his malthouse in 1856. Other breweries and brewers followed, notably Frank Jones who built a veritable empire. He owned the Rockingham Hotel, now the Library Restaurant, at 401 State St., worth peeking into just to see the magnificence of the stucco and woodcarving. You'll also pass the **Portsmouth Brewery Warehouse** at 125 Bow St. (now the Seacoast Repertory Theatre).

There are other historic highlights along the way. **The Warner House,** 150 Daniel St. (☎ 603/436-5909), a brick residence dating to 1716, contains some dramatic murals believed to be among the oldest in the nation and an exceptional collection of Portsmouth furniture. Open mid-June to mid-October, Tuesday to Saturday from 10am to 4pm.

The **Governor John Langdon House,** 143 Pleasant St. (☎ 603/436-3205), was built in 1783–85 by a wealthy merchant and patriot who was a delegate to the Constitutional Convention and later governor of the state. The interior features some very ornate wood carving, and the perennial garden and the rose garden are very inviting. Open Wednesday to Sunday, from noon to 5pm.

The Wentworth-Gardner House, 50 Mechanic St. (☎ 603/436-4406), is a handsome Georgian house (1760) that was built as a wedding gift for Thomas Wentworth, brother of the governor, by his mother. The 15-panel front door, topped with a prominent pineapple is particularly notable. The interior contains remarkable Chinese and French wallpapers plus brilliant blue and mulberry tile around the hearths. Open mid-June to mid-October, Tuesday to Sunday from 1 to 4pm.

The Rundlet-May House, 364 Middle St. (☎ 603/433-2494), was home to a textile merchant and contains much furniture attributed to Langley Boardman, dating to 1807. Open mid-June to mid-October, Wednesday to Sunday from 1am to 5pm.

The **John Paul Jones House,** 43 Middle St. at State (☎ 603/436-8420), is well worth visiting even if you don't get the real story about the life of this swashbuckling character who has become the hero of the navy. To some, the John Paul Jones house is a misnomer, since the house was built in 1758 for Sara Wentworth, niece of Governor Benning Wentworth, for her marriage to Captain Purcell. When Captain Purcell died in 1776, Sara began taking in boarders, and among them was the famous Captain John Paul Jones. John Paul Jones was born in Kirkudbright, Scotland, son of a gardener. He went to sea at age 13, and became a master mariner by the age of 21. He arrived in Portsmouth in 1777, having been appointed as commander of the *Ranger,* which was being built at Rising Castle (now Badger's Island) in Kittery. When he stayed here, he supposedly paid Sara $10 a week for room and board. He stayed here again in 1781 when he was supervising the construction of *America* (it never saw service in the American navy and was in fact given to France). He died in Paris at the young age of 45, largely because of his reckless, dissolute life.

The house is the home of the Portsmouth Historical Society. The ground floor is dedicated to a display of historical artifacts, including a superb collection of wedding gowns plus a fine textile collection. Other rooms contain Sara's furnishings. Several rooms are devoted to John Paul Jones and contain his personal mementos. There are models and pictures of the ships that he commanded, including the *Ranger*. Open by tour only, June 1 to mid-October, Monday to Saturday from 10am to 4pm and Sunday from noon to 4pm. Admission is $4 for adults, $2 for children 6 to 14.

Shopping In town around the port along Bow, Market, and Congress streets are plenty of stores worth browsing. The **N. W. Barrett Gallery,** 53 Market St. (☎ 603/431-4262), sells finely crafted glass, ceramics, and jewelry; **Macro Polo,** 89 Market St. (☎ 603/436-8338), has great toys and fashions. **Gallery 33,** on Market Street, also has quirky whimsical craft objects. If you're a book lover, there are several good stores in town: **Little Professor Book Center,** 103 Congress St. (☎ 603/436-1777), and **Stroudwater Books and Cafe,** 775 Lafayette Rd. (☎ 603/433-7168). My all-time favorite, though, is the **Portsmouth Bookshop,** 1–7 Islington St. (☎ 603/433-4406), which has a huge stock of old and rare books housed in an equally historic building.

FROM GRAND ISLAND TO THE FULLER GARDENS

From Portsmouth, you can take Route 1B to the tiny village of **Newcastle** located on Grand Island, which juts out protectively into Portsmouth Harbor on the New Hampshire side of the Maine state border. For a magnificent view of the Harbor and to revisit some American Revolutionary history, stop at **Fort Constitution,** where one of the first overt acts of the Revolution took place. You have a fine view of Portsmouth Light, and from here in the distance, 9 miles out to sea, are the **Isles of Shoals.** Today you can take a ferry to the isles (see "Special & Recreational Activities," below). Skipping over their early history, when they were settled by English fishermen and visited during the 17th century by Champlain and John Smith, their greatest claim to fame is as the **birthplace of poet Celia Thaxter.** She was the daughter of Thomas Laighton who came to White Island as the lighthouse keeper and decided to open two hotels, one on Smuttynose Island and the other, the Appledore, on Hog Island. The Appledore became a summer retreat for numerous literary lights in the late 1800s.

Southeast of Portsmouth, the coastline is occupied by the community of Rye, a fishing village that also incorporates three of the Isles of Shoals—Star Island, White Island Lighthouse, and Lunging Island. You may want to come for a stroll along **Rye Harbor** or to visit the historic town, which has some gracious homes. More likely, you'll want to picnic or hike in 330-acre **Odiorne State Park** and to see the habitat exhibits and other animals at the **Seacoast Science Center** (☎ 603/436-8043) at Odiorne Point. In the adjacent community of North Hampton, the **Fuller Gardens,** 10 Willow Ave. (☎ 603/964-5414), designed by Arthur Shurtleff, will delight horticulturists.

PORTSMOUTH AFTER DARK

The **Seacoast Repertory Theater,** 125 Bow St. (☎ 603/433-4472), presents a full season of theater in a converted brewery. Nearby, the **Music Hall** (☎ 603/433-3100) is the venue for touring dance, music, and theater companies and for film events.

The downstairs tavern at the **Dolphin Striker** is a convivial gathering place where the music starts around 9pm. **Poco Diablo,** 37 Bow St. (☎ 603/

431-5967), and **Old Ferry Landing**, 10 Ceres St. (☎ 603/431-5510), both of which have outdoor seating areas right at the water's edge, are hot cocktail spots for the after-work crowd. The **Portsmouth Brewery** (☎ 603/431-1115), marked by a large beer stein at 56 Market St., is another crowd-pleaser where you can wash down some eclectic fare with its famous ales and stouts plus Old Brown Dog, a dark ale produced by the Smuttynose Brewing Company.

PORTSMOUTH LODGING

Within walking distance of downtown, the **Martin Hill Inn**, 404 Islington St., Portsmouth, NH 03801 (☎ 603/436-2287), is a very fetching accommodation made especially so by the beauty of its gardens that extend behind the house and afford shady sitting areas from which to observe the birds splashing in the bird bath or to enjoy the water garden. The main house was built about 1820 and contains three rooms that are exquisitely furnished with handsome artifacts—ginger-jar lamps, gilt-framed pictures, and applique quilts—along with fine linens and extra touches such as potpourri. The Williamsburg-blue room has a stunning canopied bed and an inlaid armoire, plus a plush loveseat. The guest house (c. 1850) is the most private and has an attractive Indonesian-style sitting room. It contains four rooms furnished with canopy, spindle, or iron-and-brass beds. All rooms have writing tables and sofas or separate sitting areas. A full breakfast is served in a very attractive dining room featuring a collection of chinoiserie. Rates: July 1 to November 1, $100 to $125; November 1 to July 1, $90 to $100.

The Inn at Christian Shore, 335 Maplewood Ave., Portsmouth, NH 03801 (☎ 603/431-6770), is the domain of textile designer Mariaelena Koopman, who hails from Argentina via New York. The 1800 Federal-style home is full of eye-catching pieces, not all of them textiles. There are artifacts from Ecuador and Meso America, Chinese ceramics, and other objects from around the world. The six rooms (four with private baths, two with fireplaces) are furnished eclectically with some key art objects. Room 2, for example, has a brass bed, but it's the oriental art and the owl from Africa that catch the eye. Another room features a remarkable mirror and a piecrust table. Each room has at least one object of interest, and all rooms have a TV. Breakfast is served in a warm room with beamed ceiling at tables appointed with wing backs or at the long table in front of the fireplace. Rates: June 1 to October 31, $95, November 1 to May 31, $75.

The Oracle House Inn, 38 Marcy St., Portsmouth, NH 03801 (☎ 603/433-8827), is located right by Strawbery Banke in a lovely gambrel-roofed house built in 1702. There are only four rooms. Each is decorated stylishly. One is furnished with a real brass bed, which stands on wide-board floors covered with rugs. The focal point of the room is the handsome wood-burning fireplace, surrounded by sage green paneling. The Blue Room is furnished with a fine highboy and maple canopied bed plus other carefully crafted reproductions. Lighting is provided by Shaker-style tin sconces. The Richard Wibird Room features a four-poster with a crochet canopy and red gingham ruffles and a fireplace that is paneled in a dark plum color. The bathroom has a Jacuzzi. Breakfast in summer is served on the charming back flagstone patio. It's usually a continental affair of fruit salad, muffins, bagels, granola, and pastries. Rates: 139 to $149; less in winter.

The **Sise Inn,** 40 Court St., Portsmouth, NH 03801 (☎ 603/433-1200), is on a quiet downtown street and caters to a mixture of business executives and leisure travelers in search of modern accommodations with full amenities. It's located in a handsome 1881 Victorian that was built for merchant John Sise. The 34 rooms are similarly furnished with high-back oak beds and other oak furnishings, although they feature varied wallpapers. All have TV/VCRs, telephones, clock radios, and air-conditioning. The suite has a whirlpool bath and CD/stereo. A buffet-style breakfast is offered. Rates: late May to late October, $115 to $160, suites $185; late October to late May, $89 to $135, suites $160.

PORTSMOUTH DINING

Lindbergh's Crossing, 29 Ceres St. (☎ 603/431-0887), serves some of the best food in Portsmouth in a lovely atmosphere created by plastered stone or brick walls and heavy beams. A window table has a view of the bridge and harbor. Tables are plain wood, and chairs are mostly oak. Start with the fantastic clam chowder or the moules marinière. Among the main courses, the roast pork tenderloin, pan roasted and served with an almond roasted-red-pepper coulis is a successful combination of flavors. There's also plenty of great fresh seafood—sautéed trout with a lemon-caper beurre blanc served over shiitake mushrooms and leek rice or seared sea scallops in a basil tomato broth. Prices range from $12 to $18. There's a good wine list with about 20 selections available by the glass. Open Sunday to Thursday from 5:30 to 9:30pm, Friday and Saturday from 5:30 to 10:30pm. Call for hours in winter.

The Oar House, 55 Ceres St. (☎ 603/436-4025), is another attractive restaurant along the waterfront that serves first-class cuisine. Whatever you order will feature fresh ingredients and reflect careful preparation. Among the specialties, you might find a grilled duck breast with pineapple salsa or a richly flavored chicken marengo redolent with prosciutto, mushrooms, tomatoes, and artichoke hearts. Fish is featured, too, in dishes such as the Oar House Delight, which consists of shrimp, scallops, and haddock, finished with a lobster sauce. Seafood really comes to the fore in the appetizers. There's everything from baked stuffed clams to basil lobster cakes, chowder, and scallops wrapped in bacon, and a full raw bar. Prices range from $16 to $24. Open Monday to Thursday from 11:30am to 3pm and 5 to 9pm, Friday and Saturday until 10pm, Sunday from 11:30am to 9pm.

The Dolphin Striker and Spring Hill Tavern, 15 Bow St. (☎ 603/431-5222), has a formal, very shipshape, beamed dining room where the tables are polished wood and the chairs Windsor style. The room is especially alluring at night, when it's lit by whale-oil lamps. It's been one of the city's premier dining rooms for many years. Here patrons can order a $49.95 four-course prix fixe, which might begin with buffalo mozzarella and Caesar salad and proceed with a choice of sautéed lobster accompanied by sun-dried tomato ravioli in marsala cream and finished with a julienne of plum tomato, leek, and pine nuts, or grilled tenderloin of beef glazed with chèvre and finished with a chipotle roasted-red-pepper sauce. Selections on the à la carte menu feature similar dishes but are priced from $16 to $24. For dessert, try the dark chocolate truffle served with blackberry puree and ground pistachios. Open daily from 11:30am to 2pm, Monday to Friday from 5 to 9:30, Saturday from 5 to 10pm, and Sunday from 4 to 9pm.

Porto Bello, 67 Bow St. (☎ 603/431-2989), is a cozy small dining room with only 10 or so tables, located upstairs with a view of the harbor. The fine Italian fare is redolent with garlic and herbs. Many of the dishes are pastas, such as pennini with prosciutto, porcini mushrooms, and peas sautéed in oil and enriched with cream and parmesano, gnocchi napoletana, or fettuccine Bolognese. The menu is rounded out by delicious grilled meats and fish—lamb chops with garlic and rosemary, and sausages with sweet peppers and roasted potatoes. Prices range from $13 to $22. Open Wednesday to Saturday, 11am to 2:30pm; Tuesday to Saturday, 4:30 to 9:30pm.

The **Blue Mermaid World Grill,** The Hill between Hanover and Deer streets (☎ 603/427-2583), is a casual hip restaurant that serves some very appetizing food. Many of the dishes reflect an Asian or Caribbean influence. Favorite appetizers, for example, include Jamaican jerk chicken wings with salsa, and what are called "saddle bags"—wontons with barbecue dipping sauce filled with chicken, jack cheese, herbs, and spices. You can also have a good-tasting burger topped with bacon, Monterey jack cheese, and barbecue sauce, and a choice of quesadillas. The specialties of the house are the exciting pizzas—with cilantro pesto, red pepper, and romano cheese—plus Cuban spiced pork, and red snapper with Java island spices, or roasted chicken. Prices range from $10 to $18. Open Sunday to Thursday from 11:30am to 9pm, Friday and Saturday from 11:30am to 10pm.

On a trip around Grand Island, **B & G's Boathouse,** Wentworth Rd., affords an opportunity to sit out on a deck overlooking an inlet and enjoy a lobster dinner or a plate of fried clams.

KITTERY & YORK

Kittery and Kittery Point lie just across the Piscataqua River in York County, Maine. Kittery is known today for its shopping outlets, but it is in fact the oldest community in Maine, and for those interested in pastimes other than shopping, it's worth exploring this corner of the state that is so rich in history.

The Portsmouth Naval Shipyard was established here in Kittery on Seavey Island in 1800. Ever since, it has played major roles in the War of 1812, the Civil War, and World Wars I and II. Although you can't visit the shipyard today, you can visit the **Shipyard Museum** (☎ 207/438-3550) that traces the history of the yard and the many vessels that have been built there since its founding.

EXPLORING THE AREA

Drive from Kittery along Route 103 East until you reach the **First Congregational Church** on the left side of the road. Go into this church, established in 1714, and seek out the boxed pew up front on the left that belonged to the Pepperrell family. This family was one of the great seafaring families of the state. Shipping magnate Sir William Pepperrell was the first man in the colonies to make the equivalent of $1 million. He was knighted by George II. His residence stands at Kittery Point (½ mile down the road) overlooking the cove where his 150 ships plied the oceans. Because Pepperrell was a Loyalist, his property was confiscated in 1779 but was later bought back by his descendants.

Even before the establishment of the Navy Yard, the entrance to Portsmouth harbor and the Piscataqua River was vital to protecting the shipping and settlements on both sides of the river, and so **forts McClary** and Foster were built. The first is located farther along Route 103. Today, it's a state park, and the rangers have compiled some displays relating to the history of the fort, which was garrisoned from the Revolutionary War until World War I. It has an inspiring setting overlooking the Piscataqua River and a fine central blockhouse built 1844–46. **Fort Foster** (☎ 207/439-3800), which was built in the early 1900s and manned through World War II, is now a little-used and very appealing 88-acre recreational area on the southwestern side of Gerrish Island with a rush-fringed marsh, a picnic area overlooking the water, a fishing pier, a nature trail, and a shoreline walk. Windsurfing is allowed here at Whaleback Beach, and there's even a scuba diving area at Rocky Beach. There's a terrific view from the park of Whaleback Island light on the closest of the islands of Shoals.

Continue along Route 103 to the cutoff to Crescent Beach or continue on 103, which will take you by Chauncey Creek and through the **Rachel Carson National Wildlife Refuge.** From here, Route 103 continues past Seabury before crossing the York River and passing York's two town docks. Before Route 103 intersects with Route 1A, you may want to stop and walk across the Wiggly Bridge, surely the smallest suspension bridge in the world. It crosses the marsh to an island. Route 1A swings west to York Village in one direction and proceeds along the coast in the other, through York Harbor to York Beach and Cape Neddick.

It could be said that the colonial revival began in York Village, for it was here that Elizabeth Perkins (1879–1952) went to work salvaging, moving, and restoring buildings to their original condition and interior design. Clustered around the burial ground in Old York are two buildings that she rescued—the **Jefferds' Tavern** (1754), which was moved from Wells, and the **Old Schoolhouse,** which was moved from York Corner on Route 1. The last certainly looks far from inviting, having as it does only one small window. The interior, with its hard benches, is not exactly welcoming either. The graffiti on the interior shows that kids in the 18th and 19th centuries did what kids do today. Across the street the **graveyard** is worth exploring. It includes a memorial to those who died or disappeared in 1691–92 when the Abenaki Indians attacked York. They killed 40 people and took the rest to Canada. Both buildings are maintained by the **Old York Historical Society,** Lindsay Road and Route 1A (☎ 207/363-4974), along with the Old Gaol, the Emerson-Wilcox house, the Elizabeth Perkins House, and the John Hancock Warehouse and Wharf. The society leads tours of the six buildings. Open mid-June through September, Tuesday to Saturday, from 10am to 5pm and Sunday from 1 to 5pm. Admission is $6 for adults, $2.50 for children 6 to 16.

Nearby on a bank overlooking the York River, the **Sayward Wheeler House,** 79 Barrell Lane Extension, York Harbor (☎ 603/436-3205), was the home of West Indies merchant Johnathan Sayward, who participated in the siege of Louisbourg in 1745. Owned by the same family for 200 years, it has some fine original furnishings. Open June 1 to mid-October, Wednesday to Sunday from noon to 5pm. Admission is $4 for adults, $2 for children 12 and under. While you're here in the village, drop into the craft store in the **Olde Church** at

211 York St. (Route 1A) (☎ 207/363-4830) and the handful of other stores that make up the village.

The journey along Route 1A to Cape Neddick is in sharp contrast to the serenity of Old York Village. The road passes several trailer parks before entering York Beach and Heights, where clapboard and shingle houses stand cheek-by-jowl looking out across the long sand beach. **Cape Neddick Lighthouse,** or "Nubble Light" as it's called, was erected in 1879 to protect and warn mariners against the savage rocks of the coastline. At the base, **Sohier Park** is where folks gather to take photographs of this much-loved light that towers 88 feet above the high-water mark.

A short drive along Route 91 from York Village will bring you to **South Berwick** and the home of one of the state's legendary authors, Sarah Orne Jewett, who wrote *The Country of the Pointed Firs*, a quintessential novel about Maine and Mainers. The house is located at 5 Portland St. (☎ 603/436-3205). Sarah, the daughter of a country doctor, was born here in this handsome Georgian residence. You can see her small writing desk overlooking the town square, and Jewett fans will recognize some of the interior spaces from her novels and stories. Open June 1 through mid-October, Tuesday, Thursday, Saturday, and Sunday from noon to 5pm. Admission is $4 for adults, $3.50 for children 12 and under.

KITTERY & YORK LODGING

The Gundalow Inn, 6 Water St., Kittery, ME 03904 (☎ 207/439-4040), occupies an 1889 brick Victorian in old Kittery on the banks of the Piscataqua River, where the gundalows or sailing barges plied every day. It's operated by a charming music-and-literature-loving couple, Cevia and George Rosol, so it's not surprising that the parlor is filled with books and a grand piano or that there is no TV anywhere. The six rooms are furnished in country style. In one room you might find an iron-and-brass bed matched with a velvet-covered chaise lounge and an Eastlake-style desk. Another might have an iron bed and wicker chairs and table. The room named Alice has a great view of Portsmouth harbor through the skylight. A four-course breakfast of fresh juice, fruit, scones, and breads plus a meat or fish entree—anything from blintzes to codfish cakes—is served at separate tables in a sunny breakfast room with a brick fireplace. Note the half-deck of a gundalow on the wall if you're wondering what this trusty barge looks like. Guests can also rock away on the porch and gaze across to Portsmouth. Rates: mid-May to October, $120 to $135; November to mid-May, $90 to $100.

York Harbor Inn, Route 1A, Box 573, York Harbor, ME 03911 (☎ 800/343-3860 or 207/363-5119), is an entrancing accommodation located across the street from the shoreline. It has history and charm, some imaginatively furnished rooms, an excellent dining room, and an atmospheric pub. The signature room is the sitting room, which was originally a 17th-century Isle of Shoals sail loft that was brought here and is now lit with a host of tiny lights. The downstairs cocktail lounge was once the stables for horses; now it serves as a convivial pub. The original part of the house was built in 1783. The 35 rooms vary in decor and size. All have air-conditioning, a phone, and an iron/ironing board; some have a fireplace, Jacuzzi, and TV. Traditional rooms, such as Room 1, are decorated with floral wallpapers, wing chairs, and four-posters with quilt coverlets. Additional furnishings might include an Empire-style chest.

Some rooms also have spa tubs. The most appealing room is the camping-theme room; it has accents such as an antique fishing basket and old wood skis above the door that leads to a private deck with a water view. Furnishings include a bed with an L.L. Bean quilt, a twig side table, and a green rocker with gingham upholstery. The bathroom has a spa tub, and the whole room is arranged around a river-stone pillar. See below for dining. Facilities include a pretty outdoor spa-hot tub. Rates: April to November, $119 to $179 double, suite $209; low season, $109 to $149.

Dockside Guest Quarters, Harris Island Rd. (P.O. Box 205), York, ME 03909 (☎ 207/363-2868), has a stunning setting overlooking York Harbor. It has been operated by the same family since it opened. The buildings are well kept and so are the grounds, which consist of lawn and shade trees and plenty of tubs of flowers. There are 21 rooms. Five rooms are in the main house; three have a private bath. They have not been prettified and retain the air of an old fashioned seafront hostelry. The rest of the rooms are located in studio cottages, which have been plainly furnished with white-painted furniture. Some are right down by the water and have small decks. Some are efficiencies equipped with a two-burner stove, sink, coffeemaker, toaster, and dinnerware. Others are larger and can accommodate two to four people. All accommodations are simple and sparkling clean. Rates: late May to late October, $76 to $169; mid-June and late September to late October, $70 to $138; mid-May to mid-June and late October to November 1, $70 to $114; in winter, open only on weekends.

Edwards' Harborside Inn, Stage Neck Rd. (P.O. Box 866), York Harbor, ME 03911 (☎ 207/363-3037), is right down on the waterfront and has a sunporch overlooking the scene and a small lawn going down to the water's edge. The nine guest rooms are super large; two rooms share a bath. Each is furnished individually. Seascape, for example, has an Ethan Allan–style bed covered with a quilt, an oak chest, and two modern Mission-style rockers. The York Suite's bathroom has a Jacuzzi tub from which you can peer out at the water. The room itself is huge, and the wing chair, highboy, couch, and dresser are dwarfed by the space. A continental breakfast is served in the bright wicker-furnished sitting area at the front of the house. Rates: May to October, $100 to $220; November to April, $60 to $170.

KITTERY & YORK DINING

The York Harbor Inn, Route 1A, Box 573, York Harbor (☎ 800/343-3860 or 207/363-5119), has a romantic dining room looking out towards the water. It offers some fine dining with an emphasis on seafood. Try one of the signature dishes—the Maine lobster stuffed with scallops and shrimp filling, laced with thermidor sauce and baked with Parmesan; or the medallions of beef topped with asparagus, crabmeat, and béarnaise sauce. If they're a little too rich for your taste, then there's a full selection of dishes like grilled swordfish marinated in citrus and ginger and served with orange cranberry chutney or baked stuffed haddock. Prices range from $16 to $25. The inn is also a good brunch choice when the typical menu is leavened with such dishes as huevos rancheros and broiled scallops. Downstairs, there's a very convivial wine cellar–pub with a lighter menu and entertainment. Here you can order burgers, sandwiches, and dishes such as fried scallops or chicken cordon bleu. Prices range from $5 to $12. Open daily from 11:30am to 2pm and 5:30 to 9:30pm.

Dockside on York Harbor has a romantic dining room where you can sit out on a screened porch and watch the comings and goings of the harbor and see the mist drift in shore in the early evening. The cuisine could be better, but the location can't be beat. It's pretty standard fare—broiled scallops, broiled scrod with lemon butter, broiled halibut with fresh herb butter, and similar dishes. The experience, though, of sitting and watching the mist envelop each individual vessel in the harbor is magical. Prices range from $11 to $20. Open Tuesday to Sunday 11:30 to 2pm; and from 5:30 to 9pm.

Chauncey Creek Lobster Pier, Chauncey Creek Rd., Kittery Point (☎ 207/439-1030), is a great spot—bring a bottle of wine and set yourself up at one of the tables alongside the still creek in the open air or under an awning for a lobster feast. There are lobster rolls for only $9 and crab rolls for $6 plus a plentiful supply of boiled or steamed lobster sold at market price. This has to be one of the most picturesque lobster piers anywhere. Open Mother's Day to Columbus Day.

Cap'n Simeon's Galley overlooks Pepperell Cove on Route 103 at Kittery Point (☎ 207/439-3655). It's a typical seafront restaurant with captain's chairs and tables at which you can wolf down as much fried seafood as you dare— scallops, clams, oysters, haddock, shrimp. You can even order a quart of each. The seafood is also available broiled. Prices range from $9 to $14.

Fox's Lobster Pound, Nubble Point, York Beach (☎ 207/363-2643), is located at the foot of Sohier Park at Nubble Light. Here you can sit outside and enjoy a lobster or some shellfish overlooking the ocean.

The Cape Neddick Lobster Pound and Harbourside Restaurant, Shore Road between Ogunquit and York Beach (☎ 207/363-5471) offers a broad range of seafood, including a shore dinner of clams or mussels followed by a Maine lobster. There are broiled and baked fish dishes plus a bouillabaisse. The restaurant sits on a small harbor and, unlike some shoreside places, is only minimally decorated with fishing gear—some floats and an odd net or two plus some photos. There's also an outdoor deck, plus a lobster shack for live lobster, decorated with hundreds of lobster floats and worthy of a photograph.

Portsmouth, Kittery & York
Special & Recreational Activities

Beaches: In the **Hamptons,** both Hampton Beach and North Hampton State Beach are commercial sandy beaches, and so too is Long Sands at **York Beach.** Quieter beaches can be found at **Rye Harbor State Park,** Route 1A, Rye (☎ 603/436-5294), and **Odiorne State Park** (☎ 603/436-7406). At **Kittery Point,** Seapoint Beach is sandy; there's limited parking, but no facilities.

Biking/Mountain Biking: Mount Agamenticus has become a mountain-biking haven.

Birding: Brave Boat Harbor, Route 103 at Kittery Point, is a small wildlife refuge on a tidal estuary where you can walk the 2-mile nature trail through the marsh. Good bird watching.

Cruises: Isles of Shoals Steamship Co., 315 Market St., Portsmouth (☎ 603/431-5500), operates a ferry to Star Island plus cruises of the harbor and to the Isles of Shoals. It also runs reggae and dance cruises as well as whale-watching trips (see below). The ferry and harbor cruises cost $15 for adults and $8 for children 3 to 11; on some Isles of Shoals cruises you can make a stopover. Cruises operate daily from mid-June to Labor day, and on weekends from May to mid-June and after Labor Day through October. **Portsmouth Harbor Cruises** (☎ 603/436-8084) operates similar harbor, river, and island cruises for similar prices. An unusual tour is **Celia Thaxter's Garden Tour** to Appledore Island, operated by Shoals Marine Laboratory, on Wednesday only. For information about this tour and to make reservations, contact Cornell University (☎ 607/255-3717).

Fishing: Lobstering trips can be taken from York Harbor's Town Dock 2. You can see the traps being hauled and learn about the art of lobstering. The price is only $6.50 per person. For information call ☎ 207/363-3234. Fishing for blues or striped bass is offered by **Mainely Fishing** (☎ 207/363-6526) for $35 per person. Trips last about 5 hours. Charter fishing trips for tuna, and bluefish are offered from May 1 to mid-October by **Seabury Charters** (☎ 207/363-5675), which sails from York's Town Dock 2. You need to get six people together for the trip, which costs from $420.

Golf: Highland Farm Golf Club is at 301 Cider Hill Rd. (Route 91; ☎ 207/351-2727); **Wentworth by the Sea** (☎ 603/433-5010) in New Castle, is a par-70, 18-hole course with water views.

Hiking: Climb 602-foot **Mount Agamenticus,** Mountain Road, York, for the best area views. A less strenuous walk is along the **Shore Path**, beginning in York Harbor and going east along the river through the Steedman woods over the Wiggly Bridge and across Route 103.

Horseback Riding: At the summit of Mount Agamenticus, the **Agamenticus Riding Stables** (☎ 207/363-1040) offer great trail riding in a wilderness area. Open Memorial Day to Columbus Day.

Scuba Diving: York Beach Scuba in York Beach (☎ 207/363-3330) rents equipment and offers boat and guided dives. Prices begin at $25 for a single boat dive. Instruction provided.

State Parks: See **Fort McClary State Park** above (☎ 207/439-2845).

Whale Watching: Isles of Shoals Steamship Co., 315 Market St., Portsmouth (☎ 603/431-5500), offers whale-watching trips. The cost is $25 for adults and $16 for children. Cruises operate daily from mid-June to Labor Day, and on weekends from May to mid-June and Labor Day through October.

OGUNQUIT

Ogunquit means "Beautiful Place by the Sea," and that it is, with broad sand-and-dune beaches and the Ogunquit River coursing along behind them on the inland side. Given the natural beauty, it's not surprising that when Charles

Woodbury arrived here in 1890, he dubbed it an artist's paradise. He helped establish an art colony that included such famous figures as Walt Kuhn, Yasuo Kuniyoshi, and Harrison Easter Field. To see the magnificent ocean and rocky coastline views that attracted them, walk along the Marginal Way as it meanders along the coastline from Perkins Cove into Ogunquit.

EXPLORING THE AREA

Perkins Cove lies south of Ogunquit proper and was artificially created by fishermen, who cut through a narrow strip of land to create a safe haven for fishing boats. What makes the cover unusual is the draw footbridge that arches above the inlet. Today, in season, people flock to the stores and restaurants on the wharf. To get the flavor of what it might have been like when it was a true working harbor and the focal point of the art colony that flourished at the turn of the century, stroll around the perimeter of the dock, staying as close as you can to the water, and cross the bridge for a view from the other bank.

The art colony was started by Charles Woodbury, an academic painter with a circle of young women followers (the locals dubbed them "Virginal Wayfarers"). But it was the arrival in 1902 of Harrison Easter Field (1873–1922) with his French protege, Robert Laurent, that transformed Perkins Cove and Ogunquit into an avant-garde enclave of cubism and fauvism. The best-known member of the colony was Walt Kuhn (1877–1949). Art is still an important part of the scene. Artists like **Bonnie Nelson** paint and sell from their roadside studios. You'll find Bonnie's fine watercolors of irises, or of York Harbor and Monhegan Island, at her gallery-studio at Shore Road and Juniper Lane (☎ 207/361-1678).

Few of the many stores here are really worth browsing—exceptions are the jewelry at **Swamp John's** (☎ 207/646-9414) and the porcelain and stoneware at **Christ Davis** (☎ 207/646-7619).

The **Ogunquit Museum of American Art,** Shore Road (☎ 207/646-4909), offers special shows as well as a permanent collection, which contains works by a roster of leading 20th-century American artists—Thomas Hart Benton, Will Barnet, Charles Burchfield, Charles Demuth, Marsden Hartley, Rockwell Kent, Yasuo Kuniyoshi, Gaston Lachaise, Jack Levine, Reginald Marsh, Charles Woodbury, William and Marguerite Zorach, and Walt Kuhn. The museum's location on a bluff overlooking the ocean, as well as its grounds with sculptures, a reflecting pool, and a small brook, add an extra dimension to the experience. The museum is only ½ mile from Perkins Cove and 1½ miles south of Ogunquit center. Open July 1 to September 30, Monday to Saturday from 10:30am to 5pm and Sunday 2 to 5pm. Admission is $3 for adults, children under 12 are free. The Ogunquit Art Association on Bourne's Lane holds juried shows from May to October.

North of Ogunquit, Route 1 runs through **Wells,** which is famous for being a secondhand book town and having a substantial number of antique stores. It was a frontier town during the French and Indian wars, and some of its history can be gleaned at the **Historic Meetinghouse Museum** on Post Road (☎ 207/646-4775). Car lovers also know the town for its **Wells Auto Museum** (207/646-9064), a collection of 100-plus antique beauties. Wells is also the home of the **Rachel Carson National Wildlife Refuge,** Route 9 East (☎ 207/646-9226), off Route 9 on the way to Kennebunkport. The refuge encompasses 1,600 acres of wetlands. Here you can walk the 1-mile trail along the edge of a salt marsh inhabited by a variety of marine life, shore birds, and waterfowl.

OGUNQUIT AFTER DARK

For evening entertainment in the area, the famous **Ogunquit Playhouse**, about a mile south of town on Route 1, opens its season at the end of June. It has been doing so since 1933 when it was founded by Walter Hartwig; stars such as Ethel Barrymore and Laurette Taylor have walked the boards here. A few miles inland from Wells, Berwick's **Hackmatack Playhouse**, 538 Rte. 9 (☎ 207/698-1807), has been putting on a season of musicals and plays for close to 30 years.

OGUNQUIT LODGING

The **Wooden Goose Inn**, Route 1, Cape Neddick, ME 03902 (☎ 207/363-5673), may be on Route 1, but it is a very special accommodation that has been decorated with panache to give both comfort to the body and pleasure to the eye. Innkeepers Jerry Rippetoe and Tony Sienicki have created a quiet oasis for guests to enjoy. Behind the house a fountain plays at the center of a flagstone patio furnished with urns and wrought iron tables and chairs. Beyond ripples the Cape Neddick River, inviting you for a leisurely stroll along its banks. On the enclosed terrace, decorated with paintings and eye-catching objets d'art, an elaborate afternoon tea—pâté, flourless chocolate torte, and other homemade tarts—is served. The six rooms have been decorated with the finest antiques, fabrics, and linens, from plush carpeting to elaborate draperies and ruffled pillows. In the morning, a tea or coffee tray will be delivered to your door to prepare you for the superb breakfast that will soon follow. It's rumored that the innkeepers have 20 or so menus, and any one of them will knock your socks off—from the Grand Marnier custard followed by lobster quiche to the strawberries Romanoff followed by potato pancakes topped with poached egg and Hollandaise sauce. In short, it's just perfect—so perfect in fact that you'll need to book months in advance on a weekend. Rates: $140

A few hundred yards from the Marginal Way on a quiet cul de sac, midway between Ogunquit and Perkins Cove, **The Trellis House**, 2 Beachmere Place (P.O. Box 2229), Ogunquit, ME 03907 (☎ 207/646-7909), is a delightful bed-and-breakfast, located in a historic home surrounded by lovingly tended gardens. Built as a summer cottage in 1907, the house itself has only three guest rooms; the other five are in two small separate buildings. Each room has been stylishly and creatively decorated by Pat Houlihan, who has an eye for unusual objects that add the final touch to a room—a painting, a birdcage, or an architectural fragment. The Maine Suite is a lovely room, with a large bay window providing space for a sitting area. The English Suite has its own little porch and contains a carved mahogany four-poster. The Garden Room is appropriately bright and airy and has some intriguing decorative accents, such as the architrave trimmed with ivy and dried flowers. The rooms in the outside buildings have gas fireplaces. The Cottage, with its white-painted beams and sponge-painted silver walls, and the Little Field Room, with its wisteria murals and sponge-painted light-blue walls, are both charmers. Breakfast is usually served on the porch. It's a treat of items like zucchini pie and steamed herbed potatoes plus, say, pecan-ring cake and mango parfait. Chaise lounges on the lawn are surrounded by peonies, azaleas, tulips, and seasonal flowers. Rates: May to mid-June, $85 to $100; mid-June to early September, $110 to $130; early September to October, $85 to $100; November to April, $85 to $95

Hartwell House, 116 Shore Rd. (P.O. Box 393), Ogunquit, ME 03907 (☎ 207/646-7210), is a short walk from Perkins Cove. It stands on 1½ acres and beckons guests to its sunporch and shaded lawns. There are four very spacious rooms in the main house plus three suites in another building up the street, all attractively furnished with antique reproductions. The James Wilson Room contains a scallop-shell four-poster, a maple dresser, and two very beautifully upholstered chairs. It has a small private balcony, too. The Winslow Homer Room has a serpentine burled-maple canopied bed with sheer drapes plus an extravagant Victorian sofa. A full breakfast featuring dishes such as stuffed French toast with apricot/orange beurre blanc or poached eggs with artichoke hearts is served in the breakfast room at a long maple harvest table. Afternoon tea is served on the sunporch. In the off-season, a seven-course dinner and champagne reception are offered to a maximum of eight guests on Saturday night. Rates: July to mid-September, rooms $130 to $155, suites $175 to $195; May to June and mid-September to October, rooms $105 to $135, suites $155 to $175; November to April, rooms $95 to $115, suites $145.

The Beachmere Inn, (P.O. Box 2340), Ogunquit, ME 03907 (☎ 207/646-2021), is a Victorian-style place that is tucked away off Shore Road in a prime spot overlooking the ocean. It's one of those somewhat old-fashioned seafront hostelries. The rooms include an efficiency, which has a two-burner stove, a microwave, a coffeemaker, and a toaster, in the turret. Bedroom furnishings are mostly pine, set against plain white walls, although some rooms have wallpaper with floral or decorative motifs. More units, all with efficiencies, are located in another modern two-story building. The living room at the Victorian house, where coffee and muffins are taken around the fireplace in the morning, extends out to a deck that overlooks the lawn and the ocean beyond. Rates: late June to August, $90 to $190; mid-May to mid-June and September to mid-October, $70 to $145; late March to mid-May and mid-October to mid-December, $60 to $105.

The Pine Hill Inn, 14 Pine Hill S. (P.O. Box 2336), Ogunquit, ME 03907 (☎ 207/361-1004), occupies a quiet location on a back road behind Perkins Cove. It's a large house set on an acre atop a hill with a splendid wide side porch that is furnished with bamboo and glass tables. The house has some extraordinary tongue-and-groove paneling throughout, most lavishly used in the sitting room where there's a TV and a small organ. There are five rooms (two with shared bath). They are simply furnished, mostly with white-painted furniture and wicker or brass-and-iron beds. The most alluring accommodation is the two-bedroom cottage, which has a front deck with umbrella table. It has a tiny bathroom but is equipped with a full kitchen with a four-burner stove. Rates: $95 to $105; cottage, $110 per night, $700 per week.

The **Beauport Inn & Cafe,** 102 Shore Rd. (P.O. Box 1793), Ogunquit, ME 03907 (☎ 207/646-8680), is a medium walk from Perkins Cove. It's operated by a friendly couple and offers good value. The rooms, all with private bath, are attractive and very nicely maintained. There are a couple of sitting rooms with fireplaces for guests and a back deck where you can lounge and watch the birds. The cafe is a good breakfast or luncheon spot. It serves fresh salads, sandwiches and other dishes. Rates: in season, $105; off-season, $75.

The **Cliff House,** Shore Road (P.O. Box 2274), Ogunquit, ME 03907 (☎ 207/361-1000), is in a dramatic spot atop Bald Head Cliff with panoramic views of the crashing surf below. It's a venerable classic (1872) where people used to pass entire summers. The 150-plus rooms are located in modern three-story blocks along the cliff side. They're furnished in a Scandinavian 1950s style. All are appointed with color TVs and telephones and have ocean-side balconies. The dining room offers traditional New England and continental cuisine to accompany the view. Facilities include an indoor pool. Rates: late March to late May, $125 to $155; late May to early July, $160 to $190; early July to August, $190 to $220; September to late October, $160 to $190; late October to mid-December, $125 to $155. Mid-December to late March, by package plan only. Special packages and MAP rates available.

Right in town, the **Nellie Littlefield,** 9 Shore Rd., Ogunquit, ME 03907 (☎ 207/646-1692), occupies an 1889 Victorian that has been gutted and totally restored and redesigned. All the rooms have private baths and cable TVs, and four have private decks. The rooms are attractively decorated with wall-to-wall carpeting and country pieces. The George Littlefield Room, for example, is decked out in a broad candy stripe and contains an iron bed, armoire, and two easy chairs. The most luxurious room is the top floor J. H. Littlefield Suite, which has a whirlpool tub. The Grace Littlefield Room is in the turret. Facilities include a small fitness room with treadmill and step-climbing machine. Rates: July to Labor Day, $150 to $205; May, June and Labor Day to mid-October, $100 to $150; May and late October, $85 to $130.

OGUNQUIT DINING

Cape Neddick Inn and Gallery, 1233 Rte. 1, Cape Neddick (☎ 207/363-2899), is the place to eat where dramatic interiors filled with color, art, and sculptures make for an artistic dining experience. The cuisine is good-quality contemporary American, featuring dishes with assertive flavors. To get into the mood, start your meal with a smoked-fish platter of Atlantic salmon, mussels, and sea scallops or delicious grilled salmon and cod cakes with to-mato-caper mayonnaise. Follow with a wasabi sesame-crusted halibut with stir-fry vegetables or herb-rubbed and grilled venison with smashed yams, dried-cherry chutney, and Jack Daniels onion gravy. Prices range from $14 to $19. The desserts are also sublime, whether the simple pie of the day or the old port mudcake pyramid, which is built around mango buttercream and served in a pool of raspberry coulis. Open daily from 6pm to closing in summer; Wednesday to Sunday winter.

The name **98 Provence,** 104 Shore Rd. (☎ 207/646-9898), says it all. Beams, lace, and Mediterranean colors make for lovely dining rooms and con-jure a similarly inspired cuisine. There are plenty of delights among the appe-tizers—pan-seared scallops with an orange and basil sauce, lobster and fennel salad with a Campari and grapefruit vinaigrette, and shrimp and vegetable fritters served with a saffron aioli. Main courses are equally inspiring. Try the wild-flavored rabbit hunter style, the delicious halibut poached in red wine, or the beef tenderloin roasted with herbs and served with a rich and wonderfully intense Gigondas wine sauce. You'll think you're back on Provençal soil. Prices range from $15 to $24. Open Wednesday to Monday 5:30 to 9:30pm. Closed December to March.

Surprising though it may seem given its location, **Hurricane,** Oarweed Lane, Perkins Cove (☎ 207/646-6348), is one very good place to eat right down in the cove. Start with the deviled Maine lobster cakes with a fresh tomato and cilantro salsa or Penobscot Bay mussels with tomato, garlic, and basil finished with an extra touch of capers and white wine. All of the fish dishes—from the fire-roasted haddock with Maine lobster and bean salsa to the baked stuffed lobster— are worth ordering. Meat lovers will appreciate the pan-roasted pork tenderloin with a brandied whole-grain mustard cream. Prices range from $18 to $26. Open daily 11:30am to 10:30pm.

Arrows, Berwick Road (☎ 207/646-7175), has all the ingredients for a romantic dining experience—a wisteria-draped entryway, a 1765 house as a stage setting, surrounded by lovely gardens complete with pond. The chairs are lushly upholstered, and the table settings are exquisite. The chefs draw their inspiration from a variety of sources. The accompaniments of each dish are carefully selected. The menu changes daily. Start with the jumbo Maine sea scallop wrapped in pancetta and served with baked polenta, braised cipolline onions, and rosemary butter; or the house-cured prosciutto with Ranier cherries and mint crème fraiche. Salads are refreshing combinations like the timbale of avocado, mango, and celery root with a radicchio and endive salad and lemon-saffron vinaigrette. There are half a dozen main courses. For example, you might enjoy a sautéed halibut with crispy eggplant chips on a seared green-noodles pillow with a tangerine and star-anise sauce; or the delicious Maine lobster with a slow-roasted tomato sauce, tarragon oil frisé with bacon, and twice-baked potatoes. Prices range from $32 to $36. Proper dress is required. Open late April through Thanksgiving, Tuesday to Sunday from 6 to 10pm.

Jonathan's, 2 Bourne Lane (☎ 207/646-4777), is a rambling restaurant with several dining rooms arranged around a central bar. One of the rooms has a 600-gallon tropical fish tank; another looks out on the sculptures in the garden. Lilac napkins and blue glasses enliven the table settings. The specialties of the house are the oysters to start, which you can have prepared in a variety of styles—for example, Spanish with sour cream and salsa or Japanese with wasabi, pickled ginger, and soy sauce. The rest of the menu balances fish and meat with a handful of pasta dishes and Italian favorites like veal piccatta and veal marsala. One dish that really glows is the caramelized salmon marinated in Grand Marnier vinaigrette; dusted with sugar, dill, and black pepper; and then cooked and served over a lemon beurre blanc with a touch of balsamic essence. Prices range from $15 to $21.

Ogunquit Lobster Pound, Route 1 (☎ 207/646-2516), is about as far from a small shack on the shoreline as you can get. It's on a main highway in town and is a large institution with a huge tank of lobsters outside. You can dine either inside at polished wood tables or outside in the grove of trees. In addition to the specialty lobsters, steamed clams, steak, and chicken dishes are available. Prices for lobster average $12 a pound for hardshells, while the rest of the menu ranges from $10 to $29 (for surf and turf). Open in summer daily from 4 to 9:30pm, off season daily from 5:30 to 8:30pm.

Frankie & Johnny's, 1594 Rte. 1, North Cape Neddick (☎ 207/363-1909), is an odd name for a place that serves healthful and natural cuisine. It sounds more like a hamburger joint, somehow. Nevertheless, this is where you can enjoy some unique crustoli dishes that are similar to pizza but made with a round French bread crust and topped with a variety of items—chicken basil pesto, arugula and salmon, you name it. Then there are the entrees, which range from a grilled tofu served with a ginger soy sauce and rice and vegetables to grilled ostrich—the healthful meat of the moment—which is served with smoked mushrooms. Prices range from $11 to $19. Salads, burritos, and pastas are also available. BYOB. Open July to August, daily; spring/fall Thursday to Sunday from 5pm to closing.

Ogunquit
Special & Recreational Activities

Antiquing: Between Cape Neddick and Kennebunk are several group shops well worth browsing. Many are concentrated in Wells, notably **Reed's Antiques & Collectibles** (☎ 207/646-8010); **Bo-March Hall** (☎ 207/646-4116); and **D & A Country Mouse Antiques** (☎ 207/646-7334). Also try the **Blacksmith's Mall** (☎ 207/646-9643) at 116 Main St., Ogunquit, with 60-plus dealers and **The Barn at Cape Neddick** (☎ 207/363-7315) with 80 dealers.

Beaches: Footbridge Beach, off Ocean Street, is so called because you reach it via a bridge. It's a splendid stretch of sand and quieter than many. **Ogunquit Main Beach,** Route 1 to Beach Street, is a very popular sandy beach.

Biking: Rentals available from **Bikes by the Sea** (☎ 207/646-5898).

Cruises: The catboat *Cricket* sails on 1¾-hour trips from Perkins Cove along the rocky coastline to tiny coves that are accessible aboard such a small boat that takes only six passengers. The fare is $15, and reservations are needed. Two-hour sails are also offered aboard the *Silverlining* (☎ 207/361-9800), a 42-foot classic wooden sloop. Only six passengers are taken on the trip, so reservations are recommended. Tickets are $28. *Finestkind* (☎ 207/646-5227) offers several different cruises—a lobstering trip, breakfast and cocktail cruises, and a 1½-hour trip to Nubble Lighthouse. Prices range from $8 to $12 for adults, $6 to $8 for children.

Fishing: Several sport-fishing boats leave from **Perkins Cove** in search of cod, pollock, halibut, and haddock. Contact the *Bunny Clark* (☎ 207/646-2214), which carries a maximum of 30 people. A full day of fishing will cost about $50 per person, a half day, $30 per person. The *Ms Lainey* (☎ 207/646-5046) and the *Ugly Anne* (☎ 208/646-7202) are two other options.

Hiking: Walk the **Marginal Way** mile-long coastal pathway from Perkins Cove to Ogunquit. The **Old Trolley Trail,** which begins at the northern end of Pine Hill Road, is another popular walk.

Nature Reserves: Wells National Estuarine Reserve off Route 1 on Laudholm Farm Road (☎ 207/646-1555), at Laudholm Farm, offers 1,600 acres of field, forest, wetland, and beach for exploration. As you walk the trails, you might see black ducks, peregrine falcons, and piping plovers as well as a variety of wildflowers.

Tennis: There are three courts at the **Agamenticus Recreational Area**, on Agamenticus Road.

Whale Watching: From **Perkins Cove**, the *Deborah Ann* (☎ 207/361-9501) operates twice daily in summer. Rates are $30 for adults and $25 for children 12 and under.

KENNEBUNKPORT

The approach to Kennebunk-Kennebunkport is grand. When you turn onto Route 9 from Route 1, the scene changes. The road is lined with beautiful Greek Revival homes and Victorian mansions. Gooch's Beach stretches for a long way in front of handsome beachfront homes. The town itself focuses on Dock Square, from which streets lined with handsome historic homes fan out. From Dock Square, Ocean Avenue travels along the harbor and curves around beautiful Cape Arundel, past Blowing Cave and Spouting Rock where the surf crashes against the rocky coastline in geyserlike fountains to **Walker's Point.** Along the way you can gawk at the Bush's summer place in the distance. You will have already passed St. Anne's Episcopal Church, where President Bush's parents wed. Just around the corner from Walker's Point is a different kind of memorial, one to those shipwrecked aboard the *Wandby* on May 9, 1921— they ran aground and broke up off the coast here en route from Algiers to Portland.

If you continue around and pick up Wildes District Road to Route 9, you will come eventually to **Cape Porpoise,** which returns you to quiet old-world Maine. The wonderful gallery, **Silica** (☎ 207/967-0133), is located here on Pier Road. It has some terrific glass art that sells for thousands, as well as smaller, less expensive items like perfume bottles and jewelry. Also stop in at the **Wright Gallery** (☎ 207/967-5053) on Pier Road, where the art is hung in a 19th-century post-and-beam home. Farther along on Route 9 is the other Kennebunk village of **Goose Rocks Beach** with a sweep of beach facing the tiny islands of Goose Rocks.

Back in town, you'll want to visit the **Brick Store Museum,** 117 Main St., Kennebunk (☎ 207/985-4802), which focuses on the Kennebunks' history, displaying historical and decorative-arts exhibits in several 19th-century buildings. The Brick Store Museum sponsors **architectural walking tours** of the Kennebunk National Historic District, including the **Taylor-Barry House** (1803), from mid-June to mid-October, but they're only given on Wednesdays and Fridays (call for a schedule). On weekends you'll have to follow the self-guided tour through the district. The historic sites are open Tuesday to Saturday from 10am to 4:30pm. Admission is $3 ($5 to include the Taylor Barry House).

The other keeper of the resort's heritage is the **Kennebunkport Historical Society** (☎ 207/967-2751), located in the school house at 135 North St.,

Kennebunkport. It has a collection of photographs, shipbuilding records, and other memorabilia (open Wednesday to Friday from 10am to 4pm). Nearby you can visit the **Nott House,** an 1853 Greek Revival home featuring the original wallpaper and rugs and other contents belonging to several generations of the Perkins-Nott family. Open mid-June to Columbus Day, Tuesday to Friday from 1 to 4pm. The society also sponsors walking tours of Kennebunkport.

A livelier historical exhibit is found at the **Seashore Trolley Museum,** Log Cabin Road, Kennebunkport (☎ 207/967-2800). The museum has a very large collection of electric trolley cars and railroad cars, and you can catch a ride aboard one of these old, more gracious forms of transportation.

There are plenty of stores to browse in and around Dock Square. As far as art galleries go, don't miss **Mast Cove Galleries** on Mast Cove Lane and Maine Street (☎ 207/967-3453), where owner Jean Briggs features the paintings, graphics, and sculpture of nearly 100 outstanding artists. It's located in a 19th-century Greek Revival Home next door to the Graves Memorial Library, only a block from Dock Square. Other galleries to look for are **The Gallery on Chase Hill,** 10 Chase Hill Rd. (☎ 207/967-0049), and **Ocean Winds,** Ocean Avenue (☎ 207/967-2823), which also has a branch at Perkins Cove.

KENNEBUNKPORT LODGING

Even though the **White Barn Inn,** Beach Street (P.O. Box 560C), Kennebunkport, ME 04046 (☎ 207/967-2321), has no water view, it is an extraordinarily lovely place to stay and to dine—a place for celebration and romance. Guest rooms have been meticulously decorated using superb furnishings, fabrics, wallpapers, and appointments. The pool house rooms are the most alluring, each furnished with a rice four-poster, two easy chairs in front of a wood-burning fireplace, conveniences such as a secretary and Chippendale chair, and luxuries such as a marble bathroom featuring Jacuzzi and shower. They provide immediate access to the quarry stone pool with waterfall. The junior suites in the carriage house contain pretty much the same features but are larger. The most lavish space, May's Cottage, has a double granite fireplace, which faces into sitting area and bedroom, plus a TV/VCR, a double Jacuzzi, and a shower-steam bath. The rooms in the original farmhouse, which dates to the 1820s, have been decorated in a lighter style. Extra touches and services in all the rooms include plush robes, fresh flowers, nightlights, twice-daily maid service, and turndown. Poolside there's a cabana where massages are given. Breakfast, afternoon tea and cookies, and ports and brandies are provided. Perfect for a wonderful romantic weekend. See below for dining. Rates: rooms $160-$190, pool house $240, junior suite $340, and cottage $400. Special bargain packages available off-season.

The **Captain Lord Mansion,** Pleasant and Green streets (P.O. Box 800), Kennebunkport, ME 04046 (☎ 207/ 967-3141), is certainly the premier place to stay. It's located right behind the town green in an imposing and very beautiful building with an octagonal cupola. It was built for merchant-shipbuilder Nathaniel Lord in 1814. The interiors have been beautifully decorated and furnished by Bev Davis and her husband, Rick Litchfield. The gardens, too, are carefully maintained and include a 10-visit memory path made of bricks bearing the names of frequent guests. There are 16 rooms (15 with gas fireplace; some with refrigerator). They are meticulously designed for comfort as well as aesthetics, with good reading lamps over the beds, double sinks in the bathroom, and similar thoughtful details. The furnishings are very high quality. The Ship *Mary Lord,* for example, has a handsome rice four-poster with a crocheted canopy and a Victorian-style (yet amazingly comfortable) sofa, an Eastlake loveseat, and handsome oriental lamps. The Captain's Suite is astonishingly luxurious, with two bathrooms. Bathroom no. 1 has a 10-jet hydro massage body spa, a rich brown-marble tiled shower, a heated marble floor, and a bidet. Bathroom no. 2 is carpeted and has a mood-lit double whirl-pool enclosed in glass mirror, two granite Corian vanities, a stereo with a CD and tape player, a gas fireplace, and a NordicTrack from which you can watch the TV/VCR that is tucked into a cabinet. To cap it all off, there's a lavishly upholstered ottoman. The bedroom features a serpentine mahogany four-poster, an intricately carved armoire set against a rich damasklike wallpaper, and a gas fireplace. This is the top-of-the-line accommodation, admittedly, but the other accommodations are all exquisitely turned out in striking color palettes and accented with fine paintings and stenciling. Ship *Ophelia* contains the bed that originally belonged to Captain Lord. It's combined with a polished armoire and an Empire chest and is set off by peach candy-stripe wallpaper and forest-green carpeting. Bark *Dana* is dramatic in cherry-red and black. An elaborate three-course breakfast is served in the dining room at pine harvest tables; afternoon tea is also served. Naturally, guests also have a very comfortable gathering room in which to relax. Additional amenities include beach towels and umbrellas. Rates: June to October and weekends in December $159 to $259; Captain's Suite $359. Special packages and reduced rates available at other times.

Captain Jefferds Inn, Pearl Street (Box 691), Kennebunkport, ME 04046 (☎ 207/967-2311), occupies a stunning Federal-style mansion built in 1804. There are 16 rooms, all with private baths (four are in the carriage house and only available in summer). Each tasteful, traditionally decorated room has a color or a geographical theme. The Chatham Room has a spindle four-poster canopied bed piled high with burgundy pillows. The Manhattan Room has wallpaper with a New York print and Fifth Avenue hatboxes that are used as accents. The bed is a mahogany four-poster. The Monticello Room sports Williamsburg blue, while the Florida Room has a contemporary look with its skylight, watercolors, and wicker and pine elements. Some rooms have wood-burning fireplaces. The pièces de résistance are the suites like the Assisi, which has lavish tiles decorated with peacocks in the bathroom plus a large shower with double heads. The house has large sitting rooms and a dining room with a long table where a candlelit breakfast of muffins, croissants, and apricot-stuffed French toast with syrup from Jeff's family farm is served. Hot tea and cookies are offered in the garden room, which has windows on three sides; there's a TV here, too. Extra welcome is provided by Tweedledum and Tweedledee, two Guldian finches, and Katy, the Golden Retriever. Rates: $115 to $230 year-round.

Bufflehead Cove, off Route 35 (P.O. Box 499), Kennebunkport, ME 04046 (☎ 207/967-3879), is tucked back in the woods on a cove. Take a seat on the porch facing the cove or in one of the hammocks and watch for the bufflehead ducks that gave their name to this serene retreat on 6 acres. There are five spacious accommodations. Several have Jacuzzis and private decks. Hideaway has a skylit bedroom/sitting room and a deck overlooking the cove. The furnishings are country comfortable—bamboo chairs and glass tables, sofa and loveseat, plant-filled baskets, and an old trunk serving as a coffee table. The whole is enhanced by a double-sided gas fireplace and a bathroom with Jacuzzi and shower. The Cove Suite is similar, but the living area is embellished with a mural of buffleheads bobbing on the cove. It also has a double Jacuzzi on a glassed-in balcony. The Garden Studio has a separate entrance and a private slate patio shaded by a trellis. A full breakfast of pop-overs filled with fresh fruit, followed by a dish like eggs with feta and spinach, is served in an attractive dining room warmed by a wood stove. The sitting room also has an inviting fireplace and plenty of comfortable seating. Positively inspirational. Rates: June to October, $145 to $260; November to June, $105 to 175.

The Inn on South Street, South Street (P.O. Box 478A), Kennebunkport, ME 04046 (☎ 207/967-5151), has a view of the river and ocean from the kitchen table where breakfast is served. This inn, in an early 19th-century Greek Revival home, is operated by Jack and Eva Downs. Jack, a professor of American history, has written a book on the China trade, and his passion for Asian art is clear from the Korean silk paintings, Chinese ceramics, carved coffee table, and other decorative objects found in the sitting room. In addition to this comfortable room, guests have access to a balcony and to a lovely back garden landscaped with a brick terrace, pond, and gazebo. There are three guest rooms and a suite. Each is individually decorated. The Gibson Room is furnished with a brass bed, a wicker chaise lounge, and an antique trunk. Fresh flowers add that extra touch to all the rooms, and a corkscrew and glasses are supplied. The Romantic Room, tucked under the eaves, contains a painted cottage bed covered with a ring quilt that stands on painted-board floors. Wicker chairs and a pier mirror complete the furnishings. The first-floor Perkins room has a wood-burning fireplace and a stunning tiger maple four-poster with a crocheted canopy. The Garden Suite has a separate entrance, private porch, and a full kitchen. The breakfasts are special. On any day you might be greeted with minted watermelon with strawberries or blueberries, rhubarb ginger muffins, and an omelet filled with fresh seasonal ingredients or German pancakes with seasonal fruit. Afternoon tea is also served. Rates: in season $149 to $235; off-season $99 to $165.

The **Captain Fairfield Inn,** Corner of Pleasant and Green streets (P.O. Box 1308), Kennebunkport ME 04046 (☎ 207/967-4454), occupies an 1813 Federal-style home. It's a lovely home, but it is totally without pretension. There are nine guest rooms all with private baths; some have fireplaces. Rooms are decorated with chintz wallpapers, swag drapes at the windows, and might have a serpentine canopied bed. Each room contains a hair dryer, iron/ironing board, nightlight, and little extras such as wine glasses and a corkscrew along with bottled spring water. The living room is very comfortable, and here guests gather to read, play cards, or just relax in front of the fireplace. The breakfast prepared by chef/owner Dennis Tallagnon is a treat—Maine blueberry pancakes and other specialties. It's served either in the dining room in front of the open-hearth fireplace or in a breakfast room overlooking the garden.

Afternoon tea is also served. Rates: late June to late October, $149 to $235; late May to late June and late October, $109 to $235; January to late May and November to December 31, $99 to $235.

Ocean View, 72 Beach Ave., Kennebunk Beach, ME 04043 (☎ 207/967-2750), has a marvelous location looking out to Lord's Point and is a real seaside kind of place decorated in light pastels and lots of white to reflect the brilliance of the light. You can't miss it. The exterior is painted in a riot of royal and sky blue, magenta, pink, and lilac, capped off by a magenta door. Guests have the choice of two sitting rooms and a fine front porch. There are nine rooms including four junior suites that are in an adjacent building. The premier room occupies the entire third floor and has a huge bathroom. Most rooms have been furnished with white-painted furniture plus wing chairs and a chaise lounge or with pine and wicker. All have minirefrigerators, ceiling fans, telephones, TVs, clock/radios, and CD players. A full breakfast of broiled grapefruit, fresh fruit, and dishes like Belgian waffles is served. Rates: mid-June to mid-October, $175 to $235; mid-April to mid-May and mid-November to mid-December, $105 to $165; mid-May to mid-June or mid-October to mid-November, $135 to $190.

Old Fort Inn, Old Fort Avenue, Kennebunkport, ME 04046 (☎ 207/967-5353), is situated a block from the ocean on 15 acres in a prime residential area near Cape Arundel. The majority of the rooms (16, in fact) are located in a fine brick-and-stone carriage house where there is also a sitting room for guests. The rooms are large, and furnished attractively with maple four-posters, wing chairs, a sofa or loveseat, and oak chests, plus decorative accents such as Shaker boxes, a stocking maker, or other piece of Americana. The suite in the main building is striking, decorated in black and burgundy. All rooms have wet bars, color TVs, telephones, and private baths. A buffet breakfast of fruits and pastries is served in the common room around the large brick fireplace. The room, with its weighty beams, barn-board walls, decorative decoys, and dark green couches has a rustic air. Amenities include one tennis court and a large nicely landscaped pool screened by a hedge. Rates: late April to early December, $140 to $290; lower off-season.

Tides Inn by the Sea, 252 Goose Rocks Beach (R.R. 2), Kennebunkport, ME (☎ 207/967-3757), has a glorious location on the beach facing the ocean where seals bask on rocky islands. It occupies an 1899 Victorian and has a delightful homey, country ambience imparted by the mother-daughter team of innkeepers, Marie and Kristin Henriksen. There are no TVs or phones in the 22 rooms, which are furnished simply with oak and wicker pieces. The building has two porches on the first and second floors. It's a historic place, and the guest roster includes figures such as Conan Doyle and Teddy Roosevelt and more recently John Hurt and Phil Donahue. Facilities include a dining room and a pub warmed by a pot-belly stove. The dining room offers some ambitious menu items—rack of lamb in a red wine jus with pear-mint chutney or shellfish ragout, a medley of lobster, shrimp, scallops, mussels, cherry stones, and oysters that have been braised in a liquid containing tomato, fennel, garlic, and basil, served over angel-hair pasta. Prices range from $16 to $27. Reminiscent of an earlier era, it is a stately place, but not at all stuffy—a place where you can genuinely unwind. Rates: in season, $109 to $205; off-season, $85 to $205.

KENNEBUNKPORT DINING

The White Barn Inn, Beach Street (☎ 207/967-2321), is the most romantic place to dine in what was once a barn. It's wonderfully warm, with a loft that has been lavishly furnished with oriental rugs and antiques. A pianist quietly entertains, and a floor-to-ceiling window looks out onto a flower-filled garden or a snow covered landscape, depending on the season, that is illuminated at night. The beautifully orchestrated sequence of dishes brings you a meal that will leave you at peace with the world. The $58 fixed-price menu changes daily to reflect the best ingredients of the season; some come from the restaurant's own garden. You might begin with pan-seared Quebec foie gras layered with oven-dried apple and potato crisps in a pool of aged balsamic jus and golden raisins or with a lobster spring roll with carrot, daikon radish, snow peas, cilantro, and a spicy sweet sauce. A choice of six or so entrees will follow—grilled beef tenderloin topped with a potato and three peppercorn crust, bok choy, spring corn, and a rich merlot and shiitake mushroom sauce; Maine crab soufflé; or pan-seared salmon medallions with roasted-red-pepper coulis and a spiced almond-coated couscous cake. Finish with one of the irresistible desserts like the chocolate mousse structure on a cherry coulis with brandied cherry and mascarpone parfait. If you like, you can order a half bottle of Chateau d'Yquem for $179. The wine list includes a wide range of moderate to expensive bottles. Open Monday to Thursday from 6 to 9:30pm, Friday to Sunday from 5:30 to 9:30pm. Closed Monday and Tuesday in February and March.

Grissini, 27 Western Ave. (☎ 207/967-2211), will transport you to Italy in a flash. Opera plays in the background of the spacious cathedral-ceilinged room that's blessed with a large river-stone fireplace. The floors have been painted in bold black-and-white squares. Breads, flowers, olive oils, vinegars, and a huge wheel of cheese rest on a table at the center of the room. The Northern Italian cuisine is palate pleasing indeed, and the grilled dishes are outstanding. There's something for everyone, from delicious pizzas and salads to appetizers like grilled portobello mushrooms drizzled with pesto sauce or fried calamari to start. The wood-grilled chicken in savory is perfect and full of flavor. There's also osso buco and many other traditional dishes, including a wonderful bowl of local seafood featuring cod, mussels, clams, and scallops in a lobster broth. Prices range from $10 to $14. In summer, tables on the outdoor heated flagstone patio are in demand. Open daily from 11:30am to 2:30pm and from 5:30 to 9:30pm. Closed off-season.

The Saltmarsh Tavern, Western Avenue (Route 9; ☎ 207/967-4500), has an extremely pretty exterior of gardens and brick walkways and trees trimmed with tiny lights. Inside, the beamed ceiling and barn board impart warmth to the candlelit dining room. Try the Marsh pot stickers to start. They're brimming with chicken and redolent with green chilies and cumin-scented sauce. Or else select the crispy bacon-wrapped oysters. There are eight or so entrees on the menu, ranging from a sirloin with roast vidalia onions and balsamic demiglace to potato-crusted trout with lemon chive vinaigrette. Prices range from $17 to $24. The piano bar is a bonus. Open Tuesday to Sunday from 6 to 9pm. Closed January and February.

Stop by the **Chase Hill Bakery**, Chase Hill Road (☎ 207/967-2283), for lunch. You can buy a chicken burrito, veggie melt, ham-and-Swiss sandwich, or a slice of pizza for anywhere from $4 to $6. The breads and pastries are also a drawing card. Try the fresh fruit pies and bars or the decadent chocolate toffee. Open year-round.

Mabel's Lobster Claw, Ocean Avenue (☎ 207/967-2562), is President Bush's favorite place. It's small and very unassuming, a place that belongs to another era when swing was king—as it still is here. Pine walls and red tablecloths set the background for some of the greatest chowder ever. The rest of the menu is plain and simple. The house specialty is baked stuffed lemon sole with chunks of lobster and Mabel's own Newburg sauce, and this is supplemented with items such as broiled haddock and scallops in lemon butter and several lobster dishes including a complete shore dinner. A chicken dish and a couple of steaks round out the menu. Prices range from $6.95 to $30. Open May to October daily from 11:30am to 3:30pm and 5 to 9:30pm. Closed from late October to mid-April.

Arundel Wharf, 43 Ocean Ave. (☎ 207/967-3444), offers casual dining on a river wharf. A popular place in summer where folks gather around the cabana-style bar and dine off the tables decorated with navigational charts in a yacht-club atmosphere. The lobster rolls draw raves. Open daily from 11:30am. Closed off-season.

Federal Jack's Restaurant and Brew Pub, 8 Western Ave. no. 6 (☎ 207/967-4322), is the place to repair for some good ale, a game of darts or pool, and weekend musical entertainment. Open daily from 11:30am to 9pm.

LODGING & DINING AT CAPE PORPOISE

If I were headed for Kennebunkport, I'd choose to stay out at Cape Porpoise. Cape Porpoise has remained remarkably remote from Kennebunkport's summer frenzy, primarily because only working fishing boats are allowed to dock here, and there is no yacht marina.

I'd choose to stay at the **Inn at Harbor Head,** Pier Rd., (R.R. 2; P.O. Box 1180), Cape Porpoise, ME 04046 (☎ 207/967-5564), just so that I could unwind in the beautiful interiors created by artist Joan Sutter and her husband, David, and gaze at the view of harbor, water, and sky. Joan sculpted and painted when she was younger, and some of her pieces are displayed about the house. Sadly, she has not sculpted in a while, but her eye for shape and contour and for the perfect detail shows throughout the house. Comfort and convenience are key ingredients in the rooms. All have flashlights, razors, toothbrushes and toothpaste, hair dryers, bathrobes, irons/boards, beach towels, and other amenities, along with beach parking permits. It's impossible to pick a favorite. The Garden Room is inspired by a Japanese esthetic. At the entrance, you step over a small strip of rocks and tiny fountain; Japanese art hangs over the rice four-poster with its tapestry coverlet, ink-painted peach and plum blossoms float on the walls, and white porcelain lamps and figurines complete the scene. French doors lead to a private trellised deck overlooking the harbor and cape. The bathroom in the Greenery has a gardenlike painting on the tiles that Joan designed around the sunken Jacuzzi; the room's wrought-iron bed and maple armoire are accented by several works by family members, including a lily painted by Joan. The Ocean Room has a splendid carved mahogany bed with a superfine damask duvet, piled high with pillows. The mural in the Harbor Suite sitting area depicts a seascape of Cape

Porpoise, and there's another mural of lupines and foxglove in the bedroom. Tiles from local potter Lou Lipkin decorate the fireplace. The suite also has a private deck. The sitting room is really comfortable and you can admire a bronze and a terra-cotta sculpture by Joan. Guests also can sit in the library and listen to music or read. Breakfast is served in another charming room. There might be raspberry poached pears on peach coulis, followed by eggs Florentine, or chicken quiche with asparagus and apple bread. The garden slopes down to the water's edge where a swing seat and hammocks invite the muse. A great deck, too, for the guests. Definitely my kind of place. Rates: late May to late October, $190 to $285; late April to late May, $135 to $205.

Seascapes on the Pier, Pier Rd., Cape Porpoise, Kennebunkport (☎ 207/967-8500), offers great dining with an unmarred view of the harbor, but it's more casual than the equivalent fine-dining emporiums in Kennebunkport. Upholstered bamboo chairs are arranged at tables set with jade or salmon tablecloths and brightly colored contemporary china and candlesticks. The cuisine uses local seafood and organic vegetables prepared in imaginative and traditional ways. There's scrumptious roasted medallions of lobster, miso-marinated grilled swordfish with citrus tamari sauce, and grilled, maple-glazed, pecan-encrusted rack of lamb. Prices range from $18 to $29. If you're not stuck on seafood chowder or lobster and crab bisque, then try the Prince Edward Island black mussels steamed with local beer, garlic, tomatoes, and fresh herbs. The wine list is excellent, and there's a good selection of wines by the glass. A pianist entertains at the small bar up front, and there's a pub downstairs. Open daily for lunch and dinner. Closed off-season.

For a slice of real Maine, you can't beat **Nunan's Lobster Hut** on Route 9 in Cape Porpoise (☎ 207/967-4362). It's in a shack that stands on stilts at the edge of a salt marsh. You can't miss it, because it's painted bright red and yellow. Inside, people cluster at the trestle-style tables feasting on lobsters, lobster stew, lobster rolls, and steamed clams, although there are other items on the menu. Prices range from $7 to $15.

Kennebunkport
Special & Recreational Activities

Antiquing: In **Kennebunk,** Renee Bowen (☎ 207/985-7874) carries a diverse selection of 19th-century furniture; Rivergate Antique Mall, Kennebunk (☎ 207/985-7766), offers a large selection of antiques displayed by more than 100 dealers. In **Arundel,** browse at Antiques USA (☎ 207/985-7766), which features hundreds of dealers and at Arundel Antiques (☎ 207/985-7965), which has 200-plus dealers. Call Collins Auction Galleries, 35 Western Ave. (☎ 207/967-5004) for information about their regular auctions.

Beaches: Gooch's Beach is the long sandy stretch in the Lower Village perfect for families; Goose Rocks Beach is a quieter 3-mile long sandy beach around from Cape Porpoise. Parking permits for both are available at the Chamber of Commerce. **Arundel Beach** near the Colony Hotel is a small beach for those who appreciate the meeting of rock and ocean.

Biking: Rentals available from **Cape-Able Bike Shop**, Kennebunkport (☎ 207/967-4382). Bike out to Cape Porpoise and Goose Rocks or along the bridle path beside the Moussam River off the entrance road to Sea Road School.

Birding: Vaughns Island Preserve lies between Walkers Point and Cape Porpoise.

Boating: Head to **Kennebunkport Marina** for rentals of all sorts.

Cross Country Skiing: Go to **Harris Farms Cross Country Ski Center** in Dayton (☎ 207/499-2678), which has groomed trails and rentals on this 500 acre dairy and tree farm.

Cruises: The schooner *Lazy Jack* sails from **Shooner's Inn** from late May to mid-October on 2-hour coastal trips. Passenger capacity is six only. Lobster cruises are offered by **Second Chance**, Lower Village, Kennebunk (☎ 207/967-5507), aboard a former commercial lobster boat. Cruises are 1½ hours and leave from the Arundel Boatyard behind the clam Shack. In summer, cruises leave at 11am, 1, 3, 5, and 7pm; cost is $15 for adults, $6 for children 12 to 3.

Diving: The **Diver's Locker** in Lyman (☎ 207/985-3161) offers guided tours and rental equipment.

Fishing: *Deep Water II* (☎ 207/967-4938) offers full-day and half-day trips leaving by the bridge on Route 9. *Venture Inn II* (☎ 207/967-0005) also sails from here. The season is May to October. Call for prices and schedules.

Fly-fishing: For guides and fly-fishing trips on the Kennebunk and Mousam rivers, go to **Port Fly Shop**, Kennebunk (☎ 207/967-5889).

Fruit Picking: Pick your own raspberries at **Whistling Wings Farm** and purchase some products made from them.

Golf: Cape Arundel Golf Course, Old River Road, Kennebunkport (☎ 207/967-2222), is a semiprivate 18-hole course where George Bush plays. **Webhannet Golf Course**, Sea Road, off Route 9 in Kennebunk, is another semiprivate course; **Dutch Elm Golf Course**, Brimstone Road off Route 111 between Biddeford and Lyman (☎ 207/282-9850) is a 9 holer.

Kayaking: Contact **Kayak Adventures**, Kennebunkport (☎ 207/967-5243), for guided trips.

Whale Watching: Indian Whale Watch, Kennebunkport (☎ 207/967-5912), is the original. *First Chance,* Lower Village, Kennebunk (☎ 207/967-5507), was built specifically for whale watching and offers two trips daily in season plus sunset cruises on Friday and Saturday. *Nautilus* (☎ 207/967-0707) is another operator.

FROM KENNEBUNKPORT TO PORTLAND

From Cape Porpoise, the rocky coastline extends past **Goose Rocks Beach** and many small coves and rocky inlets until it reaches Biddeford Pool, the point where the river Saco empties into the ocean. Wood Island, marked by a lighthouse, lies off Biddeford Pool. If you travel Route 9 north to the Pool, it will take you past **Rachel Carson Refuge,** a stirring landscape of marsh and tidal estuary. The only way to cross the River Saco is to go into **Biddeford-Saco.** These two towns are as different in flavor and demeanor as they can be. Biddeford on the southern bank has pretensions to a certain degree of grandeur, while Saco, on the opposite bank, is blue collar, and its playground is Old Orchard Beach, famous for its 7-mile beach, amusement park, and other kitsch. The river itself is one of the state's great rivers from which so much of the lifeblood of its history and peoples has been drawn.

A short distance along the coast, at the mouth of the marsh-laden Scarborough River lies **Prout's Neck,** a beauty spot that is closely associated with the painter Winslow Homer. It's worth driving out on Route 207 to visit the **Prout's Neck Bird Sanctuary** and **Scarborough Beach State Park** farther round the point. From here Route 77 will take you along the rocky coast (although you'll have to turn off into the several state parks and beaches along the way to see it) all the way to Cape Elizabeth and Portland. Stop at **Higgins Beach, Crescent Beach State Park,** or at my favorite, **Twin Lights State Park,** which rambles around the base of Cape Elizabeth Light. It's a lovely spot to walk the trails and commune with the ocean, sky, and wind. **Portland Head Light & Museum** at Fort Williams Park, 1000 Shore Rd., Cape Elizabeth (☎ 207/799-2661), offers another great oceanscape; stop here, perhaps to fly a kite on the grassy headland or to have a lobster roll at the shack. The museum is open June 1 to October 31 daily from 10am to 4pm. Cape Elizabeth is a wealthy community, and you'll pass many a fine oceanfront residence before crossing the Fore River into Portland.

LODGING & DINING ALONG THE WAY

From a cane rocker on the long porch of the **Black Point Inn Resort,** 510 Black Point Rd., Prout's Neck, ME 04074 (☎ 207/883-4126), you look across a grand sweep of sand beach. Here you can come to relax and wrap yourself in comfort. Enjoy basking in the sun lounge, reading in the gracious sitting room, or passing time over a cocktail in the library bar. A splendid outdoor pool overlooks the ocean; there's also an indoor pool. The majority of the 80 rooms are located in clustered buildings around the property. They're furnished with wall-to-wall carpeting, pine furnishings, brass lamps, and wing chairs. All have TVs. The grounds are prettily landscaped. Facilities include an 18-hole golf course and 14 tennis courts. Rates: MAP July to August, $150 to $210; MAP June, September to October, $140 to $190; B&B May and November, $80 to $110.

PORTLAND

Portland is a seafaring town with a great degree of sophistication. The **Old Port** has been renovated in a very fetching manner and is now an area of restored warehouse and other seafront buildings, art galleries, shops, and restaurants. You'll want to spend some time browsing through this whole area.

The gem of downtown is the **Portland Museum of Art,** 7 Congress Sq. (☎ 207/775-6148), the flagship museum of this art-loving state. It displays the works of many artists associated with Maine—Marsden Hartley, Winslow

Homer, Rockwell Kent, and Andrew Wyeth. It also possesses the outstanding Payson Impressionist/modern collection, which contains works by Renoir, Degas, Monet, Picasso, and others. It's housed in an acclaimed building designed by I. M. Pei. Open Tuesday to Wednesday and Saturday from 10am to 5pm, Thursday to Friday from 10am to 9pm and Sunday from noon to 5pm. Admission is $6 for adults, $5 for seniors and students, $1 for children 6 to 12. Free Friday 5 to 9pm.

In addition to its artistic associations, the city has quite a history of its own. For insight into the subject, go to the **Maine Historical Society,** 489 Congress St. (☎ 207/879-0427), which, in addition to its display of memorabilia, mounts temporary themed history exhibits. Open June to October, from Tuesday to Sunday from 10am to 4pm; and November to May, Wednesday to Saturday from noon to 4pm. Next door is the **Wadsworth Longfellow House,** 485 Congress St. (☎ 207/879-0427), the boyhood home of the poet Henry. It also happens to be the first brick house that was built in the city. Open June to October, Tuesday to Sunday from 10am to 4pm.

For a town of its size, Portland is bursting with cultural life. The **Portland Symphony** plays at City Hall, 389 Congress St. (☎ 207/874-8300). There are two major theater companies operating plus several smaller groups: **Mad Horse Theatre,** 955 Forest Ave. (☎ 207/878-3547), which performs cutting-edge plays and classics; **Portland State Company,** 25A Forest Ave. (☎ 207/774-0465), which is the state's premier company and performs a broad repertory of comedy and drama, both classic and contemporary. The last performs at the **Portland Performing Arts Center,** 25A Forestt Ave. (☎ 207/774-0465), along with the Ram Island Dance Company. The **State Theatre,** 609 Congress St. (☎ 207/879-1112), is another large performing-arts venue. The city also boasts three movie theaters.

From Portland it's only an hour or so to **Sebago Lake** for a taste of inland Maine.

PORTLAND LODGING

The **Pomegranate Inn,** 49 Neal St., Portland, ME 04102 (☎ 207/772-1006), has to be one of the most aesthetically pleasing bed-and-breakfasts anywhere. It's a veritable feast for the eye. The house itself is a stunning Italianate mansion. Innkeepers Alan and Isabel Smiles have decorated it with an extraordinary collection of art that ranges from abstracts to landscapes and sculptures. The six rooms are similarly extravagantly decorated. Rich golden linens make up the bed in the Heidi room. The walls are hand painted with beautiful birds, and lavish fabrics upholster the wing chairs. A claw-foot tub with hand shower and pedestal sink are in the bathroom. Another room on the third floor has been hand painted with urns and pale blue flowers and furnished with choice pieces that include an oriental-style table and rug and two easy chairs. Another room has a unique modern carved bed dressed with fine fabric and a skylit bathroom. All rooms have private baths, telephones, and TVs. Art covers the walls of the sitting room so that it's filled with life, color, and beauty. Books, too, contribute to the decor, as do the brilliant hearth tiles around the marbleized mantel. Breakfast can be taken inside or out in the garden at wrought-iron tables among classical columns and other accents. Rates: late May to October 31, $135 to $175; November to late May, $105 to $135.

PORTLAND DINING

The Back Bay Grill, 65 Portland St. (☎ 207/772-8833), is among the city's top dining establishments. Beside the fine quality of the cuisine, the room has great style and drama with its soaring ceilings, track lighting, and unique mural. The menu is limited and features dishes using local organic ingredients wherever possible. Cuisine is cutting-edge American, cooked enough to release the flavor of the natural ingredients. Try the herb-crusted rack of lamb with black mission figs, maple whipped sweet potatoes, and burgundy sauce or the delicious combination of grilled salmon on porcini mushroom risotto and red wine tarragon sauce. Another great dish is the cassoulet of Maine rabbit with garlic sausage and smoked bacon. If it's on the menu, don't miss the signature gravlax purse of artichokes, mascarpone, and Maine crab with baby greens and black pepper Stolichnaya vinaigrette. Prices range from $16.50 to $24. Desserts are extravagant too—you won't forget the chocolate mousse tower or the roasted banana-rum ice cream swans in warm bittersweet chocolate sauce. There's also a $59 seven-course tasting menu available. The extensive wine list is weighted towards California and features several decent half bottles, which is rare. Open Monday to Thursday from 5:30 to 9:30pm, Friday to Saturday from 5:30 to 10pm, and in July and August only, Sunday from 5 to 9pm.

Street and Co, 2/33 Wharf St. (☎ 207/775-0887), is far and away one of the best places to go for fish. It's right down in the old port on a brick-lined street. The interior is full of atmosphere with low ceiling beams studded with drying herbs and rush-seated chairs set at plain wood tables. The kitchen is up front, and you can see the young chefs preparing everything right there. There's no menu here—just a blackboard on which the dishes, inspired by the freshest ingredients available, make their appearance. You might find mussels sautéed with lemon, white wine, and butter; sautéed calamari, lobster diavolo, sole française, scallops in pernod and cream, grilled and blackened tuna, swordfish or salmon, linguini with seafood, shrimp with butter and garlic, and lobster and crab, of course. Great stuff. Prices range from $13 to $18. Desserts are typically items like tiramisu, chocolate sin cake with a rich mousse center, or fruit pies. Open Sunday to Thursday from 5:30 to 9:30, Friday and Saturday until 10pm.

At **Fore Street,** 288 Fore St. (☎ 207/775-2717), the menu changes daily, but the methods stay the same—braising, apple-wood grilling, and roasting of prime fresh ingredients with sealed-in flavor. This is one of the city's very best dining places. The roasted fish, whether its monkfish filet, whole New England sea bass, or farm-raised Maine Arctic char, are sublime. The meats, slowly roasted on a spit—such as pork loin or organic chicken—are also great. You haven't ever tasted scallops until you've tasted the apple-wood grilled version. The selection of appetizers runs from pizzetta made with mushrooms, red peppers, eggplant, and mozzarella to Pemaquid oysters. Prices range from $15 to $18. Desserts are equally amazing. Think about it—wood-baked plum and almond tart and roasted banana mousse. Open daily from 5:30pm.

Tabitha Jean's Restaurant, 94 Free St. (☎ 207/780-8966), is sleek and elegant with its long, fine wood bar and vaguely oriental black chairs set at spacious white-clothed tables. Privacy is ensured by the wood shutters on the windows. Asian accents mark the cuisine, which emphasizes fresh seafood. All the dishes are prepared in a straightforward way to bring out the flavor of

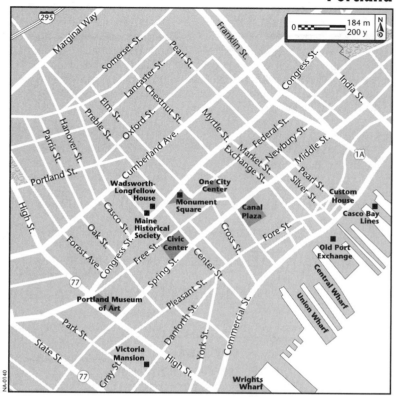

the ingredients. For a light, refreshing dish, try the filet of sole served on wilted greens and radicchio with rice pilaf in a light tomato broth. The rack of lamb is beautifully combined with a rosemary port wine sauce, and the *frutti di mare* brims with the natural flavor of mussels, shrimps, calamari, and other fresh fish. Prices range from $12 for a simple stir fry of vegetables to $20. Open Monday to Friday from 11:30am to 3pm and daily from 5pm to closing.

Zephyr Grill, 653 Congress St. (☎ 207/828-4033), is a fun, color-filled space in which you can enjoy dining at the marbleized tables and checking out the papier-mâché Mexican art. It attracts a hip crowd that comes because the food is fresh, up-to-the-minute, and reasonably priced. It offers a wide range of choices, too, from pasta and vegetarian dishes to more substantial items like rump steak with garlic, ginger, and tamari served with kimchee (a Korean dish) and roasted potatoes. Fish is not overlooked, either. Try the fresh-tasting salmon-polenta cakes with dill, celery, thyme, and shallots. They're served with a spicy tartar sauce. For a mouthwatering vegetarian dish, you can't beat the baked cornmeal crepe filled with caramelized pears, blue cheese, and spiced walnuts that's served with chopped tomatoes and olive oil, a balsamic vinegar reduction, roasted vegetables, and green salad. Prices range from $12 to $17—you see what I mean. Open from 5pm to closing.

The Pepperclub, 78 Middle St. (☎ 207/772-0531), is spicy in every way: from the food to the decor to the incredibly low prices for this quality of fare. It's one of the restaurants in Portland to which I always return. Abstract murals decorate the walls, or else they are swathed in calico blue or deep mustard or purple. Diners sit in sleek black booths. The food is always innovative and spicy. The menu changes daily and is chalked on a board. It's predominantly vegetarian with a lacing of fish and chicken. Every dish is fresh and pleasing to the palate, from the Thai shrimp cakes with a lime rémoulade to the Greek savory pumpkin phyllo pie and the mushroom walnut loaf with mashed potatoes. Prices range from $7.95 to $11.95. Open daily from 5 to 9pm.

Wharf Street Cafe, 38 Wharf St. (☎ 207/773-6667), makes a striking statement with its decor and its food. Black-and-white floors, black-and-white table settings, and white walls that are hung with art set the background for a heartwarming bistro-style dining experience. About half the menu features fresh fish. Some dishes work better than others. For example, the flavors in the pistachio-crusted salmon served with soba noodles, citrus tamari, and hot oil meld well, but the lobster and Brie cheese ravioli with roasted grapes and caramelized onion sauce seems a less fortunate marriage. As for meat, you might find grilled chicken teriyaki or beef tenderloin with wild mushrooms. Pasta dishes complete the menu. The most popular appetizer must surely be the Asian barbecue shrimp. Prices range from $11 to $18. The wine bar is upstairs. Open daily from 5:30 to 8:30pm.

Portland
Special & Recreational Activities

Boating: Sebago Lake is less than an hour from Portland. It's a very large lake with a state park at its northern end.

Cruises: Casco Bay Lines, Commercial and Franklin streets (☎ 207/774-7871), operates the ferries that deliver mail and supplies to the islands that dot Casco Bay. You can ride to Peaks Island, Diamond Cove, Long Island, Great Chebeague Island, and Bailey's Island. Prices range from $8 to $14, and the trips range from 1¾ hours to 5¾ hours (to Bailey Island). By the way, Longfellow's poem the *Wreck of the Hesperus* was inspired by the foundering of the *Helen Eliza* on the southerly coast of Peaks Island in 1869. You can visit Eagle Island and the home of Robert E. Peary on a boat that sails from Long Wharf (☎ 207/774-6498).

Olde Port Mariner Fleet (☎ 207/775-0727 or 207/642-3270) also operates cruises from Long Wharf: *Indian II* is a deep-sea party fishing boat; *Odyssey* is for whale watching, *Suellyn* is for scenic cruises, and *Casablanca,* which cruises from Custom House wharf, offers dinner cruises. Call for details.

Fishing: There's good fishing in **Sebago Lake** for trout and salmon.

Mid-Coast Maine—from Freeport to Camden

Yarmouth & Freeport ◆ *Brunswick,*
the Harpswell Peninsula & Bath ◆ *Wiscasset &*
Westport Island ◆ *Boothbay Harbor & Monhegan Island* ◆
Newcastle, Damariscotta & the Pemaquid Peninsula ◆
Rockland/Vinalhaven Island & Tenants Harbor ◆ *Camden &*
Islesboro Island

Distance from Boston in miles: Bath/Brunswick/Freeport, 125; Boothbay Harbor, 164; Newcastle, 180; Rockland, 189; Camden, 200.

Estimated driving time: 2½ hours to Bath/Brunswick/Freeport; 3 hours to Boothbay Harbor; 3½ hours to Newcastle; 3½ hours to Rockland; 3½ to 2¾ hours to Camden.

◄o►◄o►◄o►◄o►◄o►

Driving: Take I-95 to Exit 22 (Route 1) to Brunswick, Bath, Wiscasset, Newcastle, Damariscotta to Warren. Continue on Route 1 to Rockland and Camden. At Warren, you can turn off on to Route 90 and go straight to Camden.

Further Information: For more information, contact **Freeport Merchants Association**, P.O. Box 452, Freeport, ME 04032 (☎ 207/865-1212); **Bath-Brunswick Region Chamber of Commerce**, 59 Pleasant Rd., Brunswick, ME 04011 (☎ 207/725-8797); **Boothbay Harbor Region Chamber of Commerce**, P.O. Box 356, Boothbay Harbor, ME 04538 (☎ 207/633-2353); **Damariscotta Region Chamber of Commerce**, Main Street (P.O. Box 13), Damariscotta, ME 04543 (☎ 207/563-8340); **Rockland-Thomaston Area Chamber of Commerce**, P.O. Box 508, Rockland, ME 04841 (☎ 207/ 596-0376); **Rockport-Camden-Lincolnville Chamber of Commerce**, P.O. Box 919, Camden, ME 04843 (☎ 207/236-4404).

◄o►◄o►◄o►◄o►◄o►

Vacationers who fly along Route 1 through the mid-coast region, and give it only a day or so in their rush to Downeast, miss a lot, for the diverse towns along this coast are worth a lot of attention.

For a start, **Freeport** has more than just outlets. **Rockland** is a real salty town with a great sense of character. In addition, it's becoming a major art center as more and more galleries open along Main Street. From here, too, the

Events & Festivals to Plan Your Trip Around

January–February: National Toboggan Championships at the Camden Snow Bowl. Call ☎ 207/236-4404 for information.

May: Harpswell Craft Guild Sale & Studio Tours are held on several weekends from May to December. This is when the many craftspeople open their studios to visitors. Call ☎ 207/725-8797.

June: Windjammer Days, Boothbay Harbor, kicks off the summer with a tall-ships parade through the harbor. Music and fireworks plus other entertainment. Call ☎ 207/633-2353.

July: The Great Schooner Race takes place July 1 on Penobscot Bay from North Haven to Rockland. At the end of the day the schooners dock in a raft formation, enabling people to walk from one end of the fleet to the other. Live entertainment and the award ceremony complete the day. Call ☎ 207/596-0376.

Yarmouth's Clam Festival is the third weekend in July. Call 207/846-3984.

Schooner Days and Blues Festival, Rockland. The tall ships rendezvous in the harbor, putting on a grand parade. Special entertainment and waterfront events, plus a big craft show and fireworks display. Call ☎ 207/596-0376.

August: Sweet Chariot Folk Festival at Burnt Coat Harbor on Swan's Island is fast becoming a major folk music venue, with two dozen groups entertaining on windjammers followed by a big shore concert in the evening.

great revamped schooners and other seafaring vessels known as the *windjammers* depart. Everyone already thinks of **Camden** as the jewel of the mid-coast—which it is—but it has more than just a pretty face and warrants the effort to dig a little deeper. Visit Rockport Harbor or climb to the top of the Camden Hills, rather than just cruising through and checking out all the wealth in the harbor. Any one of these towns makes a great weekend destination.

YARMOUTH & FREEPORT

Most people will skip Yarmouth and go directly to **Freeport,** the headquarters of Maine's first family, L.L. Bean, and the other outlets that have grown up around this vast and famous emporium. The whole town of Freeport has been turned into one large shopping center, but it's one of the most pleasant of its type, and you can still park the car and walk around as if it's still a small town.

Maine Festival presents the works of the best of the state's crafts and arts plus performances and demonstrations at Thomas Point Beach. Call ☎ 207/772-9012.

Brunswick Highland Games. Bagpipe bands, Scottish dancing and fiddling, plus Highland events like tossing the caber and the putting of the stone. Sheep-dog demonstrations and plenty of other fun. Call ☎ 207/364-3063.

Maine Lobster Festival. A 4-day affair, during which hundreds of pounds of lobster are eaten. There are also a road race, a blindfold rowing race, and a lobster-crate race (two crates are suspended between floats and the contestants must run with them without falling down). It's topped off with a lobster-boat parade and the coronation of the Sea Goddess. First weekend of August in Harbor Park, Rockland. Call ☎ 207/596-0376.

September: Thomas Point Beach Bluegrass Festival features some of the top bluegrass bands in a 4-day festival over the Labor Day weekend. Fireworks, too. For information call ☎ 207/725-6009.

Windjammer Festival. Camden celebrates the founding of this seafaring industry in the 1930s with concerts, fireworks, and other festivities. Call ☎ 207/633-2353 or 207/236-4404.

Windjammer Rendezvous in Eggemoggin Reach, when the windjammer fleet sails into Brooklin, the headquarters of *WoodenBoat Magazine*. Music, dancing, fireworks, and a parade of sails are the main events. Call 207/359-4651.

December: Sparkle Weekend, in Freeport, when Santa Claus and a talking tree both appear. Call ☎ 207/865-1212.

L.L. Bean, Main and Bow streets (☎ 800/341-4341), is the business that launched Freeport as one of Maine's two outlet capitals (the other is Kittery). It is indeed a great place to shop for rugged country clothing and equipment and more. Best time to shop? From midnight on. There are dozens of other stores to visit, depending on what your favorite brand names are—Anne Klein, Brooks Brothers, Burberry, Calvin Klein, Donna Karan, Cole Hahn, Dansk, Villeroy & Boch, Polo, Nautica, J Crew, Bed & Bath, Dooney & Bourke, Coach—the gang's all here. In addition to L.L. Bean, there's another Maine story at **De Lorme's Maps,** Lower Main Street (Route 1; ☎ 207/865-4171), which produces terrific state maps along with software products such as Map 'n' Go and Street Atlas, USA.

Freeport has other selling points, too—**Mast Landing Audubon Sanctuary** and **Wolf Neck Woods State Park,** on the opposite side of the Harraseeket River. For a view of Casco Bay, hike or bike the trails in **Bradbury Mountain State Park.** Wander through the commercial **Desert of Maine,** on Desert Road (☎ 207/865-6962), where some of the buildings, like the Spring House, are engulfed by a 25-foot-high dune. Visit **Eagle Island** to see the summer home of the explorer Admiral Peary aboard the *Atlantic Seal* or take a trip to **Chebeague Island** from Yarmouth.

FREEPORT LODGING

Harraseeket Inn, 162 Main St., Freeport, ME 04032 (☎ 207/865-9377), is a modern accommodation, but it has character and charm and a very fine dining room. The rooms are large and well furnished. Many have fireplaces, and you may find a copper washtub holding the logs for stoking the fire. Beds have half canopies, and rooms also have a sofa, desk, and chair and amenities such as TVs, telephones, and small refrigerators. Some rooms have Jacuzzis. When I stopped by, a brand-new wing was being built; it will contain large double rooms, all with king beds and Jacuzzis, plus gas fireplaces. The buffet breakfast offers a spread of eggs, bacon, pancakes, fruit, cereals, breads, and pastries. There's a formal dining room and an attractive pub on the first floor. Lobsters, clambakes, and grilled fish and meat dishes, plus pasta are offered. Rates: mid-May to mid-July $140 to $230, suites $235; mid-July through October $155 to $230, suites $235; November to mid-May $95 to $205, suites $215.

    Atlantic Seal B&B, 25 Main St. (P.O. Box 146), South Freeport, ME 04078 (☎ 207/865-6112), is a small place down by the water. Your host is Tom Ring, a hospitable waterman who used to operate a tugboat in New York. Today he operates cruises to Eagle Island and runs this hostelry. If you want to experience the authentic Maine, then this is the place to stay. In the sitting room there is a portrait of the *Governor Goodwin,* a ship that Tom's ancestors sailed to China. You can imagine some of the interesting tales that this genuine Mainer can tell. There are only three rooms, each named after a boat that was built in the area. *Heart's Desire* contains a bed with a chenille spread and quilt and a Rumford fireplace. From the window seat there are great views of the dock and the water. Amenities include a small TV and a wood-burning fireplace. The *Glen,* which also has a small TV and a maple bed, is named after the ship that Tom's great-grandfather sailed from here to California during the Gold Rush with a cargo of prefabricated house frames aboard. The *Dash* has a brass bed and the most extras: a TV/VCR, a small refrigerator, and a Jacuzzi. At breakfast, expect to dine on blueberry pancakes, feathered eggs, or lobster omelets. There's a back deck overlooking the backyard that goes down to the waterside dock. A picnic table is available on the lawn. Rates: summer $105 to $145; winter $75 to $125.

    Kendall Tavern B&B, 213 Main St., Freeport, ME 04032 (☎ 207/ 865-1338), is a late-18th-century home that is set well back from the road on 3½ acres, some distance away from the hubbub. It has seven rooms, all furnished in country style with pencil four-poster or cannonball beds covered with quilts, combined with pine chests, armoires, and wing chairs. There are two sitting rooms, both with fireplaces. One has a TV. The breakfast—pancakes, omelets, scrambled eggs, or similar dishes, plus muffins and fruit, is served at separate tables. Rates: summer, $110 to $135; winter $85 to $105.

    Minutes from town, the **Isaac Randall House,** 5 Independence Dr., Freeport, ME 04032 (☎ 207/865-9295), is located on 6 acres in a quiet area. A Federal-style farmhouse that was built in 1823, it has had quite a varied history—it has served as a stop on the Underground Railroad, as a dance hall, and as a dairy farm. Today, it offers handsomely furnished guestrooms equipped with private baths and telephones. Some have working fireplaces, and others have cable TV/VCRs. Most have private entrances, too. The house has some very attractive public areas for guests. The sitting room is arrayed with south-western-style artifacts, from tiles and rugs to leather chairs. Breakfast is served at a long table in the beamed country kitchen where copper pots hang on the walls and from the ceiling. Rates: summer, $100 to $135; winter, weekends $85 to $100, Sunday to Thursday $75 to $90.

FREEPORT DINING

The **Harraseeket Inn** (see above) has a locally renowned dining room, and rightly so. The dining room is elegant, and tables are arranged with plenty of space between them. But the food is what matters. Start with the signature lobster stew with sherried cream or the chilled Pemaquid oysters with ginger mignonette. Among the main courses you'll note several dishes featuring local organic produce—for example, the Merrymeeting Farms chicken with portobello, leek, and sourdough pan stuffing au jus or the farm-raised Maine salmon with watercress, basil, and potato-salmon brandade. (For a full list of locally derived produce, see the menu.) One of the more fashionable dishes is the ostrich medallions with juniper, thyme, potato ravioli, and grilled asparagus. Prices range from $13 to $26. The buffet brunch on Sunday (included in the price of the room) is quite an event, when more than 20 dishes, plus half a dozen desserts, are put out for your pleasure.

Harraseeket Lunch and Lobster Company, Town Wharf, South Freeport (☎ 207/865-4888), is a fun place right down on the waterfront. Order your food at the window, pick it up, and sit outside at one of the picnic tables. Prices range from $6 to $9 for such items as lobster and crab rolls, clams, and more. Open May 1 to mid-June from 11am to 7:45pm; mid-June to mid-October from 11am to 8:45pm.

Yarmouth & Freeport
Special & Recreational Activities

Birding: Mast Landing Sanctuary, Upper Mast Landing Road, Freeport (☎ 207/781-2330). **Wolf's Neck State Park** is a good place to spot osprey.
Camping: See Bradbury Mountain State Park, below.
Cruises: Take the *Atlantic Seal,* 25 Main St., South Freeport (☎ 207/865-6112), for a 3-hour cruise to visit Admiral Peary's summer cottage or take an early morning seal-and-osprey watching cruise. Fall foliage cruises are offered, too. Cruises operate from mid-May through October. Rates are $20 for adults, $15 for children under 12. You can also sail aboard the sloop *Apogee,* 8 Cove Rd. (☎ 207/756-4329), which leaves from South Freeport Marina. Fares are $25 to $30.
Hiking: Wolfe's Neck Woods State Park, Wolfe's Neck Road in Freeport (☎ 207/865-4465), has several attractive trails, including a ¾ -mile shore-line trail that overlooks an osprey sanctuary. At **Bradbury Mountain State**

Park on Route 9 there are 6 miles of trails, including one leading to the summit of the mountain.

State Parks: Bradbury Mountain State Park, Route 9 west of Freeport, has 440 acres of forested land that offers hiking, biking, and horseback riding trails, plus 41 camp sites. In the fall, it provides spectacular foliage views. Hike to the top of the mountain or enjoy a picnic. It also offers good cross-country skiing and snowshoeing in winter.

BRUNSWICK, THE HARPSWELL PENINSULA & BATH

Brunswick, on the Androscoggin River, is a college town, home to **Bowdoin College,** and has all the assets that go with that designation—museums, art galleries, and performance venues. Bowdoin was founded in 1794, and among its more famous alumni are Nathaniel Hawthorne, Henry Wadsworth Longfellow, Senator George Mitchell, and Olympic gold medallist Joan Benoit Samuelson. The **Museum of Art,** in the Walker Art Building (☎ 207/725-3280), shows works by Winslow Homer, John Sloan, Mary Cassatt, Rockwell Kent, and other 19th- and 20th-century artists. It's open Tuesday to Saturday from 10am to 5pm and Sunday from 2 to 5pm. Exhibits in the **Peary-MacMillan Arctic Museum,** in Hubbard Hall (☎ 207/725-3416), relate the stories of the many expeditions that these two explorers made to the Arctic. It's a fascinating museum. Peary and his assistant, Matthew Henson, were the first men to reach the North Pole in 1909, without the use of mechanical or electrical devices. Donald B. MacMillan made his first trip to the Arctic in this expedition and spent the next 45 years exploring Labrador, Baffin Island, and North Greenland, taking many Bowdoin students with him on the schooner *Bowdoin.* It's open Tuesday to Saturday 10am to 5pm and Sunday 2 to 5pm.

In summer, the university hosts the **Maine State Music Theatre** in the Pickard theater in Memorial Hall and the **Bowdoin Summer Music Festival** in Kresge Auditorium and other venues. For events information, call ☎ 207/725-3253. Free guided tours of the campus leave from the admissions office. Call ☎ 207/725-3100 for a schedule.

From Brunswick, you can loop around the long double-fingered **Harpswell Peninsula,** which has 150 miles of shoreline. The **Harpswells** are on the western finger, and while you're driving along Route 123, note the old meetinghouse in Harpswell Center that was built in 1759, certainly one of the oldest in Maine. **Orrs** and **Bailey islands** are on the eastern finger, linked to the mainland by bridges. The Cribstone Bridge, which connects island to island, is unique. It was built in 1928, using great granite blocks that are laid, without mortar, lengthwise and crosswise to withstand tides and ice. Many a tall ship was built on this peninsula in the 19th century. It is rich in history and has many literary associations. Harriet Beecher Stowe summered here and wrote *The Pearl of Orr's Island.* Ragged Island was the summer home of poet

Edna St. Vincent Millay. Robert P. Tristram Coffin spent his childhood on Pond Island, which inspired his *Lost Paradise*. Today Harpswell continues to be home to many authors and artists.

If you go all the way to Land's End, you can see a moving **Memorial dedicated to All Maine Fishermen**, which was erected in 1976. The sculpted figure is kneeling down over lobster and crab, holding a fish in his hand. **Mackerel Cove** cuts into Bailey's Island. The serene harbor is dotted with lobster boats, many with old-fashioned riding sails that keep them head-to-wind while the lobstermen pluck the pots. Buoys, by the way, all get painted in the spring. Each is distinctive, and each is registered by its owner, who decides what colors to use. On Bailey's Island, don't miss the natural spectacle of the **Giant Staircase**, Washington Street—a great picnicking spot.

Bailey's and Orr are only two of the hundreds of tiny islands that lie off the coast here. Among them, **Eagle Island** is famous as the summer home of Admiral Peary. Born in Pennsylvania in 1856, he came from an old family of Maine lumbermen, and when his father died, he and his mother returned to Maine. He discovered Eagle Island when he was in high school and fell in love with it, but it was not until 1904 that he began building the Big House that sits on a rocky bluff. Among its notable features is the three-sided fireplace; each side is built of a different stone. Today the island is a state park, and you can visit it on cruises from Freeport, Portland, and Bailey's Island.

Bath, a short distance along Route 1 from Brunswick, is located at the mouth of the Kennebec River and is famous for its great shipyard and ironworks. Anyone interested in Maine's story must visit Bath's **Maine Maritime Museum and Shipyard**, 243 Washington St. (☎ 207/443-1316), which relates the story of the shipbuilding in Bath and the maritime history of Maine. It stands on the site of the Percy and Small Shipyard; between 1894 and 1920, 41 four-, five-, and six-masted schooners were constructed in several of these buildings. Start in the museum, which displays marine paintings, photographs, ships models, dioramas, and hands-on multimedia exhibits. From here, walk out to see the demonstrations and exhibits in several other buildings. In the mold loft you can see how a ship is designed and framed. Other buildings detail the processes of milling and joining and nailing and painting. A very interesting lobstering exhibit includes a video that really tells it like it is. At the waterfront, you can go aboard the *Sherman Zwicker*, a Grand Banks fishing schooner and see an additional half dozen vessels ranging from a lobster boat to a Friendship sloop. An excursion boat takes visitors out into the Kennebec River and past the Aegis destroyers being built at Bath Iron Works. Open daily from 9:30am to 5pm. Admission $7.50 adults, $4.75 children. The boat excursion costs $7 adults, $4.50 children.

From Bath, you can travel down the Phippsburg peninsula via Route 209 to Phippsburg, Sebasco, and **Popham Beach State Park**, site of two forts. You can also cross the Kennebec to Woolwich on the eastern bank and travel along Route 127 down the **Arrowsic** and **Georgetown islands**, which are joined by bridges. From Route 127, Steen Road and Bald Head Road lead to **Squirrel Point Light**. It's a 4-mile hike to the light itself.

Georgetown Island is split by Robinhood Cove, which is crossed by Route 127 and leads to **Five Islands**, a fishing village with a lobster shack. Explore the side roads that lead all the way to the southern shores. **Reid State Park**, on the eastern coast facing Sheepscot Bay and the **Josephine Newman Bird Sanctuary** are both off Route 127.

BAILEY & GEORGETOWN ISLAND LODGING & DINING

Log Cabin Lodging & Fine Food, Route 24 (P.O. Box 41), Bailey Island, ME 04003 (☎ 207/833-5546), is a restaurant, but it also has six very nice rooms overlooking the water. The most expensive room has a full kitchen and private deck with hot tub; additional amenities include a telephone, two TVs, a VCR, and stereo. The least expensive is a spacious bedroom with private bath and amenities such as a TV/VCR, telephone, and hair dryer. In addition, some of the rooms have refrigerators, microwaves, and front and back decks. All are fresh and modern, furnished mostly with pine, and designed in an open studio style with defined sleeping, kitchen, and dining areas. They represent excellent value.

The food served in the dining room is well prepared. This is the place to enjoy a shore dinner, starting with stew or chowder and followed by steamed clams, lobster, and fried shrimp. Other dishes range from a simple vegetable lasagna to broiled fish of the day. The room is furnished in country-casual style with polished wood tables and decorated with hunting trophies—bear, moose, deer, and fish. It's warmed on cold days by a gas fire. There's a full bar and a decent selection of wines by the glass. Rates: $109 to $175. Rooms available March to November.

Grey Havens Inn, Seguinland Road (P.O. Box 308), Georgetown, ME 04548 (☎ 207/371-2616), is a fantasy come true where I could cheerfully while away a whole summer. It's located on Georgetown Island, which extends along the eastern bank of the Kennebec River south of Woolwich. It's a grand old shingle-style hotel, complete with turrets, that stands right on the water with stirring views of islands; fir-clad points; and the harbor, bay, and ocean from rooms and porch. You can watch the lobstermen harvesting their pots in the cove while the sea gulls screech above them. Binoculars are provided in every room. Lace curtains hang at the windows; the bed will most likely be made of iron, and there will be a dresser and a rocker or easy chairs. The lavish tongue-and-groove woodwork is in every room. Each room has a beach bag filled with blanket and towels, ready to go. There's a spacious lounge with a large stone fireplace, huge picture windows, good books and music, plus a small, well-stocked honor bar. A continental breakfast is served in the dining room at separate tables. Rowboats are available. And what's so great about all this is that it's easy-going and unpretentious and operated by a family—the Eberhards, Bill and Haley, and five additions who are amazingly unnoticeable. Note, however, that if you can't or won't tolerate strange-tasting water and low but adequate water pressure, you may not be content here. Open April to December. Rates: $130 to $205.

For those who don't mind staying in very rustic, and I mean *very* rustic, accommodations, the **Driftwood Inn & Cottages**, Bailey Island, ME 04003 (☎ 207/833-5461), occupies a spectacular fir-clad point where the churning surf boils over the rocks. The accommodations share a living room with a wood-burning fireplace and old wicker furnishings. Rooms are spartan, and baths are shared, but the setting is Maine extraordinaire. In a nor'easter the ocean sprays over the buildings' roofs. Housekeeping cottages and meals are also available. Every summer, a watercolorist comes to teach here. Rates: late

May to mid-October $70 to $85; weekly MAP, $355 per person. Cottages from $475.

DINING IN THE AREA

The Robinhood Free Meetinghouse, Robinhood Road (☎ 207/371-2188), is indeed operating in an 1855 meetinghouse, now decorated with Shaker chairs, maple tables, wall hangings, and sculptures by local artists. The large first-floor room features random-width pumpkin-pine floors and a solid cherry bar. There are also a few tables upstairs tucked in behind the pews. This is the best dining room in the area. It also functions as a catering establishment and so offers an amazing array of entrees that are priced from $16 to $20. You can select pecan-encrusted halibut with beurre blanc, Cajun-style salmon, tournedos of beef with two sauces, or veal grenobloise with lemon butter and capers. Open daily from 5:30 to 9pm and Sunday from 10am to 2pm.

    Lobster Village, Bailey Island (☎ 207/833-6656), sits out right on Mackerel Cove. It's a great spot. The dining room is plain and simple with typical booths, or you can choose to dine outside facing the cove. A lobster dinner is about $15, or there are clam, lobster, crabmeat and shrimp rolls, plus grilled cheese sandwiches and burgers, with prices ranging from $3 to $10.

    Cook's Lobster House (☎ 207/833-2818) faces water on both sides and overlooks the Cribstone Bridge. This is the island's traditional dining spot. Cook's has been here since 1955, serving seafood purchased and processed at the wharf. In addition to the dining room, there are two outdoor decks from which you can enjoy the sunsets. The thing to order here is one of the shore dinners (there are four), which consist of clam or fish chowder or lobster stew, followed by either a serving of steamed clams or fried shrimp and a hot boiled lobster. There's also a full menu of seafood and other items including steaks, sandwiches, and salads. Prices range from $10 to $18 with shore dinners going for the market price. Open Sunday to Thursday from 11:30am to 9pm, Friday and Saturday from 11:30am to 10pm.

    Blueberry Pancake, Route 24, Bailey Island (☎ 207/833-6808), has great blueberry pancakes plus other breakfast fare like omelets and eggs Benedict. Open Monday to Friday 7am to 11am, Saturday and Sunday 7am to noon.

Brunswick, Harpswell, Bath & Georgetown
Special & Recreational Activities

Antiquing: There are several shops along Front Street in Bath.

Birding: See hiking.

Boating: Boats can be rented from Lowell's Cove Marina on Bailey Island (☎ 207/833-2810) for fishing, seal watching, or taking trips to Eagle or Whaleboat Island. Rates are $18 to $25 an hour, $45 to $65 for a half day and $75 to $115 for the full day.

Cruises: Casco Bay Charters (☎ 207/833-2978) operates a variety of trips from Mackerel Cove, Bailey Island. You can cruise to Eagle Island ($30 per couple) or view Bailey Island from the water and go on seal watches ($20 to $35, depending on the number of passengers), fishing trips ($25 for 2 hours, $40 for 4 hours), or take a sunset cruise ($20 to $35, depending on the number of passengers). Similar trips for similar prices are offered aboard the *Amanda Marie,* leaving from Cook's Lobster House (☎ 207/833-6641). The *Amanda Marie* also runs fun lobstering trips for $25 for 2 hours or $35 for a full day. All of these trips are offered by *The Ruth* (☎ 207/389-1161), which operates from Sebasco Lodge on the **Phippsburg Peninsula.** Also try **Sea Escape Charters** (☎ 207/833-5531) for fishing and seal-watching trips. The *Symbion* (☎ 207/725-0979) can be chartered for an afternoon or for several days. It sails from Cundy's Harbor, Harpswell. Call for prices and other information.

Fishing: For "wicked good fishing," as they say in Maine, for mackerel and stripers, bluefish, and more, in **Bath** contact *Obsession* (☎ 207/729-3997), which carries four passengers, departing from Waterfront Park on Commercial Street. *Kayla D* (☎ 207/443-3316) specializes in shark fishing and also operates out of Bath. In **South Harpswell**, try Captain Jerry Sullivan (☎ 207/833-5447), who operates *Happy Hooker III* from the town dock.

Golf: Brunswick Golf Course, River Road, Brunswick (☎ 207/725-8224), is an 18-hole par-72 course.

Kayaking: H2O Outfitters, P.O. Box 72, Orr's Island (☎ 207/833-5257), offers instruction and trips.

Hiking: Georgetown has three preserves for coastal and woodland hiking. **Reid State Park**, on the Seguinland Road off Route 127, offers easy and moderate walking trails to beach and marsh overlooking Sheepscot Bay. There are three beaches that protect salt marshes where you can see waterfowl and wading birds and osprey. Open May to Labor Day; admission is $2.50. The **Josephine Newman Sanctuary** between the bridges in Georgetown is owned by the Audubon Society and has shoreline and woodland trails through 119 acres. Other trails can be found in the **Ledgewood Preserve,** Legemere Road in Five Islands.

WISCASSET & WESTPORT ISLAND

Wiscassset is a pretty town on the banks of the Sheepscot River. It's worth stopping in town to browse in some of the stores along Route 1 and the side streets. Don't miss the **Wiscassset Bay Gallery** (☎ 207/882-7682) on Main Street; it has a very fine selection of paintings and is operated by youthful enthusiast, Kenneth Oehmig who is a painter himself. Other stores to explore: the **Butterstamp Workshop,** Middle Street (☎ 207/882-7825), which sells castings of antique butter molds with a variety of motifs, and **Part of the Past** on Water Street (☎ 207/882-7908). Also in town, **Musical Wonder House,** 18 High St. (☎ 207/882-7163), displays hundreds of music boxes and player pianos dating back to 1750 in elegant settings in a handsome 1852 home. Open mid-May to mid-October daily from 10am to 5pm.

There are also several historic sites to visit. The **Old Jail** on Federal Street (☎ 207/882-6817) was built in 1811 and used until 1953; you can see the cells and the jailer's house. It's open July and August, Tuesday to Sunday from 11am to 4:30pm; admission $2 for adults, $1 for children under 13.

The **Nickels-Sortwell House,** a striking sea captain's home, was built in 1807–08 for Captain William Nickels, ship owner and merchant. It's open June to September; admission is $4 for adults, $2 for children 6 to 12. The **Castle Tucker House** (1807) on Lee Street is an extraordinary looking house, mainly because of the portico that was added in 1860. It's open July to August, Tuesday to Saturday from 11am to 4pm; admission is $3.

The most photographed objects of the town's history, though, lie in Sheepscot River—the remains of two 4-masted schooner hulks, the *Luther Little* and the *Hesper,* that at one time sashayed from eastern American ports to Haiti, Lisbon, France, England, and Central and South America They wound up here in 1932 when they were bought for $600 by an Auburn, Maine, resident who planned to use them to transport timber from Boston to New York. The depression nixed his plans, and here they sit, pleading to be salvaged. Out in the river, **Fort Edgecomb** (☎ 207/882-7777), built in 1808, stands on Davis Island with its octagonal blockhouse guarding the entrance to Wiscasset's Harbor.

WISCASSET & WESTPORT ISLAND LODGING & DINING

The **Squire Tarbox Inn,** R.R. 2 (Box 620), Wiscasset, ME 04578 (☎ 207/882-7693), is a delightful, contemplative place that is operated by a thoughtful, philosophical couple, Karen and Bill Mitman, who gave up city life to experience the rhythms of nature in their daily lives by coming to this small farm. In addition to being a high-quality accommodation and restaurant, the inn operates as a farm that produces 2,000 pounds of goat cheese a year from 30 goats. There are also a donkey, a horse, and hens in the menagerie. Guests are welcome to go into the barns and see the animals, as well as to learn about the cheese-making process. The farm is located in a lovely remote area and occupies a building full of character that was originally built in 1763 and added to in 1820. The pumpkin-pine wide-board floors positively glow. The 11 rooms, all with private baths, are large and well furnished with country pieces. In any room you might find a brass bed with a quilt or candlewick spread, a braided rug, an antique trunk, or an oak or pine chest. Some of the rooms have wood-burning fireplaces, and one has a private entrance. Guests have the choice of several gathering rooms—a comfortable parlor with fireplace decorated with antique quilts and a games room in the original barn that has an antique woodstove and plenty of puzzles and books for entertainment. There's also a music room where the folks on staff gather to sing and enjoy the player piano. In addition, you can wander down a path through the woods to a screened shack on the edge of the salt marsh and take out the rowboat.

The dining room has a good reputation and is delightful, with its brick fireplace, pumpkin-pine beams, and rose-colored tablecloths. Here you'll be treated to a four-course dinner that changes daily. It might begin with crab fromage in phyllo with tomato watercress sauce and continue with Caesar salad and whey buns before proceeding to roast marinated lamb with rosemary mint sauce, finishing up with chocolate pound cake with Grand Marnier blackberry sauce. Breakfast is served in another room, buffet style. Open mid-May to the end of October. Rates: May to mid-July, MAP $149 to $199 per couple; mid-July to October, MAP $169 to $230 per couple; B&B $95 to $176 per couple.

Le Garage, Water Street, Wiscasset (☎ 207/882-5409), is by the yacht club and has a balcony on the waterfront. The high-ceilinged space is simple and elegant in Shaker style. The cuisine is typical continental-New England with dishes such as chicken pie, poached haddock with Newburg sauce, and lobster and steaks. Prices range from $10 to $16. Open daily from 11:30am to 2pm and 5 to 8:30pm.

Down on the riverfront, **Sara's Cafe,** Wiscasset (☎ 207/882-7504), is casual and fun and offers a wide menu featuring everything from more than 20 pizzas to special sandwich combinations baked with two cheeses that are called Whaleboats. The combinations are endless—why not spinach, bacon, and ham or tomatoes, onion, mozzarella, and cheddar. The rest of the menu features sandwiches, salads and pasta, and best of all, a dozen lobster delights, including a lobster burrito and lobster quesadilla. Open daily from 11am to 10am.

BOOTHBAY HARBOR & MONHEGAN ISLAND

Boothbay Harbor is much too well touristed in summer, but if you make the effort to get out of town to visit Southport Island, Ocean Point, and other regional spots, you can find quiet places to relax and savor the coastal scenery and natural life of the area. The eastern shore of the Lower Sheepscot River is particularly rewarding, from **Cape Newagen to Gooseberry Island.** This is where Rachel Carson spent much of her time pondering the ecology of the coastlands. On your way to Boothbay, you may want to stop at **Edgecomb Potters,** Route 27 (☎ 207/865-1705) to see the ceramics, glazed with brilliant colors. Also visit the **Aquarium,** off Route 27 south at McKown Point in West Boothbay (☎ 207/633-9500). The Aquarium has a shark and skate tank and displays relating to marine ecology. Open Memorial Day to Labor Day, daily 9am to 5pm; Labor Day to Columbus Day, weekdays only. Admission is $2.50 adults, $2 children 5 to 18.

While you're here, take the 1½-hour ferry ride to **Monhegan Island**—the island that has been associated with many great artists: with George Bellows, Robert Henri, Rockwell Kent, and Andrew Winter in the past; today, with Jamie Wyeth and Reuben Tam. It's a tiny island, only 1½ miles long and ½ mile wide, covering a total of 700 acres, so you don't need a car. An essential part of the island experience is visiting the studios of the resident artists. There are about 20 such studios; you can find them by checking the bulletin boards in the village, on the western side of the island.

Cliffs are the main features of the eastern side of the island. At **Black Head** and **White Head,** you'll stand face to face with roaring winds and waves and views, on a clear day, of Isle au Haut and Matinicus. The light on the island is intense and can swing from brilliant one minute to gloomy the next. The central part of the island offers 17 miles of trails for hiking through the serene beauty of **Cathedral Woods.** You can pick up a map from any island store. The island offers some great wildflower spotting and birding (the island is on the Atlantic flyway), especially during the spring and fall migratory seasons at **Lobster Cove** at the southern tip of the island.

For a view of the harbor, Manana Island, and the mainland, including the Camden Hills, climb up to **Monhegan Light** (1824). If you want to get some idea of the island's history, stop at the **Monhegan Museum,** which was once the lighthouse keeper's house, open July 1 to September 30, daily from 11:30am to 3:30pm. Each year a show honors one of the artists who have worked on the island, and a new building is being constructed to display the works of Monhegan Island artists.

Monhegan can be reached aboard *Balmy Days II* (☎ 207/633-2284) from Boothbay Harbor and aboard the *Hardy III* from New Harbor (☎ 207/677-2026). But it's more fun to take the mail boat, *Laura B,* from Port Clyde. For information, contact the Monhegan Boat Line, P.O. Box 238, Port Clyde, ME 04855 (☎ 207/372-8848).

If you want to stay on the island, you'll need to reserve well in advance at one of the two or three inns. Until recently there was no electricity on the island, and even now it's recommended that you bring a flashlight.

BOOTHBAY HARBOR LODGING

The Admiral's Quarters, 71 Commercial St., Boothbay Harbor, ME 04538 (☎ 207/633-2474), is right downtown, but because it is set on a bluff on the less trafficked side of town, it seems more quiet than most. It's operated by a very welcoming couple, Deb and Les Hallstrom. Guests gather on the front deck or in the glass-enclosed sun room around the wood-burning stove to enjoy the views of Boothbay Harbor. All of the six rooms have been pleasantly furnished, and all have private entrances, telephones, and TVs. Most are painted white and contain a bed, two wicker chairs, and a chest plus decorative accents like a basket of dried flowers or a watercolor. The two front units have great views from their private deck. Breakfast will be bountiful—fresh fruit, yogurt, coffeecake and breads, plus an egg dish like egg casserole, and pancakes or sausage. Facilities for guests include an ice machine and a laundry. Rates: $75 to $135.

The **Welch House,** 36 McKown St., Boothbay Harbor, ME 04538 (☎ 207/633-3431), is located up above the frantic action of the town amid lovely gardens and wonderful views. A fountain plays outside the entrance and a driftwood-and-wire sculpture adds interest to the garden approach. Huge lilacs and a spreading chestnut tree give a sense of serenity. From the large third-floor deck, there's a beautiful view of harbor and bay. There are 16 rooms, all with private baths, and attractively decorated with floral-motif wallpapers, serpentine canopied beds, and country pieces. Room 10, which is tucked under the eaves, has immediate access to the deck. A full breakfast featuring, say, banana pancakes, fruit, and baked goods, is served in the glass enclosed breakfast room. Rates: mid-May to mid-October, $75 to $125; mid-October to mid-May, $60 to $95.

To reach the **Albonegon Inn,** Capitol Island, ME 04538 (☎ 207/633-2521), you have to cross a wooden bridge and drive down a narrow dirt road fringed with pines. It has operated as an inn since the 1880s, when steamers brought guests here and the current owner's great grandfather was the innkeeper. It may not be for everyone—it's definitely on the rustic side, but for nature lovers and those who want repose without trappings, this is a perfect hideaway. It actually bills itself as "determinedly old-fashioned." The location is magical. From the main house and cottages there are glorious views of Burnt Island. The 11 guest rooms in the main building, some with small sitting rooms and some with balconies, are simply furnished: beds with white chenille spreads, wall-to-wall carpeting, and usually a desk and an old chest. Most appealing are those in small cottages. The Barnacle is charming with its painted blue floors, mural, and tongue-and-groove paneling. The Periwinkle Suite contains a bedroom, sitting room, kitchen, and deck. Guests enjoy a continental breakfast in the morning, and later in the day they can relax on the porch, drinking in the scene from a rocker, or on colder days, curl up in front of the fire in the large stone hearth in the sitting room. Rates: $85 to $133.

Situated on a hillside, **Five Gables Inn**, Murray Hill Road, East Boothbay, ME 04544 (☎ 207/633-4551), has views from the front porch out past the houses on the opposite side of the street to Linekin Bay. It's away from the frantic crowds of Boothbay itself. All 16 rooms except one face the bay, and five have fireplaces. Each has been attractively decorated in a light country inn style with pencil four-posters or iron beds combined with comfortable sitting chairs and country items like blanket chests. The second-floor rooms are a little larger than those on the first floor. The third-floor rooms are my favorites, with dormers and window seats. No. 16 is the smallest room, but it has a great view from the bed. Guests gather around the fire in the light and airy common room or on the enclosed or open porch that extends the full length of the house and has a hammock inviting repose. The garden is also a great place. A full breakfast—bloody Mary soup, apple pancakes, fresh breads, muesli, and fruit—is served at separate tables. Afternoon tea and cookies and evening port and sherry are available, too. Open mid-May to mid-November. Rates: $100 to $165.

Spruce Point Inn, Boothbay Harbor, ME 04538 (☎ 207/633-4152), is away from the heavily trafficked downtown scene on 15 oceanfront acres. The location is superb. It's a gracious place where the restaurant looks out on the water, and leather chairs await around the fireplace. The accommodations are in the main building or in cottages/condominiums. Most are plain paneled and casually furnished with chintz. All have telephones and cable TVs; the one- and two-bedroom cottages have stone fireplaces. The new deluxe suites offer spacious bedrooms and luxurious bathrooms with whirlpool tubs, and each has a screened private porch. In the living rooms, there are woodstoves, large TVs, and comfortable furnishings. Amenities include tennis and two swimming pools, one freshwater and the other saltwater. The saltwater pool is right down on the oceanfront and has a hot tub nearby. Rates: MAP per person late May to late June and September to mid-October, $105 to $158; late June to mid-July, $138 to $214; mid-July to late August, $142 to $208.

Hogdon Island Inn, Barter's Island Road (P.O. Box 492), Boothbay, ME 04571 (☎ 207/633-7474), overlooks Sheepscott Cove. Family portraits look down from the upstairs hallway where there are six rooms, all with private baths. They are attractively furnished with brass or Jenny Lind beds covered with colorful quilts, oak chests, loveseats, and braided rugs on the floors. The sitting room offers a TV/VCR plus board games, books, and comfortable seating arranged around the fireplace. Breakfast (muffins, granola, and a hot dish such as eggs Benedict or waffles) is served in the dining room at a large table. Facilities include a heated outdoor pool, set in the pretty gardens that have a glider/swing on a grassy knoll. There's also a porch furnished with wicker. Rates: $90 to $110 in summer, $70 to $80 in winter. No credit cards.

MONHEGAN ISLAND LODGING

The Island Inn, Ocean View Terrace (P.O. Box 128), Monhegan Island, ME 04852 (☎ 207/596-0371), faces west and offers great ocean sunsets and vistas from the long front porch. The original section of the inn was built in 1807. There are 36 simply furnished rooms of varying sizes and configurations. Only seven have a private bath. The dining room serves three meals a day in a casual setting. Rates: June 30 to August 26, $130 to $185; June 16 to June 29 and August 27 to September 21, $120 to $175; May 23 to June 15 and September 22 to October 13, $100 to $165. Closed after Columbus Day until Memorial Day.

The **Monhegan House,** Monhegan, ME 04852 (☎ 207/594-7983), was built in the 1870s. It's opposite the General Store only a short walk from the dock. Its 32 rooms have been furnished in country style with a variety of oak pieces. All rooms share baths. Rates: $85 double.

BOOTHBAY HARBOR DINING

Although the **Lawnmeer Inn & Restaurant,** Route 27 (P.O. Box 505), West Boothbay Harbor, ME 04575 (☎ 207/633 2544), has rooms, the real reason to come here is to dine in the country-style dining room overlooking the water. The menu focuses primarily on seafood dishes—potato-crusted halibut topped with caper and saffron aioli, tuna glazed with basil and sun-dried tomato pesto, and, of course, lobster. There are some good meat dishes, too, like the grilled pork tenderloin with five-spice black-bean sauce and scallions or the grilled venison with juniper-scented onion confit and cabernet sauvignon sauce. Prices range from $13 to $23. Open daily from 6 to 9pm. The rooms, by the way, are decorated in a Laura Ashley country-style, with a teddy bear on every bed.

Lobsterman's Wharf, off Route 96 in East Boothbay (☎ 207/633-3443), is a casual waterfront restaurant where you can feast outside on lobster and other fish dishes like grilled seafood or baked stuffed sole. Inside, it's a typical waterfront kind of place with wooden booths and floats hanging from the rafters. Chicken Oscar and steaks are also available. Prices range from $13 to $20.

Boothbay Harbor
Special & Recreational Activities

Biking: Rentals are available at **Auclair Cycle** (☎ 207/633-4303) and at **Tidal Transit Co.,** by the footbridge in the Chowder House Building (☎ 207/633-7140), which rents bikes for $20 a day.

Boating: Rentals are available from **Midcoast Rentals,** Pier 8, Boothbay Harbor (☎ 207/633-4188). Depending on the size, boats range from $130 to $175 for a half day and from $195 to $250 a day.

Canoeing/Kayaking: Tidal Transit Co., by the footbridge in the Chowder House Building (☎ 207/633-7140), rents kayaks for $35 a half day, $50 full day, and offers tours too.

Cruises: The *Appledore* (☎ 207/633-6598) is a traditional windjammer that sails from Fisherman's Wharf for a 2½-hour cruise to the outer islands past seal rocks. It operates from June through September. Cost is $20 per person. **Balmy Days Cruises** (☎ 207/633-2284) offers a variety of cruises, including a 1½-hour sailing trip on the *Bay Lady*. Cruises go to Monhegan Island and include a night-lights tour of the harbor and a supper jazz cruise. Balmy Days operates from Pier 8 Boothbay Harbor. Fares to Monhegan are $29 adult and $18 children under 12. Other cruises range from $8.50 to $22 adults. **Cap'n Fish's Scenic Boat Trips** (☎ 207/633-3244) offers a variety of nature trips including whale-watching and puffin-watching trips to Eastern Egg Rock. Reservations recommended.

Golf: Bath Country Club (☎ 207/442-8411) is less crowded than most golf courses in the area in summer.

Hiking: There are several reserves with trails in the region. Many of them were set aside in memory of Rachel Carson, who spent much time exploring the area and writing about it in *The Edge of the Sea* and her other books: **Porter Preserve** on Barter's Island; **Ovens Mouth,** which offers salt marsh and cove; the **Linekin Reserve** off Route 96 in East Boothbay with frontage on the Damariscotta River. For more information, contact the **Land Trust,** P.O. Box 183, Boothbay Harbor, ME 04538 (☎ 207/633-4818).

Picnicking: Ocean Point and McKown Point are both great spots.

NEWCASTLE, DAMARISCOTTA & THE PEMAQUID PENINSULA

Newcastle stands on the western bank of the Damariscotta River, and Damariscotta on the eastern bank. From Damariscotta, Route 130 leads down through the village of Bristol past Pemaquid Falls to the Pemaquid Point Lighthouse, which stands at the southern tip of the broad peninsula. It's a great place to go to just sit and look out at the rocky coastline and the pounding surf or to picnic under the fir trees. Near the lighthouse, the **Fishermen's Museum** displays lighthouse memorabilia, lobstering and fishing gear, and half models of ship hulls. Open Memorial Day to Columbus Day, Monday to Saturday from 10am to 5pm, Sunday 11am to 5pm.

On your way to the light, you can turn off on Huddle Road to see **Fort William Henry** (1689) at the entrance to Pemaquid Harbor. On the way back from the light, you can take South Side Road to Back Cove and then travel on Route 32 along New Harbor and back up the peninsula to Waldsboro. This road goes past the **Rachel Carson Salt Pond Preserve** on the shores of Muscongus Bay in Chamberlain. Carson summered on Southport Island, and this was one of her favorite coastal spots.

Another favorite spot on the peninsula is on the western side along Seal Cove off Route 129, a few miles north of South Bristol. Here you can wander in the **Menigawum Preserve.** For more information, contact the Damariscotta River Association (☎ 207/563-2196).

NEWCASTLE & PEMAQUID PENINSULA (NEW HARBOR) LODGING

The **Newcastle Inn,** River Road, Newcastle, ME 04553 (☎ 207/563-5685), is operated by Rebecca and Howard Levitan who are fine hosts and have invested much money and time into creating one of the most comfortable hostelries in the area. It's located on the banks of the Damariscotta, with lawns that sweep down to the edge of the river, lined with weeping willows. Each of the 15 rooms is named after a lighthouse. Monhegan Island contains a rice four-poster covered with a fluffy comforter and dressed with eyelet-lace linens and dust ruffles. The oak floor is covered with an oriental rug, the walls are adorned with gilt-framed still lifes, and two wing chairs and a dresser complete the decor. Winter Harbor has a private entrance leading into a room that is decorated with a lovely floral-motif Waverly wallpaper and contains a four-poster with a crocheted canopy, and a sofa and wing chair in front of the gas fireplace.

The inn also has a fine restaurant and a comfortable bar-lounge, decorated with original watercolors and paintings from the Southwest. R. C. Gorman paintings hang in the two intimate dining rooms, too, where the three- or five-course dinner is a leisurely dining experience around large, well-spaced tables. The menu changes daily. You might start with the delicious crab cakes accompanied by a rémoulade sauce, which will be followed by soup or salad, and then by a choice of duck with a raspberry cassis glaze, salmon with horseradish crust, or beef tenderloin with a Dijon rosemary mustard crust and a bordelaise sauce. No matter which you choose, it will be finely prepared and served. A multicourse breakfast is included in the room rates. Two decks set with tables under market umbrellas, a sun room, and a small TV room complete the public areas. Rates: B&B, June 1 to October 31, $105 to $180; November 1 to May 31, $85 to $160. Dining hours are Tuesday to Sunday in summer and Thursday to Sunday in winter from 6 to 7:30pm.

Flying Cloud Inn, River Road (P.O. Box 549), Newcastle, ME 04553 (☎ 207/563-2484), occupies an original Cape Cod cottage, plus a late Greek Revival addition. It does not have direct access to the river, but there are views from all rooms but one. The high-ceilinged sitting rooms are spacious and have floor-to-ceiling windows. A marine painting hangs above the mantel, and the floors are covered with Chinese rugs. There are five rooms, all with private baths. The ground-floor London Room has pumpkin-pine, wide-board floors; a carved mahogany bed; and an antique-reproduction dresser. The San Francisco Room has floor-to-ceiling windows, giving a view of the river, and a rice four-poster. The bathroom is down the hall, but bathrobes are provided. The owners have traveled extensively, and some of the rooms contain their mementos, like Aussie hats or boomerangs, as decorative accents. The Melbourne Room has a skylight, plus the best views in the house. Civil War buffs will appreciate the collection of books shelved on the landing. A full breakfast—sourdough blueberry pancakes, plus muffins and fruit—is served in the dining room or on the front deck, which has a view of the river across the street. There's a screened porch at the back of the house and a hammock waiting in the backyard. An excellent value. Rates: $65 to $100.

The **Millpond Inn**, 50 Main St., Nobleboro, ME 04555 (☎ 207/563-8014), in an idyllic location on a mill pond in a quiet inland village, was built in 1780. Friendly owners, Bobby and Sherry Whear, added the deck that overlooks the pond, where you can fish if you like and watch for the loons, otters, and even a bald eagle. Hammocks hang on the back lawn, and two canoes as well as two mountain bikes are available for guests. (Bobby will tell you where to go—he's a registered Maine guide.) There are six rooms, all with a country look, with oak dressers and rockers plus accents such as spinning wheels. Several rooms have fireplaces. The Pond View Room has a kitchen with microwave and sink. A breakfast of blueberry pancakes or cinnamon swirl French toast is served at separate tables in a dining room warmed by a woodstove. Wine and cheese are served in the late afternoon in or around the bar, where the mantel is full of photographs of Bobby Orr in action and other hockey pictures. There's also a sitting room for guests. Another very good value. Rates: $90.

The **Bradley Inn**, Route 130, HC 61, 361 Pemaquid Point, New Harbor, ME 04554 (☎ 207/677-2105), is a very appealing place with lovely gardens. The common areas are cozy and comfortable, and the furnishings all finely upholstered. There are 12 rooms in the inn, all with private baths and phones and furnished with antique reproductions. Top-floor rooms have cathedral ceilings and distant views of Johns Bay. Two suites, located in the barn, have bedrooms, sleeping lofts, full kitchens, and living rooms. There's also a cottage with fireplace and private porch overlooking the gardens. The gazebo is an ideal spot to retire to at the end of the day. The front lawn is used for croquet. Bikes are available.

The inn has marine bar and Ships, a restaurant serving fine cuisine. The menu is limited, but the ingredients are fresh and the food is well prepared. Seafood dishes are particularly satisfying—baked Maine halibut with a warm lemon and rosemary reduction and a tomato-coriander concasse, or crispy seared salmon with a mustard sauce and roasted-garlic mashed potato. Naturally there's lobster, and also a very good five-spice-crusted pork tenderloin with a cranberry and port wine reduction and sweet potato frites. Prices range from $14 to $22. For an appetizer, my choice would be the steamed Pemaquid mussels in herb broth, set off by some crispy fried leeks. A continental breakfast is included in the rates. Rates: in the inn: January to May 31, $100 to $135; June 1 to October 31, $110 to $185, November 1 to December 31, $100 to $135. Cottages: April 1 to May 31 and November 1 to Dec 31, $160; June 1 to October 31, $205. Suite: May 23 to Columbus Day, $205.

In Damariscotta, **King Eider's Pub** (☎ 207/563-6008) is an authentic English-style pub located in an old brick building just off Main Street. It serves good quality pub fare including really good fresh fish and chips.

Pemaquid Fishermen's Co-op is located in a little shack off Route 130, set on a slope up from the working dock. Here you can secure a lobster dinner for only $10.95, although the price will vary depending on the season. It also has a shore dinner featuring a 1½-pound lobster, steamed clams and mussels, corn on the cob, and cole slaw for only $14.95. Lobster rolls and hot dogs are also available. Sit right down and enjoy the view.

At **Shaw's Lobster Pound,** Route 32, New Harbor (☎ 207/677-2200), you can sit outside and enjoy fresh lobster at market prices from the dock right there. It offers an extensive menu of other fish and shellfish including fried oysters, clams, and scallops plus a variety of sandwiches. Prices range from $3 to $13. In winter, move into the long room that is warmed by a woodstove.

∏ewcastle & Damariscotta
Special & Recreational Activities

Cross-country Skiing: **Dodge Point Wilderness Area** along the Damariscotta River in Newcastle has cross-country trails.

Golf: **Wauenock Country Club,** Route 129, Walpole, is a nine-hole course.

Hiking: Walk the trails in the 300-acre **Dodge Point Reserve** along the Damariscotta in Newcastle. A 3-mile nature trail in the **Salt Bay Preserve** is accessible from Route 215 in Newcastle. It passes by the Great Salt Bay, and among the creatures you might sight are horseshoe crabs, eagles, osprey, and Great Blue and green back herons. Along the way you can see one of the treasures of the region: the oyster-shell heaps on Glidden Point, which are reckoned to be 2,400 years old. They represent the remains of many Native American feasts.

Nature and Wildlife Watching: Puffin and seal watches are operated by **Hardy Boat Cruises** (☎ 207/677-2026) from Shaw's Fish and Lobster Wharf, New Harbor. The company also offers special birding trips during migratory season to Eastern Egg Rock, where the puffins nest; to Monhegan Island; and Matinicus Rock, which is home to numerous shorebirds including puffins, razorbills, and several different terns. Audubon naturalists guide several of these trips. Prices range from $8 to $30.

ROCKLAND, VINALHAVEN ISLAND & TENANTS HARBOR

On your way from Damariscotta to Rockland, you'll pass through Thomaston. Boat lovers will also want to visit the **Maine Watercraft Museum,** on Thomaston Harbor, which displays antique boats, many of them mahogany. Visitors can take a tour of the St. George River and even rent an antique boat. It's open late May to October 1, Wednesday to Sunday from 10am to 5pm; admission is $4 adult, $2 children 5 to 16. The **Montpelier General Henry Knox Museum,** at routes 1 and 131 (☎ 207/354-8062), displays memorabilia of this Revolutionary War hero and other local history; it's open late May to mid-October, Tuesday to Saturday from 10am to 4pm, Sunday from 1 to 4pm; admission is $4.

Rockland is a salty quarrying town, and that reality gives it more flavor than many of the pretty but overrun tourist towns. The company owned 150 or so schooners that hauled the casks of lime from this port to Boston and New York. Those days ended at the turn of the century, and the port is now famous as the home of one of the windjamming fleets, while the town itself is slowly being transformed into an art town—the old main street, lined with handsome Victorian storefronts, now boasts several galleries.

The cornerstone of this development is the wonderful **Farnsworth Museum**, 352 Main St., Rockland (☎ 207/596-6457), dedicated to showing how Maine has influenced American art and artists. The galleries trace the history of art in Maine, from the arrival of Thomas Eakins, Childe Hassam, Winslow Homer, Fitz Hugh Lane, and Frederick Church to the time when Marsden Hartley and John Marin lived here to the current generation of Wyeths. A whole room is dedicated to the Wyeth family, who have become—Andrew in particular—bellwethers of popular taste. Another strength of the collection is American Impressionism with works by Frank Benson, Joseph deCamp, Maurice Prendergast, and John Twachtman. The 20th century is richly represented with works by Will Barnet, Robert Henri, Edward Hopper, Robert Indiana, Rockwell Kent, and Marguerite and William Zorach. Rockland native Louise Nevelson has a gallery of her own.

Concerts are also given at the museum. A new gallery devoted to the Wyeths and a performing arts center are being constructed in a church behind the gallery. Open Memorial Day through Columbus Day, Monday to Saturday 10am to 5pm, Sunday 1 to 5pm; in winter, Tuesday to Saturday 10am to 5pm, Sunday 1 to 5pm. Admission is $5 for adults.

Behind the museum is the **Farnsworth Homestead**, an 1852 Greek Revival house that represents the lifestyle of a wealthy Maine family in the 19th century. It was the home of William Farnsworth, a prosperous businessman who owned a fleet of schooners, a general store, and interests in limestone quarries and kilns. His daughter Lucy left the money to establish the library and art museum. It's open Memorial Day to Columbus Day, Monday to Saturday from 10am to 5pm, Sunday 1 to 5pm. Admission is included in museum admission.

Note: Wyeth fans will also want to visit the **Olson House**, Hathorn Point Road in nearby Cushing, which Andrew painted so hauntingly in many of his works, including the now famous *Christina's World*. Open Memorial Day to Columbus Day, daily from 11am to 4pm. Admission is $3 adult, $1 children 8 to 18.

Back in Rockland, stroll along Main, where you'll find several antiques stores and bookstores, the **Harbor Square Gallery**, at no. 374 (☎ 207/594-8700), and **Gallery One**, at no. 365 (☎ 207/594-5441), above the Huston Tuttle store. On a side street, **Details Mercantile**, 8 Lindsey St. (☎ 207/596-0054), specializes in salvage and sells architectural fragments—pediments, mantels, and cupboards—some of which have been taken and reworked or decorated by contemporary artists. **Caldbeck Gallery**, 12 Elm St. (☎ 207/594-5935), is another gallery worth checking out.

South of town, the **Owls Head Transportation Museum**, Route 73, Owls Head (☎ 207/594-4418), displays early pre-1930 aircraft along with some automobiles, carriages, bicycles, and motorcycles. The best time to visit is during one of the special events such as the World War I air show when the planes are flown and other vehicles used. Open daily April through October, 10am to 5pm. November to March weekdays 10am to 4pm, and weekends 10am to 3pm.

Three miles farther on Route 73, **Owls Head Light** is great for picnicking and also has a swimming beach, plus views of the Fox Islands (Vinalhaven and North Haven). From Owls Head, Route 73 will take you to St. George with a fort of the same name, and from there Route 131 rolls down through Tenants Harbor to Port Clyde and **Marshall Point Lighthouse** (1857), which stands just across the "gut" from N. C. Wyeth's summer home, Eight Bells.

As you travel the Maine coast in summer and look out over the ocean, you'll see ships with several masts that stand out among all the others. These are the famous **windjammers,** which sail from a number of ports along this coast—Rockland and Camden, in particular—for 3-, 4-, and 6-night cruises. For information, call **The Maine Windjammer Association,** P. O. Box 1144, Blue Hill, ME 04614 (☎ 800/807-WIND), which operates a fleet of nine of these wonderful craft. It's a unique experience: sailing by day—spotting seals, porpoise, whales, and puffins—and anchoring in quiet coves at night. The tone of the boat is set by the captain and crew. The food is good and hearty and often includes lobster bakes and other fun food. If you like, you can take the wheel or help hoist the sails, or you can just relax and enjoy an authentic experience of the sea. The cost of the trips ranges from $300 for a 3-night cruise to from $625 for 6 nights. Members of the Windjammer Association that sail from Rockland include the two-masted *J & E Riggin* (☎ 207/594-2923), a rebuilt 1927 oyster dredger that accommodates 26 passengers, and the three-masted *Victory Chimes* (☎ 207/594-0755), a restored lumber schooner dating to 1900, accommodating 44 passengers. It's the largest in the fleet. The *Nathaniel Bowditch* (☎ 800/288-4098 or 207/273-4062) was built in 1922 as a private racing yacht. Today it accommodates up to 24 guests. Other member vessels sail from Camden.

From Rockland there's a ferry to **Vinalhaven,** once famous for its granite quarries and canneries. The granite industry employed hundreds of men from the late 1800s to around 1930. It was a success because the stone didn't have to be hauled very far overland—a stone fleet sailed from here, carrying this valuable stone to New York for buildings like the Cathedral of St. John the Divine and to Boston for the Fine Arts Museum. The other major industry, sardine canning, was established in 1917 by H. F. Sawyer, who opened the first cannery. Today Vinalhaven is a fishing and lobstering island that gives scarcely a nod to the tourist trade. It won't take long to drive around the 9-mile-long, 5-mile-wide island, past the granite quarries—Lawson's on the North Haven Road and Booth's on the east side—which are now used as natural swimming holes. Explore **Lane's Island Preserve,** taking a picnic to one of the beaches and observing the different flora and fauna. Visit **Brown's Head Light** on the western tip of the island and **Heron Neck Light** on the outside of Green's Island. The trip on the car-passenger ferry from Rockland takes about 1½ hours. For information, contact **Maine State Ferry Service** (☎ 207/594-5543).

You can also take a ferry to a much quieter, more exclusive island, **North Haven,** that was once a summer refuge for Anne Morrow and Charles

Lindbergh. It has a year-round population of 350 (1,500 in summer) and does not attract day trippers because it has few amenities for visitors. For information, contact Maine State Ferry Service (☎ 207/594-5543).

ROCKLAND LODGING

The Captain Lindsey House Inn, 5 Lindsey St., Rockland, ME 04841 (☎ 207/596-7950), is located in a historic 1837 brick building right downtown just off Main Street. The nine rooms here are designed for convenience and comfort and have been lavishly decorated with fine-quality wallpapers and fabrics. You might find a Shaker four-poster with a tapestry bed cover set against green-striped wallpaper. There are oriental rugs on the oak floors and furnishings such as plushly upholstered wing chairs or cane rockers, desks, and drop-leaf antique-reproduction side tables. All have TVs and telephones. The sitting-room floor also has an oriental rug; couches and chairs are arranged around the fireplace. Some conversation pieces for decoration are the ornately carved lion chair from Indonesia and the Chinese ceramic horse. A continental breakfast is served to guests in the paneled dining room. Afternoon tea is also served. The Waterworks Restaurant, which is owned by the same management, is in the building next door (see below). Rates: summer, $105 to $170; winter $65 to $110.

The LimeRock Inn, 96 Limerock St., Rockland, ME 04841 (☎ 207/594-2257), occupies a lovely 1890 Victorian with a wraparound porch on a quiet residential street in town. The building, as they say, has "good bones," and the interior architectural woodwork and stained glass are extra enhancements. The rooms are large and light, and they have style—the first-floor Grand Manan contains a rice four-poster and a good reproduction highboy and has the extra attractions of a wood-burning fireplace and a double whirlpool tub. Fox Island has a lavishly carved mahogany bed combined with a carved armoire and chests, all set against striped wallpaper with rich swag drapes at the windows. In North Haven, a handsome cherry sleigh bed stands on the original linoleum. The Island Cottage room is the most private; it has its own small deck overlooking the back lawn. Dhurries rest on the gray-painted floor; walls are papered with a blue floral and a broad blue-striped wallpaper. The white-painted bed sports a blue comforter. Decoration runs to fresh and silk flowers and landscapes and reproductions of the Impressionists. The bath contains a whirlpool tub. An extraordinarily good breakfast—egg soufflé with blueberry sauce plus fresh fruit—is provided at glass-covered individual tables. The extra-large living room features some lovely stained glass, ship models, and a big-screen TV. There's another parlor for quiet conversations. Rates: $95 to $170.

Accommodations at the **East Wind Inn & Meeting House** (P.O. Box 149), Tenants Harbor, ME 04860 (☎ 207/372-6366), are in three buildings on the harbor front. The Inn was originally a sail loft, and the Meeting House a sea captain's home. There are 13 rooms in the inn (six with private bath). They are nicely decorated with iron or pineapple beds and oak desks and dressers as well as rockers. Room 1, which is a suite, has a lovely water view, is decked out with a carved pine bed and burled-maple side tables, and has a sitting room large enough to accommodate a loveseat and two chairs. All of the 10 rooms in the Meeting House have water views and private baths; some are suites. The dining room serves traditional New England cuisine. It's open for lunch daily from July 1 to mid-September only, and daily for dinner 5:30 to 8:30pm (5:30 to 9:30pm July 1 to mid-September). Tenants Harbor is on the St. George peninsula south of Thomaston. Open year-round. Rates: June to October, $80 double with shared bath, $115 with private bath, and $130 for a suite; November to May, rates are $68, $86, and $100, respectively.

Craignair, Clark Island, Spruce Head, ME 04859 (☎ 207/594-7644), opened originally as a boardinghouse for the stone cutters working the Craignair quarry. It's on 4 acres, right on the water—the lawns go down to the shore. The owner is also an antiques dealer, and the place has all the hallmarks of a collector's home. Sitting rooms are filled with all manner of eclectic pieces, poured into the room in Victorian style—fringed lamps, urns with potted ferns, oriental screens, and collections of oriental ivory and glass are all present. There are 14 rooms in the main building (all sharing 8 baths) and 8 rooms (all with private baths) in the vestry. They contrast with the public areas by being simply furnished. In one you might find an iron and brass bed with swing-arm reading lamps, an oak dresser, and a fan for a decorative accent. Vestry rooms are little more elaborate. Room 26, for instance, has a painted cottage bed, an oak dresser, an India inlay table, and a skylit bathroom. There's a restaurant on the premises decorated in pinks with plenty of ferns; tables look out over the water. Rates: July to Labor Day, $89 to $112; September to June, $84 to $107.

From the outside, the **Payne Homestead** (P.O. Box 216), Vinalhaven, ME 04863 (☎ 207/863-9963), looks like a faded Victorian beauty, and in many ways it is. It was built in 1873 by a granite magnate. Today Lee and Donna have opened it up to visitors, whom they welcome warmly. The four rooms, which are not fancy at all, share one bath. They are furnished country style, with painted floors overlaid with braided rugs. Among the furnishings there might be a brass bed and oak dresser and easy chair. In the Moses Webster Room on the first floor is a carved mahogany bed covered with a candlewick spread. The room has some nice architectural details, including a tin ceiling and a marble fireplace. Donna serves bountiful breakfasts in an attractive dining room. Great slabs of granite lay around the island, and the gardens here, which extend down to the cove, are no exception. Rates: $85 to $100.

ROCKLAND DINING

Jessica's, 2 S. Main St. (Route 73; ☎ 207/596-0770), is located in a Victorian home outside of town at Owls Head. The cuisine is inspired continental drawing on Swiss, Italian, and other traditions. Try the lobster ravioli, which is served in a delicious sauce of sherry, garlic, coriander, and tarragon. Other choice appetizers include the pizzettes or the Swiss raclette. Among the specialties of the house, a favorite is the veal Zurich, made with choice veal in a rich white wine and mushroom sauce and served with the best rosti ever. Other dishes include lamb Provençale and shrimp with garlic, sun-dried tomatoes, and green olives served over fettuccine. The fish dishes change daily to ensure their freshness. Prices range from $11 to $17. Open Tuesday to Sunday from 5:30pm to closing.

Cafe Miranda, 15 Oak St. (☎ 207/594-2034), is a casual in-town restaurant for lunch or dinner. You'll be served at wood-block tables set with multicolored napkins. The cuisine mixes Italian and Asian traditions, offering dishes such as calamari marinara or gnocchi baked in blue cheese with mushrooms, along with Fukien noodle cakes flavored with scallion, ginger, coconut, and lemongrass, or Hawaii stir fry with pineapple chili sauce. Prices range from $9.50 to $14.50. Open Tuesday to Saturday from 5:30 to 9:30pm.

The Waterworks, Lindsey Street (☎ 207/596-7950), is located in the old water plant. On one side it offers a brew pub with a great long bar and rows of trestle style tables in front of a large stone fireplace. There's entertainment here on weekends, both live and with a DJ. On the other side there's a slightly more formal dining room with captains chairs and tables. The food is pretty satisfying in either place. The options range from a hearty shepherd's pie to grilled swordfish with an herb crust and shallot sauce served over roasted red peppers. Some dishes have an Asian flavor. The real specialties of the house, though, are fish cakes, accompanied by a rémoulade sauce and schooner stew made with sautéed shrimp, scallops, and lobster in a vegetable-lobster bisque. Prices range from $6 to $22. Open daily from 11am to 1am (kitchen closes at 10pm).

On the waterfront, behind a mess of lobster pots and shrimp traps, is **Contis** (☎ 207/596-5579). Inside, the tables are covered with newsprint and are clustered around a fireplace and woodstove. Started by a fishmonger from Naples, Italy, Contis serves plain, good food, particularly fresh fish. Prices range from $9 to $15 for dishes such as coquilles St. Jacques, broiled haddock, bouillabaisse, calamari Napolitana, and shrimp marinara. Open July to October only.

Second Read, 328 Main St. (☎ 207/594-4123), is—as you already guessed—a cafe bookstore, and it's a great place for breakfast and lunch. It offers a large selection of sodas, coffees, and pastries, including raspberry Linzertorte and delicious lemon madeleines, which make perfect snacks while you're reading one of the many fine secondhand books on the shelves in the back. At lunch, the gallette (pastry shell) rustica, made with tomatoes, eggplant, mushroom, and cheese, is delicious. Other sandwiches, soups, and salads are available. Prices range from $5 to $7. Open Monday to Friday from 7:30am to 6pm, Saturday from 8am to 6pm, and Sunday from 11am to 5pm.

Rockland
Special & Recreational Activities

Canoeing: For rentals, try **Pemaquid River Canoe Rental,** P.O. Box 46, Bristol, ME 04539 (☎ 207/563-5721), 5 miles south of Damariscotta on Route 130.

Cruises: See the information about the **Maine Windjammer Association** (☎ 800/807-9463) above. Three other schooners to consider are operated by **North End Shipyard Schooners.** The *Isaac H. Evans,* P.O. Box 482, Rockland, ME 04841 (☎ 207/594-8007), built in 1886, has 11 double cabins and a captain that plays concertina. It's a shallow-draft vessel, which means that it can get in closer to the coast. Prices range from $400 to $425. The *American Eagle,* built in 1930, accommodates 28 and has an auxiliary diesel engine, allowing it to offer long-range trips. The *Heritage,* built in 1983, was designed for comfort; it can accommodate 33 passengers. Prices range from $635 to $750. These schooners sail on 3- and 6-day cruises from May to mid-October.

From **Rockland,** several other windjammers offer cruises. The *Stephen Taber*, 70 Elm St., Camden, ME 04843 (☎ 207/236-3520), is another fine 1871 schooner that accommodates 22 passengers on weeklong trips. Still another schooner, the *Flying Fish*, R.R.1, Box 670, Jefferson, ME 04348 (☎ 207/549-3908), accommodating up to six passengers, generally sails on 4-day, 3-night cruises. If you just want the windjammer experience for a day or so, the schooner yacht *Wendameen* (1912) accommodates 14 and also sails from Rockland on 1-night cruises costing $155 per person (☎ 207/594-1751). A luxury yacht, it was owned by several entrepreneurs, including the Schlitz family.

Fishing: In Rockland, **Captain Bill Wasson,** 18 Pine St. (☎ 207/354-6520), charges $300 for a day's fishing trip for two.

Golf: Samoset Resort, Rockland (☎ 207/594-1431), has a spectacular oceanside course, but you'll need to book several days in advance.

Nature Trips: Atlantic Expeditions operates a trip in conjunction with the National Audubon Society to Matinicus Rock and Seal Island from mid-June to mid-August, Wednesday to Saturday. The main focus of these trips is puffins. Prices are $35 for adults, $20 for children under 12. Sunday trips are 1½ hours longer to allow for some whale watching.

Parasailing: See the Camden Hills from a different point of view. Contact **X-treme Watersports** (☎ 207/236-7272) at Landings Marina in Rockland.

Sailing: You can charter a sailboat from **Bay Island Yacht Charters** (☎ 800/421-2492) from Journey's End Marina, Tillson Avenue in Rockland; rentals from $100 a day. Skippers and instruction also available.

CAMDEN & ISLESBORO ISLAND

Camden thinks it is the jewel of the mid-coast, and indeed it is in many ways. The harbor lies at the base of the Camden hills, a tranquil oasis filled with millions of dollars' worth of yachts. The town blends into **Rockport,** which you'll pass through first. Turn off Route 1 to the right, and you'll find yourself at the lovely little Rockport Harbor. From the harbor, the road climbs up the hill, and here you'll find several stores and an art gallery worth browsing. The **Maine Coast Artists,** 162 Russell Ave. (☎ 207/236-2875), will have a stimulating contemporary art show of different media in the three floors of galleries. Open Tuesday to Saturday from 10am to 5pm, Sunday noon to 5pm. Admission is $2. The **Maine Photographic Workshop** is a visual arts center and summer workshop. For information, write 2 Central St., P.O. Box 200, Rockport, ME 04856 or call ☎ 207/236-8581. **Anne Kilham Designs,** 142 Russell Ave., sells the artist's ultra "pretty" designs that are used on all manner of items. Rockport is also home to what have become locally known as the famous belted Galloway cows—you can see them at the Mitchell Ledge Farm on Bow Street.

In Camden, get off Main Street (Route 1) and explore the nooks, crannies, and alleys along Bayview Street. Among my favorite stops: **Meetingbrook Bookshop & Bakery,** no. 50 (☎ 207/236-6808), for new and used books; **ABCDEF Book Shop,** no. 23 (☎ 207/236-6448), for rare, beautiful antiquarian volumes; **Art of the Sea,** no. 12 (☎ 207/236-3939), for original marine art and prints; **Ducktrap Bay Trading Co,** no. 28 (☎ 207/236-9568), for all kinds of decoys and wildlife art; and **Veraya Import Gallery,** no. 40 (☎ 207/236-4481). There are some fine artists working here too like **Laurie V. Adams** on Cobb Road (☎ 207/236-4023), who creates fluid, sensual, organic-shaped porcelains that are light as a feather and glazed with iridescent surfaces.

This is where the **windjamming fleet** was first established in 1936, and many windjammers still sail from here. The *Grace Bailey* (☎ 800/736-7981), built in 1882 as a lumber schooner, and the *Mercantile* (☎ 800/736-7981), another cargo schooner, built in 1916, belonged to the original fleet. The *Lewis R. French* (☎ 800/469-4635) was launched in Maine in 1871 and is the oldest schooner in the fleet. It has no inboard engine and delivers a real sailing experience under 3,000 square feet of magnificent sail. Still other members of the fleet sailing from Camden are *Angelique* (☎ 800/282-9989); *Mary Day* (☎ 800/992-2218); *Roseway* (☎ 800/255-4449); and *Timberwind* (☎ 800/759-9250).

For a great view, drive up Route 1 to **Camden Hills State Park** and take the road to the top of Mount Battie for magnificent views all the way to Bar Harbor and Mount Desert Island. Hikers can also climb the mountain or its neighbor, Mount Megunticook.

If you appreciate fine furniture and like Windsor chairs, then stop at **Windsor Chairmakers** on Route 1 (☎ 207/789-5987) in Lincolnville Beach. Lincolnville is also home of a popular attraction for kids and adults alike— **Kelmscott Farm,** off Route 52, 4½ miles from Lincolnville Center (☎ 207/763-4088). This enterprise is dedicated to preserving rare breeds of sheep like the Cotswolds and the Katahdin Hair sheep, along with other ponies and animals. From the sheep, the Metcalfs, who own the farm, produce a line of English woolen products—scarves, blankets, and hats—which they sell here and via mail order. Special fun events include sheep-dog trials and shearing day.

For evening entertainment the **Camden Civic Theatre** (☎ 207/236-7595) produces a season of summer theater, plus performances in October and December at the Camden Opera House at routes 1 and 105. The **Bay Chamber Concerts** (☎ 207/236-2823) puts on a season of classic and jazz concerts at the Rockport Opera House in July and August. On weekends, you can also find jazz and other musical entertainment at the **Sea Dog Brewing Co.** on Mechanic Street (☎ 207/236-6863).

CAMDEN LODGING

Granite steps lead up to the **Maine Stay,** 22 High St. (Route 1), Camden, ME 04843 (☎ 207/236-9636), which is located on 2 acres right next to the state park. The owners were a navy family, and the house is filled with interesting artifacts brought back from their postings. For example, in the dining rooms there's a handsome Samurai warriors' campaign chest, along with an Amish pie safe that is used to display Waterford crystal. Classical music is piped in to all the rooms. There are eight rooms, each attractively decorated, often with personal mementos. Room 1 has twin beds made up with lace coverlets, plus wicker side chairs, a rocker, and a white-painted chest. The claw-foot tub has a hand shower. Room 8 has a gas-fired woodstove, a long window seat, and French doors that lead to a private flagstone patio. Luxuries in the Clark Suite include a gas fireplace and a Corian shower and bathtub. A full breakfast featuring egg casseroles, muffins, fruit, and granola is set out buffet style and eaten around the long harvest table. There are two parlors, both with fireplaces, and a TV room. Rates: summer, $85 to $150; winter, $70 to $110.

Whitehall Inn, High Street (P.O. Box 558), Camden, ME 04843 (☎ 207/236-3391), is a lovely old-fashioned place, dating to 1834, with very gracious hosts who have operated it for generations. As a consequence, it has great warmth, and the spaces have that lived-in air where the antiques—grandfather clocks, oriental rugs, and Queen Anne desks—are truly seasoned. It's most famous as the place where Edna St. Vincent Millay's sister worked. Edna herself first read her poem "Renascence" here, and here she met a guest who paid for her education at Vassar. A whole wall in the sitting room is dedicated to Millay memorabilia. The 50 rooms are plain and unadorned, perfect for those who seek peace and quiet. Guests enjoy a variety of sitting areas—the large room where puzzles, games, and books are available; an enclosed porch; and a long front porch. The dining room, with its windows flung open in summer, serves good cuisine. The menu changes weekly. It will always have a good balance of fish and meats and will always feature lobster. The chowders are excellent and so, too, is the seafood mousse. Among the main courses you might find veal marsala with wild mushrooms or bay scallops with cherry tomatoes and fresh basil. Prices range from $16 to $18. There's also a pretty flagstone patio with umbrella tables. A full breakfast is served. Facilities include a tennis court. Open Memorial Day to the end of October. Rates: late May to June, B&B $85 to 120, MAP $115 to $150; July to mid-October, B&B $115 to $155, MAP $145 to $185.

The Belmont, 6 Belmont Ave., Camden, ME 04843 (☎ 207/236-8053), offers one of the best, if not the best, dining experience in town. Only about eight entrees are offered, and each is superb. There will always be a fish of the day and a vegetarian dish, such as grilled portobello mushroom with beluga lentils, red pepper, and polenta. Don't expect a plain Maine lobster—instead you'll find a thrilling version made with cabbage, lime, and coconut milk broth, which is heavenly. Another pièce de résistance is the split hare—consisting of James Beard's forty cloves of garlic, braised rabbit legs, and roasted rack of saddle. Prices range from $16 to $28. Don't miss the desserts. The banana tart and caramel ice cream or the chocolate molten tart with sun-dried cherries are to lust after. Open from 6 to 9pm.

Although it's primarily a restaurant, its six rooms have not been neglected. They are spacious and very tastefully furnished. The smallest room has an elegant four-poster, two wing chairs, and a marble sink in the bathroom. Other rooms, some of which are suites, have been strikingly designed with drapes separating the bed from a sitting area.

Norumbega, 61 High St., Camden, ME 04843 (☎ 207/236-4646), is a striking and extraordinary accommodation. It stands in all its stone glory, down below Route 1 on a semi-circular drive. It was designed by the inventor of duplex telegraphy, Joseph B Stearns, in 1886. It's an exquisite place. The interior is almost entirely hand carved out of solid oak. There are 12 guest rooms including three suites. Each one is lavishly appointed and furnished with antiques and often has an extra-special architectural feature. For example, the Library Suite has a round stained glass window and paneled ceiling and a library gallery where the bed is located. The walls are painted dark green, and against them is placed a white wicker bed with two marquetry side tables. The sitting area is painted lemon yellow and has Palladian nooks, which have been painted crimson. It also has a wood-burning fireplace enclosed in beautiful floral tiles. Sandringham has an ornately carved mahogany four-poster, beautifully dressed in white and off-white linens set down in a burgundy and forest green decor. Kensington has a view of the water over the vast lawn. The Penthouse has a spectacular skylit bedroom with panoramic views from a private deck and amenities like a stocked refrigerator, TV, and fireplace. Downstairs, you'll find a billiard room with a full-size table and carved seats that were taken from an opera house. The reception room is a splendid space with an inlaid parquet floor and a carved white mantel enclosed in ornate tile work. A smaller area is lined with semicircular bookcases flanking a carved wooden fireplace decorated with gryphons. Other furnishings include a grand piano and an elegant ormulu desk. Another magnificent fireplace is the focus of the dining room, which also has an elegant carved sideboard and tables set with Chippendale chairs. A full breakfast—whatever you desire—is served in your room or on the verandah; a wine and cheese social is held in the evening. The acres of grounds contain two gazebos, and here on the lawns, croquet and badminton are played. Bicycles are available. Rates: late October to mid-May, $105 to $305; mid-May to June and mid-October to October 31, $135 to $385; July to mid-October $165 to $460.

A Little Dream, 66 High St., Camden, ME 04843 (☎ 207/236-8742), is just that—a delightfully romantic place. Hostess Joann Ball really has a knack and an eye for creating beautiful rooms and spaces. You'll want to linger in the garden sitting room among the ivy in terra-cotta pots, listening to the play of the little fountain. Even the seating on the side porch has been arranged to encourage intimate conversation. Each of the rooms is decorated in a different palette. The Master Room has a pine four-poster with fabric drapes and twig decoration, wicker armchairs, an oak dresser and a chaise lounge piled high with cushions. From the large deck (in winter only), there's a good water view. Travels contains travel accoutrements as decorative accents plus a handsome carved bed that is loaded with pillows. Two charming rooms are in the carriage house. At breakfast you might enjoy poached pears in a cranberry reduction, smoked salmon, an omelet with three fillings, or guests' favorite—stuffed French toast with peaches Amaretto. The house has 2 acres of gardens with stone walls that have been terraced into the slope. Rates: summer $105 to $205; winter $105 to $140.

The Inn at Sunrise Point, P.O. Box 1344, Camden, ME 04843 (☎ 207/236-7716), is the only accommodation in Camden that offers access to the water. It stands on a 22-acre property, but only 4 acres are developed. There are three handsomely decorated rooms in the inn. All rooms have wood-burning fireplaces, telephones, TV/VCRs, and plush bathrobes, makeup mirrors, and hair dryers. They are furnished in modern style. Four additional accommodations are located in cottages, two of which are on the waterfront. These have amenities like those in the main house, plus wet bars, refrigerators, coffeemakers, double Jacuzzis, and private porches. Guests may use a sitting area where they can gather around the fireplace and enjoy a chess game or take down a book from a shelf and read. There's also a selection of videos. A full breakfast is served—hot entrees such as lobster hash, crab croissant bake, or a delicious crème brûlée French toast, plus fruits, cereals, and bread. Open from mid-May to the end of October. Rates: $160 to $360.

The **Hawthorn,** 9 High St., Camden, ME 04843 (☎ 207/236-8842), occupies a large Victorian house that was built in 1894 for a coal merchant. It stands near the harbor on 1½ acres. Four of the 10 rooms are in the old carriage house, and these are the most attractive. From Broughman's private balcony there's a good view of the harbor through the trees. The room is furnished with a four-poster; has wall-to-wall carpeting; and is equipped with a TV/VCR, clock radio, gas fireplace, and double Jacuzzi. In the house, the Turret Room is a favorite, decked out with a wicker bed and chaise lounge and a rocker. A full breakfast of fruit, breads, pastries, cereal, and an entree like crème-caramel French toast is served, usually on the large deck or at individual tables in the dining room. Rates: $90 to $195 (higher prices for the carriage-house rooms).

The **Victorian,** Seaview Drive, off Route 1 (P.O. Box 1385), Camden, ME 04843 (☎ 207/236-3785), was built in 1881 and is tucked away on a little more than 1½ acres down a lane off Route 1. It has a wraparound porch from which there is a water view through the trees. Here Ray and Marie Donner have set up a telescope for stargazing. There are six rooms and two suites; several have wood-burning fireplaces and antique claw-foot tubs in the bathroom. Each has been nicely decorated. The Season Room has an iron bed, oak dresser, two easy chairs, and a wicker dresser, plus a claw-foot tub with shower. The Sawyer Suite fills the entire third floor. The bedroom features a brass bed, and the living room has sliding doors leading to a private balcony. Breakfast— muffins, cereal, and cranberry-orange-zest pancakes or something similar—is served in the light and airy dining room. Guests particularly appreciate the 16-window sun room, where they can bask on wicker chairs and loveseats. Rates: mid-June to mid-October, $145 to $215; the rest of the year, $105 to $155.

The **Spouter Inn,** Route 1, Lincolnville Beach, ME 04849 (☎ 207/ 789-5171), is located on 2 acres right across the road from Lincolnville Beach. It's an 1832 home that has been renovated by the owner. The seven rooms are nicely furnished; several have fireplaces. Your room might contain a carved-oak bed, a marble-top dresser, and a rocker. One of the most appealing rooms is the third-floor Admiral. It's large and has a skylight and wood-burning fireplace plus a small deck. The Helmsman has a magnificent tiger maple bed and a bird's-eye maple vanity. The Captain tops them all with its fireplace, a beaded-board tub surround, and a Jacuzzi tub, plus dresser and side tables of inlaid wood. Breakfast, which might be a crustless garden quiche plus fruit and breads, is served at a large lace-covered table in the pretty dining room. There's also a sitting area that is comfortably furnished with velvet Victorian chairs, loveseat, and blanket chest that are placed around the fireplace. Guests also like the front porch. Rates: summer $85 to $175; winter $75 to $145.

From the porch of the **Camden Harbor Inn,** 83 Bayview St., Camden, ME 04843 (☎ 207/236-4200), there's a great view of Camden Harbor with tree-covered Mount Battie behind it. The inn is located away from the frenzy of the town center, just up from the Yacht Club. There are 20 or so guest rooms, all with private bath and all decorated with good period reproductions—canopied four-posters, Federal-style lowboys, French-style sitting chairs, or Victorian rockers. Some have balconies and some have fireplaces. The original eagle-claw-footed tubs have sometimes been retained in the bathrooms. None have TVs or telephones, but both of these amenities are available in the public areas. The inn has a good dining room, Cetacea, in which the complimentary breakfast might feature delicious Maine blueberry pancakes or similar egg dishes. At dinner, the fare is continental—lobster with a saffron cream sauce or duck with black olive orange sauce. Prices range from $20 to $24. It's open from 6 to 9pm daily in summer; Wednesday to Sunday in spring and fall, and Thursday to Saturday in winter. Rates: mid-June to mid-October, $185 to $235; May to mid-June and mid-October to November, $135 to $185; December to April, $105 to $135.

CAMDEN DINING

For fine dining, also see the Belmont, White House, and Cetacea above.

Rathbone's, 21 Bayview St., Camden (☎ 207/236-3272), serves a modern American cuisine with a definite tilt to the Mediterranean. You might start with wild mushroom strudel baked and served with a spinach puree, or the oyster martini cocktail served with a champagne mignonette. Among the entrees, which are always supplemented by daily specials, you might find oven-roasted salmon with a citrus beurre blanc; or pasta with clams, calamari, and shrimp flavored with fresh farm tomatoes and garlic. Prices range from $16 to $19. The restaurant is decorated in Mediterranean colors of terra-cotta and gold, creating a warm ambience. Tables sport white tablecloths, but the atmosphere is casual. There's a bar and deck upstairs. Open Tuesday to Sunday from 5:30 to 10pm and from 10:30am to 2:30pm Saturday and Sunday.

The deck of the **Waterfront Restaurant,** Harborside Square off Bay View Street (☎ 207/236-3747), is an idyllic place on a warm summer day to while away an hour or two over lunch or drinks as you watch the yachts come and go. Luncheon fare runs to lobster and crab roll sandwiches, plus good fish and chips and salads, and much more. At dinner, the menu extends to seafood Newburg, filet mignon with a wild mushroom espagnole sauce, and salmon with a braised onion and sun-dried-tomato sauce. Prices range from $14 to $22, the last for a 1½-pound lobster with mussels in shallots white wine and flamed with cognac and served with a cognac cream sauce. Open daily from 11:30am to 2:30pm, 5 to 9pm.

The **Sail Loft Restaurant,** Town Landing, Rockport (☎ 207/236-2330) is situated right down by Rockport Harbor, but it's not a typical waterfront casual restaurant. It offers fine dining at polished wood tables. Certainly, the menu concentrates on fresh shellfish and seafood offering live lobsters and shore dinners of all sorts, along with dishes such as a fisherman's platter of clams, scallops, shrimp, fish, and steamed mussels. If you throw in a lobster, then it becomes a lobsterman's platter. Prices range from $11 to $30 (the higher price for a 2-pound lobster). Open in summer, daily from 11:30am to 2:30pm and 5:30 to 10pm; in winter, Thursday to Monday 11:30am to 2:30pm and 5:30 to 8:30pm.

The **Frogwater Cafe**, 31 Elm St. (☎ 207/236-8998), has a '60s-style atmosphere. It's small, casual, and friendly, but the food is more than the usual casual fare. At dinner, you'll find a dozen or so entrees, ranging from a baked salmon with leeks, tomatoes, red onion, and feta cheese drizzled with tarragon vinaigrette to grilled tenderloin of beef served with a roasted-shallot sauce. Prices are very reasonable, ranging from $11 to $16. Beer and wine only. Open for dinner only: 5:30pm until closing.

Chez Michel, Route 1, Lincolnville Beach (☎ 207/789-5600), is a casual and very popular local place that serves good French-inspired dishes. The fish dishes are what people come for—lobsters, scallops Provençale, haddock meunière, bouillabaisse, and poached salmon with hollandaise. But there are also classics such as beef bourguignon and steak au poivre. Prices range from $11 to $15. Open Tuesday to Sunday from 11:30am to closing.

Sea Dog Brewing Company, 43 Mechanic St. (☎ 207/236-6863), has 10 brews on tap and attracts a local and tourist crowd to its large bar or to the outdoor patio that overlooks the waterfall of the Knox mill. The decorative scale models of schooners and clippers are worth checking out, too. You can also take a tour of the brewery. Open daily from 11:30am to 1am.

Cappy's Chowder House, 1 Main St. (☎ 207/236-2254), is the town's casual woodsy pub. It has an extensive menu with a lot more than chowders. There's a raw bar, fresh fish dishes, and more. Great breakfast place, too. Open 7:30am to midnight in summer.

The **Camden Deli**, 37 Main St. (☎ 207/236-8343), is the place to pick up a sandwich (from pastrami to liverwurst and tuna salad) and dessert to go for a picnic on the coast—unless you prefer sitting out on the deck overlooking the falls. Prices range from $4 to $6.

Camden & Lincolnville
Special & Recreational Activities

Beaches: The most accessible are Martinsville Beach near **Port Clyde**; Lincolnville Beach and Laite Beach on **Camden Harbor**.

Biking: Rentals are available at **Fred's Bikes**, 53 Chestnut St. (☎ 207/236-6664) for $15. Fred's delivers to local inns and motels.

Boating: Boston whalers are available for rent from **Ocean Images** (☎ 207/236-6404) for the day or the week.

Camping: Camden Hills State Park has the best camp sites.

Cross-Country Skiing: Camden Hills State Park is a good place.

Cruises: From **Camden**, lobster fishing and nature cruises are offered aboard *Lively Lady Too* (☎ 207/236-6672), operating from Sharp's Wharf. The cost is $15, $5 for children under 15. Lobster bakes cost $40 per person. For information during winter months, call ☎ 418/839-7933. The *Betselma* (☎ 207/236-4446) cruises from the Public Landing on 1- and 2-hour trips. The 1-hour trip is $10 for adults, $5 for children 3 to 12; the 2-hour trip costs $20 and $10, respectively. See below for windjammer cruises.

Maine

Canoeing/Kayaking: Guided trips are offered by **Mount Pleasant Canoe &
Kayak,** P.O. Box 86, West Rockport, ME 04865 (☎ 207/785-4309). Prices
start at $175. This company also offers inn-to-inn paddling trips for 3
nights, starting at $600 per person.

Hiking: Camden Hills State Park (☎ 207/236-3109) offers about 20 different trails, including one leading to the summit of Mount Battie and another to an ocean lookout on the eastern slope of Mount Megunticook
before crossing the summit.

Kayaking: Maine Sports Outfitters, Route 1, Rockport (☎ 800/722-0826
or 207/236-8797), offers trips, tours, instruction, and rentals in sea
kayaking. Two-hour tours around the harbor cost $30 per person, $90 for
a day tour. Longer tours are possible. **Ducktrap Sea Kayak,** Route 1,
Lincolnville Beach (☎ 207/236-8608), gives 2-hour coastal tours ($25),
half-day tours ($50), and other custom trips as well as rentals.

Sailing: You can learn to sail at the **Camden Sailing School** (☎ 207/
236-7048). A full day for two costs $150.

Skiing: Camden Snow Bowl has great ocean views plus two T-bars and a
chairlift. There is also good tobogganing. National tobogganing championships are held here in early February (see " Events & Festivals to Plan
Your Trip Around," earlier in this chapter).

Windjammer Cruises: Members of the **Windjammer Association** are the
Mary Day (☎ 800/992-2218); the *Angelique* (☎ 800/282-9989); the *Lewis
R. French* (☎ 800/469-4635 or 207/236-9411); and the *Roseway* sail from
Camden. The first was built especially for passengers and can accommo-
date 30 people. Extra features include a parlor organ and a fireplace. The
second was designed for windjamming and accommodates 31 passengers.
The 1925 *Roseway* sails from Camden in August and September, carrying
36 passengers.

Day sails are offered aboard the *Surprise*, a 1918 schooner that carries
18 passengers. It sails from Memorial Day through mid-October from
Camden Public Landing. Cost is $25 per person. Two-hour sails can be
taken aboard the Schooner *North Wind* (☎ 207/236-2323) for $20 per
person from Sharp's Wharf at Camden Town Landing. The windjammer
Appledore (☎ 207/236-8353), built in 1978, also offers 2-hour day sails
from Camden.

East Penobscot & Downeast Maine

Searsport ◆ Castine, Brooksville & Deer Isle ◆ Blue Hill,
Sedgwick & around Blue Hill Bay ◆ Bar Harbor ◆ Acadia
National Park ◆ Seal Harbor & Northeast Harbor ◆
Southwest Harbor/Bass Harbor ◆ Hancock,
the Schoodic Peninsula & Jonesport

Distance in miles from Boston: Deer Isle, 290; Bar Harbor and Mount Desert, 276.

Estimated driving time: 5½ hours to Deer Isle, 6 hours to Bar Harbor and Mount Desert.

━◀○▶━◀○▶━◀○▶━◀○▶━◀○▶━

Driving: Take I-95 to Exit 22 and take Route 1 to Searsport and then routes 1 and 3 to Ellsworth and Route 3 into Bar Harbor. Or you can take I-95 to Bangor and then Route 395 to Route 1A East to Ellsworth and Route 3 into Bar Harbor.

Further Information: For more information, contact the **Belfast Area Chamber of Commerce,** P.O. Box 58, Belfast, ME 04915 (☎ 207/338-5900); **Searsport and Stockton Springs Chamber of Commerce,** P.O. Box 139, Searsport, ME 04974 (☎ 207/548-6510); **Bar Harbor Chamber of Commerce,** P.O. Box 158, Bar Harbor, ME 04609 (☎ 207/288-5103).

For **Acadia National Park** information write to Acadia National Park, P.O. Box 177, Bar Harbor, ME 04609 (☎ 207/288-3338).

━◀○▶━◀○▶━◀○▶━◀○▶━◀○▶━

This is the rocky coastline that visitors rush to see—where surf pounds against the granite rocks and mountains soar above the coastline, ponds and lakes mirroring them at their base. Much of this spectacular scenery has been saved for future generations in Acadia National Park. Facilities and services are available to park visitors in Bar Harbor, the former gracious seaside resort town; as a result, Bar Harbor is literally overrun in summer. You may want to consider anchoring at other smaller and quieter villages around Mount Desert Island.

From here, you can just as easily foray into the park to hike, bike, canoe, or climb and to enjoy the whole range of outdoor adventures and pastimes. But

Events & Festivals to Plan Your Trip Around

Fishermen's Day in Stonington at the tip of Deer Isle. This is when lobster-boat races over a ¾-mile course are held, showcasing lobstermen's skills—hauling traps, swimming to a life raft, and flaking or moving gill nets so that the floats don't entangle in the mesh.

June: Quiet Side Festival in Southwest Harbor celebrates with a flea market and arts and crafts fair, followed by dancing in the evening.

July: Bar Harbor Music Festival ranges from jazz and chamber to pop and orchestral music. It includes a New Composers series and afternoon tea concerts. Call ☎ 212/222-1026 or 207/288-5744 for information. It lasts until the first week of August.

August: Blue Hill Fair. A classic country fair. Call ☎ 207/374-9976. Late July to late August.

Mount Desert Festival of Chamber Music. Call ☎ 207/288-5103.

December: Bonfire and sleigh rides and the arrival of Santa by lobster boat in Northeast Harbor.

before you head off to this admittedly stunning meeting of land and sea there are a couple of stops you might consider along the way. One in particular, the Penobscot Marine Museum, will give you insight into Penobscot Bay and what it has meant down the years. And don't miss exploring Castine, Brooksville and Cape Rosier, Deer Isle, and Stonington, and the whole peninsula extending from Blue Hill down to Brooklin with its spectacular coastlines and historic towns. So pause before you rush pell-mell to Bar Harbor—there are other weekend possibilities to enjoy.

SEARSPORT

The important **Penobscot Marine Museum,** Church Street, at Route 1, Searsport (☎ 207/548-2529), is a wonderful place to learn about the life and history of the region. Penobscot Bay alone has 2,000 miles of shoreline if you include the 1,700 islands. The museum displays are exhibited in several historic buildings. In the Captain Jeremiah Merithew House, exhibits focus on the natural and the working life of those who lived along this shore, shipbuilding, lumbering, fishing, and quarrying for granite and lime.

Another exhibit traces Castine's economic growth from its settlement in 1626 as a fishing station to the 1880s when the first "rusticators" arrived by steamer. First to arrive were the artists, Robert Cole and Frederick Church, who were soon to be followed by wealthy society.

Don't miss the film, made in 1929, about a trip round Cape Horn aboard a schooner. The commentary is hilarious, the trip harrowing and thrilling, and the photography extraordinary. It shows the terrible trials and tribulations of seafarers and what it was really like to work as a sailor aboard a ship that had 32 acres of sail, 350 lines, and a bottom sail that weighed 1 ton when it was dry.

In the old Town Hall, the story of the Down Easters is told. Developed after the Civil War, from 1875 to 1885, Down Easters hauled wheat from California to the East Coast and Liverpool; rice from India; sugar from Hawaii; and tea, silk, and porcelain from China. Down Easters were more economical than clippers because they had fewer and smaller sails and consequently could be handled by a smaller crew. Open from Memorial Day to mid-October, Monday to Saturday from 9:30am to 5pm and Sunday from 1 to 5pm. Admission is $5 adults, $1.50 children from 7 to 15.

Antiquing Searsport is also a well-known antiquing ground. Stop in at one or other of the antiques centers, notably **Robert Davis Antiques,** a barn filled with art, china, glass, and furniture at decent prices, and **Pumpkin Patch** where there are 26 dealers offering a good selection of tools, marine instruments, furniture, jewelry, art, rugs, and much more.

On Route 1, book and art lovers will want to stop at **Penobscot Books,** a wonderful art specialist who also sells some reasonably priced cultural objects, many of which are Japanese or religious objects.

SEARSPORT LODGING & DINING

The **Homeport Inn,** Route 1 (P.O. Box 647), Searsport, ME 04974 (☎ 207/548-2259), is located in a wonderful 1861 Victorian that has two cupolas. The interior is splendidly arrayed with fine English, Far Eastern, and American antiques. In the front parlor, large urns from China are combined with Japanese lamps and a screen and a table from India. Another sitting room is decorated with British-royal-family memorabilia and portraits, including one of the British queen in a carriage with Saudi King Faisal that was taken by the innkeeper. Furnishings are suitably rich and include a richly carved library table set under the sky-blue dome. Eye-catching objects—from clocks and pictures to ivory carvings and bronzes—are everywhere. There are 10 guest rooms; some share baths. In one, a carousel figure hovers behind and above the sleigh bed, while a pine chest, desk, and rockers complete the furnishings. One room has a pencil four-poster covered with a Battenburg lace coverlet set against a bird-motif wallpaper. Breakfast is taken at separate tables on an enclosed porch. From the back of the house you can walk down to the water, but there is no view per se. Peacocks and swans are a part of the scene, and at certain times of the year create quite a ruckus. Rates: $70 to $95 (lower rates apply November 1 to April 30).

The **Nickerson Tavern,** Route 1 (☎ 207/548-2220), is a typical New England dining room with its Windsor chairs set at white-clothed tables. The cuisine is traditional continental with some minor variations. For instance, you might find roast duck with orange, currant, and honey cassis sauce; salmon baked in rice paper and served with three citrus, ginger, and sherry vinaigrette; veal piccata Milanese; and hazelnut-crusted chicken with a raspberry-shallot butter sauce. Prices range from $13 to $20. Open summer and fall, Tuesday to Sunday from 5:30 to 9pm. Closed from December to Easter.

Penobscot Bay

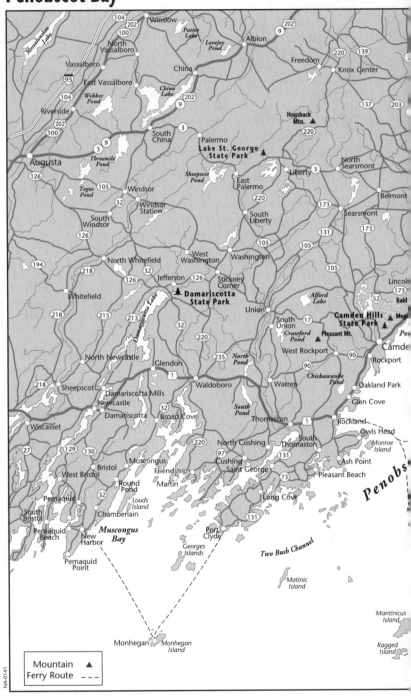

Mountain ▲
Ferry Route – – –

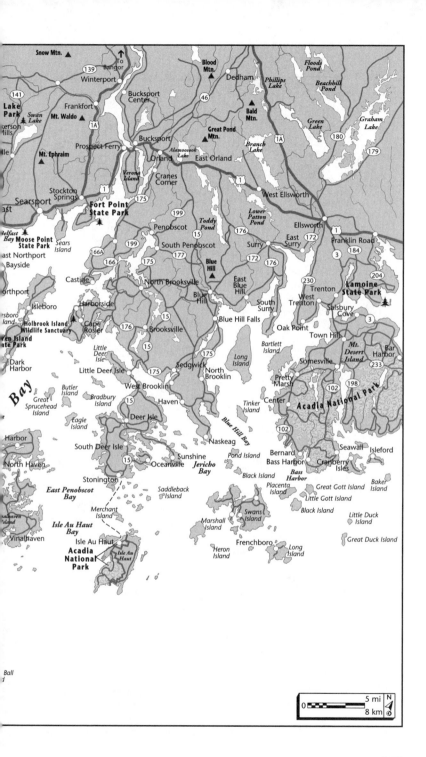

THE PENOBSCOT PENINSULA—CASTINE, BROOKSVILLE & DEER ISLE

Castine is a historic community. What makes the town special is its ocean-front location and beautiful old homes. It's also unusual because it has remained largely unchanged—if you look at old photographs, they will show buildings that can still be seen today. In the early 19th century, it was one of the wealthiest towns of its size in the United States, and it has retained that air of well-being and comfort. Today you can stroll along the streets that are lined with handsome early-19th-century homes.

You'll also find some shops worth visiting in town and on the outskirts. Book collectors will want to stop at **Barbara Falk** (☎ 207/326-4036) on Route 166A, who sells wonderful antiquarian books. In town, you may want to purchase one of **Chris Murray's** intricate bird carvings from the studio behind his house on upper Main Street (☎ 207/326-9033). **Leila Day Antiques,** Main Street (☎ 207/326-8786), has some beautiful pieces of furniture and decorative objects—porcelain, paintings, rugs, quilts, and folk art.

In summer you may want to visit the **Wilson Museum,** Perkins Street (☎ 207/326-8545), which was founded by geologist and anthropologist John Howard Wilson who summered here. It features marine and mineral exhibits and artifacts relating to local history. Hours: Memorial Day to September 30, Tuesday to Sunday from 2 to 5pm. Free admission.

From town, the road loops around to Fort Madison and Dice Head Light where you can get right down to the bay and enjoy a picnic on the grassy knoll, which is all that remains of the fort.

From Castine, take Route 166 to 199 and then Route 175 south down to Brooksville. From Brooksville, you can explore the coastline along Eggemoggin Reach, a wonderful strip of sailing water, and then head west to remote Cape Rosier. In South Brooksville, seek out the studio of **Janet Redfield** (☎ 207/326-8449) who makes windows, bowls, panels and platters, all in stained glass. After circling Brooksville, take routes 175 and 15 south to Deer Isle. Before you cross the bridge to the island, you might want to stop in Sargentville to look at the stock in **Wayward Books,** Route 15 (☎ 207/359-2397). Deer Isle is famous for the **Haystack Mountain School of Crafts** (☎ 207/348-2306) and the numerous arts and crafts studios that are located here. Stop at the **Blue Heron Gallery,** Route 15 (☎ 207/348-6051); the **Turtle Gallery,** Route 15 (☎ 207/348-9977); **Eastern Bay Gallery,** Main Street, Stonington (☎ 207/367-5006); the **Deer Isle Artists Association** (no phone); **Maine Crafts Association** (☎ 207/348-9943) to see representative examples of local crafts, and also at **Harbor Farm** (☎ 800/342-8003) to look at the architectural fragments and other decorative items including ceramic floor tiles, hand-marbled papers, porcelain, stoneware, and pewter. Some notable studios to visit include **William Mor,** Box 409, Reach Road, off Route 15 (☎ 207/348-2822), who makes fine-quality pots; jeweler **Ronald Hayes Pearson** (☎ 207/348-2535); **Doug Wilson** (☎ 207/348-6871) for hand-forged ironwork. For specialty foods, stop at **Nervous Nellie's Jams & Jellies,** Sunshine Road, Deer Isle (☎ 800/777-6845). Call ahead to find out if the artists are available and for studio locations.

Stonington Village at the tip of Deer Isle is a working harbor. Drive down and along the harbor in both directions. At the west end are a couple of galleries. At the eastern end are a couple of restaurants. Down by the harbor there is a moving sculptural tribute by William Muir to the stonecutters who made Deer Isle granite known the world over. A ferry-mail boat (☎ 207/367-5193) departs from here to Isle Au Haut, which is part of Acadia National Park. It leaves four times a day with maximum sailing times of an hour each way. The island has no facilities, and it can be windy and chilly, so come prepared. Still, this is maritime and island beauty at its rawest and best.

CASTINE, BROOKSVILLE, & DEER ISLE LODGING & DINING

It's worth staying at the **Castine Inn,** Main Street (P.O. Box 41), Castine, ME 04421 (☎ 207/326-4365), just for the opportunity to sample the brilliant cuisine of young chef Tom Gutow who has worked with David Bouley and also Michel Guerrard. The setting is delightful. A lovely mural envelops the whole room, depicting what you would see if the wall were not there. In summer you can have dinner (and breakfast, which is included in the room rate) at one of the wrought-iron and glass tables on the terrace with a view of the gardens and the water.

The cuisine is zestfully prepared and beautifully presented and served. The menu changes frequently. Depending on the season, you might enjoy a wonderfully redolent steamed cod in lemongrass broth with braised fennel or an olive-crusted salmon with caponata and yellow pepper grapefruit sauce. In winter the aged beef tenderloin with a red wine Madeira sauce will hit the spot. To start with, the lobster corn chowder is nectar to the soul, and even as simple a dish as red and yellow tomato terrine with green beans and balsamic vinegar can prove satisfying because it's so full of freshness. The desserts are not pretentiously extravagant. Instead, they contain the best ingredients: peach tart, apple tart, strawberry-rhubarb cobbler—all delicious. Prices range from $15 to $26. Open from 5:30 to 8:30pm.

In 1997 when the new owners were just getting into their stride, the 20 rooms were plain, bland, and unadorned, but Tom and Amy have plans for sprucing them up. Guests can relax in the comfortable sitting room, where Amy has placed a family-heirloom chime box along with other attractive pieces like the secretary and the nest of Chinese tables. The bar pub is a cheery room with painted dark-red floors and forest-green walls. The tables have been painted too, with flowers and birds. The gardens are lovely and have been landscaped into several different areas—a woodland fern area, an azalea bank, a Concord grape arbor, and a clematis trellis. A little bridge arches over a pond and brook leading to another garden and eventually to a "garden rug," designed with pebbles and shells and patches of hissop and thyme. Open May to late December. Rates: $95 to $145.

Oakland House, R.R. 1, Box 400, Brooksville, ME 04617 (☎ 207/359-8521), has been operating since 1889, and it's still owned by the same family that started it. It offers well-kept cottages that have stunning views. The cottages have been built over several decades; some are log-cabin style, while others are more contemporary. The resort encompasses 50 acres so that the accommodations are spread out, which affords guests great privacy. Oak Grove, for example, was built in 1950, but it has great character, bestowed by the pine beams and walls and the stone fireplace. Homestead West was built later, in 1963, but it too has an attractive living room with stone fireplace plus a kitchenette equipped with microwave, coffeemaker, refrigerator, and hotplate. Some individual rooms are in a building called Shore Oaks. A stone and shingle home, it was built in 1907, and has a large porch overlooking the water. Many of the attractive rooms have fireplaces. Hooked rugs are under foot, and furnishings might include an iron or cannonball bed and a maple dresser and rocker. The Lone Pine cottage has been winterized for year-round living. It's located back in the woods and has a great atmosphere. A sofa and maple rocker are arranged around the stone fireplace, and there are plenty of good books in the bookcases. The bedrooms have twin iron beds and a double. The kitchen is fully equipped with stove and microwave. Meals can be enjoyed in the old original building at the entrance to the resort. Menus are limited, but offer good food with fresh ingredients—dishes like broiled sea bass with red pepper coulis or fettuccine with sun-dried tomatoes in a scampi-style sauce. There's half a mile of shorefront with a swimming beach, where a lobster picnic is held every Thursday. Videos are shown in the barn. Rates for B&B, from early May to mid-June, $61 to $84 per room; September to late October, $78 to $125 per room; MAP, mid-June to late July, $66 to $90 per person; late July through August, $70 to $96 per person.

Hiram Blake Camp, Harborside, P.O. Box 59, Blake's Point, Cape Rosier, ME 04642 (☎ 207/326-4951), is located on Stand Cove. It's remote and very rustic indeed—a cottage with somewhat worn furnishings and a plain, paneled, somewhat gloomy bedroom. What makes it worth considering is the magnificent shore setting and the main lodge and dining room, which are loaded with character. It was founded by Captain Hiram Blake in 1916, and his descendants still run it. It was Hiram who started collecting all the books that line the walls and are stacked between the beams and the rafters of the dining room. A stone fireplace, deer trophies, marine paintings, and ship's lanterns add to the spirit of the place. Here many ingredients of the meals come from organic gardens on the property, along with lobsters from the traps that family member Paul Venno sets, right here from his own dock. Dishes are simple: baked ham, roast turkey, or fish served family style. In summer, the camp attracts a lot of family regulars. Accommodations are in 14 cottages, all with woodstoves or stone fireplaces. CawCaw Lodge has a stone fireplace and a wood stove, and under a cathedral ceiling are such furnishings as a Mission chair, desk, and sofa, as well as a wicker rocker. It has a fully equipped kitchen, which directly overlooks the cove, and a pine table for dining. The twin and double bedrooms are dark, however, and have well-used furnishings, and the bathroom has a tiny sink and shower. Rowboats available. Summer rates are $500 to $750 per week for a one-to-three bedroom cottage, plus $165 per person for meal plan; winter B&B, $350 to $550 for cottages.

Eggemoggin Reach separates Deer Isle from Brooksville and Sedgewick peninsulas. It's a magnificent stretch of sailing water, and here Mike and Susie Canon who are delightful hosts, have located the bewitching bed-and-breakfast, **Eggemoggin Reach,** Box 33A, Herrick Road, Brooksville, ME 04617 (☎ 207/359-5073), on 6½ acres looking out across the Reach to Pumpkin Island Lighthouse and beyond to the Camden Hills. The sunsets are spectacular. The property has 1,900 feet of shoreline and a floating dock, plus row boat and canoe for guests' use. The 10 very spacious rooms are all on the water. Six of the rooms are located in Bay Lodge. They are fresh and modern and have been decorated tastefully with fine fabrics and furnishings. Spruce, for example, contains a pickled-pine bed, pine chest and side table plus a sitting area furnished with a pickled-pine couch and chest. The unit also has a woodstove and a kitchen with refrigerator, microwave, and electric frying pan/burner, toaster, and coffeemaker. The screened deck with table and chairs is an appealing addition and so, too, is the library sitting room with telephone that is shared with another unit. Vinalhaven is the largest and offers a sitting room furnished with sofa, wing chair, and rocker plus a kitchen with a Mexican-tile floor. Two of the units are located in another cottage that has a cathedral ceiling and a two burner stove. Tuckaway Cottage makes a wonderful retreat. It's furnished with pine and kilims and filled with books. The kitchen has granite counters and cherry cabinets, and the bedroom features a Stickley bed. All have decks overlooking the water. Guests gather in the super-comfortable post-and-beam living room in the main house around the old brick fireplace, which is flanked by bookcases. The decor combines fine American antiques—inlaid sideboard, Federal bull's-eye mirror, Chippendale chairs, and cherry table—with some modern features like the pickled-pine paneling. Breakfast is served in the dining area or on the long, covered porch, which is a favorite spot at any time of day. The meal might consist of baked French toast with blueberries or Mexican eggs with chilies cilantro plus breads, fruit, cereals, and yogurt. Rates: $150 to $175.

The **Pilgrim's Inn,** Deer Isle, ME 04627 (☎ 207/348-6615), which is set on 2½ acres, overlooks Northwest Harbor in Penobscot Bay and a picturesque mill pond. Built in 1793, it's a delightful place to stay and made especially so by the public areas—the post-and-beam dining room warmed by a woodstove, a parlor with settles and a huge inglenook beehive fireplace and a sitting room–library. The 13 rooms have been furnished comfortably (some share baths). One might contain a brass bed and wing chairs, another an iron bed or a pencil four-poster. Guests dine in a converted barn on creative dishes that use fresh local products, many of them organic. The menu will feature one item, depending on the day of the week. For example, salmon is featured on Wednesday (sautéed, grilled, poached, or roasted), while on Friday it's lobster and crab, and on Saturday rack of lamb and quail. Cocktails and hors d'oeuvres are served before the meal, which is priced at $29.50 for the full dinner. The grounds extend around the pond and include a brick grill for guest use. Open mid-May to mid-October. Rates: MAP, $185 for two; $160 for two with shared bath.

Goose Cove Lodge, Deer Isle, Sunset, ME 04683 (☎ 207/348-2508), is a very fine waterside lodging that also has 20 cottages available. The guest sitting room is wonderfully cozy—a place where you can read in front of the large stone fireplace or enjoy some conversation, around the blacksmith's workbench table, about what you can see through the telescope, which innkeeper Dominick Parisi cheerfully shares with guests. The cottages are the most appealing accommodations. Lookout has a fully equipped kitchen and a sitting room with a wood-burning stove and comfortable seating. The bedroom has two skylights. Mayflower lacks a kitchen but has a stone fireplace, a deck with a great view, and a small fridge among its amenities. Furnishings are pine and maple with braided rugs on the floors. The lodge is famous for its breakfasts, and Sunday brunch, lunch, and dinner are also offered. There are ocean and island views from the back deck. Facilities include a game room with Ping-Pong and a video library. Open mid-May to mid-October. Rates: MAP, summer, $95 to $140 per person per day; MAP, winter, $85 to $120 per person ; B & B, $90 to $170 for a double.

Inn at Ferry Landing, Old Ferry Road, Deer Isle, ME 04683 (☎ 207/348-7760), occupies a great waterfront location on Eggemoggin Reach. You'll get a warm and friendly reception from your hosts, Gerald and Jean Wheeler. For people who love music, this is the place to stay. Gerald is a pianist and organist, and the living room contains two Steinways on which impromptu chamber concerts are given on summer weekends. Outside, the living room windows sweeps the grand blue Eggemoggin Reach, a perfect setting for listening to Debussy's *La Mer,* say. The five rooms are very attractively furnished with cottage-style beds and oak dressers. The most magnificent is the Suite which has a skylit sunken tub under a cathedral ceiling and a great ocean view. The bedroom also has skylights and a brass bed, plus a sitting area furnished with a loveseat and with a wood stove. The Annex, which has a full kitchen, private deck and sunroom, sitting room, and two bedrooms, rents by the week only in July and August. Gerald has given recitals all over the world at Westminster Abbey and at Christ Church in Montreal, and the house is decorated with programs and musical souvenirs. The walls are also adorned with Jean's work—nature and other photographs. The setting is out of this world. A very special place. Rates: $105 to $140; annex is $1,000 per week.

CASTINE & STONINGTON DINING

For the best dining in Castine, see the **Castine Inn** above.

Dennett's Wharf (☎ 207/326-9045) in Castine is located in a sail loft right down on the water. It's a large and lofty restaurant with outdoor dining. The bar has several microbrews on tap. Note the ceiling is studded with dollar bills—you can ask the waiter how they got there, and if you have a bill, he'll doubtless show you. Naturally, oysters, clams, mussels, and lobsters are on the menu, but so are burgers, sandwiches, and barbecue dishes. Prices range from $5 to $20. Open daily from 11am to 3pm and 5 to 9pm.

The Landing, S. Brooksville (☎ 207/326-8483), is located right by the yacht club, and the upstairs dining room has a great view of Buck's Harbor. It's certainly one of the best dining experiences available in the area, providing contemporary American cuisine that is full of flavor and prepared with verve. The menu ranges from pasta dishes like plank-roasted salmon on a bed of fettuccine with dried-cranberry salsa to main dishes such as duck with boysenberry and shiitake gratin, thyme-crusted grouper, or roasted rack of lamb. The room has a woodsy warmth with lots of pine and a cathedral ceiling. Open Tuesday to Sunday, 5 to 10pm.

The Lobster Deck & Restaurant, Sea Breeze Avenue, Stonington (☎ 207/367-6526), is right down on the waterfront where you can secure a lobster dinner for $16.95 and a plate of clams or shrimp for anywhere from $7 and up. Open 5am to 9pm.

PENOBSCOT PENINSULA—BLUE HILL, SEDGWICK & AROUND BLUE HILL BAY

A real charmer of a town, **Blue Hill** is known as a gathering place for musicians and artists. There are at least six art galleries, and one of them, the **Leighton Gallery**, Parker Point Road (☎ 207/374-5001), may well be the best (certainly one of them anyway) in Maine. Linger in the galleries and in the beautiful sculpture garden out back. Don't miss the **Hartmann Gallery** either, at 110 Main St. (☎ 207/374-9917), which has fantastic bronze sculptures of East Coast Indians inspired by historical events like the massacre at Deerfield. The sculptures are remarkable and all the more extraordinary because Hartmann is self-taught and obviously has a divine gift.

Craftspeople have also been drawn to the area. **Rackliffe Pottery**, Ellsworth Road (☎ 207/374-2297), is worth visiting, but the most fascinating place is **Rowantrees Pottery**, 9 Union St. (☎ 207/374-5535), which was started by Adelaide Pearson, who was inspired by Gandhi to take the art of pottery seriously. She established the pottery in 1939, and it was from here that the Eisenhowers selected the service for their Gettysburg farm. The quality of the product is very fine, and some items, like the unusual napkin rings, make nice small gifts for only $5 to $8 each. To view the studio and the ceramics on sale, go through the garden to the back of the house. Outside of town, another brilliant potter, **Mark Bell**, 1½ miles south of Blue Hill (☎ 207/374-5881), crafts delicate shell-shaped bowls and other classical Japanese-style pots and bowls. Some are glazed a brilliant blue that is stunning. Main Street also has several antiques stores worth browsing—try Blue Hill Antiques or Emerson Antiques. Other interesting stores worth stopping in include the **Tea and Tobacco Shop** (☎ 207/374-2161), at the junction of routes 176 and 15, which stocks teas, tobaccos, coffees, and wines.

For evening entertainment, go to the **Left Bank Cafe** or, during July and August, check out the weekend chamber music concerts that are given in **Kneisel Hall** (☎ 207/374-2811), named for Franz Kneisel, who founded the famous chamber music summer school that has operated here since the 1920s.

If you'd like to picnic on a weekend, pick up the fixings at the **Blue Hill Farmers Market,** held on Saturday mornings. Then from Blue Hill take Route 175 south to Blue Hill Falls where the Salt Pond runs out into Blue Hill Bay. This is a beautiful spot, with the water crashing down under the bridge between two fir-lined points. You can picnic along the edge of the Salt Pond, although there are no tables. Or continue to Brooklin and then take the road from there down to Naskeag Point, another great place to enjoy a picnic, either at one of the tables provided or else on the boulder-strewn beach.

BLUE HILL LODGING & DINING

Blue Hill Farm Country Inn, P.O. Box 437, Blue Hill, ME 04614 (☎ 207/374-5126), is located just outside of town on 48 acres that incorporate a duck pond, spacious lawns, and a vegetable and herb garden. Walking trails crisscross the property. The inn consists of the original farmhouse plus a barn that has been converted to accommodate rooms. There are seven rooms in the farmhouse (three sharing baths). They are furnished in country style with blanket chests and floral wallpaper. Beds are covered with quilts, and the closets are Shaker-style with pegs. The barn has seven rooms, all with private bath, decorated with braided rugs and oak or pine furnishings combined with iron or similar beds. Guests love the post-and-beam common room, which is warmed by a woodstove and is broken up into several sitting areas. There's also a second sitting room in the farmhouse. Breakfast is continental—fruit, yogurt, breads, and muffins. Watch out for the geese and the angora goats. Rates: June 1 to October 31, $85 to $100; November 1 to May 31, $70 to $80.

Blue Hill Inn, Union Street (P.O. Box 403), Blue Hill, ME 04614 (☎ 207/374-2844), is right in town, just up from the general store. It's owned by Mary and Don Hartley, who know a lot about the area and take time to point their guests toward the delights of the area. The inn was built in 1830 and has plenty of character. The 11 rooms are tastefully furnished. A room might contain a cherry, pencil four-poster, two wing chairs, and an Empire dresser. The painted wide-board floors have oriental rugs, and the tub in the bathroom might be a claw foot. Some of the rooms have fine antiques. The Cape House Suite is in a separate building. It's large and has a brick fireplace, sitting area, a deck, and a full kitchen. Amenities include TVs and telephones. The breakfast is especially appealing because you can choose from among five or more dishes—waffles with strawberries or omelets cooked to order, all served in the attractive dining room at separate tables. The inn also offers a five-course candlelight dinner that begins with wine and hors d'oeuvres in the parlor before continuing in the dining room, perhaps with chilled asparagus soup with sorrel. The main course might be a choice of either rack of lamb with green peppercorn crust or scallops with white wine, tomatoes and fennel, mesclun salad, and in conclusion, a chocolate gâteau. There are several parlors, each containing finely upholstered chairs and sofas and authentic antiques with lovely patinas. One of the parlors is set apart as library and games room; the other has a fireplace. Special packages available. Rates for MAP are $130 to $200; B&B, $20 to $25 less per person.

If you want splendid water views, then **John Peters Inn,** Peters Point, Blue Hill, ME 04614 (☎ 207/374-2116), is the place to stay. It occupies a grand plantation-style Greek Revival mansion set on 27 acres at the crest of a hill with views of Blue Hill and Peter's Point. There are eight rooms in the main house, all attractively furnished with good quality furnishings—wing chairs, rockers, Empire chests—but the rooms in the carriage house are particularly appealing because they have kitchens, decks, and fireplaces. The parlor is decorated in style with antiques and accented with a spinning wheel, fine art, and shelves of books flanking two fireplaces. Guests take breakfast (a full menu, offering such items as lobster omelet or blueberry waffles) in a light and airy room or enclosed porch. French doors lead out to the pool. There are also a canoe, a sailboat, and a rowboat for guests' use. Rates are $115 to $175.

BLUE HILL DINING

The **Firepond,** Main Street, Blue Hill (☎ 207/374-9970), has two dining rooms. Both are romantic. Downstairs is a post-and-beam room with tables on the enclosed porch overlooking a running brook. Upstairs there's a very inviting bar room containing oak tables dressed with table runners. Decorative accents include book-lined shelves, large fresh-flower bouquets, and a classical nude statue or two. The cuisine is first-class classic continental. If you like scallops, try the sea scallops sautéed with pancetta, sun-dried tomatoes, spinach, and fresh sage. The sage gives the dish a subtle, distinct flavor. Or there's roast duckling with a raspberry Chambord sauce that is cooked to a crisp nonfatty finish. Fresh fish is always available; the variety depends on what is fresh at the market. Prices range from $14.95 to $22.95. Open daily from 11:30am to 2:30pm and 5:30 to 9:30pm. Closed November to Easter.

Jonathan's, Main Street, Blue Hill (☎ 207/374-5226), has a plain and spare decor with captain's chairs set around tables covered with forest-green cloths, but it serves some surprisingly good food. For example, you might find Jamaican fish stew, a happy conglomeration of shrimp and salmon simmered in a yellow curry and coconut cream sauce with yams, avocados, tomatoes, peppers, and spiced peanuts. The eight entrees available will always include fish of the day and boiled lobster. Really satisfying is the braised lamb shank in a brew of local beer, bourbon, and maple barbecue sauce. It's a house favorite that keeps folks returning. Prices range from $14 to $18. Open summer, daily from 5 to 9pm; spring and fall, Thursday to Sunday from 5 to 8:30pm; winter Wednesday to Sunday from 5 to 8:30pm. Closed March.

Penobscot Peninsula (from Castine to Blue Hill)
Special & Recreational Activities

Birding: **Holbrook Island Sanctuary** on Cape Rosier is a good place to start.

Canoeing/Kayaking: The **Phoenix Center** (☎ 207/374-2113) at Blue Hills Falls offers 2½-hour, half-day, and full-day canoe and kayak tours. It also offers a variety of other activities from climbing to backpacking.

Cruises: Captain Gil Perkins will take you either on a sailing trip or under power on a trip around Penobscot Bay. The maximum number of passengers is six people. Cost is $35 per person for a half day; $65 for a full day. Call ☎ 207/326-8839. He sails from South Brooksville.

The mail boat operates from Stonington to Isle au Haut. Other cruises also operate from Stonington.

Hiking: Hike Blue Mountain and visit Blue Hill Municipal Park for a view of the bay.

BAR HARBOR

Bar Harbor is the resort that immediately comes to mind when people think of Maine. It is, of course, the gateway to the 40,000 acre Acadia National Park, the only national park on the East Coast, and in the summer its streets are super crowded, with its 3 million annual visitors. The main reason for coming here is to bask in the natural spectacle of mountain and ocean and to bike, canoe, hike, kayak, and climb in the park, whose features were carved by glaciers 2 to 3 million years ago.

By all means stroll along Main Street. Around the corner from Main Street, you can pop into **St. Saviour's Church** and see the 10 stained glass windows that were made by Louis Tiffany. Across the street, on the lower floor of the handsome wood-paneled Jessup Memorial Library, the **Bar Harbor Historical Society Museum** at 34 Mount Desert Street (☎ 207/288-4245) displays a pictorial history of the town from its early days to the devastating fire of 1947, which burned for 10 days and destroyed 17,000 acres of forest and 250 of the summer cottages.

About ¾ of a mile south of town on Route 3, the **Jackson Laboratory,** which engages in genetic research, is a major employer in Bar Harbor. Physicians and scholars come here every summer for intensive study programs. Tours are offered on weekdays only; call ☎ 207/288-6000 for information.

As you come onto the island, the **Bar Harbor Oceanarium,** Route 3 (☎ 207/288-5005), will answer all the questions you ever had about lobsters. It also displays specimens from around the world as well as exhibitions on the life of the lobsterman, how traps are built, and other lobster lore. Nature walks are given from here to Thomas Bay Marsh. Here, too, you can visit the lobster hatchery and learn why these creatures are being raised and released into the seas. The oceanarium is open Monday to Saturday from 9am to 5pm; admission is $6 for adults, $4.50 for children 4 to 12. The hatchery is open Monday to Saturday 9am to 5pm; admission is $3.95 for adults, $2.75 children 4 to 12.

Another kind of experience can be enjoyed a few miles down the road at the **Bar Harbor Brewing Company** (☎ 207/288-4592) on Otter Creek Road (Route 3) where you can taste great brews with great names like Thunder Hole Ale and Cadillac Mountain Stout.

From Bar Harbor, take a cruise to the **Cranberry Islands.** On Little Cranberry Island the Isleford Historical Museum will give you some insight into island life in the 19th century (open daily mid-June to Labor Day). Nearby Baker Island is where you can see the extraordinary slab of smooth granite called the "Dance Floor." The lighthouse can also be visited in summer. Call **Isleford Ferry Company** (☎ 207/276-3717) for information.

Don't expect to find stylish stores stocking fine-quality goods—most Bar Harbor stores sell tourist trinkets. Notable exceptions are **J.H. Butterfield & Co,** 152 Main St., which stocks gourmet items and is an old-fashioned store where you can purchase Maine's seasonal delicacies, like blueberries, and the local beers (Blueberry Ale, Cadillac Mountain Stout), pickled fiddleheads, and maple syrup. **Island Artisans,** 99 Main St. (☎ 207/288-4214) stocks good-quality craft items, including ceramics, jewelry, baskets, and tiles. The **Eclipse Gallery,** 12 Mount Desert St. (☎ 207/288-9048), and **Spruce Grove Gallery,** 43 Cottage St. (☎ 207/288-2002), are two worthy galleries. **Cool as a Moose** sells good-quality shorts, shoes, and other casual wear. Outside town you may want to stop at the MDI Workshop on Route 3 to look at the wooden products that this nonprofit facility manufactures. Prices are reasonable.

In the evening, head to the **Lompoc Cafe and Brew Pub,** 36 Rodick St. (☎ 207/288-9392). It has local and British ales, plus thin crust pizza and other fare to go with them. There's also live entertainment, and it's a place to make friends. Other cultural avenues to investigate include the **Criterion Theater** (☎ 207/288-3441); the **Second Stage Dinner Theater**

(☎ 207/288-4989); and the **Acadia Repertory Theater** in Mount Desert (☎ 207/244-7260), a resident group based in Somesville that performs half a dozen popular plays during its July to August season.

BAR HARBOR LODGING

Miramonte Inn & Suites, 69 Mount Desert St., Bar Harbor, ME (☎ 207/288-4263), is one of those extraordinary inns where the owner has listened carefully to what her guests want and then delivered it. It's the kind of place where you can choose whether or not to socialize and where you can be sure that every possible comfort and convenience will be provided in your room. It's located right in Bar Harbor and occupies a historic home that was built in 1864 and now has 2 acres of landscaped grounds. There are 15 rooms. Each one has been decorated in a different palette, but certain amenities will be on hand in all—good reading lights; an umbrella in the closet; extra shelving in the bathroom; and cable TV, telephones, and clock-radios. Each room is named after one of the grand hotels that once existed in Bar Harbor. Rockaway is furnished with a wicker bed and chaise lounge set against blue floral pattern wallpaper. French doors lead out to a deck, and there's a woodstove. Belmont is richly decorated in blues and greens with a fainting couch covered in forest-green velvet as one of the focal points. Atlantic has a tented treatment above a brass bed and two charming tufted chairs, plus a semicircular deck overlooking the gardens. Some of the suites have bathrooms with double Jacuzzis, kitchens equipped with a two-burner stove and microwave, and sitting rooms with fireplaces, and TV/VCR. Breakfast is served buffet style. You can pop the batter into the waffle iron yourself, help yourself to muffins and fruit, and take it back to your room or onto the back brick patio or porches, or you can join other people at the table. The choice is yours, and that's what the owner Marian has learned that her guests want—options. Even though it's right in the heart of Bar Harbor, the place still manages to seem quiet and spacious. Rates are $130 to $160; suites $190.

The **White Columns Inn,** 57 Mount Desert St., Bar Harbor, ME 04609 (☎ 207/288-5357), incorporates many architectural and other features from a salvaged mansion. Step from the impressive porch with its portico and columns into the foyer and sitting room. There are 10 rooms (3 with private balcony), all with cable TV. All are decorated in a very pretty manner, with rose wallpaper and wicker furniture and attractive fringed bedside lamps. Meadowbridge has an iron bedstead. Forest has a rice four-poster with lace canopy and a Winged Victory on the mantel. Some rooms have private sheltered porches. Guests can enjoy the side porch that overlooks the gardens. A continental breakfast is served, and wine and cheese are available in the late afternoon. Rates in July and August are $80 to $115; in May, June, September, and October, $65 to $95.

Balance Rock Inn, 21 Albert Meadow, Bar Harbor, ME 04609 (☎ 207/288-2610), is right down on the water. As you enter through the fan-lighted door of this 1903 mansion, you encounter a glorious view through the French doors of the living room. Much care has been taken to make the rooms comfortable and eye appealing. Room 105 is particularly spacious, large enough to accommodate a nice four-poster with a fabric canopy and one wing chair, plus a sofa and three wing chairs in the sitting area. Amenities include a wood-burning fireplace, TV/VCR and CD player, and a whirlpool tub and full-length mirror in the bathroom as well as private deck with an umbrella table. A buffet breakfast of yogurt, cereal, and fruit plus waffles and egg dishes is offered. There's a gracious sitting room, but the spot to be in summer is on the large covered porch with a water view across the lawns. Facilities include an outdoor pool set into a flagstone apron. Rates: summer, $225 to $465; spring and fall, $185 to $405 (higher prices for suites or ocean views). Closed late October to May 1.

Breakwater, 45 Hancock St., Bar Harbor, ME 04609 (☎ 207/288-2313), was built for the great grandson of John J. Astor, so you can imagine the luxury of the interior of this Tudor gabled building. Guests enter via a grand lobby into a great hall with a magnificent water view and a minstrels' gallery. Everything about the decor is grand and lavish, from the tapestry upholstered chairs around the large dining table to the marble sideboard and ornate scallop shells that adorn the fireplace. As you go up the grand staircase to your room, you'll pass a suit of medieval armor on the landing. The second floor also has a guest parlor with a fireplace; French doors lead to a large deck with a carved banister. There are seven guest rooms; four have fireplaces. Each room is different, but most contain a rice four-poster and oriental rugs. There are also unique furnishings—like the fainting couch and the ormolu and marquetry French desk in Mrs. Kane's chamber, or the leather sofa and demi-lune chests in Ambassador Jay's room. The billiard room, which has a secret staircase leading to another room, provides a touch of intrigue. An elaborate breakfast is served in high style. Open late April to November 11; rates are mid-June to mid-October, $205 to $340; late May to mid-June and mid-October to late Oct, $175 to $285; late April to late May and late October to mid-November, $155 to $245.

Inn at Canoe Point, Route 3 (P.O. Box 216), Bar Harbor, ME 04609 (☎ 207/288-9511), has a fabulous location right down on the rocks overlooking the ocean with a front deck that literally hangs off the cliff. In an 1889 Tudor-style building that stands on 2 acres, there are five rooms, with crystal candlesticks provided for that extra dash of romance. Each room is nicely furnished with a wicker bed and wicker furnishings or with a rice four-poster and pieces like an Empire chest. The Master Suite has a gas fireplace and access to a shared deck. The Garret Suite takes up the entire third floor. Guests enjoy relaxing around the granite fireplace and lolling on the Adirondacks on the wraparound porch. A full breakfast is served with hot dishes such as eggs Benedict or omelets or quiche. Afternoon refreshments are also served. Rates from late May to October 31 are $145 to $255; November 1 to late May, $90 to $255.

Ullikana B&B, 16 The Field, Bar Harbor, ME 04609 (☎ 207/288-9552), is located in an enclave off the main street in Bar Harbor in a lovely granite half-timbered summer cottage that was built in 1885. It's run by a very warm and friendly couple. The public areas are grand but cozy, and throughout the house, you'll find very fetching kilims and fine art. The lobby opens to an oak staircase with a stained glass window, accented by sculpture and a very large urn of dried flowers. Each of the seven rooms has been decorated in rich color palettes. Three have a fireplace. In Room 1, gray-blue floors are covered with braided rugs, and the walls have been painted a mustard yellow. Room 3 is a large room that contains a painted cottage bed and dresser plus a sofa, needle-point chair, and table. Room 4 has a dramatic carved four-poster, while Room 5 has its own covered porch and a bed made up with a Battenburg lace cover-let and red gingham ruffle. Breakfast (puff pancakes, lemon soufflé with peaches, or chocolate crepes with oranges) is served in the dining room or on a gravel courtyard at the back of the house. Guests also have use of a comfortable sitting room. Open May 1 to October 30; rates are $150 to $205.

Bar Harbor Inn, Newport Drive, Bar Harbor, ME 04609 (☎ 207/288-3351), is located in town, right on the water, and has a great view from the open garden dining area of the harbor and the vessels passing in and out. It's a full-service hotel with typical modern accommodations in several wings. All are equipped with minibars, TVs, telephones, coffeemakers, and hair dry-ers. The decor is unremarkable. The semicircular dining room overlooks the water and is furnished in French style. The cuisine is traditional with a twist. Popular signature dishes are the lobster pie, which has chunks of lobster meat in a rich sauce with a buttered crumb topping, and seafood mixed grill, a platter of lobster tail, crabmeat, and scallops wrapped in bacon. Meat dishes run to steaks and pan-seared lamb loin in a wild mushroom demiglace or oven-roasted breast of chicken with a raspberry peppercorn sauce. Prices range from $17 to $22. Lunch outside overlooking the harbor is a pleasant experi-ence, too. Try the clam chowder or the lobster bisque, which are both full flavored, and follow with a crab roll, sandwich, or salad. Open daily 11:30am to 2:30pm and 5:30 to 9:30pm. Five nights a week there's entertainment in the Reading Room. Rates: late May to mid-June, $105 to $199; mid-June to August, $125 to $275; September to mid-October, $125 to $255; mid-Octo-ber to early November, $85 to $189; mid-November to closing date, $69 to $109; late March to late May, $69 to $159.

The Tides, 119 West St., Bar Harbor, ME 04609 (☎ 207/288-4968), is another in-town Greek Revival beauty, on 1¼ acres with a magnificent view of the ocean and Bar Island. From the lawns at low tide, you can even step out and cross over the sandbar to the island. The wide veranda has the same great view and also offers a unique wood-burning fireplace, along with a ship's wheel for guests to play with, keeping the house on an even keel. It's owned and operated by Joe Losquadro, an ex-navy man, and Judy, his wife, who love welcoming and caring for guests. The three guest suites are spacious and at-tractive. All have cable TV. The most luxurious is the Master Suite, furnished with a French country cherry bed and made more romantic by the gas fire-place, a claw-foot tub and shower in the bathroom, and a sitting room. The Ocean Suite has its own private balcony, while the Captain's Suite features a carved oak bed and dresser and a sitting area that is large enough for a sofa and a wing chair. It has the most commanding view of the bay. The Mate's Room is more modest, but it still has plenty of space. The full breakfast fea-tures entrees such as eggs Dijon or cinnamon French toast. On warm days it's taken on the veranda; on colder days it's served by candlelight in a dining room warmed by a fire. Rates in summer are $135 to $275; winter $105 to $175. Closed from mid-October to Memorial Day.

Inn at Bay Ledge, 1385 Sand Point Rd., Bar Harbor, ME 04609 (☎ 207/288-4204), has a spectacular location atop Cathedral Rock, a scenic spot above the caves that folks have been visiting for hundreds of years. On a sunny day, to sit out on the twig chairs and gaze at the cliff face opposite, and the expanse of blue ocean beyond, is sheer heaven. Similar joy can be found in the hammock or down on the beach, reached by a wooden staircase. The inn was built in the early 1900s. The rooms have four-poster beds, made up with fine linens and down comforters. The cottages are a little more rustic. Some of the rooms have Jacuzzis, and some of the cottages have fireplaces. Breakfast is served either on the deck overlooking Frenchman Bay or inside before a roaring fire. Jeani Ochtera tends to the perennial gardens, and both she and Jack love entertaining their guests. The deck is great for lounging and so is the pool. There's also a sauna and a steam room. Rates: mid-June to October, rooms are $160 to $260 and cottages are $140 to $160; May to mid-June, rooms are $95 to $160 and cottages $85 to $105.

Stone's Throw Cottage, 67 Mount Desert St. (☎ 207/288-3668), is an 1860 cottage located in town. It has seven rooms, all with telephones and whirlpool tubs. The bathroom fixtures are super decorative—artist's-edition sinks, toilets, and cisterns, all with floral decoration. Beds are made up with lovely linens, and walls are decorated with botanical prints and fine wallpapers that range from a green bow-tie pattern to lemon candy stripes. Room 5, for example, has a carved bed covered with a floral duvet. The most luxurious room is Room 1, which has a double Jacuzzi located in the turret area so that you can look out of the window from the tub. A full breakfast is served, including dishes such as scrambled egg casserole or blueberry bread pudding, plus breads and fruits. The sitting room has a double fireplace and comfortable seating arrangements. The front and back porches are nice extra spaces where guests can relax. Rates are $145 to $185.

The **Ledgelawn Inn,** 66 Mount Desert St., Bar Harbor, ME 04609 (☎ 207/288-4596), is operated more like a hotel than an inn, with nonintrusive service. The Colonial Revival town house, that sits back from the street, was built at the turn of the century for a wealthy shoe manufacturer. From the lobby, a grand staircase leads up to the rooms. They are furnished in a cottage-style mixture, and often feature the original fixtures like the elegant sinks with turned porcelain legs in the bathrooms. All rooms have private baths, TVs, and telephones. The carriage house rooms have Jacuzzis, fireplaces, porches, and air-conditioning. Guests enjoy the use of a spacious common room, which has a bar at one end, and they can also enjoy drinks on the back veranda overlooking the gardens. Facilities include an outdoor pool and hot tub, plus admission (for a fee) to the Bar Harbor Club, where guests can play tennis on clay courts or swim in the Olympic-size pool. A buffet breakfast is available for an extra charge. Rates are $115 to $270 in summer; $95 to $170 spring and fall. Closed from late October to May 1.

BAR HARBOR DINING

George's, 7 Stevens Lane (☎ 207/288-4505), is hard to find but worth seeking out, for it is the most romantic, elegant dining room serving the best French/fusion food in the area. Dishes make the best use of local ingredients; for example, the crab cake with a corn puree, blueberry relish, and roasted chili slaw. The menu changes daily but you'll always find dishes to excite your palette—the duck breast with blueberries and zinfandel or the cioppino, which is brimming with shrimp, crab, scallops, fish, and mussels. The appetizers are also stimulating. Try smoked salmon quesadilla if it's on the menu or the steamed mussels in a spicy mustard broth. Grazers will appreciate the jump-seared tuna with spicy, soy-glazed pickled ginger and wasabi. Entrees are $25, or you can opt for the three-course fixed-price menu at $33. George's opens in mid-June and closes in late October. Sometimes there's classical guitar entertainment.

Cafe Bluefish, 122 Cottage St. (☎ 207/288-3696), is a neat restaurant. It's a small and unadorned dining room but it serves some great fish dishes that are quite innovative and filled with flavor. The menu will usually feature five or so fish dishes, which have been carefully cooked to retain the moisture of the fish, such as the poached salmon which is served with a sherried mustard sauce. Steamed lobster is pretty much always available, and there will also be a couple of vegetarian dishes and several strudels, which are a specialty. Try the lobster strudel made with chunks of lobster meat, caramelized onions, sherry, and a homemade boursin cheese. Prices range from $13 to $20. Open from 5:30pm to closing.

Park Side, at Main and Mount Desert streets (☎ 207/288-3700), is open and airy and great for people watching. It has an extensive menu that is meant to please everyone—everyone, it seems, will dine here at least once. There's plenty of fish to choose from. Several lobster dishes lead the lineup, but there's also baked halibut with lemon herb vinaigrette and almond-breaded crab cakes. The meats range from rack of lamb with cilantro-mint chutney to filet mignon with a sauce béarnaise or bordelaise. Prices range from $14 to $20. There's a good selection of wines by the glass. Open early May to mid-October, daily from 11am to 3pm, Sunday to Thursday from 5 to 9pm and Friday and Saturday from 5 to 10pm. Closed mid-October to April.

Galyn's Galley, 17 Main St. (☎ 207/288-9706), is a casual place with plain wood tables and chairs. The fare is traditional and will satisfy diners looking for lobster or steak or items like baked stuffed shrimp or baby back ribs. Prices range from $12 to $20. Open daily 11am to 10pm.

ACADIA NATIONAL PARK

Before you visit the park, stop by one of the visitor centers: **Thompson Island Information Center** (☎ 207/288-3411), which is on Route 3 where you cross over to Mount Desert Island; **Hulls Cove Visitor Center** (☎ 207/288-5262), which is on Route 3 before you enter Bar Harbor (open daily May 1 to October 31, 8am to 4:30pm); or the **park headquarters** on Route 233 between Bar Harbor and Somes Sound (☎ 207/288-3338), which stays open year-round. You can also write for information before arrival to **Acadia National Park,** P.O. Box 177, Bar Harbor, ME 04609 (☎ 207/288-3338). While you're in the park, pick up *Acadia Weekly,* which lists daily activities in the park, including naturalist cruises. Entrance to the park is $5 per car for 1 day; $10 for a 4-day pass.

Mount Desert Island drops down into the ocean like a giant hand. Somes Sound cuts deeply into the island dividing Acadia National Park into two sections, an eastern section around Bar Harbor and a western section that is less trafficked and extends west from Southwest Harbor. The park was not carved out of public lands; it was created by a visionary group of people who wanted to save the spectacular landscape from development. Among them were textile magnate George B. Dorr; Charles W. Eliot, a former president of Harvard; and John D. Rockefeller who donated 11,000 acres. Rockefeller also built the gravel carriage roads (as a defense against the motor car) that wind around Jordan and Eagle lakes and Sargent and Penobscot mountains and lead to magnificent vistas of Somes Sound and Frenchman Bay.

Before the arrival of the French and English, the land was inhabited by Abnaki Indians, and their heritage and artifacts can be viewed at the small **Abbe Museum** off the park loop road about a mile south of Bar Harbor (open daily May 1 through October, admission $2 adult, 50¢ children).

SEEING THE PARK

To really see the natural landscape with its granite cliffs and ledges, basalt dikes, some 17 mountain peaks, close to a dozen ponds and lakes, and the fjordlike beauty of Somes Sound, you need to hike some of the trails and get out on the water. You can also drive the scenic Loop Road on the eastern side of Somes Sound, stopping at the lookouts along the way. The so-called Quiet Side, on the western side of Somes Sound, is more authentically Downeast.

To orient yourself, first drive the **Park Loop Road,** which winds 20 miles around the perimeter of the park's eastern section. Start at the Hulls Cove Visitor Center and proceed to the entrance where you'll pay an entrance fee. About 5½ miles from the visitor center, the **Wild Gardens of Acadia** will give you some idea of the flora in the park, featuring 400 species of plants native to the park. They're divided into different habitat gardens—meadow, mountain, bog, and so on—and are especially fine in late spring.

Farther along the route are several stops where you can pull off to enjoy vistas of the ocean and rocks: Bear Brook picnic area, Schooner Head Overlook, and Sand Beach, the only sand beach in the park. Along this coastline you might be able to see the speck of Egg Rock Light, marking the entrance to Frenchman Bay between Mount Desert Island and the Schoodic Peninsula. Make sure you stop at **Thunder Hole** where the surf smacks into walls of granite creating a resounding boom that is louder or softer depending on the tide and the weather. The most dramatic sound effects can be heard on a rising tide about midway between low and high tide. It's hard to believe, but the constant perseverance of the ocean does break off pieces of granite creating narrow channels like this one. From here the road loops out around the Otter Cliffs, pink granite buttresses that drop 100 feet to the ocean. The road then crosses Otter Cove, and just beyond Little Hunters Beach is one of the more serene spots in which to linger.

The road cuts behind Day Mountain and up to the **Jordan Pond House** (☎ 207/276-3316), which is the only restaurant in the park with the Bubbles as the backdrop. From the observation deck, there's also a view of the pond. The restaurant has been operating since the 1870s, although not in the current building, which dates to 1979. It's popular for afternoon tea, taken on the lawns, and famous for its popovers and strawberry jam. The birch-bark dining rooms have massive stone fireplaces, and here diners can enjoy lobster and crabmeat rolls and salads plus steaks and delicious Maine salmon. Prices

Mount Desert Island/Acadia National Park

range from $9.50 to $17.50. It's open daily, mid-May to October, from 11:30am to 8pm.

From here the road goes past Eagle Lake and climbs up Cadillac Mountain (1,532 ft.) for extraordinary panoramic views of Frenchman and Blue Hill bays, the islands, and Bar Harbor, often with islands of floating clouds below. The best visibility is usually in fall and winter; sunrise and sunset are moments of epiphany. For a great view of **Somes Sound**, take Sargent Drive south (off Route 198), which hugs the shore of this narrow 168-foot deep gorge.

The western section of the park is less crowded and the mountain peaks are lower, but it offers the rewards of a remote and rocky coastline, a series of lakes and ponds, and the inviting traditional fishing communities of Southwest Harbor and Bass Harbor.

To reach the other sections of the park, you need to drive back to two other peninsulas. **Isle au Haut** lies 15 miles southwest of Mount Desert and is reached via mail boat (45 min.) from Stonington at the tip of Deer Isle, which is at the foot of the Penobscot Peninsula. The 2,000-acre **Schoodic Peninsula** lies east of Mount Desert Island. It's little visited, even though it's only an hour from Bar Harbor, but it's worth a visit for its spectacular meeting of rock, pine, cobblestone, and ocean. Drive the 6-mile park road and stand at the point of the peninsula facing the sound and fury of ocean and wave—a thrilling experience. The closest community here is Winter Harbor, so called because the harbor remains ice free in winter.

Acadia Park
Special & Recreational Activities

Biking/Mountain Biking: Carriage roads in the park are open to bicyclists except where they extend onto private land. Rent from **Bar Harbor Bicycle Shop,** 141 Cottage St. (☎ 207/288-3886), which charges $14 to $18 a day or at **Acadia Outfitters,** 106 Cottage St. (☎ 207/288-8118), or at **Acadia Bike and Canoe,** 48 Cottage St. (☎ 207/288-9605), which offers a guided tour down Cadillac Mountain and rents mountain bikes for $16 a day.

Birding: The park offers some great birding for both woodland and shore birds. More than 300 species have been spotted in the park. Blagden Reserve at Indian Point and Ship Harbor Nature Trail, off Route 102A near Sea Wall, both in the western section of the park, are two places to take those binoculars.

Boating: Boat rentals are available from **Harbor Boat Rentals,** Bar Harbor (☎ 207/288-3757).

Camping: Acadia has two campgrounds: Blackwood, 5 miles south of Bar Harbor (☎ 207/288-3274), which is open all year (reservations necessary June to September) and has 300 sites. The fee is $13, and you can reserve by calling **Mistix** at ☎ 800/365-2267. Seawall is in the western section of the park on the coast near Southwest Harbor (☎ 207/244-3600). It has 200 sites and is open May to September on a first-come-first-served basis for $11 a night. Isle au Haut also has five lean-to shelters, which can accommodate a total of 30 people. Shelters are available only by written reservation, which must be postmarked after April 1. Send to **Acadia National Park** Isle au Haut Reservations, P.O. Box 177, Bar Harbor, ME 04609.

Canoeing: Contact National Park Canoe Rentals located at the north end of Long Pond just outside Somesville (☎ 207/244-5854). Rates are $20 a half day, $30 per day. Rentals are also available from Coastal Kayaking, 48 Cottage St. (☎ 207/288-9605), for $20 to $25 a day.

Schoodic Tours and Kayaking (☎ 207/963-7958) offers 3- and 4-hour tours along the shores of the peninsula.

Climbing: There are no outfitters in the park, but you can secure a guide and instruction at **Acadia Mountain Guides,** 137 Cottage St. (☎ 207/288-8186), or **Atlantic Climbing** at 24 Cottage St. (☎ 207/288-2521). Then you can climb Otter Cliffs or the South Wall of Champlain mountain.

Cross-Country Skiing: This is allowed along the carriage roads in the park, which make ideal trails.

Cruises: In addition to specific nature cruises, there are several others. From Bar Harbor Town Pier you can take the three-masted windjammer *Natalie Todd,* a 1941 Grand Banks fishing schooner, which sails daily on 2-hour trips and includes a sunset cruise with live music. The motor vessel *Chippewa* offers 1½-hour cruises. For information, call ☎ 207/288-4585 or 207/288-2373.

From Northeast Harbor you can take the mail boat to the Cranberry Isles (☎ 207/244-3575). There are five islands. The boat stops year-round at Great Cranberry and Isleford. In summer, it also stops at Sutton Island.

There are limited services on the islands, so you may want to brown bag it and bring a bike to ride the lanes and explore island way of life. Fare is only $10 round-trip, $5 children 3 to 12. A ferry to the islands also operates from Southwest Harbor for $9 adult, $5 children round-trip.

The Blackjack sailing sloop also leaves Northeast Harbor on 1½-hour trips carrying a maximum of six passengers. Call ☎ 207/276-5043 or 207/288-3056 for information.

From Bass Harbor, Island Cruises (☎ 207/244-5785) operates a lunch cruise to Frenchboro and an afternoon nature cruise for $17 adults, $8 children 4 to 11, and $14 and $8, respectively.

Fishing: Freshwater fishing is not that great, and you need a license.

Golf: Kebo Valley Golf Club (☎ 207/288-2200) is among the nation's top 50 courses.

Hiking: In Bar Harbor it's fun to walk out to Bar Island, which is reachable at low tide (allow 1½ hr.).

There are 120 miles of trails in Acadia National Park; some are easy and some are grueling, like the Precipice Trail on Champlain Mountain that requires negotiating iron rungs and ladders, or the Dorr Mountain Trail, which takes you up a steep granite ladder. Trails interconnect so that hardy hikers can climb to the summit of several peaks in a single day if so inclined. **Cadillac Mountain North Ridge Trail** (3⁸⁄10 miles/2½ hr.) and **Gorham Mountain Trail** (2 miles/1 hr.) are both moderate and immensely rewarding. **Acadia Mountain Trail** (2 miles/1¼ hr.) provides the best views of Somes Sound. The **Ocean Trail** (3⁶⁄10 miles/2 hr.) along Frenchman Bay is level and easy and offers some wonderful ocean experiences. Easy walks are available around Jordan Pond and at the top of Cadillac Mountain.

The old Carriage Roads (50 miles of them), except those on private land, can also be hiked. Hiking is popular in winter, too. For additional information talk to the rangers.

Kayaking: Guided tours are offered by **Coastal Kayaking Tours,** 48 Cottage St. (☎ 207/288-9605). They range from 2½-hour and half-day trips to full-day and multiple-day tours. Prices are $29, $43, $65, and from $175 per person, respectively. Kayaks can be rented for $45 a day. Also try **National Park Sea Kayak Tours,** 137 Cottage St. (☎ 207/288-0342), which charges $45 for a half-day tour, or **Acadia Outfitters,** 106 Cottage St. (☎ 207/288-8118). The last offers tours and rentals.

Nature Cruises: Several cruises are led by park rangers. You can take a 4½-hour cruise from Northeast Harbor to Baker Island. Call ☎ 207/276-3717 for information. Cost is $16 adults, $9 children 4 to 12. From Northeast Harbor, a 3-hour cruise aboard the *Sea Princess* to Isleford on Little Cranberry Island includes a visit to the museum. For information, call ☎ 207/276-5352. Cost is $13 adult, $9 children 4 to 12. The Frenchman Bay Nature Cruise lasts 2 hours and goes spying for eagles, osprey, and porpoises from Bar Harbor. Call ☎ 207/288-3322 or 207/244-5882. The fare is $15 adult, $12 children 5 to 15.

The following cruises are also available. *The Acadian* operates nature cruises from the Town Pier in Bar Harbor. The 10am cruise is narrated by a park ranger. The same company (☎ 207/288-3322) also operates *The*

Katherine which sails on 1½-hour lobstering trips from the Town pier in Bar Harbor. The *Sea Princess* (☎ 207/276-5352) also sails from Northeast Harbor on Somes Sound Cruise and Sunset Dinner cruise. Prices are $11 adult, $7 children under 12, and $10 and $7, respectively.

Ranger Programs: Check the visitor center for evening and other nature programs that include nature walks, star watches, lobstering and whale-watch cruises, and much more.

Sailing: Rentals and instruction are available at **Mansell Boat Company** in Manset (☎ 207/244-5625). Sixteen-foot sloops rent from $85 a day to $400 for several days. Larger boats with outboards also offered.

Snowmobiling: It's allowed along Park Loop Road.

Soaring: For a thrilling ride above the island, contact **Island Soaring** at ☎ 207/667-SOAR. It operates from Hancock County Bar Harbor Airport on Route 3.

Swimming: In summer, lifeguards are on duty at **Echo Lake** and **Sand Beach,** but the water's mighty cold at the ocean beach (rarely reaching 55 degrees). You can also try swimming in Long Pond in the western section of the park.

Tours: Carriage rides are given by **Wildwood Stables** (☎ 207/276-3622).

SEAL HARBOR & NORTHEAST HARBOR

If I were planning a trip to Bar Harbor, I'd stay out on the less trafficked parts of Mount Desert Island, either in Northeast Harbor (20 miles from Bar Harbor) or still farther out at Southwest Harbor. Just outside Northeast Harbor on Route 3, do visit the **Asticou Terraces and Thuya Gardens** (☎ 207/276-3344). Here you can climb up a pathway via the giant granite steps through the fir trees to the Curtis Memorial and eventually to the Thuya Gardens. The memorial is dedicated to the landscape architect who was the vigilant protector of these hills and who, upon his death in 1928, left his property to the locals for their enjoyment. The gardens are especially lovely in spring when the rhododendron are in bloom and later in the summer when the perennial beds come into their own. Just around the corner the **Asticou Azalea Gardens** on routes 3 and 198 are extraordinary gardens that were created in the 1950s by Charles Savage for John Rockefeller. Beautifully laid out, they are obviously influenced by Japanese garden style.

The town of **Northeast Harbor** is a great place to browse. Although it has the air of a village, its main street is lined with interesting shops stocking fine-quality items. The **Kimball Shop** has good looking china, glass, tableware, and kitchenware; **Redfield Artisans Gallery** displays fine art and sculpture plus photography; **Local Color** has some really lovely fashions including silk dresses, chenille sweaters, and unique accessories; **Fourteen Carrots** showcases jewelry plus some crafts from Mexico. **Wikhegan Old Books,** Main Street (☎ 207/276-5079) is a good general bookstore that has an exceptional collection of old rare Maine books.

NORTHEAST HARBOR LODGING

The Asticou Inn, Route 3, Northeast Harbor, ME 04662 (☎ 207/276-3344), has a spectacular location overlooking the harbor. It's set on 38 acres. The lawns sweep down to the water, and on the same grounds there are an outdoor heated pool and clay tennis court. It's the only historic hotel still standing. As such, it has an important role to play on Mount Desert, and staff members take their roles very seriously, paying attention to all your needs in a warm and hospitable way. The public areas are very comfortable and cannot be duplicated elsewhere in the area. The large back deck is a beautiful spot to linger over lunch or cocktails in summer at the umbrella tables. The rooms are not spectacular, but the views from them are, and the management is currently investing money to give them some sparkle. The most modern and attractive units are in a couple of additional buildings on the property. In addition to the sitting room, there is a games room with a large screen TV. Massage therapy is another special treat available.

The dining room has a good reputation for its brunch spread of carved meats, smoked seafoods, and egg dishes and it's also famous for its Thursday night buffet, which has been held regularly for the last 20-plus years. It always features poached salmon in aspic, seafood Newburg, and cold cracked lobster with a number of different sauces, plus a selection of carved meats. On other nights, you can dine very well from a traditional continental menu featuring dishes such as chicken marsala, halibut amandine, and rosemary-and-Dijon-crusted rack of lamb served with a minted glaze with prices ranging from $17 to $33. The setting is quite beautiful, too—made so by the view and also the murals depicting birds of paradise and an array of flowers. During the summer, there's also nightly entertainment.

Rates: late June to early September, MAP $274 to $309, EP $207 to $242; mid-May to late June and early September to mid-October $194 to 259 and $127 to $192, respectively.

Harbourside Inn, Northeast Harbor, ME 04662 (☎ 207/276-3272), is located up on a hillside away from the roadside. It occupies two shingle-style buildings dating to 1888, which stand surrounded by 4 acres of wooded property. There are 14 guest rooms, all within one building. Some have fireplaces; some have kitchenettes. Throughout the house are some interesting decorative elements, from the historic maps of the region to the ornithological prints. Some of the rooms have unique furnishings, too, like the Wallace Nutting bed in one room. In the suite you'll find a teak chaise lounge from the *Queen Elizabeth* plus a drop-leaf desk. The largest suite has an extra-large porch, too. The best views are from the third-floor rooms tucked under the eaves. These rooms have shower only. Rates include a continental breakfast. Rates: summer $100 to $185, with most in the $135 range. Open mid-June to mid-September.

The **Maison Suisse Inn,** Main Street (P.O. Box 1090), Northeast Harbor, ME 04662 (☎ 207/276-5223), is right on the main street but distanced from it by the rock garden with ponds, irises, ferns, and lilies. The inn has an interesting history. The name was given to the property by the Swiss hairdresser who became Mr. Fred of Hollywood, who also operated a hair salon here in the 1950s. Today the owners don't prepare breakfast for guests, but do invite them to go to the Colonel's on Main Street and select whatever breakfast they please. There are 10 rooms, all of which are furnished in attractive country style with such additional amenities as TV. Many of the rooms have rice four-posters that are combined with Empire chests and similar pieces. The living room draws guests to the seating around the brick fireplace or to the good reading on the bookshelves. Rates: May from $75, June from $85 to $95, July to October, $135 to $185. Closed from late October to late May.

SEAL HARBOR & NORTHEAST HARBOR DINING
The Bistro at Seal Harbor, Route 3 (☎ 207/276-3299), is the place to come for some really fine, carefully prepared cuisine that is served in a small dining room with only seven tables in two sittings. Just to give you some idea of the imagination that goes into the cuisine, you might find among a rich potpourri of flavors in appetizers such as scallops with heirloom beans, preserved lemons, and parmigiana-reggiano or the fried artichoke with fennel and lemon with aioli. Among the main dishes there might be potato-crusted salmon with celeriac puree, a lamb chop with rosemary au jus, or crab cakes with a spicy creole mustard sauce. Prices range from $16 to $21, but it's worth it. Open June to mid-October, Tuesday to Sunday from 6pm to closing. Closed mid-October to May.

At **Redfield's,** Main Street, Northeast Harbor (☎ 207/276-5283), the menu changes nightly so that you're always assured of the freshest of fresh ingredients prepared in some very innovative ways. For example, there might be breast of duck with cranberry port compote or rare tuna with wasabi and fresh tomato sauce. To start, the roasted red pepper and crab bisque has an extra kick, while the soft-shell crab is enhanced with a basil rémoulade. It's a lively small restaurant with small bar. Tables are combined with chairs that are locally crafted, and the art on the walls has the same provenance. Prices range from $16 to $23. Open summer, Monday to Saturday from 6pm to closing; fall and winter, Friday and Saturday from 6pm to closing. Closed March and April.

You can't beat the lobster at **Abel's Lobster Pound** (☎ 207/276-5827) off Route 198 en route to Northeast Harbor, overlooking Somes Sound. Enjoy your feast at one of the picnic tables or inside while you watch a sunset. The lobster comes in five different ways—boiled, Newburg, sautéed, as a stew, or in a Caesar salad. Open Memorial Day through June, noon to 9pm; July to August, noon to 10pm; and September to Columbus Day, 5 to 9pm.

SOUTHWEST HARBOR & BASS HARBOR

Southwest Harbor is a fishing town looking out over Somes Sound. Visit Southwest Harbor to see the **Mount Desert Oceanarium** on Clark Point Road (☎ 207/244-7330), for a hands-on lesson about the ocean and its inhabitants. There are 20 tanks, including a touch tank in which the kids love to handle the sea cucumbers, moon snails, and crabs. Open mid-May to late October, Monday to Saturday from 9am to 5pm.

The **Wendell Gilley Museum,** on Main Street, Southwest Harbor (☎ 207/244-7555), is a fascinating museum dedicated to a master carver of birds and decoys. Southwest Harbor resident Gilley was a master plumber who did his first carving at age 26 but made it his career at age 52. Today you can see the splendid works that he created from single blocks of wood. They are incredibly true to life, and he painted each one carefully to replicate the plumage of each species. In addition to the beautiful lifelike birds, there's likely to be a temporary exhibit of paintings or artwork on display that are for sale. Open June through October, Tuesday to Sunday from 10am to 4pm; May, November, and December, Friday to Sunday from 10am to 4pm. Closed January to April. Admission is $3 adult, $1 children 5 to 12.

Manset just south of Southwest Harbor is home to the famous **Hinckley Boatyard** (☎ 207/244-5531), where some of the greatest and most expensive yachts in the world are made.

At **Bass Harbor** you can drive down to **Bass Harbor Head Lighthouse,** which marks the entrance to Blue Bay, and from Bass Harbor you can take **ferries** to Swans Island and Long Island.

From Bass Harbor you can loop around the coast on Route 102 by Seal Cove and Seal Cove Pond. Bring a picnic and enjoy it on the beach at **Pretty Marsh** and then continue into Somesville, the original (1761) settlement on the island. Today it's a gracious historic town that looks much as it did in 1850. The **Mount Desert Island Historical Society Museum,** Oak Hill Road and Route 102, displays cultural artifacts that include shipbuilding tools, kitchen gadgets, toys, costumes, china, furniture, and historic photographs of island life. Open June through October, Tuesday to Saturday 10am to 5pm. Admission $1.

SOUTHWEST HARBOR LODGING & DINING

From the porch at **The Claremont,** Claremont Road, Southwest Harbor, ME 04679 (☎ 207/244-5036), you can look out onto beautiful Somes Sound. The main hotel sits on 5 acres and offers privacy and some 24 rooms (20 with private bath). The nicest accommodations, though, are in the adjacent Phillips House, which is part of the property. The six rooms here are furnished with brass beds, braided rugs, maple dressers, plus sitting chairs. Two rooms have fireplaces. There's a comfortable common room with plenty of books to read, a grand piano, and seating arranged around the stone fireplace. Other accommodations are in traditional log cottages with stone fireplaces and in more modern cottages ranging from studios to two bedrooms with Franklin stoves and decks with ocean views. Facilities include a tennis court, rowboats, bikes, plus a croquet lawn where a championship is held in August. Guests also have access to a TV parlor and library/game room with another fireplace. The dining room has crisply attired tables, fresh flowers, and candlelight service. Lunch is served daily between July 4 and Labor Day. The cuisine is fine and eclectic. Among the entrees, you might find pan-seared duck with redcurrant, cherry, and port wine reduction served with red onion confit or sirloin steak with morel, chanterelle, and shiitake mushrooms with sauce espagnole, as well as boiled lobster and bouillabaisse. Lunch is noon to 2pm and dinner 5 to 9pm.

Rates: $130 bed-and-breakfast, $205 MAP in summer (July 1 to Labor Day); $90 bed-and-breakfast and $185 MAP mid-June to July 1 and Labor Day to October 17. Closed winter. Cottages range from $163 to 193 in summer and from $100 to $145 winter.

Lindenwood Inn, 118 Clark Point Rd. (P.O. Box 1328), Southwest Harbor, ME 04679 (☎ 207/244-5335), has five nicely furnished rooms. There are decorative accents from South and Central America and the Pacific—you'll pass a Maori shield on the way up the staircase. Room 3 has a wrought-iron canopied bed that is dressed with eyelet-lace linens. The most luxurious accommodation is the penthouse suite, which has huge skylights, a fireplace, and a large deck with a hot tub from which you can see a panoramic view. The suite's sitting room has been decorated with fun pieces from Mexico, along with a comfortable sofa and other furnishings. There are also some cottage accommodations. Breakfast is served in a dining room brightly painted in yellow and lime, decorated with masks and totems from the South Pacific. There's also a sitting room for guests, and a restaurant with full bar is on the premises. Facilities include a small pool and hot tub. Rates: July 1 to Labor Day, $95 to $205; Labor Day to mid-October, $85 to $195; mid-Oct to June 30, $75 to $185.

If you want to enjoy a real experience of Maine, then stay at the **Pointy Head Inn,** Route 102A, Bass Harbor, ME 04653 (☎ 207/244-7261), and pass some time talking with Captain Warren Townsend, a Mainer who still goes out on the water, but whose great love and gift is woodcarving. The inn occupies a lovely spot overlooking Bass Harbor. The heart of the home is the kitchen with its potbelly stove and old slate sink and beams. You'll notice a number of decoys, carved by Captain Warren, that are tucked around the walls—puffins, cardinals, jenny wrens, chickadees, loons, and ducks. They are really beautiful—not to be compared to the machine-made decoys imported from Taiwan and sold in Bar Harbor at inflated prices. If you're looking for a beautifully crafted bird or decoy, this is the place to come for the real thing.

The six rooms in the house are not fancy, but they are clean and comfortable, with country furnishings: iron beds covered with a quilts, pine side tables, oak dressers, and armchairs. There are several sitting rooms, one of which is more formal than the rest. The floors are covered with dhurries and easy chairs are arranged in front of the brick fireplace. The most beautiful objects in the room, again, will be Warren's carvings—a life-size osprey, a lighthouse scene carved out of a single piece of wood, a carved black bass or brook trout, or a ship's model in which everything works. Rates: $65 to $105.

The dining room at the **Preble Grill,** 14 Clark Point Rd. (☎ 207/244-3034), has plain pine tables and chairs and some booths set around a fireplace. The eclectic cuisine served here melds different cooking traditions from Mexican to Italian. The menu offers dishes such as quesadilla with cranberry salsa along with cioppino and pasta dishes. And, of course, there are also traditional New England shore specialties like Maine crab cakes and lobster stew. Open daily 5pm to closing.

Beal's Lobster Pier, Clark Point Road (☎ 207/244-7178), is right down overlooking Southwest Harbor—a great place to enjoy a boiled or steamed lobster, crab rolls, fish and chips, or burger. Wine and beer available. Prices run from $2 to $12.95. Open 9am to 8pm in summer, 9am to 5pm after Labor Day.

Keenan's, Route 102A, Bass Harbor (☎ 207/244-3403) is a real Maine experience. It's located in a little old shingle shack with a rough-and-ready interior of Formica tables and kitchen-style chairs. It's a lovable dive with a warm and engaging atmosphere and good spicy Louisiana-style cuisine—really hearty seafood gumbo that is filled with chunks of lobster and crab, shrimp étouffée, barbecue ribs, and flavorsome crab cakes. You'll step into another world when you open the doors to this small room with a beat up old woodstove just inside the door. Open Wednesday to Sunday from 5 to 9pm. Closed winter.

HANCOCK, THE SCHOODIC PENINSULA & JONESPORT

From Bar Harbor, take Route 3 to Route 1 and continue east to Ellsworth and Hancock. From Hancock, drive south to Hancock Point. Return to Hancock and travel east on Route 1 to Sullivan. En route, don't miss stopping in North Sullivan at the **Barter Family Gallery,** 2½ miles off Route 1 (☎ 207/422-3190), in Sullivan. Primitive colorful woodcarvings of animals stand outside in the yard of this home-gallery. Inside, there are some brilliant colored landscapes painted by Phillip Barter and priced from $1,800. Barter is a fisherman turned painter who began painting about 20 years ago and gained a reputation for painting in the early style of Marsden Hartley. Over the years, he has moved beyond his original folk art–style landscapes into strong, highly charged, almost abstract landscape canvases. Painted furniture and animal carvings, plus some clothing items, are for sale, too.

Another stop worth making is at **Pine Tree Kiln,** Route 1, West Sullivan, which sells fine art and watercolors by Doris Holman, plus woodcuts; jewelry; and ceramic bowls, lamps, and vases.

At West Gouldsboro, turn south on Route 186 to Winter Harbor and Schoodic Point. After exploring the park, take Route 186 east to Prospect Harbor, where it links up with Route 195, which will take you to the small fishing community of Corea. Return to Route 1 and continue east to Columbia Falls and turn south on Route 187 to Jonesport, gateway to Beals and Great Wass islands. These islands are made for time traveling. You may just not want to return to the 20th century. From here, Route 1 runs on to the Canadian border to **Campobello Island,** which was FDR's family's summer home.

HANCOCK & COREA LODGING

The Crocker House Country Inn, Hancock Point Road, Hancock, ME 04640 (☎ 207/422-6806), is on a quiet lane a short distance from Hancock Point. It's a comfortable place with a first-rate dining room. Rooms are nicely decorated in a country style with floral wallpapers, hooked rugs, and oak pieces; beds are iron or brass or four-posters. The bed in Room 12 has an attractive star quilt, and Room 7 has a bay window overlooking the front lawn. The diamond-pane windows add a touch of romance to the dining room. The cuisine is excellent—good-quality ingredients enhanced by knowledgeable cooking. You might have a wonderful rack of lamb with mustard crust served with vegetables and luscious potatoes dauphinoise, or poached salmon Florentine (with spinach and hollandaise). Prices range from $18 to $20. At breakfast you can select from the menu—eggs, omelets, pancakes—and they'll be cooked to order. Rates: August, $110 to $150; mid-June through

July and September to mid-October, $100 to $140; mid-October to mid-June, $85 to $105.

Le Domaine Restaurant and Inn, Route 1 (P.O. Box 496), Hancock, ME 04606 (☎ 207/422-3395 or 207/422-3916), is an elegant place that has been serving some of the finest French cuisine in Maine since opening in 1946. It's decorated in a rich, warm red and has a large brick fireplace at one end of the dining room. The menu changes frequently to reflect what is fresh at the time. Many of the dishes are inspired by Provence, once home to the mother of current owner-chef Nicole Purslow. Olive oil, garlic, thyme, and rosemary are often used in this superb French country cooking. The three or four main dishes might range from grilled salmon with a shallot red-wine butter to rabbit served in a prune sauce. Prices range from $21 to $25. Desserts are such classics as crème brûlée or *coupe aux marrons glacé* (vanilla ice cream with chestnuts marinated in a vanilla-rum sauce). The restaurant has a 5,000-bottle wine cellar and a list that is notable for its earthy Rhones and fine Burgundies. Open Wednesday to Monday from 6 to 9pm.

There are seven light and airy rooms upstairs. They are tasteful, but lack such features as TV and focus instead on the substantial comforts of good beds, carpeting, and thick towels. Rates: late May to mid-October, MAP $210.

The Black Duck, Crowley Island Road (P.O. Box 39), Corea, ME 04624-0039 (☎ 207/963-2689), is located on a remote lobstering cove. It's operated by Barry Canner and Bob Travers who have furnished the house with their personal collections and paintings created by friends or family. In one sitting room, for example, hang watercolors by Barry's sister; in another is Bob's collection of oil lamps and a mechanical toy collection. Guests gather around the TV in front of the pebble-stone fireplace in one of the rooms or relax and get to know one another around the brick fireplace in the other. The four rooms in the main house have been attractively decorated. In one, you'll find an iron bed on a white painted floor with marbelized side tables and an acorn chest. My favorite is the cottage, which has a full kitchen, a sitting room, and a skylit bedroom upstairs. A full breakfast with main dishes such as blueberry pancakes or baked French toast with orange glaze is served on lovely plates from Lee Glass in Winter Harbor. Rates: $75 to $105.

NEW HAMPSHIRE

The Monadnock Region

The Villages by the Mountain: Temple, Rindge,
Fitzwilliam & Jaffrey ◆ *Henniker, Hillsborough, Antrim,*
Hancock, Peterborough, Dublin & Harrisville ◆ *Along the*
Connecticut River from Hinsdale to Walpole

Distance from Boston in miles: Mount Monadnock, 75; Peterborough, 80; Keene, 100; Hillsborough, 120.

Estimated driving time: 1½ hours to Peterborough; 2 hours to Keene; 2½ hours to Hillsborough.

◄o►◄o►◄o►◄o►◄o►

Driving: I-93 north to Route 128 south and then Route 3 north to Nashua. Take Exit 8 and head west on Route 101A to Milford and then take Route 101 to Peterborough.

Bus: Vermont Transit operates from Boston to Keene and Fitzwilliam (☎ 800/451-3292 or 617/526-1800).

Train: Amtrak has trains to Brattleboro (☎ 800/872-7245).

Further Information: For more information, contact the **Hillsborough Chamber of Commerce** (☎ 603/464-5858); **Jaffrey Chamber of Commerce** (☎ 603/532-4549); **Monadnock Travel Council**, Keene (☎ 603/355-8155); **Peterborough Chamber of Commerce** (☎ 603/924-7234); **Rindge Chamber of Commerce** (☎ 603/899-6040).

◄o►◄o►◄o►◄o►◄o►

The solitary 3,165-foot-high Mount Monadnock, called by the Indians "one that stands alone," dominates this "quiet corner" of New Hampshire. Many a literary figure has been moved by the beauty of the mountain and inspired by the surrounding landscape as Ralph Waldo Emerson was when he wrote on a visit to the Halfway House on the slopes of the mountain:

> Every morn I lift my head,
> See New England underspread
> South from St. Lawrence to the Sound,
> From Katskill east to the sea-bound.

Southwest New Hampshire

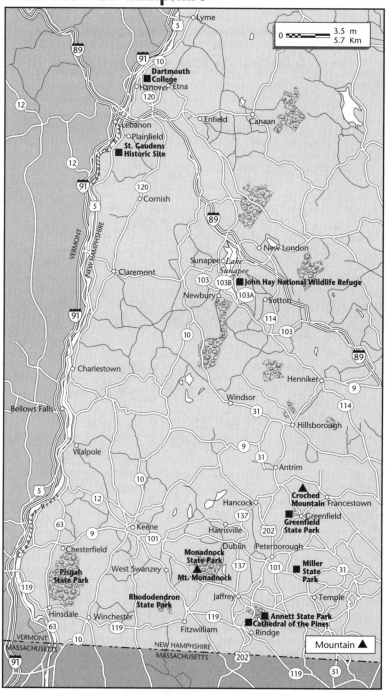

On clear days you can still see a 150-mile panorama of the six New England states from the summit of this aerie citadel—north to the Presidential range and Mount Washington and west to mounts Tom and Greylock in the Berkshires, and to Vermont's Green Mountains. Ever since Captain Samuel Ward made the first ascent of Grand Monadnock in 1725, it has drawn climbers, seekers, writers, artists, and poets to its barren crags. It's still a most-climbed mountain; if you want to climb it, the best access is from Monadnock State Park outside Jaffrey. Even if you don't climb it, you should take the road up to the summit to get a real impression of the beauty of this region and the somnolent towns that lie at its base.

THE VILLAGES BY THE MOUNTAIN: TEMPLE, RINDGE, FITZWILLIAM & JAFFREY

The hilltop town of **Temple** will return you to the 18th century. It's notable for its triangular common and the rows of historic buildings that face it. On one side is an old stagecoach inn that contains murals painted by itinerant artist, inventor, and journalist Rufus Porter. Stroll down into the graveyard on one side of the common, where the stones evoke memories of the past—among those resting here is the boy Frances Blood Moses, who was sent by General Washington on a spying mission to Nova Scotia, and Ebenezer Edwards, who fought at Concord Bridge. Temple was the location of the first glassmaking factory in New Hampshire, founded in 1780 by Robert Hewes, who employed Hessian mercenaries from the British army.

It seems that Grand Monadnock can be seen from every vantage point in the region. One of the best views is from the outdoor altar at the national **Cathedral of the Pines,** off Route 119 in Rindge (☎ 603/899-3300). The Cathedral was created by Dr. and Mrs. Douglas Sloane in memory of their son, who died in World War II. It's open daily, from May through October.

Other peaks thrust up around Grand Monadnock, including Little Monadnock, which looms above the picturesque village of Fitzwilliam. It's a classic New England village with a steepled church and Federal-style homes facing the small green. At one time it was a quarry town. To get a sense of local history, stop in at the small **Amos J. Blake House Museum** on the Common (☎ 603/585-7742), which has 13 rooms filled with collections of toys, early farming tools, glass, and pottery. The house itself dates to 1837. Open from Memorial Day to October 1, on weekends only. If you visit Fitzwilliam in spring, you'll want to stroll along the paths that wind through a mass of huge rhododendrons in nearby Rhododendron State Park.

Jaffrey Center is another pretty village and is home to Monadnock State Park. Pilgrims of a different stripe visit the Old Burying Ground behind the classic Jaffrey meetinghouse where Willa Cather is buried. She is resting here, far from her Nebraska home, because she used to summer in Jaffrey at an inn where she wrote much of *My Antonia* (1918) and *One of Ours* (1922). If you wander around this old graveyard, you'll discover some other remarkable memorials, like the one created by artist Count Vigo Brandt Erickson to his infant daughter and his first wife, a Jaffrey native who loved to sit here and read. Amos Fortune is another celebrated local name, and he, too, is buried here. Amos was a slave who secured his freedom and amassed a substantial sum of money, some of which he left to a local school. It is said that he was an African prince and maintained great dignity of bearing and dress, always appearing at church in fine black suit and top hat. Even so, he was not allowed to take communion, and it's somewhat ironic that he donated a communion plate to the church. For additional insights into local history, visit the **Jaffrey Historic District Melville Academy Museum,** Thorndike Pond Road, Jaffrey Center (☎ 603/532-7455). Local railroad magnate Jonas Melville financed the academy, which was founded in 1843. He subsequently lost his fortune, and the school was closed in 1857. It now houses a fine small museum that has notable collections of Hannah Davis bandboxes among other objects. Open July to August on Saturday and Sunday; admission is free.

TEMPLE, RINDGE, FITZWILLIAM & JAFFREY LODGING

Ram in the Thicket, Maple Street, Wilton, NH 03449 (☎ 603/654-6440), reflects the entertaining, fun personality of the Reverend Andrew Tempelman and his wife, Priscilla. It's a delightful white clapboard Victorian home, set on a little hill in a very quiet area. The rooms are all tastefully decorated with wicker, chintz, ruffled curtains, and brass-and-iron beds with country comforters; some of the rooms have four-posters with canopies. The ground floor houses several small intimate dining rooms, candlelit at night, which offer fine food to a classical music background. The menu might feature dishes such as chicken mulligatawny, chunks of chicken in a mildly spicy coconut milk sauce, or roasted pork wrapped in bacon and sprinkled with brown sugar. Prices range from $16 to $20. For summer dining there's a screened-in porch overlooking the garden. Open Wednesday, Thursday, and Sunday from 5:30 to 8:30pm, Friday and Saturday from 5:30 to 9:30pm. Whatever else you do, be sure to take a seat at the tiny bar and listen to the ex-reverend as he serves up a few bons mots along with an ounce or two of alcohol. Rates: $80 double with private bath, $65 double with shared bath.

The Birchwood Inn, Route 45, Temple, NH 03084 (☎ 603/878-3285), is an old brick coaching inn dating to 1800 that overlooks the green in Temple. The seven rooms (five with private baths) have been decorated in country style with quilts and chintz and oak. The innkeeper is a train buff, and one room has been decorated with photographs of trains and reliefs of locomotives. The most notable historic room is the dining room, which has murals by Rufus Porter portraying a clipper ship scene. There's also an atmospheric tavern. The menu changes daily, and is listed on a blackboard; the menu includes roast duck; filet mignon; and usually a chicken, veal, and fish dish. The tavern is filled with eye-catching objects from puzzles and games to china and model trains. Rates: $70 to $80. Open Tuesday to Saturday from 6 to 8pm.

The **Amos A. Parker House**, Route 119 (P.O. Box 202), Fitzwilliam, NH 03447 (☎ 603/585-6540), is a lovely place to stay not just for the richness of the accommodations and the historic home in which it's located but also for the heavenly gardens that owner Freda B. Houpt has created over the years. Laced with fountain and ponds, the garden beds contain 1,500 plants and are completely entrancing, and they alone are reason enough to stay here. The circa 1780 house itself is filled with character, especially the post-and-beam sitting room, which is thought to date to 1700. Throughout, Freda has decorated with sumptuous personal collections. The most obvious are the oriental rugs, but there are other eye-catching accents, including delightful flower stencils. There are two rooms and two suites (three of the units with wood-burning fireplace). One suite has a sitting room with a sofa, two wing chairs, and a table and Windsor chair; the bedroom has an iron-and-brass bed. One room has a striking four-poster with a lace canopy and toile bedspread and a wing chair upholstered with the same beautiful fabric. A full breakfast is served in a very handsome dining room that has a fireplace with a baking oven. Guests also have the pleasure of gathering in a gracious sitting room. Rates: $90 to $100.

Innkeepers Mike and Kaye Terpstra at the **Hannah Davis House**, 186 Depot Rd. (Route 119), Fitzwillliam, NH 03447 (☎ 603/585-3344), extend a warm greeting to their guests. The 1820 home has fine architectural elements such as random-width pumpkin-pine floors and chair-rail wainscoting. There are three rooms and three suites all nicely decorated (four of the guest accommodations have wood-burning fireplaces). Even though Hannah's Room is small, it accommodates an iron bed, oak chest, wing chair, and iron floor lamp. The Canopy Room, of course, has a canopied bed, while Chauncey has an iron-and-brass bed dressed with lace-trimmed linens and a striped ruffle. The most fetching room is actually above the garage. Here, the ceilings are high, and there's a sitting area with enough room for a table and four chairs. The bed is an antique cannonball, and the suite has its own private deck and entrance. A small TV/VCR is available in the inn's sitting room, and there's also an upright piano if guests want to entertain. The heart of the house is the large country kitchen. Rates: $70 to $145.

The **Fitzwilliam,** on the Common, Fitzwilliam, NH 03447 (☎ 603/585-9000), dates back to 1796. Old family portraits and wedding certificates hang in the beamed dining room; an adjoining room displays the family's huge basket collection. The country dining room overlooks the pool and garden and also exhibits some handsomely painted corner cupboards. The food is traditional—steaks, salmon with lemon hollandaise, roast duck, chicken marsala—and priced from $11 to $20. It's open daily from 8 to 9:30am; Monday to Saturday from noon to 2pm and 5:30 to 9pm, Sunday from noon to 8pm. In the winter, you'll likely find three fireplaces blazing, one in the dining room, another in the library (where there's also a TV), and another in the tap room. There are 25 guest rooms, 12 with private bath, all differently furnished in simple country fashion. For example, Room 5 has chintz wallpaper and stenciling, and a sage-green painted chest, while Room 16 sports a pink gingham coverlet and curtains set against rose-colored wallpaper. Rates: $70 to $80 double.

Benjamin Prescott Inn, Route 124 East, Jaffrey, NH 03452 (☎ 603/532-6637), is in a Greek Revival home, dating to 1853, which is surrounded by a 700-acre dairy farm. The inn has nine rooms, all attractively decorated with country furnishings. One room has a cottage painted bed, drop-leaf side tables, an acorn dresser, and Eastlake chair. Others might have brass beds or a marble-top dresser or Victorian chairs. The most luxurious accommodation is the third-floor suite, which has a skylit sitting area with French doors leading to a private balcony with pastoral views. It's equipped with a refrigerator, wet bar, and small TV. In the bedroom is a canopied bed plus two beds ingeniously tucked under the eaves. Breakfast dishes run to temptations like peach French toast and multigrain waffles. While you're eating, you can contemplate the collection of sand from around the world displayed in glass jars—begun by Barry's grandfather, it comes from 31 different countries and 30 states. There's a comfortable parlor for guests. Rates: $75 to $140.

RINDGE DINING

Lily's on the Pond, Route 202 (☎ 603/899-3322), has a warm country feel with its wagon-wheel lamps and wood-burning stove. The food is good and reasonably priced, and the variety of selections will satisfy everyone whether you want burgers or sandwiches or more interesting fare like Cajun-style sirloin. My choice would be one of the many daily fish specials, for example, the red snapper with mushrooms, tomatoes, and garlic. Prices range from $10 to $15. There's an attractive post-and-beam tavern room, too. Open Tuesday to Saturday from 11:30am to 9pm; Sunday from 10am to 8pm.

HENNIKER, HILLSBOROUGH, ANTRIM, HANCOCK, PETERBOROUGH, DUBLIN & HARRISVILLE

Henniker is a pretty, historic town nestled by the Contoocook River. It has a couple of appealing inns, and the stores along Main Street are worth browsing. Nearby **Hillsborough** is made up of four villages: Bridge Village, an old mill town on the banks of the Contoocook, is the commercial center; Hillsborough Center has a cluster of early American homes arranged around a green; the upper village is the home of the Fuller Library; and the lower village is on Franklin Pierce Lake. Hillsborough was settled in 1748, and many of the original old homes are still standing in Hillsborough Center. Visit **Gibson Pewter Workshop** (☎ 603/464-3410) just off the common or attend one of the many auctions that are held under tents on the green during the summer. For information on the latter, contact Richard Withington, 590 Center Rd. (☎ 603/464-3232).

The Franklin Pierce Homestead Historic Site at routes 9 and 31, Hillsborough (☎ 603/478-3165) is the childhood home of Franklin Pierce, the rather bland 14th president of the United States. Built in 1804 by his father, General Benjamin Pierce, who was twice governor of New Hampshire, the home reflects the atmosphere of wealth in which the young president grew up. The rooms are spacious and have stenciled walls and fine imported wallpapers. Upstairs there is a ballroom where Benjamin drilled the local militia and entertained such figures as Daniel Webster. After serving terms as a congressman and senator, the young Franklin was nominated to run for the presidency at the Democratic Convention of 1852 and was elected largely because he supported the Fugitive Slave Law that won him the votes of the South. During his term, pre–Civil War social conflict intensified, and he did little to calm it. Open June and September to Columbus Day, Saturday 10am to 4pm and Sunday 1 to 4pm; July to August, Monday to Saturday 10am to 4pm and Sunday 1 to 4pm.

Hancock is another delightful village that was once an old mill town. Nearly every building on Main Street is in the National Register of Historic Places. The old clapboard and brick homes, four-room schoolhouse, town market, and classic steepled church evoke an earlier era. If you're interested, stop in at the **Hancock Historical Society** (☎ 603/525-9379). Open July to August, Wednesday and Saturday; June and September, Saturday only; winter, Wednesday only. Admission free.

In this region, **Peterborough** is the biggest town and has the most to see. The red brick buildings cluster along the banks of Goose Brook and the Contoocook River, which were both lined with mills at one time when this town was a center of Yankee ingenuity. It was settled largely by Scotch-Irish folk who left Londonderry, New Hampshire, because they could not scratch a living from the stubborn soil there.

Many an enterprising and successful inventor-entrepreneur set up business here or in the surrounding towns in the 19th century, and the factories turned out everything from textiles and paper to machinery and precision instruments. The Phoenix Mills operated from 1793 to 1908, and at one time employed 200 people; Goodell cutlery was made in nearby Antrim. Charles Wilder started making thermometers in North Peterborough and later sold his company to an instrument manufacturer in Troy, New York. These industries have long gone, but today the town is well known for the 40 or so special-interest magazines that are published in the town or nearby—from *CD Review* to *Byte Magazine,* which occupies the former site of the Phoenix factory. The biggest building in town at one time was the Guernsey Cattle Club, which kept the genealogical records of the nation's Guernsey herds here until it moved out to Ohio. **The Peterborough Historical Society,** 19 Grove St. (☎ 603/924-3235), has a whole floor of exhibits tracing town history and also some beautifully crafted New Hampshire furniture. It also provides a walking-tour map of the main buildings along Grove Street on request. Open daily Monday to Friday from 1 to 5pm.

Peterborough was the model for Thornton Wilder's play *Our Town,* which he wrote while he was staying at the famous **MacDowell Colony,** 100 High St., Peterborough (☎ 603/924-3886), a retreat for artists, musicians, and writers on the northwestern edge of town. Just before composer Edward MacDowell died, he dreamed of establishing a place to which creative artists could retreat to write and paint in solitude surrounded by natural beauty. He died before he could realize his dream, but his wife, concert pianist Marian Nevins MacDowell, took on the task at the age of 50 and built the colony on the 450 wooded acres. Since then it has nurtured more than 4,500 artists—writers Stephen Vincent Benet, Edward Arlington Robinson, Willa Cather, James Baldwin, Alice Walker, Spalding Gray, Barbara Tuchman, Padraic Colum, and Maxwell Bodenheim: composers Aaron Copland, Virgil Thomson, Leonard Bernstein, and Mrs. H. H. Beach; and artists Milton Avery and Jules Feiffer.

The artists work in the 32 studios on the property, where they are free to follow their own inspiration. They may be inspired, or discouraged, as the case may be, by the studios' previous occupants, whose names are displayed upon the walls. The studios are for work only—they sleep elsewhere. Breakfast and dinner are taken at the red barn; lunch is delivered in a pannier to the porch of each studio. Ask for the key to the Savidge Library if you want to see all the books and scores of those that have spent time here. It's an inviting space, lit by Palladian windows and furnished with oriental rugs, a fireplace, and wing chairs.

Other in-town entertainment includes browsing and shopping, especially at Dock Square where there are several galleries, including a branch of the famous **Sharon Arts Center** (in nearby Sharon), plus **Haskell Russell Antiques** and other interesting stores. Four miles south of town, the **Sharon Arts Center,** Route 123, Sharon (☎ 603/924-7256), operates two galleries exhibiting fine arts and crafts—pottery, jewelry, prints, furniture, textiles, glass, wood, and metal sculptures—plus the well-known craft school, which offers a variety of lectures and workshops throughout the year in painting, weaving, jewelry, stained glass, sculpture, and pottery. Open Monday to Saturday from 10am to 5pm; Sunday from noon to 5pm.

Entertainment can be enjoyed at the **New England Marionette Opera,** Main Street, Peterborough. (☎ 603/924-4333), a rare marionette theater devoted primarily to opera. Patrons climb up a narrow spiral staircase to the 135-seat theater that has velvet and mahogany seats and a state-of-the-art sound system to see performances by 32-inch-tall personalities in full costume on elaborate sets. Tickets are $24 for adults; shorter shows geared to children are $14 for adults, $10 for children 11 and under. Open in spring and fall; call for schedules.

A better-known company is the **Peterborough Players,** Hadley Road (☎ 603/924-7585), off Middle Hancock Road, which has provided summer theater since 1933 at the 125-acre Hadley Farm. Alumni of this venerable theater company include Avery Brooks, Jean Stapleton, and James Whitmore. On weekends, tickets range from $21.50 to $24.50 for such productions as Shakespeare's *Romeo & Juliet,* Neil Simon's *Broadway Bound,* and A. R. Gurney's *Sylvia.*

From Peterborough, Route 101 will take you to the hill town of **Dublin,** which is the highest town in the region and offers great views of Monadnock and Dublin Lake. It has been a summer resort for more than 150 years, attracting a number of authors, musicians, artists, and executives. Among them were poet Amy Lowell, artist and naturalist Abbot Thayer, and artists George de Forest Brush and Joseph Lindon Smith. Today it's home to *Yankee Magazine.*

A side road off Route 101 will bring you to **Harrisville,** a classic mill village incorporated in 1870, huddled beside a pond. Unlike the other villages in the region, which were largely agricultural, Harrisville was at one time a thriving industrial enclave of mills, warehouses, and worker's housing, all made of brick. Today the town is a National Historic Landmark (☎ 603/827-3722) in which the buildings have been restored and reused (more than 200 are landmarks). At the center stands a wool storage building that is now home to **Harrisville Designs,** a mecca for weavers who come to take instructional courses and to purchase looms, yarn, or finished clothing. Stay awhile and take in the setting of the old buildings standing in a wooded valley beside reed-rimmed Harrisville Pond and Goose Creek.

AREA LODGING

Colby Hill Inn, P.O. Box 778, Henniker, NH 03242 (☎ 603/428-3281), is a 1795 farmhouse charmer in an idyllic setting with 6 acres of beautiful gardens and weathered barn. There are 16 rooms (10 in the main house and 6 in the carriage house). They are decorated in a country style. One might have a brass bed combined with an Empire chest and club chairs, all set against striped wallpaper with a decorative tassel border pattern. Another might contain a sleigh bed and a Victorian-style sofa against a cabbage-rose patterned wallpaper. Some have gas fireplaces. Carriage house rooms are a little smaller but still attractive. There are two wonderful old barns on the property, one 110 years old and the other 190. The pool, with a flagstone apron, is shaded by maples and has great views of tree-clad hills. The garden is shaded by honeylocust and black-and-white birch and has a fountain and colorful flower beds, too. The gazebo is a romantic place in the evening. Dinner is served daily, and the food is well prepared. The traditional menu features dishes such as filet mignon with roasted garlic and shallot peppercorn sauce or chicken saltimbocca pie, which consists of chicken sautéed with mushrooms, red peppers, and prosciutto, baked under a pastry. The minted red wine sauce with rack of lamb is delicious, and the shrimp and fennel, flamed with Pernod, is a perfect blend of flavors. Prices range from $16 to $24. Dining hours are Monday to Saturday from 5:30 to 8:30pm, Sunday 4:30 to 7:30pm. Rates: $95 to $125.

Meetinghouse Inn & Restaurant, 35 Flanders Rd., Henniker, NH 03242 (☎ 603/428-3228), is a charming accommodation made even more so by the trellis and gardens along the front, the hot tub, and an excellent restaurant. The post-and-beam dining room is a romantic candlelit trysting place with cabbage-rose decor and an occasional cherub for good measure. The plastic bags of sand on one wall look more down to earth, but they are equally sentimental in their way—the collection began 15 years ago when some local students returned from Bermuda with the first sample. The classically prepared food is great, and there's a full selection to choose from. Tenderloin of beef is served with a rich cassis sauce with blackberries and green onions, or you can order beef Wellington. On the seafood side, the shrimp Alfredo is cooked in a blend of basil, wine, and cheese; and the plain broiled halibut is delicious. Prices range from $16 to $22. The rooms are also charming, with canopied oak or brass beds and wide-board floors. A full breakfast is served. Dining hours are Wednesday to Sunday from 5 to 9pm. Rates: $75 to $115.

The Inn at Maplewood Farm, 447 Center Rd., Hillsborough (☎ 603/ 464-4242), is a beautifully situated landmark farmhouse on 14 acres that is operated by an engaging young couple, Jayme and Laura Simoes. There are four suites—two with sitting rooms and two with two bedrooms. Each is large and nicely furnished. One room has a canopy bed and marble-top side tables, pine furnishings, and a wood-burning fireplace. Kilims and dhurries enhance the floors. In the barn room, the floor has been painted to look like a rug and then furnished with a four-poster and oak pieces. In each room, you'll find an old radio that plays old radio shows. Jayme is a passionate collector of old radios and enjoys sharing them with guests. In the parlor where guests relax, Jayme has his collection of radios on display, and there's an abundance of reading material and comfortable places to sit. The breakfasts are superb, served in a light and airy dining room where Laura displays her collection of teapots. Expect dishes such as peach soup followed by the lightest quiche you've ever tasted or spinach wrap containing scrambled eggs and fresh salsa with stuffed pattypan. It's a serene place where you can sit on the front porch or at the tables by the apple orchard.

The Hancock Inn, Main Street, Hancock, NH 03449 (☎ 603/525-3318), is a seasoned inn, in continuous operation since 1789. The staircase creaks as you step up to the 11 guest rooms, all with private baths and all furnished with antique country pieces set against stenciled walls or striking murals. Room 16 has a pastoral scene painted by the famous itinerant painter Rufus Porter. Its furnishings include a pencil four-poster canopied bed, matched with a painted blanket chest, maple dresser, rocker, and wing chair. Most of the wide-plank floors are covered with braided area rugs. The ground floor features an inviting tavern room that serves as a common room for guests. The dining room positively glows at night. Its walls are sponge painted in red with Colonial-blue trim, and tin wall sconces and candles on the tables provide the lighting. The fare is traditional New England: baked Boston scrod, Nantucket seafood casserole (scallops, shrimp, and lobster), filet mignon, chicken amandine, and lamb chop mixed grill. The specialty is Shaker cranberry pot roast that's so tender it just flakes onto the fork. Prices range from $16 to $22. Open Monday to Saturday from 6pm to closing, Sunday from 5pm to closing. Rates: $108 to $160 double.

The Inn at Crotched Mountain, Mountain Road (off Route 47), Francestown, NH 03043 (☎ 603/588-6840), a brick building covered with ivy, has a magnificent setting on a mountainside overlooking a valley and wooded hills—a surprising, delightful hideaway and a great place for skiers. The ceilings are low in parts of the 1822 building. There are 14 rooms, 8 with private baths. Room 9 is my favorite—it has a door that leads out to the pool and also offers a dramatic view. Three of the rooms have fireplaces; one has a woodstove; and all are nicely furnished with maple pieces, braided rugs, in country style. Guests are free to use the comfortable living room, with wing chairs and a sofa around two fireplaces. The dining room is crisply turned out with white and red napery and maple Windsor chairs. There's also the cozy Winslow tavern where you can snuggle up by the fireside at tables made from old wagon-wheel hubs. The menu features filet mignon with béarnaise, cranberry port pot roast, and lamb chops with apple mint jelly, priced from $13 to $17. Open May to October, Friday and Saturday only, from 6 to 8pm. Facilities include a large swimming pool, two clay tennis courts, and 5½ miles of cross-country skiing trails. Rates: $80 to 90 double. Closed for 3 weeks in November.

The Greenfield Inn, at routes 31 and 136, Greenfield, NH 03047 (☎ 603/547-6327), 10 minutes from Greenfield State Park, is run by friendly Victor and Barbara Mangini. The old Victorian house has a wraparound veranda leading onto a spacious deck that overlooks Mount Monadnock. Guests have use of a hammock, a TV room, parlor, and a breakfast room where a full buffet breakfast—ham and egg soufflé plus muffins and granola—is served to the strains of Mozart and his contemporaries. Photos of Bob Hope adorn the walls in a nook of the sitting room—he's a good friend of the couple.

The 12 rooms, 9 with private bath, are attractively furnished with chintz wallpapers and oak and pine furnishings. The most alluring accommodation is the Honeymooner's Hideaway, which is tucked away under the house with stone foundation walls. In the Samson and Delilah Room, a brass bed covered with a rose-and-cream eiderdown shares space with a rocker, a table with a mirror, and a rush-seated stool. Fringed lamps and lace curtains and other accents add a touch of romance to all the rooms. Rates: $59 to $109 double.

Harrisville Squires Inn, Keene Road, Harrisville (☎ 603/827-3925), is located on a quiet, little-traveled road in a wooded valley in a mid-19th century homestead. The owners, Pat and Doug McCarthy, have been hosting guests for the last 14 years. The house is set on 50 acres, with more than 6 miles of ski trails across 30 acres. Since Doug runs Monadnock bike touring, he's really familiar with all the back roads. There are five rooms, all furnished in a country style with iron and brass beds with quilts, wing and Windsor chairs, acorn chests, and wicker or oak furniture. Room 3 has a Jacuzzi, and the bedroom has been sponge painted and furnished with a high-back cottage bed, a wicker rocker, and an oak dresser. The garden contains a tiny meditation garden by the pond-fountain. Breakfast is served in an attractive dining room, where baskets hang from the beams and French doors lead out to a tree-shaded area with tables. Facilities include 30 acres of ski trails and a store, which sells dried-flower arrangements, stained glass, and wooden bowls that Pat has made. Rates: $80 to $90.

PETERBOROUGH & DUBLIN DINING

Latacarta, 6 School St., Peterborough (☎ 603/924-6878), occupies an old movie theater.

The restaurant decor is simple: crisp white tablecloths and kitchen chairs set against peachy–terra-cotta-colored walls hung with choice Japanese kimonos. The food is prepared with spiritual consciousness and is primarily Japanese inspired. You can begin with gyoza or nori rolls (gyoza are dumplings filled with meat or shrimp; nori rolls are sushi-like) along with a sea chowder filled with fresh fish. Ginger chicken over linguini or salmon in a creamy dill sauce are among the main courses, but the signature dish is the Latacarta dinner—a stuffed artichoke steamed with garlic tofu and basil filling and served with zucchini and summer squash that has been simmered with soy sauce and sherry. Prices range from $16 to $19. Open Monday to Friday from noon to 2pm, Monday to Thursday from 5 to 8:30pm, Friday and Saturday from 5 to 9pm.

Del Rossis Trattoria, Route 137 at Route 101, Dublin (☎ 603/563-7195), is a fun place to dine especially if you like bluegrass. Some of the best bluegrass artists, like Kate Campbell, appear in the back room. The smaller dining rooms are more formal with their beamed ceilings, wide-board floors, and

Windsor chairs. To start, try the polenta Gorgonzola, a perfect combination of flavors topped with a little marinara sauce. Or there's the very popular cream of garlic soup. The traditional Italian fare includes a number of refreshing dishes—for example, try Butter's chicken, a Ligurian dish that features breast of chicken sautéed with pancetta, onion, mushroom, garlic, fresh sage, red pepper, and pine nuts; simmered with Chianti and tomato; and finished with a splash of balsamic vinegar. Another unusual dish is the Sicilian-style pork, which is breaded with a special mixture and finished with lemon. Prices range from $9 to 18. The owners operate a store upstairs that sells acoustic stringed instruments. Saturday night there is always entertainment. Open Monday to Friday from 11:30am to 2pm, Saturday 11:30am to 5pm, and Sunday 4 to 8pm. Closed Wednesday in winter.

Aesop's Tables, 12 Depot St., Peterborough (☎ 603/924-1612), occupies a corner of the Toadstool Bookstore. The main staples are sandwiches—turkey, egg, and BLTs, all under $5, plus soup, pastries, and breads. Open Monday to Saturday from 7am to 5pm.

Twelve Pines, 11 School St., Peterborough (☎ 603/924-6140), has great takeout—salads, pizza, soups, and sandwiches. Prices run from $2 to $5.50. Open Monday to Friday from 8am to 7pm; Saturday and Sunday from 9am to 4pm.

ALONG THE CONNECTICUT RIVER FROM HINSDALE TO WALPOLE

Keene is the major town of the Monadnock region. Here art lovers will want to visit the **Thorne-Sagendorph Art Gallery** at Keene State College, 229 Main St. (on Wyman Way; ☎ 603/358-2720). The collection focuses on local and regional artists and contains works by Alexander James, Richard Meryman, Joseph Lindon Smith, and Barry Faulkner. Contemporary artists include Robert Mapplethorpe, Vargian Bogosian, and Jules Olitski. From Keene, it's easy to reach **Pisgah State Park** and the small towns that cluster around its perimeter from West Swanzey to Winchester via Route 10. From Winchester, Route 119 will bring you to the river town of Hinsdale and then north through the mountains to Chesterfield and eventually via Route 12 to Walpole. Chocolate lovers make this little village a destination just to visit **Burdick Chocolates,** where customers can select their own choices and have them put into the hallmark cigar box that is then tied with a bow and closed with a wax seal. They are absolutely wonderful chocolates. Or you can relax at one of the tables and enjoy a cappuccino or chocolate espresso and a pastry.

CHESTERFIELD & WALPOLE LODGING
The Chesterfield Inn, Route 9 (P. O. Box 155), Chesterfield, NH 03443 (☎ 603/256-3211), is an exquisitely decorated lodging that offers 13 guest rooms, all with private baths, telephones, and TVs (8 have fireplaces). Rooms in the new Johanna Wetherby Building have private garden patios. Nine rooms in the restored 1787 farmhouse/carriage house have great character, with their handsome beams and many fine antiques. Each room is tastefully decorated.

In Room 14 you'll find a round Empire-style table, a scallop-shell secretary, and attractive oak side tables, along with wing chairs, all set against a pretty blue-and-rose floral wallpaper. Carved Victorian love seats, desks with decorative inlays, and drop-leaf tables are just some of the fetching antiques that are found throughout. A full breakfast is served. The dining room serves American/continental cuisine—for example, duck with raspberry sauce, grilled gingered swordfish, lamb shanks with rosemary and zinfandel. Prices run $16 to $22; open daily from 5:30 to 9pm. Rates: Summer, $135 to $160, suites $175; winter, $135 to $185, suites $190 suites.

The Josiah Bellows House, Walpole, NH 03608 (☎ 603/756-4250), occupies a lovely 1813 house that has a back flagstone patio and gardens that offer views of wooded hills. It's a center-hall building with large rooms and some very distinctive interior details—Belgian blue tiles around the fireplace in the parlor and wood floors with patterned borders crafted from maple and cherry. The four rooms (two sharing a bath) are furnished with iron and brass beds, rugs spread over wide-board floors, and pieces such as marble-top dressers and Victorian button chairs. One room features a half-poster and an Empire chest. Breakfast is served at a lace-covered table in a room that is flooded with light from the Palladian-style windows. Guests have the use of two parlors furnished with a sofa and armchairs. Rates: $70 to $80.

AREA DINING

The best dining is to be found across the river in Bellows Falls, Vermont, at **Leslie's** in Rockingham (☎ 802/463-4929). There's a series of country dining rooms furnished with polished wood tables; in summer an outdoor dining area is open. Ingredients are fresh, and the food is tasty and reasonably priced. There might be salmon in a Beaujolais cream sauce or Boston scrod baked in wine and lemon, plus meat dishes like veal marsala or roast duckling served with raspberry Chambord sauce. Prices range from $13 to $17. Service is casual. Open Wednesday to Friday 11:30am to 1:30pm and Wednesday to Monday 5:30 to 9pm.

Also on the Vermont side in Saxtons River is **Averill's**, Route 121 (☎ 802/869-2327). It has a tavern on one side and a more formal dining room on the other. The food is good, and you can expect to find daily specials such as salmon with a Caribbean sauce along with steaks and other items. The Cuban bread is a great start to the meal. Prices run from $14 to $18. Open summer, Monday to Saturday from 5:30 to 10pm; winter, Wednesday to Saturday from 5 to 9pm.

Monadnock
Special & Recreational Activities

Biking: Although the terrain is somewhat hilly, it's a scenic region to bike. For information and tours contact, **Monadnock Bicycle Touring Center** (☎ 603/827-3925); rentals are available at **Spokes and Slopes** (☎ 603/924-9961). Temple Mountain is the place for mountain biking.

Cross-Country Skiing: Several of the inns listed (like the Fitzwilliam) have facilities, or you can head into **Monadnock State Park** (☎ 603/532-8862),

Greenfield State Park (☎ 603/547-3373), or to the facility at **Temple Mountain. Road's End Farm,** Jackson Hill Road, Chesterfield (☎ 603/363-4703), also has 32 kilometers of trails.

Fishing: Licenses are available from town clerks and sporting goods stores. Nonresidents can contact the **New Hampshire Fish and Game Department,** 34 Bridge St., Concord, NH 03301 (☎ 603/271-3421).

Golf: Bretwood Golf Course, East Surry Road, Keene (☎ 603/352-7626); **Keene Country Club,** R.R. 2, Box 264, Keene (☎ 603/352-9722); **Monadnock Country Club,** Peterborough (☎ 603/924-7769); and **Angus Lea** in Hillsborough (☎ 603/464-5404) are places to try.

Hiking: There are plenty of hiking trails at **Rhododendron State Park** and other reserves. **Grand Monadnock** itself is the most-climbed mountain in the country. A round-trip hike to the top up the popular **White Dot Trail,** which begins at the entrance to Monadnock State Park in Jaffrey, will take about 3 hours. For information about the five main trails, call **Monadnock State Park** at ☎ 603/532-8862.

At **Crotched Mountain** there are three trails to the summit. The sign-posted **Bennington Trail** starts 3 miles north of Greenfield on Route 31 and is probably the easiest to find. The **Francestown Trail** begins at the base of what was Crotched Mountain ski area. For additional information, call the **New Hampshire Division of Forests and Lands** (☎ 603/271-2214).

Other trails and hikes include the **Monadnock-Sunapee Greenway Trail** and several in **Shieling State Forest.** From **Miller State Park** you can also hike to the summit of **Mount Pack Monadnock.** For additional hiking, see "State Parks."

Skiing: Day and night Alpine, cross-country, and snowboarding can be enjoyed at **Temple Mountain,** off Route 101, Peterborough (☎ 603/924-6949), which has a quadruple–chairlift, snow-making capability, night skiing, and 35 miles of cross-country skiing.

State Parks: Rhododendron State Park, off Route 119, 2½ miles west of Fitzwilliam (☎ 603/532-8862), consists of 16 acres where you can stroll under these wild majestic shrubs (some as tall as 20 feet). The park itself is 494 acres and offers fine views of Monadnock. Visit in July for the rhododendrons in bloom. **Annett State Park,** Cathedral Road, off Route 119, Rindge (☎ 603/532-8862), is a 1,336-acre park for hiking and picnicking. **Monadnock State Park,** off Route 124, 4 miles west of Jaffrey (☎ 603/532-8862), has 40 miles of trails. It provides the easiest access to the summit of Grand Monadnock. The park offers hiking, camping, and ski touring.

Fox State Forest, School Street, Hillsborough, 2½ miles from Hillsboro Center (☎ 603/464-3453), is a 1,432-acre forest with 20 miles of trails and roads. **Miller State Park,** off Route 101, 3 miles east of Peterborough (☎ 603/924-3672), provides access to the summit of Pack Monadnock Mountain (2,290 ft.). Named after General James Miller, hero of the Battle of Lundy's Lane in the War of 1812 at Niagara, this park offers picnicking, hiking trails, and great views of the Green Mountains.

Wapack National Wildlife Refuge, off Route 101 at Miller State Park, Peterborough, is a wilderness area of bog, rock, and swamp on Pack Monadnock Mountain. It's great for hawk spotting and other wildlife observation and has ski touring. **Pisgah State Park,** Chesterfield, Hinsdale, Winchester, off Route 63 or Route 119 (☎ 603/239-8153), affords 13,000 acres of wilderness for hiking, hunting, and fishing, and ski touring and snow-mobiling in winter. **Greenfield State Park,** off Route 136 (☎ 603/547-3373 or 603/547-3497) shelters Otter Lake for swimming. Picnicking and camping are also available in this 400-acre park.

Tennis: Courts are available at the **Inn at Crotched Mountain** in Francestown (☎ 603/588-6840) and at **Monadnock Country Club** in Peterborough (☎ 603/924-7769).

Laconia & the Lakes of New Hampshire

Laconia, Wolfeboro & Lake Winnipesaukee ◆
Holderness & Squam Lake ◆ *Plymouth, Rumney, Bristol &*
Newfound Lake ◆ *Moultonborough, Center Sandwich, the*
Tamworths, Chocorua, Silver Lake & Eaton Center ◆
Loudon & Canterbury

Distance in miles from Boston: Laconia, 95; Holderness and Moultonborough, 125; Wolfeboro, 100.

Estimated driving times: 2 hours to Laconia; 2½ hours to Holderness and Moultonborough; 2 hours to Wolfeboro.

◄○►◄○►◄○►◄○►◄○►

Driving: I-93 to Exit 20 to Route 11/3 into Laconia; I-93 to Exit 24 for Holderness; I-93 to the Everett Turnpike, then Exit 7 to 101 east, and then the first exit to the 28 bypass north to Wolfeboro. Or for Wolfeboro you can take I-95 to Route 16 north to Route 109 to Route 28. To Loudon take I-93 north to Concord. Then take Exit 3 to Route 106 north.

Further Information: For more information, **Laconia Chamber of Commerce** (☎ 800/531-2347); **Wolfeboro Chamber of Commerce**, P.O. Box 547, Wolfeboro, NH 03864 (☎ 603/569-2200); **Meredith Chamber of Commerce**, Route 3, P.O. Box 732, Meredith, NH 03253 (☎ 603/279-6121); **Plymouth Chamber of Commerce**, P.O. Box 65, Plymouth, NH 03264 (☎ 603/536-1001); **Newfound Region of Commerce**, P.O. Box 454, Bristol, NH 03222 (☎ 603/744-2150).

◄○►◄○►◄○►◄○►◄○►

The focal point on any map that you look at of this region is quite obviously Lake Winnipesaukee with its irregular cut and crevassed shape. And it makes an impression in reality—a large 23-mile-long-by-14-mile-wide lake divided into a series of bays at one end; dotted with close to 30 islands; and ringed with inlets, coves, promontories, and other natural features. Sadly, it has paid for its beauty with overdevelopment, but that doesn't mean that there aren't loads of places along its shores where you can have a glorious time picnicking and contemplating and just plain enjoying the dancing sparkle of the sun on water. And there are also lesser trafficked lakes to meander around—but not

---

Events & Festivals to Plan Your Trip Around

July: New Hampshire Music Festival is a 6-week series of symphonic and chamber concerts given at different venues in New London and Plymouth. For information, call ☎ 603/524-1000.

Antique Classic Boat Show, Weirs Beach, is when more than 100 shining and silky smooth antique wooden boats gather at the public docks to be judged in a competition. A nostalgic event.

---

before you've seen the big one, as they say. Once you've done that, you can seek out your own golden pond. In addition to the lakes, weekenders can also take the back roads to the strings of somnolent historic villages that fan out west along the Baker River Valley and east into the foothills of the White Mountains, especially alluring during foliage season.

Laconia is the major town in the region. It's not much to look at, except for the library and the riverfront, but it does sit between Lake Winnisquam and Lake Winnipesaukee, affording access to both as well as to the whole region of lakes and mountains. From Laconia, you can travel around the southern tip of Lake Winnipesaukee to Wolfeboro on the eastern shore via routes 11 and 28. Or you can travel north on Route 3 to Meredith and Holderness on Squam Lake. From here, you can turn west to Plymouth, Rumney, and Bristol and the unspoiled Newfound Lake, or you can turn east at Meredith to Center Harbor, sandwiched between Squam Lake and the northern shores of Lake Winnipesaukee. Beyond Center Harbor along Route 25 lie the small towns of Moultonborough and Center Sandwich, and beyond them the Tamworths, Chocorua, Silver Lake, and Eaton Center, which is located only a short distance away from Conway, gateway to the White Mountains. Laconia is also close to one of the area's most fascinating attractions, the **Canterbury Shaker Village,** which can be reached via Route 106 south to Belmont and Shaker Road.

LACONIA, WOLFEBORO & LAKE WINNIPESAUKEE

The Winnipesaukee River flows around downtown **Laconia** and adds some interest to the town. You can stroll and browse in the shops along Main Street in Laconia, but by and large you should save the town for a rainy day when you feel like going to the cinema or dropping into the handsome library. In good weather, weekenders in their right minds will only want to find a marvelous bed-and-breakfast inn with a hammock by the lake and settle in for some R & R and water sports.

In any tour around the lake, it's worth stopping in **Wolfeboro** to bask at the side of the lake on one of the many restaurant waterfront decks. The town also a vital arts and crafts community, and you'll find some worthwhile browsing at galleries, craft, and gift stores on North Main Street. Off Main Street, you may want to seek out custom-cabinetmaker **England's** at 3 Depot Rd. (☎ 603/569-9241), or the **Blue Shutter Gallery** at 19 Lehner St. (☎ 603/569-3372). Stop at **Hampshire Pewter,** 43 Mill St. and 7 North Main St. (☎ 603/569-4944), which offers tours of its pewter-making facility from Memorial Day to Labor Day on weekdays only. The **League of New Hampshire Craftsmen** store is in Wolfeboro Falls (☎ 603/569-3309).

Better yet, take Route 28 round to **Wentworth State Park** (☎ 603/569-3699) where there is a swimming beach. The park is so named, by the way, because royal governor Wentworth built his summer home here. Wolfeboro also has some evening theater provided by the **Village Players** (☎ 603/569-5726).

North of Wolfeboro you'll discover lovely **Mirror Lake** and the **Libby Museum of Natural History.** Off Route 109 you can stop to see the **Castle in the Clouds,** Route 171, Moultonborough (☎ 603/476-2352), a major regional landmark. The mansion is home to the Castle Springs Brewing Company and is also the source of Castle Springs water. There are great views of Lake Winnipesaukee from the grounds, and you can picnic, hike, or ride horseback ($25 per hour) here. Open weekends from May 10 and daily from June 7 to Labor Day, from 9am to 5pm; Labor Day to October 19, from 9 am to 4pm. Admission to the grounds is $4 for adults, free for children 10 and under; admission including the castle tour is $10 for adults, $7 for students.

Back on Route 109 and farther on around the lake, the **Marcus Wildlife Sanctuary** is just outside Moultonborough. The drive down Moultonborough Neck, which extends from Moultonborough into the lake area, will bring you to a marshland at Langley Cove. From Moultonborough, Route 25 coasts into Center Harbor and then to Meredith. Center Harbor was the first tourist destination to develop on the lake, when passengers having crossed from Weirs Beach began to stop overnight on the way to the White Mountains before boarding the stage. Starting in the 1860s, other towns also entered the tourist business.

Before Route 25 enters Meredith, you can turn off to **Stonedam Island Natural Area,** a 112-acre reserve that has several loop trails and a picnicking area. For more information, write to Lakes Region Conservation Trust, P.O. Box 1097, Meredith, NH 03252 or call ☎ 603/279-3246. Meredith is a busy commercial center with plenty of shopping centered in **Mill Falls Marketplace,** plus some minor attractions like the **Historical Society Museum** (☎ 603/279-1190), open Wednesday to Saturday from noon to 5pm. You can take a ride on the **Winnipesaukee-Pemigewasset Valley Railroad,** which departs from South Main in Meredith for Weirs Beach, taking you on a trip along the lake.

From Meredith, Route 3 will bring you to Weirs Beach and Route 11B round to Belknap Point. From Weirs Beach you can **cruise** aboard the M/S *Mt. is Washington II* (☎ 603/366-5531). The original M/S *Mount Washington* was a wooden side-wheeler that was built by the Boston and Maine Railroad Company in 1872 to ferry passengers and cargo from Weirs Beach to the other side of the lake. Back then, the lake was filled with steamer traffic and folks on their way to the White Mountains. At Weirs Beach there was even a grand

The White Mountains & Lake Country

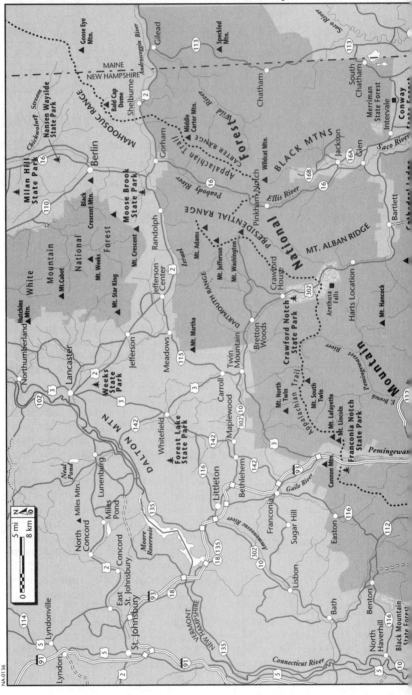

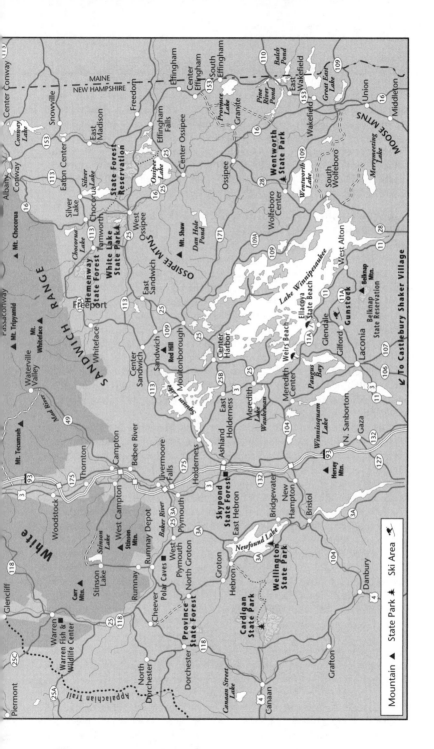

Mountain ▲ State Park ≜ Ski Area ⛷

299

hotel, which attracted many summering people from Boston until it burned in 1924. The M/S *Mt Washington* was the king of the steamers and remained so until it caught fire in 1939. It was replaced by a Champlain vessel, which was launched in 1940. Over the years, this vessel has seen many modifications and now sails under the grand title M/S, but it still delivers a lake experience reminiscent of the earlier days, without the steam and coal-speck-filled smoke. Fittingly, Weirs Beach is also home to the **Antique and Classic Boat Museum**, Route 11B, at the Weirs Bridge (☎ 603/524-8989), where you can wax nostalgic over these varnished wooden beauties and the social life that surrounded them.

LODGING & DINING IN LACONIA, WOLFEBORO & AROUND LAKE WINNIPESAUKEE

The **Ferry Point House**, 100 Lower Bay Rd., Sanbornton, NH 03269 (☎ 603/524-0087), is a pretty Victorian overlooking Lake Winnisquam across the road. Guests return here year after year to enjoy the convivial company of innkeepers Joe and Diane Damato and their family, Eric and Danielle, and to cross the road to loll in the hammock or the gazebo and to listen to the lap of the lake. On cold evenings and in winter, guests can sit in the comfortable living room, which has a dramatic fireplace made of all kinds of stone—mica, quartz, and schist. There are seven guest rooms, all with private baths and all attractively decorated in country style with high-back oak beds or sleigh beds or similar pieces. A terrific breakfast is served at a large table in the dining room. Fruit quiche might be featured one morning and stuffed French toast another. Afternoon refreshments are also served. Open May to the end of October. Rates: $85 to $105.

The **Wolfeboro Inn**, 90 N. Main St., Wolfeboro, NH 03894 (☎ 603/569-3016), is a larger accommodation than most in this book. It's in the center of Wolfeboro and has 44 modern rooms decorated with antique reproductions and equipped with telephones and TVs in cabinets. Some rooms have fireplaces. Pewter tankards hang from the beams in the Wolfe's Tavern, which has more than 50 international beers available and also offers outdoor dining on the brick patio. The dining room serves traditional New England dishes as well as more contemporary American fare. At the end of the long narrow garden, the gazebo affords views of Lake Winnipesaukee. Rates: $119 to $179.

The **Red Hill Inn**, Route 25B (R.F.D. 1, Box 99M), Center Harbor, NH 03226 (☎ 603/279-7001), sits on a hill on 60 acres with a distant view of Squam Lake. It's a very appealing inn, with sweeping views of lawn, meadow, and the White Mountains, and in the winter, cross-country ski trails and sleigh rides add to the fun. The 1850s red brick farmhouse at the center of the property contains the dining room and sitting rooms. The 25 rooms in five different buildings have been tastefully decorated; all have telephones and some have fireplaces and balconies, too. Passaconaway, for example, has a carved mahogany bed combined with an oak dresser and two wing chairs arranged in front of the wood-burning fireplace. Kancamagus features a bold floral wallpaper plus a pineapple bed, a desk, and two wing chairs. Some accommodations are located in cottages. The Ossipee has a double whirlpool and a Franklin stove. Three out of the four rooms in the farmhouse also have double whirlpool tubs and Franklin fireplaces for extra romance. A favorite gathering place is the Runabout Lounge, where a 1948 Chriscraft Sportsman à la *On Golden*

Pond serves as the bar, and the walls are lined with owner Don Leavitt's collection of license plates. There are also spacious, comfortable sitting rooms warmed by fires. The dining room emphasizes traditional American/continental cuisine—duck à l'orange, filet mignon wrapped in bacon, and chicken Shaker style (made with Vermont apples in a light cider cream sauce). Prices range from $14 to $23. Open Monday to Saturday noon to 2pm, Sunday 11am to 2pm, and daily from 5pm. The inn is actually about 1¼ miles along Route 3 from Meredith. There are 9 miles of cross-country ski trails on the property. Rates: late May to October and February, $115 to $175; March to late May and November to January, $88 to $134. Special packages available.

Hickory Stick Farm, 60 Bean Hill Rd., Belmont (☎ 603/524-3333), is located out in the country and offers country charms—slate floors, colonial furnishings, fireplaces, and a screened gazebo dining area. It's known for the duckling, but it also offers a full range of dishes. Among desserts, the favorite is the frozen hickory stick, consisting of vanilla ice cream rolled in chocolate cookie crumbs and served on hot fudge and garnished with toasted almonds. Prices range from $10.95 to $18.95. Open Memorial Day to Columbus Day, Tuesday to Sunday from 5 to 8pm; weekends only off-season. Call for directions.

It's strange to find **Las Piñatas**, 9 Veterans Sq. (☎ 603/528-1405), in Laconia—and indeed it was established only because a member of the Lezama family got to know the area as an exchange student. The restaurant is located in the old Boston and Maine Railroad Station, to which an outside deck has been added. The atmosphere is established by photographs, piñatas, and most of all by the music—old favorites like Los Tres Diamantes, Los Panchos, and Jorge Negrete. The food is good—the recipes are traditional and as authentic as possible. Try the chilies rellenos, the fajitas, or the enchiladas de mole. Prices range around $8 to $11. Open Monday to Thursday from 11am to 2pm and 5 to 9pm, Friday and Saturday from 5 to 9:30pm, Sunday from 5 to 8pm. Reduced hours in winter, and closed Tuesday.

Lake Winnipesaukee
Special & Recreational Activities in Weirs Beach, Meredith, Center Harbor & Wolfeboro

Boating: Rentals are available from **Thursdayton's Marina** on Route 3 (☎ 603/366-4811) and from **Winnisquam Marina** (☎ 603/524-8380) at the bridge on Route 3 in Winnisquam.

Birding: **Markus Wildlife Sanctuary**, Lee's Mill Road in Moultonborough, is the headquarters of the Loon Preservation Committee started by the state Audubon society. The sanctuary sits on 200 acres that include 3,000 feet of lakefront, and the trails lead through woodland and marsh to the lakeshore. The center is open July through Columbus Day, daily from 9am to 5pm.

Canoeing/Kayaking: For rentals, go to **Wild Meadow**, Route 25, Center Harbor (☎ 603/253-7536).

Cruises: The M/S *Mount Washington* (☎ 603/366-BOAT) cruises from **Weirs Beach** and **Wolfeboro**. For 2½-hour lunch and Sunday brunch cruises, prices are $15 for adults and $7 for children 4 to 12; dinner/dance cruises range from $29 to $39, depending on day. The much smaller Doris E cruises from docks on Route 3 in **Meredith**. They both operate from May to October.

Golf: Courses in the area are **Highland Links Golf Course**, Mount Prospect Road off Route 175, Holderness (☎ 603/536-3452); **Kingswood Golf Course**, Wolfeboro (☎ 603/569-3569); the golf course at **Kona Mansion Inn**, Moultonborough (☎ 603/253-4900); **Laconia Golf Course** (☎ 603/ 524-1274); **Oak Hill Golf Course** (☎ 603/279-4438); **Waukewan Golf Course**, Waukewan Road, Meredith (☎ 603/279-6661).

Parasailing: Contact **Weirs Parasail** (☎ 603/366-7723) for reservations.

State Parks: Ellacoya State Park, Route 11 (☎ 603/293-7821) is on the edge of Lake Winnipesaukee.

HOLDERNESS & SQUAM LAKE

Everyone thinks of *On Golden Pond* when **Squam Lake** is mentioned—the images of Jane Fonda and Henry Fonda playing themselves in this romantic, melancholic movie come to mind. On any weekend, you'll want to take a boat of some sort out on the lake. Back on land, you'll also want to hike the nature trails that wind through the 200-acre property of the **Science Center of New Hampshire at Squam Lake**, Route 113, Holderness (☎ 603/968-7194). The center has exhibits featuring local ecology and fauna, and along the nature trails you might spot deer, fox, otters, hawks, and even a bald eagle if you're really lucky. One trail leads to the summit of Mount Fayal for grand views of Squam Lake. Open May 1 to November 1; July to August, daily from 9:30am to 4:30pm; other months, Monday to Friday from 9:30am to 4:30pm and Saturday and Sunday from 1 to 4pm. Admission is $4 for adults, $2 for children.

From **Holderness**, Route 113 travels around the shore of Squam Lake past West Rattlesnake Mountain Natural Area and the University of New Hampshire's **Five Finger Point Natural Area.** Five Finger Point is one of the most scenic spots on the lake. The 71 acres separate Rattlesnake Cove from True Cove. The trail that loops around the peninsula goes past a swamp; it's best reached by boat, but it can be accessed by a 1-mile trail off Pinehurst Road, just off Route 113. For more information and directions, contact **Squam Lakes Association**, P.O. Box 204, Holderness, NH 03245 (☎ 603/968-7336).

From Center Sandwich you can turn back toward the lake and take Bean Road to Sandwich Landing and then continue on it into Center Harbor. The **Proctor Wildlife Sanctuary** off Center Harbor Neck Road is a pleasant woodland stop. You can also take Route 25B around to the **Chamberlain-Reynolds Memorial Forest**, one of the quietest, least used areas on the lakeshore at Dog Cove. Return via Route 3/25 to Holderness.

HOLDERNESS & SQUAM LAKE LODGING & DINING

The Manor on Golden Pond, Route 3, Box T, Holderness, NH 03245 (☎ 603/968-3348), is a super-luxurious inn, appropriately named, and operated by very hospitable owner-innkeepers David and Bambi Arnold. A gracious tree-lined drive leads to the 1904 residence that is set on 14 acres high above Lake Squam. Interiors are richly decorated. Everywhere you look, there are fine fabrics and beautiful objects. In the lobby-foyer, the carved mantel above the handsome marble fireplace supports two porcelain roosters and a lovely basket of dried flowers. Beyond is the luxuriant sitting room. In addition to the Three Cocks Pub, where a grand piano supports a cock and a hen, there are several formal dining rooms with tables covered with burgundy tablecloths with white overlays and graced with small silver candle-lamps, set against a background of rich wood paneling, gilt mirrors, and gilt-framed landscapes. Here you can enjoy a leisurely five-course dinner that is beautifully presented and served. The menu changes daily. Your meal might begin with a nori warp of sticky rice with cream cheese and cucumber, followed by a choice of teamed Prince Edward Island mussels in Thai green curry broth or chicken liver mousse pâté with toast and cornichons. A salad or soup follows. There will be three choices of main course—for example, pork tenderloin with mango salsa, blackened swordfish with fresh lime, or pesto-crusted organic chicken in Holland orange-pepper sauce. Four dessert selections might include banana caramel cake with banana chocolate chip ice cream or vanilla crème brûlée with berries. Prices range from a three-course meal for $38 to a five-course meal for $50. Open by reservation only, from 6:30 to 8pm.

There are 17 guest rooms in the main house and 4 in the carriage house. Ten have fireplaces, and some have private decks and/or double whirlpools. The rooms are named after English counties, and each incorporates lavish wallpapers, fabrics, and fanciful decorative accents. Dorset has a rich-looking red panel behind the bed and American painted side tables. A collection of musical instruments—clarinet, mandolin, and cornet—decorates the walls. Devon is decked out in blue and gold. Wellington proffers a double whirlpool and private deck plus a raised hearth. Some rooms are in the carriage house, and a few are in cottages. Dover is the only one down by the lake. A trellis of wisteria runs along one side of the house, and there's a nicely landscaped pool. Down at the lake there's a private beach, canoes, and paddleboats. A clay tennis court, a badminton court, and a croquet lawn are on the grounds. A full breakfast is served, and also a grand afternoon tea, using silver service and bone china. Rates: MAP $200 to $335 double.

The Pressed Petals Inn, Shepard Hill Road, Holderness, NH 03245 (☎ 603/968-4417), is a very fetching place, run by delightful hostess Ellie Dewey. It's an old farmhouse that has been transformed into a light, airy, and pretty inn. There are eight rooms all with private baths. Each has been named after a different flower, which inspires the decor. The candlelight breakfasts, served in a spacious dining room at separate tables, are extra special. Ellie can really cook, and whatever she makes will be delectable. Afternoon tea is also served, and there are hors d'oeuvres on Saturday evenings. Rates: $109 to $128.

Inn at Bay Point, Route 3, Meredith, NH 03253 (☎ 603/279-7006), is located in the busy hub of Meredith, directly on the lake with most of the 24 rooms facing the water. They are furnished with antique reproductions and contain all the modern amenities—TVs, two phones, and hair dryers. Some have balconies, gas fireplaces, and Jacuzzis. There is a small lawn alongside the lake and a private dock. Facilities include the Bar & Boathouse Grill which affords great water views and offers a weekly changing menu featuring such items as soft shelled crabs with mustard greens and aioli. Rates: late October to late May, $79 to $245; late May to late October, $89 to $259.

Squam Lake
Special & Recreational Activities

Boating: Canoes, kayaks, sunfish, and Boston whalers are available from **Squam Boat Livery,** Route 3 at the bridge, Holderness (☎ 603/968-7721). Daily rates range from $40 to $125.

Cruises: This is the place to do your 2-hour Golden Pond tour. Call ☎ 603/279-4405 to reserve a place aboard the **pontoon boat** that takes you to the movie's Thayer cottage and Purgatory Cove, and to Church Island, while the captain gives you plenty of loon lore. Boats leave daily from Memorial Day through foliage season from Squam boat docks on Route 3 at the bridge in downtown Holderness. Tickets are $10 for adults, $5 for children.

Fishing: Fishing for salmon and lake trout can be enjoyed with **Squam Lakes Fishing Guide** (☎ 603/968-7577). The cost is $150 for one to three persons for 4 hours.

PLYMOUTH, RUMNEY, BRISTOL & NEWFOUND LAKE

From Holderness, Route 3/25 west runs along the northern shore of Little Squam Lake into Ashland, which has a couple of attractions for a rainy day unless you happen to be an enthusiastic historian. The **Pauline E. Glidden Museum** is a personal collection of toys displayed in five rooms in a historic home. Many of them are household or school related—stoves, laundry items, antique teddy bears, and dolls including classics like Shirley Temple and Little Orphan Annie. The **Whipple House Museum,** 4 Pleasant St., is the birthplace of Nobel Prize winner in medicine George Hoyt Whipple, who discovered a cure for pernicious anemia in the 1930s. Both are open July to August, Wednesday to Saturday from 1 to 4pm. Admission $1 for anyone 12 or over.

Route 3/25 will take you to Plymouth, which is the gateway town to the Polar Caves and the old historic and remote small towns along the Baker River Valley, notably the Rumneys. The **Polar Caves,** Route 25, Plymouth (☎ 603/536-1888), are so called because of the icy air that emanates from the ice caverns below the caves. The caves at the bottom of Haycock mountain, along the Pemigewasset River, are in a forested area that has been turned into a commercial recreational park complete with a "glacial boulder maze," petting animals, and trails. Open mid-May to mid-October, daily from 9am to 5pm. Admission $9 for adults, $4.50 for children 6 to 12.

Rumney is a historic valley town, which has changed hardly at all since the 19th century. Here, in this inspirational landscape of mountain pasture, river, and stream, Mary Baker Eddy, founder and organizer of the Christian Science Movement and one of the most remarkable women of the 19th century, spent her early years in two different homes in Rumney and North Groton. The headquarters for both sites is the **Mary Baker Eddy Historic Homes,** Stinson Lake Road, Rumney (☎ 603/786-9943). Mary Baker Eddy lived in North Groton (1855–60) and in Rumney (1860–62) during the pivotal period in her life: Her family took her son away from her, and her husband eloped with another woman. Both these events and her constant physical afflictions led her to try alternative therapies such as homeopathy, spiritualism, and hydrotherapy and eventually led her to develop the idea of Christian Science. The North Groton home is perched on the side of a small mountain in a lovely remote location. Open May 1 to October 31, Tuesday to Sunday. Free admission.

From Rumney depot you can loop back south to North Groton and Groton. Just outside Groton, off North Groton Road, is the **Sculptured Rocks Natural Area.** Here, trails lead down to the Cockermouth River where, beneath the shade trees, bathers can drop down from granite overhangs into a series of pothole pools created by waterborne stones and sediment during the last ice age. Their cries of excitement as they do so echo through the rocky canyon across the splashing falls.

Return to the Groton Road, which will bring you into Hebron. Naturalists will want to visit the **Hebron Marsh Wildlife Sanctuary** or take a short detour east of Hebron along the northern shores of Newfound Lake to the **Paradise Point Nature Center,** North Shore Road, Newfound Lake, Hebron (☎ 603/744-3516), which has some nature exhibits plus lakeshore trails. Then return to the West Shore Road of Newfound Lake and travel down to **Wellington State Park** and beach, off Route 3A (☎ 603/744-2197). Even though the beach gets crowded on weekends in summer, you can still find a secluded picnicking place on the fir-clad point. From here, West Shore Road will bring you into the little town of Bristol, and Route 104 will then take you back to Meredith and 3/25 to Holderness.

If you want to extend the trip, you can continue on to Franklin to the **replicated birthplace of Daniel Webster,** off Route 127 in Franklin (☎ 603/ 934-5057). (His actual home is a private residence along Route 3.) One of New Hampshire's dynamic personalities, Daniel Webster's (1782–1852) voice and energy still resonate in this part of New Hampshire where he was born, educated, and labored to save the Union. His tall, powerful frame and mane of jet black hair earned him the name "Black Dan," and in his time he was a folk hero whose presence and oratory were electrifying. This native son did remarkably well for a farm boy, rising to become congressional representative, senator, and secretary of state. Born in 1782 in Salisbury, New Hampshire, he always exhibited a combination of wit, laziness, and brilliance. It's said that on one occasion, he and his brother Ezekiel were taken to task by their father for not completing a particular chore. The father asked Ezekiel what he had been doing. "Nothing, sir," he replied. "Well, Daniel what have you been doing?" asked his father. "Helping Zeke, sir," came the quick reply. Locally he is held in high esteem for his defense of Dartmouth against government encroachment. Ever a diehard Federalist and staunch protector of the Union, he opposed states rights but supported the compromise of 1850, upholding the fugitive slave law "not as a Massachusetts man, nor as a northern man but as an American defender of the Constitution." For this he was denigrated by many, including John Quincy Adams who described Webster as a "gigantic intellect, envious temper, ravenous ambition, and rotten heart." From this verdict others demurred—Theodore Parker declared on Webster's death that even "the coal heavers and porters of London looked on him as one of the great forces of the globe: they recognized a native king." Here at his replicated home, you can see memorabilia of the life of this extraordinary man whose name is still used liberally in this region. Open mid-May to mid-October, daily from 9am until 5pm. Admission is $10 for adults, $4.50 for children 6 to 12.

NEWFOUND LAKE AREA LODGING & DINING

To reach **Cliff Lodge Country Dining and Tavern,** P.O. Box 199, Bristol (☎ 603/744-8660), you climb up a winding drive to the top of the knoll situated at the southern end of Newfound Lake. The main building is a turn-of-the-century structure that is now a country dining room plus a warm and inviting tavern complete with mahogany bar. The views from the dining room and from the outdoor dining brick courtyard of this less crowded lake are beautiful. The food is eclectic, to say the least, lurching from wiener schnitzel to pad thai to chicken Alfredo to cheese fondue, plus grilled and broiled fish and daily specials like pork tenderloin with a lemon ginger glaze. On cool nights there's a fire in the large stone fireplace. There are also seven seasonal cottages situated in the woods. They are rustic, but each has a kitchen and bathroom and deck. Open July to August, daily from 5 to 9pm, Sunday 9am to 12:30pm; in winter, Thursday to Monday from 5 to 9pm and Sunday 10:30am to 1:30pm.

MOULTONBOROUGH, CENTER SANDWICH, THE TAMWORTHS, CHOCORUA, SILVER LAKE & EATON CENTER

Beyond Center Harbor along Route 25 lie the small towns of Moultonborough and Center Sandwich, and beyond them the Tamworths, Chocorua, Silver Lake, and Eaton Center, which is located only a short distance away from Conway, gateway to the White Mountains.

Center Sandwich stands encircled by mountains. It has long been a favorite summer place and was a favorite haunt of sentimental poet John Greenleaf Whittier (1807–92). Today the main street is lined with many crafts stores, a development that was fostered back in the 1920s when Mr. and Mrs. J. Randolph Coolidge, who sold hand-crafted items made in Sandwich (baskets, woodenware, jewelry, and pewter) founded the Sandwich Home Industries.

A short distance away in North Sandwich, the **Alice Bemis Thompson Wildlife Refuge** consists of woodland, marsh, and brook and is a fine bird-spotting place, especially for warblers and marsh birds. It's also a likely place to spot some moose.

Route 25 skirts Ossipee Mountains to Tamworth that shelters a piece of theatrical history. **The Barnstormers** is one of the oldest professional summer theaters in the country. The company performs a series of comedies and mysteries in summer. For information, write the Barnstormers, Box 434, Tamworth, or call ☎ 603/323-8500.

AREA LODGING & DINING

Old Orchard Inn, Lee Road, Moultonborough, NH 03254 (☎ 603/476-5004), is a colonial-and-brick Georgian. The owners have traveled extensively, and many of the decorative objects reflect their experiences. Kilims, Russian dolls, and other objects d'art decorate the sitting room. The original part of the house dates to 1790, and the brick section to 1810–12. Rooms are attractively furnished. The Gray Room contains an oak bed covered with a richly colored Indian coverlet. In the Pink Room, the bed is piled high with pillows, while the Blue Room features a high-back oak bed with a lovely blue quilt. One room has a Jacuzzi. There is a sitting room and also a deck that has mountain views. Breakfast is included in the rates. Rates: $75 to $130.

The **Woodshed,** Lee's Mill Road, Moultonborough (☎ 603/476-2311), is an atmospheric dining room in a post-and-beam barn with a dining loft decorated with farm implements. It's a large enterprise, and sometimes the service can seem rushed, but it is a favorite of many locals and visitors including celebs. Your meal will start with a piping-hot loaf of bread served in a clay pot. The premier dish is the prime rib, supplemented by such fish as orange roughy and mahimahi, plus Cajun pork tenderloin with a Dijon-peppercorn sauce or barbecue ribs. Prices range from $13 to $19. Open Tuesday to Sunday from 5 to 9pm.

The **Tamworth Inn,** Tamworth, NH 03886 (☎ 603/323-7721), stands on 3 acres and has pastoral views, even though it's in the heart of this tiny village right across from one of the oldest running summer stock theaters in the country. There are 16 very nicely decorated rooms. Room 3, for example, has a Shaker canopied bed plus an acorn chest, loveseat, and pier mirror. Another room might have an iron-and-brass bed combined with wicker chairs and a painted dresser. Guests enjoy the comforts of the sitting room with its fireplace and the TV/VCR and the games in the library. The post-and-beam pub's ceilings are studded with antique sleighs. The beamed dining room serves traditional continental/American cuisine, featuring dishes such as roast leg of lamb with mint jelly or grilled salmon with a dill cream sauce. Prices range from $10 to $17. Facilities include an outdoor pool with a concrete apron where there are loungers. Rates: B&B, $105 to $130; MAP, $130 to $155.

Stafford's in the Field, off Route 113 between Chocorua and Tamworth (☎ 603/323-7766), is a large, rambling place set on 36 acres amid golden hayfields and woodlands. Here, you'll be welcomed by Ramona Stafford, a gracious hostess who is well known locally for the quality of her cuisine. The main building dates back to the 1700s. There are 13 guest rooms (7 sharing baths). Each has its own personality, and those extra touches like the stenciling were done by the sons of the family. Some rooms have wall-to-wall carpeting dressed with hooked rugs; others have braided rugs on wood floors. Rooms in the so-called L are special—one contains an iron four-poster draped with paisley fabric, two armchairs in front of the brick fireplace, and a pine desk. There are also three attractive cottages available, with fireplaces or wood-burning stoves. The library is a retreat for guests, along with the enclosed porch.

The dining room offers fine European and American cuisine prepared by Ramona. A five-course fixed-price dinner for $33 features main dishes such as cassoulet (the traditional French casserole of white beans, sausage, pork, and confit of duck), grilled salmon with chipotle aioli, or roast duck with black currant and roasted garlic sauce. Soup, salad, intermezzo, and dessert complete the meal. Depending on the season, soup could be mock turtle or Creole onion, while the dessert could be a rich peppermint angel food cake served with dark chocolate sauce, or tarte tatin. Guests who stay at the inn are treated to a superb breakfast that may have Southwestern or Mexican accents. Meals are served in a warm and welcoming country dining room that has a pressed tin ceiling and tables covered with floral cloths; it's warmed by a fire on cool days and decorated with antique butter molds and similar cooking artifacts. Open summer, Friday to Saturday from 6:30 to 8pm; otherwise, Tuesday to Sunday from 6 to 8:30pm. There's also a small pub with a carved boar's head above the bar. Rates: MAP mid-September to mid-October and Christmas to New Year, $170 to $250; off-season, $150 to $190.

Rockhouse Mountain Farm Inn, Eaton Center, NH 03832 (☎ 603/447-2880), is a working farm that occupies a lovely location among wooded hills and pastureland. The spirit of the place is still set by 83-year-old Libby, who began taking in guests 52 years ago. She still bakes the fresh-fruit pies that are served in the dining room. It's a great place to bring the kids. During the week, a variety of events are arranged—a canoe trip on Thursday, a picnic on Swift River, or a barbecue. A dinner of homemade breads and soups followed by beef stroganoff or curried lamb or a roast, accompanied by fresh vegetables from the garden, is served in an attractive dining room. Children have their own separate adjacent dining room. Rooms are simply decorated with floral wallpapers and furnished with beds with candlewick spreads, braided rugs, and pine furniture. Open mid-June to the end of October. Rates: MAP $62 to $70 per person.

Snowvillage Inn, Snowville, NH 03849 (☎ 603/447-2818), is a beautiful place that is a little off the beaten track, offering cross-country skiing and snowshoeing in winter. Situated on 10 acres, with Crystal Lake at the bottom of the road, the house affords wonderful views of Mount Washington and the Presidential Range. The house was originally built in 1915 by author Frank Simonds and later turned into an inn by an Austrian couple, which accounts for the traces of Austrian decor that still exist, most obviously the knotty pine Austrian-style chairs, the stenciling, and the large porcelain stove in the dining room. There are 18 attractive rooms. The Robert Frost Room has a pine bed with a tented treatment and two easy chairs from which you can relish the view. Short Stories boasts beams and pine furnishings. Four rooms are in the chimney house, which was built in the late 1980s. They share a large central sitting room with a brick fireplace. Here, Michener contains a canopied four-poster and two club chairs among its comforts, plus a wood-burning fireplace. There are also eight equally appealing rooms in the carriage house. The inn has 10 miles of cross-country trails plus snowshoeing trails, and in winter the fire in the brick hearth in the beamed sitting rooms welcomes visitors coming in from the outdoors. The dining room serves a classic menu with such dishes as duck à l'orange, poached salmon with ginger beurre blanc, or rack of lamb with herbes de Provence. Prices range from $16.50 to $24. Open summer, Wednesday to Monday from 5:30 to 9pm; closed Tuesday all year, and on Monday in winter. Rates: MAP, $139 to $229 double.

LOUDON & CANTERBURY

The outstanding attraction in the area is the **Canterbury Shaker Village,** 288 Shaker Rd., Canterbury (☎ 603/783-9511). It's worth a full day's exploration. From the very knowledgeable guides, you will really learn something about the philosophy and way of life of the Shakers, a once-successful Utopian group, who practiced equality of the sexes, common ownership of goods, celibacy, and pacifism. The village is a serene and beautiful spot, surrounded by meadows and woods and mountains—a perfect place for what the Shakers conceived as a heaven on earth. This particular community was founded in the 1780s, sixth of the 19 Shaker communities that were established in North America. The tour begins at the Gateway to the World, where the community connected to the larger world. The Shakers did not shun the world—they sold their seeds, medicines, tools, and furniture to the outside world. In fact, they welcomed people and took in orphans, whom they educated for free.

The Shakers were a splinter Quaker group, started in England and brought to America by Mother Ann Lee, who arrived in 1774 and established the communities that stretched from the east to Kentucky and Tennessee. This particular community began on the Witcher family farm in 1792 with 48 believers. At its height, around the time of the Civil War, there were 300 members working and living on what was then a 4,000 acre farm. After the war, urban growth and industrialization destroyed the basis for the communities, and they went into steady decline. By 1953, only 13 sisters were living here, and the last Shaker member here died in 1992.

There are 25 buildings to see. Highlights include the Meeting House, dating to 1792, where the Shakers entered through separate doors, brothers on the left and sisters on the right, and where they sang and danced in worship. The women worked in the Sisters Shop, which shows how extremely organized and efficient they were. The laundry was also very streamlined—in fact, it was the Shakers who devised the first washing machines. The one-room school house was originally built for Shaker children, with boys attending during the winter and girls during the summer, but eventually local children attended too.

Workshops are held throughout the summer in basket weaving, broom making, oval box making, and other crafts. There's an excellent selection of fine-quality Shaker items in the store. Two restaurants are on the property: the Creamery, for lunch or for a candlelit Shaker dinner, and the Summer Kitchen, which offers soups, sandwiches, and similar snacks. The restaurants are open April to December; May through October, daily for lunch and Friday and

Saturday for dinner; lunch only on weekends in April, November, and December. The village is open May to October, daily from 10am to 5pm; April, November, and December, Friday to Sunday only. Admission is $8.

In dramatic contrast, the other big attraction in this area is the **New Hampshire International Speedway** (☎ 603/783-4961) at Loudon. The season gets going in April, swinging into full gear in summer with car and motorcycle racing every weekend. Tickets range from $10 to $30, depending on the event.

LOUDON LODGING

Lovejoy Farm, 268 Lovejoy Rd., Loudon, NH 03301 (☎ 603/783-4007), is a 1790 farmhouse set on 12 acres where Art Monty still raises sheep and pigs. It has seven very comfortable rooms furnished with antiques. Two suites have fireplaces. Some, like the Lovejoy, which is the largest, have wood-burning fireplaces. Each has been decorated with an eye for color and style. One room has a brass bed set against mustard-colored walls that are the backdrop for a cherry chest and desk and an easy chair. Four spacious rooms are in the carriage house. Art seems to have a passion for elephants, and they make many appearances in the decor. The kitchen, in which cooking is done on a wood-burning stove, radiates warmth and bonhomie with its hanging copper pots, herbs, and baskets. A full breakfast, featuring delights such as the Lovejoy casserole of eggs with three cheeses, ham, onion, peppers and home fries, is served in a dining room in front of the fire on chilly days. A brick patio set with umbrella tables is a lovely spot to sit and look out at the meadows. There are cross-country ski trails, too. Rates: $79 to $87.

Wyman Farm, 22 Wyman Rd., Loudon, NH 03301 (☎ 603/783-4467), is a beautifully situated farmhouse on 55 acres, operated by very warm and hospitable owners. Guests are catered to in every way to ensure that their particular personal needs are met, even to the point of placing books that the hostess believes return visitors will enjoy in their rooms. There are only three rooms, each furnished with antiques. The largest has a comfortable sitting room with a decorative fireplace, and the bedroom contains a serpentine canopied bed, two wing chairs, and a pine chest on good rugs. One room has a private entrance. Breakfast brings a spread of fresh fruit (kiwi, melon, oranges, bananas, and blueberries) plus yogurt and cooked-to-order dishes of scrambled eggs with terrific hickory-smoked bacon. The setting, with its mountain views, is beautiful, and guests can enjoy it all from the screened gazebo furnished with Victorian wicker sofa and chairs. Rates: $60 to $90.

The White Mountains

Lincoln, Woodstock, the Waterville Valley &
the Kancamagus Highway ◆ *The Conways, Jackson (Pinkham*
Notch) & Fryeburg ◆ *Crawford Notch (Route 302 from Glen*
to Littleton via Bretton Woods & Bethlehem) ◆ *Franconia &*
Sugar Hill ◆ *Bethel*

Distances in miles from Boston: Franconia-Bethlehem, 115; North Conway and Mount Washington, 140; Bretton Woods, 165; Gorham, 180.

Estimated driving times: 2¼ hours to Franconia-Bethlehem; 2½ hours to North Conway and Mount Washington; 2¾ hours to Bretton Woods; 3½ hours to Gorham.

Driving: To Franconia take I-93 to Exit 37. To North Conway take I-95N to Spaulding Turnpike (Route 16). To Bethel take I-95N to the Maine Turnpike, and then Exit 11 to Route 26 north to Bethel.

Bus: Concord Trailways (☎ 800/639-3317) provides service from Boston and Logan Airport to Conway, North Conway, Jackson, and Pinkham Notch.

Train: Closest **Amtrak** service is to White River Junction, Vermont (☎ 800/640-1412).

Further Information: For more information, contact the **Office of Travel and Tourism Development**, P.O. Box 1856, Concord, NH 03302 (☎ 603/271-2343); **White Mountain Visitor Center**, P.O. Box 10, North Woodstock, NH 03262 (☎ 603/745-8720); **White Mountain National Forest** (☎ 603/466-2727).

   Mount Washington Valley Chamber of Commerce, P.O. Box 2300, North Conway, NH 03860 (☎ 603/356-3171); **Jackson Chamber of Commerce**, P.O. Box 304, Jackson, NH 03846 (☎ 603/383-9356); **Twin Mountain Chamber of Commerce**, P.O. Box 194, Twin Mountain, NH 03595 (☎ 603/846-5407); **Franconia-Eaton-Sugar Hill Chamber of Commerce**, P.O. Box 780, Franconia, NH 03580 (☎ 603/823-5661); **Waterville Valley Chamber of Commerce**, RFD 1, Box 1067, Campton, NH 03223 (☎ 603/726-3804).

   The **central White Mountain** office is at 719 Main St., Laconia (☎ 603/466-2721); it's supplemented by the following ranger stations: **Saco** (☎ 603/

447-5448), on the Kancamagus Highway west of Route 16; **Androscoggin,**
80 Glen Rd., Gorham (☎ 603/466-2713); **Evans Notch** (☎ 207/824-2134)
on Route 2 north of Bethel; and **Ammonoosuc** (☎ 603/869-2626), on Trudeau
Road in Bethlehem. **Bethel Chamber of Commerce,** P.O. Box 439, Bethel,
ME 04217 (☎ 207/824-2282).

Events & Festivals to Plan Your Trip Around

January: Jackson Winter Carnival is a weeklong celebration of winter. Call ☎ 603/383-9356.

June: Lupine Festival, Sugar Hill, celebrates the fields of lupines
that are found along Route 117 and elsewhere in the area. It includes glider rides, art exhibits, garden workshops, and more.
Call ☎ 603/823-5661.

Mount Washington Footrace, and the **Mount Washington
Hillclimb** has a parade, time trials, a classic car show, and other
activities. Call ☎ 603/745-8720.

July: Bluegrass Festival in Franconia is held the July 4 weekend.

Native American Cultural Weekend brings song, dance, and
art to Twin Mountain Recreation Field. Call ☎ 603/846-5407.

Poetry Festival at the Frost Place in Franconia. Call ☎ 603/
823-5510.

July–August: Arts Jubilee brings an assortment of free concerts including a Symphony Pops Concert that features the 1812 Over-
ture with fireworks. Call ☎ 603/356-3171.

Music in the White Mountains sponsors performances of
chamber music at Loon Mountain and at the Meetinghouse in
Sugar Hill. For information, call ☎ 603/444-0309.

August: The White Mountain Jazz and Blues Festival hosts international jazz and blues artists at the Fields of Attitash. Call
☎ 603/745-8720.

The **Double R Rodeo** brings cowboys and cowgirls to compete in steer wrestling, calf roping, and Brahma bull riding. It
takes place at Attitash.

The **Professional Lumberjack Festival** at Loon Mountainpark is a 2-day festival featuring cross-cutting, axe-throwing,
springboard-chopping, and other competitions plus burling and
tree-climbing demonstrations.

September: Mount Washington Auto Road Bicycle Hillclimb to
the mountain's summit.

New Hampshire Highland Games at Loon Mountainpark is
one of the largest Scottish festivals in the East, celebrated over 4
days. It includes piping, Scottish dancing, Scottish games, and
more.

The first sight of the Presidential Range and of **Mount Washington** in particular is a stirring experience. Unlike other so-called mountains on the East Coast, Presidential Range peaks really do look like mountains, scraping the sky with bald boulder-strewn peaks. Mount Washington, the second highest peak in the East, rises 6,288 feet, making it the only place on the East Coast that offers true Alpine terrain that was shaped by glaciers moving at a rate of 100 feet per day. It's surrounded by a 780,000-acre playground—the **Green Mountain National Forest** where you can hike, bike, ski, and climb. Here you can encounter deep-cut gorges, boulder-strewn ravines and ledges, lush forest glades, and iridescent cascades dropping into fast-flowing rivers. No wonder this thrilling landscape has been drawing visitors for close to 200 years, ever since Thomas Cole painted a *View of the White Mountains* in 1827 and the *Notch of the White Mountains* in 1839. Soon, people were flocking to the region to enjoy the fresh air and get back to nature. Large mountain resorts catered to their needs and provided a full range of activities—tennis, croquet, golf, billiards, and social mixers, plus hiking, mountaineering, and fishing. Initially people came via stagecoach and ferry, later by train. Today about 4½ million visitors per year come by car, largely for the very same reasons—fresh air, recreation, and rejuvenation.

LINCOLN, WOODSTOCK, THE WATERVILLE VALLEY & THE KANCAMAGUS HIGHWAY

One of the must-do's in the White Mountains, other than drive or ride to the summit of Mount Washington, is to drive the **Kancamagus Highway** (Route 112), a National Scenic Byway that runs 34½ miles from Lincoln to Conway between the Pemigewasset River at one end and the Saco River at the other. Driving the highway on a clear day is magnificent, but when it's foggy and damp it's hard to see the natural beauty. Wait for the weather to cooperate if you can; otherwise, save the drive for another visit.

On your way to the highway, you'll pass **Loon Mountain** and the commercial development around it. It's the focal point for special events, and while you're here you may want to take the gondola to the summit ($10 adult, $5 children 6 to 16), although there are better views than those from Loon. Nearby Lincoln is also home to the **Papermill Theatre** (☎ 603/745-2141), which produces several musicals during the summer.

Before traveling the highway, stop at the **Lincoln Information Center** just off I-93 to secure maps of trails and other information about the route. You can also stop at the eastern end of the highway at the Saco Ranger Station Visitor Center in Conway. There are dramatic views and outlooks along the entire route, which climbs 3,000 feet as it flanks Mount Kancamagus. The mountain is named, by the way, after a Penacook Sagamon, Kancamagus "The Fearless One," who tried to keep peace between his people and the encroaching white settlers at the end of the 17th century. The road was opened only in

1959. There are at least a half dozen campgrounds and several picnic areas along the highway and numerous overlooks and trailheads.

About ¾ mile past the Otter Rocks Rest Area, the **Greeley Ponds Scenic Area** can be accessed by hiking the Greeley Ponds Trail (a half-day hike). About 3¾ miles farther on, the Sawyer River trail leads off on another half-day hike to the **Sawyer Pond Scenic Area,** where overnight camping is allowed in a shelter at the pond. At **Sabbaday Falls,** 2 miles or so farther on, there's a picnic area, and the short trail is an easy walk to see the lovely falls. About 3 miles farther, on the eastern side of Passaconaway, the Champney Falls Trail leads off to the **Chocorua Scenic Area.** From here it's about ¾ mile to **Rocky Gorge Scenic Area,** where the Swift River has cut a narrow cleft in the rock. Here you can cross the gorge via a footbridge to Falls Pond and take the short trail around the pond. A little farther on, at the Covered Bridge Campground the **Boulder Loop Trail** is a pleasant 2½-mile hike.

Ten or so miles south of Lincoln, Route 49 provides access to the **Waterville Valley** recreation area, which is surrounded by the White Mountain National Forest and the Sandwich Range Wilderness Area.

Kancamaǥus Highway & Waterville Valley
Special & Recreational Activities

Biking: Waterville Valley Base Camp (☎ 800/468-2553) has mountain bike rentals. Also try **Loon Mountain Bike Center** (☎ 603/745-8111), which has down-mountain trails plus 22 miles of cross-country trails. Rentals range from $20 for 4 hours to $30 a day.

Cross-Country Skiing: Loon Mountain (☎ 603/745-6281) has 22 miles of trails along the Pemigewasset River.

Camping: For hiking and camping information, contact the **White Mountain's National Forest Saco District,** Saco Ranger Station, 33 Kancamagus Hwy., Conway, NH 03818 (☎ 603/447-5448), or The Supervisor's Office, 719 Main St., Laconia, NH 03246 (☎ 603/528-8721). There are many campgrounds along the Kancamagus Highway.

Golf: The **Waterville Valley Golf Club** is the best in the area.

Hiking: See camping for information and suggested trails above. At **Waterville Valley,** hike the Mount Tecumseh Trail.

Horseback Riding: Trail rides are offered at **Loon Mountainpark** (☎ 603/745-8111). Prices start at $26 an hour.

Skiing: Waterville Valley (☎ 603/236-8311) covers 255 acres and has a vertical drop of 2,020 feet. The 49 trails are accessed by 12 lifts, and the resort has a high 98% snowmaking coverage. **Loon Mountain,** Kancamagus Highway (☎ 603/745-8111) has a vertical drop of 2,100 feet and offers 43 trails that are accessed by 8 lifts, including a high-speed quad and a four-passenger gondola. It also has 97% snow coverage.

Tennis: The **Waterville Tennis Center** (☎ 603/236-4840) has 18 courts and offers a full range of clinics and private instruction.

THE CONWAYS, JACKSON (PINKHAM NOTCH) & FRYEBURG

The Kancamagus Highway brings you directly into **Conway** or into North Conway if you turn off at Bear Notch Road (which links via Bartlett and Route 302 into North Conway). North Conway is one huge bottleneck in summer when the main street is clogged with the cars of shoppers at the long mall of outlets that have accumulated in this town. When you've exhausted all the possibilities from Lenox to Dansk and Ralph Lauren to J.G. Hook and paid your compulsory visit to the headquarters of **Eastern Mountain Sports** (☎ 603/356-5433), it's time to get out of town as far as I'm concerned. The preferred lodging place is Jackson, a much quieter village a few miles north of North Conway, or at one of the inns closer to Conway like the Snowhill (see "Laconia and the Lakes").

In **North Conway,** there are some attractions besides shopping. The **Conway Scenic Railroad** (☎ 603/356-5251) offers trips through the valley from North Conway to Conway or from North Conway to Bartlett. The first takes only an hour and costs $8 for adults and $5.50 for children 4 to 12; the second takes 1¾ hours and costs $13.50 for adults and $8.50 for children. The railroad also operates a 5½-hour trip from North Conway to Crawford Notch, a spectacular route in fall (when you'll need advance reservations). The price is $32 for adults, $17 for children 4 to 12. North Conway also offers some evening entertainment at the **Mount Washington Valley Theatre Company,** Route 16 (☎ 603/356-5776), which stages popular musicals during the summer.

From North Conway, Route 16 will take you to the turnoff for **Jackson** and Jackson Falls. Jackson has a couple of appealing inns and good restaurants. While you're here, take the time to drive the so-called 5-mile circuit along Route 16B past Jackson Falls. It climbs through farmland and affords some lovely views before looping back to Jackson at Whitney's Inn.

The next stop is the **AMC Pinkham Notch Visitor Center,** Route 16 (P.O. Box 298), Gorham, NH 03581 (☎ 603/466-2727), which is the focal point for hikers in the Presidential Range. Here you can secure information about trails and weather conditions, plus lodgings, supplies, books, and maps and food at the cafeteria. From here, it's only 4.1 miles to the summit of Mount Washington, but it's a grueling 4.1 miles. Tuckerman Shelter is a closer 2.4 miles. Across Route 16, **Wildcat gondola** (☎ 603/466-3326) will transport you to the summit of Wildcat Mountain.

Farther north, Route 16 brings you to the **Mount Washington Auto Road** at Great Glen (☎ 603/466-3988). Don't miss the experience of going to the top unless the weather is bad (which is often; there are on average 300 days of fog per year). On a clear day you can see 100 miles. Visibility is posted at the office at the base of the mountain. If you don't suffer from vertigo or fear of heights, then drive the road yourself. It's a hair-raising thrill—more terrifying on the ascent than the descent because all you see is the sky above and the land sheering off at the roadside. It takes you 8 miles and 6,288 feet up to the summit, twisting and turning all the way with no crash barriers to prevent you from careening off the road. If you drive it yourself, you'll be given a tape to play that relates the history and early exploration of Mount Washington. Alternatively, you can take one of the jitneys that go to the top (1½ hr. round-trip including 30 min. at the summit).

The first road was opened in 1861, and the first auto to make the climb was driven by F. O. Stanley in 1899. Then there's the cog railway that arrives from Crawford Notch (see "Crawford Notch" below). It's exciting to watch the tough little steam train belching black smoke as it struggles to the summit and then to see it slipping away into the distance down the mountainside whistling as it goes.

At the summit there's an observatory weather station and a broadcasting facility plus several attractions to view. The premier attraction is, of course, the view. The **observation facility** and the **museum** (☎ 603/356-8345) at the summit display some very sobering information, including a list of people who have died hiking or climbing in the Presidential Range. The average temperature at the summit in June is 44°F, and in August, 47°F; in winter it's 4°F, with winds gusting to 70 mph. And in 1968–69, a record of 566.4 inches of snow fell. The second hotel that was built on the mountain in 1853 is still standing, and you can visit to get some idea of what staying here was like. It has walls that are 4 feet thick, small windows, and rooms containing bunks made up with lichen moss—not exactly a luxury accommodation. The road is open from mid-May to late October, from 7:30am to 6pm throughout most of the summer. Private car toll is $16 for car and driver, plus $7 for each adult passenger and $3 per child 5 to 12. Guided tours are $40 for adults, $20 for children 5 to 12.

NORTH CONWAY & JACKSON LODGING

Stonehurst Manor, Route 16 (P.O. Box 1937), North Conway, NH 03860 (☎ 603/356-3271), is a grand accommodation that was once the summer home of carpet magnate Erastus Bigelow. Even though it's on Route 16, it's set on 33 secluded acres up a steep driveway in a grove of evergreens. It's a large shingled residence that has 24 guest rooms (7 with wood-burning fireplaces). The architectural features of the house are eye-catching indeed—solid oak staircase and pocket doors, Tiffany windows in the bar area, and magnificent turned wood columns in the library-lounge. The rooms are elegantly decorated. Room 22 is a suite with a rice four-poster set against a rich dark blue wallpaper on wall-to-wall dark carpet. Furnishings include a pier mirror, a sofa, and a Chippendale chair at a sizable desk. In another room, a damask coverlet graces the rice four-poster, and there's a small balcony as well as a fireplace. There are three dining rooms—one is a terrace with bamboo seating and brick flooring, where tables sport floral cloths; the other two are more formal. The patio is also very inviting with its Mexican tile and wrought-iron and glass tables. There's even a wood-fired pizza oven out here for pizza and other meat and fish items. Other fare consists of dishes such as wood-fired duck with blackberry sauce, filet mignon with black truffle and wild mushroom bordelaise, and grilled salmon with roasted-red-pepper coulis. Prices range from $15 to $23. Open daily from 5:30 to 9pm. Facilities include an outdoor pool, hot tub, tennis court, and hiking and cross-country ski trails. Rates: MAP $63 to $93 per person double; B&B $50 to $80 per person.

The Buttonwood Inn, Mount Surprise Road, North Conway, NH 03860 (☎ 603/356-2625), is set back in the woods well away from the madness of

Route 16. It's a charming hostelry operated by Claudia and Peter Needham, a very hospitable couple who make all the difference. The nine rooms (five with private bath) are on the small side and decorated in an unaffected country style with all the necessary comforts. You might find a high-back oak bed in your room along with cloth covered side tables and a teardrop pine dresser. Or you might find a bed covered with a star quilt, combined with side tables and an oak dresser. Room 2 is particularly pretty with its mural depicting a farmhouse and horses. The sitting room has comfortable seating and fireplace, but the favorite haunt of the house, especially in winter, is the downstairs lounge with another large stone fireplace and a TV/VCR plus film library. Guests also have access to their own fridge, and Claudia and Peter even provide day packs and picnic blankets that have been donated by local businesses. Breakfast is served at individual tables in a pretty dining room. Choices are always available, but if the raspberry pancakes are served when you stay there, don't miss them. The backyard has an outdoor pool. Rates: in season (early January to late March, late June to mid-September, late October to end October [foliage season]), Christmas $80 to $140; April to late June and November to late December, $70 to $110; mid-September to mid-October, $95 to $160.

Carter Notch Inn, Carter Notch Road (P.O. Box 269), Jackson, NH 03846 (☎ 603/383-0630), has a great location on a quiet road in Jackson overlooking the Wildcat River valley. Hosts Jim and Lynda Lovell and Tucker, their chocolate lab, love what they're doing and welcome guests into what they consider their home. There are seven rooms, five with private bath. Each has been individually and attractively decorated. Room 1, for example, has a high-back maple bed with a quilt coverlet, combined with twig side tables, an oak chest, and a wicker loveseat. Other rooms might contain an iron bed and a painted cottage dresser. Guests enjoy the living room with its fireplace, the wraparound porch, and outdoor hot tub. Rates: summer, $89 to $99; fall/winter, $89 to $119.

The parking lot at the **Wentworth Resort Hotel,** Carter Notch Road (Box M), Jackson, NH 03846 (☎ 603/383-9700), is located across the road from the Wildcat River and a short distance from Jackson Falls. The 1869 turreted building has been thoroughly restored and updated with modern cluster accommodations. All rooms have cable TVs; some rooms have fireplaces and/or Jacuzzis. There's a heated outdoor pool, an 18-hole golf course, and access to the Jackson Ski touring trails. The dining room offers some good cuisine. There are only six main courses, and these use the freshest ingredients prepared in a contemporary American fashion. You might find a roasted leg of lamb with black-currant gravy or grilled salmon with summer corn–tomato salsa. Prices range from $16.50 to $20; hours are Sunday to Thursday from 6 to 9pm, Friday to Saturday from 6 to 10pm. Rates: early January to mid-June, $159 to $249; mid-June to late September, $169 to $259; late September to mid-October, $179 to $269; late October to mid-December, $159 to $249; mid-December to early January $179 to $269. Special golf and other packages available.

The **Christmas Farm Inn,** Route 16B, Jackson, NH 03846 (☎ 603/383-4313), celebrates Christmas year-round, and while this may seem hokey, it actually translates into some very warm hospitality. The inn has a fine location up on a hill near Wildcat River and is operated by very friendly innkeepers. There are nine rooms in the main house and nine rooms in The Saltbox facility. The rooms in the main house are decorated in comfy country fashion with chintz, Jenny Lind beds, Hitchcock rockers, and similar furnishings. Five rooms have a Jacuzzi. The Saltbox rooms are more deluxe in style and might feature a canopied bed, wing chairs, and a double Jacuzzi. There are also 5 two-bedroom cottages plus a two-room honeymoon cottage and four family suites. The cottages are extraordinarily attractive. Livery Stable has a comfortable living room with a wood-burning fireplace, and large bedrooms decorated with floral motifs. Amenities include a refrigerator and a TV. The inn is set on 14 acres and has cross-country ski trails, an outdoor pool with cabana, plus a restaurant that is lit at night with tiny white lights. It's very appealing and offers good meals (open to the public by reservation only) that feature dishes such as veal Dijon, pork tenderloin with cranberry apple compote, or baked stuffed sole, priced from $15 to $19. Dinner is daily from 5:30 to 9pm. Two parlors are available for guests. The favorite has a raised slate hearth and a TV. There's also a game room with a large TV, table tennis, and foosball. The gardens are beautiful in season. Facilities also include an outdoor pool. Rates: MAP $88 to $120 per person double.

The Inn at Thorn Hill, Thorn Hill Road (Box A), Jackson, NH 03846 (☎ 603/383-4242), is a lovely accommodation with a quiet location. Built in 1895, it was designed by Stanford White. There are 19 rooms (10 in the main house). The views of Mount Washington from the porch and the property are inspiring. The rooms are attractively furnished in Victorian country style with iron or brass beds, oak or pine dressers, and easy chairs. The rest of the rooms are in the carriage house, which has its own living room with a large raised brick hearth. The rooms here are a little more rustic, but some have Jacuzzis. There are also three cottages that have double Jacuzzis, gas fireplaces, and decks. The guests enjoy the library with TV, the inviting sitting room, and the pub, which sells a range of single malts and several hundred wine selections. New American cuisine is served in the dining room, where the menu changes daily. You might find medallions of venison with red wine juniper-berry sauce and parsnip pancakes, or salmon marinated in sake, mirin, and soy and then pan seared and served in a ginger broth. Prices range from $16 to $24. Rates: MAP mid-September to mid-October and late December to early January, $196 to $235 double; cottages $280 to $310; off-season, $160 to $200 double; cottages $240 to $260. Subtract $30 for B&B rates.

Darby Field Inn, Albany, NH 03818 (☎ 603/447-2181), is miles away in spirit from the main street of North Conway. It's located on 9 acres and offers a full restaurant and tavern dining, too. The house was built in 1826 and has served as a farm, a boys' camp, and an inn. It is, of course, named after the man who, in 1642, made the first ascent of Mount Washington. There are 16 rooms (14 with private baths), all furnished with assorted country pieces. For example, Room 6 has a carved mahogany bed combined with two cane-seated chairs and white-painted side tables plus 1850s-style lighting. Some rooms are more stylish than others, like Room number 2, which has a cottage-style carved mahogany bed and a loveseat with intricately carved arms and a matching chair, plus a marble-top cottage dresser. The dining room, where a full breakfast is served, has a grand view of Mount Washington. At dinner, a short menu features items such as filet mignon, duck with orange glaze, and veal with a sauce of scallions, mushrooms, tomatoes, and fresh basil. In summer, some dishes are prepared on the outdoor stone fireplace-grill. The sitting room offers a large-screen TV and comfortable seating around the great stone hearth. Guests enjoy the patio, the two hammocks, and the outdoor swimming pool. There are cross-country ski trails. Rates: MAP, $75 to $110 per person double; B&B, $55 to $90. In peak season, mid-September to mid-October, add $10; subtract $10 from rates in January, March, May, early June, November, and early December.

NORTH CONWAY & JACKSON DINING

Thompson House Eatery, routes 16A and 16, Jackson (☎ 603/383-9341), is a very pleasant restaurant. In summer, you can dine out on the terrace under an awning lit with colored lights and gaze at the silhouetted mountains. The dining room is also charming with its tables set with floral tablecloths. The food is fresh and delicious and an excellent value. The smoked chicken with pineapple and peach barbecue alone will make you want to return, but there are plenty of other tasty dishes like pork tenderloin piccata, or hickory bay shrimp and scallops broiled with sweet red peppers in roasted-garlic olive oil and white wine. Prices range from $13 to $17. Open Wednesday to Monday from 11:30am to 3:30pm and 5:30 to 10pm. Closed in November.

Prince Place at the Bernerhof, Route 302, Glen (☎ 603/383-4414), is the place to head if you want to enjoy some Alpine-inspired cuisine like wiener schnitzel, *émince de veau Zurichoise,* and middle-European classics. Other dishes include ginger-plum chicken and sirloin steak marinated with maple syrup, horseradish, and mustard and then grilled. The setting is casually elegant. Prices range $17 to $20. Fondue, bratwurst, and other dishes that deviate from the usual typical tavern fare are served in the Black Bear Pub for prices ranging from $6 to $10 (fondue is $17.95). Open Tuesday to Sunday from 5:30 to 9:30pm. Closed Monday.

Bellini's, 33 Seavey St., North Conway (☎ 603/356-7000), is not the place for a quiet romantic meal. It's a popular bustling scene—it's casual and fun, the food is good, and there's always enough for three in one portion. You'll sit on black leatherette booths at copper-topped tables and enjoy hearty Italian dishes. In addition to a full selection of pastas—fettuccine Alfredo; lobster ravioli; gnocchi marinara; manicotti; and cappellini with shrimp, sun-dried tomatoes, garlic, and oil—there are dishes such as braciola (a thin slice of beef rolled and stuffed with prosciutto), vegetables, garlic, mozzarella, and Romano, baked in marinara sauce. Naturally, there are also chicken marsala and parmigiana and other expected specialties. Portions really are huge. Prices range from $10 to $16. Open Wednesday, Thursday, and Monday 5 to 10pm; Friday and Saturday 5 to 11pm. Closed Tuesdays and for 2 weeks in November.

LODGING & DINING ACROSS THE BORDER IN MAINE

The Admiral Peary House, 9 Elm St., Fryeburg, ME 04037 (☎ 207/935-3365), is situated in town on a quiet street. It has extensive gardens so that there is plenty of privacy. There are five rooms, all of which are attractively decorated with antiques or antique reproductions. For example, one might have a rice four-poster and wing chairs among the furnishings, another a brass bed with an Empire chest and loveseat. Decorative accents include stenciling, quilted pieces, and brass-candlestick lamps or iron floor lamps. In North Pole, the quilt was made by Nancy's grandmother and great aunt. Breakfast is served in an inviting kitchen warmed by a woodstove and is likely to include hot dishes such as Belgian waffles with strawberries or blueberries, and Peary's penguin pie, a crustless quiche. There's also a more formal dining room. The sitting room has French-style furnishings and is decorated with family portraits. Guests love the well-stocked floor-to-ceiling bookcases in the library. Rates: in season, $108 to $118; winter, $80 to $90; foliage add $10.

Quisisana, on Lake Kezar, Center Lovell, ME 04016 (☎ 207/925-3500), or in winter at ☎ 914/833-0293, means a place for healing, and this lakeside resort is certainly that. It's a serene place on the shore of Lake Kezar, but what makes it more special is the music, provided by a musical staff, that fills the air all summer. The staff members are recruited from the best music conservatories in the country; they serve meals and clean cabins by day and then sing arias and play sonatas at night. Performances are given an hour or two after dinner in a lakeside building. Sundays are devoted to chamber music, Mondays to musical theater, Tuesdays to piano recitals, Wednesdays to one-act operas, Thursdays to a musical revue, and Fridays to a concert of arias. On Saturday, the musical welcome previews the week's offerings. There are 37 guest cottages that are plainly but comfortably furnished. They are pine paneled, and the living rooms, with stone fireplaces, are furnished with wicker pieces. Some cottages are literally on stilts on the lake, others are lakeside, and still others off in the woods. A full breakfast is served, and at that time you can make your dinner selections. A typical dish is salmon leek roulade or scampi in white wine. At the lake, there's swimming, canoeing, kayaking, sailing, windsurfing, waterskiing, and fishing. Other facilities include a pool and three clay tennis courts. It's a magical place, and guests return year after year to enjoy both nature and music—as close to heaven as you can get. Rates: full American plan, $97 to $188; B&B, $78 to $108. Open mid-June to the end of August. A minimum 1-week stay is required except for a couple of weekends in June.

Area of North Conway, Jackson & Gorham
Special & Recreational Activities

Biking: There are extensive mountain biking trails in the **White Mountains** along logging and fire roads and at **Attitash** and **Mount Cranmore** (off Kearsage Road in North Conway; ☎ 603/356-5543). Rentals are available at **Great Glen Trails** (☎ 603/466-2333) near Mount Washington and at both mountains. Rentals are also available at **Joe Jones Ski and Sport,** Main Street, North Conway (☎ 603/356-9411). **Northern Extremes,** Route 302, Glen (☎ 603/383-8117) rents bikes and offers tours. Prices average $20 a day for bikes. **Mountain Road Tours** (☎ 603/532-8708) offers inn-to-inn tours.

Camping: The **White Mountains Forest** contains 20 campgrounds. Reserve ahead (depending on the campground, you're allowed to reserve anywhere from 11 to 180 days in advance) to avoid disappointment. The camps are usually full on summer and fall weekends. Camping is also available in state parks like **Moose Brook** (☎ 603/466-3860).

Canoeing: The **Androscoggin River** has class I-II whitewater upstream from Berlin; there's also good whitewater on the Saco River. Rent canoes from **Saco Canoe Rental,** Route 16, Conway (☎ 603/447-2737); **Saco Valley Canoe** in Conway on Route 302 or in Fryeburg on Route 302 (☎ 603/447-2444); **Joe Jones North Shop** in Intervale (☎ 603/356-6848) or in North Conway (☎ 603/356-9411). **Saco Bound** on Route 302, Center Conway (☎ 603/447-2177), offers rentals and overnight trips in New Hampshire and Maine. Average rates are $23 a day on weekends plus $8 to $10 for shuttle service. Most companies also offer trips.

Climbing: **Eastern Mountain Sports Climbing School** in North Conway (☎ 800/310-4504) offers instruction as well as guided trips.

Cross-Country Skiing: Jackson Ski Touring has 150 kilometers of trails and is rated number 1 in the East by several skiing magazines. **Great Glen Trails,** Gorham (☎ 603/466-2333), offers rentals and snowshoeing and ice skating, too. Additional facilities include Bretton Woods (☎ 603/278-5181).

Fishing: Contact **New Hampshire Fish and Game Department,** 2 Hazen Dr., Concord, NH 03301 (☎ 603/271-3211), for detailed information. **Great Glen Trails** (☎ 603/466-2333), near Mount Washington offers courses in fly-fishing.

Golf: Wentworth Golf Club is on Route 16A in Jackson (☎ 603/383-9641); **Eagle Mountain Golf,** Carter Notch Road (☎ 603/383-9111), is a nine-hole course with some hazards along the Wildcat River. **North Conway Country Club** (☎ 603/356-9391) is highly rated in the state and has great mountain scenery. The state PGA championships are held here.

Hiking: The White Mountains have 1,200 miles of trails. Serious hikers will want to secure a copy of the Appalachian Mountain Club's *White Mountain Guide.*

For guided trips and information about hiking huts and lodges, contact the **Appalachian Mountain Club,** Pinkham Notch Visitor Center, Route 16, Box 298, Gorham, NH 03581 (☎ 603/466-2727). The club operates eight huts in the White Mountains, and it also offers hut-to-hut packages. Overnight rates, including breakfast and supper at the huts, are as low as $65 in peak season for nonmembers. Similar low rates ($50 with breakfast, supper; $60 in private rooms; and $30 in dorms for lodging only) prevail at the lodge at Pinkham Notch where you can stay in private rooms or bunk rooms accommodating up to five. There are several short hikes near Pinkham Notch to **Glen Ellis Falls** (0.3 miles, 20 min.); to Lost Pond (1 mile, 30 min.); and to **Square Ledge** (½ mile, 30 min.). For additional information, contact **Androscoggin Ranger Station,** 300 Glen Rd., Gorham, NH 03581 (☎ 603/466-2713).

Horseback Riding: For horse, pony, and wagon rides, go to the **Stables at the Farm by the River,** 2555 West Side Rd., North Conway (☎ 603/356-4855). The charge is $25 an hour.

Skiing: For downhill beginners, **Mount Cranmore** in North Conway Village is great (☎ 603/356-5544); **Black Mountain** in Jackson (☎ 603/383-4490) is a family mountain with 30 trails as well as a snowboard

park, snow tubing, and sleigh rides; **Wildcat,** Route 16, Pinkham Notch
(☎ 603/466-3326), offers challenging skiing on a 2,100-foot vertical drop
with 100% snowmaking. **Tuckerman Ravine** is famous for its spring skiing and for the daredevils that ski it.

State Parks: Moose Brook State Park outside of Gorham on Route 2
(☎ 603/466-3860) offers camping, fishing, swimming, hiking, and
picnicking.

Snowmobiling: Contact **New Hampshire Snowmobile Association,**
722 Rte. 3A, Bow, NH 03304 (☎ 603/224-8906).

Swimming: For fun swimming holes you can't beat **Diana's Baths** along Lucy
Brook where you can frolic under falls and waterspouts in granite basins.
It's located west on River Road from North Conway about ½ mile before
the turnoff to Cathedral Ledge. **Jackson Falls** is another lovely sunny spot
to swim in pothole pools; it's on Carter Notch Road (Route 16B) off Route
16A in Jackson.

Wildlife Viewing: AMC offers programs from the **Pinkham Notch Visitor
Center** throughout the summer. From September to June, **Tin Mountain
Conservation Center** offers nature programs.

CRAWFORD NOTCH — FROM GLEN
TO LITTLETON VIA BRETTON WOODS
& BETHLEHEM

Although Timothy Nash first discovered the Notch in 1771 while he was track-
ing a moose, it wasn't until 1790 that the man who gave it its name struggled
through the Notch. Subsequently, it became a major summer resort area with
grand hotels to which people flocked to take the air in the mountains. Crawford
House was one of the most famous hotel destinations, and it counted Daniel
Webster; Nathaniel Hawthorn; and presidents Pierce, Grant, Hayes, Garfield,
and Harding among its guests. It was built in 1828 by Abel Crawford and his
son Ethan Allen Crawford but was twice destroyed by fire, in 1856 and again
in 1859. A third Crawford House was erected in 1859. Today as you drive on
Route 302 through the Notch, it's still mind-boggling to conceive what an
effort must have gone into cutting this road through the mountains.

In **Glen,** families may want to stop at **Heritage** (☎ 603/383-9776), where
a Disney-like history of New Hampshire is offered, and **Storyland** (☎ 603/
383-4293), a park featuring close to 20 themed rides. Heritage is open mid-
May to mid-June, daily from 9am to 5pm; and mid-June to Labor Day, from
9am to 6pm, Labor Day to mid-October 9am to 5pm. Admission $10 for
adults, $4.50 for children 6 to 12. Storyland is open daily from early June to
September 1 and on weekends only from September 2 to mid-October. Admission is $16 for unlimited rides.

From here, the road leads west to Attitash and Bartlett. At **Attitash Bear
Peak** (☎ 603/374-2368) in the summer, it's fun to ride either the Alpine or

water slide or simply to take the chairlift to the top of the mountain. You can ride the slides all day for $18, which is the best deal, or you can enjoy two rides for $12. Open daily from 10am to 6pm.

Just west of Bartlett, Route 302 enters **Crawford Notch State Park,** winding between the mountains to Notchland and then to **Arethusa Falls** and **Willey House** where you will want to stop. The falls are the highest in the state at about 176 feet. They're reached via a 1.3-mile trail off Route 302 near the Crawford Notch State Park entrance sign. You pass through the Notch surrounded on both sides by several peaks.

Right here in the Notch at **Bretton Woods** is where you can climb aboard the **Mount Washington Cog Railway** (☎ 603/278-5404) that will take you on a 3-hour round-trip to the summit. Don't miss it. The railway was an engineering marvel in 1869, and it still is. It's the second steepest railway track in the world, and in one spot the grade is so steep that the heads of the people at the back of the train are 13 feet below those of the folks at the front. The train uses coal-fired steam and on the 3-mile trip to the summit consumes an amazing 1 ton of coal and 1,000 gallons of water. The railway operates from early May through October. Tickets are $39 for adults, $26 for children 6 to 12. On the western side of the Notch, you come upon the marvelous view of the **Mount Washington Hotel & Resort** at Bretton Woods, the only truly grand hotel left from the earlier days when the whole of society, as it seemed then, flocked to the resorts in the White Mountains.

From Bretton Woods, the road continues past **Sugarloaf Mountains** into Twin Mountain and then skirts along the White Mountain National Forest to Bethlehem and Littleton. **Bethlehem** was a popular mountain resort in the late 19th century, and several prominent writers and poets summered here, including Helen Hunt Jackson, author of *Ramona,* and Robert Frost. Back then there were more than 30 resort hotels in town. Folks gathered at places such as the Maplewood Casino that housed a bowling alley, ballroom, theater, and secret gambling casino. Any White Mountains vacation always included Bethlehem's annual Coaching Parade, when Concord coaches, surreys, and buggies, drawn by four- and six-horse teams, jammed the mile-long Main Street. Today the casino serves as a golf clubhouse, and the coaches have long since disappeared from our lives. Today Bethlehem consists of one main street (Route 302), which has a cluster of antique stores (there's also a summer flea market on the green). Before you reach town, **Bethlehem Flower Farm,** Route 302, East Bethlehem (☎ 603/869-3131), specializes in daylilies, which are best seen blooming in July and August. There's a typical gift barn for visitors and a garden shop. Open daily from 10am to 6pm.

West of Bethlehem, it's worth visiting **The Rocks** (☎ 603/444-6228) to see the view of Mount Washington and the Vermont hills from the road that leads up to the estate. The property was once owned by John Glessner, vice president of International Harvester, who came to the mountains in search of fresh healthy air for his son. Today it's an educational center operated by the Society for the Protection of New Hampshire Forests, which also operates a tree farm. This is the place to harvest your own Christmas tree in December or to visit and tag one in September or October for shipping later.

Gepetto's Barn, Blaney Road (☎ 603/444-2187), is another Bethlehem landmark. It started when Gepetto's wife asked him to move his woodworking hobby to this barn, which is now filled with all kinds of wooden stuff fashioned by Gepetto himself—blanket chests, miniature castles and forts, desks, coffee tables, jelly cabinets, and more. His real name is Win Brebner. Take Brook Road off Route 302 west of Bethlehem.

For evening entertainment the **Weathervane Theatre,** on Route 3 in Whitefield (☎ 603/837-9322), performs popular Broadway shows in July and August.

LODGING & DINING ALONG THE ROUTE

The **Bernerhof,** Route 302, Glen, NH 03838 (☎ 603/383-4414), is located in a Victorian right on Route 302. The nine rooms have been decorated with brass beds and country furnishings, and several have double Jacuzzis. This is certainly one place to dine in the valley (see above), either at the Black Bear Pub or in the more sophisticated dining room where classics such as wiener schnitzel and *émince de veau* are on the menu. Rates: $99 to $149 weekends and holidays; $79 to $129 midweek.

Notchland Inn, Hart's Location, Bartlett, NH 03812 (☎ 603/374-6131), is a lovely accommodation that is set on a side road off Route 302. It's a granite mansion with wood posts and gables located on 400 acres. The gardens are well tended and incorporate a pond and gazebo. The seven rooms are very nicely decorated with high-back oak beds, candle-stand lamps, wing chairs, or similar pieces. In addition, there are five suites, all of which have fireplaces. Guest areas include the front parlor, which was designed by Gustav Stickley, where guests gather around the hooded fireplace. There's also a music room with piano and stereo, library, and sun room. In the evening, a five-course dinner is served in a romantic fireplaced dining room. There are choices at each course, with three entrees offered. They might be beef tenderloin with portobello-and-Madeira sauce; shrimp with tomato, asparagus, and saffron; or roast duck with blackberry Chambord sauce. For those not staying at the inn, dinner is $32 per person. The dining room is open Wednesday to Sunday from 7pm. Rates: MAP $190 to $235 double; $220 to $275 during foliage season and on holidays.

It might seem more appropriate to draw up at the porte cochere of the **Mount Washington Hotel & Resort,** Route 302, Bretton Woods, NH 03575 (☎ 603/278-1000), in a coach and four rather than in a car. It's a majestic grand hotel—the only one left from the Gilded Age when hotels like this one thrived as they hosted and cosseted the rich and famous. It's a historic place that was opened by Joseph Stickney, a Pennsylvania coal and railroad magnate, on August 1, 1902. It's most famous for hosting the 3-week meeting held here in July 1944 between Winston Churchill and Franklin Roosevelt, which led to the Bretton Woods Agreement that effectively established the International Monetary Fund. Step through the pillared lobby and out through the soaring rotunda-lounge to the back porch that sweeps around the rotunda and extends along the whole building, affording great views of Mount Washington. The front porch looks out across the golf course. The rooms in this building are not as spectacular as the setting, furnished as they are with uninspired Ethan Allan beds and decor. Other accommodations are located in the Bretton Arms, which offers more privacy and nicely appointed rooms plus a dining room that serves continental cuisine. The most luxurious rooms are in the one-to-five bedroom town houses, which have fireplaces, decks, and full kitchens. Another 50 rooms are located in the motor inn on a knoll overlooking the hotel.

Jackets are required in the dining room, where you can dine and dance in grand Edwardian style. The four-course meal might start with shrimp bisque and move on to either roast sirloin of beef with bourbon-roasted onion demiglace or peppered salmon over sautéed artichokes with red wine garlic sauce. Downstairs, the Cave Lounge is just that—a cavelike space with rough-hewn walls, brick floor, and arches—the backdrop from some live entertainment. There are also additional more casual restaurants around the property. Facilities include 12 clay tennis courts, indoor and outdoor pools with deck aprons, a croquet lawn, and two golf courses. There are children's programs and babysitting, too. Rates: hotel: MAP, $195 to $325 double. Bretton Arms: room only, late June to mid-October, $109 to $159 and $99 to $139 off-season; motor inn: room only, late June to mid-October $99 to $139 and $79 to $105 off-season; town houses: room only from $139 to $199 for one bedroom to $329 to $379 for five bedrooms. Special packages available.

It's a beautiful approach off Route 302 through a stand of firs and down a curvaceous drive past a pond to **Adair**, Old Littleton Road (P.O. Box 850), Bethlehem, NH 03574 (☎ 603/444-2600). The house, a Dutch gambrel beauty, was built in 1927 by Frank Hogan the Washington attorney who successfully defended Edward Doheny in the Teapot Dome Scandal. It's surrounded by 200 acres of gardens that were laid out by Frederick Olmsted and offer magnificent views of Mount Washington and the Presidential Range. This perfect bucolic retreat also has nine very attractively decorated accommodations. Each has been individually furnished and has some distinctive accent. In Waterford, it's the carved beds and the fern motif wallpaper; in Kinsman it's the bookcases in the entryway, the bold iris patterned wallpaper, and amenities such as a gas woodstove and a small balcony. Concord has a lovely burled maple dresser plus a tufted bed that is lit by sconces. The coziest public space is the Granite Tap Room, which has a grand old Oliver Briggs Boston pool table, an upright piano, a TV/VCR, stone fireplace, guest pantry, and plenty of comfortable seating. There's also a more formal sitting room decorated with Chinese rugs, handsome mirrors, and richly carved furniture. The dining room has a hearth, too, and for summer dining, the flagstone terrace furnished with wrought iron is a favorite spot. A full breakfast featuring eggs Benedict, blueberry pancakes, or similar dishes is served. The grounds flow down a hillside studded with rock outcroppings all the way to a pond. Facilities include a tennis court.

The inn's restaurant, the **Tim Bir Alley**, Old Littleton Road, Bethlehem (☎ 603/444-6142), is a great favorite in the area. The cuisine is exciting and innovative. For example, you might find salmon with peach Hoisin barbecue sauce and spiced pecans; catfish with Parmesan-basil crust and sun-dried tomato vinaigrette; or tournedos of beef with smoked bacon, grilled leeks, and a cabernet-thyme sauce. The desserts are legendary—dark and white chocolate tart with frozen chocolate-Kahlúa mousse and strawberry mousse. Dinner is served seasonally from 5:30 to 9pm. Rates: $145 to $230. For dinner add $35 per person.

Spalding Inn, Mountain View Road, Whitefield, NH 03598 (☎ 603/837-2572), is off Route 302 in a secluded location where you're likely to be greeted by one of the Springer Spaniels in residence. It occupies a gracious

1865 home that stands on 200 acres and has 24 accommodations. The rooms in the main house are simply furnished with chintz, and most have white-painted furniture—beds, dressers, and side tables. The largest and nicest rooms are in the carriage house. These have hardwood floors covered with rugs, beds made up with quilts, and loveseats and wicker chairs. Cottages are also available with fully equipped kitchens, screened porches, and fireplaces. Facilities include four clay tennis courts, an outdoor pool with a concrete apron, and pitch-and-putt golf. The clubhouse has a Ping-Pong table and other games, while there's always a volleyball net set up on the lawn. The guest sitting room is divided into an area for conversation and a games area where puzzles, books, and a TV/VCR are readily available. The dining room menu changes nightly, but on Friday nights there's always lobster. Rates: late May to June, $109 to $139, cottages from $210; July to mid-September, $129 to $160, cottages from $160; mid-September to October $139 to $160, cottages from $310. MAP rates available.

The **Jefferson Inn,** Route 2, Jefferson, NH 03583 (☎ 603/586-7998), is operated by a warm and welcoming couple. The original home was built in 1896. There are 11 accommodations, all decorated in a pleasant fashion, with sleigh or brass beds, floral coverlets, and braided rugs. The New England Room has a claw-foot tub in the bathroom. There is also a unit that is ideal for families; it has a double and a twin bed, and a small fridge and TV. The Colonel Whipple is a handsome room with a carved bed and a wing chair and dresser. The most romantic rooms are the tower rooms—Monticello, in particular, with its mahogany bed and ornately carved easy chairs. Marla, the innkeeper, loves making breakfast, and will appear with delights such as bacon cheddar quiche, stuffed orange French toast, and Southwestern eggs. Afternoon tea is also served. The breakfast room has separate tables and overlooks the backyard where birds gather around the bird feeders and the owners' horses graze. The house has a wraparound porch but it's not screened from Route 2. Rates: $80 to $120, suite $150.

Grand Depot Cafe, Cottage Street, Littleton (☎ 603/444-5303), is located in the old railroad station. It's very popular with the locals because the cuisine is fine and it has a comfortable casual atmosphere. At dinner, there are about 10 or so entrees. Each is carefully prepared. Try the pork stuffed with jalapeño au gratin and finished with mushroom and diced pepperoni reduction or the shrimp with prosciutto and sun-dried tomatoes served on linguine and finished with a garlic and lemon butter sauce. Prices range from $15 to $22. Open Monday to Friday from 11:30am to 2pm and daily from 5:30 to 9pm.

Crawford Notch
Special & Recreational Activities

Biking: There's mountain biking at **Bretton Woods** (☎ 603/278-5000).
Camping: The **White Mountain National Forest** has numerous campgrounds. For information and reservations, call ☎ 800/280-2267. **Crawford Notch State Park** (☎ 603/374-2272) has 30 primitive sites at Dry River Campground.

Cross-Country Skiing: Bretton Woods, Route 302, Bretton Woods (☎ 603/278-5181), has 62 miles of groomed trails.

Golf: Bethlehem has two PGA golf courses, both designed by Donald Ross, at the **Bethlehem Country Club** (☎ 603/869-5745) and the **Maplewood Casino and Country Club** (☎ 603/869-3335 or 603/869-2113).

Hiking: Bretzfelder Memorial Park in Bethlehem has some trails and is a great place to picnic and enjoy nature and observe wildlife.

Skiing: At **Attitash/Bear Peak** (☎ 603/374-2368), the first mountain has a vertical drop of 1,750 feet, the second 1,050 feet. The resort has 46 trails accessed by 10 lifts, including a high-speed super-quad.

   Bretton Woods, Route 302, Bretton Woods (☎ 603/278-5000), has a 1,500-foot vertical drop and 32 trails serviced by five lifts, including a high-speed quad.

State Parks: Crawford Notch (☎ 603/374-2272) offers camping and hiking.

FRANCONIA & SUGAR HILL

The road through **Franconia Notch State Park** (☎ 603/745-8391) on the western side of the Green Mountains, that runs from the Flume Gorge to Echo Lake has to be one of the most scenic in the East.

Your first stop coming from the south will be at the **Flume Gorge** at the base of Mount Liberty. The gorge extends for 800 feet, with granite walls rising 70 to 90 feet above it. You can walk to it yourself along a long trail or take the bus, which will deposit you 500 yards from the entrance to the gorge. You'll cross a covered bridge and then pass huge, dramatic boulders and outcroppings until you reach the Flume at the base of Mount Liberty. Here you'll have a close-up view of the 45-foot **Avalanche Falls.** From the Flume, a trail continues past another cascade to the **Sentinel Pine Bridge and Pool,** a deep basin surrounded by cliffs. It is 40 feet deep and 150 feet in diameter. At the visitor center (☎ 603/745-8391), you can view photographs and other displays relating the history of the Notch and watch a video program about the park. Open mid-May to late October from 9am to 5pm; admission $7 for adults, $4 for children 6 to 12.

The next natural spectacle to stop and see is the **Basin,** a huge granite pothole, 20 feet in diameter, at the bottom of a splendid waterfall on the Pemigewasset River. North of the Basin, **Lafayette Place** is the camping and hiking hub of the park. Stop here at the visitor center for information on trails and weather conditions (☎ 603/823-9513). Just beyond, you'll enter the Notch. Cannon Mountain will be on your left, and you'll soon see the **Old Man of the Mountain,** a granite profile of a great stone face, first discovered in 1805 and immortalized by Nathaniel Hawthorne and Daniel Webster. Scientists estimate that it was formed 200 million years ago. Five granite ledges form a man's profile that, from chin to head, measures 40 feet. It hovers 1,200 feet above **Profile Lake,** which is often referred to as the Old Man's Washbowl. It's open for fly-fishing and is known for its trout.

At **Cannon Mountain,** take the **Aerial Tramway** (☎ 603/823-5563) to the summit for magnificent views over the White Mountains. The first passenger aerial tramway in North America began operation here in 1938. Today it's only a 5-minute ride to the 4,200-foot summit. Walking trails will take you from the aerial station to an observation tower at the summit. A round-trip costs $9 for adults, $7 for children 6 to 12. Back at the base of the mountain, check out the **New England Ski Museum** (☎ 603/823-7177) where you can see and trace the development of ski bindings from leather-bamboo to the high-tech safety bindings of today. Other exhibits trace the history of cross-country and downhill skiing or focus on the ski champions that have made it what it is. Open daily from noon to 5pm; closed Wednesday December 1 to March 31. Admission is free.

Echo Lake, a lovely lake at a high elevation, with views of Mount Lafayette and Cannon Mountain, makes an ideal place for a picnic, a swim, or a little canoeing and fishing. From the lake, it's a short hop into Franconia, either along I-93 or Route 18. The town itself isn't that prepossessing, but the surrounding countryside is beautiful.

Robert Frost is associated with Franconia, and **The Frost Place,** where he lived from 1915 to 1920 and summered until 1938, is on Ridge Road off Route 116 in Franconia (☎ 603/823-5510). It's a center for poetry and the arts, and each summer a resident poet is invited to occupy the house and give poetry readings in the old barn. You can hike the poetry trail, which is marked with plaques featuring Frost's poems. First editions of his works, photographs, and other memorabilia are on display in the house where he wrote many of his best-loved poems. Open Wednesday to Monday in summer, weekends only in spring and fall from 1 to 5pm. Closed Columbus Day to Memorial Day. Admission $3 for adults, $1.25 for children 6 to 15.

From Franconia, Route 117 winds west to Sugar Hill, a charming village that was settled in 1780. Before you reach the center of the village, stop at the **Sugar Hill Sampler** (☎ 603/823-8478), not only because it's an above average gift store but also because it has a fine museum that tells visitors about Sugar Hill and its early settlers. The store sells fine crafts—reverse paintings, lampshades, wood toys, candles, and quilts, plus candy and foodstuffs, including a spiced tea specialty.

More about the town's history can be learned at the **Sugar Hill Historical Museum,** Main Street (☎ 603/823-8142). This very fine small museum creates interesting themed temporary exhibits along with its well-conceived permanent exhibits. Sugar Hill became the nation's first ski resort in 1931 when the first ski school was organized here at the famous Peckett's hotel. The school was organized by Katherine Peck, who brought over an Austrian ski instructor. The hotel was already famous for hosting Bette Davis, who later married the hotel's manager. In the museum is a photograph of Bette herself wearing, of all things, hiking boots! Open July 1 to mid-October, Thursday, Saturday, and Sunday from 1 to 4pm. Admission $2 for adults, free for children 11 and under.

Also on Main Street, **Harman's Cheese & Country Store** (☎ 603/823-8000) is the place to purchase pure maple syrup, berry preserves, honey, and other northern New England products. Just off Route 117, **P C Anderson** makes fine solid-wood furniture at 253 Center District Rd. (☎ 603/823-5209) using oak, cherry, and other hardwoods.

FRANCONIA & SUGAR HILL LODGING & DINING

Bungay Jar B&B, Easton Valley Road (Route 116), Franconia, NH 03580 (☎ 603/823-7775), is an extraordinarily beautiful place. A Shangri-La created by a landscape architect, it's not just the gardens that are stunning—it's the whole place. From the outside, the house looks like a Little Red Riding Hood cottage with raspberry-colored shutters. Step into the delightful living room, built out of 200-year-old timbers, brought from nearby Littleton, that were put together by local craftsmen. The ceiling soars above the huge timbers, and below, the room is wonderfully casual, even though it's decorated with early American hutches and oriental rugs and has wing chairs and a sofa set in front of a wood-burning fireplace. It's obviously been created with loving personal care using an assortment of special objects—quilts, farm implements, books, and toys. The living room flows into the dining area, which features an intricately carved Flemish sideboard and a long table with a runner. Here a breakfast buffet, consisting of local fresh fruits (raspberries and blueberries in season), popovers, smoked meats and fish, plus such items as calendula biscuits and cheddar dill strata or decadent French toast and a chocolate baguette with raspberry sauce, is served.

There are only seven rooms, and each is decorated in an inspired, creative fashion. The most extravagant is the Garden Suite, which has a double Jacuzzi, dimmer switches throughout, a white painted bed covered with a pink fan quilt, and tables with covers in rich embroidery. The ceiling is trellised, and the kitchenette has a microwave, fridge, toaster, and coffeemaker. All of the decorative accents are garden related—seed boxes, garden tools, and more. It also has a private deck. A carved-oak bed graces the Saffron Room. The Rose Room is decked out in rose and green, furnished with a wicker chaise lounge and a dresser with a taffeta fringe, and has a tiny interior balcony overlooking the living room. The bathroom in the Cinnamon Suite boasts Benny Goodman's 6-foot-long bathtub plus a very alluring red-and-yellow gas lamp hanging over the bath. Hand-hewn stairs lead to the Star Gazer Suite that has not only two skylights with views of mountain peaks but also has a telescope. Golden stars decorate the ceiling, and there's another skylight over the bed. A twig loveseat and a gas fireplace add a little extra. Kate Kerivan has an eye for the unusual piece or for the adaptive use of a particular object. For example, the landing railing is made of lightning rods, while the doors came from a church in Boston. A wide deck with wood furniture and herb- and flower-filled barrels overlooks the magnificent terraced gardens (all of the plants are labeled). Winding pathways lead down to a waterlily-filled pond; a wrought-iron bench sits among a small field of sunflowers; more pathways lead down to the river. Shangri-La for sure. Rates: $85 to $160; foliage season $95 to $205.

Jim and Barbara Quinn at the **Sugar Hill Inn,** Route 117, Franconia, NH 03580 (☎ 603/823-5621), have been innkeepers for 12 years. They love what they're doing and go out of their way to welcome and provide comfort to their guests in this 1789 farmhouse. There are 16 rooms available. Those in the main house are decorated in a country style with half-posters, chintz wallpaper, braided rugs, wing chairs, and similar pieces. Room 7 has a Shaker four-poster with a crocheted canopy that is combined with a wing chair and rocker. The cottages contain two units each. They have been attractively decorated and also have gas fireplaces. The sitting room has a woodstove inserted into a brick fireplace, and the dining room is also warmed by a brick hearth. Dinner is offered from Thursday to Monday. The specialty of the house is rack of lamb with a rosemary crust. Prices are $16 to $21. Rates: $100 to $165; foliage season $225 to $265.

The **Foxglove Inn,** Route 117 at Lovers Lane, Sugar Hill, NH 03585 (☎ 603/823-8840), is operated by gracious hosts Walter and Janet Boyd. The house has been very prettily decorated by interior designer Janet in a very feminine and comfortable manner with plenty of lace, silk, heart-shaped boxes, flower motifs, potpourri, silk-flower arrangements, and such extra touches as fragrances in the bathrooms for guests. It's a delicate decor and one that warrants the sign on the bed that asks people kindly not to place their luggage there and to refrain from eating in the bedrooms. Each of the four rooms and one suite is individually decorated; two are equipped with TVs. In one room you might find an upholstered bed piled high with an eiderdown and cushions, a dresser with a silver brush and mirror, wicker chairs, and a table covered with lace, all set against floral wallpaper. Lace curtains hang at the windows. The glass-topped tables in the dining room overlook the back garden, and here a super breakfast, which might feature French toast with corn cob-smoked ham or banana pecan pancakes with smoked turkey, is served. Dinner is also offered and is a very beautifully prepared and served meal. It might begin with cauliflower soup and a salad with a rich walnut vinaigrette and then follow with a dish like shrimp with peppers and oil on linguini or poached salmon on a bed of kale with fresh basil, ginger, and lime sauce. It will close with an equally delicious dessert like the chocolate torte with raspberry sauce. There are two living rooms, and on cool days you'll find a fire blazing in the hearth. Rates: $95 to $145 (on request, dinner is additional).

Sunset Hill House, Sunset Hill Road, Sugar Hill, NH 03585 (☎ 603/823-5522), is set on 10½ acres at the top of a hill with fine mountain views. It was built in 1882 and was one of the famous resorts in the area. Today it has a definite Irish flavor with the tavern and a dining room where you can find a filling camp-fire breakfast. There are 30 rooms available. About 24 have been recently renovated and furnished with antique reproductions—rice four-posters swathed in Waverly fabrics, desks, and chests. All rooms have telephones, and some have Jacuzzi tubs and decorative fireplaces. Guests have the use of three parlors, each with a fireplace. One has an upright piano, and another has games and a TV. The dining room serves modern American cuisine featuring dishes such as double-cut lamb chops with blackberry Chambord sauce, poached salmon with a guava compote, and roast duck with caramelized onions and a zinfandel risotto cake. Facilities include an outdoor pool and a nine-hole golf course that is across the road from the inn. Cross-country skiing is available in winter. Rates: B&B $100 to $160; MAP, $157 to $217; fall foliage MAP only $172 to $242.

Polly's Pancake Parlor, Hildex Maple Sugar Farm, Route 117, Sugar Hill (☎ 603/823-5575), is always crowded and for good reason. It makes great pancakes (and has been doing so since 1938) and waffles and sells them for reasonable prices in a warm country dining room. You can select buckwheat, whole wheat, cornmeal, or oatmeal, along with blueberry walnut or coconut waffles. Everything is $6 or under. For those who don't want the pancakes, there are always sandwiches. Open Mother's Day to mid-October, Monday to

Friday from 7am to 3pm and Saturday and Sunday from 7am to 7pm. Open
weekends only in early spring and late fall.

Franconia Notch
Special & Recreational Activities

Antiquing: There are antique shops in Bethlehem.

Biking: Rent a bike at **Cannon Mountain** and follow the path around Echo
Lake. There's also a bike path from Flume Center to Skookumchuk trailhead.
Rentals are also available at **Franconia Sport Shop**, Main Street, Franconia
(☎ 603/823-5241). Prices start at $19 for a full day. In-line skates are also
available.

Camping: The **White Mountain National Forest** has numerous campgrounds.
For information and reservations, call ☎ 800/280-2267. In **Franconia
Notch State Park** there are 97 wooded tent sites at Lafayette Place
(☎ 603/823-9513).

Cross-Country Skiing: About 50 miles of trails surround the **Franconia Village Cross-Country Ski Center** at the Franconia Inn (☎ 603/823-5542).
Rentals and instruction available.

Fishing: Fly-fishing for trout is good at **Profile Lake.**

Golf: Sunset Hill Golf Course in Sugar Hill is a par-33, nine-hole course.

Hiking: The **Appalachian Trail** cuts right through the park. For **Franconia
Notch State Park** information, call ☎ 603/823-5563. Among the trails
that are most accessible are the Basin-Cascades, Falling Waters, and
Greenleaf. Bald Mountain Artists Bluff Path leads to some glorious views.
The Coppermine Trail from Franconia leads to Bridal Veil Falls on Cannon
Mountain.

Skiing: Cannon Mountain, Franconia Notch Parkway, Franconia (☎ 603/
823-5563), has a 2,146-foot vertical drop and 38 trails accessed by five
lifts, plus an 80-passenger aerial tramway.

Soaring: Route 116, Franconia (☎ 603/823-8881), offers **glider rides** from
May to October.

State Parks: Franconia Notch State Park (☎ 603/823-5563) covers 6,440
acres and offers swimming, picnicking, biking, hiking, and camping.

ACROSS THE BORDER: BETHEL

This historic town across the border in Maine is on the Androscoggin River
about 22 miles east of Gorham. It makes a good base for accessing **Sunday
River** and **Grafton Notch State Park** as well as the White Mountains to the
west and in the Evans Notch area.

The town itself is down to earth. Its most famous institutions are the **Gould
Academy,** which dates back to 1836, and the more recent **National Training**

Laboratories Institute (☎ 800/777-5227). The institute was founded in 1947 and conducted the first experimental human relations program. Today many executives come to the institute to develop leadership skills and study human dynamics. In nearby Newry, the **Hurricane Island Outward Bound School** (☎ 800/341-1744) conducts similar leadership-development courses, but in a wilderness setting. The forerunner of these two establishments was a clinic, operated in the early part of the century by Dr. John Gehring and his two partners. The major anchor on the town green is the **Bethel Inn & Country Club,** which opened in 1913 to house Dr. Gehring's patients. He put Bethel on the map with his successful program of treating nervous disorders through healthy country living.

There are a couple of stores worth browsing on Main Street, notably **Bonnema Potters** (☎ 207/824-2821), and several stores in Philbrook Place. Rock hounds will want to visit **Mount Mann,** 57 Main St. Place (☎ 207/824-3030) to see the artistry of this gem collector and gemstone cutter and jeweler. He has an inventory of Maine's gems—tourmaline, amethyst, aquamarine—as well as stones from around the world, including lapis lazuli and opals.

The **Moses Mason House Museum** (☎ 207/824-2908) is the home of the historical society. It has been restored to reflect the period when physician, civic leader, and entrepreneur Dr. Moses Mason lived here in the early 19th century. The house contains murals by itinerant painter Rufus Porter and an autograph collection. Open July 1 to Labor Day, Tuesday to Sunday from 1 to 4pm.

SCENIC DRIVES

Any White Mountain visit in Bethel starts at the Wild River Valley in **Evans Notch,** which is reached via Route 2 west to Gilead and Route 113 south. You can travel all the way to Fryeburg and then turn back up Route 5 via **Center Lovell** and by **Kezar Lake** to Bethel.

For another scenic tour, drive north through **Grafton Notch State Park** to Errol, New Hampshire, and loop back to Bethel via Berlin. From Bethel, drive north along Route 26, which parallels the Bear River. It will take you to Step Falls and finally into the State Park. Here in the park, there are several falls and gorges in quick succession, notably **Screw Auger Falls, Mother Walker Falls Gorge,** and **Moose Cave Gorge.** The first is a 23-foot-deep gorge where you can swim and picnic; the second is twice as deep and 980 feet long; and the third has a 45-foot-deep slot and a 200-foot-long gorge. Route 26 also accesses **Old Speck Mountain Trails,** which offer some tough hiking, and **Table Rock Trail,** an easier trail that takes you to a huge granite overhang. Outside the park, Route 26 continues into New Hampshire, affording great views of **Umbagog Lake.** As you leave the park, keep an eye out for moose, which are often spotted here. At Errol, turn back south along Route 16, which parallels the Androscoggin River, to Berlin and Gorham and then take Route 2 to return via Shelburne to Bethel. If you don't want to go that far, outside Grafton State Park you can turn right on East B Hill Road to see a couple of Maine's most spectacular waterfalls, **Dunn Falls,** and about a mile farther on the **Cataracts.** In Andover where you can see two turn-of-the-century octagonal buildings, pick up Route 5 south, traveling alongside the Ellis River. Just outside Andover, you'll find the **Lovejoy Covered Bridge**, built around 1867, spanning the Ellis River. Continue on Route 5 and then take 5/2 back into Bethel.

BETHEL LODGING & DINING

The Bethel Inn & Country Club, Bethel, ME 04217 (☎ 207/824-2175), is in the heart of town. This 200-plus-acre resort offers a full range of recreation and a choice of accommodations either in the four buildings that constitute the main inn or in town houses. All rooms have TVs and telephones; some have fireplace and Jacuzzis. The town houses have fully equipped kitchens, living areas with fireplaces, decks, and even washer/dryers. Both types of accommodations are furnished with antique reproductions. The dining room provides a gracious dining experience. The cuisine is continental-American. You might find maple-walnut-scented venison medallions served with a red wine sauce or broiled duck breast with cranberry port wine sauce. Seafoods are simply prepared to bring out the flavor—oven-baked haddock with a citrus sauce or broiled swordfish with a balsamic vinegar sauce. Prices range from $15 to $21. Facilities include a PGA golf course that is among the top rated in the Northeast; 25 miles of groomed cross-country ski trails; a health club with an outdoor heated pool; and swimming, sailing, and canoeing at the Lake House. Rates: MAP mid-June to mid-October: $139 to $199 per person; town houses $169 per person (add $35 for meal plan in town houses); winter $99 to $160 per person; town houses $119 to $140 per person double (add $35 for meal plan in town houses). Deduct $20 per person before mid-June and after mid-October. Special packages available.

Although **The Sudbury Inn**, Lower Main Street, Bethel, ME 04217 (☎ 207/824-2174), has 16 basic country rooms, people come to dine because it has one of the best dining rooms in Bethel. It's not fancy or elegant. It's just a country dining room with an enclosed porch overlooking the street, but the food is good and reasonably priced. You might find grilled loin of lamb with balsamic roasted shallots and a Dijon rosemary sauce, or lobster Sudbury, a roasted lobster that has been shelled and is presented with tomato and tarragon butter sauce over linguini. Prices range from $16 to $19. Downstairs, **Suds Pub** (☎ 207/824-6558) offers micro brews, pizza, and live entertainment 5 nights a week. Open daily for lunch and dinner.

The Telemark Inn, RFD 2, Box 800, Bethel, ME 04217 (☎ 207/836-2703), is an extraordinary place for those who are enthusiastic about nature, conservation, and discovering a better way to live on the earth. Here, in a remote location miles down a dirt road, Alpine ecologist Steve Crone operates his own 360-acre Shangri-La, where he raises Siberian and Alaskan huskies, offers llama treks (he has 15 llamas), and generates his own power. The pine lodge, built 100 years ago by Leo Blanchard, who owned Prudential Insurance, features some extraordinary woodwork and architectural details such as the built-in birch-twig cabinets and birch-root shelving in the bedrooms. The fireplace in the living room incorporates gilded mica quartz into the stonework. There are six rooms, furnished simply with iron or cannonball beds, wall-to-wall carpeting, pine chests, and other pieces. Meals are served at the huge round cherry table that Blanchard himself crafted, in the dining room lit by oil lamps. The food is always health oriented, and many of the ingredients come from the organic garden. If you sign up for a llama trip, you'll arrive the night before; the next day, after a llama orientation, you'll go into the forest and camp by the swimming hole. Trips are led by fully qualified outdoors educators. Winter fun means riding in an antique sleigh, cross-country skiing on 12 miles of groomed trails, plus unlimited backcountry skiing. A remarkable, inspiring place; a place for self-restoration and reawakening to nature. Llama treks are 1 to 4 days; there's also a combination canoeing/trekking 6-day trek. Rates: $100; llama trekking $90 per adult a day; 3 days $450. Other packages available.

For a good brew and entertainment, go to the **Sunday River Brewing Company,** Route 2 and Sunday River Road (☎ 207/824-4ALE). It offers steaks and barbecue, plus sandwiches and burgers that can all be washed down with the beer that's brewed on the premises. Open daily from 11:30am to 9pm.

Bethel
Special & Recreational Activities

Adventure Outfitters: Bethel Outdoor Adventures, Inc., 121 Mayville Rd. (☎ 207/824-4224), offers canoe, kayak, windsurfer, and mountain bike rentals as well as guided hiking and canoe trips on the Androscoggin.

Biking: Sunday River (☎ 207/824-3000) has a lift-served park and some of the best terrain and vistas for this sport. Rentals are available at **Great American Bike Renting Company** (☎ 207/824-3092) at the park.

Boating: Kezar Lake Marina, West Lovell Road, Lovell (☎ 207/925-3000), rents pontoon, power boats, fishing boats, and canoes.

Camping: There are five campgrounds in this region of the White Mountain National Forest. For information, contact **Evan's Notch Visitor Center,** 18 Mayville Rd., Bethel, ME 04217 (☎ 207/824-2134). They are open from mid-May to mid-October only and cost $12 a night.

   Moose Brook State Park (☎ 603/466-3860), off Route 2 west of Gorham, has 42 sites.

Cross-Country Skiing: Telemark Inn (☎ 207/836-2703) in West Bethel; **Bethel Inn & Country Club,** on the Common, Bethel (☎ 207/824-2175); **Sunday River Inn,** Sunday River Road, Bethel (☎ 207/824-2410), has 25 miles of groomed trails.

Fly-Fishing: Rapid River Flyfishing (☎ 207/392-3333) offers courses and trips.

Golf: The course at the **Bethel Inn & Country Club,** on the Common, Bethel (☎ 207/824-2175), is among the top 20 in the East. The **Androscoggin** (☎ 603/466-9468) in Gorham is located along the banks of the Androscoggin River.

Hiking: For trail and other information, contact **Evan's Notch Visitor Center,** 18 Mayville Rd., Bethel, ME 04217 (☎ 207/824-2134). In the Evans Notch region alone there are more than 160 miles of trails.

Horseback Riding: Speckled Mountain Ranch, Flat Road (☎ 207/836-2908).

Llama Trekking & Dog Sledding: Both are offered at **Telemark Inn** (☎ 207/836-2703).

Picnicking: Great locations are available in **Grafton State Park** at Step Falls and Screw Auger Falls.

Skiing: Sunday River (☎ 207/824-3000) is a large and fast-growing resort with 121 trails and 16 modern lifts, including four super-quads. There are eight interconnected mountain peaks and very good snowmaking (92% coverage) for skiing through November to May. Accommodations range from dorms to condos to the Jordan Grand Hotel and Crown Club.

   Mount Abram, Route 26, Locke Mills (☎ 207/875-5003), is a family-oriented resort with 35 trails. It also has a snow-tubing park and an out-door ice-skating rink as well as the ski slopes.

State Parks: Grafton Notch State Park is out along Route 26, north of Bethel. It's a very scenic park with great views of the White Mountains. The Appalachian Trail is just one of the hiking trails that passes through the park. It's also a good place for picnicking or fishing.

Hanover (Dartmouth) & Lake Sunapee

Lake Sunapee Area ✦ *Along the Connecticut River*
from Charlestown to Hanover ✦ *Hanover* ✦ *Lebanon, Enfield,*
Canaan, Etna, Lyme & Orford

Distance in miles from Boston: Lake Sunapee, 110 miles; Hanover, 135.

Estimated driving times: 1¾ hours to Lake Sunapee; 2 hours to Hanover.

Driving: I-89 to Exit 9 (Route 103) to Bradford and Newbury (from Bradford via Route 114 to the Suttons and New London; or Exit 18 and Route 120 north into Hanover.

Further Information: For more information, contact the **Hanover Chamber of Commerce,** P.O. Box 5105, Hanover, NH 03755 (☎ 603/643-3512); **Lebanon Chamber of Commerce,** 2 Whipple Place, Lebanon, NH 03766 (☎ 603/448-1203); **New London Chamber of Commerce,** P.O. Box 532, New London, NH 03257 (☎ 603/526-6575).

Hanover sits at the center of the Upper Connecticut River and is the focal cultural point of reference for the New Hampshire and the Vermont towns that are strung along the river between the White Mountains in the east and the Green Mountains in the west. It has a lot to recommend it to the visitor, and the surrounding area, which is dotted with somnolent villages in pastoral-river landscapes at the base of the foothills of the White Mountains, is ideal back-roading country, perfect for weekend exploration. And only half an hour away is lovely Lake Sunapee.

LAKE SUNAPEE AREA

Lake Sunapee is a small lake that you can easily drive around. Sunapee, on the west side of the lake, is an appealing place, although it is the most commercial town on the lake. The other anchor point for any weekend is New London, an attractive town a few miles inland from the eastern shore.

Events & Festivals to Plan Your Trip Around

February: **Dartmouth Winter Carnival** is an ice-sculpture fest, laced with sporting events and winter-related activities. Call ☎ 603/646-1110.

Chocolate Festival in New London. One of the highlights is the Chocolate Challenge in which a dozen chefs compete with each other to make the most elaborate chocolate concoctions. Call ☎ 603/526-6575.

April: **Pajama Party in New London,** when anyone on the streets in his or her pajamas between 6:30 and 8:30am on Saturday morning can secure 20 percent off at participating stores. Call ☎ 603/526-6575.

August: The **Annual Craftsmen's Fair,** in Newbury, brings together hundreds of artisans who display and sell their works in a series of tents at Mount Sunapee State Park. The quality is high, and the exhibits include ceramics, textiles, jewelry, wood, stained glass, pewter, and much, much more. Workshops and entertainment make it even more fun. Call ☎ 603/526-6575.

Lake Sunapee Antique and Classic Boat Parade in Sunapee Harbor.

The **Cornish Fair** is a traditional country fair with 4-H exhibits and competitions as well as other demonstrations of horse and oxen pulling. Fireworks cap it all off. Call ☎ 603/643-3512.

Muster Field Farm Days are held at a historic farm in a lovely bucolic spot. Here more than 100 demonstrations of agrarian skills are given—coopering, spinning, tanning, dowsing, sheep shearing, stone-wall building—plus a grand parade, roast-beef dinner, and more. For information, call ☎ 603/927-4276.

On your way to New London, stop at the **Mount Kearsarge Indian Museum** (☎ 603/456-2600), Kearsarge Mountain Road in Warner. It's a very rewarding museum, and the guides who lead the 90-minute tours help to give you real insight into Native American culture and the harmony that existed between Native Americans and their world. You'll learn how the Native Americans made their birch bark canoes, how they secured porcupine quills for their baskets without harming the porcupine, and many other facts about aspects of the many different Native American cultures. You'll also see how they adapted to white culture. Take some time to read the quotations from Lakota Chief Luther Standing Bear and others. They're worth pondering. Open May through October, Monday to Saturday from 10am to 5pm and Sunday from noon to 5pm; November to the weekend before Christmas, weekends only.

From Warner, Route 103 brings you to Bradford where you can turn off on Route 114 to the Suttons. At North Sutton, **Lake Kezar** is an ideal stop for a picnic. Near the lake, **Musterfield Farm Museum** (☎ 603/927-4616) has a bucolic setting in North Sutton. It's an old farm dating back to the late 18th century when it was settled by a Matthew Harvey, who built the homestead in 1784. There are numerous farm buildings to see—barns, an ice house, corn cribs, a blacksmith shop, the 1810 schoolhouse—which tell the story of the evolution of farming in this region. It's still a working farm, and there's a farm stand that sells produce. Open Sundays in July and August from 1 to 4pm.

New London is a pretty town with a village green where many community events are held. Wander along Main Street and browse in the stores. Anyone interested in history will want to drop in to the **New London Historical Society,** Little Sunapee Road, and view the 10 or so buildings that have been relocated here and reflect earlier forms of architecture and ways of life.

Evening entertainment includes the **New London Barn Playhouse,** 209 Main St. (☎ 603/526-4631), which presents a summer season of musicals and comedies. Concerts are also arranged during the summer by **Summer Music Associates of New London.** Call ☎ 603/526-8750 for information.

From here, you can take Route 11 to nearby Lake Sunapee. Lake Sunapee was always a smaller quieter resort area than the White Mountains and Lake Winnipesaukee, and it remains quieter and less frantic to this day. On the way to the lake, antiques lovers will want to take a detour to **Prospect Hill Antiques,** Prospect Hill Road, Georges Mills (☎ 603/763-9676). It's a pleasant mile drive to an old barn filled with all kinds of country furniture—pine, oak, and walnut armoires; carved mahogany Victorian pieces; hand-painted German chests; and other decorative items. Open May to October, daily from 10am to 5:30pm; November to April, Tuesday to Saturday only. Continue on Route 11 to Sunapee Harbor from which boats sail on the lake. There are some interesting stores to browse here. **Small Change Kilims,** 71 Lake Ave. (☎ 603/763-9177), sells gorgeous Turkish tribal rugs at reasonable prices. Open Wednesday to Sunday in summer.

From Sunapee, take routes 103B and 103 to reach Newbury. If you want a panoramic view of the region, take the chairlift to the top of **Mount Sunapee** (☎ 603/763-2356). It operates daily from late June to Labor day, and weekends in May, early June, and October, charging $5.50 for adults, $2.50 for children 6 to 12. From Newbury, take Route 103A up the eastern shore of the lake. Newbury was the chosen summering place of the retired author and statesman John Milton Hay who served under President Lincoln and three subsequent presidents including Teddy Roosevelt. He built **The Fells,** on 103A, in 1890–91. Between 1914 and 1940, John's son Clarence and his wife, Alice Appleton Hay, landscaped the property, laying out a walled garden, a rose terrace, a perennial garden, an Alpine garden, rockeries, and water gardens, all with views of Lake Sunapee. Today the property serves as the **John Hay National Wildlife Refuge.** The house has few furnishings except for its fine wood paneling and is used primarily for classrooms. There are more than 60 acres with 5 miles of hiking trails, one leading to the top of Sunset Hill for great views of the lake. It's great to visit in May when the lilacs and azaleas are in bloom. July is the month for rhododendron, while the perennial borders are at their peak in August and September. Fall is spectacular. The grounds are open year round from dawn to dusk; the house from Memorial Day to

Columbus Day, weekends only from 11am to 5pm. Admission $3 for adults, $1 for children 6 to 15.

AREA LODGING

The **Follansbee Inn**, Route 114 (P.O. Box 92), North Sutton, NH 03260 (☎ 603/927-4221), is right across the street from Kezar Lake. It's a welcoming, old-fashioned country inn, dating to 1840, where guests return year after year to renew their friendship with innkeepers Dick and Sandy Reilein. The 23 rooms are small and modestly furnished—beds with candlewick spreads, chintz wallpaper, a dresser, and an upright chair. Some rooms share baths. Guests gather at several tables in the morning for a breakfast of pancakes and bacon or a similar hot dish plus all the trimmings. There's a dock and a beach for swimming at the lake. It's a very warm, convivial place and an excellent value. Rates: $85 to $115.

The **New London Inn**, 140 Main St. (P.O. Box 8), New London, NH 03257 (☎ 603/526-2791), dates to 1792. It sits in the center of town, its long front porch overlooking a pretty garden border. It is currently being restored and renovated by the new owners, who have redecorated 9 of the 27 rooms. In these rooms, guests will find high-back oak beds set against chintz-patterned wallpaper, combined with pine or Empire chests and wicker or wing chairs. The owners have retained the wide-board floors, and each room has been given a spacious light and airy feel. The inn has a comfortable sitting room and library. The dining room is one of the best places to dine in the area. The menu is limited, offering eight or so main courses. For example, there might be New England lobster cakes with horseradish tomato cream, roast duck with wild-berry sauce, or loin lamb chops with mint sauce. Prices range from $12 to $18. A buffet breakfast is served. Dining hours are Tuesday to Sunday from noon to 2pm and 5 to 9pm. Rates: $80 to $140.

Dexter's Inn & Tennis Club, Stagecoach Road, Sunapee, NH 03782 (☎ 603/763-5571), is a pleasant country resort that has 20 acres of beautifully landscaped grounds and splendid mountain views. The 17 accommodations are somewhat old-fashioned but they are well maintained. There are two sitting rooms, one with a stone fireplace, plus a screened porch. Facilities include three tennis courts, an outdoor pool with a deck, and lawns for sitting and playing. Rates: May to October, MAP $67.50 to $87.50 per person double. Closed November to May 1.

The Inn at Pleasant Lake, 125 Pleasant St., New London, NH 03257 (☎ 603/526-6271), is situated on a knoll with a clear view of the lake and the mountains behind. There are 12 rooms, about half of them with views of the lake and Mount Kearsarge. They are furnished in country style with brass and four-poster beds, and one room has a rope bed. The one suite has a whirlpool tub in the bathroom. There are two sitting rooms for guests' leisure. Afternoon tea and a full breakfast are served. Facilities include a tennis court and a beach.

The young new owners have developed a good reputation for the dining room, which is the prime reason to visit. Here a five-course fixed-price meal is served. At a premeal reception, Chef Brian MacKenzie explains the technique and ingredients used in preparing the dinner. Menus change daily. The meal might begin with a savory lobster bisque garnished with diced lobster. To follow comes a salad of organic baby spinach with a balsamic vinaigrette, pumpernickel croutons, and edible pansies, along with country French bread with herb butter. An entremezzo of fresh citrus sections with a splash of sherry or something similar comes next. There will be two entrees to choose from: for example, oven-roasted leg of lamb served with a roasted-garlic rosemary demiglace and watercress salad or pan-seared mahimahi with an exotic mushroom salad and yellow-pepper oil. The meal might close with a rosette of white chocolate mousse in a lace cookie cup with a trio of sauces. The price is $38 per person. The dining room is closed Tuesday. Rates: $105 to $145. Open for 7pm seating, in summer from Wednesday to Monday, in winter, Wednesday to Sunday.

AREA DINING

See above for the notable dining rooms of the **Inn at Pleasant Lake**, which offers a six-course fixed-price dinner, and the **New London Inn.**

    Peter Christian's Tavern, 186 Main St., New London (☎ 603/526-4042), is a fun place to go for some convivial dining and plentiful portions of hearty fare at reasonable prices. Wooden beams and wood tables and high-back wooden booths establish the pubby atmosphere. The menu ranges from a good shepherd's pie, enhanced by whole kernel corn, to huge sandwiches like Peter's Russian Mistress, which is roasted turkey breast, tomato, bacon and spinach topped with Swiss cheese and Russian dressing. There's also a huge burrito. The great crocks of soup are a meal in themselves. Prices range from $6 to $11. Among the desserts, the apple berry crisps made with berries of the season are legendary, and so is the carrot cake with pineapple and walnuts and the brownie sundae. Open daily 11am to 10pm.

Lake Sunapee, New London, Kezar Lake & the Suttons
Special & Recreational Activities

Beaches: There's a beach at **Mount Sunapee State Park** and at Kezar Lake at **Wadleigh State Park** in North Sutton (☎ 603/927-4724).

Biking: Mountain bikes can be rented at **Village Sport** in New London (☎ 603/526-4948). There's lift-served mountain biking at Mount Sunapee State Park.

Canoeing: Rentals available at **Alden's of Sunapee** in Sunapee Harbor (☎ 603/863-5327). Kayaks and paddleboats, too. Canoes are also available at **Mount Sunapee State Park** beach.

Cross-Country Skiing: Nineteen miles of trails plus skating and snowshoeing await the visitor at **Eastman Cross-Country** in Grantham, NH (☎ 603/863-4500). Cross-country trails are also at **Norsk Cross-Country Ski Center,** Route 11, New London (☎ 603/526-4685).

Cruises: M/V *Mt Sunapee II* cruises around the lake for a cost of $10 for adults and $6 for children under 12. M/V *Kearsarge* offers buffet supper cruises (☎ 603/763-5477). Both operate from mid-May to mid-October.

Golf: The Country Club of New Hampshire in North Sutton (☎ 603/927-4246) is one of the best courses in the state.

Hiking: In **Mount Sunapee State Park** there are miles of hiking trails.

Kayaking: Instruction is provided on the Black Water River by **Quickwater Kayak Tours** (☎ 603/526-4685).

Moose Spotting: Prime spying area is along Route 114 between Bradford and Hennicker.

Nature Reserves: Beaver pond and trails are available at **Esther Currie Wildlife Management Area** at Low Plain, Route 11, New London. In New London, off Newport Road, boardwalk trails cut across the **Philbrick Cricenti Bog.**

Scuba Diving: LaPorte's SkinDiving, Route 103, Box 53, Newbury (☎ 603/763-5353) offers lessons in the lake.

Skiing: Mount Sunapee, Route 103, has 30 trails, eight lifts, and 95% snow-making capability (☎ 603/763-2356).

State Parks: Mount Sunapee State Park offers swimming, boating, mountain biking, hiking, and picnicking. At **Rollins State Park,** off Route 103 (☎ 603/456-3808), 4 miles north of Warner, an auto road climbs to the summit of Mount Kearsarge for picnicking, with great views. A trail leads to the very top.

ALONG THE CONNECTICUT RIVER FROM CHARLESTOWN TO HANOVER

From Sunapee, Route 11/103 leads to the Upper Connecticut Valley and the towns of Claremont and Charlestown. About a mile north of Charlestown off Route 11, the **Fort at No 4,** Springfield Road (☎ 603/826-5700), recalls the time when this was the frontier during the French and Indian wars of the 1740s and 1750s. It's a reconstruction of a settlement that was turned into a fort. The log stockade encloses houses, a great hall, and watch tower, while outside stand workshops and barns. Costumed staff members lead tours, and musket loading and other skills are demonstrated daily. Open Memorial Day to Labor Day, Wednesday to Monday from 10am to 4pm; weekends only the first 2 weeks in September, and then Wednesday to Monday until Columbus Day. Admission: $6 for adults, $4 for children 6 to 12.

From the fort, return to Route 12/11 and travel north to the junction of Route 12A, which runs along the eastern side of the Connecticut River. About 14 or so miles along this route, you'll come to the **Cornish-Windsor covered bridge** spanning the Connecticut River. It was built in 1866 for $9,000, and at 460 feet it is not only the longest wooden bridge in the United States but also the longest two-span covered bridge in the world. The current bridge is the fourth version.

In the 19th century, Yankee ingenuity and enterprise were legendary, and across the river in Windsor, Vermont, at the **American Precision Museum,** 196 Main St. (☎ 802/674-5781), you'll encounter some of it. You'll be standing in an armory that was at the center of the development of the modern system of industrial design and production. Here at the Robbins, Kendall &

Lawrence Armory, the first mass-produced rifles using the new concept of interchangeable parts were manufactured. The company exhibited them at the famous Crystal Palace Exhibition in London in 1851 and secured an order from the British government for what was, at the time, a highly innovative product. When the demand for arms diminished after the Civil War, the plant adapted its mass-production methods to produce consumer products like typewriters and sewing machines. The historic building now houses the National Machine Tool collection, which may not excite everyone, but will fascinate budding engineers and those interested in technological development. Here are the tools that made the Sharps, Enfield, and Springfield rifles; the cars that Henry Ford produced; and the inventions of Thomas Edison. There are also scale models, photographs, blueprints, and other documents on view. Open Memorial Day to November 1, Monday to Friday 9am to 5pm, Saturday and Sunday from 10am to 4pm. Admission is $5 for adults, $2 for students and children over 6.

Back on the New Hampshire side of the river, a few miles north of the Cornish-Windsor bridge, don't miss the **St. Gaudens Historic Site** in Cornish, off Route 12A (☎ 603/675-2175). It has a most beautiful setting and terrific views of Mount Ascutney. Noted sculptor Augustus St. Gaudens and his wife, Gussie, arrived here to summer in 1885 and rented this old abandoned tavern. Later they purchased the tavern, together with 23 acres, for $500 and named it Aspet after his father's French birthplace. The couple lived here full time from 1900, when Augustus developed cancer, until his death in 1907.

After training at Cooper Union and at the École des Beaux Arts in Paris, St. Gaudens began his career as an apprentice cameo carver in 1861, working for Jules LeBrethon at his studio at Broome and Broadway in Manhattan. You can see some of St. Gaudens's lovely cameo portraits of figures such as writer Robert Louis Stevenson, artist Bastien La Page, and Mary Queen of Scots. It followed naturally from his cameo expertise that St. Gaudens would go on to make remarkably fine relief portraits—virtually delicate drawings made in stone. You can see some of those works here, too. He also designed some of the most beautiful coins ever made—the $10 and $20 pieces during the Teddy Roosevelt administration.

The gardens are entrancing, and here a series of settings has been created for some of his masterworks. One is dedicated to the moving memorial that he created for Marian Hooper Adams, wife of Henry Adams, who committed suicide. Another contains the most famous piece of all, the extraordinary Robert Shaw Memorial, which took years to accomplish. St. Gaudens used 40 different models for the heads of the black soldiers—he was the first artist in America to bother to individualize blacks. The most beautiful garden salon has been created for the panel of *Ceres,* one of four that St. Gaudens made for Cornelius Vanderbilt's Fifth Avenue mansion. *Ceres* stands in emblazoned glory at the end of a small lily pond surrounded by a classical atrium-arcade. It's an extraordinarily moving place and a fitting memorial to a man who said as a justification for the time and care that it took to complete the Shaw monument: "There is something extraordinarily irritating, when it is not ludicrous, in a bad statue. A poor picture goes into the garret, books are forgotten, but the bronze remains to accuse or shame the populace and perpetuate one of our idiocies. It is plastered before the world to stick and stick for centuries while man and nations pass away."

St. Gaudens attracted in his wake a number of creative artists who settled in the community of Cornish where they could find low-cost accommodations in a beautiful mountain landscape. The **Cornish Colony** lasted roughly from 1885 to 1935. Its 75 or so members included actress Ethel Barrymore; artists Everett Shinn, Kenyon Cox, and Stephen and Maxfield Parrish (who lived in nearby Plainfield); sculptors Frederic Remington, William and Marguerite Zorach, Paul Manship, and Herbert Adams; plus landscape architects Rose Nichols and Ellen Shipman, novelist Winston Churchill, and poet-dramatist Percy Mackaye. The commentators Herb Croly and Finley Peter Dunne, founding editor of the *New Review*, were also part of the group.

Few traces except the mill and some markers along Route 12 remain to recall this group of bohemians who frolicked and summered here and indulged their creative spirits by performing dramas and masques. They produced *The Gods and the Golden Bowl* in 1905 in a pine grove at Aspet to celebrate St Gaudens's 20th year in Cornish. The temple stage set was later re-created in marble, and St. Gaudens and his family rest beneath it on the grounds at Aspet. Open daily late May to late October from 9am to 4:30pm. Admission: $4 for adults 17 and older, under 17, free.

CORNISH & PLAINFIELD LODGING

The **Chase House,** Chase Street (Route 12A), Cornish, NH 03745 occupies two 18th-century homes, one dating to 1766, the other to 1775. They stand on 160 acres (11 of them along the Connecticut River) with fine views of Mount Ascutney. The inn is named after Senator Salmon P. Chase (of Chase Manhattan fame), who was also secretary of the treasury in Lincoln's cabinet and chief justice of the Supreme Court. He was born in 1808 in the older house, in what is currently the dining room. Today, Bill and Barbara Lewis welcome guests to eight rooms, all of which have been very tastefully decorated using striped wallpapers; serpentine canopied beds; oriental rugs; and good-looking chests, desks, and wing and armchairs. Swag drapes grace the windows. Breakfast is served in the dining room at a large table set with Hitchcock chairs. Main course for the day might be buttermilk pancakes, egg strata, or French toast plus all the usual trimmings, including some extra-special wicked popovers. There's also a comfortable sitting room with a fireplace for guests. The other marvel on the property, a magnificent post-and-beam gathering room taken from the second story of an 1810 Garrison Colonial house; it is now used as a function room. It has a super-large stone fireplace with a raised fieldstone hearth and a minstrel loft. The entire space is lit by tin Shaker-style candelabras. Rates: $105 to $135.

Home Hill Country Inn, River Road, Plainfield, NH 03781 (☎ 603/675-6165), is a splendid 1763 mansion set behind wrought-iron gates and surrounded by gardens. It has great style and savoir faire throughout, from the elegant and renowned dining room to the attractively appointed guest rooms. The inn is set amid 25 acres of wonderful gardens, and in summer the terrace is the place to dine at the tables with their attractive market umbrellas. There are four guest rooms and a two-bedroom suite in the main house, plus two rooms and a suite in the carriage house. The pool house is only available seasonally. The rooms are furnished in country style with oak dressers, stenciling, and blanket chests along with oriental rugs. Candlelit dinners are served in three intimate dining rooms. The four-course fixed-price menu costs between $32 and $38, depending on the entree selection. On the menu you'll find updated classics such as the pan-seared duck with a citrus sauce, fresh ginger, and currants or the rack of lamb roasted with a rosemary and brandy sauce. The tuna, seared rare and served with a warm sherry and caper vinaigrette, is a lovely fresh dish. To start, you might enjoy scallop mousse surrounding a ragout of prawns in a lobster sauce, finished with light saffron cream. End with a fresh cherry flan or chocolate and hazelnut tart with raspberry sauce. Open Monday to Saturday for one 7pm seating. Rates: $135 to $185.

WINDSOR (VERMONT) LODGING

Juniper Hill Inn, R.R.1, Box 79, Windsor, VT 05089 (☎ 802/674-5273), is set on a hill outside Windsor with magnificent views of Mount Ascutney and the Connecticut River Valley. This 28-room mansion was built in 1902 as the centerpiece for a 350-acre estate. Since then it has served both as a school and a nursing home, but today it makes a wonderful inn, with 16 spacious rooms. They are handsomely furnished with pencil four-poster canopied beds, pretty floral wallpapers, and Empire dressers or Eastlake wing chairs. Some have woodstoves and porches. The sitting rooms are very large. Both library and sitting room have wood-burning fireplaces, and both have rich honey-oak paneling and detailed molding. There are attractive gardens in front and back. The brick porch, supported by Ionic columns, overlooks the gardens and offers views of Mount Ascutney. A full breakfast is served, and meals are offered for overnight guests and to the public from Monday to Saturday. A four-course dinner will feature a short selection of poultry, fish, and meat dishes—chicken marsala, halibut with pineapple salsa, or tenderloin tips. Rates: $105 to $165 (dinner is about $30 per person additional).

HANOVER

Arranged around a central green that has a white steepled church on one side, Hanover is a classic New England town. It was chartered by Benning Wentworth, governor of New Hampshire, in 1761. What brought the town its greatest fame was the arrival in 1769 of a school for Native Americans, originally established in Connecticut by Congregationalist minister Eleazar Wheelock. Subsequently, the school became Dartmouth College.

Today **Dartmouth College** (☎ 603/646-1110) has a 200-acre campus and a student body of close to 6,000. On campus there are some treasures that you won't want to miss. My favorites are the extraordinary frescoes, *The Epic of American Civilization,* painted by Mexican artist Jose Clemente Orozco in 1932–34 on the walls of the lower floor of Baker Memorial Library. These frescoes condense 3,000 years of American history into two parts. The pre-Columbian themes are explored in the west wing of the hall and post-Columbian in the East Wing.

The Hood Museum of Art on Wheelock Street (☎ 603/646-2426 or 603/646-2808), is one of the oldest and largest university collections. It was begun in 1773 when Governor Wentworth donated a large engraved silver bowl in honor of the college's first commencement in 1770. From then it has expanded prodigiously. Among the highlights of the collection are Assyrian reliefs from the palace of Ashurnasirpal II, dating to the 9th century B.C., along with fine Cypriote, Egyptian, Greek, and Roman antiquities. European art is also well represented, particularly such French artists as Boucher, Chardin, Watteau, and Fragonard. Chinese paintings, ceramics, and bronzes are a major part of the collection and so too are the pottery, baskets, textiles, and clothing from Africa, Oceania, and Native North America. The American collection is also very strong, containing works by Gilbert Stuart, Thomas Eakins, John Sloan, Maurice Prendergast, William Merritt Chase, John Copley, George Inness, Thomas Doughty, and James McNeill Whistler. Other famous names in the collection include Picasso, Braque, Gris, Lipchitz, Leger, Botero, Kenneth Noland, Alex Katz, Mark Rothko, and Sol Le Witt. Open Tuesday to Saturday from 10am to 5pm, Wednesday until 9pm, and Sunday from noon to 5pm. Admission is free.

The **Hopkins Center for the Arts** (☎ 603/646-2422) was designed by the architect who went on to create Lincoln Center. In addition to the theater space, it contains design workshops, drama classrooms, and a cafeteria. Other cultural performances are found at the **Claremont Opera House** (☎ 603/542-4433), which features everything from Irish cabaret and Gilbert & Sullivan operettas to the Vienna Boys Choir. The season runs from September to May.

Browse along Main Street and drop into the **Dartmouth Bookstore** (☎ 800/624-8800, or 800/675-3616 in New Hampshire). This store has been on the west side of Main Street since it was founded in 1883 by the Storrs family, who still run it today. It's a large and wonderful bookstore.

HANOVER LODGING & DINING

The **Hanover Inn,** Wheelock Street (P.O. Box 151), Hanover, NH 03755 (☎ 800/443-7024 or 603/643-4300), faces the green and is the place to stay for parents and others visiting the university. A tavern-hotel has stood here since 1780, but the core of the current building was built in 1889 although it has been extended frequently since then. It's a typical comfortable, modern hostelry, with a low-key atmosphere and 92 rooms equipped with cable TV and telephones. The lobby is a pleasant place to sit. The Terrace Cafe is quite lovely in summer when diners can look out over the outdoor cafe's cheery window boxes to the green beyond. The dining room is named after Dartmouth graduate Daniel Webster and is decorated in appropriate Federal style. The cuisine is finely prepared in a contemporary yet traditional style. For example, the menu will feature a plain aged sirloin alongside a grilled rack of lamb with a martini sauce or yellowfin tuna with caramelized onions and toasted pine nuts and grilled salmon in a champagne sorrel sauce. Open Tuesday to Friday from 7 to 10:30am, 11:30am to 1:30pm, and 6 to 9pm; Saturday from 7 to 10:30am and 6 to 9pm; Sunday and Monday from 8 to 10am and 11am to 1:30pm. Prices range from $15 to $26. Rates: $227 to $237; suites $287 to $297.

Cafe Buon Gustaio, 72 S. Main St. (☎ 603/643-5711), is an intimate place to dine. It's small, and the low ceilings and beams only add to its charm, as does the tiny bar with its peach-colored walls. The kitchen uses only the freshest ingredients. A house-made mozzarella is featured in several dishes; for example, the cannelloni of smoked chicken, asparagus, mushrooms, mozzarella, and ricotta with d'Abruzzi red sauce. Another very rich pasta dish is the spinach pasta lasagna of lobster, fresh grilled eggplant, leeks, Vidalia onions, peppers, ricotta, and mozzarella in a fontina cream sauce. The rest of the menu offers pizzetta and dishes such as grilled rib eye with mushrooms, peppers, and roasted red onions or pan-seared red snapper with putanesca sauce and asparagus. These dishes are accompanied by six or seven grilled vegetables. As an appetizer, the cioppino is really good. Prices range from $12 to $19. Fifteen wines are available by the glass. Open Tuesday to Saturday from 5:30pm to closing.

Lou's, 30 S. Main St. (☎ 603/643-3321), is a must for breakfast. It's a classic diner-deli with a counter, but it has a little more "decor" provided by prints and photos of local scenes. Good sandwiches, plus burgers, fish and chips, quesadillas, and other things that the college kids like. Open Monday to Friday from 6am to 3pm, Saturday from 7am to 5pm, and Sunday from 7am to 3pm. Prices range from $5 to $7.

LEBANON, ENFIELD, CANAAN, ETNA, LYME & ORFORD

From Hanover, you can take Route 120 southeast to Lebanon, picking up Route 4 to Route 4A, which will take you to the **Enfield Shaker Museum,** Route 4A, Enfield (☎ 603/632-4346). This museum is located in the Shaker "Chosen Vale," a beautiful valley between Mount Assurance and Mascoma Lake. The Shakers settled here in 1793 on the slopes of Mount Assurance. In 1923 the Shakers closed their community and sold the property to the La Salettes, an order of Catholic priests who established a seminary and high school. The museum retains 13 Shaker buildings, which you can tour on your own to view the exhibits of their furniture, tools, and clothing. Highlights include the great stone dwelling, the largest and most expensive building erected by any Shaker community, and the wooden Shaker barn. Open Memorial Day to mid-October, Monday to Saturday from 10am to 5pm, and Sunday from noon to 5pm; November to Memorial Day, Saturday from 10am to 4pm and Sunday from noon to 4pm. Admission $5 for adults, $2.50 for children ($1 off in winter).

While you're on the museum property, go over and watch the Dana Robes's woodcrafters and other artisans, who fashion furniture, wooden bowls, ceramics, baskets, and textiles. During the summer, craft demonstrations and workshops are offered. For information about the workshops of these **Meetinghouse Artisans,** call ☎ 603/632-5385.

CANAAN, ETNA & LYME LODGING & DINING

Moose Mountain Lodge, Moose Mountain Highway (P.O. Box 272), Etna, NH 03750 (☎ 603/643-3529), is on the western slope of the mountain in an absolutely magnificent setting with glorious views of the Connecticut River Valley and the Green Mountains. Relaxed, warm, and friendly, this is a real haven—an extraordinary retreat on 350 acres—the perfect place for a summer or winter weekend. It was built in the 1930s as a ski lodge and has a wonderful woodsy air. The acreage connects with the Appalachian Trail for extended hikes and ski tours. The present owners, Kay and Peter Shumway, have lived here for 22 years—they love it so. From the long front porch there are magnificent views, and you may spot a moose at the beaver pond. The sitting room is extremely cozy and has plenty of good books to while away the evening hours. Twig rockers and other log cabin–style furnishings cluster in front of the large stone fireplace in the sitting room; there's also a grand piano. The 12 rooms, sharing 5 baths, are small and simple, but with all the essentials—good reading lights over the bed, oak desks, Shaker-style pegs, pine side tables, and the extra special touch of some fine art. Kay designed the great log beds with the help of a local carpenter. There's a huge game room downstairs, equipped with Ping-Pong, a player piano, and a great stone fireplace. In winter, breakfast, lunch, and dinner are served; in summer, just breakfast and dinner. Kay makes her own breads, pastas, and maple syrup; much of the produce comes from the gardens. Buffet-style meals are taken at a long library table in a warm and inviting dining room. Rates: June 1 to October 24, MAP $90 per person per day (deduct $20 if you don't take dinner); December 26 to early March, AP (three meals a day) $100.

Sweet Tomatoes Trattoria, 1 Court St., Lebanon (☎ 603/448-1711), celebrates Italy and all things Italian. The decor is classic modern Italian and so, too, are the dishes. The specialty is wood-fired cuisine. Try the pizza made with wood-fired roasted mushrooms, tomatoes, garlic, olive oil, and mozzarella or the wood-fired roasted sausage with the same accompanying ingredients. There are also several pasta and seafood dishes, which are very popular. *Fruit di mare* is a combination of shrimp, calamari, and scallops sautéed with plum tomatoes, garlic, lemon, parsley, olive oil, and white wine and served over linguine; the sautéed zucchini, wood-fired roasted red peppers, spinach, garlic, and olive oil are tossed with *penne ziti rigate*. Great panini are also available. They do takeout, if you want a picnic. Prices for dinner entrees range from $7 to $13. Open Monday to Friday from 11:30am to 2pm, Monday to Thursday from 5 to 9pm, Friday and Saturday from 5 to 9:30pm.

Hanover & the Upper Connecticut River Valley
Special & Recreational Activities

Canoeing: For rentals and to take a canoe trip, including overnight tours, contact **North State Livery,** R.R. 2, Box 894, Cornish, NH 03745 (☎ 603/542-5802). Canoes rent for $30 a day. Daily trips start at $17 per person.

Fishing: For information on where the fish are, and for guided trips and classes in fly-fishing, go to **The Lyme Angler** in Hanover, 8 S. Main St. (☎ 603/643-1263). Guided trips for trout on the Upper Connecticut River are offered by **River Excitement,** P.O. Box 65, Hartland Four Corners, VT 05049 (☎ 802/457-4021).

Hang Gliding: Morningside Flight Park, R.R. 2, Box 109, Claremont (☎ 603/542-4416) is well known among practitioners of this sport. You can take an introductory lesson or a comprehensive course in the art. Prices begin at $100 for an introductory lesson, which provides simulated experience only.

Skiing: Dartmouth Skiway, Lyme Center (☎ 603/795-2143), attracts students to its 16 trails. The vertical drop is only 900 feet, and there is one quad and one double chair.

State Parks: Cardigan State Park (☎ 603/763-2356) has access points in Orange off Route 4 and Route 118, 4½ miles east of Canaan, has a road that leads to a picnic spot on the western slope of Mount Cardigan. The park has extensive hiking trails, including several trails leading to the summit.

VERMONT

Wilmington, Mount Snow &
the Southeast Corner

Brattleboro & Marlboro ◆ *Ludlow, Londonderry,*
Weston & Landgrove ◆ *Wilmington, West Dover, & Mount Snow*

Distance in miles from Boston: Brattleboro, 102; Grafton, 152.

Estimated driving times: 2¼ hours to Brattleboro; 3¼ hours to Grafton.

◄◊►◄◊►◄◊►◄◊►◄◊►

Driving: To Brattleboro, take I-90 west to I-91 north to Exit 1 or Exit 2 or take I-93 to I-89 to Route 2 west to I-91 north to Brattleboro.

Further Information: For more information, on Vermont in general: **Vermont Department of Travel & Tourism,** 134 State St., Montpelier, VT 05602 (☎ 802/828-3236); **Vermont State Chamber of Commerce,** P.O. Box 37, Montpelier, VT 05602 (☎ 802/223-3443). For state park camping information: **Department of Forests, Parks & Recreation,** 103 S. Main St. (10 South), Waterbury, VT 05670 (☎ 802/241-3655).

For specific town information: **Brattleboro Chamber of Commerce,** 180 Main St., Brattleboro, VT 05301 (☎ 802/254-4565); **Grafton Information Center,** Grafton, VT 05146 (☎ 802/843-2255); **Chester Chamber of Commerce,** P.O. Box 623, Chester, VT 05143 (☎ 802/875-2939); **Ludlow Area Chamber of Commerce,** P.O. Box 333, Ludlow, VT 05149 (☎ 802/228-5830); **Londonderry Chamber of Commerce,** P.O. Box 58, Londonderry, VT 05148 (☎ 802/824-8178); **Mount Snow Valley Chamber of Commerce,** West Main Street (P.O. Box 3), Wilmington, VT 05363 (☎ 802/464-8092).

◄◊►◄◊►◄◊►◄◊►◄◊►

This corner of Vermont has much to offer the visitor. The major town of **Brattleboro** is still hip and friendly, a town where the '60s lingers on in an updated form. Walk the streets and drop into the stores and galleries. Take a look at the restored Latchis Hotel and the movie theater next door—an art deco extravaganza where the ceiling is emblazoned with the zodiac. The town is at the confluence of the West and Connecticut rivers, making it an ideal location for canoeing and other outdoor pursuits. Four mountains are within a 45-minute drive—Mount Snow, Okemo, Stratton, and Bromley. The first is a major Vermont mountain and is blessed with some wonderful inns and

Events & Festivals to Plan Your Trip Around

February/March: Brattleboro holds a large carnival with more than 50 events, including an ice-fishing derby and a 70-meter ski jump. Call ☎ 802/254-4565.

March/April: Easter Weekend at Mount Snow, when a sunrise service is held at the summit along with a variety of other events including parades and egg hunts. For information, call ☎ 802/464-3333.

July: Art on the Mountain at Haystack Mountain, which is in its 35th year, displays the works of New England's finest artists and craftspeople. The show includes pottery, glass, quilts, watercolors, photographs, furniture, and jewelry all of terrific quality. Don't miss it. Usually the third weekend.

July/August: Marlboro Music Festival. Weekend concerts from mid-July through mid-August at Marlboro College's Persons Auditorium. To book tickets, call ☎ 802/254-2394 between June 15 and August 15; ☎ 215/569-4690 before June 15.

August: Vermont State Zucchini Festival in Ludlow celebrates this humble vegetable with competitions for the largest specimen grown, plus cooking contests, a hill climb, golf tournament, and other events. Call ☎ 802/228-5830.

bed-and-breakfasts scattered through the Deerfield Valley. The anchor town here is Wilmington, which has been experiencing a mini-renaissance in the last few years, sprouting interesting stores and galleries of its own.

Quiet, tiny villages sit in the valleys surrounded by forest—**Marlboro**, famous for its music festival, and **Newfane, Grafton**, and **Chester**, each one worth some time and each possessing some choice places to stay.

BRATTLEBORO & MARLBORO

Brattleboro is an old, historic industrial town, southeastern Vermont's major shopping and service center, and one of the state's larger cities. In its heyday, it was full of Yankee vigor and was home to men such as Jacob Estey, who founded an internationally famous company that manufactured parlor organs; Peter Latchis, the movie theater mogul; and Jubilee Jim Fisk, partner of railroad baron Jay Gould, the man who defrauded hundreds of investors in his get-rich-quick schemes. Fisk is buried in Brattleboro under a gaudy memorial depicting, among other things, semiclad beauties clutching and stroking bags and bags of money.

Brattleboro has a casual, relaxed air. In fact, the town is often referred to as the college town without a college. Today there's a large concentration of paint-

Southern Vermont

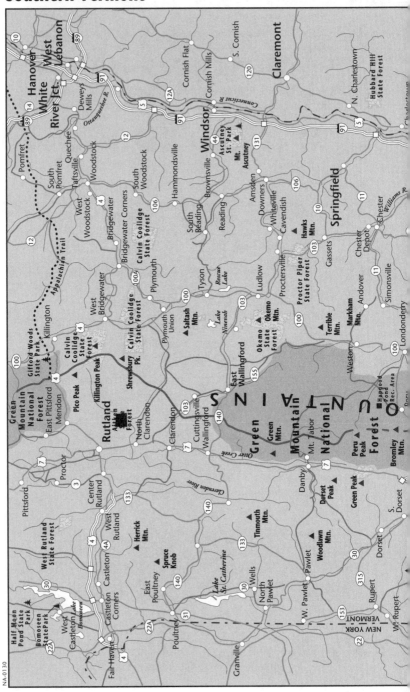

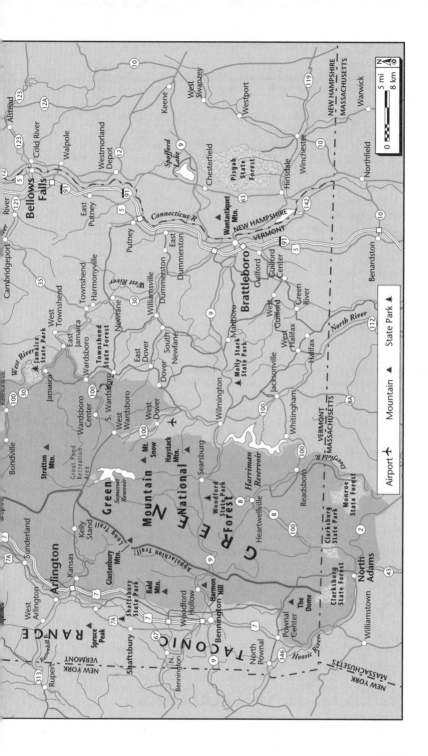

353

ers, potters, writers, musicians, sculptors, and performers of all sorts tucked away in the surrounding hills—painters Wolf Kahn and David Utiger, comedy team Gould & Stearns, and many others.

You can occasionally catch local regional exhibits along with national shows at the **Brattleboro Museum & Art Center,** Old Union Station (☎ 802/257-0124). It also contains a collection of Estey organs. Open May to November, Tuesday to Sunday from noon to 6pm. Other works by local artists can be seen at **Vermont Artisan Designs** at 115 Main St. (☎ 802/257-7044) and at the **Hays Gallery,** 103 Main St. (☎ 802/257-5181).

Outside Brattleboro, on the way to Wilmington, book lovers will want to stop at the **Bear Book Shop** off Route 9 (R.D. 4, Box 446), Brattleboro (☎ 802/464-2260), where you'll find 30,000 categorized books housed in a big old barn. The owner, John Greenberg, was at one time a professor of philosophy in Montreal. The store is open by chance or appointment during the warm weather. Beyond the book barn is one of my favorite craft studios, the **Gallery in the Woods,** Butterfield Road (off Route 9, 1 mile east of Hogback Mountain; ☎ 802/464-5793), which is home to cabinetmaker and woodcarver Saturday Singh and potter Saturday Kaur Khalsa of Hawkwings Pottery. Their furniture is exquisite, and the pottery is very original and strikingly glazed. Other artists and sculptors also display their works here. Another studio worth visiting is **Malcolm Wright,** on the Turnpike Road in Marlboro (☎ 802/254-2168), who crafts wood-fired traditional Japanese-style pieces.

Just 9 miles outside of Brattleboro, **Marlboro** is more a state of mind than an actual place, for when you arrive at the dot on the map you'll find only a church, a post office, a few houses, and an old inn right next door to the church. This little village is home to the famous **Marlboro Music Festival,** founded in 1951 by Rudolf Serkin and others. Each summer, dozens of the most talented musicians from the United States and abroad gather for 7 weeks of intensive chamber music study and rehearsal. Weekend concerts are presented from mid-July through mid-August at Marlboro College's Persons Auditorium. If you wish to attend the concerts, you must book tickets early. Write or call Marlboro Music, Box K, Marlboro, VT 05344 (☎ 802/254-2394 between June 15 and August 15; ☎ 215/569-4690 before June 15).

Naturalists will want to stop at the **Southern Vermont Natural History Museum,** Route 9, Marlboro (☎ 802/464-0048), to see the collection of 500 mounted birds arranged in more than 50 dioramas. The museum was started by local taxidermist Luman Ranger Nelson and affords an opportunity to observe species close up. Open Memorial Day to October 31, daily from 9am to 5pm. Admission is $2 for adults, $1 for children under 18.

While you're in Marlboro, take a drive to the top of **Hogback Mountain** for the spectacular 100-mile view. The **Skyline Restaurant,** Route 9 (☎ 802/464-5535), is at the summit and makes a great spot for a Vermont breakfast of waffles and real maple syrup. Open Monday and Tuesday from 7:30am to 3pm; from 7:30am to 8 or 9pm on other days.

BRATTLEBORO & MARLBORO LODGING & DINING

Your best bet is to stay outside Brattleboro in Saxtons River, Chester, or Marlboro where you'll find attractive inns. In Brattleboro itself, with one major exception, the options are primarily motels.

If you want to be in town, then the **Latchis Hotel,** 50 Main St., Brattleboro, VT 05301 (☎ 802/254-6300), is the place to stay. When it was built in 1938, it was the town's social center with the largest ballroom in the state, a solarium cocktail lounge, and the Latchis Theatre, an extravagant art deco movie palace. The hotel is still owned by the Latchis family, whose members have restored this historic landmark to its former chrome-and-terrazzo glory while keeping the original simplicity of the rooms. All have private baths, phones, TVs, refrigerators, and coffeemakers. The hotel dining room, the Latchis Grille, overlooks Whetstone Brook and serves an innovative American cuisine. Don't miss seeing a movie in the gem of a theater with its Greek murals and star-studded ceiling. Rates: $65 to $100.

The glorious old inn by the church in Marlboro is the **Whetstone,** Marlboro, VT 05344 (☎ 802/254-2500). Here Jean and Harry Boardman welcome guests into their living room, which is lined with interesting books (from Rabelais to *Moby Dick*) and houses a piano and a bar and a fireplace that is well used on cold Vermont days. Built in 1786, this venerable building has nearly always flourished as a tavern. Many of the musicians performing at the Marlboro Festival stay here, so you'll enjoy interesting company. In addition, fascinating conversation is likely to flow from Harry, who spent a decade at the Salk Institute in California educating professionals about new biological developments and their effects on our society. Rooms vary in decor and size, although most are furnished in keeping with the colonial atmosphere of the inn. Most have private bathrooms, and all look out on meadowed and forested grounds. Meals are served in what was originally the big old kitchen in the back, with a fireplace large enough to accommodate a cooking crane. Full breakfasts are $7 to $9; complete dinners run $18 to $25. Although Jean will accommodate friends of yours at table, dining is really only for guests. In summer, dinner is served on concert nights—Wednesday to Saturday; in winter, only on Saturday. Dishes will be homemade, from the cheddar-cheese soup and roast leg of lamb or pork to the Brandy Alexander pie. Rates: $70 to $80 double without bath, $75 to $90 double with bath. Rates go up in July and August during the music festival, when priority is given to weekly rentals. In winter, the inn is ideal for cross-country skiing, sledding, and snowshoeing.

T.J. Buckley's, 132 Elliot St., Brattleboro (☎ 802/257-4922), is an unlikely local dining favorite—an old diner, now looking avant-garde, that seats 16 people maximum. Michael Fuller, who runs it, is a creative cook. He prepares a different menu daily, consisting of four entrees made with local and often organic ingredients. You might find roasted chicken stuffed with *bucheron* with black truffles under the skin, served with flageolets and a caramelized cumice pear and parsnip-porcini sauce; or striped bass in a roasted-lobster stock with carrots, celery, fresh horseradish, and rosemary, served with risotto; or shrimp and clams in two sauces (parsley pesto and sweet red pepper). The $25 price includes salad and rolls. Desserts are prepared daily. On weekends, you'll need to reserve at least a week in advance. Open late May to mid-February, Tuesday to Sunday from 6pm to closing; mid-February to early May, Thursday to Sunday only.

Peter Havens, 32 Elliot St., Brattleboro (☎ 802/257-3333), has also been gaining a reputation for carefully prepared cuisine. It's a tiny restaurant where original art by local artists adds warmth to the spare white walls of the dining room. The menu is short with a definite emphasis on seafood, which plays to the chef's particular strength. Try the scallops sautéed with fire-roasted red peppers, crabmeat, and light cream sauce or the broiled salmon with smoked pesto butter. In both, the flavor of the seafood shines through. For meat dishes, you might find filet mignon with a Roquefort walnut butter, or a duck breast roasted with a fresh fig and merlot sauce. Prices range from $16 to $22. To start, try the delicious smoked lemon-pepper trout. Open Tuesday to Saturday 6pm to closing. Closed 2 weeks in July, March, and November.

The other local spot is **Common Ground**, 25 Elliot St., Brattleboro (☎ 802/257-0855), where many of the craftspeople can be seen lingering over vegetarian and natural foods on the second-floor enclosed terrace in summer. Downstairs, the entryway and stairwell serve as the town's alternative bulletin board. The menu is strictly vegetarian, with items such as cashew burgers, lentil stew, lasagna, bean and cheese burritos, and stir fries made with vegetables, plus tofu, tempeh, and seitan (a soy-based bean curd substitute). Prices range from $4 to $10. Open Sunday from 10:30am to 2:30pm and 5:30 to 9pm; Monday to Thursday; Friday and Saturday from 11:30am to 9pm.

NEWFANE, GRAFTON, CHESTER & SAXTONS RIVER

From Brattleboro, it's only about 12 miles or so, following Route 30 and the West River, to **Newfane,** a quintessential Vermont village blessed with two fine inns and a steepled Congregational church clustered around a green with the Windham County Courthouse at the center. As you travel the route, there are plenty of antique shops for you to explore, and east of Newfane, Putney is a major center for crafts lovers.

If you continue farther along Route 30, you'll come to the Townshends and Windham, where you can turn off to **Grafton,** taking Route 121. From there, a 7-mile drive north along Route 35 will bring you to **Chester,** or you can continue along Route 121 for about 6 miles east to **Saxtons River.** Grafton and Chester are both picture-book New England villages. The first was settled in 1780 and grew throughout the 19th century. Farming, milling, and soapstone quarrying were the major occupations of the villagers, and in 1850 there were about 10,000 sheep grazing in the surrounding meadows. The town was on the Boston-Montreal stage route, and the Phelps Hotel (now the Old Tavern) serviced overnight travelers. Around the turn of the century, the town declined as people were lured west or moved to the cities. By 1940, many of the buildings in the community were in a decrepit condition, and it wasn't until the Windham Foundation was founded in 1963 that the serious work of restoration was undertaken. Today, in Grafton, stroll (or take a narrative tour in a horse and carriage) through the beautifully restored town. Don't miss visiting the **Grafton Village Cheese Company,** ½ mile south on Townshend Road (☎ 802/843-2221). It makes its very own Covered Bridge Cheddar, and you can watch the process and take a few tangy samples home. Open June to October, 8:30am to 4pm weekdays, on Saturday from 10am to 4pm.

History buffs will want to stop at the **Grafton Historical Society Museum,** Main Street (☎ 802/843-2489), just down from the post office. Old photographs, memorabilia, historical objects, and genealogical books reflect the town's story. Open Memorial Day through Columbus Day, Saturday and Sunday from 1:30 to 4pm.

Chester is a Victorian-style New England classic with a village green and a wide main street lined with handsome late-19th-century homes and commercial buildings. Among them are more than 20 pre–Civil War buildings faced in gleaming mica schist. Take a stroll along both sides of the street to view these remarkable buildings. Examples are the MacKenzie House, with its marble newel posts and ornamental metal roof crest, and the fanciful Eastlake–Queen Anne Sherwins House at Depot and Maple streets.

Stores to browse in are **Century House Interiors** (☎ 802/875-4872), **Carpenter's Emporium** (☎ 802/875-3267); **Vermont Country Store** (☎ 802/463-2224), **Vermont Stone Works** (☎ 802/875-4141), and **Reed Gallery** (☎ 802/875-6225), which is tucked away off the main street.

Chester is a terminus for the Green Mountain Railroad's (☎ 802/463-3069) **Green Mountain Flyer** that steams 26 miles round-trip from Bellows Falls. Trains operate in summer and during special holidays. Tickets cost $12 for adults, $10 for seniors and children 3 to 12, and $3 for under 3's.

Saxtons River is more gritty. There's not an awful lot to do in any one of these towns, but that's the whole point—this is biking and rambling country, havens for those who just want to enjoy the bounties of the mountains and the back roads.

AREA LODGING & DINING

The **Four Columns Inn,** on the Common at 230 West St., Newfane, VT 05345 (☎ 802/365-7713), occupies an 1832 building fashioned after a southern mansion, whose Greek Revival columns give this marvelous country inn its name. It's complete with trout pond and swimming pool, flower and herb gardens, and hiking trails. The dining room is exceptional as well as being appealing, with its large brick fireplace, old beams, Windsor chairs, and decorative kitchen and farm utensils. The cuisine is always exciting, incorporating American, Mediterranean, and Pacific Rim flavors and techniques. Among the appetizers, you may find a quail rubbed with Thai spices, crunchy watercress and vegetable salad or a sautéed foie gras with leeks, Napa cabbage, and balsamic vinegar. Specialties include poached salmon with a spicy tamarind-sesame sauce and shrimp wontons and aged Black Angus sirloin with a horseradish-chervil sauce. Prices range from $21 to $27. Hours are Wednesday to Monday from 6 to 9pm; closed April. In the front building, there are nine rooms, and several more are in the renovated barn. All have private baths and are decorated in an elegant country style with chintz on the walls, quilts on the brass beds, and assorted items like armoires and wicker chairs. Some have gas fireplaces, and deluxe rooms have Jacuzzis. Rates: B&B winter, spring, and summer, $120 to $205 double; fall, $150 to $235; MAP, fall foliage season, $220 to $305.

Old Newfane Inn, Route 30, Newfane, VT 05345 (☎ 802/365-4427). Eric and Gundy Weindl run this typical New England inn with uneven floors, beamed ceilings, and flocked wallpaper. The dining room possesses a large warming brick fireplace and pewter lamps and offers food that runs from fillet of sole amandine and frog's legs Provençale to veal marsala, duck á l'orange, and a variety of steaks. Desserts include the classic cherries jubilee, crêpes suzette, and baked Alaska. Main dishes go for $16 to $26. Dining hours are Tuesday to Sunday from 6 to 9pm. The inn's 10 guest rooms are furnished with pleasant oak pieces, rockers, and wing chairs. Rates (including continental breakfast): $115 to $155 double. Closed November to mid-December and April to mid-May.

West River Lodge, R.R. 1, Box 693, Newfane, VT 05345 (☎ 802/365-7745), has a beautiful setting indeed. It sits on 30 acres and possesses 1,200 feet along the West River. People come primarily for the English riding stables, which offer dressage instruction and other riding clinics. There are also other kinds of workshops—watercolor painting, for example. Innkeepers Jack and Gill Winner, former college biology teachers, gladly share their intimate knowledge of the area. The eight rooms (two with private baths) are simply furnished with half-posters and other country pieces. Guests gather around the hearth in the living room. A full breakfast is served in the pine-paneled dining room. Dinners are also available. Trail rides are offered at the stable for $20. Rates: B&B, $90 to 100 double; MAP, $130 to $140.

At the center of the idyllic, meticulously kept New England village of Grafton, the **Old Tavern,** routes 35 and 121, Grafton, VT 05146 (☎ 802/843-2231 or 802/843-2245), is a town landmark dating from 1801. It occupies a main building as well as a number of historic homes in the village and has a long and proud tradition dating back to 1788. Among the famous visitors who have stayed here are Henry David Thoreau, Ralph Waldo Emerson, Nathaniel Hawthorne, Teddy Roosevelt, and Rudyard Kipling. Today, the tradition of attracting celebrities continues.

The main building contains 14 guest rooms, all with private baths, some with canopied beds. Behind it, in what was originally the livery stable, is a bar with an upstairs gallery, a slate fireplace, and beams and barn siding. Most of the accommodations in the beautifully furnished cottages—White Gates, Barrett House, Tuttle House—contain canopied beds, mahogany chests, comfortable armchairs, candle-stand tables, and sitting rooms ideally furnished for quiet reading. They have accents like broken-scroll mirrors and demi-lune tables set with a Staffordshire or similar vase filled with fresh flowers. A couple of the cottages are reserved primarily for families and are furnished appropriately. There are no telephones or TVs in any of the rooms. The place is filled with authentic antiques (and a few reproductions). A number of really tasteful antiques-filled guesthouses, sleeping 7 to 16, with full kitchens are also available.

There are several choices of dining rooms: first a formal room, whose oak tables are set with place mats and Mottahedeh china; second, the pine room, with a beamed ceiling, fireplace, and Windsor chairs; and third, the garden room, with a brick floor and flowers and plants in pots. The food in all is traditional New England fare—New England lobster pie, rack of lamb with a minted Madeira sauce, plus some lighter entrees like the salmon with a fresh yellow-pepper puree. To start, try the smoked rainbow trout with horseradish sauce or the classic escargots with garlic butter. To finish, there's a selection of parfaits, along with strawberry shortcake and white chocolate mousse. Entree prices run from $18 to $26. Dining hours are Monday to Saturday from noon to 2pm, Sunday from 11:30am to 2pm; daily from 6 to 9pm.

The Old Tavern is not the place to visit if you're looking for nightlife—come in search of peace and quiet, a comfortable chair, a good book and a brandy in front of a crackling fire, and you'll find contentment. The inn also offers 20 miles of cross-country ski trails, sleds and toboggans, and a natural swimming pond. Two tennis courts just down the street are free to guests. Platform tennis and a game room with billiards and Ping-Pong complete the facilities. Rates: rooms and cottages, $130 to $250 double; $525 to $730 per day. Closed April.

Chester House, 266 Main St., Chester, VT 05143 (☎ 802/875-2205), sits on the main street overlooking the green. This charming 1780 house is operated by Paul and Randy, who have renovated and furnished it with style. They are experienced innkeepers, having operated a similar place on Cape Cod. The rooms are furnished with antiques and decorated with stenciling. The largest room has a canopied bed and bathroom with a double Jacuzzi. Some rooms also have decorative fireplaces. A superb breakfast is served in summer outside on the side porch. It's exquisitely presented and will consist of fresh fruit and a delicious entree. Rates: $95 to $125.

The Inn at Long Last, Main Street (P.O. Box 589), Chester, VT 05143 (☎ 802/875-2444), has welcoming public areas—a lobby with a stone fireplace and a scattering of sofas and armchairs and a library-bar that also has a flagstone hearth. The dining room features a contemporary American menu with main courses such as grilled chicken breast with roasted red peppers and ginger salsa or roasted veal chop with merlot and wild mushrooms. Prices range from $12 to $18. Open Tuesday to Sunday. There are 26 rooms and four suites, all with private baths. They are plainly furnished with brass or Jenny Lind beds and painted furniture. The owners are sprucing them up, but it's a slow and arduous process. Facilities include two tennis courts and a garden that extends down to a fishing stream. The inn has recently been sold, and the new owners will open in mid-summer. Call for information.

What makes **Inn Victoria,** Box 788, On the Green, Chester, VT 05143 (☎ 800/732-4288), special is the dedication of its innkeepers to afternoon tea. The inn was built in the 1850s and is furnished in Victorian style. Parlors have Empire-style couches and Victorian armchairs. There are nine rooms and suites, several with double Jacuzzis and gas fireplaces. The beds are highback carved Victorians with plenty of pillows and cushions. A family loft accommodates six and has a full kitchen, a wood-burning fireplace, and a TV. The innkeepers set a lovely table with elegant bone china and lace place mats at breakfast and at afternoon tea. They also operate the Tea Pot Shoppe, and many a guest carries home one of their handsome international teapots. Rates: $105 to $170.

Halfway to Londonderry from Chester on Route 11 in Simonsville is **Rowell's Inn,** R.R. 1, Box 267D, Chester, VT 05143 (☎ 802/875-3658), a very beautiful and elegant inn. The 1820 brick building with double porches served originally as a coaching inn. Step through the front stained-glass doors, and you'll find yourself in a lovely historic home with cherry and maple floors and a tin ceiling. The sitting room has lavish carpeting, a brick hearth flanked by bookcases, and a Remington sculpture. The tavern is warmed by an old woodstove inserted into the inglenook fireplace and is decorated with suitable scenes of debauchery plus a special rendering of the local jackalope. There are six rooms. None has a phone or TV, but all have been carefully decorated with choice pieces. In one, you might find a canopied brass bed, oak dresser, Victorian sofa, and desk and chair in a setting of blue chintz. Room 5 occupies a barrel-vaulted space and has a bed with a tent treatment supported by a carved top of an armoire, an Empire dresser, and another single sleigh bed. A full breakfast is included in the rates, and you can also enjoy a very fine five-course dinner. No credit cards are taken and no children under 12 allowed. Rates: MAP $170 to $185.

At the heart of Saxtons River, you'll find the very Victorian **Inn at Saxtons River,** Main Street, Saxtons River, VT 05154 (☎ 802/869-2110), a friendly idiosyncratic place where you can loll on the front porch or enjoy afternoon tea in the garden. It's not your precious perfectly coifed New England inn, but it has great character. Throughout the house are Southern pine door frames and woodwork. The 16 rooms are decorated in a handsome Victorian country style with antique furnishings. At the end of the day, guests gather in the Victorian pub where there is piano entertainment Friday and Saturday night, or else around the hearth in the very comfortable lounge. There's also a tucked away TV/VCR room. The dining room has harvest tables and Windsor chairs. Food is updated traditional—pork medallions with an apple and juniper-berry sauce, chicken marengo over fettuccine, roast duck with raspberry-red wine sauce, and scampi in lemon-garlic cream sauce. Prices range from $17 to $20. Appetizers are equally popular; try the smoked trout with Dijon honey dill mayonnaise or the steamed mussels in white wine, shallots, garlic butter, and fresh herbs. Dining hours are Tuesday to Sunday from 11:30am to 2pm; Sunday and Tuesday to Thursday 5 to 9pm, Friday and Saturday 5 to 10pm. Rates: $82 to $102 double ($112 in October). Closed in March and April for 5 weeks.

LUDLOW, LONDONDERRY, WESTON & LANDGROVE

From Chester, Route 103 north will take you through Proctorsville, home of the **Joseph Cerniglia Winery,** Route 103 (☎ 802/226-7575), which has been producing wines for 10 years, to Ludlow, an old milling town that is right at the base of **Okemo Mountain,** the state's fastest growing resort. From Ludlow, it's a short cruise down Route 100 to the little village of Weston, a charmer indeed with a famous summer theater, and—to catalog aficionados—the hometown of the Vermont Country Store.

Stop at the **Weston Bowl Mill & Annex** (☎ 802/824-6219) for some reasonably priced woodware; at the **Vitriesse Glass Gallery** (☎ 802/824-6634); and also at **Susan Sargent Designs** (☎ 802/824-3184), where exuberant designs are woven into colorful unique pillows, rugs, and throws. **Todd Gallery** (☎ 802/824-5606) is the studio of watercolorist Robert E. Todd, who also shows works by other Vermont artists.

The **Farrar-Mansur House** (☎ 802/824-4399) has some fine furniture that has survived in remarkable condition. Among the highlights are silver items made by Bailey of Woodstock, a Rawson shelf clock made in Saxtons River, and paintings by folk artists Asahel Powers and Aaron Dean Fletcher. Murals in the parlor were painted by WPA artist Roy Williams in the 1930s. The house was built in 1797 and served as home and tavern to several generations of the Mansur family until it was donated to Weston in 1932. Next to the house, the **Old Mill Museum** displays collections of tinsmithing, woodworking, and agricultural tools. Open July to August, Wednesday to Sunday from 1 to 4pm, and on fall weekends.

The **Weston Playhouse** (☎ 802/824-5288 in season; 802/824-8167 off-season), is the oldest professional theater in the state and one of the finest. It's a handsome Greek Revival theater in a lovely riverside setting with a downstairs restaurant and bar where you can secure a fine dinner before the show. Comedies and musicals are its stock in trade and there's also after hours cabaret.

AREA LODGING & DINING

The **Castle,** Route 103 at Route 131 (P.O. Box 207), Proctorsville, VT 05153 (☎ 802/226-7222), occupies a unique turn-of-the-century mansion that was modeled on a Cotswold manor house. It's located on a hillside overlooking the Black River Valley with views of Okemo Mountain. It was built in 1904 for lumber-quarry baron and Vermont governor Allen M. Fletcher. The interior woodwork and detailing is extraordinary, from the elaborate stucco ceiling in the sitting room to the boiserie in the dining room. There are 10 very spacious rooms, all with CD players; six have fireplaces and two have Jacuzzis. Even the smallest room (Room 9) is larger than most accommodations at other places, and it has a gorgeous fireplace. Each room is decorated in a different palette, from cranapple red to moss green. Room 8 is predominantly deep blue and has a wood-burning fireplace. Room 4 is dramatic—it has a black Chinese Aubusson rug, a carved bed, and a red and gold brocade sofa. The largest room, Room 11, is 420 square feet and has been decorated in deep purple. A Chinese screen hangs on the wall above the bed. A full breakfast is served as well as afternoon tea. You can dine either in the oak-paneled former billiard room or in the elegant smaller oval dining room, which has superb boiserie. The contemporary American cuisine has obvious Asian traces. On the menu, you might find sautéed salmon with black-bean cakes and lemongrass beurre blanc or pork tenderloin with a pesto marsala sauce. In fall and winter, expect to find game dishes like venison with juniper berries and red wine. Prices range from $15 to $24. A splendid conclusion to any meal would be the chocolate Grand Marnier torte. Rates: $160 to $210; MAP is an additional $60 per couple per night. Open summer, Wednesday to Sunday from 5 to 9pm; rest of year, Friday to Sunday from 5 to 9pm.

A trellis gate hung with fuchsias leads into the garden entrance of the **Three Clock Inn,** R.R. 1, Box 59, Middletown Road, South Londonderry, VT 05155 (☎ 802/824-6327). This secluded establishment is best known for its restaurant, which is very good indeed. The dining room has a warm ambience and a glass-enclosed wine cellar plus a lounge with a fireplace. It offers a $35 three-course fixed-price menu. The updated French/continental cuisine features fresh local ingredients. You might find duck breast with a wild-berry sauce, pistachio-crusted swordfish, or rack of venison with risotto galette. Prices range from $18 to $23. To start, there might be smoked salmon with buckwheat crepes and horseradish cream or pâté maison. Desserts include classics like crème brûlée, hot apple tart, and profiteroles. Open Tuesday to Sunday from 5:30 to 8:30pm.

Upstairs, four rooms are available, including a small suite with two bedrooms. The largest has a canopied bed and a fireplace. The guests also can use a colonial-style living room, also with a fireplace. At breakfast, the gracious proprietors will serve whatever you fancy. Rates: $95 to $130 double. Closed April and November.

Brattleboro & the Southeastern Corner of Vermont
Special & Recreational Activities

Auctions: Contact the **Townshend Auction Gallery** for its schedule. The gallery is located on Route 30 in Townshend (☎ 802/365-4388).

Biking: Grafton Ponds Mountain Bike Center at the Old Tavern (☎ 802/843-2400) has 19 miles of trails. Rentals available. Rentals are also available from the **Brattleborough Bike Shop** (☎ 802/254-8644).

For tour information, contact **Bike Vermont,** P.O. Box 207, Woodstock, VT 05091 (☎ 802/457-3553). It offers inn-to-inn bicycle touring from May through October, on weekend and 5-day trips. Or try **Vermont Bicycle Tours Worldwide Active Vacations,** P.O. Box 711, Bristol, VT 05443 (☎ 802/453-4811). It will also supply bikes. Note, too, that the company also offers hiking holidays.

Camping: Two state parks in the area offer camping: **Fort Dummer** (☎ 802/254-2610) in Brattleboro and **Townshend** (☎ 802/365-7500), which has 34 sites as well as trails up Bald Mountain for great views.

For information, write to **Department of Forests, Parks and Recreation** Waterbury, VT 05602 (☎ 802/241-3655).

Canoeing: This can be done along the Connecticut and West rivers. Rentals available at **River Safari** (☎ 802/257-5008).

Cross-Country Skiing: This is great terrain for cross-country skiing, which is available at **Grafton Ponds Cross-Country Ski Center** at the Old Tavern (☎ 802/843-2400) with 20 miles of trails. In **Ludlow, Fox Run,** 89 Fox Lane (☎ 802/228-8871), has 12 miles of trails. Rentals are available.

Fishing: For information, contact the **Vermont Fish and Wildlife Department,** Waterbury, VT 05676 (☎ 802/241-3700). Licenses are available by mail, but allow plenty of time. A useful guide to fishing and a booklet outlining state laws and regulations are also available.

Golf: Tater Hill Country Club, R.R.1, Chester (☎ 802/875-2517), has an 18-hole course with some fine mountain views.

Hiking: Grafton Ponds Center offers some decent hiking.

Horseback Riding: English riding, including trail rides, are offered at the **West River Lodge. Jack's Horse Farm,** Westminster West Road in Putney (☎ 802/387-2782), also offers trail rides. In Proctorsville, contact **Cavendish Trail Horse Rides,** 20 Mile Stream Road (☎ 802/226-7821). The average price is $25 per hour.

Picnicking: Good picnicking sites are available in **Townshend State Park.**

Shopping for Crafts: Many craftspeople have settled in the area, and their works are displayed in many locations. At the **Marlboro Craft Studios,** Lucy Gratwick (☎ 802/257-0181) exhibits her hand-weaving, the Applewoods (☎ 802/254-2908) their furniture and wood pieces, and Malcolm Wright (☎ 802/254-2168) his wood-fired pottery. Call any of them to make an appointment.

Skiing: The star of the region is **Okemo** (☎ 802/228-4041), which has developed a reputation for challenging expert skiers, since 50% of its 88 trails are considered "more difficult." It has a vertical drop of 2,150 feet, 485 acres with 95% snowmaking coverage, and 13 lifts, including seven quads (two high speed). A 2-day lift ticket is $90.

Ascutney Mountain (☎ 802/484-7711) in Brownsville has great views from the top. It's much less challenging, with a vertical drop of 1,530 feet. There are 31 trails accessed by three triples and a double chair.

State Parks: For information, contact the **Department of Forests, Parks, and Recreation,** 103 S. Main St., Waterbury, VT 05671 (☎ 802/241-3655).

Swimming: Try Newfane's **Townshend State Park.**

Tennis: There are **municipal courts in Brattleboro. Tater Hill Country Club** in Chester (☎ 802/875-2517) has two clay courts.

WILMINGTON, WEST DOVER & MOUNT SNOW

From Brattleboro, it's only about a dozen or so miles to Wilmington, a small town that is undergoing a sort of renaissance. This can be seen very clearly at the **Young & Constantin Gallery** in the church (☎ 802/464-2515), which makes a perfect backdrop for some exquisite hand-blown art glass. Jewelry, ceramics, wood sculpture, and paintings and pastels are also on sale. Photographs, watercolors, and paintings are shown at **Roseate Creations,** 7 N. Main St. (☎ 802/464-1466). There are also several worthy antique stores in town. Around the corner on Route 9, **John McLeod** (☎ 802/464-3332) sells beautifully turned woodware and also offers fine crafts in the **Eclectic Eye** on the same premises. About 10 miles west of town on Route 9, book lovers will want to seek out **Austin's Antiquarian Books** (☎ 802/464-3727), which sells books, prints, and maps.

For evening entertainment, check out what's happening at the **Memorial Hall Center for the Arts** on West Main Street. Recitals, chamber music concerts, and jazz are also given at the **Shield Inn.**

From here, Route 100 begins its winding journey north through the Green Mountains to the first of Vermont's major ski areas, **Mount Snow,** Mount Snow, VT 05356 (☎ 802/464-3333), in West Dover. In summer, take the chairlift to the summit for the four-state view. Beyond this resort, the road continues on its way to the villages of Wardsboro, Jamaica, Londonderry, and Weston. In Wardsboro, don't miss **Anton of Vermont Fiber Art Gallery & Quilts,** where

Judith Anton creates her richly colored Vermont quilts. Much of her inspiration comes from Japan, which she visits frequently. Call ☎ 802/896-6007 for location and availability of the artist.

Evening entertainment in the winter is largely confined to having a drink and dinner in a cozy spot like the **Hermitage Inn** (see below). During the summer, **Mount Snow Playhouse** (☎ 802/464-3333 or 802/295-7016) offers summer stock theater.

There's plenty of après-ski at the main base lodge at Mount Snow and at the **Snow Barn** on the access road. Other favorite spots include **Deacon's Den**, the **Dover Bar & Grill**, and **The Pub** in Wilmington.

WILMINGTON LODGING & DINING

For an ideal weekend, I'd head for the warm and idiosyncratic hospitality of Jim McGovern and Lois Nelson at the **Hermitage Inn**, Coldbrook Road, Wilmington, VT 05363 (☎ 802/464-3511). Jim certainly has his very own way of doing things. He's a renegade Connecticut gent, who more than 25 years ago fled the South to the 24 acres he now owns. Here he can indulge his own particular hobbies and enthusiasms without too much interference.

From the minute you cross the bridge over the tiny stream onto the property, you know you're somewhere special. Off to the left stand a series of farm structures. After investigation, these turn out to be houses for the game birds—goose, pheasant, duck, and wild turkey—that Jim raises specifically for the table and for which his dining room is famous. He also has collected some 35 species of rare beauties that are worth far too much to put on any table—gold and silver pheasants, India blue peacocks, New Zealand and Arctic snow geese, to name a few. Walk up toward the house at the top of the hill, and you'll discover a whole run full of wild turkeys, an area where Jim and Lois raise English setters, and a sugar house where every spring 5,000 buckets of maple sap are turned into 700 gallons of pure maple syrup. The syrup is sold in the store, along with jams, jellies, and other McGovern favorites, notably decoys and fine wines. You can also rent ski equipment in the store to ski 25 miles of cross-country trails or the downhill slopes at Mount Snow. A clay tennis court and a trout pond complete the picture.

The inn itself dates back 100 years. Wide pine floors and chairs cozily placed in front of the hearth in the bar engender a convivial atmosphere conducive to conversation. Check out the gallery, too, where Jim has assembled a huge collection of Delacroix lithographs. In the dining rooms, you'll enjoy some of the finest dining in the area, enhanced by really fine wines from Jim's virtuoso wine cellar (2,000 labels with many vintages over 30 years old). Start with mushrooms Hermitage, stuffed with caviar. I can heartily recommend the pheasant braised in white wine cream sauce. Prices range from $14 to $25. Dining hours are daily from 5 to 11pm.

The inn was once the home of Mrs. Bertha Eastman Barry, the redoubtable editor of the *Social Register,* and retains some of her original furnishings, most notably the four-poster in Room 4. In the mid-1980s, Jim added a new wing, carefully constructed in the same architectural style. All of the 15 rooms have private baths, working fireplaces, and telephones, and all are furnished differently, some in mahogany, some in honey oak. A typical large room contains a pineapple half-poster, a chest of drawers with a broken-scroll mirror, a Stickley love seat, and a comb-back Windsor chair. From most of the rooms, there's a glorious view looking toward Haystack Mountain. Additional rooms are located a short distance down the road in Brookbound. Here guests can use a pine living room with fieldstone fireplace, TV, and an upright piano. Brookbound rooms vary in size. The largest, Room 42, possesses a high carved-oak bed, a needlepointed Victorian rocker, a Stickley chair, a Chippendale side table, and a brick fireplace. Most have private baths.

This may not be the ultimate designer-stamped, $4-glossy-magazine quality establishment, but it offers a deeply satisfying sense of honesty, character, and individuality—it's a place where you can relax and be yourself. In winter, you can enjoy the miles of ski trails; hunters appreciate the sporting clays and hunting preserve.

It's located 2 miles north of Wilmington; from Route 100, turn left at Coldbrook Road and continue for about 2 miles. Turn left at the sign marking the inn. Rates: spring and summer, MAP $230; fall and winter, MAP $260. In winter in Brookbound, MAP $150 to $220; in summer, B&B $70 to $130.

You won't miss the **Nutmeg Inn,** Route 9, Wilmington, VT 05363 (☎ 802/464-3351), a Chinese-red clapboard house whose long front porch always supports some colorful floral display—roses in summer; potted bronze, yellow, and orange mums in fall. The place is very lovingly cared for, and everything is spick and span at this comfortable, homey 180-year-old farmhouse. The special warmth is most evident in the large living room in the carriage house where guests gather either to read in front of the fire or play cards or games or to enjoy a drink at the BYOB bar. Out back, there's a lawn where you can sit under the apple trees by the brook. Throughout the house, pine furnishings add special coziness. Each of the 10 rooms, all with private bath and air-conditioning (most with fireplace), is decorated in country fashion with pine or oak pieces, tables draped with Laura Ashley prints, brass beds or four-posters, and so on. There are also 3 two-room suites with fireplace, TV/VCR, and double Jacuzzi.

There are two cozily furnished dining rooms—one containing a Norman Rockwell plate collection, the other warmed by a woodstove, giving a hillside view. Rates (including breakfast): summer $100 to $150, suites $165 to $198; fall $120 to $170, suites $210 to $250; winter $135 to $190, suites $205 to $235. These are weekend rates; weekday rates are $10 to $15 less.

Tall maples, manicured lawns, and a vegetable garden surround the white clapboard **Red Shutter Inn,** Route 9 (P.O. Box 84), Wilmington, VT 05363 (☎ 802/464-3768). The house on 5 acres was built in 1894, and inside there are five guest rooms, all with private bath, and most furnished in chintz country fashion. Deerfield is a corner room with a whirlpool tub. Chimney Hill is furnished in wicker, and Jenny's Room has a four-poster. The largest is a two-room suite with fireplace, color TV, and private deck. In the carriage house behind the inn are three rooms plus a fireplace suite, which also features a double whirlpool bath. The dining room with its stone fireplace is a welcoming retreat on a winter's night. In summer, there's alfresco dining on the awning-covered porch. Guests also enjoy the woodstove's warmth in the living room–pub. Rates (including breakfast): $110 to $130 double. Dining hours: summer, Wednesday to Sunday 6 to 9pm; open only on Friday and Saturday in winter.

Set atop a hill with a great view of the Deerfield Valley, the **White House,** Route 9, Wilmington, VT 05363 (☎ 802/464-2135), was built as a private summer home in 1914 for a lumber baron and possesses a gracious Georgian-style portico and rows of dormers jutting from the roof line. As you might expect, the 16 rooms in the main inn are extra-large—all with private baths. Nine of the rooms have fireplaces, and two have double whirlpool tubs. Seven additional rooms are located in the guest house, which has a common living room with a fireplace and cable TV. The public areas include large, antique-filled sitting rooms, a dining room with rich mahogany paneling, and a bar, which was sunken, especially so as not to impair the view of sunsets across the valley. An outside terrace also takes advantage of the vista. The grounds are delightful. Roses climb around a trellis by a garden fountain, creating a romantic arbor; beyond, there's an outdoor swimming pool. In winter, 27 miles of ski trails are available. There's also a spa with small indoor pool, whirlpool, and sauna. The restaurant offers a selection of continental dishes—chicken marsala, veal piccata, filet mignon with a bordelaise sauce, and salmon with a country glaze, priced from $18 to $22. Dinner hours are daily from 5:30 to 9pm; Sunday from 11:30am to 2:30pm in addition. Rates: $138 to $188 double; $150 to $205 on holidays. Guest house rooms are $118 and $128, respectively.

Le Petit Chef, Route 100 (☎ 802/464-8437), is a local favorite for superb food served in homey country surroundings. Although the dishes change frequently, you might find rack of lamb, filet of beef with a merlot wine sauce and morels, veal chops marinated in balsamic vinegar, *poisson Méditerrané* (fish, clams, mussels, and shrimp poached in tomato broth with aromatic sea herbs), or venison with cranberry demiglace and chutney; there's always a vegetarian dish. Desserts are tantalizing—especially the crunchy meringue pie (if it's available), chocolate torte, and any of the fresh homemade fruit pies. Main-course prices run $21 to $27. Open Sunday, Monday, Wednesday, Thursday from 6 to 9pm; Friday and Saturday from 6 to 10pm. Closed Tuesday, and mid-April to mid-May, November until Thanksgiving.

MOUNT SNOW/WEST DOVER LODGING & DINING

Close to 100 lodges, inns, and motels are clustered near the ski area, and one or two of them are quite exquisite. I've already mentioned the Hermitage Inn. The other accommodation, the **Inn at Sawmill Farm,** Route 100 (P.O. Box 367), West Dover, VT 05356 (☎ 802/464-8131), created by Rodney Williams and his wife, Ione, from an old farmhouse and barn, has international renown and is a Relais & Châteaux property. It's famous for its classic dining room, the designer-perfect quality of its rooms and cottages, and the understated elegance of its grounds. The dining room positively glows. Copper pots adorn the walls, fresh flowers add color and life, and fine crystal and china grace the tables in a cathedral-ceilinged room that has been carefully designed to provide small, intimate dining areas. Their son, Brill, creates the cuisine. At dinner, there's a selection for every palate—pan-seared salmon with crispy skin and saffron sauce, breast of pheasant with forestière sauce, rack of lamb with mint sauce, or steak au poivre. Prices run from $27 to $35. Appetizers are equally tempting—coquille of crabmeat au gratin; delicious local trout with white wine, lemon, and capers; or sautéed chicken livers with bordelaise sauce, for example. The wine list proffers 900 selections. Jackets are required for men after 6pm. The garden dining room has a sun atrium filled with huge ferns and hydrangeas. Pine hutches, Windsor chairs, and burgundy floral wallpaper complete the summer atmosphere. A pianist quietly entertains in the evening. Hours are daily from 6 to 9:30pm.

In winter, the living room is especially welcoming, as guests gather around the large fireplace and settle into the couches and wing chairs. The upstairs gallery overlooking the living room contains games, chess, books, and a large TV. Tea is served at 4pm, classical music making the announcement. The 10 guest rooms in the main inn are very large and individually decorated with antiques and bright chintzes, combined with cannonball, pencil post, or similar beds. Some have balconies and some have sitting areas. The prime accommodations, though, are in the cottages. For example, Farmhouse 2 is decorated in peach tones and possesses a full-canopied bed and fireplace, handsome china lamps, a desk tucked into the bay window, a candle-stand table, and floor-to-ceiling drapes. The Woodshed, Mill House, and Spring House offer rooms with fireplaces, sitting areas, and views of the beautifully land-scaped grounds and ponds. All of the rooms are richly appointed with fine linens and fabrics, original art work, and fresh flowers plus extra treats such as Godiva chocolates at nightly turndown.

On the grounds are a swimming pool, a pond with canoes, a tennis court, and two trout ponds. The Mount Snow Golf Course is conveniently located up the road. No children under 10 are allowed. Rates: MAP, $370 to $480 double. Higher prices are for lodgings with fireplaces. Closed Easter to mid-May.

The **Deerhill Inn,** Valley View Road (P.O. Box 136), West Dover, VT 05356 (☎ 802/464-3100), is my personal favorite. It's tucked away off Route 100 and offers inspirational rooms, great food, serene gardens, and great views of the valley and Haystack Mountain. Thanks to owners Michael and Linda, it also has a warm and wonderful feel. The 17 guest rooms, all with private baths, have been creatively decorated in different palettes, using the finest fabrics, linens, and other furnishings without making the rooms seem precious or too beautiful for comfort. One room, decked out in rose-lavender, features a four-poster with a canopy and a floral dust ruffle. It has French doors lead-ing to a balcony overlooking the attractively landscaped pool. Room 4 has been sponge painted sea blue. A picket-style headboard crowns the bed, which is made up with broad-stripe blue linens. The walls, painted by the staff, de-pict shore and sailboat scenes, while the furnishings are light wicker. Another room has been dramatically decorated with a bamboo four-poster, a Korean armoire, side tables, and a chest. Still another room looks as if the stenciling of a trellis and potted plants is three-dimensional. A gentle moss-green theme creates the serene atmosphere of Room B-3, which has all the comforts you could possibly seek—a beautifully dressed iron bed, two ultracomfortable wing chairs, a built-in TV, and books. Around the house and pool, Linda has planted a gorgeous array of wonderful plants including many unique scented flowers. Guests also have the use of a large upstairs sitting room complete with a brick fireplace, a variety of seating, plus a supply of books as well as a TV. Another, more formally furnished parlor downstairs serves as a waiting area for diners. A new swimming pool opened in the summer of 1998.

The inn offers a romantic dining experience. One dining room has a lovely mural of an English garden and a slate-and-brick hearth. Both offer a view of the valley that is equally lovely in winter or summer. The art that adorns the walls of both rooms is for sale. The menu is limited and changes seasonally, but it will likely feature some signature dishes like the five-layered veal (composed of three layers of veal interspersed with a layer of caramelized onions, mushrooms, and artichokes and a layer of mozzarella and tomatoes). Fish is emphasized; a favorite dish is the candy-stripe fish, made by alternating layers of a white fish such as bass with salmon fillet. Among the appetizers, the mussels and the shrimp K-Paul are the chief draws. As for dessert, if you don't select the homemade ice cream, then opt for the white chocolate and pumpkin cheesecake with caramel sauce. Prices range from $18 to $24. A full breakfast is served. Hours are Sunday to Thursday from 6 to 9pm, Friday and Saturday from 6 to 9:30pm. Rates: weekends, B&B $120 to $185; MAP $190 to $255; midweek, B&B $105 to $170; MAP $175 to $240. Holiday rates, B&B $160 to $224; MAP $230 to $295. Closed Wednesday off-season.

Doveberry Inn, Route 100 (P.O. Box 1736), West Dover (☎ 802/464-5652), is a favorite valley dining room that also has eight rooms to rent, all with private baths and TVs. They are decorated in simple style with tartan walls; the bathrooms have copper counters. The rooms are comfortable and represent good value. The dining room is decked out in tartan, too, and uses wine storage bins as decorative accents. The specialties include a wood-grilled veal chop served with a host of mushrooms and fillet of salmon grilled and served over orzo with tomatoes, garlic, and mixed herbs. To start, there's homemade gnocchi tossed with fresh sage, garlic, and Parmesan or a delicious Gorgonzola salad. Prices range from $18 to $28. Finish with a bittersweet chocolate crème brûlée or the peach Napoleon, which is made with peaches poached in Chianti and cinnamon and served with mascarpone cream. Open Wednesday to Monday from 6 to 9pm. Rates: $85 to 160.

If you're looking for an Alpine-style ski lodge, there's the nicely kept **Kitzhof,** on Route 100 in West Dover, VT 05356 (☎ 802/464-8310), only ½ mile from Mount Snow. Here no two rooms are alike except in their comfort and cleanliness. Knotty-pine boards, logs, and a fieldstone fireplace impart a mountain coziness; a mahogany hot tub is an added luxury. There's a BYOB bar with setups and a full-service restaurant. Facilities include a heated swimming pool. Rates: summer $68 double; fall $90 double. In winter, $75 double midweek or weekend package for $128 double. During the summer, many bus tours stop here.

WEST DOVER & MOUNT SNOW DINING

Prime dining spots I've already mentioned are the **Inn at Saw Mill Farm,** the **Deerhill Inn,** and the **Hermitage.**

Two Tannery Road (☎ 802/464-2707) has a fine reputation locally. Its name comes from its location on the old site of two saw mills and a tannery. The original old frame building, with plank floors and a piano for impromptu entertainment, offers a comfortable, romantic candlelit setting for dinner, while the high-ceilinged barnlike extension is most inviting in summer, though it's warmed by a woodstove in winter. Specialties include veal Tannery, made with a marsala sauce; chicken Roosevelt flavored with crumbled bacon, spinach, shallots, and a Madeira wine sauce; shrimp Provençale; and desserts like mud pie and baklava à la Nancy. Prices range from $18 to $25. Open Sunday to Thursday from 6 to 9:30pm, Friday and Saturday from 6 to 10pm (Thursday to Sunday only in November and April). Take the left fork off Route 100 about 2 miles north of West Dover.

Wilmington & Mount Snow
Special & Recreational Activities

Biking: Mount Snow operates a mountain-bike park with a 100-mile trail network. Rentals (from $38 to $52 a day) and instruction are available (☎ 800/245-SNOW). The all-day lift is $28, and trail access is another $9. Rentals are also available at **Bonkers Boardroom**, Route 100, West Dover (☎ 802/464-2536), and the **Cupola Ski and Bike Shop**, Route 100, West Dover (☎ 802/464-8010).

For information on touring, contact **Bike Vermont**, P.O. Box 207, Woodstock, VT 05091 (☎ 802/457-3553). It offers inn-to-inn bicycle touring from May through October, on weekend and 5-day trips. Rentals are available. Or try **Vermont Bicycle Tours Worldwide Active Vacations**, P.O. Box 711, Bristol, VT 05443 (☎ 802/453-4811). It will also supply bikes. Note, too, that the latter organization also offers hiking holidays.

Boating: At Lake Whitingham you can rent a sailboat from **Green Mountain Flagship Co.**, 389 Rte. 9, Wilmington (☎ 802/464-2975). Boats are also available in Woodford State Park.

Camping: Two state parks in the area have campsites: **Molly Stark**, Rte 9, Wilmington (☎ 802/464-5460), has 34 sites; **Woodford State Park**, Route 9, Woodford (☎ 802/447-7169), between Wilmington and Bennington, has 104 sites.

For information write to **Department of Forests, Parks and Recreation**, Waterbury, VT 05602 (☎ 802/241-3655).

Canoeing: At Lake Whitingham, also known as Harriman Reservoir, south of Wilmington, you can rent a canoe from **Green Mountain Flagship Co.**, 389 Rte. 9, Wilmington (☎ 802/464-2975). Rentals are also available at **Equipe Sports**, Mount Snow Access Road (☎ 802/464-2222).

Cross-Country Skiing: Mount Snow's cross-country centers are at the **Hermitage**, P.O. Box 457, Wilmington, VT 05363 (☎ 802/464-3511), with 30 miles of trails; **Sitzmark**, East Dover Road, Wilmington, VT 05363 (☎ 802/464-3384), with 25 miles of trails; and the **White House**, P.O. Box 757, Wilmington, VT 05363 (☎ 802/464-2135), with 28 miles of trails.

Fishing: There's freshwater fishing in Lake Whitingham and Lake Raponda for trout, bass, perch, salmon, and pickerel. For information, contact the **Vermont Fish and Wildlife Department**, Waterbury, VT 05676 (☎ 802/241-3700). Licenses are available by mail, but allow plenty of time. You can pick them up usually at general or tackle stores. A useful guide to fishing and a booklet outlining state laws and regulations are also available.

Golf: **Mount Snow** is also famous for its golf school and championship course (☎ 802/464-4184). **Haystack Golf Club,** R.R. 1, Box 173, Mann Road, Wilmington (☎ 802/464-8301), has a fine course, too. At the **Mount Snow Country Club** (☎ 802/464-3333) the fourth hole has been named one of the most beautiful in North America. There's also an 18-hole course at the **Sitzmark Lodge,** East Dover Road, Wilmington (☎ 802/464-3384). Mt. Snow and several inns, including the Hermitage (see above), offer golf packages.

Hiking: Among the legendary mountain trails are the **Long Trail,** the **Molly Stark Trail,** and the **Appalachian Trail.** Mount Snow has a hiking center and there are also trails in Molly Stark and Woodford State Parks. Haystack mountain has trails, too.

For detailed information and maps, contact **Appalachian Trail Conference,** P.O. Box 236, Harper's Ferry, WV 25425. Long Trail information can be obtained from the **Green Mountain Club, Inc.,** R.R. 1, Box 650, Route 100, Waterbury Center, VT 05677 (☎ 802/244-7037). Information is also available from **Green Mountain Forest** at ☎ 802/362-2307.

Horseback Riding: **Flames Stables,** Wards Cove Road, Wilmington (☎ 802/464-8329), has trail rides for $25 an hour.

Llama Trekking: **Green Mountain Expeditions** offers llama trips around Lake Whitingham. Call ☎ 802/368-7147.

Skiing: Only 9 miles north of Wilmington in West Dover, **Mount Snow** (☎ 802/464-3333) is one of the state's largest ski resorts and draws great crowds from the metropolitan areas of Boston, Hartford, and New York. The trails are myriad (130 plus), serviced by 24 lifts. You'll find good skiing for beginners and intermediates, and on the North Face, skiing for experts, with 85% snowmaking capability. Lift passes are about $50 on weekends. Facilities include a nursery, bar, cafeteria at the summit, rentals, ski school, and 40 miles of cross-country trails.

Besides Mount Snow/Haystack, there's more modest **Hogback** in Marlboro, VT 05344 (☎ 802/464-3942), which has 12 trails and four T-bars.

State Parks: For information, contact the **Department of Forests, Parks, and Recreation,** 103 S. Main St., Waterbury, VT 05671 (☎ 802/241-3655).

Swimming: There are a couple of beaches at Lake Whitingham at **Mountain Mills,** off Fairview Avenue, and at **Ward's Cover,** off Route 100. There's also a beach at **Lake Raponda,** north of Route 9 between Wilmington and Brattleboro. The **Deerhill Inn, Sitzmark Lodge,** the **White House,** and several other accommodations have swimming pools.

Bennington, Arlington & Manchester

Bennington & Arlington ◆ *The Manchester-Dorset Valley*

Distance in miles from Boston: Bennington, 142 miles; Manchester, 160.

Estimated driving times: 3 hours to Bennington; 3¾ hours to Manchester.

◄○►◄○►◄○►◄○►◄○►

Driving: To reach Bennington, take Route 9 west from Brattleboro; from Bennington, take Route 7 north to reach Manchester.

Further Information: For more information on Vermont in general, contact **Vermont Department of Travel & Tourism**, 134 State St., Montpelier, VT 05602 (☎ 802/828-3236); the **Vermont State Chamber of Commerce**, P.O. Box 37, Montpelier, VT 05602 (☎ 802/223-3443); **Vermont Division for Historic Preservation**, Division 4, National Life Building, Drawer 20, Montpelier, VT 05620 (☎ 802/828-3051); the **Department of Forest, Parks & Recreation**, 103 S. Main St., Waterbury, VT 05670 (☎ 802/241-3655), for state park camping information.

For specific town information, contact the **Bennington Chamber of Commerce**, Veterans Memorial Drive, Bennington, VT 05201 (☎ 802/447-3311); **Manchester and the Mountains Chamber of Commerce**, R.R. 2, Box 3451, 2 Main St., Manchester Center, VT 05255 (☎ 802/362-2100); **Dorset Chamber of Commerce**, P.O. Box 121, Dorset, VT 05251 (☎ 802/867-2450).

◄○►◄○►◄○►◄○►◄○►

Southern Vermont was home to Ethan Allen and his Green Mountain Boys who stalked the British and turned the tide to victory at the Battle of Bennington. Historic it may be, but today the area offers an incredible variety of both summer and winter activities, although Vermont is at its shining best in winter when the ski slopes at Stratton, Bromley, and Magic Mountain are dotted with colored parkas streaming down the trails, the inns and lodges are warmed by blazing hearths, and people return burnished from the slopes to enjoy an evening's entertainment. During the summer, there's a variety of events and performances to watch at the Southern Vermont Arts Center and at Hildene Meadowlands, as well as plenty of antiquing and craft studios to visit, for here in this region (especially around Bennington), many of the '60s generation settled down to practice their crafts. Fall brings an even-greater glory, when

371

Events & Festivals to Plan Your Trip Around

February/March: Winter carnivals are held at Bromley Mountain and at Stratton Mountain, featuring ice skating, snow sculptures, fireworks, ski races, and more.

March/April: U.S. Open Snowboarding Championships at Stratton Mountain. Call ☎ 802/297-2200 for information.

May: Bennington County Horse Show at Hildene in Manchester. Call ☎ 802/362-1788 for information.

June: The **Dorset Theatre Festival** opens in June and continues through Labor Day. For information, call ☎ 802/867-5777.

　　Vintage Car race up Mount Equinox over a 3,140-foot change in elevation. The record was set by John Meyer over the 5.2 mile course of 4 minutes 8.8 seconds. Call ☎ 802/362-2100.

July: Old-Fashioned Fourth, a celebration complete with square dancing. Vermont Symphony concert. Polo season opens and continues every third weekend. Hildene and Dorset Antiques shows. Call ☎ 802/362-1788 or 802/867-2450.

　　Stratton Summer Music Series, which includes the Vermont Symphony and jazz and blues groups in a series of concerts performed as the sun goes down over the mountains. Call ☎ 802/297-2200.

　　Vermont Race for the Cure. This day is an emotional one for Manchester and area communities when people of all ages and from all walks of life celebrate the survival of those fighting breast cancer by running or walking in the race to raise money. Call ☎ 802/362-2100.

August: The **Acura Tennis Tournament** at Stratton. Call ☎ 800/787-2886 for information.

　　Hildene Crafts Fair exhibits work by 250 craftspeople, along with an array of Vermont food specialties. Call ☎ 802/362-1788.

September: Stratton Arts Festival. Call ☎ 802/297-2200 for information.

December: Prelude to Christmas is a series of celebrations with the signature event being a huge pot-luck supper at which whole communities donate the food. Appetizers are usually served at Hildene, main courses at the Equinox, and desserts and coffee followed by dancing at a local Congregational Church. Call ☎ 802/362-2100.

the mountains are turned into great pyramids of color. And then there are the quiet villages, perfectly groomed town greens, inviting inns, and white clapboard churches that offer the visitor the gentle relaxation of another, much quieter era. In short, it's a lovely area for any weekender to explore at any time of year.

BENNINGTON & ARLINGTON

From Wilmington it's only about 21 miles to Bennington, a town that is divided into several different sections. There's a commercial downtown plus a historic area west of town and the tiny village of North Bennington, home to the progressive Bennington College whose curriculum emphasizes the creative arts and gives this village a certain hip air. The college also has one of the best dining rooms in the area.

In **Bennington** itself you may want to stop by **Williams Smokehouse,** 1001 E. Main St. (☎ 802/442-1000), and pick up some fine smoked hams or bacon (without nitrates) plus many other fresh Vermont products. Also visit **Bennington Potter's Yard** (☎ 802/447-7531), a shopping and gallery complex at School and Country streets where you'll find Bennington Pottery selling its new ceramics and seconds, plus **McCleod Woodwares** selling all kinds of wood items from toys and pegs to cutting boards and salad bowls. The company makes the latter for Williams-Sonoma, and you can purchase them here at a substantial discount. **Cinnamons** stocks kitchenware and **Terra Sua** has assorted ethnic crafts. Open Monday to Saturday from 9:30am to 5:30pm; noon to 5pm on Sunday.

Much of the history and the crafts of the area can be reviewed at the **Bennington Museum,** West Main Street (Route 9), Old Bennington (☎ 802/447-1571), which is filled with an assorted collection of glass, stoneware (including that of the famous Bennington potters), early-American paintings by Erastus Salisbury Field, furniture, military items, and other household wares from the 19th century. Most appealing of all, though, is the gallery devoted to Grandma Moses, or Anna Mary Robertson, a New York farm girl who turned her full attention to art at age 78 and put on her first show at age 80 at the Gallerie St. Etienne in New York in 1940. She became a legendary figure, who continued to paint until she died in 1961 at the age of 101, an inspiration to all aspiring artists for her late start and her untutored natural gift. Here you can view a collection of her refreshing, delightful farm and country scenes and a display of family memorabilia. Open daily from 9am to 5pm. Closed Thanksgiving and major holidays. Admission is $5 for adults, $4.50 for students, free for children under 12.

From the obelisk of the 306-foot **Bennington Battle Monument,** you can stroll past gracious 18th- and 19th-century homes through Old Bennington, past the **Old First Church burial ground,** where some Hessians who fell in the battle are buried in a mass grave. Here, too, Robert Frost is buried. If you wish, you can pick up a walking tour map of the area at the Bennington Chamber of Commerce, on Veterans Memorial Drive (Route 7 north).

The **Park-McCullough House** (☎ 802/442-5441) is an extremely well-kept Victorian mansion at the corner of West and Park streets in North Bennington. Besides the house itself, which is filled with period furnishings and personal effects, be sure to see the miniature "manor," used as a children's playhouse, and a cupola-topped carriage house, complete with century-old carriages. Open late May through October, daily from 10am to 4pm. Admission is $5 for adults, $4 for seniors, and $3 for students 12 to 18.

Bennington also has its own theater company, **The Oldcastle** (☎ 802/447-0564), which plays a summer season that mixes new and modern dramas. One of the best around.

Arlington has quite a history of its own. It was the seat of the first governorship under Thomas Chittenden, and it was here, supposedly, that the seal of the state was created by an officer on a mission to Chittenden. He drew the view of the mountain to the west of Arlington, and so it remains today. The resident chronicler of the village was Dorothy Canfield Fisher, who attracted other creative artists, like her friend Carl Ruggles, to the area. To most visitors today, however, it's famous as being Norman Rockwell's hometown from 1939 to 1953, and fans of his will want to visit the **Norman Rockwell Exhibition & Gift Shop,** on Route 7A (☎ 802/375-6423). Hundreds of *Saturday Evening Post* covers are on display in the gallery, which is hosted by former models and neighbors of Rockwell. A 20-minute film is also shown. Open in summer daily from 9am to 5pm, in winter from 10am to 4pm. Admission is $2 for adults, free for children 6 and under. Another artist who also lived in Arlington for a time was Rockwell Kent, and many of his woodcuts were inspired by the landscape around Arlington.

BENNINGTON LODGING & DINING

South Shire Inn, 124 Elm St., Bennington, VT 05201 (☎ 802/447-3839), is on a quiet residential street, 1 block off Main. It's a handsome Victorian, dating to 1879, with a semicircular front porch. It possesses some handsome interiors, like the mahogany-paneled sitting room with its mahogany leadglass bookcases and the breakfast room, which has much intricate molding. There are nine rooms—five in the main house and four in the carriage house. All have telephones; some have fireplaces and charming window seats. Each is decorated differently. The Peach Room, for example, has a cottage-style carved bed, in contrast to the Gold Room where a handsome rice four-poster is the main feature. All four rooms in the carriage house have Jacuzzis and fireplaces and are furnished with four-posters, armoires, and other antique reproductions. The Sleigh Suite has a pine sleigh bed and side tables, plus a pine desk and dresser and a chaise lounge, all set under a cathedral ceiling with a skylight. Breakfast is served at separate tables and will likely bring fresh fruit, muffins, and entrees such as apple sesame pancakes, eggs Benedict, and waffles. Rates: in season $105 to $160; foliage season $125 to $175; off-season $90 to $140.

Molly Stark Inn, 1067 E. Main St., Bennington, VT 05201 (☎ 802/442-9631), occupies an 1890 Queen Anne–style Victorian with a wraparound porch set on 1 carefully tended acre. Six rooms are available, decorated in country style with quilts, oak, and other pieces, and claw-foot tubs in the bathrooms. The most private accommodation is in the guest cottage that contains a brass bed set in the loft, a Jacuzzi, wet bar, woodstove, and many other creature comforts. Guests also may use the den and parlor, warmed in winter with a wood-burning stove. A hearty breakfast is served. Rates: $75 to $100 double; cottage $150.

The **Brasserie,** in Potter's Yard, 325 County St., Bennington (☎ 802/447-7922), is a pleasant outdoor dining spot in summer and a fine luncheon or dinner spot year-round. At lunch, have the Yard Special, a platter with Danish pâté, French bread and butter, and a Boston lettuce salad. Or you can choose from a variety of salads, omelets, and sandwiches under $9. At dinner, the dining room is candlelit for romance, and the short menu proffers a spicy seafood putanesca made with scallops, shrimp, clams, and halibut in broth spiced with tomatoes, olives, capers, and anchovies; lamb chops with an apple mint chutney; or steak au poivre. Prices range from $15 to $18. Turn off Main Street at Dunkin Donuts (at 460 Main). Open in summer daily from 11:30am to 8pm; in winter Sunday to Thursday from 11:30am to 3pm.

Alldays & Onions, 519 Main St. (☎ 802/447-0043), is a casual place with plain wood tables and chairs. It's the place to come for breakfast or lunch, when you can create your own sandwich using a variety of great fresh breads—pumpernickel, marble, sourdough—and assorted fillings that include corned beef and pastrami. In addition, there are soups, salads, quiches, and vegetarian specialties. At dinner, the room takes on a more intimate ambience with candles and cloths on the tables. The food is well prepared and very reasonably priced. About 10 entrees are offered, always including a fish, a pasta, and a beef or game dish of the evening. You might find roasted chicken breast with lingonberries or a rack of lamb with honey-rosemary sauce. Prices range from $11 to $15. Open Monday to Saturday from 7:30am to 5:30pm and Wednesday to Saturday from 6 to 8:30pm.

The **Publyck House,** Route 7A, Harwood Hill (☎ 802/442-8301), is a remodeled barn that has been filled with 18th-century decor and has an indoor greenhouse. Good beef and seafood are the staples here, priced from $11 to $16. There might be grilled halibut with an herb butter, salmon with dill-hollandaise, and chicken teriyaki, as well as several steaks and surf-turf combinations. Open Monday to Thursday from 5 to 9pm, Friday to Saturday from 5 to 10pm, Sunday from 4 to 9pm.

ARLINGTON LODGING & DINING

The **West Mountain Inn,** ½ mile west of Arlington on Route 313, Arlington, VT 05250 (☎ 802/375-6516), is one of my favorite retreats for several reasons, but primarily for the spirit and character of its owners, Wesley and Mary Ann Carlson. Both love animals and tend a menagerie of Netherland dwarf lop-eared rabbits, goats, and several llamas. Both are caring individuals, and on the ground floor, they have created Gwendolyn's Room, a *really* accessible room for people with disabilities, where all the switches are placed low, as are the bars in the closet. The bathroom is fully and properly equipped and even has an open-style shower to accommodate a wheelchair. The room itself is one of the nicest, with a brick fireplace, ebony sculptures on the mantel, a Stickley love seat, and a comfy chair. The 150-acre setting is lovely. Cornflowers and iris and other flowers bloom. The house looks out onto Red Mountain, and the grounds are filled with hemlocks, pine, and maple. To get there, you'll have to cross the Battenkill and take a dirt road to the top of a hill. There are 14 rooms (plus the special one), each named after a favorite historical figure. In each, guests will find a chocolate bar and a bowl of fruit. The Robert Todd Lincoln Room has a carved-oak lace-canopied bed covered with a hand-loomed 1830 quilt—"snowflakes on evergreen," a special Vermont pattern. Oak furnishings, including a rocker, complete the decor. In the Daniel Webster Suite there are sleigh beds; Grandma Moses's small pale-blue room has a fireplace, a rocker, and of course, her farm scenes; the Robert Frost Room has its own porch with wicker chairs overlooking the llama pasture; the Carl Ruggles Room, with fireplace and deck, features a carved high-backed oak bed, a Stickley couch, and a rope rug. The largest room of all is the Rockwell Kent suite. It has a native pine cathedral ceiling and a loft bed, a brick fireplace, an Indian rug as a wall hanging, and an eclectic mix of pine and Victorian furnishings. There are still other accommodations, including a Booker T. Washington Room with original pine paneling. In addition, there are three millhouse suites, each with living room, kitchen, and two bedrooms and bath. Two have wood-burning stoves.

The dining room is basically for inn guests, who receive a six-course dinner that changes daily. As a main course, it might feature veal marsala and a chicken and a shrimp dish. The fireplace makes it cozy in winter, and the orchids and other plants and color photos of the inn in all seasons give it a homey feel. Adjacent, there's a bar with Windsor-style bar stools and, oddly enough, a tank full of exotic tropical fish, along with plenty of books and magazines. Other popular gathering spots for guests are the game room, equipped with cribbage, backgammon, and other board games, and the sitting room, warmed by a Franklin stove and offering plenty of couches and armchairs and a piano at which guests entertain each other. In summer, the enclosed flagstone porch, set with cushioned bamboo chairs, is a favorite lounging spot. At breakfast, eggs Benedict, omelets, and vanilla crepes with butterscotch sauce are all likely choices. Rates: fall, $182 to $254 double; winter, $162 to $194 double; summer, $186 to $234 double; spring $176 to $234 double. Mid-March to mid-June, midweek $155 double.

Occupying a cream-colored Greek Revival building with rust-colored shutters, the **Arlington Inn**, Route 7A, Arlington, VT 05250 (☎ 802/375-6532), stands behind a row of stately maples. A marble path fringed with flowers and ferns leads to the central portico. Inside, the hallway, handsomely decorated with oriental carpets, carved Chippendales, and color engravings of London scenes dating back to 1848, is a refreshing change from colonial New England style.

It's both an inn and a restaurant. In the main dining room, tables are elegantly covered in white and set with crystal candlesticks and gold-rimmed china. A rather Empire-style ambience is created by a couple of classical urns and an ornate clock that stands on the fireplace mantel. A meal here might start with a strudel of pheasant in a cream sauce with sun-dried cranberries or a sauté of Maine crab cakes with cilantro and orange and green peppercorn beurre blanc. Among the main courses, priced from $17 to $22, might be pan-roasted breast of duck with port and currant game sauce, or rack of lamb with garlic and cumin red wine sauce. A lighter menu is offered in the tavern. Breakfast offers eggs, bagels, omelets, and pancakes. If you have to wait for your table, relax in the cozy forest-green Sylvester Deming Tavern, decorated with stoneware and hunting prints, while a pianist entertains (Friday and Saturday only). Don't miss the two huge (you'll see what I mean) Canadian rawhide rockers on the adjacent porch. There's also a greenhouse dining room that looks very summery with its green, peach, and pink color scheme and marble floor. Open in summer Tuesday to Sunday from 5:30 to 9pm; in winter Tuesday to Saturday from 5:30 to 9pm.

The accommodations are variously decorated in a 19th-century style; some have fireplaces. For example, the Pamela Suite features flounce pillowcases, valanced windows, a Madame Recamier sofa, an oriental throw rug, and a marble Victorian dresser in one room. The Martin Chester Room contains a broken-scroll bed, needlepointed side chairs, a camelback sofa, an armoire, a carved wood table, orange-and-green-macaw and bird-of-paradise wallpaper, and a huge with turnip-foot sideboard. The tongue-and-groove ceiling makes it very cozy and different. Some of the rooms are tucked under the eaves. Many of the bathrooms have claw-foot tubs; and quilts, Victorian prints, and period pieces like spinning wheels are found throughout the rooms. Guests have the use of the parlor, furnished Stickley style, and most comfortable in winter when the fire is lit. Active folks will like the tennis court out back. Rates (including breakfast): July 1 to August 15, $90 to $170; August 16 to October 31, $100 to $195; November 1 to June 30, $80 to $160 (the higher price is for fireplace rooms).

Fans of Norman Rockwell will want to stay at the **Inn on Covered Bridge Green**, R.D. 1, Box 3550, Arlington, VT 05250 (☎ 802/375-9489). This was once his home and studio. Another attraction is its remote location on the Battenkill on 5 acres of grounds, with picturesque views from the front porch of the covered bridge and a small church etched against the mountains. Granite steps mount up to the front of this 1792 house with its historic outdoor brick smokehouse. There are five rooms in the inn and two cottages in the back that Rockwell used as studios. Narrow doors lead into the rooms, decorated in typical country style with floral-patterned wallpapers and braided rugs. The Bicentennial Room, for example, has a maple four-poster and a pine chest, plus two wicker chairs and a fireplace. The bathroom has a whirlpool tub. The large studio cottage has two bedrooms and a kitchen and incorporates the room where Rockwell painted. The low-ceilinged parlor is a comfy room where people can browse through books and maps, watch TV, and look at Rockwell's paintings, *The Four Freedoms*. A breakfast of French toast, eggs baked in tomato, or a similar dish is served at a communal table. Facilities include a tennis court. Rates: $120 to $155.

Bennington & Arlington
Special & Recreational Activities

Boating: Rental boats are available in **Woodford State Park,** east of Bennington on Route 9.

Canoeing: Battenkill Canoe, Arlington on River Road (leading to West Arlington), off Route 313 (P.O. Box 65; ☎ 802/362-2800), will rent a canoe for $44 a day and pick you up at the end of the trip. It also offers interpretive nature trips on the river and guided day trips, plus many other longer trips in the Northeast (also even farther afield in places like Costa Rica).

Cross-Country Skiing: Prospect Ski Mountain Touring Center, Woodford, near Bennington, VT 05201 (☎ 802/442-2575), with 40 kilometers of trails.

Fishing: Woodford State Park has some great trout fishing.

Golf, Swimming & Tennis: Mount Anthony Country Club, Bank Street, below the Battle Monument, in Bennington (☎ 802/442-2617).

Horseback Riding: Valley View Horse & Tack Shop, Northwest Hill Road (Box 48A), Pownal, VT 05261 (☎ 802/823-4649), offers trail rides and such specialty rides as Haunted Halloween rides. Take Route 346 off Route 7.

THE MANCHESTER-DORSET VALLEY

A beautiful region, the area is bordered on each side by mountains and cut through by the famous Battenkill River. Manchester Village has always attracted visitors, often wealthy ones, especially to its grand old hotel, the Equinox. People came in the mid-19th century to take Dr. Sprague's famous water cure. Hotel owner Frank Orvis capitalized on the popularity of the cure when he advertised that he had piped the precious water from the mountain and bottled it—his advertisements appeared briefly in subway cars and on buses in New York City until a federal agency intervened. Today people come to the area to climb Mount Equinox; attend the events held at the Hildene Meadowlands and the Southern Vermont Arts Center; and to fish, cycle, ski, canoe, or just plain relax. The current winning pastime, though, seems to be shopping the 125-plus outlets in and around Manchester.

Just 6 miles up Route 30, Dorset is a far more somnolent village, but also well endowed and sought after—it boasts the Dorset Playhouse, several fine inns, plus an evocative country store. Beyond are two villages that are much rougher around the edges—the Pawlets and Danby, both of which have some appealing, worthwhile surprises.

MANCHESTER & DORSET AREA ATTRACTIONS

The prime sightseeing destination in the valley is **Hildene,** off Route 7A, 2 miles south of Route 30 (☎ 802/362-1788), which was the home of Robert Todd Lincoln, eldest son of Abraham Lincoln. He first discovered Vermont in 1863 when his mother brought him to the Equinox House on a summer retreat. A visit to Hildene begins in the carriage house, where a video show records the highlights of Robert Todd Lincoln's life and successful career—born in August 1843, he served in the army (he was present at Appomattox), and later became a partner in the Chicago law firm of Isham and Lincoln. Under President Garfield, Robert was appointed secretary of war and served as minister to the Court of St. James under President Harrison. Later, he became chairman of the board of the Pullman Palace Car Company. In 1902, he purchased these 500 acres and built his Georgian Revival home overlooking the Battenkill Valley.

Hildene means "hill" and "valley." During both Robert Lincoln's working and retirement years, he and his family summered here—he was involved in local affairs until he died at Hildene in 1926. His widow summered at Hildene until her death in 1937. It was briefly occupied by her daughter, Mary Lincoln Isham, and later by her granddaughter, Mary Lincoln Beckwith, daughter of Jessie Lincoln Beckwith. Peggy Beckwith was a fascinating, outspoken woman who flew her own biplane; painted, sculpted, studied piano and guitar; and tried to operate the property as a working farm. She died in 1975. Her younger brother, Robert Todd Lincoln Beckwith, last of the Lincoln line, died in 1985. The property is now owned by the Friends of Hildene.

On the house tour, you can view the room where Robert Todd died and his office, containing one of Abe Lincoln's stovepipe hats and all of the original furnishings. The original rolls are also played for visitors on the 1908 Aeolian player pipe organ. From the top-floor rooms, you can look down onto the restored formal garden, designed after a stained-glass window. It contains 25 varieties of peonies—the best time to visit is in mid-June, when they're in bloom, but the garden is beautiful throughout the season.

Being able to walk through the rooms makes the house tour particularly appealing. In the toy room, note the screen depicting fairy tales that Robert Todd Lincoln commissioned for his grandchildren. Make sure to go down to the garden terrace for the view of the Green Mountains on one side and the Taconics on the other. Stroll the nature trails, enjoy a picnic, or visit the kitchen/cutting garden as it is being restored. Open mid-May through October, daily from 9:30am to 5:30pm. Admission is $7.

Don't miss driving up **Mount Equinox Sky Line Drive** (☎ 802/362-1114) for the glorious views of the valley and the Green Mountains. *Ekwanok* means "where the top is," and here the top is 3,816 feet. It's said that Ethan Allan lived on the eastern slope, and it's believed that the settlers who lived on the southern and northern slopes built logging roads and climbed to Lookout Rock where they carved their names. There's a hotel on the summit and a bar-restaurant that was built by Dr. J. G. Davidson, an organic chemist who founded Union Carbide and who was also an enthusiastic hiker. He acquired 8,000 acres here in 1939, and when he, and later his wife, died, they left the grounds to the Carthusian monastery located on the mountainside so that the whole mountain might be preserved for the public's enjoyment. The cost is $6 per car and driver and $2 for each additional passenger, $1 for children 6 to 12.

The **Southern Vermont Art Center,** West Road, off Route 7A (P.O. Box 617), Manchester, NH 05254 (☎ 802/362-1405), is worth a visit for its setting alone. Here against a woods-and-meadow backdrop, a Festival of the Arts is celebrated from early June to mid-October on the slopes of Mount Equinox. Paintings, sculpture, and photographs are displayed; and music, dance, and voice recitals are given in the performance barn. Open: Galleries and gardens are open in summer, Tuesday to Saturday from 10am to 5pm, Sunday noon to 5pm; in winter, Monday to Saturday from 10am to 4pm. Closed after Columbus Day to early December.

Even non-anglers and those who've only read Izaak Walton on fishing might find the **American Museum of Fly-Fishing,** Route 7A at Seminary Avenue in Manchester (☎ 802/362-3300), interesting. Tying a fly to lure a fish is a very delicate art indeed, and an exotically colorful one. The museum also has 18th- and 19th-century fly rods, some 20 feet long, the earlier ones made from ash, hickory, lancewood, and greenheart, and the later (mid-19th century on) from bamboo. Today, of course, fiberglass, graphite, and boron are used, and these, too, are displayed. Exhibits also include the fly-fishing tackle of many famous Americans: Winslow Homer, Arnold Gingrich (founder of *Esquire*), Dwight Eisenhower, Daniel Webster, and Ernest Hemingway. Open daily from 10am to 4pm. Admission is $3, free for students.

It's fun also to drop in and browse among the hunting and fishing gear at the **Orvis Company Store** (☎ 802/362-3750) on Route 7. Orvis operates a fly-fishing school near Manchester from April to October. A 2-day course will cost from $450 to $475 per person and will teach you the intricacies of tying flies and casting and all the other skills of the sport. Orvis offers a variety of packages, including one for parents and children and another for women only. Orvis also operates a shooting/hunting school.

Many people come to Manchester just to shop the outlets, and along Route 7 you'll find such famous brand names as Anne Klein, Bass, and Van Heusen. There are in fact about 125 such stores in the area, including Cole Haan, Ralph Lauren, Liz Claiborne, Brooks Brothers, Giorgio Armani, and many more. **Dexter Shoes** (☎ 802/362-4810) is at routes 11 and 30, and the **Hathaway Outlet** (☎ 802/864-4828) is located in the Equinox Shops. Stock up, too, on Vermont specialties—ham, cheese, and maple syrup—at **Harrington's** (☎ 802/362-2070) at the junction of routes 7, 11, and 30. On Route 7A, **Coffee, Tea, and Spice** has a wide selection of gourmet items. At **Mother Myrick's Confectionary and Ice Cream Parlor,** stop by to savor ice cream or fantastic pastries and cakes that you can enjoy out on the awning-shaded deck. The **Jelly Mill,** on Route 7A (☎ 802/362-3494), shelters a number of stores offering everything from handmade lamps to gourmet cookware, from crafts to foodstuffs. The **Woodcarver** is special here. The town also possesses two terrific bookstores—**Johnny Appleseed Bookshop** (☎ 802/362-2458) and the **Northshire Bookstore** (☎ 802/362-2200), both on Route 7A. Most stores are open daily from 9am to 6pm.

North on Route 7, the **Enchanted Doll House** (☎ 802/362-1327) welcomes all ages to its 12-room toy shop featuring all kinds of dolls, miniatures, stuffed animals, books, games, and creative toys. Open daily from 9am to 5:30pm.

In **Dorset,** on Route 30, the **J. K. Adams Company Factory Store** (☎ 802/362-2303) stocks a whole line of gourmet woodware—spice racks, knife racks, butcher block, and other home accessories. Dorset also has a very atmospheric country store called **Pelletier's Market** where you can pick up a picnic lunch.

From Dorset, you can continue up Route 30 to the less touristed and more authentic small village of **Pawlet.** Here several interesting workshops, studios, and stores have been opened. On School Street, step into potter **Marion Waldo McChesney's** studio (☎ 802/325-3039) to see her whimsical and unusual ceramics that include a series of raku pieces that she calls roadkill, plus some lovely floaters and organic art nouveau–style polished ceramic sculptures. Across the street, **Judy Sawyer Lake** (☎ 802/325-6308) makes lampshades using wallpapers with such fun motifs as sunflowers, cats, fish, and ladybugs as well as the more traditional cutout-style shades, too. Don't miss stopping into **Mach's Market** (☎ 802/325-6113) where you can see the "river in the box." Other artists working in the area who are worth stopping to see are **Rosalind Compain,** who creates contemporary stone sculpture (☎ 802/325-3231), and **Roy Egg,** who paints wild and whimsical canvases. Also contact the **Jay H. Connaway Studio** (☎ 802/325-3107) to see marine paintings created by this contemporary of Winslow Homer (by appointment only).

From Pawlet, you can take Route 133 to Danby and then turn south back to Manchester. **Danby** is also sprucing up, and there are some artisans and galleries to visit here, too. **The Peel Gallery** (☎ 802/293-5230) on Route 7, 2 miles north of Danby, represents 50 artists and has launched a few of them—Martin Carey, Betty Ann MacDonald, Yale Epstein—onto national recognition tracks. The gallery represents artists only, on an exclusive-in-Vermont basis, and it's a great spot to capture the cultural pulse and just to browse even if you don't buy. Price range from $35 to $30,000. Also in Danby, **Robert Gasperetti** makes Shaker- and Craftsman-inspired furniture (☎ 802/293-5195); and the **Danby Marble Company,** Route 7 (☎ 802/293-5425), offers high-quality marble items from bookends to candlesticks, soap holders, and wine coolers.

Six miles east of Manchester, **Bromley Mountain Ski Resort,** Route 11 (☎ 802/824-5522), offers winter skiing, and summer fun, too, when you can fly down the Alpine Slide or the DeValkart dirt track in a go-kart. A ride on the Alpine slide is $5.50 for adults and $4.50 for children 7 to 12; three rides cost $15 and $12, respectively; five rides cost $23 and $18; and its $42 and $33 for 10 rides. The go-kart ride is $6; $16 for three rides. The slides are open weekends only from late May to mid-June and then daily through early October. You can also take the chair to the summit for $5.50 for adults and $4.50 for children 7 to 12.

Before you reach Bromley, there's a turnoff at Route 30 that will take you to the major ski resort of **Stratton** (☎ 1/800-STRATTON). Even if you're not a skier, you may want to visit this resort that has been built to resemble a Tyrolean village and manages to achieve a charm in winter that almost makes you believe you're in the Tyrol. There are plenty of shops and restaurants to browse in, and in summer, it's fun to take the gondola up the mountain. The gondola runs from 9:30am to 4pm and costs $10 per ride.

For evening entertainment, the **Dorset Theater Festival** presents a series of plays from mid-June through Labor Day at the Dorset Playhouse, Dorset Village (☎ 802/867-2223).

MANCHESTER LODGING & DINING

Antiques lovers will adore the **1811 House,** Route 7A, Manchester Village, VT 05254 (☎ 800/432-1811 or 802/362-1811), a salmon-and-beige clapboard structure situated in the center of Manchester. It was, in fact, built as a farmhouse in the 1770s. In 1811 the roof was raised, and it was turned into a tavern. Later, Mary Lincoln and Charles Isham, President Lincoln's granddaughter and her husband, resided here until she died in 1939. Today it is run by Marnie and Bruce Duff. The 14 rooms, all with private baths, are exquisitely furnished. The Robert Todd Lincoln Room contains a canopied pencil fourposter with a candlewick bedspread and a Federal-style slate-blue mantel and fireplace; chintz curtains hang at the pelmeted windows. Most of the rooms have desks, and all have comfy chairs for reading, plus such extra touches as clocks, makeup mirrors, and nightlights. In each, you'll find a personal touch— for example, in the Grace Hoyt Singer Room is a cross-stitch rug, a small glass case filled with china cats and birds, and a handsome porcelain figure on the chest of drawers; or the framed, pressed flowers in the Franklin Orvis Room. The Henry Ethel Robinson Room possesses a great bathroom containing a claw-foot tub with a sunflower-size old-fashioned shower-head. The Robinson room has a private balcony with a glorious view of the mountains. In the Hidden Room the 12-over-12 windows are original; so, too, are the beams in the Burr Room.

The tavern is authentic to a T. Pewter mugs hang from the old beams, horse brasses adorn the fireplace and bar, brass candlesticks stand on tables smoothed by long use, and Windsor chairs and bar stools complete the scene. Here guests can select from a superb collection of 50 single malts, including some mighty rare ones, and enjoy it in a crystal glass (Marnie and Bruce both have Scottish ancestry). A breakfast of fresh fruit, breads, and an entree like

French toast with Canadian bacon or eggs Benedict is elegantly served at the Duncan Phyfe table, which is set with fine silver and china. For relaxing, there are two sitting rooms. One has a couch set on an oriental carpet before a mantel with carved plaster reliefs. Homelike touches include photos placed on a claw-foot table. The other has book-filled built-in bookcases, two couches, a wooden chess set, and a TV for guests' pleasure. The basement also contains a game room with table tennis and a billiard table. The gardens (7 acres) are lovely and have been landscaped with a pond. In spring, they burst into full color with flowering trees and azaleas, and later with lilacs, peonies, and perennial flowering plants. From the lawn, the view extends across the Equinox golf course to the Green Mountains beyond. Rates (including breakfast) $180 to $230 double.

The owners of the **Inn at Manchester,** Route 7A (P.O. Box 41), Manchester, VT 05254 (☎ 802/362-1793), go out of their way to welcome their guests and inform them about the area. The 1880 house has 14 rooms and four suites. The Primrose Suite has a spacious bedroom, furnished with a maple bed, and a separate sitting room with a working fireplace. The Woodlilly Suite is dramatically decorated in Chinese red and features an iron and brass bed. The Garden Suite, decorated with country pine and oak furniture, pretty comforters, frilled curtains, and chintz wallpaper, also has a wood-burning fireplace.

There are four rooms in the carriage house that offer mountain and meadow views. Here Columbine has a handsome carved cherry bed with a Ralph Lauren blue-and-white comforter and matching drapes at the windows. The antique Tiffany-style floor lamp and a beautifully carved lion's-head chair immediately catch the eye. These rooms are large and will likely contain a brass bed, bold chintz wallpaper, or a Victorian-style mahogany chest, cherry side table, and wing chairs. The full country breakfasts are delicious. Stanley and Harriet whip up great apple-buttermilk pancakes with Vermont maple syrup, omelets, and homemade granola. Afternoon tea is also served. Rates: $100 to $150; foliage season and holidays, $120 to $175.

From the road, you can't help noticing the celery and mauve splash of color, and the hanging flower baskets that adorn the front porch of the **Village Country Inn,** Route 7A, Manchester, VT 05254 (☎ 802/362-1792). It's run by Anne and Jay Degen. Anne is the one who has the natural flair for interior decoration, and here she has created a magical full-scale romantic retreat filled with flowers and lace. Celery and mauve are the predominant colors in the large front parlor area, which offers an array of seating arrangements—a corner furnished with Stickley, a high-backed Victorian love seat and a mauve camelback sofa—all set around a fieldstone fireplace in a room accented with a gilt mirror and stained-glass door.

The 31 accommodations, all with private bath, are highly individual. Room 111 is large and features a carved oak bed set under a tented effect of cream lace, a wicker chaise lounge, oak dresser, lace-draped table, bold chintz wallpaper, and inviting window seats. Room 107 is a small country space furnished primarily with oak pieces. Other rooms might come in pale blue with wicker, in Laura Ashley country style, or in gray and lavender with a lacy swag above the bed. There are also a couple of garden rooms in the back by the pool. All rooms have fluffy towels and pretty eyelet linens.

In the dining room, the lattice trellises, floral-green wallpaper, and pink and forest-green napery create a romantic gardenlike effect. Here, even the fireplace is mauve. The menu is continental and changes seasonally. You may find medallions of veal with wild mushrooms, shallots, and Madeira; fish of the day grilled with oil, oregano, garlic, and lemon; breast of chicken sautéed with shiitake mushrooms, garlic, parsley, and lemon; or charcoal-broiled venison with caramelized onions and red wine sauce. To start, there might be roasted onion tart with merlot-thyme sauce or a trio of smoked seafoods with lemon-chive and horseradish sauce; to finish, a crème brûlée or pears poached in red wine. Prices run $16 to $24. A pianist entertains softly at the grand piano. There's also a comfortable tavern that opens onto a summer patio furnished with wrought-iron celery-colored furniture set among fountains and flowers. The gardens are brimming in spring with pink mountain laurel, golden coreopsis, and white Virginia spiderwort, and they make the outdoor pool an even more inviting place to relax. Anne also offers different weekend packages—including one called "A Blooming Affair" that includes a champagne picnic delivered to the garden's gazebo at a prearranged hour. Always inquire about her latest idea. Rates: MAP $150 to $235 double; suites and larger rooms $215 to $360.

You can't miss the purple-and-cream clapboard building that's called **The Reluctant Panther Inn,** Route 7A (P.O. Box 678), Manchester Village, VT 05254 (☎ 802/362-2568), known for its fine restaurant as well as its accommodations. The Greenhouse dining room seats 60 in a highly colorful, almost tropically inspired setting of plants, flagstone floor, and brilliant orange, yellow, and peach napery. The stone fireplace makes it cozy in winter, while in summer, the marble terrace dotted with flowers, plants, silver birches, and stone ornaments with a view of Equinox Mountain makes a lovely spot for cocktails. Or you can enjoy drinks in the unique bar. Green-leather low chairs on casters are set at Vermont marble tables; ceiling, paneling, and shutters are a brilliant purple; and in one corner, a full bear trophy, his teeth bared, stands ready to party no matter what. Elsewhere, carved gryphons are placed in niches. A fire adds warmth in winter.

The menu, which changes daily, offers a dozen or so entrees. The seafood is finely prepared—grilled or poached salmon with orange butter sauce or grilled trout finished with lemon, parsley, and almonds—and so too are meat dishes such as flank steak marinated in dark beer and honey reduction, or pan-seared duck breast with raspberry demiglace. Prices range from $21 to $27. Among the appetizers, try the raclette, a Swiss specialty of melted cheese, boiled potatoes, and pickles; or the delicious Prince Edward Island mussels steamed with white wine and saffron. Dining hours in summer, daily from 6 to 9pm; in winter, Thursday to Monday from 6 to 9pm.

There are 12 rooms in the main house, all with private baths, air-conditioning, color TVs, and phones; six have working fireplaces. Each is dramatically and differently decorated. A half bottle of wine is placed in each for guests to enjoy. The wallpapers are quite extraordinary: mushroom in Room A, purple poppies in Room C, Queen Anne's lace in Room E, for example. Room G is exceptionally attractive: Eyelet pillows grace the bed, which is covered with a light-purple comforter and adorned by a draped lace curtain effect. Comforts include two steel-gray wing chairs, a fireplace, dusky-rose carpet, marble-top table, oak dresser, and a bathroom with a claw-foot tub and pedestal sink. Room J is exceptionally large and possesses a Victorian oak bed and furniture in a matching style, while Room L contains a cherry Stickley bed, carved oak Victorian chair, a chestnut armoire, black-walnut chest of drawers, and two wing chairs covered in salmon-pink fabric. In the adjacent Mary Porter House, there are also four suites that have whirlpools and fireplaces and four-poster beds. Rates: MAP: summer/fall weekends, $210 to $360; midweek $180 to $310; foliage season (mid-August to late October), $245 to $385; winter/spring weekends, $210 to $390; holidays, $265 to $405. B&B only: midweek $120 to $290.

The famous old resort, the **Equinox,** Route 7A (P.O. Box 46), Manchester Village, VT 05254 (☎ 800/362-4747 or 802/362-4700), which once welcomed Mary Todd Lincoln and other dignitaries in its heyday, has been restored to its former glory in partnership with the Guinness family. Although on the site of a pre-Revolutionary tavern, its life as a fashionable summer resort was really begun by the Orvis family in 1854. Behind the facade with its stately columns and veranda stretching a full block along the marble sidewalk, you'll find a small lobby and a tavern-restaurant.

All of the 183 rooms have air-conditioning, TVs, and telephones and have been decorated in a light modern style using bleached pine, Audubon prints, and richly textured fabrics. The most luxurious rooms are located down the street in the Charles Orvis Inn, which dates to 1812 and which Charles Orvis himself owned. It contains six 2-bedroom and three 1-bedroom suites. Each features a marble bathroom with Jacuzzi, a cherry-paneled kitchen, and a handsome sitting and living room with a gas fireplace. The amenities include a CD stereo, TV, and telephone. In true club style there's a bar and a luxurious billiard room for guests.

The most impressive public space is the main dining room, the Colonnade. Designed in 1913, this domed room with a semicircular series of Palladian windows provides splendid mountain views. The menu features about six expertly prepared entrees, such as poached lobster and mussels with saffron basil risotto; medallion of hickory smoked beef tenderloin with cabernet demiglace; veal loin medallions with crabmeat custard, asparagus, fresh morels, and a cognac demiglace. Prices range from $21 to $25. Dining hours: June to October, daily from 6 to 9pm, November to May, Friday and Saturday from 6 to 9:30pm. The Marsh Tavern is authentic and original, dating back to 1769. Today it's furnished with Windsor chairs and polished wood tables and is open for breakfast, lunch, and dinner. The menu offers a variety of dishes like Yankee pot roast, shepherd's pie, and pan-seared trout in a Dijonnaise sauce, priced from $9 to $20. Open daily from 7am to 9:30pm.

What sets the inn apart from many other resorts is the **British School of Falconry** and the **Land Rover Driving School.** At the first, you can don a glove and learn how to hunt with a magnificent Harris hawk; at the second, you can learn how to handle this beguiling vehicle over all kinds of terrain under all conditions. Other facilities on the 1,100-acre property include two swimming pools (indoor/outdoor), three clay tennis courts, a fitness center and spa (with massages, wraps, and scrubs available), and the Gleneagles Golf Course, a recent update by Rees Jones of the original 1927 Walter Travis course. You can dine at the Dormy Grill at the clubhouse, or outside under an awning and enjoy the glorious view. In winter, there are 22 miles of cross-country ski trails plus ice skating and snowshoeing; rentals are available. Services include concierge, valet, and room service. While you're here, you can also stroll across and down the street to the Equinox shops. Rates: $179 to $319; suites from $479; Charles Orvis rooms $679 to $939. Special packages available.

The Inn at Ormsby Hill, R.R. 2, Box 3264, Manchester Center, VT 05255 (☎ 802/362-1163), is a restored manor house standing on 2½ acres of landscaped grounds with mountain views. Legend has it that Ethan Allen took refuge here from the English, and the innkeepers will happily show you the secret room where he is said to have hidden. Spectacular hand-tooled staircases and woodwork and other handsome architectural elements are found throughout the house. Part of the house dates back to 1764, with the remainder added in the 1800s by Isaac Isham. Guests enjoy two comfortable sitting rooms, both decorated in warm style using damask wallpapers and other rich fabrics and rugs. There's also a splendid flagstone terrace with glorious mountain views. The 10 rooms are all luxuriously furnished with antiques and original artwork. Nine have fireplaces and heart-shaped Jacuzzis equipped with candles, potpourri, and a rubber duck. The Library Room has built-in bookcases with decorative dental molding and offers a rice four-poster decorated with good-looking Waverly fabric. The beamed tongue-and-groove ceilings add an extra glow. Other furnishings consist of an armoire, a rocker and wing chairs, and an old steamer trunk. Frances has the best view and is also elegantly decked out with a toile wallpaper and furnished with a richly upholstered chaise lounge and loveseat, a burled maple chest, plus oriental lamps on the side tables. The Ethan Allen has a private entrance and sports a beautiful carved-mahogany four-poster along with candy-stripe wallpaper and armchairs upholstered in plaid and other beautiful fabrics. In this accommodation, one can sit in the Jacuzzi and enjoy the glow of the gas fireplace. The large size, the jade-and-lemon decor, and the daylight brilliance of the dining room-conservatory will beguile you, and so will the view beyond of Hildene and the Green Mountains. An excellent breakfast is served here with such relishing items as white chocolate pound cake, bananas with cream and almonds, and bread-and-butter pudding with fresh fruit. On Friday evening, a casual supper is served (linguine with shrimp and vegetables, say), but on Saturday there is a four-course single-entree dinner. It might begin with a leek, bacon, and Stilton polenta with tomato sauce, followed by a tenderloin of pork with port and dried cranberries, and finish with a triple-chocolate torte with white chocolate sauce. The supper is $20 for two; the dinner $65 for two. Afternoon tea is also served. Delicious cookies are also provided in the rooms—poppy-seed madeleines, triple-chocolate chip, and almond crescents—plus extras such as terry-cloth robes and turndown service. Guests also have access to a treasure chest of amenities such as toothpaste and other items that they might have forgotten to bring. The innkeepers pamper guests in every way possible. Rates: $125 to $245.

The **Seth Warner Inn,** Route 7A (P.O. Box 281), Manchester, VT 05255 (☎ 802/362-3830), is a more modest accommodation, but one that is very well kept and operated by a warm and welcoming host. It's set on 4 acres and has a lovely pond with resident ducks, plus inviting gardens and lawns furnished with Adirondack chairs. All five rooms are attractively decorated with stenciling and braided rugs and furnished with oak and wicker country pieces. The Seth Warner Room has a four-poster with a crocheted canopy that is made up with a star quilt and accessorized with iron lamps on the side tables. Breakfast is served by candlelight at separate tables. It might be delicious German-style pancakes, baked eggs, or something similar. Chinese rugs, a sofa, and wing chairs, clustered around the mantel, await in the sitting room, which also has a small TV. Guests appreciate the library nook where they can enjoy playing chess or reading. Afternoon tea and wine are served in the late afternoon. This has to be one of the best values in the valley. Rates: $100 in summer; $110 in fall; and $95 off-season.

The **Equinox Mountain Inn,** Skyline Drive (☎ 802/362-1113), is the place to stay if you want the thrill of being at the summit of a mountain with glorious views plus the opportunity to experience all kinds of weather "up close and personal," as they say. It's a great place for stargazing, and on clear nights owner Tim Cunningham takes a star finder down into the parking lot. In spring, you might also spot cougar, bobcats, or bears. Don't expect fancy accommodations. The place was built in the 1940s by Union Carbide president Dr. Davidson, and the 18 rooms are plain and simple, furnished in maple motel style and equipped with TVs. Some have small balconies. In a large living room with a stone fireplace, guests gather around the piano or else play a board game at one of the tables. A full breakfast of eggs, pancakes, and bacon is served in the dining room. There's also a lounge with the original circular bar and green vinyl stools. It opens at 4pm, and folks gather to enjoy the views of Stratton, Bromley, Mount Mansfield, and other peaks. The original Thonnet chairs are still in the dining room. A fine dinner is served. Among the favorite dishes on the current menu are the Mount Inn duck, made with spring onions and ginger, and the veal sweetbreads with a caper and wine sauce. To start, the duck livers sautéed with caramelized onions, mushrooms, bacon, and a hint of vermouth are something to write home about. Open mid-May to the last weekend in October. Rates: $100 to $150.

The **Chantecleer,** Route 7A, Manchester Center (☎ 802/362-1616), is considered the premier local restaurant. The fieldstone fireplace, rafters, and barn siding give a pretty country atmosphere to the room, filled with captain's chairs and tables covered in pink tablecloths. The inspiration is distinctly Swiss, but with other tones, too. For example, you might find specialties such as veal tenderloin that has been marinated in truffle oil, roasted, sliced and layered with truffle pâte and shallot confit, and finished with a Chardonnay velouté, served over wild-mushroom mashed potatoes with a drizzle of balsamic-maple reduction. Other dishes are equally inspired and executed in high style, such as the filet mignon Grand Marnier or the superb whole Dover sole served with a choice of classic sauces. Don't overlook the delicious Swiss-inspired accompaniments, whether it's rosti or spaetzle. Among the appetizers, the trademark dish is the Escargot Chantecleer, which is simmered with garlic and wine as usual but is then glazed with hazelnut garlic butter with a hint of Pernod. Prices run from $21 to $28. It's located about 4 miles north of Manchester on Route 7A. Open Wednesday to Monday from 6 to 9pm; Sunday from 11:30am to 2pm (winter only). Closed mid-April to mid-May and mid-November to mid-December.

Mistral's at Tollgate, Tollgate Road (☎ 802/362-1779), is definitely one place to plan on for dinner on any weekend. It has a very pretty setting by a stream that you can hear cascading over and around the large boulders. Picture windows look out onto the scene. There are two small dining rooms and a bar with cushioned banquettes where you can enjoy a cocktail. The menu balances meat and fish, and there will likely be a fillet of salmon with black sesame seeds and warm honey mustard vinaigrette or a roast duckling with Beaujolais and bing cherries. Classic appetizers include a rich French onion soup, escargots bourguignonne, and delicious smoked salmon with blinis and horseradish cream sauce. Prices range from $19 to $26. Open Thursday to Tuesday from 6pm to closing.

Bistro Henry, Route 11/30, Manchester (☎ 802/362-4982), is a fun, upbeat kind of place with a jazzy background. It's light and airy and furnished in a casual welcoming style with French posters for decoration. The food is fresh and memorable, and there's a well-rounded list of wines at reasonable prices. Duck prepared with a spiced green peppercorn sauce is a favorite, and so, too, is the grilled orange shrimp sorrentina, flavored with orange, balsamic vinegar and basil. Other dishes might include roasted salmon with an almond crust and red-pepper sauce or grilled veal chop with a flavorsome pinot noir sauce accompanied by roasted yams. Prices range from $14 to $19. To finish, there are any number of delights, from the mandarin Napoleon to the crème brûlée and the banana strudel. But best of all is the flourless chocolate Chambord cake. Open Tuesday to Sunday from 6pm to closing, and for Sunday brunch from 9am to 1:30pm.

The Black Swan, Route 7A, Manchester (☎ 802/362-3807), offers some good country dining in its two small dining rooms where tables are set with pink undercloths and windows are decorated with chintz fabrics. The cuisine is good. Specials enliven the menu, and you might find appetizers such as oriental spring rolls with plum sauce, grilled portobello mushrooms with onion marmalade, or an avocado and tomato soup. Much of the fare is New England traditional—roast rack of lamb with mint jelly, apple glazed pork chop, and fried chicken with pan gravy. Some dishes are more successful than others; in the salmon piccata, the sauce overwhelms the fish. Prices range from $13 to $22. Desserts run to apple pie and raspberry chocolate cheesecake, which are presented on a tray for your selection. Open 5 to 8:30 or 9pm, depending on the traffic. Closed Wednesday.

The **Perfect Wife,** Route 11/30, Manchester Center (☎ 802/362-2817), offers two dining options downstairs. One dining room is a plant-filled atrium, and the other is more formal with stone walls that are decorated with original art. In addition, there's an upstairs tavern featuring about 50 bottled beers plus a number on tap. Many of the dishes have a mixture of flavors and cuisines. For example, you might find a classic garlic-basted grilled salmon with a tarragon horseradish mayonnaise alongside a sesame-crusted tuna with a spicy oriental sauce. Or there could be pork chops slathered with barbecue sauce that is made with achiote paste, honey, and dark rum. Prices range from $13 to $17. Appetizers are similarly internationally inspired. The tavern serves a light menu of burgers and sandwiches. Open Tuesday to Sunday from 5 to 10pm; the tavern is open later.

DORSET LODGING & DINING

Standing at the center of a quiet community, the **Dorset Inn**, on the Green, Dorset, VT 05251 (☎ 802/867-5500), is a genuine country inn. Ferns, lupins, and geraniums add a splash of color to the borders by the crazily paved marble paths and steps that lead into the white clapboard building. Operating as an inn since 1796, it has recently been extensively renovated. The upstairs accommodations and decor vary: Room 24 (with private bath) is invitingly arrayed with brass bed, ruffled curtains, floral wallpaper, comfortable Martha Washingtons, and a chest of drawers. A cannonball-style bed dominates Room 26, while Room 28 offers a four-poster, a Martha Washington chair, and a view of the center green. Third-floor rooms under the eaves are interestingly and cozily shaped.

Besides the lovely accommodations, the inn has an excellent reputation for its food—and it's well deserved. The same menu is served in both the tavern and the dining room and affords ample choice—from simple turkey croquettes served with mashed potatoes to crispy duck confit served with plum chutney. Prices range from $10 to $20. Green paint, plank floors, plaid tablecloths, and white shutters provide the country dining atmosphere. The tap room is a cozy supper spot, especially in winter when a fire flickers. A broad selection of beers and a fine selection of wines are offered. Open: summer, daily from 11:30am to 2pm and 5:30 to 9pm; winter, Wednesday to Sunday only. Guests can also enjoy the two comfortable stenciled parlors with fireplaces, furnished with thick rugs, books, and country objects such as an old spinning wheel. Rates: MAP, $100 to $150 single, $130 to $235 double.

The **Barrows House**, Dorset, VT 05251 (☎ 800/639-1620 or 802/867-4455), is a large rambling property on 11 acres that retains a warm country feel. The grounds are quite beautiful and fragrant, bursting with lupins, iris, cornflowers, tulips, honeysuckle, and lilacs shaded by hemlocks, weeping willows, and silver birches. There are eight rooms in the white clapboard black-shuttered inn, originally built as a parsonage in 1804. Each is decorated in a simple country style with pine or oak furnishings, perhaps a four-poster, slip-covered chairs, and a desk. The rest of the 28 rooms and suites are dotted around the property in eight buildings. Six similar rooms are in the Hemlock House. The Truffle House contains three double rooms and a large living room with a fireplace. The upstairs suite is especially attractive, with its window seat and canopied four-poster. The Schubert House holds one double room and two suites with fireplaces. The Stable suites are pleasantly rustic with plank floors, pine hutches, and Windsor chairs. Each has a kitchenette and living room with a TV. The carriage house contains ideal accommodations for a family. The Truffle House contains five bedrooms plus a spacious living room with fireplace. Ping-Pong and a billiard table are located in the basement. All the accommodations are attractively furnished and very well kept.

The outdoor pool is idyllically situated and surrounded by grass. A sauna is located in the stables. So is the bicycle and cross-country ski shop, where bikes and equipment are available for rent. There are also two tennis courts. In the dining room, fresh flowers grace the tables along with atmospheric hurricane lamps. The whole room is fresh and gardenlike, but when you're sitting in the atrium it's as if you're sitting in a garden. The Tap Room gleams with polished wood, and here people gather to chat, entertain at the piano, or play backgammon. The food is regional New England. At dinner, you might find veal tenderloin with pancetta, tomatoes, and shiitake mushrooms; grilled swordfish on chipotle pepper and roasted corn puree; or rack of lamb with a three-mustard sauce. Among the appetizers, don't miss the crab cakes Chesapeake style. Prices range from $15 to $24. Dining hours are daily from 6 to 9pm. Rates: MAP, $210 to $270 double. B&B rates are available.

The **Inn at West View Farm**, Route 30, Dorset, VT 05251 (☎ 802/867-5715), has enjoyed a fabled reputation for its **Auberge** dining room. Here contemporary American cuisine is offered. Among the appetizers, there might be escargots in garlic butter and white wine, baked Brie in phyllo with poached pears and a port sauce, and always an appetizer of the day. Among the 10 or so entrees, try the sautéed sesame shrimp with sweet-red-pepper agnolotti, served with a ginger and apricot beurre blanc; the loin of pork served with fresh-fruit salsa on wilted scallions and a semisweet puff crouton; or the herb-crusted rack of lamb topped with a pear-bourbon sauce, served au jus. Prices range from $19 to $24. In the tavern, you can enjoy dishes such as crab cakes, grilled bratwurst, or marinated rosemary chicken in a spiced tomato-herb sauce, priced from $10 to $14. For dessert, there are homemade sorbets and ice creams, tarts, chocolate mousse, and crème caramel. Tables are arrayed with Villeroy and Boch table settings and hurricane-style lamps; choice tables are set in the large bay window. Dining hours are Tuesday to Sunday from 6 to 9pm; Friday and Saturday only in winter. If you have to wait, there's a small bar in which you can study the 1920s news photos from the *New York Times* that cover the walls. There are also 10 guest rooms available, all with private baths. The nicest, in my opinion, has a pineapple-style bed covered with a star quilt, a cane-seated rocker, a chest, and side table. In the carriage house, the suite has two double rooms, one with a turned four-poster sans canopy. Rates: MAP, $165 to $210 double; B&B $95 to $150 double. Closed April and November to December 11.

Cornucopia of Dorset, Route 30 (Box 307), Dorset, VT 05251 (☎ 802/867-5751), is an attractive bed-and-breakfast that offers guests those extra little services, such as a champagne welcome, a wake-up tray with coffee or tea and fresh flowers, evening turndown, and a library of VCR movies. There are four rooms, all with private baths, phones, and air-conditioning, plus a cottage suite that has a skylit loft bedroom, a living room with a cathedral ceiling and fireplace, a fully equipped kitchen, and a private patio. All the rooms have sitting areas, and three have fireplaces. Most have canopied beds that are covered with down comforters in winter and quilts in summer. The ground-floor offers a living room and study, both with fireplaces, and a sunroom overlooking the grounds. A full breakfast is served. Rates: weekends, $135 to $165, weekdays $125 to $150; cottage on weekends, $235; weekdays, $210.

LODGING & DINING IN THE JAMAICAS & TOWNSHENDS

The **Windham Hill Inn**, Windham Hill Road, West Townshend, VT 05359 (☎ 802/874-4080), takes some finding, but it's worth the trouble. It's set on 150 secluded woodland-mountain acres overlooking Rattle Snake Mountain and has a peaceful garden filled with iris, roses, poppies, pansies, and a redolent fringe tree. There are 13 guest rooms in the restored 1825 farmhouse and 8 rooms in the white barn annex. All have private baths and telephones; some have fireplaces or stoves. Most of the rooms have beds with candlewick spreads, country maple furnishings, and chintz wallpapers. My favorites are in the barn—a real barn, where chamber concerts are performed. Here, most rooms have high, beamed ceilings, and best of all, decks that have gorgeous views; some rooms are low beamed, like Matilda's Room, which is furnished with a bed, rocker, trunk, and floor lamp, plus that deck and the glorious view. Three new rooms at the "loft level" have extra lavish appointments—fireplaces and sunken bathrooms with double soaking tubs or Jacuzzis. The cupola in Marion Goodfellow is a great reading nook.

Guests can choose among three parlors, two comfortably furnished with antiques; the third, an outside deck, is furnished more casually with wicker pieces. Each one has either a fireplace or wood-burning stove. In the small dining room, oak tables are covered with pink tablecloths, and wall niches display china. A five-course meal is served and might feature wild-mushroom ravioli in a savory forestière bouillon to start, followed by five-onion soup with lentils and a salad of mesclun greens. Among the five or so main courses might be pan-seared Arctic char in a light Provençal broth flavored with pernod; breast of duck with wild berry–juniper sauce; and a vegetarian and a pasta dish. A full country breakfast is served. In summer, guests can enjoy a heated outdoor pool, a tennis court, and hiking trails that lead to a brook with a swimming hole. In winter, the trails are for cross-country skiing. Rates: MAP $255 to $335 double (the higher price is for rooms with whirlpool tub). Loft rooms, MAP $380 double. Add $50 to all rates during foliage season and Christmas week.

Manchester-Dorset Area
Special & Recreational Activities

Biking: **Stratton** has a mountain-bike park. An all-day pass is $20.

Boating: **Emerald Lake State Park** is on Route 7 (☎ 802/362-1655); **Lake Shaftsbury State Park** is 10 miles north of Bennington (☎ 802/375-9978); the **Hapgood Pond Recreation Area** in Peru, is about 6 miles from Manchester (☎ 802/362-2307).

Camping: **Emerald Lake State Park,** Route 7 (☎ 802/362-1655) has campsites; **Hapgood Pond Recreation Area** in Peru, about 6 miles from Manchester (☎ 802/362-2307), has 28 sites.

Cross-Country Skiing: **Hildene Ski Touring Center** (☎ 802/362-1788) has 30 miles of trails. It's open daily from 9am to dusk if there's sufficient snow (usually from the third week in December to March 1). The **Viking Ski Touring Centre,** R.R. 1, Box 70, Little Pond Road, Londonderry, VT 05148 (☎ 802/824-3933) has 25 miles of trails and also offers inn-to-inn tours and guided tours.

Fishing: The **Battenkill** is one of the East's great fishing rivers. See information above for the famous **Orvis Fly-Fishing School** (☎ 800/548-9548).

Golf: The **Dorset Field Club** (☎ 802/867-5553) has a course, as does the **Equinox** (see above). The **Stratton Mountain Country Club** hosts the **McCall's LPGA Classic Golf Tournament.**

Horseback Riding: Stratton offers 1- and 2-hour trail riding at the Sunday Bowl Ranch for $30 to $55.

Skiing: Bromley, off Route 11 in Bromley, is a full-facility resort offering 39 trails serviced by nine lifts. Slope-side accommodations are available at **Bromley Village.** For information, call ☎ 802/824-5522 or write to P.O. Box 1130-B, Manchester Center, VT 05255.

     Stratton, Stratton Mountain, VT 05155 (☎ 802/297-2200), is a full-facility resort complete with a sports center that also offers tennis, badminton, swimming, and more. At the base of the mountain, the Alpine Village is amazingly reminiscent of the Tyrol. There are 90 trails on 563 acres, serviced by 12 lifts, including one high-speed 12-passenger gondola, one high-speed 6-passenger chair, and four quads. Accommodations include the Stratton Mountain Inn, Stratton Village Lodge, and Stratton Mountain Village, as well as Liftline Lodge and the Birkenhaus. For reservations, call ☎ 800/787-2886. For snow conditions call ☎ 800/297-2211. To get there, from Manchester take Route 7 to Route 11 east to Route 30 south to Bondville. The entrance to Stratton is located in the village center. Follow the Stratton Mountain Road for 4 miles.

Swimming: Emerald Lake State Park, Route 7 (☎ 802/362-1655), and **Lake Shaftsbury State Park,** 10 miles north of Bennington (☎ 802/375-9978), have beaches. **Hapgood Pond Recreation Area** in Peru, about 6 miles from Manchester (☎ 802/362-2307), has a shallow swimming area.

Tennis: The **Stratton Tennis School,** site of the **Acura Women's Tennis** tournament during the summer, has 15 Har-Tru and Deco Turf II courts, four indoor courts, three racquetball courts, and other athletic facilities. Special packages including accommodations in a variety of room types are available. Call ☎ 800/787-2886 or 802/297-2200. From Manchester, take Route 7 to Route 11 east to Route 30 south to Bondville. From the center of the village, follow the Stratton Mountain Road to the resort. Courts are also available at the Equinox.

Middlebury, Burlington &
the Champlain Valley

Middlebury ◆ *From Middlebury to Vergennes* ◆ *Burlington* ◆
The Champlain Islands

Distance in miles from Boston: Middlebury, 192; Burlington, 225.

Estimated driving times: 3¾ hours to Middlebury; 4¼ hours to Burlington.

◄o►◄o►◄o►◄o►◄o►

Driving: To reach Middlebury, take I-93 to I-89 to Exit 3 for Bethel and then Route 107 west to Route 100 north. Take Route 100 north to Route 125 west and then to Route 7 north, which enters Middlebury. For Burlington, take Exit 13.

Bus: Vermont Transit (☎ 800/451-3292) operates to Middlebury, Vergennes, and Burlington.

Further Information: For more information, contact **Addison County Chamber of Commerce**, 2 Court St. Middlebury, VT 05753 (☎ 802/388-7951); **Brandon Area Chamber of Commerce**, P.O. Box 267, Brandon, VT 05733 (☎ 802/247-6401); **Lake Champlain Regional Chamber of Commerce**, 60 Main St., Burlington, VT 05401 (☎ 802/863-3489).

◄o►◄o►◄o►◄o►◄o►

Sandwiched between the Green Mountains and the Adirondacks across the border in New York State, mid-Vermont is blessed with another stunning geographical feature, the magnificent Lake Champlain. This huge lake, which is often called the sixth Great Lake, stretches for 136 miles, from Whitehall, New York, to the Quebec border, and at its widest point is 12 miles wide. Along its 580 miles of shoreline, coves and bays abound, inviting recreation and relaxation. In addition, it is fed by two major rivers, the Lamoille and the Winooski, that also offer opportunities for canoeing, kayaking, and other water sports. In the early history of the nation, Lake Champlain was very important strategically, and on this body of water and around its banks, the struggles between the nations for North America were fought. As a consequence, the lake holds the secret of many a shipwreck, including the most recently found member of Benedict Arnold's fleet, scuttled during the American Revolution. Get out on the lake to fish or canoe, and you enter a world where porcupines

Events & Festivals to Plan Your Trip Around

May: Lilac Festival at the Shelburne Museum. In addition to the palette and aroma of the 400 plus lilacs themselves, there are lawn games, music, dance, food, and more. Call ☎ 802/985-3346.

June: Lake Champlain Balloon & Craft Festival. A colorful event when 50 hot-air balloons float above the lake. It's accompanied by a crafts fair, fireworks, rides, and other entertainment. Call ☎ 802/863-3489.

Vermont Vintage Auto Exhibition gathers 300 antique cars at a meet on the Shelburne Museum grounds. Call ☎ 802/985-3346.

Discover Jazz Festival is a 6-day festival that brings jazz to the theaters, streets, beaches, and parks of Burlington. It features international artists plus a Latin dance party, gospel tent, and other events. Call ☎ 802/863-3489.

At the **Lake Champlain International Fishing Derby** in Burlington, folks compete in 14 categories for cash and other prizes. Call ☎ 802/863-3489.

Vermont Food Fest, or **Green Mountain Chew Chew,** is a 3-day food marathon in Burlington's waterfront park that features everything from Belgian waffles swathed in strawberries, bananas, and Vermont maple syrup to chicken sate prepared with garlic, ginger, cilantro, and lime juice. Call ☎ 802/863-3489.

July: Vermont Mozart Festival takes place in a beautiful setting on the lawns of the Inn at Shelburne Farms in a series of concerts starting mid-July to early August. Call ☎ 802/985-8686.

August: Champlain Valley Folk Festival is a 3-day festival of folk music and dancing that includes workshops, jam sessions, and other activities on the UVM campus in Burlington. Call ☎ 802/863-3489 or 802/524-6501.

Champlain Valley Fair in Essex is the state's biggest country fair with midway rides, culinary attractions, art, and commercial exhibits plus entertainment and agricultural contests and demonstrations. Call ☎ 802/863-3489.

September: Fine Wine and Food Festival at the Inn at Shelburne Farms when more than 20 international vineyards and more than 30 Vermont food producers participate. Call ☎ 802/985-8498.

October: Essex Fall Craft Show is a large festival featuring close to 400 artists from the region. It includes demonstrations and other entertainment. Call ☎ 802/863-3489.

Central Vermont & the Champlain Valley

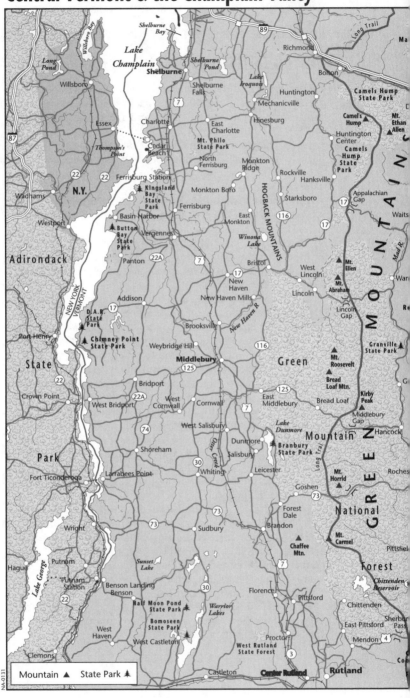

Mountain ▲   State Park ⚓

NA-0131

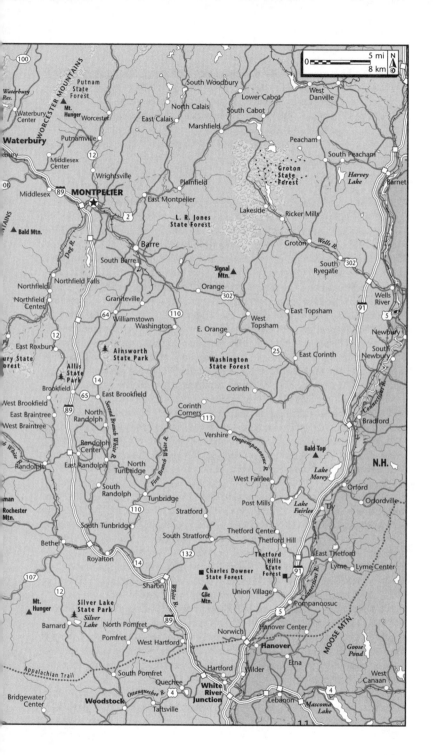

appear on the banks while hawks and eagles soar above. Today, Burlington is the Vermont city on the lake, but in earlier times, towns like Vergennes, where the American fleet was built, were the important centers. And at the southern end of the Champlain Valley there's Middlebury, an appealing college town with plenty of attractions of its own.

MIDDLEBURY

Middlebury is a college town and as one would expect has a degree of sophistication. What also makes it appealing is its location straddling Otter Creek. The square, village green, and courthouse are on one bank, and the Frog Hollow Mill on the other. You can cross from one side to the other via a footbridge, which gives a great view of the Otter Creek falls. These falls generated the power that fueled the grist and woolen mills, foundries, and other industries that once thrived here. The town was chartered in 1761 and settled in 1773 and soon became a center for marble quarries, farms, especially sheep farms, and rural industries. One famous native son, who is recalled by a marker, was John Deere, the inventor of the "plow that broke the plains." He apprenticed here as a blacksmith before moving to Illinois and achieving success on the plains.

If you enter town via Route 7, you can stop at the **Vermont Folk Life Center**, 2 Court St. (☎ 802/388-4964), which is likely to have a fascinating display relating to the folk arts and rural traditions of the region—blacksmithing, quilting, wood carving, fiddling, boatbuilding, or basket making, and more. This organization is dedicated to preserving traditional arts and crafts, and when I visited, the exhibit documented several different ethnic arts with audio-visual presentations of master artists teaching young apprentices, in an effort sponsored by the organization to preserve these dying arts. Open Monday to Friday from noon to 4pm and on Saturday from Memorial Day to the end of October.

Stroll from the square down Main Street. Browse in the well-stocked **Vermont Book Shop** (☎ 802/388-2061) where Robert Frost used to shop. Stop by **Skihaus** (☎ 802/388-6762), which sells a full range of sportswear and ski gear, plus classic and casual fashions. **Calvi's Ice Cream** (☎ 802/388-9038) is an old-fashioned soda fountain. Turn down Mill Street and don't miss Frog Hollow Alley where you'll find the gallery store of the **Vermont State Craft Center at Frog Hollow** (☎ 802/388-3177), which exhibits and sells very high-quality crafts—pewter, glass, jewelry, ceramics, textiles, furniture, wooden bowls, lithographs, and folk art—by more than 250 artists. Open Monday to Saturday from 9:30am to 5:30pm and also on Sunday from May through December. Across from the alley on Park Street, another store worth visiting is **Dan Freeman's Leatherworks** (☎ 802/388-2515), where you can secure a pair of custom-made shoes. Men's oxfords run about $800 for the first pair and $500 thereafter.

As you travel Vermont, you'll see that black-and-white cow everywhere, representing the state it seems. The artist who originated this image has a store here in Middlebury called **Woody Jackson's Cow Store**, 52 Seymour St. (☎ 802/388-6739), where he displays his new originals plus other cow-inspired designs for light switches and more.

Just up the street, the **Sheldon Museum,** 1 Park St. (☎ 802/388-2117), displays a historical collection in an 1829 marble merchant's house bordered by gardens. The museum conducts walking tours of downtown during the summer. Open weekdays from 10am to 5pm and Saturday in summer 10am to 4pm. Admission is $4 for adults, $1 for children 6 to 12.

Double back to Mill Street and cross the footbridge to the **Marble Works,** which has been converted into a shopping mall of sorts. Visit **Danforth Pewter** (☎ 802/388-0098), a company that was begun back in the 18th century in Middletown, Connecticut, by the ancestors of the current Danforth family. Fred Danforth founded the current company in 1975 in Woodstock and moved it to Middlebury in 1989. Even if you don't purchase anything, you can observe demonstrations in the workshop and admire the beautiful satin finish of each bowl, oil lamp, candlestick, vase, and key ring. You can picnic by Otter Creek on one of several marble slabs that grace the banks.

Middlebury also has a popular brewery, **Otter Creek Brewing Company** (☎ 802/388-0727), located a mile from the square on Exchange Street. Here you can taste and purchase its various ales and lagers—Copper Ale and Helles Alt Beer—along with other seasonal brews that include a tasty weiss beer. Open Monday to Saturday from 10am to 6pm and Sunday from 11am to 4pm. Tours are given daily at 1, 3, and 5pm.

From downtown, take College Street (Route 125) out to the campus of **Middlebury College,** a liberal arts college that has some claims to admiration. It became co-ed in 1883 and graduated the first African-American student in 1823. The 350-acre campus itself is worth a stroll, and you can take a student-led tour Monday to Friday (and Saturday in October and November) except during examinations and vacations. Assemble at the admissions office in the Emma Willard House on South Main Street (Route 30). Don't miss the **Middlebury College Museum of Art** (☎ 802/443-5007). The permanent collections have some singular pieces, including fine Chinese ceramics, stoneware and bronzes, the bust of a Greek slave by Hiram Powers (that caused a controversy because of its nudity), and sculptures by turn-of-the-century artist Bessie Potter Vonnoh. Don't miss the albumen print of Gateway Garden of the Gods and Pike's Peak taken by William Henry Jackson. The museum will also have temporary exhibits worth viewing, like the brilliant glass sculptures by Dale Chihuly that were on display when I visited. Open Tuesday to Friday from 10am to 5pm and Saturday to Sunday from noon to 5pm. Admission is free.

To reach the **UVM Morgan Horse Farm** (☎ 802/388-2011), another popular attraction, take Weybridge Street (Route 23) off College Street for about 2½ miles. You could say this strong, efficient, and adaptable horse was the horse that broke the plains, for it was this ideal light horse that helped clear the forests and herd the cattle from east to west. The story of the breed is a quintessential American Horatio Alger story along the lines of the "little colt that could." The progenitor of the line was a stallion called Figure, who was brought from Springfield, Massachusetts, by schoolteacher Justin Morgan. Morgan believed in his stallion, who went on, against the odds, to gain fame for his strength, endurance, and speed even against more thoroughbred racehorses. Figure sired others with his characteristics, and soon his descendants were being used on the ranch, in the city, and at the trotting track.

Champions like Edna May, Bourbon King, and Wing Commander all trace their lineage back to him. Today the Morgan still works the range from Montana to Wyoming to New Mexico. This Vermont facility has been the home of the Morgan breeding farm since the late 1800s, when it was begun by Colonel Joseph Battell, who compiled the original Morgan Horse Register and worked to save the breed from extinction. Today the farm breeds and sells about 70 horses at a time. Tour the stables, see the video, and enjoy a picnic among the rolling hills of Vermont. The UVM, by the way, stands for *Universitas Viridis Montis* meaning the "University of the Green Mountains." Open daily May 1 to October 31, from 9am to 4pm. Admission is $4 for adults, $3 for students, $1 for children 5 to 12.

Do take the time to drive scenic Route 125 east to **Bread Loaf**, Middlebury college's graduate school of English that is famous for its 11-day writers conference and summer program. Most people associate the school with Robert Frost, and if you go inside the facility, you can see the marble sculpture of Frost and also the signatures of such luminaries as Sinclair Lewis, Bernard deVoto, Louis Untermeyer, and publishers Alfred and Blanche Knopf, who attended the conference or taught here. The 1-mile **Robert Frost Memorial Trail**, where you can wander and ponder quotations from his poetry, is just down the road.

In Brandon, ski enthusiasts will want to visit the **Vermont Ski Museum** on Route 7 (☎ 802/247-8080), which traces the history of the sport in the area from the first ascent in 1914 of Mount Mansfield at Stowe and the early days in the 1920s when only the hardy clambered up mountains for the pleasure of skiing down. The skiing revolution began in 1934 when the first ski tow in New England was established on a hillside outside Woodstock. Soon other areas were developed at Stowe; Suicide Six and Bromley, Pico, and Middlebury soon followed, and Mad River Glen later in the 1940s. Other areas like Mount Snow, Killington, and Sugarbush came in the next decade. The museum displays a collection of memorabilia that invokes nostalgia and amazement at how far and how fast the skiing industry in the United States has traveled. Open May through October, Tuesday to Sunday from 9am to 4:30pm. Admission is $2 for adults, 50¢ for children 12 to 18.

Several local artists are worth seeking out in **Brandon,** notably basket maker Joyce Heath, watercolorist Bob Miller, and sculptor James Dunn. Folk artist Warren Kimble paints rural Vermont scenes and highly stylized animals that have been used on ceramics, wooden accessories, wall and floor coverings, and calendars. His gallery stocks both originals and prints, plus other items carrying his images. His gallery is located off Route 73 East on Country Club Road (☎ 802/247-3026) and is open daily in summer, weekdays only in winter.

Being a college town, Middlebury offers a variety of cultural events at the **Middlebury College Center for the Arts** (☎ 802/443-3168), which houses a concert hall, an experimental theater, and a dance theater. The main theater group performing here is the **Middlebury Community Players** (☎ 802/388-7951).

MIDDLEBURY LODGING & DINING

The Inn on the Green, 19 South Pleasant St., Middlebury, VT 05753 (☎ 802/388-7512), which opened in 1997, was needed in Middlebury. The inn stands just off the square and offers 11 rooms, all with private baths. It's located in a restored 1803 bracketed and turreted Victorian that is filled with light. Each room has been decorated in a different palette. The Cornwall boasts peach walls, a Chinese rug, and a cannonball bed with a tapestry-style bed cover; room furnishings include a small desk, an oak chest, and two easy chairs placed in the bay window. Watercolors and photographs by local artists grace the walls. The Addison Suite is decorated in a dark blue and has a modern bed plus a daybed. New Haven is one of the nicest rooms, with its four-poster and maple dresser, plus a tilt-top breakfast table and two small wing chairs. Some wheel chair–accessible rooms are in the carriage house. A breakfast of croissants, cinnamon rolls, and baguettes, along with fruit and scones is put out for guests, or you can opt to have breakfast delivered to your room. Rates: $80 to $185.

The **Middlebury Inn and Motel,** 14 Courthouse Sq., Middlebury, VT 05753 (☎ 802/388-4961), is old-fashioned, but it sits facing the green and has plenty of history behind it—you can view historic photographs of the town in the lobby and pictures of Morgan horses in the Morgan tavern. Some of the 75 rooms have been renovated; they are furnished with antique reproductions and equipped with air-conditioning, phones, TVs, and hair dryers. The motel rooms also have coffeemakers. Ten rooms in the Porter House mansion with decorative marble fireplaces have more character. The inn has a restaurant and tavern. Rates: Sunday to Thursday $88 to $156; Friday to Saturday $100 to $166.

Woody's Restaurant, 5 Bakery Lane (☎ 802/388-4182), is a multilevel art deco–style restaurant with an outdoor deck over Otter Creek. Woody's features Vermont products, and its dishes range from traditional to innovative. For example, you'll find eggplant parmigiana as well as leg of lamb with roasted garlic, tomato, and herb demiglace and bourbon shrimp with shallots, garlic, scallions, cream, and a hint of mustard served over linguini. Prices range from $11 to $16. The menu changes monthly. Open Monday to Saturday from 11:30am to 3pm, Sunday from 10:30am to 3pm, and daily from 5 to 10pm.

Mister Up's, on Bakery Lane on the river (☎ 802/388-6724), has an attractive summer terrace overlooking Otter Creek. It's a pleasant luncheon spot for sandwiches and other light fare. Dinner consists of grilled steaks and seafood, supplemented by pasta dishes. Open from 11:30am to midnight and Sunday brunch from 11am to 2pm.

LODGING & DINING IN NEARBY BRANDON & GOSHEN

The dozens of lilac bushes that grow along the front porch give **The Lilac Inn,** 53 Park St., Brandon, VT 05733 (☎ 802/247-5463), its name. Architect Melanie Shane and her husband, Michael, have transformed this 1909 mansion into a luxurious modern inn, building on the original architectural assets like the marvelous grand gallery of the first floor. It's designed around a U-shaped cobblestone patio, which is furnished with umbrella tables and opens onto rock and water gardens. There are nine rooms, all furnished differently. Some have fireplaces. Farr's Room is huge, 600 square feet, accommodating a bed, a wicker daybed, two lilac-colored wing chairs, an oak table, a chest, and dresser, plus two large built-in armoires. Silver-framed wedding invitations grace the side tables, and in the bathroom there's a double Jacuzzi furnished with pillows and candles. Fretzel's has a carved French country iron bed and a cherry armoire and is decorated in green and lemon-yellow hues. Albert's Room contains a pine four-poster, a dresser, and armoire, and two wing chairs are placed in front of the fireplace. Throughout the house there are dolls, part of Melanie's large doll collection, plus baskets, paintings, and other works of art by local artists. A butler's pantry leads to the inn's casual Tavern restaurant and more formal Garden Room. The restaurant, which is particularly lovely in summer, has a fine reputation locally and is certainly a handsome room, where tables are set with white and dark green cloths and chairs are either Windsor or wing style. The menu is very focused. You might find rack of lamb with rosemary and red wine reduction or a poached salmon *en croûte* with lemon-dill cream sauce. There will always be an appealing vegetarian dish. Prices range from $17 to $22. Open May to October, Wednesday to Saturday from 5:30 to 9pm, Sunday from 10am to 2pm. Black wicker chairs await guests on the front porch, which is also lined with dozens of lilac bushes. Rates: $115 to $260 (most rooms cost $140 to $185).

The **Blueberry Hill Inn**, R.R. 3, Ripton-Goshen Road, Goshen, VT 05733 (☎ 802/247-6735), is one of my all-time favorite inns for a variety of reasons, but number one is the innkeeper, Tony Clark, a warm, caring Brit with a good sense of humor. He has created a perfect 110-acre retreat here at the base of Romance Mountain between Hogback Mountain and Mount Moosalamoo in the Green Mountain National Forest. The 1813 farmhouse has a magical setting, beautiful organic gardens, top-notch food, comfortable accommodations, and an unpretentious atmosphere that is infused with soul, for want of a better word. In summer, it offers miles of hiking and is a cross-country skiing facility in winter. The greenhouse where you can loll over coffee in the morning is filled with positively healthy plants, including gigantic jade plants and a rose that seems to bloom in all seasons. Good books line the parlor, which is warmed in winter by a fire, and throughout the rooms and the public areas there are original paintings and watercolors. The 12 rooms offer many comforts—warm quilts on the beds, good reading lights, a well-lit desk, and a built-in dresser with makeup lighting above. Extra touches include the hot-water bottle hanging in the bathroom, fresh wildflowers, and a small bowl of fresh fruit. The decor is usually wicker with iron and brass beds or similar furnishings. North Sky, however, contains a carved cottage-style bed. Some rooms are located in what used to be an old barn, and family rooms are available.

The kitchen is the heart of the place with its copper pots, dried herbs hanging from the beams, and an old Glenwood stove. Blueberries, herbs, and organic vegetables come from the gardens. In the dining room, guests are seated at long tables in front of the huge stone hearth and served a four-course meal by candlelight. If you wish to accompany the meal with wine, you'll need to provide your own. Whatever you receive will be fresh and fine tasting. A recent meal began with a delicious smoked trout accompanied by small toasts and squash filled with dill crème fraiche. This was followed by a salad of organic greens and mozzarella. The main course was organically raised beef accompanied by peapods and potatoes. The meal finished with a light and creamy cheesecake. The fixed-price menu costs $35, and there is only one seating at 7pm daily. In summer, the meadows across the road serve as volleyball and croquet playing fields. Facilities include a complete cross-country skiing center with 47 miles of trails. Rates: MAP winter mid-December to March, $130 per person double, midweek January to March $105; April to mid-August and October to mid-December $105; mid-August to mid-October $130.

FROM MIDDLEBURY TO VERGENNES

En route to Vergennes, you can turn off at Addison onto Route 17 and drive by the Dead Creek Wildlife Management Area and across Dead Creek to two historic spots on the shores of Lake Champlain. The first is the **home of Revolutionary patriot John Strong** (☎ 802/759-2309). It was built in 1795 and contains period furnishings and memorabilia of the Strong family. Open Friday to Sunday from 9am to 5pm.

The second is **Chimney Point State Historic Site and Park** (☎ 802/759-2412) down on the shores of the lake. Chimney Point was once an inn. Part of the building dates back to the late 1780s, and locals say it's in this taproom that Ethan Allen planned the capture of Fort Ticonderoga. The exhibits here will give you a good idea of the historical background of the period.

The name "Chimney Point" refers to all that was left after the British destroyed Hocquart, the French settlement that was here in the 1760s. Other exhibits deal with later 19th- and 20th-century history. Even if you're not interested in history, this is a quiet and pleasant retreat by the lake, and the park offers camping. Open Wednesday to Sunday 9:30 to 5:30pm Memorial Day to Columbus Day.

Vergennes sits at the head of Otter Creek, which opens into the great Lake Champlain. The lake is a magnificent body of water for recreation today, but in the early history of the United States, it played a major role in the power struggles between the British and the Americans. It was here on the shores of the creek that Commodore Thomas MacDonough built his fleet of gunboats that defeated the British in a crucial battle during the War of 1812. As you pass through the inland port of Vergennes, now filled with summer boaters and other fun seekers, you might want to peek into one of the striking buildings that date to earlier times when the town was a thriving industrial center. In the grand Greek Revival **Bixby Memorial Library** (1911) (☎ 802/877-2211), go inside to marvel at the Tiffany rotunda and enjoy the view from the second-floor porch. Another *belle dame* in town is the **Vergennes Opera House,** the major cultural center in the region when it was built in 1897 long before Burlington or Middlebury emerged as such. It has been restored to its lavish glory and was reopened in 1997.

One of the best ways to have fun and gain some insight and perspective on the lake's ecology and its history is to visit the **Lake Champlain Maritime Museum** on Basin Harbor Road (☎ 802/475-2022), 7 miles west of Vergennes near the entrance to the Basin Harbor resort. The museum offers a fascinating series of displays relating to the lake's strategic importance in both the Revolutionary War and the War of 1812.

In another building you can see a sea horse ferry—the ferry was operated by horses, who turned a large wheel that drove the paddlewheel. The story of steamboats on the lake is also told, and you'll learn about such legendary women as Louis Daniel's wife, who became the first woman to hold a license as a master and pilot of a steam vessel. The last of the steamers plied the lake until 1953. Open daily from 10am to 5pm from early May through mid-October. Admission is $7 for adults, $3 for children 6 to 15.

From Vergennes it's a short drive north on Route 7 to Shelburne. A mile north of Ferrisburg, you can stop at the **Rokeby Museum** (☎ 802/877-3406). It traces the history of the town through the several generations of the same family that have lived in this house from the 1790s to the 1960s. At one time, this home was a major stop on the Underground Railroad, and its owner, Rowland Thomas Robinson, assisted slaves by employing and educating them. Open Thursday to Sunday for tours at 11am and 12:30 and 2pm.

About ¾ mile up Route 7, food lovers will want to stop at **Dakin Farm** (☎ 802/425-3971) to pick up some cheese, maple syrup, or corncob ham. You can also watch the making of these products. Another popular stop is the **Vermont Wildflower Farm,** Route 7, Charlotte (☎ 802/425-3500), whose catalog is familiar to many people. Here you can stroll through 6 acres of wildflower gardens (admission $3) and buy some seeds for your own garden. Open daily from early May to late October from 10am to 5pm.

From Route 7, turn off to the small village of **Charlotte,** which largely consists of an old brick general store, dating to 1853. Here you can pick up deli sandwiches or picnic fixings and take them to Mount Philo State Park. From Charlotte, take the back road, CR 22K, with its glorious views of the Adirondacks across the lake. Turn right onto Mouth of River Road and Bostwick Road, which will return you to Route 7.

If you wish to visit the factory that makes the latest phenomenon to sweep the country, then you may want to visit the **Vermont Teddy Bear Company,** 2236 Shelburne Rd. (☎ 802/985-3001), a short distance south on Route 7. People flock to this place. The tour guides are young and sassy, and it all makes for an amusing interlude for $1.

The highlight of Shelburne is the **Shelburne Museum,** Route 7 (☎ 802/985-3346), a remarkable complex of 37 buildings dedicated to preserving the arts and crafts of New England.

The museum was established in 1947 by Americana collector Electra Havemeyer Webb, and her first collection of dolls, given to her by her grandmother, is here. There are peddler dolls carrying their wares, jointed wooden Queen Anne dolls, a mechanical monkey doll, and many more. The Beach Gallery is dedicated to Native American arts—baskets, beadwork, and other artifacts from many different tribal traditions—and here also are the bronzes of Native American subjects by Harry Jackson, Charles Merion Russell, James Lippitt Clark, and James Earl Fraser, creator of the moving *End of the Trail.*

Don't miss the Circus Building, which was especially designed to accommodate the 3,500 Kirk circus figures fashioned by jigsaw and penknife over 50 years by a railroad brakeman. Exotic and evocative, it offers an astonishing series of tableaux of elephants, giraffes, and lions, plus traditional subjects such as the Old Woman Who Lived in a Shoe and Mother Goose, plus mythical representations of America, Europe, Africa, and Asia, all assembled into one grand parade.

The museum offers classes in printing, blacksmithing, and similar arts, and hosts a number of special events. Open late May through late October, daily 10am to 5pm. Late October to late May a tour of selected buildings is given at 1pm daily. Admission is $17.50 for adults, $7 for children 6 to 14, and includes free admission for the second consecutive day.

Shelburne Farms (☎ 802/985-8686) is another popular stop, especially for children who love to observe the animals in the barns and to help with the chores. You can also watch cheese being processed in the plant and enjoy the magnificent setting and buildings that make this farm so stunning. Guided tours from mid-May to mid-October. The Welcome Center and farm store is open daily year-round.

VERGENNES LODGING & DINING

Basin Harbor Club, Vergennes, VT 05491 (☎ 802/475-2311), is an extraordinary and magical place. It's one of the few independently owned resorts that has managed to keep pace with the times and to provide a vacation experience to those who have been coming here for years and also to those who are seeking a romantic experience. In summer, it's something of a traditional lakeside family resort, but in spring and fall it becomes a couples place. It has a superb 700-acre setting on the eastern shore of Lake Champlain. Accommodations are in the main lodge, where there are 16 rooms, or in one- to three-bedroom cottages. Brother and sister Pennie and Bob Beach have upgraded all of the rooms and accommodations in the last few years and made them very modern and comfortable. In any one of the rooms in the main lodge you might find a brass bed and oak furnishings and wall-to-wall carpeting. The cottages were all built at different times, some as far back as the 1930s, but they are all fresh and modern and finished with attractive carpeting and candy-striped wallpaper, plus comfortable beds, easy chairs, desks, and porches. Anchorage has a living room with marble fireplace, a bedroom with pine beds, and sliding doors that lead to a furnished deck. Sunny Pines has a fantastic view of the dock and lake from its deck plus an attractively furnished living room and bedroom. Whitecaps 2 has a brick fireplace and a fridge/bar; a pine bed is in the bedroom and wicker chairs and a sofa in the living room. The deck has a tree growing through it. The resort has a wide array of facilities. Unlike what's found at many resorts, the main dining room serves superior cuisine. Any daily menu will certainly list traditional favorites like veal marsala and roast turkey, but most of the dishes will be more adventuresome—pan-roasted breast of duck with raspberry bordelaise, shallot-crusted halibut with port wine beurre rouge, or herb Dijon roast rack of lamb with merlot-rosemary *jus*. The five-course meal costs $28. Open Sunday to Friday from 6:30 to 8pm, Saturday 6 to 8:30pm. The Red Mill is a more casual bar and restaurant located in an old sawmill, a handsome post-and-beam building. Red gingham cloths cover the tables. Breakfast and a buffet lunch are served in the Range Room. There's an L-shaped outdoor Olympic-size pool with a marble and grass apron, plus swimming and boating at lakeside. Canoes, outboards, kayaks, Daysailers, Windsurfers, and water skis may be rented for a modest fee. Facilities include an 18-hole golf course, five tennis courts, and hiking trails. Bikes are available for rent. Open mid-May to mid-October. Rates: mid-May to mid-June, B&B $129 to $159, $185 cottage double; MAP, $189 to $219, $245 cottage per couple; Labor Day to mid-October, B&B $199 to $229 double, $260 cottage, MAP $199 to $229, $260 cottage per couple. AP is available mid-May to mid-October, $205 to $265 rooms, $290 to $330 cottage. Special packages are available.

The Strong House, 82 W. Main St., Vergennes, VT 05491 (☎ 802/ 877-3337), is located just outside of town in a farmhouse on 6 acres. The bed-and-breakfast has some extras available, like Swedish massage. Activities like quilting are offered in special packages. There are eight rooms (four with fireplaces or some extra feature). Guests are welcome in the kitchen, the heart of the house, where tea, coffee, and cookies are constantly available. The rooms are attractively furnished in a country style. The Vermont Room has a high-back pine bed plus a pine armoire, a small desk, a chaise lounge, and an armchair. The inn has a liquor license, and there is a small closet where you can select beer and wine. At breakfast, you can expect entrees like frittatas, quiches, omelets, or sour cream pancakes, along with fresh fruit and baked items. The pond is great for winter skating. The gazebo is a welcome place to sit and view the Adirondacks in the distance. Gourmet dinner baskets are available for those who don't want to venture outside. The living room has comfortable seating around the fireplace, plus board games and an upright piano. Rates: $85 to $175.

Christophes on the Green, 5 Green St. (☎ 802/877-3413), in Vergennes is a surprise, although less so when you really think about it. It's a classic country French restaurant where copper pots decorate the upstairs bar and pristine white tablecloths cover the restaurant's tables. A harpsichordist provides background music.

The menu is limited, and all entrees are the same price ($19.50). It changes frequently, but you might find grilled halibut with parsnip potato puree and braised scallions or sautéed sea scallops with a hard cider sauce served over a bed of ruby chard and pearl barley. The sautéed lamb with a *paloise* sauce made with mint shallots and butter is extraordinarily good. To start, try the signature Malpeque oysters broiled in the shell with a leek sabayon. It's hard to choose among the desserts; all are superb, whether it's the lemon mousse with wafers, candied lemon slices, and blueberry coulis or the chocolate tart flavored with smoked tea and served with a coffee sauce. You can order à la carte or choose the $28 fixed-price menu, which gives a choice of any appetizer and entree, and cheese or dessert. An excellent value. Open Tuesday to Saturday from 5:30 to 9:30pm. Closed mid-October to Easter.

LODGING IN NEARBY STARKSBORO

The **Millhouse,** Route 116 (P.O. Box 22), Starksboro, VT 05487 (☎ 802/ 453-2008), is located in an inspiring spot beside a millstream that makes a rushing sound as it cascades down over the rocks. The 1831 homestead is built in a chalet style with a lower floor of stone. It sits among lovely gardens of foxgloves, hollyhocks, marigolds, and nasturtiums. Accommodations are in three buildings that include a tiny and very beguiling cottage. It's called the Pighouse and is warmed by a wood-burning stove and decorated in early-American style with pie chests, Hitchcock chairs, and antique quilts that are draped over the loft railing. The floors have been painted in a salmon hue and are covered with braided rugs. It has a full kitchen and loft bedroom. The main house is entered through a country kitchen, painted in burnt orange and pumpkin tones and lit by Shaker tin candelabras and warmed by a woodstove. Guest rooms are furnished in country style with maple beds and comforters. Some rooms share a bath. Attached to the house is a barn, open on three sides that serves as a sitting and dining room. Here guests enjoy a tasty breakfast that Pat makes, using no eggs or meat. In the house dining room there are collections of pitchers and teapots, and a collection of porcelain is displayed in the comfortable living room. All in all it's a beguiling place—and one of the best values in the state. Open mid-May to mid-October. For information off-season, call ☎ 800/859-5758 or 617/837-3646. Rates: $40 per person with shared bath, $45 per person with private bath; $100 for cottages.

SHELBURNE LODGING & DINING

The Inn at Shelburne Farms, Shelburne Farms, Shelburne, VT 05482 (☎ 802/985-8498), is a glorious place to stay because of its setting by the lake and the grandeur of its interior. It was built originally by Dr. William Seward Webb and Lila Vanderbilt in the 1880s as a 14,000-acre model agricultural estate. Today there are a more modest 1,400 acres, which is still enough to support the environmental education center that attracts 10,000 children per year. The farm buildings were dramatically designed by Robert Henderson Robertson in a Renaissance style with copper roofs and witch's turrets.

The inn opened in 1986 and has 24 huge rooms that have been extravagantly decorated. The Rose Room, once daughter Frederica's room, contains a carved mahogany four-poster along with an Empire-style mahogany chest. The chaise lounge is upholstered in a pink shade picked up from the pink tile of the fireplace; a desk and an ormolu pier mirror complete the decor. The Dutch Room features a brilliant blue fireplace of tiles depicting Dutch scenes, while the Oak Room's main feature is, of course, the oak leaf–carved bed, plus the burgundy tiles around its fireplace. The Brown Room has beautiful marquetry twin beds and a marquetry lamp. A basket of Shelburne Farms cheddar, mustard, and fruit, plus a bouquet of fresh flowers, is placed in each room.

The public areas are furnished in grand style befitting the large spaces. The library retains many books original to the house plus fringed easy chairs in which to read them. In the Tea Room, an ornately carved table serves as a bar. Everywhere you look there are stunning and authentic antiques. The original red damask wallpaper brings a richness to the formal dining room where breakfast, dinner, and Sunday brunch are served at tables set with silver candlesticks and white linens. The cuisine is first class. About six entrees are offered at dinner, ranging from grilled filet of beef tenderloin with grilled wild mushrooms and cabernet sauvignon sauce to pan-roasted sea bass with spinach, leeks, and a light tomato broth. Open Monday to Saturday from 7:30 to 11:30am and 5:30 to 9:30pm; Sunday from 8am to 1pm and 5:30 to 9pm. Prices range from $20 to $27.

Outside, the flagstone patio, overlooking the lawns and the Italianate gardens, is a favorite retreat. Even though the garden is laid out with parterres, it is filled with plantings inspired by Gertrude Jekyll's designs—roses, peonies, and a lily pond. Beyond in the distance rise the Adirondack peaks. Still, the pièce de résistance of the whole place has to be the Game Room where an antique billiard table holds sway. A brass-studded leather bench extends around the perimeter of the huge sandstone fireplace, and hunting trophies stare down from the walls. Magnificent dragon-head settles and chairs with carved bisons, plus a bishop's chair, add to the splendor of the room.

"Today at the Farmyard" is the daily program that tells everyone what's going on at the farm, from chicken chores to milking the cows. In addition, guests and visitors can observe the cheese-making process that converts 7,000 pounds of milk into 700 pounds of cheese a day. There are 8 miles of trails on the property for hiking. The Vermont Music Festival is held here on the south lawn. It opens with an impressive dressage demonstration. Breakfast and dinner are included in the rates. Open mid-May to mid-October. Rates: $105 to $195 for double with shared bath; $205 to $360 for double with private bath.

Cafe Shelburne, Route 7, Shelburne (☎ 802/985-3939), is a classic country French restaurant, even down to the copper bar. The chef hails from the coast just south of Brittany, and he really knows how to prepare seafood. The fillet of lotte on a bed of spinach and mushrooms in a shrimp coulis is one of his particular specialties, but there are plenty of other fine fish dishes. Steamed salmon is served with spaghetti squash charlotte and a sun-dried tomato and virgin olive oil emulsion. Among the meat dishes, try the delicious roasted rack of lamb with a red wine sauce. Prices range from $18 to $20. To finish, linger over the warm crepe filled with caramelized pineapple, served with a pineapple and dark rum sauce, vanilla ice cream, and toasted coconut flakes. Open Tuesday to Saturday from 5:30 to 9:30pm.

The Village Pumphouse, On the Green, Shelburne (☎ 802/985-3728), is an intimate country dining room with pristine white walls and bentwood chairs set at comfortable tables. The menu changes frequently and is supplemented with daily specials. To start, you might enjoy a flavorful smoked-salmon roulade or mushrooms stuffed with sausage and Parmesan. You could follow with a dish like poached red snapper and sea scallops with leeks and tomatoes in dry vermouth or roast leg of lamb finished with port and shallots. Prices range from $19 to $23. The restaurant features a good wine list that includes 13 wines by the glass as well as a full selection of bottled beers (25 in all), fine tequilas, rums, and single malts that you won't usually find at other establishments of this size. Open Tuesday to Thursday from 5 to 9pm, Friday and Saturday from 5 to 10pm.

Middlebury & Lower Lake Champlain Valley
Special & Recreational Activities

Birding: For information, contact the **Otter Creek Audubon Society,** P.O. Box 938, Middlebury, VT 05753 (☎ 802/388-4082). **Dead Creek** is a great birding spot especially in spring. The refuge consists of 2,900 acres of water marsh and adjacent land. It's home to geese and waterfowl—black duck, blue-winged teal, wood duck, hooded merganser, goldeneye, and Canadian geese.

Cross-Country Skiing: The **Inn at Blueberry Hill** (☎ 802/247-6735) has a full-scale facility in the heart of the beautiful Moosalamoo Area. At the

Bread Loaf campus of Middlebury College, **Rikert's Ski Touring Center** has 42 kilometers of groomed trails on Route 125 in Ripton (☎ 802/388-2759).

Golf: Ralph Myhre Golf Course at Middlebury College is an 18-hole course open to the public on Route 30 (☎ 802/443-5125).

Hiking: Mountains, lakes, and streams and diverse wildlife make for great recreation in the **Moosalamoo Area** and the **Green Mountain National Forest.** For information, contact the Forest Supervisor, 231 N. Main St., Rutland, VT 05701, or the Middlebury Ranger District R.R. 4, Box 1260, Route 7, South Middlebury, VT 05753 (☎ 802/388-6688). **Rattlesnake Trail** in East Middlebury loops 7¾ miles around Rattlesnake Mountain with great views along the route. **Button Bay State Park** also has trails. And don't forget the **Robert Frost Trail,** mentioned above.

Nature Reserves: Visit **Dead Creek Wildlife Management Area** (see above). For back-to-nature activities in Moosalamoo and elsewhere, contact **Vermont Ecology Tours,** P.O. Box 210, Killington, VT 05751 (☎ 800/368-6161).

Skiing: Middlebury College Snow Bowl, Route 125, Hancock (☎ 802/388-4356) has two double and one triple chairlift and snowmaking on six trails.

State Parks: Button Bay State Park sits right on the shore of Lake Champlain south of Basin Harbor and offers camping, plus the beauties of the lakeshore. North of Basin Harbor, **Kingsland Bay State Park** also adjoins the lakefront at Grosse Pointe, and is backed by marshlands along Otter Creek. It also adjoins the **McDonough** marshlands along Otter Creek and the **McDonough Point Natural Area.**

Mount Philo State Park lies between Ferrisburg and Charlotte on the eastern side of Route 7, away from the lake. It also has camping.

BURLINGTON

Burlington is the biggest metropolis for miles around, and it's become a lively scene in the last decade. The lakefront has been rescued and turned into a waterfront park, while downtown Church Street has been closed to traffic and shops and restaurants flourish along its several blocks. On weekends, entertainers play to the crowds, and you might see anything from a bicycle stunt man to a magician or musician.

More action and recreation can be found down on the waterfront. Here you can cycle the 8.2 mile bike path or take a cruise aboard several motor vessels and sailing boats from the King Street dock. The **Lake Champlain Basin Science Center** (☎ 802/862-7777) features ecological exhibits, and there's also an **Aquarium** that focuses on the lake's aquatic life, displaying huge catfish, eels, crayfish, and other species. Open May through October.

The **Robert Hull Fleming Museum** at the University, 61 Colchester Ave., is worth visiting. The museum's collection ranges across many cultures and periods—Asian, Middle Eastern, and Egyptian, as well as American. Highlights include an outstanding collection of Northern Plains Indian art and early 20th-century American drawings plus some rare examples of Rookwood pottery. Paintings by Vermont artists, including Francis Colburn and Ronald Slayton, ring the balcony. Open Tuesday to Friday from 9am to 4pm, Saturday and Sunday from 1 to 5pm. Admission is by $2 donation.

Ethan Allen's Homestead (☎ 802/865-4556) is just outside Burlington. It was the last home of this flamboyant founder of Vermont who captured Fort Ticonderoga and Crown Point and made sure that Vermont became a state, separate from New York or New Hampshire. The homestead occupies a serene pastoral setting with views of the Winooski. The exhibits address both the man and the myth and help visitors arrive at some measure of truth about the man and his place in Vermont history. Picnicking is available. Open mid-May to mid-June, daily from 1 to 5pm; mid-June to mid-October, Monday to Saturday from 10am to 5pm, Sunday from 1 to 5pm. Take Route 7 north and turn left on Pearl Street; then turn right on North Champlain Street and take it to the end. Turn right onto Route 127 north. Take the first exit marked NORTH AVENUE BEACHES and then follow the signs.

Although many of the stores here are generic—April Cornell, the Yankee Candle Company, the Nature Company, and the Vermont Trading Company—there are some gems like the **Vermont State Craft Center** at 85 Church St. (☎ 802/863-6458) and **North Country Books,** 2 Church St. (☎ 802/862-6413). There are also some other appealing shops around town. At King and St. Paul, **Courtyard** sells gorgeous Italian majolica and other home furnishings, including finely crafted cherry furniture. Visitors enjoy tasting the brews at the **Magic Hat Brewery,** 189 Flynn Ave. (☎ 802/658-2739), which is open for tours Wednesday through Saturday and daily for sales and tastings.

There are plenty of bars for evening entertainment in Burlington. The **Flynn Theatre,** 180 Flynn Ave. (☎ 802/863-5966), presents a season of performances by national and international dance and theater companies, plus individual musical artists. The Theater at Magic Hat sponsors the **Growling Pup Theatre Festival**, a series of new and classic plays from late June to Labor Day. Other concerts and plays are performed at UVM's **Royall Tyler Theatre** (☎ 802/656-2094). The **Vermont Symphony,** 2 Church St. (☎ 802/864-5741), does pops performances with fireworks during the summer (both here and around Vermont), and in the winter moves indoors for classical concerts.

BURLINGTON LODGING & DINING

Willard Street Inn, 349 S. Willard St., Burlington, VT 05401 (☎ 802/651-8710), occupies a striking redbrick Victorian in a residential neighborhood. The interior has magnificent cherry paneling and intricate woodwork throughout. There are 15 rooms (7 with private bath). Each has been attractively decorated with eclectic furnishings. In one room there might be an iron and brass bed matched with chintz wallpaper and an Ethan Allan–style dresser. Another, like Room 4, might contain a four-poster canopied bed with a green-striped duvet, a marble-top dresser, and easy chairs. Some rooms have decorative fireplaces. Top-floor rooms have sloping ceilings. Room 12 is particularly appealing because of its seven-sided sitting area with a view of the lake. The bathroom is across the hall, but it's private and robes are provided.

The conservatory is a delightful place to enjoy a breakfast of cereal, juice, and muffins, followed by whatever you select from the spoken menu. There's also a sitting area with a grand piano for the use of guests. Rates: $85 to $210 (rate depends on the size of the room and the view).

Trattoria Delia, 152 St. Paul St. (☎ 802/864-5253), has really good Italian cuisine supplemented by the use of local products. For example, Vermont rabbit arrives marinated in white wine, herbs, juniper, garlic, and olive oil and slow roasted with potatoes; wild boar is braised in red wine, tomatoes, rosemary, sage, and other aromatics and served over polenta. Other dishes are cooked over the wood-fired grill, or you can choose the more traditional dishes, pasta, osso buco, or saltimbocca à la Romana. Good Italian wine list, too. Prices range from $9 to $14. Open daily from 5 to 10pm.

The Five Spice Cafe, 175 Church St. (☎ 802/864-4045), is my favorite dining spot in Burlington. It's a tiny place with a bar downstairs and a dining room upstairs where the tables are covered with purple and lilac oilcloth. The cuisine ranges across all the fiery and subtle flavors of Vietnamese, Chinese, Indonesian, Thai, and Burmese traditions. On Sunday, it offers terrific dim sum—turkey wrapped in grape leaves, a corn fritter served with Thai sweet sauce, shrimp with soy and vinegar, or Serendipity Shrimp with lemongrass and garlic—each one a delicate and tasty morsel. The dinner menu presents dishes such as Thai red snapper, Indonesian beef, chicken curry, and several vegetarian dishes. Prices range from $10 to $15. Finish with the chocolate doom, a luscious and lethal combination of chocolate walnut cookies, amaretto, white and dark chocolate truffles with Cointreau and rum, topped by a chocolate chip cookie capped with melted chocolate. The bar is no slouch either, turning out the latest of flavored margaritas, or a concoction called a Golden Dragon that consists of citrus vodka, apricot brandy, and pineapple and apricot juice. It's a great place to hang your hat for a while. Open Monday to Thursday from 11:30am to 10pm, Friday and Saturday from 11:30am to 11pm, and Sunday from 11am to 10pm.

Isabel's on the Waterfront, 112 Lake St. (☎ 802/865-2522), doesn't hang out over the water as you might expect because it's set back behind the railroad tracks, but it does still offer a view of the lake and the Adirondacks. In summer, you can sit out under the awning and the maples and enjoy some tasty popular dishes like the signature maple ginger chicken or the Caribbean shrimp. Prices range from $12 to $22. It has a good Sunday brunch, too. The dining rooms are spacious and airy and decorated with brilliant watercolors. Open Monday to Friday from 11am to 2pm, Saturday and Sunday from 10:30am to 2pm, and daily from 5:30 to 9pm.

Pauline's Cafe & Restaurant, 1834 Shelburne Rd., South Burlington (☎ 802/862-1081), is on Route 7. In summer, it's particularly nice to have lunch under the vine-covered trellis. Inside, the dining room features polished oak tables lit by hurricane lamps and walls accented with posters. There's a small bar. The food is well prepared and draws on several different culinary traditions. You might find roast rack of lamb with red wine sauce alongside Thai tuna served on a Thai-style vinaigrette, as well as a dish like Mediterranean veal topped with artichoke hearts, sun-dried tomatoes, Kalamata olives, capers, leeks, and garlic in a lemon-parsley butter. Prices range from $17 to $23. A lighter menu is served in the cafe area. Open Monday to Saturday from

11:30am to 2pm and 5 to 9:30pm, Sunday from 10:30am to 2pm and 5 to 9:30pm.

Sweetwaters at Church & College, 120 Church St. (☎ 802/864-9800), is a scene on Saturday nights, as people jam into this dramatic space with its banquettes accented with purple and gold cushions and its sexy sybaritic murals. It also has an attractive outdoor dining area. The food runs to mesquite-grilled entrees and pizzas, stir fry and pasta dishes, wraps, sandwiches, burgers, and salads. There's a delicious grilled shrimp with gazpacho sauce and the signature chicken with sun-dried tomatoes and shiitake mushrooms. Prices range from $10 to $15. Open Monday to Friday from 11:30am to 2am, Saturday from 11:30 to 1am, Sunday from 10:30am to midnight.

Leunig's, 115 Church St. (☎ 802/863-3759), is another crowd-pleasing bistro café. It draws a lively group of young professionals to its marble-top bar and its tables under market umbrellas. The inspiration is Mediterranean. Pastas, flatbread pizzas, and grilled fish and meat are specialties. Low-fat dishes are flagged on the menu; examples are the slow-roasted chicken with tomatoes, mushrooms, olives, wine, and herbs or the grilled pork tenderloin with green peppercorn–apple cider sauce. Prices range from $9 to $23; the higher price is for an herb-crusted rack of lamb with pan *jus* and Vermont chèvre medallions. Open daily for breakfast from 7:30 to 11am, for lunch from 11am to 4pm, and for dinner from 4 to 10pm.

Daily Planet, 15 Center St. (☎ 802/862-9647), is a popular bar-restaurant because of its innovative food, and attracts a young crowd. In the dining room, with Windsor chairs and an atrium dining area, an innovative bistro-style menu is offered. Soul-warming dishes like roast salmon with a honey rosemary glaze and herb-crusted rack of lamb with slow-roasted garlic and preserved lemon *jus,* accompanied by mashed potatoes, are just a couple of examples. Prices range from $10 to $19. Open Monday to Friday from 11am to 2:30pm, Saturday and Sunday from 11am to 3pm, Sunday to Thursday from 5 to 10pm, Friday to Sunday from 5 to 11:30pm.

Sakura, 2 Church St. (☎ 802/863-1988), offers some good traditional Japanese cuisine, including decent sushi and sashimi as well as teriyaki, sukiyaki, and tempura dishes. Prices range from $10 to $17, with lower prices for the individual sushi-sashimi. Open Monday to Saturday from 11:30am to 2pm, Monday to Thursday from 5 to 9:30pm, Friday and Saturday from 5 to 10:30pm, and Sunday from 5 to 9pm.

Sweet Tomatoes Trattoria, 83 Church St. (☎ 802/660-9533), is an appealing and very popular restaurant with a cavernlike atmosphere. Cutouts of tomatoes festoon the space, along with glass jars filled with pasta and beans of all sorts. Folks come here for the many wood-fired pizzas, which range from simple margheritas to one that has prosciutto, provolone, mushrooms, artichokes, and sliced tomatoes. There are also at least 20 different pastas, like linguine with sautéed shrimp in a surprisingly good horseradish, tomato, and basil sauce. Daily specials are also offered. Prices are super-reasonable, ranging from $8 to $12. Open Monday to Saturday from 11:30am to 4pm and 5 to 9pm; Sunday from 5 to 9:30pm.

The Ice House, 171 Battery St. (☎ 802/864-1800), is an atmospheric dining room of post and beam with stone walls. In summer, there's a large awning-covered deck with a view of the lake. The cuisine is pretty traditional.

Start with oysters or clams on the half shell or crab cakes and follow with a dish like lemon chicken or New York sirloin topped with wild-mushroom salad and tarragon butter. Prices range from $13 to $19. Open Monday to Friday from 11:30am to 3pm and 5 to 10pm; Saturday from 11am to 3pm and 5 to 11pm; Sunday from 10:30am to 2:30pm and 4 to 10pm.

Mona's, 3 Main St. (☎ 802/658-6662), is at the lakefront end of Main Street and has a dining room looking out across the rooftops of the boatyard to the lake. There are also outdoor dining areas. This is the place to come for brunch—a whole spread of appetizers, salads, and entrees are put out, and the cost is only $12.95. At dinner, the cuisine is modern American with all the latest accents and tones. For example, grilled shrimp with a hot lime habanero base is served with a cucumber-ginger relish, and Asian chicken is basted with sesame hoisin glaze. More traditional dishes, like veal marsala and prime rib are also available. Prices range from $12 to $18. There's live jazz in the bar. Open Sunday to Wednesday from 11:30am to 10pm, Thursday to Saturday from 11:30am to midnight.

ESSEX LODGING & DINING

The main reason to stay at the **Inn at Essex**, 70 Essex Way, Essex Junction, VT 05452 (☎ 802/878-1100), is to experience the dining room, which is operated by the New England Culinary Institute. It's always fun, and diners can be assured of a fine food experience at a price that will be less than you would pay elsewhere. The 96 rooms are spacious and comfortably furnished with antique reproductions—four-posters, tilt-top tables, wing chairs, colonial-style brass candlesticks, Queen Anne chairs and desks, and pier mirrors. Some rooms have fireplaces and Jacuzzis, and all are equipped with telephones and TVs, plus hair dryers in the bathrooms. Behind the building, lawns and gardens surround the outdoor pool with its brick apron. In addition to the formal dining room with its elegant banquettes and food-themed paintings, there's the Chimney Point Lounge, furnished with pine tables and Windsor chairs. A meal in Butler's Restaurant is a real treat. It might start with a duck and chicken liver pâté or a shrimp bisque with tomato oil and Armagnac and then proceed to a subtly flavored, crisp-skin salmon with fennel risotto or a full-flavored rack of lamb served with a Mediterranean lamb sauce. Prices range from $16 to $21. Dining hours are Monday to Saturday from 6 to 10pm. Visitors can also drop in downstairs at the bakery and see student chefs put the finishing touches to their fancy creations. Facilities include a heated outdoor pool and bike rentals. Rates: $139 to $149 double; room with sitting room and fireplace, $189.

THE CHAMPLAIN ISLANDS

From Burlington, you can take Highway 89 or Route 7 to Route 2, which loops through the islands in Lake Champlain all the way to the Alburgs just south of the Canadian border. Water and sky, marsh and woodland make this ideal bird and wildlife territory, and along the route you'll encounter many wildlife refuges where ducks and other waterfowl abound. Route 2/7 splits just north of Colchester and provides access to **Sandbar State Park** before crossing the lake to South Hero Island, a marshy haven for wildlife. At the northern end of the island, you'll pass **Grand Isle State Park** and the **Hyde Log Cabin** (☎ 802/828-3501) believed to be the oldest surviving log cabin in the nation. It was built in 1783 by Jedediah Hyde. Open Wednesday to Sunday from 9:30am to 5:30pm. Admission is $1, no charge for children 14 and under.

The road then crosses to North Hero. There's a great opportunity to see the **Royal Lipizzan Stallions,** Route 2 (☎ 802/372-5683), perform at their summer home. The dramatic white stallions perform their gracious ballet four times a week, from mid-July to late August, Thursday and Friday at 6pm, and Saturday and Sunday at 2:30pm. Tickets cost from $8.

From North Hero, the road traverses a marshy neck of land to the northern end of the island, which consists largely of **North Hero State Park** (camping available). Route 2 then crosses to the town of South Alburg where you can pick up Route 129 to **Isle La Motte,** a remote island with its very own coral reef. Little wonder that **St. Anne's Shrine** (☎ 802/928-3362) is located out here on the site of an old French fort (1666) where the first mass in Vermont was celebrated. You can picnic and enjoy the lake or attend services. Also view the granite statue of Samuel Champlain outlined against lake and sky. Open mid-May to mid-October daily from 10am to 5pm.

From here, return to Route 2 and continue north to Route 78, which passes right through the **Missisquoi National Wildlife Refuge** and follows the Missisquoi River. Farther east at Sheldon Junction, Route 78 links up with Route 105 and later with Route 108 at Enosburg Falls. This route will bring you south into the small town of **Jeffersonville.** Visit the excellent art gallery, where you can view works by Mary and Alden Bryan as well as good quality temporary exhibits. Another favorite stopping place in town is the old-fashioned **Dinner's Dunn at the Windridge Bakery,** a great place to head for breakfast or lunch, where you can sit on the maple seats at the counter or in one of the tongue-and-groove booths and enjoy sandwiches made on bakery breads, turkey pot pie, chili, or waffles with a variety of fruit toppings. Don't miss the extra-special grilled maple bread. Open from 7am to 3pm daily. From here, it's a short drive through dramatic Smuggler's Notch to Stowe (see the next chapter).

CHAMPLAIN ISLANDS LODGING

Thomas Mott Homestead, Blue Rock Road (RFD 2, Box 149B), Alburg, VT 05440 (☎ 802/796-3736), is located on Lake Champlain in an old farmhouse that has several porches where visitors can sit and gaze at the lake and mountain view. There are five attractively and comfortably decorated guest rooms, one with a fireplace. The living room is a cozy gathering place with plenty of reading material. A full breakfast is served. Rates: $79 to $99 double.

Burlington & Champlain Islands
Special & Recreational Activities

Biking: The terrain is flat and although wind can be a problem, it's still good biking country. **Champlain Island Cycling,** Old Quarry Road (Box 32),

Isle La Motte, VT 05463 (☎ 802/928-3200), offers rentals as well as guided tours.

Birding: Good spring and fall birding can be found at any of the state parks and refuges described above.

Boating: Rentals are available at the **Community Boathouse** (☎ 802/863-5090) on the waterfront in Burlington. There are also rentals at **Tudhope Sailing Center and Marina** on Grand Isle (☎ 802/372-5320). **Winds of Ireland** (☎ 802/863-5090) rents boats and Sea-Doos from here. The last cost $55 an hour, while other boats start at $100 for half day.

Cruises: From **Burlington** the *Champlain* and the *Essex* sail on cruises that explore the history of the lake; there are also Sunday brunch cruises and dinner cruises. You can cruise aboard the *Spirit of Ethan Allen II* which offers brunch, dinner, and sunset cruises. The *Winds of Ireland* sails from Burlington Community Boathouse (☎ 802/863-5090).

Fishing: Walleye, lake, rainbow, and brown trout and salmon are the targets of any fishing trip on the lake. Contact **Captain Paul H. Boileau** (☎ 802/899-3104), who operates aboard *Champ IV* from the Burlington Community Boathouse. A 6-hour trip with one to four people costs $300.

Golf: Essex Country Club (☎ 802/879-3232) has an 18-hole course with pastoral and mountain views.

Kayaking: For rentals of kayaks, sailboats, and Windsurfers contact **Inland Sea** (☎ 802/862-3487). **Umiak Outfitters** (☎ 802/253-2317) also offers canoeing and kayaking trips and rentals. Tours are operated by **True North Kayak Tours** (☎ 802/860-1910) and **Paddleways,** Burlington (☎ 802/660-8606). Both offer themed nature tours.

Sailing: Sailboat rentals are offered at the **Burlington Community Boathouse** (☎ 802/863-5090).

Sugarbush, Stowe & Montpelier

Montpelier ◆ *Stowe* ◆ *Sugarbush*

Distance from Boston in miles: Sugarbush/Stowe, 205; Montpelier, 195.

Estimated driving times: 3½ hours to Sugarbush/Stowe; 3¼ hours to Montpelier.

◄○►◄○►◄○►◄○►◄○►

Driving: To Stowe, take I-93 to I-89 Exit 10 to Waterbury and then Route 100 north. For Sugarbush, take Exit 9 (Middlesex) and go east on Route 2 to Route 100 south. For Montpelier, take Exit 8 off I-89.

Bus: Vermont Transit and Greyhound service Stowe, Waterbury, and Montpelier

Train: Waterbury is served by Amtrak's Vermonter, with daily departures from New York (☎ 800/872-7245).

Further Information: For more information, contact **Central Vermont Chamber of Commerce**, P.O. Box 336, Barre, VT 05641 (☎ 802/229-5711); **Stowe Area Association**, P.O. Box 1320, Stowe, VT 05672 (☎ 802/253-7321); **Sugarbush Chamber of Commerce**, P.O. Box 173, Waitsfield, VT 05673 (☎ 802/469-3409).

◄○►◄○►◄○►◄○►◄○►

Sugarbush and Stowe are two of the magical names in Vermont skiing. Stowe certainly is a gem, and it has so much to offer in addition to the skiing and the mountain—great inns, fine dining, and a rich cultural and recreational life. Sugarbush has some great skiing and is a terrific terrain for summer recreation, but it doesn't have quite the energy and ancillary attractions of Stowe. For some people, this makes Sugarbush all the more appealing. Both are gems and will provide numerous wonderful weekend possibilities. And Montpelier has to be one of the liveliest and civilized small towns anywhere, with great access to nearby recreational areas.

MONTPELIER

Montpelier is one of New England's most appealing state capitals. It's nestled into the hills on one side of the Winooski River. It's quite a sophisticated town, thanks to Vermont and Goddard Colleges, the New England Cooking School (that operates several fine restaurants in town), the many creative folks who live in the area, and—who knows, maybe even to the state government.

There are also a couple of sites to visit but only if you're genuinely interested. The dome of the **State House**, State Street (☎ 802/828-2228), positively glows after its recent regilding. Outside, Ethan Allen stands guard. Inside you'll find memorabilia from Vermont's political past as well as the legislative chambers and the governor's reception room, which has a large painting of the *Battle of Cedar Creek* on the wall. Open Monday to Friday from 8am to 4pm; admission is free. Also on State Street, at no. 109, the **Vermont Historical Society Museum** (☎ 802/828-2291), you can trace the history of the state's people from the Abenaki to the Yankees and their descendants. Open Tuesday to Friday from 9am to 4:30pm, Saturday from 9am to 4pm, and Sunday from noon to 4pm. Admission is $2 for adults, $1 for students.

Art lovers will want to visit the **Thomas Waterman Wood Art Gallery** in College Hall on the Vermont College campus. Wood was an American 19th-century genre painter who was born and lived in Montpelier. The permanent collection has many of his portraits and landscapes plus some works by 20th-century artists. Temporary shows display works by contemporary painters and sculptors, usually those who have some connection with Vermont. Open Tuesday to Sunday from noon to 4pm. Admission is $2 for adults, children under 12 are free.

A couple of attractions outside town can be visited. In nearby Barre, the working E. L. Smith granite quarry allows visitors to observe skilled quarriers taking out huge blocks of granite from the rocks. Open June to mid-October, Monday to Friday from 9:30am to 3pm. Admission is $4 for adults, $1.50 for children 6 to 12. For information, write to Rock of Ages Tours, P.O. Box 482, Barre, VT 05641 (☎ 802/476-3119). The **Cabot Creamery** (☎ 802/563-2231) is located in the town of the same name. It manufactures more than 450 different shapes and flavors of dairy foods including its very famous and good cheddar cheeses. Visitors can tour the factory and see the entire process.

In town, the following stores are worth browsing: the **Artisan's Hand**, which sells fine crafts; **Bear Pond Books**, and the well-known **Vermont Trading Company.** If you're interested in film, the Savoy shows art and foreign films.

And also nearby, less than 30 miles away are the two prime ski resorts, Stowe and Sugarbush.

MONTPELIER LODGING & DINING

Inn at Montpelier, 147 Main St., Montpelier, VT 05602 (☎ 802/223-2727), is located in town near the library. It occupies two Federal-style buildings from the early 1800s. One has an extravagant wraparound porch. There are 19 rooms, all with telephones and cable TVs. Several rooms have wood-burning fireplaces. The rooms are attractively decorated with fine fabrics and antique reproductions—four posters, desks, and Chippendale chairs, and more.

Events & Festivals to Plan Your Trip Around

January/February: **Winter Carnival at Sugarbush** is a 9-day festival that includes skiing, dogsledding, and skijoring races, a torchlight parade, sugar-on-the-snow parties, and much more. Call ☎ 802/583-2381.

February: **Jeep King of the Mountain Downhill Race** brings international teams to Sugarbush to compete for a rich purse. Call ☎ 802/583-2381.

    Stowe Derby is the oldest downhill/cross-country race in the nation. Call ☎ 802/253-3423.

April: The **Sugarbush Triathlon** is a race combining running, canoeing, kayaking, biking, and cross-country skiing. It's all topped off with a barbecue and an awards ceremony. Call ☎ 802/583-2381.

May: **Annual Basketry Festival** in Stowe is a weeklong event with displays and workshops by talented weavers. Call ☎ 802/253-7321.

June: **Stowe Flower Festival** blossoms with more than 30 events, including horticultural workshops, tours, and demonstrations plus a crafts fair. Call ☎ 802/253-7321.

    Moonlight in Vermont previews all the summer shows accompanied by dancing to the "Swingin' Vermont Big Band" in Stowe. Call ☎ 802/253-7321.

    Ben and Jerry's **One World One Heart Festival** in Sugarbush lines up big-name bands and entertainers for 2 days of entertainment plus crafts and food and, of course, Ben and Jerry in the flesh. Call ☎ 802/244-8687.

June/July: **Music in the Meadow** presents a series of concerts in the Trapp Family Lodge Concert Meadow—a glorious setting to listen to music as the sun sets over the mountains. The Vermont Symphony and other groups perform. Call ☎ 802/253-8511.

July: Stowe's **World's Shortest Marathon** is very short—a fun 1.7 mile run. Call ☎ 802/469-3409.

    Fourth of July Parade and Air Show in Warren. It's wacky and zany, and a street dance follows supplemented with a variety of entertainment from puppet shows to beer tasting.

The bathrooms are tiled and have pedestal sinks. Accents include stenciling and original art. A continental breakfast of breads, fruit, and cereal is served. Bar service is offered in the sitting room, which is very comfortable indeed. There's also a game room that is popular in winter. Guests have access to a pantry. Rates: $108 to 153

    The **Main Street Grill and Bar,** 118 Main St. (☎ 802/223-3188), is operated by the New England Cooking School and is its moderately priced casual-to-fine restaurant. It's great for lunch and dinner or brunch. Downstairs, there's

The **International Food & Wine Expo** brings recognized chefs, wine masters, food writers, and health experts to a food-and-wine appreciation with entertainment in Stowe. Call ☎ 802/ 253-7321.

The **Stoweflake Balloon Festival** sees the launching of dozens of hot air balloons at the resort of the same name. Call ☎ 802/ 253-7355.

Sugarbush Cricket Festival at Brooks Field is a 2-day event in which eight teams participate in a competition for the Sugarbush Trophy. It's a fast-paced version of the game with six player teams and round robin games. Call ☎ 802/583-2381.

Vermont Classic Horse Show at Kenyons Field in Sugarbush lasts from late July to mid-August. Call ☎ 802/469-3409.

August: Stowe Antique & Classic Car Meet assembles more than 800 antique cars. It includes a parade, car corral, and antique car–related flea market. Call ☎ 802/253-7321.

Vermont Icelandic Horse Show at the Luman Wadham Stable in Sugarbush. Call ☎ 802/496-7141.

September: Stowe Oktoberfest with traditional oompah bands, much beer tasting, and Bavarian style food and family activities. Call ☎ 802/253-7321.

National Traditional Old-Time Fiddlers' and Step-Dancing Contest in Barre keeps this kind of music alive.

The **Stowe British Invasion** is a 4-day celebration of the British Motorcar—the Bentley, Morgan, Jaguar, the Austin Healey, MG, Rolls, and all those other celebrated names. This classic-car meet is also an excuse to indulge in other British entertainment from sheepdog trials to tailgate picnics and tug-o-wars. Call ☎ 802/ 253-7321.

October: Foliage Festival of Antiques in Stowe. Call ☎ 802/ 253-7321.

Stowe Foliage Craft Fair draws more than 200 artisans to display their wares in elegant heated tents. Call ☎ 802/253-7321.

a bar. The dining room upstairs has striking black-and-white floors and a combination of booths and tables. In summer, a few tables are put outside. The menu is limited but offers a reasonable range of dishes. You might find grilled salmon niçoise or delicious pan-seared pork medallions served with peach-apricot chutney, potato ravioli, and grilled asparagus. To start, try the mussels in a green curry broth with lemongrass or the sweet pepper and sausage flatbread with fontina cheese and caramelized onion. Prices range from $10.50 to $14. Sometimes the service can be a little shaky, but remember these are culinary students, after all. The brunch is an excellent value at $12.95. The spread is exceptional, from the appetizers to the desserts. Open Monday to Friday from 7 to 10am and Saturday from 8 to 10am for breakfast, Sunday from 10am to 2pm for brunch, Monday to Saturday from 1:30 to 2pm for lunch, daily from 5:30 to 10pm for dinner.

The **Chef's Table**, 118 Main St. (☎ 802/229-9202), is the school's premier restaurant. It's located upstairs in an intimate and formal space. Tables are set with damask cloths, and gilt-framed art is displayed on the burgundy-colored walls. There are only three or four main courses. You might start with a warm duck salad of arugula, frisée, peaches with blackberry vinaigrette, or a fresh shrimp seafood gazpacho of shrimp and sea scallops. One of the main courses will be a vegetarian dish; the others might be seared pork loin in a port reduction accompanied by Stilton potato gratin; or yellowfin tuna with wasabi-orange butter sauce. Prices range from $15 to $19. A three-course tasting menu is also offered for $25. Open Monday to Saturday from 6 to 10pm.

Sarducci's, 3 Main St. (☎ 802/223-0229), is at the other end of town in the converted railroad station. It's a happening place that always seems to be crowded. Antiqued columns, sponge-painted walls, and a mural depicting an Italian market help transport diners in their imagination to Italy. So will the food. Start with the calamari fritti in a truly spicy marinara sauce or a grilled portobello mushroom marinated in garlic and sherry. There are about 20 pasta dishes, from the sharp and tangy fettuccine putanesca to the smooth and creamy fettuccine Alfredo that has brandy in it. The specialties are typical favorites like chicken marsala and saltimbocca, with some surprises, like the wood-roasted salmon with lemon, artichokes, red peppers, and capers in a white wine sauce. Pizzas are also available. Prices range from $11 to $14. Open Monday to Saturday from 11:30am to 10pm; Sunday from 5 to 9pm.

La Brioche, 89 Main St. (☎ 802/229-0443), is another outlet of the New England Cooking School, and it's the place to go for some of the best croissants and other baked goods anywhere. Open Monday to Friday from 7am to 7pm; Saturday from 8am to 5:30pm, Sunday from 8am to 3pm.

STOWE

This town is considered one of Vermont's jewels and warrants its status. In winter, Stowe offers top-of-the-line skiing plus the attractions of the town itself and a raft of fine-quality lodging and dining choices. It's beautiful in summer and fall, too, when the emphasis switches to summer sports—mountain biking, canoeing, hiking, and the thrills and spills of the **Alpine Slide** at Little Spruce (☎ 802/253-3000). There are also cultural events and festivals. Take some time in summer to drive the toll road up Mount Mansfield or to take the gondola to the summit and enjoy dinner at the Cliff House Restaurant.

The town is attractive and lively, and you'll want to wander the main street and browse in **Shaw's** old-fashioned general store and in the Old Depot housing **Bear Pond Books** (☎ 802/253-8236), the **Green Mountain Pantry,** and **Vermont Furniture Works** (☎ 802/253-5094), which makes handcrafted period

Northern Vermont

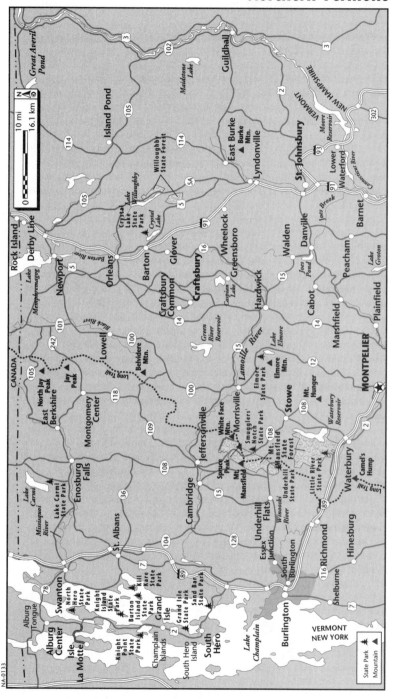

beds and other furniture in tiger maple and other fine woods. Also stop at **Stowe Gems,** 70 Pond St. (☎ 802/253-7000), for beautifully crafted jewelry made with finely cut stones and at **Blue Heron Gallery** in the Swissspot Building on Main Street (☎ 802/253-8701), which sells Vermont folk art. For Vermont foods, you can't beat **Harrington's** at 166 S. Main St. (☎ 802/253-4121), for that superb cob-smoked bacon and fine maple syrups and cheeses.

The road that goes out to the mountain has several small shopping complexes. Here you'll want to have a look at **Clarke Galleries,** 123 Mountain Rd. (☎ 802/253-7116), for fine 19th- and 20th-century art; **Robert Paul Galleries** (☎ 802/253-7282) for contemporary art, sculpture, and prints, including some delightfully whimsical ceramic sculpture; and the **Emotional Outlet Gallery** (☎ 802/253-7407), which sells contemporary crafts and assorted gifts.

The hills may be alive with the sound of music but they are also certainly alive with the sound of craftspeople working. There are plenty of studios and galleries in the area to visit. In Moscow, **Schoolhouse Pottery** (☎ 802/253-9838) showcases the work of Susan Whitehair Hydusik who creates serious and whimsical pieces. Also in Moscow on the Moscow Road, there's the **Little River Hot Glass Studio** (☎ 802/253-0889). On Route 100 just south of Waterbury Center, visit **Ziemke Glass Blowing Studio** (☎ 802/244-6126) and watch Glenn Ziemke twirling and rolling his stunningly brilliant pieces—vases, bowls, glasses, paper weights, perfume bottles, and candlesticks. Demonstrations are given Thursday to Monday. Farther afield, **Vermont Rug Makers** weave colorfully contemporary rugs at their studio on the Gihon River in East Johnson (☎ 802/635-2434). Johnson also draws people to **Johnson Woolen Mills** (☎ 802/635-2271) to shop for scarves, sweaters, hats, gloves, and blankets, as well as Johnson's own sportswear and Woolrich and Columbia brands.

And while you're in Vermont, there are some special state attractions that folks feel compelled to visit, like Ben & Jerry's, Cold Hollow Cider Mill, the Green Mountain Chocolate store, and other local food purveyors. The first three are easily reached via Route 100 South. At **Cold Hollow Cider Mill** (☎ 802/244-8771) you can view the cider-making process and pick up a jug or two along with some cider jelly or apple butter. It's open daily from 8am to 6pm. Right here between Waterbury Center and Waterbury on Route 100, **Green Mountain Chocolate** (☎ 802/244-1139) sells more than 200 different kinds of chocolates, truffles, cookies, and candies. See the chocolate sculptures crafted by expert chocolatier Albert Kumin, former White House pastry chef, who uses his Swiss family recipes to make these luscious chocolates. Continue your ruination at the **Cabot Annex Store** (☎ 802/244-6334), which sells its cheeses and other Vermont gourmet items and shares space with the **Green Mountain Coffee Roasters** (☎ 802/244-8430). And finally, like everyone else, go take a factory tour of **Ben & Jerry's** (☎ 802/244-8687), the legendary company with the affable owners and idealistic entrepreneur-founders. It's fun, and you'll learn how two childhood friends created an ice cream business that shares its success with its employees. At the end of it all, you can sit down and select your favorite flavor from more than 30 possibilities. How about some Chunky Monkey or one of their other zany combinations!

And for evening entertainment, head for the following venues: **Stowe Performing Arts** (☎ 802/253-7792); **Town Hall Theatre** (☎ 802/253-3961); **Helen Day Art Center** (☎ 802/253-8358); and **Hyde Park Opera House** (☎ 802/888-4507). There's also a triplex **cinema** in town on Mountain Road (☎ 802/253-4678). Or you can head, like all the expatriate Brits do, to **Mr. Pickwick's** (☎ 802/253-7558), which offers 150 local and international brews plus the chance to chat around the fire or enjoy a game of darts.

STOWE LODGING & DINING

Edson Hill Manor, 1500 Edson Hill Rd., Stowe, VT 05672 (☎ 802/253-7371), is an exquisite secluded accommodation on 225 acres on a mountainside overlooking a lake. The manor was built in 1940, and the current owners have imbued it with warmth and hospitality. The manor has cross-country ski trails and stables. It's furnished elegantly throughout with fine antiques and decorated with fine fabrics and wallpapers, and extensive trompe l'oeil work. The living room has pine paneling, many original oils and pastels, plus many seating clusters around the fireplace. There are nine rooms in the main house. One room features pine paneling and beams and is furnished with a four-poster, an oriental rug, a burled walnut chest, and two wing chairs, placed before the wood-burning fireplace. Decorative touches are trompe l'oeil hanging plants. Similar decoration depicting chickadees and porcupines are found in the bathroom of another room. Up the hill there are 16 carriage-house rooms in four buildings. The dining room is equally elegant with slate floors, white tablecloths, brass candlesticks on the tables, and ivy decoration on ceiling and walls. The cuisine is high quality and offers some traditional as well as more innovative dishes. Among the appetizers there might be warm stuffed poblano pepper with feta cheese, black-bean puree, and spicy papaya compote or shrimp and andouille sausage gumbo. For entrees, the seared venison scallopini and fried fruit balsamic *jus* is perfect, and the peppercorn-seared swordfish is moist and served with a tangy Provençal vinaigrette. A vegetarian dish is always available. Prices range from $15 to $23. Open Monday to Saturday 6 to 9pm. Closed Monday off-season. Paintings of grouse and pheasants decorate the downstairs bar, which has beams and a brick fireplace. Rock steps lead down to a kidney-shaped pool with a grass and brick apron. The terrace and lawns are pleasant, relaxing areas for guests. In winter, there are extensive cross-country ski trails as well as a ski center, and there are sleigh rides for two. Summer offers horseback riding. Rates: mid-June to late October, B&B $65 to 95 per person; MAP $85 to $115 per person.

Ten Acres Lodge, 14 Barrows Rd., Stowe, VT 05672 (☎ 802/253-7638), is under the same management as the Edson Hill Manor, and dining at either property is included in the MAP. Ten Acres is a well-seasoned intimate country inn where the lavishly furnished, low-beam parlors bestow an immediate sense of well-being. The eight guest rooms in the main house that have been furnished comfortably with canopied beds, inviting armchairs, and similar furnishings. The more modern hill-house rooms all have fireplaces, cable TVs, and sitting areas. The dining room is among Stowe's top 10 for sure, and here you can be assured of fresh ingredients that have been cooked to reveal all of their flavor. Among the appetizers, you might find a local specialty such as fiddlehead soup with fennel, black olive crostini, and roast pepper cream; or a fiery grilled quail with crispy wonton salad and Thai red curry sauce. There are only six or so entrees. If it's offered, try the melt-in-the-mouth, moist fillet of salmon baked in parchment with fennel, artichokes, and tomato-garlic confit served on saffron couscous. The pistachio-crusted tenderloin of beef served with dried-cherry horseradish mashed potatoes is another good choice. Prices range from $17 to $23. There's an extensive wine list. Rates: B&B $65 to $80 per person; MAP $85 to $100 per person. Special packages are available.

The **Green Mountain Inn,** Main Street (P.O. Box 60), Stowe, VT 05672 (☎ 802/253-7301), is right in the center of town, yet it manages to retain a quiet demeanor and offers some very comfortable rooms indeed, as well as a pool and a fitness club. In fact, it would be my first choice just because everything you could possibly need is in the rooms. The suites are particularly appealing. The Peter Lovejoy Suite is decorated in rose, lemon, and pale green. It has a sitting area with a raised wood-burning fireplace flanked by bookcases plus a small refrigerator. Molded woodwork adds a touch of luxury to the built-in cupboards and bookcases. There are two telephones and a TV/VCR, an ultra comfortable couch, and a wing chair with ottoman. Robes are provided; the bathroom has a double Jacuzzi. Standard rooms are furnished with canopied four-poster covered with handsome quilts, two easy chairs, a chest, and a wrought-iron floor lamp. The tasteful accents—stenciling, wainscoting and ceramic lamps—add to the ambience. Superior rooms might have a gas fireplace, a TV/VCR, a small refrigerator, and an easy chair with a footrest. Some of the rooms are located in the annex by the pool; others, called club rooms, are behind the pool in the health club building. These last are extra large and have double Jacuzzis, but the same furnishings as the other rooms. Guests have use of a library-sitting area with a fireplace. The main dining room is open only for breakfast except in foliage season, when it also serves dinner. Downstairs, the Whip Bar and Grill is a popular gathering place, with high-back settles around the wood-burning fireplace. It offers soups, salads, sandwiches, and grilled specialties like steak, swordfish, and herbed lamb chops. Facilities include an outdoor swimming pool with a concrete apron and the fitness club. Rates: mid-October to late December $99 to $169; January to mid-April $125 to $204; mid-April to early June $99 to $160; mid-June to mid-September $109 to $179; foliage mid-September to mid-October $139 to $219. Christmas rates are from $182 to $329.

Stowehof Inn, Edison Hill Road (P.O. Box 1139), Stowe, VT 05672 (☎ 802/253-9722), is a lovely Tyrolean-style accommodation that has great charm and style and offers lots of outdoor activities. It's filled with nooks, crannies, and alcoves and boasts several fireplaces where guests can gather in the winter season. It was used by Alan Alda to film the sleigh ride in the film, *The Four Seasons.* It was created by architect Lawrence Hess in 1950, and he is responsible for one of its most alluring effects—the sculptured trees that have been allowed to grow up through the interiors and are lit with fairy lights. In the sitting room, seating has been built around the trunk of the tree. The whole place is filled with eye-catching collections: folk art and antiques, from a Norwegian painted church bench to the paneled oak door at the entrance that came from a church on Fifth Avenue. The rooms have been very attractively decorated. In Room 41 you'll find an iron four-poster made up with Battenburg lace; in Room 43 is a rice canopied four-poster, a marble-top chest, a drop-leaf desk, and mirrored armoires, plus a bidet and handsome marble bath in the bathroom. Some rooms have glorious views of the mountains. The Seasons Dining Room, with its lovely mountain views, serves a classic menu that always includes a vegetarian dish, plus such main courses as grilled lamb chops with a port sauce, or broiled fillet of red snapper with shaved scallion caviar butter. The house specialty is Wienerschnitzel served with spaetzle. Prices range from $18 to $23. Open summer, daily from 6 to 9pm; October to early December and mid-April to mid-June, Friday and Saturday only. Downstairs is a bar with painted tables and a brick fireplace accented with a big, old bellows. Facilities include an outdoor pool with brick apron and umbrella tables; four tennis courts, cross-country skiing trails, hiking trails, and golf privileges at a local club. Rates: summer and winter, B&B $148 to $250, MAP $196 to $298; holiday and foliage seasons, MAP $188 to $310; spring and late fall, B&B $85 to $150; MAP (weekends only) $134 to $194.

Topnotch at Stowe Resort & Spa, P.O. Box 1458, Stowe, VT 05672 (☎ 802/253-8585), a luxury property on 120 acres, is a top tennis resort with a spa and fitness center. There are 90 rooms plus 15 town houses that have two or three bedrooms, and service is first-class. Rooms are handsomely decorated, using sponge painting, plaids, or chintz, and are well equipped with two telephone/modem hookups, hair dryers, and TVs in armoires. Furnishings include a plain bed, plus easy chairs with ottomans. The town-house accommodations range from one-bedroom, accommodating three, to three-bedroom, accommodating six. Many of them have fireplaces, decks, and sauna. There are two dining rooms and a bar. The Buttertub bar and bistro has a fireplace, comfy banquettes, and barn-board paneling. Its menu leans to such traditional dishes as New York steak topped with garlic butter or ribs served with an exquisite maple-barbecue sauce. Prices range from $14 to $16. In Maxwell's, the excellent cuisine is far more sophisticated. You'll relish the roasted rack of lamb with a macadamia crust and bourbon shallot sauce or the Hunan breast of duck with wilted scallions, leeks, corn, and red peppers. In season, don't miss the venison with a potato and peppercorn crust, cranberry and currant chutney, and juniper sauce. Prices range from $20 to $34. To start, the smoked salmon wonton napoleon with watercress, roasted peppers and saffron crema is extraordinarily good; so, too, is the chilled Gulf shrimp with mango jalapeño and traditional cocktail sauces. Afternoon tea with cookies is served in the sitting room, which has an open hooded fireplace and stone walls studded with moose trophies. The grounds are beautifully landscaped and studded with sculptures. The pool has been well designed, with stone walls, hedges, and flowers, and in summer there's a gazebo cabana where you can order meals and grills. The facilities are extensive and include 10 outdoor and four indoor tennis courts, making it one of the major tennis resorts in the nation. The fitness center features Cybex equipment, a treadmill, and more, and guests can sign on with a personal trainer. The spa has a 60-foot indoor lap pool and an indoor pool, plus 20 treatment rooms. It offers a full array of treatments. Facilities also include 20 miles of cross-country skiing and snowshoe trekking trails, an equestrian center, and an ice-skating pond. Bike and in-line skate rentals are available. Rates per person: early April to mid-June, $70 to $105, town houses $235; mid-June to mid-October, $115 to $145, town houses $310; mid-October to mid-December, $85 to $120 per person, town houses $235; mid-December to early April $95 to $123, town houses $280. Special packages are available.

Trapp Family Lodge, Luce Hill Road, Stowe, VT 05672 (☎ 802/253-8511), has the best situation of any accommodation in Stowe—22,000 acres right on the mountainside with panoramic views of the Green Mountains and Stowe Valley. It is, of course, the home of the Trapp family, Baron Georg von Trapp and Baroness Maria, who discovered Stowe in 1942 and began welcoming guests in 1950. It's still run by members of the family. The large, modern, and chalet-style main building, is built into the hillside. The main lodge has 73 rooms that have been pleasantly decorated, and most have small balconies and great views. The balconies on the second floor are larger. Additional rooms are in a lower lodge. The main dining room is spacious and takes full advantage of the view. There's also an Austrian tea room, located quite a distance from the main building, and here you can taste great Sacher torte and linzer torte, which are as luscious as they should be and far from the usual dried-up versions served elsewhere. Wurst plates are also available. It's an ideal place to enjoy lunch and the mountain vistas. Facilities include an outdoor and indoor pool and a fitness center. There's a fine cross-country skiing facility that begins right outside, with 65 miles of groomed trails. Rates: late June to mid-September, $130 to 200 double; mid-September to late October, $130 to $200; late October to mid-December, $100 to $148; early January to mid-March, $150 to $220; mid-March to mid-June, $108 to $165. Certain holidays and in the early fall MAP rates apply for an additional $45 a day.

WalkAbout Creek Lodge, 199 Edson Hill, Stowe, VT 05762 (☎ 802/253-7354), has some unique features traceable to an earlier owner who hailed from Australia. It's a charmer from the large, long barn-board living room with a rough-hewn stone wall and fireplace to the twig-furnished living room and the outdoor deck with a hot tub. In the back, there's a pool with a cabana bar plus a tennis court. Twig chairs and a hammock dot the lawns, too. Rooms are rustic in style, with pine paneling, pine furnishings, braided rugs, and iron lamps. They access a common balcony. Downstairs, there's a pub with beamed ceilings and a stone fireplace where guests can gather at the copper bar or play a game of pool. Pancakes, omelets, and other such dishes are offered on the breakfast menu. Rates: $100 to $140.

Siebenes, 3681 Mountain Rd., Stowe, VT 05672 (☎ 802/253-8942), is located on the mountain road on the way to the ski resort. There are 10 rooms in the inn and two suites in a building out back. The rooms are decorated country style, with such accents as straw bonnets and dried flowers. Furnishings are mostly oak, maple, and pine. In Room 5, you'll find a pencil four-poster made up with Battenburg lace. The units in the back have Jacuzzis and fridges; furnishings are similar. There are six bikes available free, plus an outdoor pool surrounded by lawns. The Norwegian owners are very hospitable and will offer guests *mormusen,* a Scandinavian specialty, as well as chocolate kisses. Guests choose from a full breakfast menu in a pretty, floral-inspired room. In the sitting room, sofas and chairs are arranged around the large stone wood-burning fireplace, and there's also a large TV. Rates: April to late June and late October to mid-December, $80 to $140; late June to mid-

September and early January to late March, $100 to $170; mid-September to late October and Christmas season, $120 to $190.

Andy Aldrich restored **The Brass Lantern Inn,** 717 Maple St. (Route 100), Stowe, VT 05672 (☎ 802/253-2229), to its original 19th-century ambience, and he keeps it in meticulous style. The inn has nine rooms (three with whirlpools and three with whirlpools plus fireplace). They are decorated in a traditional colonial country fashion, with quilt-covered beds, oak dressers, wing chairs, and candle-stand lamps. Everything is spic and span. There's a sitting room that has plenty of reading material, a brick fireplace, and an upright piano for those who want to entertain. From the square oak table in the dining room, you can see the mountains in the distance. Here a full breakfast of delicious waffles with strawberry rhubarb sauce or apple crepes and ham is served. Rates: $85 to $210 double.

Ye Olde England Inn, 433 Mountain Rd., Stowe, VT 05672 (☎ 802/253-7558) is a remake of a complete British pub by a British couple who fell in love with Stowe on vacation. The post-and-beam dining room and the pub, Pickwick's, attract the Brit crowd in the valley. It's a homey place with its beams and copper lamps, pint pots hanging above the bar, and an array of bottles and playing cards tacked onto the ceiling. This is the local polo-players haven and the place for dart-playing enthusiasts. Behind the restaurant, there's an outdoor pool and hot tub under an enclosed gazebo. A path through the lych-gate leads to Bluff House, where most of the rooms are located. They're furnished nicely, with rice four-poster or canopied beds and antique reproductions. Most have fireplaces and whirlpool tubs. Rates: spring and summer, $98 to 305; fall, $160 to $410.

The **Golden Eagle Resort,** Stowe, VT 05672 (☎ 802/253-4811), is just off Mountain Road in town. It has a fitness center and a variety of outdoor pursuits. Its accommodations and facilities are very appealing to families. The rooms are differentiated by size or additional features such as fireplaces, efficiencies, or Jacuzzis. There are also two-bedroom cottages available, plus some very nice rooms in a farmhouse on the property. This last contains a very attractive minisuite equipped with TV, refrigerator, coffeemaker, wood-burning fireplace, and a double Jacuzzi; it's furnished with pine and has a balcony. There's a casual restaurant plus a game/sitting room warmed by a ceramic-tile German stove. Facilities include two outdoor pools, a fitness center with an indoor pool, a clay tennis court, nature trails, and a stocked pond where guests can fish or, in winter, ice skate or even ice fish. Rates: winter $94 to $189 (holidays $149 to $249); early spring/late fall $79 to $134; late spring/early summer $89 to $144; mid-season $99 to $159; foliage $129 to $184. Suites summer from $164; winter from $169; cottages summer from $164, winter from $179.

Stoweflake, Mountain Road (P.O. Box 369), Stowe, VT 05672 (☎ 802/253-7355), is a modern accommodation arranged around a broad expanse of lawn. The 94 rooms are not superdecorated, but they have everything you need—half-posters, wing chairs, a table, a desk and chest, plus phones, and TVs tucked into armoires. Some have kitchenettes and fireplaces, and there, are also 24 town houses with fully equipped kitchens, fireplaces, and decks. Dining facilities include Winfields and Charlie B's pub, where après skiers gather around the wood-burning fireplace to hear the live entertainment given

Tuesday and Wednesday and Friday and Saturday. Facilities include an exercise room, a chip-and-pitch course, two tennis courts, complimentary bikes, and an outdoor and an indoor pool. Rates: mid-October to Christmas and mid-March to early May, $78 to 190, town houses from $120 to $345 (depending on size); early January to mid-March, $88 to $285, town houses from $160 to $490; early May to early June, $84 to $190, town houses $120 to $385; early June to mid-October, $94 to $290, town houses $175 to $505.

Gables Inn, 1457 Mountain Rd., Stowe, VT 05672 (☎ 802/253-7730), occupies a farmhouse that was built in the 1850s and has been an inn since the 1930s. It's located by the main road behind a small front lawn. There are 19 guestrooms decorated in chintz and furnished comfortably with country pieces. One might have a serpentine canopied bed, a mahogany dresser, a desk, and two easy chairs, while another could have a cannonball bed or a cottage painted bed and similar furnishings. The four most private, modern, and attractive units are located in the carriage house. These are large, cathedral-ceiling rooms with wood-burning fireplaces, Jacuzzis, and TVs. Across the lawn and across a little footbridge, Riverview contains the most spectacular accommodation, with a living and dining area plus a balcony, and a small kitchen equipped with microwave, fridge, sink, and coffeemaker. The double fireplace faces into both living room and bedroom, while the bathroom has a double Jacuzzi set into a cedar deck. The inn is a favorite breakfast place where people come to enjoy everything from French toast to kippers and sautéed chicken livers. Facilities include a downstairs game room with a stone fireplace and a BYOB bar plus an outdoor kidney-shaped pool with grass apron. Rates: April to late June and late October to late December, $75 to $150; late June to early September, $100 to $195; early September to late October, $105 to $210.

Grey Fox Inn, 990 Mountain Rd., Stowe, VT (☎ 802/253-8921), is a great place to head for breakfast and enjoy its array of Dutch pancakes. It also has 30 or so modern accommodations. The most luxurious are the suites at the back of the property that are furnished with pine and fully equipped with TVs, air-conditioning, gas fireplaces, coffeemakers, and a decent-size sitting area. Facilities include an indoor pool and a game room. Rates: B&B $76 to $179. Special packages available.

STOWE DINING

See above for the dining rooms at Topnotch, Edson Hill Manor, the Trapp Family Lodge, Stowehof, and the Green Mountain Inn.

In winter or summer, it's romantic to take the gondola to the top of Mount Mansfield to dine at the **Cliff House** (☎ 802/253-3665) in a simple room looking out at the winter moon or the sun setting over the mountains. Tables are set with white linen and a single flower, and candles glow throughout the room. The food is better than most of us have come to expect at such "come for the view and not the food" establishments. The menu is a $39 prix fixe and uses fresh local ingredients in such simple dishes as strip steak with mushrooms, Yukon gold potatoes, and artichokes; sea scallops in a brown butter vinaigrette; and chicken paillard with porcini bread pudding and caramelized onions. To start, there might be smoked salmon with potato pancakes, American freshwater caviar, or mushroom escargot bruschetta. Open daily from 11:30am to 2pm, Thursday to Saturday for two dinner seatings at 5:30 and 7:30pm. Closed March to mid-June.

Isle de France, 1899 Mountain Rd. (☎ 802/253-7751). This outpost of France is divided into two: the Pierre Bonnard, which delivers superior classic French cuisine and service, and Claudine's Bistro, with more casual-style dishes and atmosphere. In the classic restaurant, the Dover sole meunière is fresh and moist, the duck comes with classic orange sauce, and the sirloin is served with either a red wine butter and shallot sauce or a béarnaise sauce. Prices range from $14.50 to $23. The bistro offers a shorter, simpler menu, featuring dishes such as poached salmon with hollandaise and a filet mignon with béarnaise sauce. Prices range from $13 to $14. Open 6 to 10pm, Tuesday to Sunday.

The Blue Moon Cafe, 35 School St. (☎ 802/253-7006), is a great bistro-style place to dine. It offers spacious tables, set in a sleek, modern softly lit room that has a small marble bar where diners can wait for tables. The food is some of the best in Stowe. The menu changes every week and always features local organic and seasonal ingredients. If there're on the menu, don't miss the Maine crab cakes with roasted summer squash and sweet-pepper coulis to start. The chef really knows how to prepare fish to allow the flavor to shine through, and the menu is weighted towards seafood dishes—striped bass baked in parchment with fennel and picholine olive relish and slow-roasted tomatoes or grilled yellowfin tuna with mango black-bean salsa and harissa. There are meat dishes, too, like braised rabbit with garlic, mint, and wide noodles or chicken breast with champagne grapes and watercress. Prices range from $15 to $17. Among the desserts, you will always find seasonal fruit pies, tarts, and cobblers along with such delights as chocolate peanut terrine or a really fine crème brûlée. Open daily from 6 to 9:30pm; November to Thanksgiving, Thursday to Sunday and week after Easter to mid-May also. Closed Thanksgiving to Easter.

If you're a fish lover or if you just like plain good food, then don't miss a meal at the **Partridge Inn**, Mountain Road (☎ 802/253-8000). The specialty of the house is Cape Cod and Maine seafood—lobsters included. It's a low-key place with a stone fireplace and Windsor chairs set at white-clothed tables, but the seafood dishes are inspired. The cioppino is brimming with clams, mussels, oysters, scallops, scrod, and shrimp in a spicy tomato broth served over linguine; the Thai shrimp is enhanced by the red curry sauce. In addition, there's a raft of broiled and baked fish—haddock, sole, trout, swordfish, and, of course, stuffed lobster. Prices range from $14 to $20. To start, the smoked trout is perfect. Open daily from 5:30 to 9:30pm.

Trattoria de la Festa, 4080 Mountain Rd. (☎ 802/253 8480), is one of those glowing mountain restaurants that you might find in the Dolomites. It occupies a restored barn and has a long bar on one side. Red oil cloth and green napkins make the table settings festive. Little wonder that Pavarotti chooses to eat in this warm Italian spot whenever he's in town. There's even a dish named after him—the 12-ounce sirloin stuffed with prosciutto and smoked mozzarella and then topped with roasted peppers, mushrooms, onions, and wine demiglace. It's not thrilling cuisine insofar as it sticks to the tried and true—veal marsala, chicken parmigiana, and the fish of the day, but it's heart-warming. Prices range from $12 to $18. Open from 5 to 10pm.

Whiskers, 1652 Mountain Rd. (☎ 802/253-8996), is reckoned to have the best salad bar in the valley, displaying 40-plus items. This popular restaurant encompasses a series of dining rooms where there are flowers everywhere along with an eclectic assortment of objects used in the decor. The source of the flowers are the adjacent gardens, which have been beautifully laid out with foxgloves, lilies, petunias, geraniums, astilbe, poppies, bee balm, and many more plantings, including a variety of herbs. There's even a field full of poppies and another field of sunflowers to make you think of France. The restaurant serves traditional fare—prime rib, Maine lobster, steaks, broiled scallops, and some pasta dishes all priced from $9 to $19. Open Sunday to Thursday from 5 to 9:30pm; Friday and Saturday from 5 to 10pm.

For a decadent breakfast, go to the **Dutch Pancake Cafe** (☎ 802/ 253-5330) at the Grey Fox Inn. Here you can select from more than 60 different pancakes filled with either savory or sweet ingredients. There's chocolate chip and pineapple and cream as well as the more traditional blueberry and bacon and cheese. Prices range from $7 to $9. Open May through October from 7:30 to 10:30am, and July through October, 10:30am to 12:30pm. Weekends only, off-season.

For lunch or afternoon tea, go to the **Austrian Tea Room** at the Trapp Family Lodge (☎ 802/253-5705). It offers soups, sandwiches, and sausages at lunch and the best Sacher torte and linzer torte outside Austria, along with spectacular mountain views to enjoy. Open daily from 10:30am to 5:30pm.

Stowe
Special & Recreational Activities

Antiquing: There are two multi-dealer showcases near Stowe. **Early Vermont Antiques** in Waterbury has 10 dealers, and **Smuggler's Notch Antiques** in Jeffersonville has 35 dealers. In Stowe itself, the **Stowe Antiques Center** is on Route 100 south.

Ballooning: For balloon trips, try **Stoweflake Resort** (☎ 802/253-7355).

Biking: There's a 5½-mile **recreation trail** that starts in the village, winds along beside Mountain Road, and crosses West Branch River. It's easy and leisurely and suitable for families with kids. For serious mountain biking, take the lift to the park at **Spruce Peak**. Rentals are available at **Mountain Bike Shop** on Mountain Road (☎ 802/253-7919); **Action Outfitters** (☎ 802/253-7975); and **A.J.'s Mountain Bikes** (☎ 802/253-4593).

Canoeing: Contact **Action Outfitters** (☎ 802/253-7975) and **Umiak Outfitters** (☎ 802/253-2317). Tours on the Lamoille are operated by **Smuggler's Notch Canoe Touring** (☎ 802/644-8321).

Climbing: Contact **Umiak Outfitters** (☎ 802/253-2317).

Cross-Country Skiing: Trapp Family Lodge has a great facility with 65 miles of trails.

Fishing: There's good fishing in the **Lamoille** and **Winooski** Rivers. In Stowe itself, **Sterling Pond,** on top of Spruce Peak, and **Sterling Brook** are local favorites. **Beaver Lake Trout Club** (☎ 802/888-3746) has a 14-acre trout-stocked lake that you can fish. **Fly Fish Vermont** (☎ 802/253-3964) offers fishing tours.

Golf: Golf courses are at **Stowe Country Club** (☎ 802/253-4893) and **Stoweflake Resort** (☎ 802/253-7355).

Hiking: Mount Mansfield, Smuggler's Notch, and the **Long Trail** that crosses from Sugarloaf to Mount Mansfield and Spruce Peak from south to north afford great hiking opportunities. Some rewarding hikes include the trail to Sterling Pond, which begins at Smuggler's Notch (2½ miles/2 hr.). For information, contact the **Green Mountain Club,** Route 100, Waterbury Center (☎ 802/244-7037). Other options are offered by **Stowe Nature Walks** (☎ 802/253-4468).

Horseback Riding: Trail rides are available at **Edson Hill Manor** and **Topnotch Resort.** Wagon rides are offered at Stoweflake.

In-line Skating: There's a skate park at the base of **Spruce Peak** (☎ 802/253-3000). Rentals are available at **A.J.'s Ski & Sports** (☎ 802/253-4593), **Action Outfitters** (☎ 802/253 7975), and **Boots 'n' Boards,** 430 Mountain Rd. (☎ 802/253-4225).

Kayaking: Contact **Umiak Outfitters** (☎ 802/253-2317) for rentals and trips.

Llama Trekking: Between June and October, **Stowe Llama Ranch** (☎ 802/253-5118) offers treks.

Skiing: Mount Mansfield at 4,393 feet is Vermont's highest peak, and Stowe its premier resort overall, especially for skiing. Stowe straddles two mountains and has 47 trails (59% intermediate, 25% expert) and 11 lifts, including an eight-person high-speed gondola and a high-speed quad. The vertical drop is 2,360 feet, and there's 73% snowmaking coverage. It also links to Smuggler's Notch, allowing skiers a true Alpine-style experience. A 2-day adult pass is $90. Facilities include some fine lodges and dining on the mountain and the dramatically situated Cliff House. Smuggler's Notch caters to families by offering a lot of additional water recreational facilities and other programs. It's spread over three peaks, has a 2,610-foot vertical drop, and features 60 trails (including the Black Hole triple black diamond trail).

Soaring: Whitcomb Aviation, Inc. (☎ 802/888-7845) offers the experience for $48 for 10 minutes, or $169 per hour.

Swimming: Pools are available at the following resorts—Golden Eagle, Green Mountain Inn, Stoweflake, Topnotch, and WalkAbout Creek.

Tennis: Courts are available at the inns and resorts described above: Stoweflake, Stowehof, Topnotch (including indoor courts), and WalkAbout Creek Lodge. The **Smuggler's Notch Tennis Center** has eight outdoor clay courts, two outdoor hard courts, and two indoor hard courts.

SMUGGLER'S NOTCH

To most of us, Smuggler's Notch is a ski resort, but the Notch itself was here long before the resort, and it's a remarkable piece of nature's handiwork, cutting between Mount Mansfield and Sterling Peak. Today the road (Route 108) that winds through the Notch is lined with gigantic boulders, and when you reach the top of the Notch, you'll see many oddly shaped outcroppings that locals have named everything from "Elephant's Head" to "the Hunter and his Dog." The name "Smuggler's Notch" supposedly came from its use by smugglers, who carried contraband between the United States and Canada along this route whenever trade was interrupted by war or political interference (notably during Prohibition). Today Smuggler's Notch State Park is a protected natural area to which peregrine falcons have returned and where there are many rare ferns, orchids, and other flora and fauna residing.

Smugglers Notch Resort, VT 05464 (☎ 800/451-8752 or 802/644-8851), has established itself as a top-of-the-line family resort. Families can cross-country or downhill ski in the winter and mountain bike and hike on the trails in summer. There's also canoeing on the Lamoille River. Accommodations here range from studios with fireplaces to five-bedroom condos. Rates: winter and holidays, $95 to $159 per person. Call for information about special and family packages and summer rates.

SUGARBUSH

In the 1970s **Sugarbush** was dubbed mascara mountain because it attracted a glitzy, fashionable crowd that included the Kennedys and other jet setters who have since moved on to Aspen. Today it may be less fashionable, but the mountains and rivers are just as beautiful and the skiing is still just as good. Nearby **Mad River Glen** is a skiers' cult mountain. It has an old-fashioned wooden chairlift, and no snowmaking, but the trails are narrow and steep at the top of the mountain and are well maintained so that the snow doesn't blow off. It's currently owned by a skiers' consortium, a group that is passionate about Mad River Glen's remaining as it is and wants to prevent it falling into the hands of the multiresort ski corporations.

Sugarbush sits between the two villages of Waitsfield and Warren. About 1 mile south of Warren, on the right side of Route 100 (going south), **Warren Falls** is a local, unmarked swimming hole where the falls cascade down a series of pools. While you're in Warren, be sure to visit one of the few traditional wood-fired sugarhouses that's left—the **D. Ernest Ralph Sugarhouse** on West Hill Road. Here Arnold Livingstone produces roughly 250 gallons of maple syrup per year. He's a licensed maker, and he makes the syrup in his 20-year-old sugaring house, using the traditional wood-fired method. At the end of February, when the days are warm and the nights are freezing, he has about 950 taps on his trees, which run for anywhere from 2 to 6 weeks. Once the trees bud, the flavor of the sap changes, and it can't be harvested for syrup. It takes roughly 40 gallons of sap to make 1 gallon of syrup. The sap is boiled down in "the arch," or firebox, a process that takes about 15 cords of wood. Most other producers use gas or oil. Enjoy one of the very few remaining honest-to-goodness sugar houses that is still around.

For cultural and evening entertainment, check out what's happening at **The Players Theater** (☎ 802/496-3485) or see what the **Phantom Theater**, an experimental group, is performing at the Warren Town Hall (☎ 802/496-2826). There's also a **cinema** on Route 100 in Waitsfield. There's plenty of après ski and other bar entertainment at **The Blue Tooth**, Sugarbush Access Road (☎ 802/583-2656), which features live bands; **Mad Mountain Tavern**, at routes 17 and 100, for big-screen sports watching, darts, and billiards; and the **Back Room** at Chez Henri (☎ 802/583-1172) for dancing. **Gallagher's Tavern** is a popular brew pub that also features live music and dancing.

AREA LODGING & DINING

Inn at Round Barn, East Warren Road (R.R. 247), Waitsfield, VT 05673 (☎ 802/496-2276), obviously has its beautiful round barn going for it, but it also has a lot more. It's set on 85 acres, surrounded by meadows where cows graze. Throughout the inn, guests will find eye-catching decorative objects, rich fabrics, and striking wallpapers. The 11 rooms are furnished with antiques; each has special features. One of the ground-floor rooms has a tongue-and-groove ceiling and a painted pine bed with a decorative vine and floral duvet that's matched with a chest that has grape decoration. Joslin has a lovely four-poster with a tulle canopy, a handsome highboy with a fine patina, and an extra-large bathroom with a heart-shaped Jacuzzi. Richardson has a cathedral ceiling, a bed with a tented effect, and a loveseat and chaise lounge. The bathroom contains a Jacuzzi set by the window and a hand-painted porcelain sink. Oriental rugs and built-in bookcases are in the sitting rooms, while the flagstone terrace, furnished with wicker, serves as a summer extension. Breakfast will bring a fresh fruit salad, banana-nut muffins, and cottage cheese pancakes with raspberry maple syrup or some similar dish. The barn, of course, is spectacular. It served as a dairy barn until 1960 but is now the venue for art shows and concerts. Downstairs in the barn are lap pools and a game room with billiards and a TV/VCR. The grounds and gardens have been terraced, and there's a pretty pond, plus a sty for Pignelope, the resident pet pig. Rates: mid-week $125 to $205; weekends $145 to $215.

Millbrook Inn, Route 17 (R.F.D. 62), Waitsfield, VT 05673 (☎ 802/496-2405), is a charming small accommodation with a very fine dining room where you can enjoy one of the best lodging and dining values near Sugarbush. The tables in the intimate dining room are set with floral tablecloths and hurricane lamps, and classical music plays in the background. Your meal might start with a fresh gazpacho followed by a salad of fresh organic greens. The meats are organically raised, and the lamb will be some of the tenderest and finest quality you'll find anywhere. Desserts, like the blueberry and raspberry pies, incorporate fresh local produce. There are seven rooms with private baths. All rooms have serious stenciling and are decorated in country fashion. In the Rose Room, floors are painted gray, and the walls are papered with cabbage roses. The top of the painted chest has been marbleized. Jack Dana has a brass bed covered with a quilt; the nicest rooms are the Wedding Ring Room, which has a carved pine bed, and the Perkins Henry Room, with a carved oak bed. You can order what you like for breakfast and enjoy it outside on the patio or in the dining room. The sitting room and warming room complete the comforts. Rates: mid-week, MAP $60 to $70 per person; weekends, $70 to 80. Closed April, May, and November.

West Hill House, West Hill Road (R.R. 1, Box 292), Warren, VT 05674 (☎ 802/496-7162), occupies an 1860s farmhouse in a secluded location on 9 acres with mountain views. It's only a mile from Sugarbush. The seven rooms are very inviting and comfortable. For example, you might stay in a room with exposed beams and dormer windows on both sides that has been furnished with a bed piled with pillows. Some rooms have gas fireplaces and/or whirlpool tubs. The library is large and filled with books that you can take down and read in front of the inglenook fireplace. A stone fireplace is also the focal point of the main living room. In addition, there's another sitting room and a large outdoor deck. Guests have access to a pantry, fridge, and wet bar. Rates: mid-week $100 to $135; weekends, $110 to $145.

The Beaver Pond Farm Inn, Golf Course Road (R.D. Box 306), Warren, VT 05674 (☎ 802/583-2861), is in a great location overlooking the golf course. The comfortable living room contains some choice decorative objects, especially the embroidered scene above the mantel. It opens to a large wide deck overlooking the golf course. There are six rooms, four with private baths. They are attractively decorated with wall-to-wall carpeting and striped wallpapers. Side tables are draped with floral fabric, and good reading lights hang above the beds. One room upstairs has two skylights, while another has a lively decor of red polka dot linens and red gingham ruffles and is furnished with oak and wicker pieces. Breakfast choices range from scrambled eggs with smoked salmon, or eggs Benedict with sweet-red-pepper sauce, to such delicious eye openers as orange-yogurt pancakes. It's served in the beamed dining room at a large oval table. Guests have access to a bar and also to a golf driving range. Rates: mid-week, $46 to $54 per person double, weekends $53 to $62.

The Common Man, German Flats Road, Warren (☎ 802/583-2800), is a great place to dine, and very atmospheric. At one end of the post-and-beam room rises a huge fieldstone fireplace. Wilton carpets line the walls, tables are of polished pine, and hundreds of Dom Perignon bottles stand at attention along the beams. The bar is large and crowded during the ski season. The food represents a variety of European traditions. For example, you might find a ravioli calabrese made with a sauce of sun-dried tomatoes, pine nuts, garlic, olive oil, basil, and pecorino cheese or a sliced duck breast with peach and brandy sauce. Some even are inspired by North Africa, like the tagine of game hen sweetened with onion, honey, dried plums, and almonds or the vegetarian couscous. Prices range from $13 to $18. The wine list offers 130 or so selections. Open mid-December to mid-April, daily 6:30 to 10pm. Closed Monday from mid-April to mid-December.

Chez Henri at Sugarbush Village (☎ 802/583-2600) is tucked away at the base of the mountain. It has a very romantic, Alpine-French ambience and a warm welcoming hearth in winter. In summer, it's especially beguiling because tables are set out under an awning by the brook. There's also a small wine bar furnished with round marble tables and the Back Room, which is a favorite après ski venue. The cuisine is classic, from the bouillabaisse to the veal Normande and the coq au vin. Appetizers are also French, like *moules marinière* and escargots in garlic butter. Prices range from $11 to $20. Open Thursday to Tuesday from 5 to 12pm; Sunday and holidays for brunch from 11am to 2pm. Closed Wednesday. Open weekends only April to June.

Big World, Route 100 at Madbush Falls, Waitsfield (☎ 802/496-3033), is John Egan's place, a clubhouse for skiers where the walls are covered with signed pictures of skiing greats and daredevils going down the sluice at Tuckerman Ravine or other equally terrifying terrain. Skis are even under glass on the bar. It's a comfortable place with a hip atmosphere; the sign over the door sets the tone: Always welcome. Sit long. Talk Much. Food is appropriately hearty and Alpine in flavor. The goulash will warm you up, and the wood-grilled leg of lamb in a rich lamb sauce will do the same. The chicken is nicely spiced with Vermont cider, ginger, and lime. Burgers and steaks complete the fare. Trademark appetizers include "dog bones," made with Polish sausage wrapped in puff pastry and served with kraut and mustard. Prices range from $6 to $17. Open Tuesday to Sunday from 5 to 10pm.

American Flatbread at Lareau Farm Country Inn, Route 100, Waitsfield (☎ 802/496-8856), is a fun place with a '60s flavor, captured in the earnest signs about Creation and Resurrection that are posted above the oven. During the week, flatbread is turned out from the Quebec-style wood-fired stone bread oven, but on Friday and Saturday night, the place is opened up to diners who sit either in the factory itself, alongside the giant mixer, or outside in the gardens bursting in summer with marigolds and bee balm that are also the source of the organic salad greens and other herbal ingredients. The breads are delicious and topped with everything from homemade sausage and sun-dried tomatoes to chicken and shrimp. An inspiring place. Open June to October and Christmas to Easter, Friday and Saturday from 5:30 to 9:30pm; spring and fall on Fridays only.

Sugarbush
Special & Recreational Activities

Biking: Sugarbush operates a mountain-bike center. Unlimited chairlift rides and trail access cost $22. Bikes rent for $35 to $45. The center is located in the **Gate House Lodge** at Lincoln Peak. Rentals are also available from **Clearwater Sports**, Route 100, Waitsfield (☎ 802/496-2708), and **Mad River Bike Shop**, routes 100 and 17, Waitsfield (☎ 802/496-9500). **Madbush Falls Mountain Bike Clinics & Adventures** (☎ 802/496-3033) offers clinics and tours.

Canoeing/Kayaking: Paddle your way down the Mad River, the Winooski, or at the Waterbury Reservoir. **Clearwater Sports,** Route 100, Waitsfield (☎ 802/496-2708), rents the gear and also offers guided trips.

Cross-Country Skiing: Blueberry Lake Nordic Ski Trails, Plunkton Road, East Warren (☎ 802/496-6687), has 15 miles of groomed trails and charges only $10 for a day pass. The **Inn at Round Barn** also has 20 miles of trails (☎ 802/496-2276). Also at **Ole's Cross-Country Center,** at the Sugarbush-Warren Airport (☎ 802/496-3430).

Golf: Sugarbush operates the **Mountain Golf School,** which offers intensive training programs. The **Sugarbush Golf Course,** Golf Course Road, Warren (☎ 802/583-6725), was designed by Robert Trent Jones, Sr. and is a challenging mountain course with lovely mountain vistas.

Hiking: For information, contact the **Green Mountain Club** (☎ 802/244-7037) or purchase a copy of the club's guide to the Long Trail. Hike the trails at Sugarbush's Lincoln Peak. The Long Trail runs along the ridge of the mountains. You can take day hikes up Mount Ellen or take the chairlift up and hike the ridge. Mount Abraham and Stark Mountain are tougher hikes. Mount Abraham can be accessed off the Lincoln Gap Road. From here, you can take the Long Trail south to Sunset Rock, which is a short easy hike, or north to the summit of the mountain. Stark Mountain is accessed from Route 17.

Horseback Riding: Vermont Icelandic Horse Farm (☎ 802/496-7141) in Waitsfield offers great trekking on their sturdy and comfortable Icelandic horses. Treks go from inn to inn through meadow and woodlands and range from 2 to 5 nights. Day and half-day rides are also available. A 2-day, 2-night trip will cost about $400. In winter, you can also try skijoring, which is like water-skiing behind a horse instead of a boat.

Ice Skating: Rentals are available at **Inverness Ski Shop** on Route 100 in Waitsfield (☎ 802/496-3343) and at **Clearwater Sports,** Route 100, Waitsfield (☎ 802/496-2708). Use them at the Skatium in Waitsfield.

Polo: This thrilling, punishing sport has been played at Sugarbush since 1962. Today, it's played practically every weekend during the summer at several fields in East Warren and Waitsfield. For information, call ☎ 802/496-8938 or 802/496-8922.

Skiing: Sugarbush, R.R. 1 (Box 350), Warren, VT 05674 (☎ 802/583-2381), offers skiing on six interconnected peaks. It has a vertical drop of 2,650 feet, 112 trails, and 18 lifts, including four super quads. It has a high proportion of expert skiing on Castle Rock and good glade skiing. More than 30% of the trails are rated black diamond.

Mad River Glen, Route 17, Fayston, VT 05673 (☎ 802/496-3551), is the only ski area owned by a cooperative of loyal skiers who banded together to protect it forever. It's pristine, has some topnotch expert skiing, and has not been marred by snowboarding and other extraneous distractions. It has 43 trails, three double chairlifts, and a diesel-powered single chairlift.

Soaring: For a serene view of the mountains and valley, contact **Sugarbush Soaring** in Warren at 802/496-2290. Trips operate from Sugarbush-Warren Airport. A 20-minute single ride costs $73, a 40-minute single ride is $99.75; double rides are $104 for 20 minutes and $135 for 30 minutes. Lessons are available.

Swimming: The **Sugarbush Sports Center** has an indoor and outdoor pool. Call ☎ 802/583-2391.

Tennis: The **Sugarbush Sports Center** has a complete racket sports facility, including squash, racquetball, and 24 indoor and outdoor tennis courts. For information, call ☎ 802/583-2391.

Quechee, Woodstock & Killington

Plymouth ◆ *Weathersfield* ◆ *Quechee Gorge* ◆ *Killington-Pico*

Distance in miles from Boston: Quechee, 143; Woodstock, 148; Killington, 158.

Estimated driving times: 2¾ hours to Quechee; 2¾ hours to Woodstock; 3¼ hours to Killington.

Driving: Take I-93 North to I-89, which goes into Vermont. Take Exit 1 (Woodstock-Rutland) to Route 4 west to Quechee and Woodstock.

Bus: Vermont Transit from Boston to White River Junction and then to Woodstock.

Train: Amtrak has service from New York to White River Junction (☎ 800/872-7245).

Further Information: For more information, contact **Quechee Chamber of Commerce**, 15 Main St. (☎ 802/295-7900); **Woodstock Area Chamber of Commerce**, 18 Central St., Woodstock, VT 05091 (☎ 802/457-3555); **Killington and Pico Areas Association**, P.O. Box 114, Killington, VT 05751 (☎ 802/773-4181).

QUECHEE & WOODSTOCK

The natural spectacle that draws visitors to Quechee is the beautiful **Quechee Gorge**. From the bridge above, you can peer down into the 165-foot gorge and then follow one of the trails down to the bottom. Trails leave from the campground on the south side of Route 4. Or enjoy a picnic at the overlook on the northern side of the Route 4 bridge.

From Route 4 take Waterman Hill down through the covered bridge (modernized by the way) and turn left on Main Street. Quechee looks pretty today, but when the last mill closed in 1958, the town had fallen on hard times. It

Events & Festivals to Plan Your Trip Around

May: Rage Weekend kicks off the summer at Killington with a ski-bike-run triathlon, plus kayak races across Snowshed pond and lots of musical entertainment.

June: Quechee Balloon Festival. Call ☎ 802/295-7900.

August: The **Quechee Scottish Festival** assembles massed pipe bands and includes solo piping and Highland dancing competitions, sheepdog trials, rugby, Scottish arts and crafts, and other Celtic entertainment. At Quechee Polo Field. Call ☎ 802/295-7900.

Killington Stage Race is a 5-day cycling race when professional and amateur cyclists race wheel to wheel.

December: Woodstock Wasail Celebration. Parades, dances, and classic English grog celebrate this annual event. Call ☎ 802/457-3555.

had thrived when such companies as Dewey and Company were producing thousands of yards of fabric a day. In fact, a whole village of 63 buildings, known as Dewey's Mills, grew up around this particular company, which had been started in 1836 and made the material that was used in the uniforms for the Boston Red Sox and New York Yankees. Today the centerpiece of the renaissance of the late '60s is **Simon Pearce Glass,** which now occupies Downers Mill on Main Street (☎ 802/295-2711) and sits overlooking the falls on the Ottauquechee River. Pearce was raised in County Cork, Ireland, and attended the Royal College of Art in London before going to work for some of Europe's renowned glassmakers. He is also a potter, and comes, in fact, from a family that is famous for Shanagarry Pottery and Stephen Pearce Pottery in Ireland. He established his glassmaking operation in Vermont in 1981. Here he has harnessed the hydro power of the river to fuel his glass furnace, and on the lower level of this historic building you can view the hydroelectric turbine and observe the teams of glassblowers and potters at work. Upstairs, the store sells the plain, crystalline, and beautiful glass, both first- and second-quality pieces, along with his full line of pottery. The shop also stocks fine-quality handcrafted furniture, baskets, linens, clothing, and jewelry. There's also a very fine restaurant (see below). Before leaving Quechee, swing along Dewey's Mills Road to Dewey's Pond, which loops back to Route 4.

Both Hanover and Woodstock are only 10 or 15 minutes away from Quechee, with Woodstock only 6 miles to the west. On the way to Woodstock, stop in the **Taftsville Country Store,** Route 4, a genuine old-fashioned general store that stocks a variety of Vermont-made foods.

Cradled between hills, **Woodstock** has an air of wealth and prosperity that many rural towns in Vermont lack. It has some very rich patrons and millionaire residents, including associations with the Rockefeller family. The town's residents have been active conservationists and a balanced relationship between commerce and historical preservation has developed that has created a very charming and picturesque town. It will soon become the home of Vermont's first national historical park—Mary Rockefeller's ancestral home and surrounding 550 acres of gardens and woodlands are scheduled to be opened to the public by the year 2000 as the Marsh-Billings National Historical Park.

Wander the streets and browse in the quality boutiques on Elm and Central streets. Stop by the green to view the gracious Federal-style homes (many on the National Historic Register) that face it. There are a number of good antiques shops. On Pleasant Street, **Wigren and Barlow** at no. 29 (☎ 802/457-2453) displays all kinds of country and formal furnishings, including garden appointments; **Praxis Antiques** at no. 51 (☎ 802/457-2396) has a good selection of country and primitive furniture and tools; and **Pleasant Street Books** (☎ 802/457-4050) has more than 10,000 antiquarian books, including special collections on the Civil War, children's books, art, and Vermontiana. On Central Street, **Windsor Galleries/Lamp Shop** at no. 20 (☎ 802/457-1702), is filled with porcelain, silver, decorative accessories, and great lamps; **Who Is Sylvia?** at no. 26 has terrific vintage clothing from the Victorian period to the '60s plus antique linens, lace, curtains, and bedspreads. At no. 71, **American Classics in Woodstock** (☎ 802/457-4337), has an elegant display of 18th-, 19th-, and 20th-century Americana. If you like folk art, stop at **Stephen Huneck Gallery,** 49 Central St. (☎ 802/457-3206), to see his carved and painted furniture, sculpture, and wall reliefs. **Gallery on the Green** (☎ 802/457-4956) displays works by local artists, many of them landscapes in oil, pastel, and watercolor. **Church Street Antiques Gallery,** Route 4 (☎ 802/457-2628), is filled with everything from spinning wheels and butter churns to majolica and Quimper. **Polo Antiques,** 25 South St. (☎ 802/457-5837), has four rooms of paintings and prints as well as furniture, pewter, and silver.

To appreciate the seasonal round that once propelled rural Vermont life, visit **Billings Farm & Museum,** Route 12, north of town (☎ 802/457-2355), which is named after Frederick Billings, builder of the Northern Pacific Railroad and one of the nation's early conservationists. This farm celebrates the life of the farmer and is a serious working farm with Southdown sheep and a herd of Jerseys that are milked twice daily—an operation that can be observed in the dairy barn. Throughout the summer, special events are held on weekends. For example, there's Cow Appreciation Day, which celebrates the gifts of milk, butter, and ice cream, and introduces everyone to the processes in making these products. The displays in the museum and other buildings depict the round of activities that shaped the lives and culture of Vermont's farm families around 1890. Displays focus on the tools, processes, and traditions that were central to planting and harvesting, dairying, maple sugaring, and ice cutting. You'll learn, for example, about the rural custom of pouring hot maple syrup onto a platter of fresh snow to make a candy that is traditionally eaten with doughnuts and pickles. Another barn contains historic wagons, and here you just might see a man making horse whips. The farmhouse is decorated to reflect the 1890s, and the gardens are planted with appropriate plantings and vegetables. Open May 1 to October 31, daily from 10am to 5pm; November and December, weekends only from 10am to 4pm. Closed December to April.

You can also visit **Sugarbush Farm** on Hillside Road in Taftsville (☎ 802/ 457-1757), a working farm where you can watch the family make cheeses and maple syrup and other agricultural products, depending on the season.

Nature takes over at the **Vermont Institute of Natural Science**, Church Hill Road (☎ 802/457-2779). If you want to see raptors close up, this is the place to come. The organization operates a clinic devoted to treating injured raptors for rerelease into the wild. Those that are too injured remain here in outdoor cages. You'll see bald eagles, peregrine falcons, snowy owls, and more than 20 other species. It's an intense experience to peer into the eyes of these fearless birds of prey. Naturalists perform demonstrations with the birds. There are also trails to walk and a small museum with turtles, snakes, and other exhibits. Open May to October, daily from 10am to 4pm; October to April, Monday to Saturday from 10am to 4pm. Admission is $5 for adults, $2 for children.

Evening entertainment is provided at the **Woodstock Town Hall Theatre**, which also shows movies. Concerts and community theater productions are also presented in the **Little Theater.**

From Woodstock it's about 15 miles to Plymouth. En route, stop at the old mill in Bridgewater Corners that has been converted into a large antiques center (☎ 802/672-3049) with restaurants on the first floor. Plymouth Notch is home to the **Calvin Coolidge Homestead** (☎ 802/672-3773), the village where Calvin Coolidge was born and grew up. His father ran the general store, and he was born in the house behind it on July 4, 1872. The complex has a lovely rural setting and preserves not only his home but also the community church, the cheese factory, and schoolhouse. The tour of the buildings starts in the museum where his life is summarized in a photographic exhibition with quotations from his memoirs. First stop is the barn, containing 19th-century farm implements and vehicles, including a summer hearse and a horse treadmill. The Wilder House is where Coolidge's mother grew up, and next door is the homestead in which he was inaugurated while on vacation on August 3, 1923, at 2:47am as 30th president of the United States. He swore the oath on the family bible after receiving news of President Harding's death in San Francisco on August 2. The rooms are furnished exactly as they were in 1923. This house stands across from the house where he was born. Coolidge's death was attributed to eating tainted fish in Alaska, and he is buried in the hillside village cemetery that lies across Route 100A. The Plymouth Cheese Factory is still owned by the Coolidge family and still produces the granular, curd-type cheese that you can see being processed, and which you can purchase in 3- or 5-pound wheels. See also the lovely Carrie Brown Garden, planted originally by Coolidge's stepmother. Open late May to mid-October, daily from 9:30am to 5:30pm. Admission is $5 for adults, free for children under 14.

If, instead of turning south at Bridgewater Corners, you continue on Route 4 to Route 100 you'll come to **Killington** (☎ 802/422-6200), which is only 20 miles west of Woodstock. Killington has become a front-runner resort in the East. In summer, it's fun to ride the **chairlift** from the base lodge to the 4,241-foot summit and to use the mountain-bike park. The gondola, also known as the **Skyeship,** goes to the top of Skye Peak leaving from a station 1 mile west of U.S. 4 and Route 100. It affords great vistas in fall. The chairlift is $10 round-trip for adults, $5 for children 6 to 12. The Skyeship costs $16 round-trip for adults, $9 for children 6 to 12.

Pico is another few miles up Route 100 and west along Route 4. Pico's summer diversions include a chairlift ride ($5 round-trip, $4 for children 6 to 12), the **Alpine Slide** ($5 for a single ride, $4 for children 6 to 12, a five-ride card $20 and $15, respectively), a bungee-type experience called the **Bungee Thing** ($5 and $4, respectively), miniature golf, and a driving range. All-day passes at Pico cost $35 adults and $25 children 6 to 12. Pico attractions operate daily from late June to September 1 from 10am to 6pm and from late May to late June and September to Columbus Day weekends only 11am to 5pm.

QUECHEE LODGING & DINING

The Pippin Inn, 188 Dewey's Mills Rd., Quechee, VT 05059 (☎ 802/296-3646), is set back behind a very high hedge. It's a striking residence that has been turned into a superb inn. There are three 2-room suites that have been dramatically decorated by Patricia with fine quality wallpapers and fabrics. The back room has a view of hills, lake, and pond and features a Tudor-style canopied bed covered with a damask quilt that is set against a single wall of delicious dark purple. The front suite has been decorated in jade-teal and also has a four-poster. Another suite has an ornately carved mahogany four-poster, with decorative accents such as fringed lamps. The bathroom has the luxury of double sinks. The suite's sitting room contains a comfortable sofa and an easy chair with an ottoman. Downstairs by the entrance, the equestrian room, decorated with horse prints and riding regalia, contains a magnificent antique pool table. The sitting room runs the full length of the house and has a variety of seating clusters arranged around the fireplace. Breakfasts are served in a stylish way. Rates: $150 to $205.

The Country Garden Inn, 37 Main St., Quechee, VT 05059 (☎ 802/295-3121), is set up above the road and has many extra-special features. There are five rooms, all attractively decorated with fine quality Bukhara or similar rugs. Lily of the Valley contains a rice canopied bed plus two Victorian side chairs and a chest and armoire. In Rosebud, the floors are painted jade, and a sleigh bed is the main focus of the room. Daffodil is furnished predominantly with wicker, while the Rose Room has furniture that has been hand painted by a local artist. The hallmarks of this accommodation, though, are all the amenities and extras that are provided to guests—a guest telephone, a fridge stocked with soft drinks, turndown service, electric blankets, room service, and in each room, extra-thick towels, a full selection of toiletries, a hair dryer, a curling iron, and scented candles. A three-course breakfast is served in the plant-filled atrium on glass tables. There are two comfortable furnished parlors that feature some original art by Dalí and others and some fine Russian dolls, icons, and a beautiful balalaika. The gardens are lovely. Stone steps lead down to a natural pool landscaped with waterfalls. Swing seats, Adirondack chairs, and umbrella tables dot the lawn in summer. More than 300 videos are available to guests. Rates: May to September 15, $130 to $180; September 16 to October 31, $150 to $200, November 25 to April 30, $110 to $160. Closed November 2 to 24.

Quechee Inn at Marshland Farm, Clubhouse Road, Quechee, VT 05059 (☎ 802/295-3133), occupies a series of farm buildings in a rustic setting across from some wetlands. There are 24 rooms all decorated in typical country fashion with chintz, braided rugs, and antique reproductions. Some might have serpentine canopied beds or four-poster beds. The public areas are inviting. Games and a grand piano are found in the post-and-beam living room that's warmed in winter by a fire in the brick hearth. The dining room is typically colonial, with Windsor chairs; in summer, tables are placed outside under an awning. Original art that is for sale is displayed on the walls. A breakfast buffet is offered from 8 to 10am, and iced tea, cookies, and lemonade from 3 to 5pm. Rates: MAP $150 to $270 depending on the season. Deduct $40 for B&B rate.

Simon Pearce Restaurant, The Mill (☎ 802/295-1470) is a popular place, especially on weekends, so make a reservation if you want to eat here. It's well worth it. The setting overlooking the mill falls and the covered bridge is romantic, the Pearce table settings are beautiful, and the cuisine is outstanding. Start with the chilled shrimp with mango citrus salsa and wonton chips, or the grilled portobello mushrooms with shaved Parmesan, fennel, and watercress. Among the entrees, a simple dish like the horseradish-crusted cod with crispy leeks and herb mashed potatoes can be amazing, and the grilled pork tenderloin with ancho chili sauce, corn, and black-bean salsa is another winner. Prices range from $16 to $20. Open daily from 11:30am to 2:45pm and 6 to 9pm.

If you can't secure a table at the Pearce Restaurant, then try the **Parker House,** 16 Main St. (☎ 802/295-6077). It has a series of intimate country dining rooms and some excellent cuisine. If it's available, choose the roast rack of lamb, which is super tender and served with a rich, full-flavored rosemary-cabernet sauce. In season, the oven-roasted loin of venison served with a reduction of port, balsamic vinegar, and dried cranberries is another delight. Seafood lovers will find dishes such as striped bass in a piccata sauce or pan-seared scallops wrapped in bacon and served with a lemon beurre blanc. Prices range from $17 to $22. Open summer, Wednesday to Monday from 5:30 to 9pm; winter, Friday and Saturday only from 5:30 to 9pm.

WOODSTOCK LODGING

The Jackson House Inn, 37 Rte. 4 W., Woodstock, VT 05091 (☎ 802/457-2065) is a lovely accommodation set back on a little loop off Route 4. The house and the 11 rooms are beautifully furnished. The house itself has some striking interior features: There is maple and black-cherry wainscoting in the parlor and bird's-eye maple in the hallways. Each of the rooms is tastefully decorated with fine wallpapers, fabrics, and linens. The Mary Todd Lincoln has a carved, high-back Victorian cottage bed that is matched with a tufted brocade Victorian chair and a marble-top table. Maple predominates in the Ms. Gloria Swanson (she stayed here in 1948) with a tiger-maple four-poster, plus desk, chest, and side tables all of maple. A fine brocade loveseat and a spectacular Chinese lamp and Chinese sculptures are two features in Francesca's, which also has a deck and is lit by chandeliers on a dimmer switch. A three-course breakfast is served, and there are afternoon cocktails also. The gardens stretch a long way behind the house and accommodate a pond for swimming. Arbors and trellises and an ornamental maze are part of the landscape. Facilities include an exercise room with treadmill, weights, and other equipment. There's also a large TV/VCR. The owners plan to add four suites, which should be equally gorgeous. Rates: $170 to $205.

Woodstock Inn & Resort, 14 The Green, Woodstock, VT 05091 (☎ 802/457-1100), is very much at the heart of Woodstock physically and socially. It stands behind lawns and hedges by the green, has been providing hospitality for 200 plus years, and offers a full program of sports and outdoor pursuits as well as a health and fitness center. The present building was constructed by Laurence Rockefeller in 1969 with extensions and renovations made in 1990. The lobby has a country air with its slate floors and flagstone fireplace. The 144 rooms are spacious, modern, and comfortable and equipped with TVs and telephones. Some have TV/VCRs, safes, and refrigerators, and a few have fireplaces. The beds are covered with handmade quilts; Vermont scenes accent the walls. The most attractive rooms are in the tavern wing. The main dining room has an ambulatory overlooking the gardens and serves a continental menu featuring prime local ingredients. You'll find Vermont rack of lamb in a natural *jus*, roasted natural chicken breast in natural *jus* with sweet summer corn, and citrus-and-herb-crusted Chilean sea bass with merlot butter. Prices range from $18 to $30. Richardson's Tavern welcomes visitors with wing chairs and upholstered stools and offers a lighter tavern menu, while the Eagle Cafe has porch dining. The dining room is open daily from 6 to 9pm, the Eagle Cafe from 5:30 to 9pm. Complimentary morning coffee and afternoon tea are served to guests. Services include room service, laundry, valet, and concierge. In the back, there's a pool with a sandstone apron surrounded by privet hedges and a smooth sward of croquet lawn. Facilities include Alpine skiing at Suicide Six; cross-country skiing with 38 miles of trails; hiking trails up Mount Tom; and a health and fitness center with 2 indoor and 10 outdoor tennis courts, squash, racquetball, and a swimming pool; golf is available at the Woodstock Country Club, which belongs to the inn. Rates: $179 to $315. Special golf, tennis, and skiing packages are available.

Charleston House, 21 Pleasant St., Woodstock, VT 05091 (☎ 802/457-3843), is an 1835 brick house with black shutters. It's set back from the road in the town's historic district. It offers nine attractive rooms, all with private baths. Some have fireplaces and Jacuzzi tubs. Mount Peg, for instance, is a large room with a gas fireplace, furnished with a four-poster and wing chairs and a chest. Mount Tom is an attic room that has been sponge painted and features a brocade-covered Victorian chair, wicker chairs, and oriental lamps. The sitting room is inviting with its sofas and wing chairs arranged around a fireplace flanked by bookcases. Breakfast—French toast, egg casserole, and similar dishes—is served at a long table by candlelight. Rates: $135 to $185.

The Ardmore Inn, 23 Pleasant St., Woodstock, VT 05091 (☎ 802/457-3887), occupies a Greek Revival house that was built in 1830. Each of the rooms is attractively decorated. Kerrigan features a hand-carved walnut bed combined with two armchairs and a kneehole dresser. A rice four-poster covered with a floral spread is found in Tully. There's a comfortable sitting room and a porch in the back, but it overlooks the parking lot. Breakfasts are hearty. You might receive the Woodstock sunrise—a mixture of asparagus, Vermont flatbread, eggs, oyster mushrooms, and tomatoes with cheddar cheese and Hollandaise. Rates: $120 to $160.

The Kedron Valley Inn, Route 106, South Woodstock, VT 05071 (☎ 802/457-1473), is a comfortable and unpretentious place on 15 acres. It's run by Max and Merrily Comins, who have a keen sense of history. The main house was built in 1828 and contains the dining room, where most of the owner's antique quilt and linen collection is displayed. Many of the quilts we're made by Merrily's great-great-grandmother. Acute observers will note that the valances are made of antique petticoat bottoms. In summer, the garden room with its slate floors is particularly appealing. The 26 rooms, all with private baths and TVs, are spread between the main house and a couple of other buildings. Most have wood-burning fireplaces; some have Franklin stoves. Two have double Jacuzzis, and four have private decks. The rooms are decorated with serpentine canopied beds, marble-top dressers, wicker sofas, and similar pieces. In the Tavern Building, Room 22 is extra large and has a three-sided fireplace, plus a 22-foot-long deck. The room has a drop-leaf desk, two wicker chairs, and an interesting decorative touch is an Edwardian dress that is a family heirloom. The Log Lodge was added in 1968, and the rooms here are located beside a brook and have log cabin–style interiors; all have wood-burning fireplaces, and furnishings are similar to the other rooms. The mood in the dining room is casual, but the cuisine is not. Among main courses, maple-glazed duck breast, vegetarian Wellington, and oven-roasted rack of lamb might follow appetizers such as roasted butternut acorn squash bisque or smoked venison sausage on a bed of red onion confit. There's a large private swimming lake on the property. Rates: $130 to $225.

WOODSTOCK DINING

In addition to the **Woodstock Inn** (see above), there are several other good choices.

The Prince and the Pauper, 24 Elm St. (☎ 802/457-1818) offers a convivial bar plus dining room that is definitely colonial in style with its Hitchcock chairs and high-back settles along the wall. The restaurant offers a three-course $34 fixed-price menu that changes daily. It features local fresh ingredients and might include dishes such as lobster and corn chowder or smoked pheasant ravioli with forest mushroom sauce to start. To follow, there might be a choice of grilled filet mignon with peppercorns and zinfandel sauce or crispy red snapper with horseradish crust. A lighter bistro menu is served in the tavern and on the patio. The menu features traditional New England favorites such as chicken pot pie, along with Jamaican spiced pork chop or grilled salmon with Thai ginger sauce, plus a selection of pizzas. Prices range from $10 to $16. Open daily from 6pm to closing.

Bentley's, 3 Elm St. (☎ 802/457-3232), is the place to repair for breakfast or for a soda-fountain specialty, which you can enjoy at one of the marble tables out front. There's also a dining room decorated with potted ferns, and bentwood chairs. The massive mahogany bar and fringed lampshades give the place a certain 1930s air. The menu is broad enough to satisfy every taste—from chicken served with a mustard and maple-syrup sauce to the New York strip steak flamed with Jack Daniel's whiskey. A lighter dish is hot sausage, spinach, onions, and three cheeses baked in puff pastry. Prices range from $9 to $20. There's dancing on Friday and Saturday nights and a Sunday jazz brunch in winter months. Open Sunday to Thursday from 11am to 9:30pm, Friday and Saturday from 11am to 10pm; open later for drinks and dancing on weekends.

Caffe Mill (☎ 802/457-3204) is a great place for lunch. Here you can enjoy hearty hot soups and grilled panini sandwiches stuffed with maple ham,

Swiss cheese, tomatoes, and more, or tuna and cheese on *pane bello*. They can be accompanied by a variety of coffees or teas. It's a country place with stucco walls, polished wood pine tables, and Windsor chairs.

Pane Salute, 61 Central St. (☎ 802/457-4882), has all the great Italian breads (which it bakes daily) and pastries, plus Italian- and American-style coffees. At lunch, there's a selection of inspired sandwiches featuring such ingredients as Florentine beef, roasted vegetables, and fresh mozzarella as well as soup, salads, and pizza. Prices range from $4.50 to $5.50. Open Sunday from 8:30am to 2:30pm; Monday, Tuesday, and Thursday to Saturday from 7am to 5:30pm.

BARNARD LODGING & DINING

Barnard is a convenient place to stop, about 10 miles north of Woodstock.

Barnard Inn, Route 12, Barnard (☎ 802/234-9961), has four country dining rooms with fireplaces. Here, at tables covered with pink cloths and lit by hurricane lamps, beautifully presented, superb French-continental cuisine is served. Choices range from roast duck with a seasonal sauce to smoked pork tenderloin served with Vermont apple chutney. The tournedos of beef with roasted shallots, veal demiglace, and balsamic vinegar sauce are classic and tender beyond belief. To start, try the smoked scallops or the portobello mushrooms and goat cheese. Prices range from $19 to $25. Open year-round, daily during foliage season, from 6 to 9pm. Closed Monday in summer and Sunday and Monday in winter.

The Inn at Twin Farms, Barnard, VT 05031 (☎ 802/234-9999), has become a kind of Holy Grail for inn lovers, especially the wealthy and famous in search of a totally secluded retreat where complete privacy is ensured behind the electronically controlled gates. At Twin Farms, they can stay in one of 10 individual cottage-suites on the 300 acres, or they can stay less privately in the four rooms in the main house. The interior design and decor of the entire place is lavish, to say the least, representing a massive investment by the Hawaiian owner. In the main house, stunning murals adorn the walls and butternut paneling burnishes the reception-sitting room. Fringed tufted ottomans, a Tramp-art sideboard, and a Milton Avery are just a few of the decorative objects found in the bar room. Guests can help themselves to any of the selections in the 13,000-bottle wine cellar at any of the bars on the property.

The main dining room features a stone fireplace at each end, and here guests are treated to a superb dinner. It might start with roasted jumbo sea scallops served on a coulis of leek and Parma ham, followed by sweet pea-tendril salad with baby fennel and a tomato-basil dressing. The main course might be roasted breast of pheasant on potatoes whipped with sweet corn, with roasted chanterelles and an apricot madeira *jus,* followed by fresh pineapple sorbet under a crispy phyllo teepee with medjool dates and toasted cumin. From the flagstone patio, there are lovely views of the perennial gardens with Mount Ascutney as a backdrop.

All the rooms in the main house have been decorated with great flair in very different styles, ranging from folk art Americana to French toile to vaguely Russian dacha style and more. The largest of the cottage suites is the Studio, at 2,000 square feet; the smallest is 1,000 square feet. The most distant cottage is ¼ mile from the main house. The Japanese-inspired Orchard Cottage is particularly serene with its split-ash herringbone woven ceiling and white-ash floors and cabinetry. The space itself is dominated by two imposing hand-carved granite fireplaces. Meadow Cottage is the most voluptuous, inspired by Morocco, with terra-cotta floors and a magnificent tented ceiling in the bedroom. Log Cabin is fashioned out of hickory and oak, and here a whimsical dog theme prevails. There are canine references everywhere. A large tile above the twig bed announces CAVE CANEM, carved dog heads adorn the arms of an easy chair, a Dalmatian sits on the mantel above the stone fireplace, a sofa upholstered in brilliant red has a dog-patterned throw, and the carpet even has paw prints. The exquisite furnishings, however, save the place from being banal. The cabin has a screened porch that can be enclosed with glass in winter. The bathroom has granite counters, a shower with a granite seat, plus a bidet.

There are other gathering places for guests beside the main house. The pine-paneled pub features a pool table, bar, and jukebox, plus a video collection. A Cy Twombly hangs above the mantel, while leather sofas and a grand piano are assembled under the cathedral ceiling. Facilities include a pool and Japanese furo bath, plus a gym with treadmills and other equipment. A stocked trout lake, canoes, and two tennis courts are also available. Much of the food that is served in the dining room comes from the inn's certified organic farm and gardens, where raspberries, herbs, vegetables, and pumpkins are grown. Rates: main house $825 to $975; cottages $1,000 to $1,650. Rates are daily and include breakfast, lunch, afternoon tea, all beverages (except wine, available any time from honor bars), and unlimited use of all on-site recreational facilities.

CHITTENDEN LODGING

The Mountain Top Inn, Chittenden, VT 05737 (☎ 802/483-2311), is a remote and lovely place with plenty of facilities for sports and outdoor pursuits, and an extensive riding program. It occupies a terrific setting at the top of a mountain. It's operated by Mike and Maggie Gehan, a delightful couple from California. There are 35 rooms in the inn plus six cottages. A typical deluxe room will have two queen-size half-poster beds, wing chairs with ottoman, a rocker, a desk, and a closet. All rooms are attractively decorated and well maintained and many have great views. The cottages are charming. Wren, for instance, has a sitting area with a stone fireplace and a beamed ceiling, plus a bedroom with a two-poster bed and a second fireplace. The brick patio at the back of the inn takes full advantage of the view of Chittenden Reservoir. The post-and-beam dining room is decorated in Shaker style. The cuisine is excellent, fresh and uncomplicated and featuring dishes such as chicken breast with roasted red peppers, capers, white wine, and fresh lemon; beef bourguignon; rack of lamb with sun-dried cranberry *jus*; and sole meunière. Prices range from $15 to $21. There's also a bar and a game room with a Ping-Pong table, a pool table, and foosball. Horses are part of the experience. At the paddock, there are 50 horses and a lesson barn where guests can take instruction in dressage, jumping, and polo. Facilities also include a fly-fishing pond, a golf driving range, a clay-bird shooting area, and 56 miles of groomed cross-country ski trails (used for training by the U.S. Olympic team). There's also a nicely landscaped pool; a tennis court; and canoes, kayaks, and rowboats down at the reservoir. Rates: early May to late June and September 1 to 23, $178 to

$231; late June to late August and late September to October 30, $206 to
$256; winter, midweek $186 to $216; weekends/holidays $206 to $236. For
MAP add $47.

Tulip Tree Inn, Chittenden Dam Road, Chittenden, VT 05737 (☎ 802/
483-6213), is located in a lovely bucolic setting on 7 acres. There are eight
rooms (five with Jacuzzis). Each is nicely decorated with stenciling, braided
rugs, wing chairs, and country oak pieces. The largest room has a four-poster
and an antique dresser plus two wing chairs and a gas fireplace. Guests have
the choice of two living rooms with plenty of comfortable seating. Breakfast
and dinner are included in the rates. At dinner, you might enjoy a meal of
soup and salad followed by a choice of either medallions of pork with apricot
and orange sauce or swordfish with pesto. The conclusion could be ice cream
pie with chocolate sauce. Breakfast consists of breads, cereal, and yogurt plus
a main dish such as blueberry pancakes or waffles. Rates: MAP $140 to $299
for two, depending on the season.

Quechee & Woodstock Area
Special & Recreational Activities

Note: If you stay at one of the inns or bed-and-breakfasts in Quechee, you will
also have access to the amenities at the **Quechee Lakes Resort,** which include
indoor and outdoor pools, tennis courts, two golf courses, and recreations at
Lake Pinneo.

Antiquing: Woodstock has a number of antique stores that are mentioned
above. Along Route 106 are several shops, including **Yellow House Antiques** (☎ 802/484-7799), specializing in Shaker furnishings and other
high-quality antiques, and **Mill Brook Antiques** (☎ 802/484-5942) with
Americana for everyone. Another large stomping ground is **Antiques
Collaborative** (☎ 802/296-5858) in Quechee, which has fine furniture,
oriental rugs, and vintage quilts.

Biking: Rentals are available at **Wilderness Trails** at the Quechee Inn
(☎ 802/295-7620) on Clubhouse Road for $17 a day; in Woodstock at
Woodstock Sports, 30 Central St. (☎ 802/457-1568); and **Cyclery Plus,**
Route 4 West (☎ 802/457-3377). The best mountain biking is at **Killington**
(☎ 802/422-6232), where lift access is provided to 41 miles of trails. Bike
rentals are available, starting at $40 a day. Unlimited access to lift and trails
costs $25 for adults. Guided tours and instruction are offered.

Camping: In Quechee, campsites can be found at **Quechee State Park**
(☎ 802/295-2990); in Barnard at **Silver Lake State Park** (☎ 802/
234-9451); in Plymouth at **Calvin Coolidge State Park** (☎ 802/
672-3612).

Canoeing/Kayaking: Wilderness Trails (☎ 802/295-7620) at the Quechee
Inn on Clubhouse Road rents canoes for $12 for a half day, $18 for a full
day. The **Quechee Club** also has facilities at Lake Pinneo. In Woodstock,
rentals are available at **Silver Lake State Park** (☎ 802/234-9451). **Kayak
King,** in Killington (☎ 802/422-3070), rents kayaks for $15 an hour ($5
each additional hour).

Cross-Country Skiing: Wilderness Trails operates a full facility with 12 miles of groomed trails at the Quechee Inn (☎ 802/295-7620); the **Woodstock Ski Touring Center** (☎ 802/457-6674) has 37 miles of groomed trails.

Fishing: Wilderness Trails at the Quechee Inn (☎ 802/295-7620) on Clubhouse Road operates a fly-fishing school.

Golf: The Quechee Club has two courses: The **Highland Course** is reckoned the best in the state (☎ 802/295-6245); the course at the **Woodstock Country Club** (☎ 802/457-6674) was designed by Robert Trent Jones, Sr. and is another that's highly ranked. **Killington** operates a golf school and has a par-72 course designed by Geoffrey Cornish.

Hiking: From Barnard, you can hike to Luce's Lookout, which has great views. Other good hikes will take you to the summit of Mount Tom (off Route 4) and Ascutney Mountain in Weathersfield off Route 131. Killington has more than 20 trails covering 50 miles and operates a hiking center that offers guided hikes and weekend hiking adventures that include overnight lodging. Call ☎ 802/422-6708.

Horseback Riding: Kedron Valley Stables, South Woodstock (☎ 802/457-1480), offers 1-hour trail rides from $20 to $30 per hour, plus inn-to-inn riding vacations. The **Mountain Top Inn** (see above) has stables and offers instruction in dressage and polo. For additional information about riding in the region, contact the **Green Mountain Horse Association and Youth Center**, South Woodstock (☎ 802/457-1509).

Polo: Attending a polo event on a balmy afternoon is a pleasant way to pass the time and thrilling, too, if you've never seen this vigorous sport played. The polo field is off Dewey's Mills Road in **Quechee.**

Skiing: Killington-Pico (☎ 800/621-6867) is the East's largest resort, covering 1,200 acres, and it has the steepest vertical drop (3,150 feet) of all the New England ski areas. Since it joined with Pico, the area offers a dizzying 212 trails sprawled over seven peaks and accessed by 33 lifts, including 10 high-speed quads. Lift passes start at $84 for 2 days. It's frequented by a lot of college students and offers a pretty rambunctious après ski scene. **Suicide Six** (☎ 802/457-1666) has a vertical rise of 650 feet, 19 trails, and two double chairs; a day pass is $35.

State Parks: Quechee State Park (☎ 802/295-2990) has camping and is the major park in the area.

Swimming: Quechee Club (☎ 802/295-9356) offers facilities; swimming is also available at **Silver Lake State Park** (☎ 802/234-9451) in Barnard and at pools in Woodstock under the control of the **Woodstock Recreation Department** (☎ 802/457-1502).

Tennis: Try the **Quechee Club** (☎ 802/295-6069). Tennis instruction is available at the tennis school in **Killington.**

St. Johnsbury, Craftsbury & Burke Mountain

East Burke ◆ *Lake Willoughby* ◆ *Lyndonville* ◆
Greensboro ◆ *Lower Waterford*

Distance in miles from Boston: St. Johnsbury, 160 miles; Craftsbury, 196 miles.

Estimated driving times: 3¼ hours to St. Johnsbury; 3¾ hours to Craftsbury.

◄o►◄o►◄o►◄o►◄o►

Driving: I-93 to I-91 to Exit 21 to St. Johnsbury and Craftsbury. For Hardwick, Exit 21, and then Route 2 west to Route 15, and Route 14 north to Burke Mountain Area. Exit 23 to Lyndonville, and then 114 North; or Exit 25 to Barton and Crystal Lake.

Further Information: For more information, contact **Northeast Kingdom Chamber of Commerce**, 30 Western Ave., St. Johnsbury, VT 05819 (☎ 802/748-3678); **Lake Willoughby Chamber of Commerce**, R.R. 1, Box 124, Barton, VT 05822 (☎ 802/525-4496); **Hardwick Chamber of Commerce**, P.O. Box 111, Hardwick, VT 05843 (☎ 802/472-6894); **Lyndon Area Chamber of Commerce**, P.O. Box 886, Lyndonville, VT 05851 (☎ 802/626-9696).

◄o►◄o►◄o►◄o►◄o►

This is remote country where towns are small and farms, forest, mountains, and lakes can be enjoyed in their close-to-pristine state. It's great country for getting out into nature either on foot or skis, on bicycle, or in a canoe.

EXPLORING THE AREA

From Montpelier, you can either take the main routes 2 and then 14 to the town of **Hardwick** or, better yet, follow the back roads via Kents and Maple Corners to Greenwood Lake and then pick up Route 14 a little south of Hardwick. Hardwick itself is not an especially pretty town, but it does have a couple of attractions, notably a secondhand bookstore. From Hardwick, Route 14 leads north to **Craftsbury** and **Craftsbury Common,** both charming villages, the last of which is famous for its **Outdoor Center,** P.O. Box 31, Craftsbury Common, VT 05827 (☎ 802/729-7751). Or from Hardwick you can take Maple Street to Center Road, which leads into **Greensboro,** an attractive

Events & Festivals to Plan Your Trip Around

July/August: Craftsbury Chamber Players play a series of concerts under a tent at Burke Mountain. Call ☎ 802/748-3678 or 802/626-9696.

  Circus Smirkus performs under the Big Top in Greensboro. Old-Time Fiddler's Contest at Hardwick. Call ☎ 802/472-6894.

August: The Caledonia County Fair at Lyndonville is an old-fashioned country fair. Call ☎ 802/626-9696.

  The annual pageant, at the Bread and Puppet Theater barns in Glover, usually takes place the first weekend in August, but call ☎ 802/525-3031 for information, since dates change.

September: Oktoberfest at Burke Mountain begins with a *Volksmarch* that is followed by German food, music, and *schuhplattler* dancing. Call ☎ 802/748-3678.

village, by Caspian Lake, that is anchored by the usual general store. Across the street, the **Miller's Thumb** (☎ 802/533-2960) occupies an old grist mill displaying a wonderful collection of house and garden accessories including colorful Italian and Portuguese majolica bowls, mugs, platters, and tureens.

From Greensboro, you can access Route 16 north to **Glover,** then to **Barton** at the northern end of Crystal Lake, and farther on to **Lake Willoughby.** Don't miss the general store in Glover. It's filled with trophies of all kinds—deer, turkey, pheasant, fox, and more.

Outside Glover, stop to visit the **Bread & Puppet Theater Museum,** Route 122, Glover (☎ 802/525-3031). It's a shrine to actor and puppeteer Maurice Blanc and the troupe that was founded in 1963 on Delancey Street in New York City by sculptor, dancer, and musician Peter Schumann. The company subsequently moved first, in 1970, to Goddard College in Plainfield and finally to Glover in 1974. In the 1960s, the theater concentrated on social protest and presented morality plays as well as circus celebrations. Here in the barns at this farm, you can see close up more than a thousand puppets, paintings, and masks that have been used in the productions of this famous troupe. They are presented in a dramatic and often ghoulish series of tableaux. They depict all kinds of characters from all walks of life—soldiers and saints, crones and clowns, salesmen and butchers. They are built from Schumann's clay originals using a mixture of found materials like brown paper, cardboard, rummage-sale rags, and baling twine. Among my favorites are those created for The Dangerous Kitchen of Ronald Reagan. In the huge upstairs barn loom the giant figures of Yama, King of Hell, and his demons and the huge Domestic Resurrection goddess who must be 30 feet tall. Photographs capturing the group's anti-war demonstrations in 1966–68 in New York City, Washington D.C., and Paris are also on display. Scattered among the exhibits are excerpts describing Vermont life from the writings of Daisy Dopp, who owned this farm and barns with Jim Dopp until 1970. Posters, programs, and woodcuts are available. Bonuses are the political art in the psychedelically painted Cheap Art Bus across the street and the serendipitous loaves that may be available from the three clay ovens on the premises. Open mid-May through October, daily from 10am to 5pm. Admission is free, but a donation would help toward the museum's survival.

Lake Willoughby is a beautiful lake stretching between mounts Pisgah and Hor. From here, routes 5 and 5A cut south via Lyndonville to **St. Johnsbury**, a place that could be said to be the capital of the Northeast Kingdom. Before you reach Lyndonville you can turn off along Route 114 to **East Burke** and **Burke Mountain** and take the toll road to the 3,267-foot summit for some grand Vermont views. In East Burke, stop in at **Bailey's Country Store** ☎ 802/626-3666) and at the **Trout River Brewing Company. Lyndonville** has a collection of historic homes, framing the town green.

In St. Johnsbury, don't miss two startling attractions: the **Fairbanks Museum,** at Main and Prospect streets (☎ 802/748-2372), and the **St. Johnsbury Athenaeum,** 30 Main St. (☎ 802/748-8291). The first is an extraordinary natural history collection in an equally fine building. It's named after Franklin Fairbanks, the nephew of Thaddeus Fairbanks, inventor of the platform scale. Franklin began the collection as a boy. It's displayed in a Victorian manner, with many of the birds exhibited in simulations of their natural habitats. The dioramas were created by William Everard Balch, who was a pioneer in creating lifelike dioramas. If you want to see a particular species of bird up close and in detail, then this is certainly a place to come. You can study birds from many different continents. Among the most beautiful are the impeyan pheasant with its iridescent feathers, the trumpeter swan, the case of birds of paradise, and a whole case of hummingbirds. The upper galleries are devoted to anthropological displays of artifacts from Oceania, the Philippines, West Africa, and Japan plus crystals and minerals. Open Monday to Saturday from 10am to 4pm and Sunday from 1 to 5pm; admission is $4.

The **Athenaeum,** a public library and art gallery, was built for the town by Horace Fairbanks, another nephew of Thaddeus, in 1873. The interior is lavish indeed. The library shelves are made of black walnut; ash alcoves and doorways are beautifully crafted, and elegant spiral staircases lead to the upper bookcases. The focal picture of the art gallery is Albert Bierstadt's *Domes of the Yosemite*, a huge 10-by-15-foot canvas that John Davis Hatch's brother acquired for $5,000 from Connecticut industrialist Lockwood Mathews, who had paid $25,000 to commission it. On the walls around it are works by other celebrated American artists—Asher B. Durand, Joseph Cropsey, Samuel Colman, and Worthington Whittredge. Open Monday and Wednesday from 10am to 8pm; Tuesday, Thursday, and Friday from 10am to 5:30pm; Saturday 9:30am to 4pm.

This is the region of Vermont in which to find legions of genuine, individual producers of **maple syrup** tucked away in the hillsides and hollows. Here are a few sugar makers to drop by: in Barnet, **Gordon Goss,** RFD 1, Box 52 (☎ 802/633-4743); in Lyndonville, **Dave Dolloff,** H.C.R. Box 33A (☎ 802/626-5825); and in St. Johnsbury, **Broadview Farm,** P.O. Box 621 (☎ 802/748-6560), and **Sugar Ridge Farm,** R.F.D 2, Box 149 (☎ 802/748-2318). If you don't have time to seek out any one of these producers, then you can always stop in St. Johnsbury at **Maple Grove Farm,** 167 Portland St. (☎ 802/ 748-5141), the contemporary version of the original Carey Maple Sugar Company that was founded here in 1904. Open daily from 8am to 4pm with tours every 15 minutes. Admission is $1, free for children 12 and under.

GREENSBORO, CRAFTSBURY & CRAFTSBURY COMMON
LODGING & DINING

The Highland Lodge, R.R. 1 (P.O. Box 1290), Greensboro, VT 05841 (☎ 802/533-2647), spreads over 123 acres, and from the front porch there's a lovely view of Caspian Lake. The setting is inspiring, and guests can hike the trails and explore the wetlands as well as cross-country ski in winter. It's a down-to-earth country place where the meals served are hearty if not particularly refined. The dishes feature many local products—goat cheese from Rivendell, Swiss cheese and Brie from Kingset, and, of course, cheddar from Cabot. Venison comes from Wylie Hill and lamb from Hirsel. Some of the rooms are in the main house but the nicest accommodations are the cottages. Most of them were built in the 1930s, and they have a wonderful rustic feel but have been thoroughly modernized. Schuyler's Cottage is set well back into the pine forest and has a beamed sitting room with a wood-burning stove and wicker rockers standing on an oriental rug. It has a kitchen and dining room plus a deck and four bedrooms upstairs. Other cottages are smaller but similarly equipped. Numbers 3 and 4 have the best lake views. Not all of them have full kitchens, and only four are winterized. Facilities include a clay tennis court and a beach and boathouse where guests can use rowboats, canoes, and pedal boats without charge and sailboats for a rental fee. Bikes are also available for rent. In summer, Monday night is traditionally beach-picnic night. Rates: MAP $100 to $125 per person double; cottages $122.50 to $125 per person.

    The Inn on the Common, Craftsbury Common, VT 05827 (☎ 802/ 586-9619) sits on a hilltop with 15 acres of land around it. The main building dates to 1795 and contains a library lounge and several guest rooms. Furnishings throughout are high quality and comfortable, and the decor is striking. For example, a sitting room has a slate floor, stained glass, and a bold deep purple stripe on the walls. There are 16 rooms in three different historic buildings. Room 14 has a brass bed set against a stag-pattern wallpaper, combined with a blue leather chair, a bamboo chest, and built-in bookcase. Room 12 is extra large; its loveseat and armchair are upholstered in gingham, and the bathroom is outrageously decorated with flora from Hawaii. For entertainment, guests have 270 videos to choose from. They also have their own guest kitchen. The elegant dining room in the main inn has fine woodwork, oriental rugs, and gorgeous Scalamandre wallpaper. Crystal and china grace the tables. A five-course candlelit dinner is served. The menu changes nightly, but will always offer a choice of appetizers, a soup, three entrees, a salad, and dessert. Start with shrimp quenelles au gratin and follow with a dish like loin of pork with sweet figs or tiger shrimp stuffed with scallops and dill and baked in sherry sauce. Dessert might be lemon tart with apricot glaze or a flourless chocolate cake with maple whipped cream. In summer, wrought-iron tables are set outside overlooking the gardens where foxgloves, delphiniums, day lilies, and other flowers bloom. A gracious row of arbor vita stretches to a pergola, and beyond that an all-white garden is laid out, with Lutyens teak benches under the trellis. In the adjacent meadows sheep are bleating, and in the spring, guests can walk on carpets of wildflowers. Facilities include an outdoor sculptured pool with a brick apron and a clay tennis court. Rates: winter, MAP $230 to $250; summer, MAP $230 to $250; foliage season (late September to mid-October), $270 to $290. Special packages are available.

The **Craftsbury Inn**, Route 14, Craftsbury, VT 05826 (☎ 802/586-2848), is right in the tiny village across from the general store. It offers 10 rooms (six with private baths). Furnishings include serpentine canopied beds, armchairs, and oriental rugs. Handmade quilts grace the beds. There's a sitting room with TV and a woodstove, a game room, and a restaurant that looks out onto the gardens. The cuisine is continental-American, with dishes such as pork medallions with an apricot demiglace or poached salmon with cucumber-caper sauce. Prices range from $11 to $18. Dining hours are Wednesday to Saturday from 11:30am to 2pm, Sunday from 11am to 2pm, and Wednesday to Saturday from 6:30 to 8pm. Rates: B&B $100 to $120 double; MAP $150 to $170 double.

LAKE WILLOUGHBY & EAST BURKE LODGING

Fox Hall, Willoughby Lake, Barton, VT 05822 (☎ 802/525-6930), sits in solitude on 80 acres. It has 800 feet of lakeshore, where two canoes, paddle boats, and a swimming dock are available for guests. There are eight guest rooms in this handsome 1890 Victorian. Four have private baths. They have all been decorated in a similar country style. Room 1 has chintz wallpaper, a Jenny Lind bed, an oak dresser, a rocker, and a bathroom with a claw-foot tub. The winning turret room has a great view of the lake and features a wicker bed and decorative fireplace. Other rooms have brass or cottage-style beds. A full breakfast featuring dishes like strawberry-banana pancakes, muffins, and fruit is served at separate tables. Someone in the Pyden family that runs the inn is moose crazy—these creatures are a decorative motif throughout the house. There's a real trophy over the mantel in the sitting room. Fox Hall is home to a Music at Lake Willoughby series of chamber concerts that are held outdoors under a pavilion. Rates: July to October 15 and Christmas week, $80 to $100; rest of the year, $70 to $84.

The **Inn at Mountain View Creamery**, Box 355, Darling Hill Rd., East Burke, VT 05832 (☎ 802/626-9924), is located at the top of a hill in a lovely series of farm buildings at the heart of 440 acres of rolling hills and meadows. The elegant farm courtyard is framed by a carriage barn and an imposing Morgan horse stable. The inn itself is located in the restored 1890 redbrick creamery. There are 10 guest rooms, all tastefully but simply furnished with country antiques and handmade quilts. Some rooms have four-posters; others have sleigh beds. Guests have use of a comfortable parlor, and there's a game room with table tennis. The dining room where breakfast is served was once the center of the creamery's production area. Afternoon tea is also served. Facilities include cross-country skiing and hiking trails. Rates: $120 to $150.

LOWER WATERFORD LODGING

The **Rabbit Hill Inn**, Route 18, Lower Waterford, VT 05848 (☎ 802/748-5168), is the kind of place people turn to again and again for the quiet and beauty of its location, the luxurious accommodations, and the personal attention that they receive. It's a classic 1795 inn and pillared 1825 house that have been joined together, restored, and furnished lavishly with fine-quality antique reproductions. There are 21 rooms, 12 with gas fireplaces and some with whirlpool tubs. Each has been individually decorated with fine fabrics and linens and wallpapers. For example, you might find a cottage-style bed with a tented effect, combined with marble-top side tables, wicker chairs, and a pier mirror. Another room might have sponge-painted walls and a carved oak bed. Victoria's Chamber features a bold, bird-motif wallpaper plus a finely upholstered Victorian sofa, an Empire chest, and an iron-and-brass bed with a tent treatment. The most fetching room is the Nest with its wrought-iron bed swathed in sheer drapes and piled high with pillows, side tables draped in Battenburg lace, and a large bathroom with a black-and-white floor and a double Jacuzzi. It also has a private balcony. Some of the rooms have absolutely stunning views of the Presidential Range. Breakfast is a four-course affair that begins with a buffet spread of granola, fruit, and baked goods and continues with a choice of two entrees like stuffed French toast or blackberry waffles. Afternoon tea is served from 2 to 5:30pm. In the dining room, the polished cherry tables are set with crystal and fine china and lit by candles. Here, a five-course fixed-price menu is served. It changes frequently but always features a choice of appetizers—inn-cured mackerel gravlax with pickled asparagus and a white radish rémoulade or a chorizo–wild-mushroom waffle with pistachios and goat cheese accompanied by a fresh currant jam—followed by a choice of salad. About eight entrees are offered, ranging from grilled beef tenderloin with a tamarillo barbecue sauce to fresh trout wrapped in cucumber, poached in an herb vinaigrette, and served with lemon, ginger linguine, and a compote of tomatoes, capers, and black olives. Open daily from 8:15 to 10am and 6 to 8:45pm. Closed April and November. The Snooty Fox pub is a cozy nook where guests can enjoy a pint and a game of darts or chess. There are two sitting rooms for guests. Rates: MAP $189 to $279 double.

St. Johnsbury & the Northeast Kingdom
Special & Recreational Activities

Biking: Rentals available from the **Village Sport Shop,** Route 5, Lyndonville (☎ 802/626-8448), for $15 a day. Try the trails at **Burke Mountain,** which also has rentals at the base lodge. Backcountry riding and rentals are available at **Craftsbury Outdoor Center,** P.O. Box 31, Craftsbury Common (☎ 800/729-7751).

Canoeing: Rentals available from the **Village Sport Shop,** Route 5, Lyndonville (☎ 802/626-8448) for $25 a day. Head for Crystal Lake or Groton State Park. Craftsbury Center also has access to Lake Hosmer.

Cross-Country Skiing: Craftsbury Outdoor Center, P.O. Box 31, Craftsbury Common (☎ 800/729-7751), has a first-rate cross-country center with 62 miles of groomed trails. Rentals and instruction are available.

Fishing: Head for **Crystal Lake** or **Lake Willoughby** or **Greensboro's Caspian Lake.**

Golf: St. Johnsbury Country Club (☎ 802/748-9894) offers good golfing value at $30 on weekdays and $35 on weekends.

Hiking: Hike around **Caspian Lake** in Greensboro or on the mountain trails at **Burke Mountain.** There's also hiking at Mount Pisgah and Mount Hor at **Lake Willoughby.**

In-line Skating: Rentals available from the **Village Sport Shop**, Route 5, Lyndonville (☎ 802/626-8448), at $10 a day.

Nature Reserves: Barr Hill is in Greensboro. The **Victory Bog** to the east of Burke Mountain, accessed via Route 2 and Victory Road from St. Johnsbury, is good moose-spotting country.

Rowing: The **Craftsbury Outdoor Center**, P.O. Box 31, Craftsbury Common (☎ 800/729-7751), is well known for its sculling weekends, which are conducted on Lake Hosmer. Many national teams train here.

Skiing: Burke Mountain and **Jay Peak** are the main areas. Jay Peak has a 60-person aerial tramway that takes you up 3,800 feet.

INDEX

Page numbers in italics refer to maps.

FROMMER'S® COMPLETE TRAVEL GUIDES

(Comprehensive guides with selections in all price ranges—from deluxe to budget)

Alaska
Amsterdam
Arizona
Atlanta
Australia
Austria
Bahamas
Barcelona, Madrid & Seville
Belgium, Holland &
  Luxembourg
Bermuda
Boston
Budapest & the Best of
  Hungary
California
Canada
Cancún, Cozumel & the
  Yucatán
Cape Cod, Nantucket &
  Martha's Vineyard
Caribbean
Caribbean Cruises &
  Ports of Call
Caribbean Ports of Call
Carolinas & Georgia
Chicago
China
Colorado
Costa Rica
Denver, Boulder &
  Colorado Springs
England
Europe
Florida

France
Germany
Greece
Hawaii
Hong Kong
Honolulu, Waikiki & Oahu
Ireland
Israel
Italy
Jamaica & Barbados
Japan
Las Vegas
London
Los Angeles
Maryland & Delaware
Maui
Mexico
Miami & the Keys
Montana & Wyoming
Montréal & Québec City
Munich & the Bavarian Alps
Nashville & Memphis
Nepal
New England
New Mexico
New Orleans
New York City
Nova Scotia, New
  Brunswick &
  Prince Edward Island
Oregon
Paris
Philadelphia & the Amish
  Country

Portugal
Prague & the Best of the
  Czech Republic
Provence & the Riviera
Puerto Rico
Rome
San Antonio & Austin
San Diego
San Francisco
Santa Fe, Taos &
  Albuquerque
Scandinavia
Scotland
Seattle & Portland
Singapore & Malaysia
South Pacific
Spain
Switzerland
Thailand
Tokyo
Toronto
Tuscany & Umbria
USA
Utah
Vancouver & Victoria
Vermont, New Hampshire &
  Maine
Vienna & the Danube Valley
Virgin Islands
Virginia
Walt Disney World &
  Orlando
Washington, D.C.
Washington State

FROMMER'S® DOLLAR-A-DAY GUIDES

(The ultimate guides to comfortable low-cost travel)

Australia from $50 a Day
California from $60 a Day
Caribbean from $60 a Day
England from $60 a Day
Europe from $50 a Day
Florida from $60 a Day
Greece from $50 a Day
Hawaii from $60 a Day
Ireland from $50 a Day

Israel from $45 a Day
Italy from $50 a Day
London from $70 a Day
New York from $75 a Day
New Zealand from $50 a Day
Paris from $70 a Day
San Francisco from $60 a Day
Washington, D.C., from
  $60 a Day

FROMMER'S® MEMORABLE WALKS

Chicago
London

New York
Paris

San Francisco

FROMMER'S® PORTABLE GUIDES

Acapulco, Ixtapa/
  Zihuatanejo
Bahamas
California Wine
  Country
Charleston & Savannah
Chicago

Dublin
Las Vegas
London
Maine Coast
New Orleans
New York City
Paris

Puerto Vallarta, Manzanillo
  & Guadalajara
San Francisco
Sydney
Tampa Bay & St. Petersburg
Venice
Washington, D.C.

FROMMER'S® NATIONAL PARK GUIDES

Grand Canyon
National Parks of the American West
Yellowstone & Grand Teton

Yosemite & Sequoia/
  Kings Canyon
Zion & Bryce Canyon

THE COMPLETE IDIOT'S TRAVEL GUIDES

(The ultimate user-friendly trip planners)

Cruise Vacations
Planning Your Trip to Europe
Hawaii

Las Vegas
Mexico's Beach Resorts
New Orleans

New York City
San Francisco
Walt Disney World

SPECIAL-INTEREST TITLES

The Civil War Trust's Official Guide to
  the Civil War Discovery Trail
Frommer's Caribbean Hideaways
Israel Past & Present
New York City with Kids
New York Times Weekends
Outside Magazine's Adventure Guide
  to New England
Outside Magazine's Adventure Guide
  to Northern California

Outside Magazine's Adventure Guide
  to the Pacific Northwest
Outside Magazine's Guide to Family Vacations
Places Rated Almanac
Retirement Places Rated
Washington, D.C., with Kids
Wonderful Weekends from Boston
Wonderful Weekends from New York City
Wonderful Weekends from San Francisco
Wonderful Weekends from Los Angeles

THE UNOFFICIAL GUIDES®

(Get the unbiased truth from these candid, value-conscious guides)

Atlanta
Branson, Missouri
Chicago
Cruises
Disneyland

Florida with Kids
The Great Smoky
  & Blue Ridge
  Mountains
Las Vegas

Miami & the Keys
Mini-Mickey
New Orleans
New York City
San Francisco

Skiing in the West
Walt Disney World
Walt Disney World
  Companion
Washington, D.C.

FROMMER'S® IRREVERENT GUIDES

(Wickedly honest guides for sophisticated travelers)

Amsterdam
Boston
Chicago

London
Manhattan

New Orleans
Paris

San Francisco
Walt Disney World
Washington, D.C.

America
Britain
California

Florida
France
Germany

Ireland
Italy
New England

Scotland
Spain
Western Europe